UNFADING LIGHT

UNFADING LIGHT

Contemplations and Speculations

Sergius Bulgakov

Translated, edited, and with an Introduction by

Thomas Allan Smith

WILLIAM B. EERDMANS PUBLISHING COMPANY
GRAND RAPIDS, MICHIGAN / CAMBRIDGE, U.K.

Originally published in Moscow in 1917 under the title
Svet nevechernii. Sozertsaniia i umozreniia.

This English translation © 2012 Thomas Allan Smith
All rights reserved

Wm. B. Eerdmans Publishing Co.
2140 Oak Industrial Drive N.E., Grand Rapids, Michigan 49505 /
P.O. Box 163, Cambridge CB3 9PU U.K.

Library of Congress Cataloging-in-Publication Data

Bulgakov, Sergei Nikolaevich, 1871-1944.
[Svet nevechernyi. English]
Unfading light: contemplations and speculations / Sergius Bulgakov;
translated, edited, and with an introduction by Thomas Allan Smith.
p.   cm.
Includes bibliographical references and index.
ISBN 978-0-8028-6711-7 (pbk.: alk. paper)
1. Religion — Philosophy. I. Smith, T. Allan. II. Title.

B4238.B83S813   2012
230'.19 — dc23

2012022174

www.eerdmans.com

*This book is dedicated to the memory of my father,
Nikolai Vasilievich Bulgakov, archpriest of Livny,
And my mother Aleksandra Kosminichna née Azbukina
With the sentiment of spiritual fidelity*

Contents

A Note from the Translator — x

Translator's Introduction:
Bulgakov's Journey towards the Unfading Light — xx

From the Author — xxxvii

Introduction: The Nature of Religious Consciousness — 1
  I. How Is Religion Possible? — 1
  II. Transcendent and Immanent — 20
  III. Faith and Feeling — 39
  IV. Religion and Ethics — 47
  V. Faith and Dogma — 53
  VI. The Nature of Myth — 63
  VII. Religion and Philosophy — 79

First Section: Divine Nothing — 103
  I. The Fundamental Antinomy of Religious Consciousness — 103
  II. Negative (Apophatic) Theology — 111
    1. Negative Theology in Plato and Aristotle — 111
    2. Plotinus (Third Century A.D.) — 114
    3. Philo of Alexandria (First Century) — 118
    4. The Idea of Negative Theology in the Alexandrian School of Christian Theology (Third Century) — 119

Contents

    A. Clement of Alexandria — 119
    B. Origen — 120
  5. Fathers of the Church: St. Basil the Great, St. Gregory the Theologian, St. Gregory of Nyssa (Fourth Century) — 121
  6. Areopagitica — 125
  7. St. Maximus the Confessor (Seventh Century) — 129
  8. St. John Damascene (Eighth Century) — 130
  9. St. Gregory Palamas (Fourteenth Century) — 131
  10. Johannes Scotus Eriugena (Ninth Century) — 134
  11. Nicholas of Cusa (Fifteenth Century) — 137
  12. Jewish Mysticism: Cabbala — 140
  13. Negative Theology in German and English Mysticism — 143
    A. "German Theology" *(Das Büchlein vom vollkommenen Leben von Deutschherr)* ca. Fifteenth Century — 143
    B. Meister Eckhart and His School (Tauler, Suso) — 143
    C. Sebastian Frank (Sixteenth Century) — 146
    D. Angelus Silesius (Seventeenth Century) — 147
    E. Jacob Böhme (Sixteenth-Seventeenth Centuries) — 148
    F. John Pordage (Seventeenth Century) — 149
  14. Kant and Negative Theology — 150
III. Divine Nothing — 152
  1. Johannes Scotus Eriugena — 165
  2. Meister Eckhart — 167
  3. Jacob Böhme — 170

Second Section: The World — **181**
  I. The Creatureliness of the World — 181
    1. Creation — 181
    2. Creaturely Nothing — 186
    3. The World as Theophany and Theogony — 195
    4. Time and Eternity — 202
    5. Freedom and Necessity — 207

Contents

  II. The Sophianicity of the Creature — 214
    1. *Sophia* — 214
    2. What Is Matter? — 239
    3. Matter and the Body — 250
    4. The Nature of Evil — 266

Third Section: The Human Being — **285**
  I. The First Adam — 285
    1. The Image of God in the Human Being — 285
    2. Sex in the Human Being — 294
    3. Human and Angel — 311
    4. The Likeness of God in the Human Being — 315
    5. The Fall of Humankind — 318
    6. Light in the Darkness — 326
    7. The Old Testament and Paganism — 336
  II. The Second Adam — 342
    1. The Creation of the World and the Incarnation of God — 342
    2. The Salvation of Fallen Humankind — 350
  III. Human History — 359
    1. Concrete Time — 359
    2. Economy and Art — 363
    3. Economy and Theurgy — 370
    4. Art and Theurgy — 382
    5. Power and Theocracy — 404
    6. Society and Ecclesiality — 416
    7. The End of History — 424
  IV. Completion — 427
  Notes — 437
  Index of Names — 505
  Index of Scripture References — 509
  Index of Liturgical Texts — 512

A Note from the Translator

Bulgakov used standard editions of classical Greek and Latin texts and Russian translations of the same. He relied on the current editions of patristic texts gathered by J. P. Migne, *Patrologiae cursus completus. Series Latina,* 221 vols. (Paris, 1844-1890) (abbreviated as PL) and *Patrologiae cursus completus... series graeca,* 161 vols. (Paris, 1857-1912) (abbreviated as PG), as well as Russian translations of the same. He made use of the most recent editions of texts produced by medieval, early modern, and modern authors, as well as Russian translations and paraphrases. I have endeavored to provide the appropriate references for all of his sources, despite Bulgakov's inconsistent bibliographical apparatus. Where possible I have corrected mistaken references and supplied missing ones. For the benefit of readers, I list Bulgakov's sources below. Works in Russian are provided with the original title and an English translation; works in other languages, notably German, are cited in the original. The translation reflects Bulgakov's own versions of these texts, not English translations that may be more familiar to readers. Bulgakov peppered his text with sentences and phrases in the original Greek (transliterated in the translation), Latin, and German. These are retained, and where he did not translate them himself, I have provided a translation in square brackets after the word or phrase in question. His lengthy quotations of original sources in the notes have been omitted when they merely duplicate the Russian translation also provided in the notes. Bulgakov enjoyed coining new words and using abstract nouns that are not easily transferrable into English. At times, his prose becomes nearly impenetrable, and for these situations I have benefited

A Note from the Translator

greatly from the French translation by Constantin Andronikoff, *La lumière sans déclin* (Lausanne: L'Age d'Homme, 1990). In transliterating Russian I have used a slightly modified version of the Library of Congress system; proper names that have become standardized in English, such as Dostoevsky, Soloviev, and Florensky, are used instead of Dostoevskii, Solov'ev, or Florenskii. Orthography has not been modernized except for equating *iats* with *e* and dropping the hard sign at the end of words.

Bulgakov's Sources

Aleksii, Bishop. *Vizantiiskie tserkovnye mistiki 14-go veka* [Mystics of the Byzantine church of the fourteenth century]. Kazan', 1906.
Apuleius. *Metamorphoses.*
Aristotle. *Metaphysics.*
Athanasius of Alexandria. *Opera omnia*. PG 26.
Athanasius of Alexandria. *Tvoreniia izhe vo sviatykh ottsa nashego Afanasiia Velikago, Arkhiepiskopa Aleksandriiskago* [The Works of Saint Athanasius the Great, Archbishop of Alexandria]. 4 parts. Trinity-St. Sergius Lavra, 1902-1903.
Augustine of Hippo. *Confessions*. In *Tvoreniia blazhennago Avgustina* [The works of blessed Augustine]. Part 1. Kiev: Izd. Kievskoi dukh. Akademii, 1907.
Basil of Caesarea. "Against Eunomius." "Letter 190 to Amphilochius." In *Tvoreniia izhe vo sviatykh ottsa nashego sv. Vasiliia Velikago* [The works of our father among the saints Basil the Great]. Translated by Moskovskaia Dukhovnaia Akademiia. St. Petersburg, 1911.
Berdiaev, N. A. *Smysl tvorchestva. Opyt opravdaniia cheloveka* [The meaning of creativity. An attempt to justify humankind]. Moscow, 1916.
Bischoff, Erich. *Die Elemente der Kabbalah. Übersetzungen, Erläuterungen und Abhandlungen.* Berlin, 1913.
Bischoff, Erich. *Die Kabbalah. Einführung in die jüdische Mystik und Geheimwissenschaft.* Leipzig, 1903.
Böhme, Jacob. *Aurora ili utrenniaia zaria* [Aurora or the morning dawn]. Trans. A. S. Petrovskii. Moscow: Musaget, 1914.
Böhme's sämmtliche Werke. Edited by K. W. Schiebler. Leipzig, 1832.
Brilliantov, A. *Vliianie vostochnago bogosloviia na zapadnoe v proizvedeniiakh Ioanna Skota Èrigeny* [The influence of eastern theology on

western theology in the works of Johannes Scotus Eriugena]. St. Petersburg, 1891.

Bruno, Giordano. *Von der Ursache, dem Prinzip and dem Eine*. Translated by Adolf Lasson. Philosophische Bibliothek, vol. 21. Leipzig, 1902.

Bulgakov, S. N. *Filosofiia khoziaistva. Chast' I: Mir kak khoziaistvo* [Philosophy of economy. Part I. The world as household]. Moscow, 1911.

Bulgakov, S. N. "Khristianstvo i sotsial'nyi vopros" [Christianity and the social question], "Khoziaistvo i religioznaia lichnost'" [Economy and the religious person], "Osnovnye motivy filosofii khoziaistva v platonizme i rannem khristianstve" [Basic motifs of a philosophy of economy in Platonism and early Christianity], "Religiia chelovekobozhiia u L. Feierbakha" [The religion of deified humanity in L. Feuerbach]. In *Dva grada* [Two cities]. Moscow, 1911.

Bulgakov, S. N. *Ot marksizma k idealizmu* [From marxism to idealism]. St. Petersburg, 1903.

Bulgakov, S. N. "Smysl ucheniia sv. Grigoriia Nisskago ob imenakh Bozhiikh" [The meaning of St. Gregory of Nyssa's doctrine on the names of God]. *Zaprosy Zhizni* (Easter 1914). Moscow.

Carlyle, Thomas. *Sartor Resartus*. 1831.

Claassen, Johannes. *Einführung in Jacob Böhme*. Stuttgart, 1885.

Claassen, Johannes. *Franz von Baaders theosophische Weltanschauung als System oder Physiosophie des Christenthums*. Stuttgart, 1887.

Claassen, Johannes. *Jacob Böhme, sein Leben und seine theosophischen Werke im geordneten Auszuge mit Einleitungen und Erläuterungen*. 3 vols. Stuttgart, 1885.

Clement of Alexandria. *Stromateis*. In *Die griechischen christlichen Schriftsteller der ersten drei Jahrhunderte*. Vols. 2 and 3. Leipzig: Prussian Academy of Sciences, 1906.

Clement of Alexandria. *Stromateis*. Iaroslav Eparchial Gazette, 1891, No. 36.

Cohen, Hermann. *Logik der reinen Erkenntnis*. Berlin, 1902.

Das Büchlein vom vollkommenen Leben (Eine Deutsche Theologie) in der ursprünglichen Gestalt herausgegeben und übertragen von Herrman Büttner. Jena: Diederichs, 1907.

Denzinger, Heinrich Joseph Dominicus. *Enchiridion Symbolorum et Definitionum*. 1st ed., Würzburg, 1854. Bulgakov may have used the sixth edition, the last edited by Denzinger, or the tenth, which appeared in 1908 in Freiburg.

A Note from the Translator

Des Angelus Silesius Cherubinischer Wandersmann, nach der Ausgabe letzter Hand von 1675 vollständig herausgegeben. Jena: Diederichs, 1905.
Dieterich, Albrecht. *Eine Mithrasliturgie.* Leipzig: B. G. Teubner, 1903.
Dionysius the Areopagite. *Opera omnia.* PG 3.
Dobtrotoliubie. 5 volumes. St. Petersburg, 1793. This is a Slavonic version of the *Philokalia* made by Paissii Velichkovskii.
Dostoevsky, F. M. *Besy* [Demons]. 1872.
Dostoevsky, F. M. *Brat'ia Karamazovy* [The brothers Karamazov]. 1880.
Dostoevsky, F. M. *Idiot* [The idiot]. 1869.
Dostoevsky, F. M. *Son smeshnogo cheloveka* [The dream of a ridiculous man]. 1877.
Drews, Arthur. *Die Religion als Selbstbewusstsein Gottes.* Jena, 1906.
Drews, Arthur. *Plotin und der Untergang der antiken Weltanschauung.* Jena, 1907.
Elert, Werner. *Die voluntaristische Mystik Jacob Böhmes.* Berlin, 1913.
Epifanovich, S. L. *Prepodobnyi Maksim Ispovednik i vizantiiskoe bogoslovie* [St. Maximus the Confessor and Byzantine theology]. Kiev, 1915.
Èrn, V. *Rozmini i ego teoriia znania* [Rosmini and his theory of knowledge]. Moscow: Put', 1914.
Ershov, M. N. *Problemy bogopoznaniia v filosofii Mal'bransha* [Problems of divine cognition in the philosophy of Malebranche]. Kazan', 1914.
Fet, Afanasii Afanasievich. *Polnoe sobranie stikhotvorenii* [Collected poetry]. St. Petersburg, 1912.
Fichte, Johann Gottlieb. *Anweisung zum seligen Leben.* 1806.
Fichte, Johann Gottlieb. *Appellation an das Publikum.* Jena, 1798.
Fichte, Johann Gottlieb. *Die philosophischen Schriften zum Atheismusstreit. Über den Grund unseres Glaubens an eine göttliche Weltregierung.* Jena, 1798.
Florensky, Pavel. "Khishcheniem nepshcheva" [He did not consider it theft]. Sergiev Posad, 1915.
Florensky, Pavel. *Kosmologicheskiia antinomii I. Kanta.* [The cosmological antinomies of I. Kant]. Sergiev Posad, 1909.
Florensky, Pavel. "Obshchechelovecheskie korni idealizma" [The universal human roots of idealism]. Sergiev Posad, 1909.
Florensky, Pavel. *Smysl idealizma. Sbornik statei v pamiat' stoletiia Imperatorskoi Moskovskoi Dukhovnoi Akademii* [The meaning of idealism. A collection of articles in honor of a century of the Imperial Moscow Theological Academy]. Sergiev Posad, 1915.

Florensky, Pavel. *Stolp i utverzhdenie istiny.* [The pillar and ground of the truth]. Moscow, 1914.
Florensky, Pavel. *Sushchnost' idealizma.* [The essence of idealism]. Sergiev Posad, 1915.
Forberg, Friedrich Karl. "Entwicklung des Begriffs der Religion." *Philosophisches Journal,* 1798.
Franck, Adolphe. *La Kabbale.* Paris, 1843.
Franck, Sebastian. *Paradoxa.* Edited by H. Ziegler. Jena: Diederichs, 1909.
Gilbert, Otto. *Griechische Religionsphilosophie.* Leipzig, 1911.
Goethe, Johann Wolfgang von. *Faust.* Part One, 1808; Part Two, 1832.
Gregory Nazianzenus. *Tvoreniia izhe vo sviatykh ottsa nashego sv. Grigoriia Bogoslova, Arkhiepiskopa Konstantinopol'skago* [The works of our father among the saints Gregory the Theologian, Archbishop of Constantinople]. 3rd ed. Moscow, 1889.
Gregory of Nyssa. *Tvoreniia izhe vo sviatykh ottsa nashego sv. Grigoriia Nisskago* [The works of our father among the saints Gregory of Nyssa]. 8 parts. 1862-1872.
Gregory Palamas. *Opera omnia.* PG 150, 151. Paris, 1865.
Hartmann, Eduard von. *Religionsphilosophie.* Teil 2: *Die Religion des Geistes.* Berlin, 1882.
Hartmann, Eduard von. *Schelling's philosophisches System.* Leipzig, 1897.
Hartmann, Nicolai. *Plato's Logik des Seyns.* Giessen, 1909.
Hasse, Karl P. *Nikolaus von Kues.* Berlin, 1913.
Hegel, Georg Wilhelm Friedrich. *Encyclopädie der philosophischen Wissenschaften im Grundrisse.* 2nd ed. Berlin, 1840.
Hegel, Georg Wilhelm Friedrich. *Phänomenologie des Geistes.* Bamberg & Würzburg, 1807.
Hegel, Georg Wilhelm Friedrich. *Religionsphilosophie.* Jena: Diederichs, 1906.
Hegel, Georg Wilhelm Friedrich. *Vorlesungen über die Geschichte der Philosophie,* 3rd part, 2nd ed. Berlin, 1844.
Hegel, Georg Wilhelm Friedrich. *Wissenschaft der Logik.* 1st part, 2nd ed. Berlin, 1841.
Herrmann, W. "Die religiöse Frage der Gegenwart." In *Das Christenthum.* 1908.
Herrmann, W. *Ethik.* Tübingen, 1909.
Hinton, Charles Howard. *Chetvertoe izmerenie i novaia èra mysli* [The fourth dimension and the new era of thought]. Petrograd, 1915.

A Note from the Translator

Jacobi, Friedrich Heinrich. *Werke*. Leipzig, 1812-1825.
James, William. *The Varieties of Religious Experience*. New York, 1902.
Johannes Scotus Erigena. *Ueber die Eintheilung der Natur*. Translated by Ludwig Noack. Berlin, 1870-1874.
Johannes Scotus Eriugena. *Opera quae supersunt omnia*. Edited by H. J. Floss. PL 122. Paris, 1853.
John Cassian. *Pisaniia prep. Ioanna Kassiana Rimlianina* [Writings of St. John Cassian the Roman]. n.d.
John of Damascus. *Tochnoe izlozhenie pravoslavnoi very* [Exact exposition of the orthodox faith]. Translated by Aleksandr Bronzov. St. Petersburg, 1894.
Kant, Immanuel. *Die Religion innerhalb der blossen Vernunft*. Königsberg, 1794.
Kant, Immanuel. *Kritik der Urtheilskraft*. Leipzig: Reclam, 1878.
Kant, Immanuel. *Kritika chistago razuma* [Critique of pure reason]. Translated by N. M. Sokolov. St. Petersburg, 1896-1897. Other translations available to Bulgakov were by M. Vladislavlev, 1867, and N. Lossky, 1907.
Kant, Immanuel. *Kritika prakticheskago razuma* [Critique of practical reason]. Translated by N. M. Sokolov. S. Petersburg, n.d.
Khomiakov, Aleksei Stepanovich. *Polnoe sobranie sochinenii* [Complete collection of works]. Moscow, 1900.
Khomiakov, Aleksei Stepanovich. "Vecherniaia pesnia" [Evening song]. 1853. *Stikhotvoreniia Alekseia Khomiakova*. Moscow, 1868, 1888.
The Koran. Translated by Gordii Sablukov. 2nd ed. Kazan', 1895.
Leroy, Édouard. *Dogmat i kritika* [Dogma and criticism]. Original French version — Paris: Librairie Bloud, 1907.
Loofs, Friedrich. *Leitfaden zum Studium der Dogmengeschichte*. Halle a.d. Saale, 1906.
Lossky, Nikolai Onufrievich. *Obosnovanie intuitivizma* [The intuitive basis of knowledge]. 1906.
Makovel'skii, Aleksandr. "The Imitation of Heraclitus in Hippocrates." In *Dosokratiki* [The pre-socratics]. Volume 1. Kazan', 1914.
Maximus Confessor. *Opera omnia*. Edited by F. Combéfis. PG 90 and 91. Paris, 1865.
Maximus Confessor. *Scholia*. Edited by Corderius. PG 4. Paris, 1899.
Maximus Confessor. *Voprosootvety k Thalassiiu* [Questions and answers for Thalassius]. Translated by S. L. Epifanovich. *Bogoslovskii Vestnik*, II. 1916.

A Note from the Translator

Meister Eckeharts Schriften und Predigten. Translated and edited by H. Büttner. Leipzig: Diederichs, 1903.

Meister Eckhart. *Dukhovnyia razsuzhdeniia i propovedi Meistera Èkgarta* [Spiritual discourses and sermons of Meister Eckhart]. Translated by M. V. Sabashnikov. Moscow: Musaget, 1912.

Metner, Emilio. *Razmyshleniia o Gete* [Meditations on Goethe]. Moscow, 1914.

Michelangelo. *Sonnets*. In the edition by Carl Frey, *Die Dichtungen des Michelangelo Buonarroti*. Berlin, 1897.

Müller, Max. *Natürliche Religion*. Leipzig, 1890

Muretov, Mitrofan. *Filosofiia Filona Aleksandriiskago v otnoshenii k ucheniiu Ioanna Bogoslova o Logose* [The philosophy of Philo of Alexandria in relation to the teaching of John the Theologian on the Logos]. Moscow, 1885.

Muretov, Mitrofan. *Uchenie o Logose u Filona Aleksandriiskago i Ioanna Bogoslova v sviazi s predshestvovavshim istoricheskim razvitiem idei Logosa v grecheskoi filosofii i iudeiskoi teosofii* [The doctrine of the Logos in Philo of Alexandria and John the Theologian in conjunction with the preceding historical development of the idea of the Logos in Greek philosophy and Jewish theosophy]. Moscow, 1885.

Natorp, Paul. *Plato's Ideenlehre*. Leipzig, 1903.

Nesmelov, Viktor. *Dogmaticheskaia sistema Grigoriia Nisskago* [The dogmatic system of Gregory of Nyssa]. Kazan', 1887.

Nicholas of Cusa. *De docta ignorantia*. Edited by Paolo Rotta. Bari, 1913.

Nicholas of Cusa. *Des Cardinal und Bischofs Nicolaus von Cusa wichtigste Schriften in deutscher Uebersetzung von F. A. Scharpff*. Freiburg im Breisgau, 1862.

Nilus, Sergei Aleksandrovich. *Velikoe v malom i antikhrist, kak blizkaia politicheskaia vozmozhnost'* [The great in the small, and antichrist, as an imminent political possibility]. Tsarskoe Selo, 1902, 1905.

O tseli khristianskoi zhizni. Besedy prep. Serafima Sarovskago s A. N. Motovilovym [On the goal of the Christian life. Conversations of Saint Seraphim of Sarov with A. N. Motovilov]. Sergiev Posad, 1914.

Origen. *Commentary on John. Commentary on Matthew. Exhortation to Martyrdom. On First Principles*. Kazan': Kazanskaia Dukhovnaia Akademiia, 1899.

Pausanias. *Descriptio Graeciae*. Various editions of this text would have been available, including Leipzig, 1875, and Berlin, 1896-1910.

Penny, A. I. *Studies in Jacob Böhme*. London, 1912.

A Note from the Translator

Pfleiderer, O. *Geschichte der Religionsphilosophie*. 3rd ed. Berlin, 1893.
Philo of Alexandria. *Philonis Judaei Opera Omnia*. Leipzig: E. B. Schwickerti, 1828-1829.
Pisarev, Leonid. *Uchenie blazh. Avgustina, ep. Ipponskago, o cheloveke v ego otnoshenii k Bogu* [The doctrine of blessed Augustine of Hippo on the human being in relation to God]. Kazan', 1894.
Plato. *Sochineniia Platona* [The works of Plato]. Translated by Vasilii Nikolaevich Karpov. St. Petersburg, 1841.
Plotinus. *Enneads*.
Pordage, John. *Godly and True Metaphysics*. A three-volume collection of his writings published as *Göttliche und wahre Metaphysica, oder, Wunderbare durch eigene Erfahrung erlangte Wissenschaft der unsichtbaren und ewigen Dinge nemlich von denen unsichtbaren Welten*. Frankfurt and Leipzig, 1715.
Porfirii, (Uspenskii) Bishop. *Istoriia Afona* [A history of Athos]. St. Petersburg, 1892.
Pushkin, Aleksandr Sergeevich. *Sochineniia A. S. Pushkina. Polnoe sobranie* [The works of A. S. Pushkin. Complete collection]. St. Petersburg, 1899.
Rose, Valentin. *Aristotelis qui ferebantur librorum fragmenta*. Leipzig, 1886.
Scharpff, Franz Anton von. *Nicolaus von Cusa als Reformator in Kirche, Reich und Philosophie des XV. Jahrhunderts*. Tübingen, 1871.
Schelling, Friedrich Wilhelm Joseph. *Darstellung des philosophischen Empirismus*. 1830.
Schelling, Friedrich Wilhelm Joseph. *Philosophie der Mythologie*. Schellings sämtliche Werke, vol. 2. Stuttgart, 1856-1861.
Schelling, Friedrich Wilhelm Joseph. *Philosophie der Offenbarung*. Schellings sämtliche Werke, vol. 2. 1858. Stuttgart, 1856-1861.
Schleiermacher, Friedrich. *Rechi o religii k obrazovannym liudiam, ee preziraiushchim* [On religion. Speeches to its cultured despisers]. Moscow, 1911.
Schmidt, Anna Nikolaevna. *Iz rukopisei A. N. Shmidt. S pis'mami k nei V. S. Solov'eva* [From the manuscripts of A. N. Shmidt, with letters to her from V. S. Soloviev]. Moscow, 1916.
Schwarz, Hermann. *Der Gottesgedanke in der Geschichte der Philosophie*. Heidelberg, 1913.
Sefer Jetzirah. Das Buch der Schöpfung. Warsaw, 1884. Translation, notes, and introduction by Lazarus Goldschmidt. Frankfurt a. M., 1894.

A Note from the Translator

Sertillanges, Antonin Gilbert. *Saint Thomas d'Aquin*. 2 volumes. Paris, 1912.
Seuse, Heinrich. *Deutsche Schriften*. 2 volumes. Edited by Walter Lehmann. Jena: Diederichs, 1911.
Soloviev, Vladimir Sergeevich. *Sobranie Sochinenii* [Collected works]. St. Petersburg, 1901-07.
Spasskii, A. A. *Istoriia dogmaticheskikh dvizhenii v èpokhu vselenskikh soborov* [A history of dogmatic movements in the epoch of the ecumenical councils]. Vol. 1. Sergiev Posad, 1906.
Spinoza, Baruch. *Ètika* [Ethics]. Translated by N. A. Ivantsov. 1892.
Steiner, Rudolf. *Die Geheimwissenschaft im Umriss*. Leipzig, 1910.
Steiner, Rudolf. *Iz letopisia mira* [From a chronicle of the world]. Moscow: Dukhovnoe Znanie, 1914. [This is the Russian translation of the original *Akasha Chronik* — the *Akasha Chronicle*.]
Steiner, Rudolf. *Put' posviazshcheniia ili kak dostignut' poznanii vysshikh mirov* [The path of initiation, or how to attain knowledge of higher worlds]. Kaluga, 1912. This was the first Russian translation of *Wie erlangt man Erkenntnisse der höheren Welten* [How to know higher worlds. A modern path of initiation], 1904.
Stöckl, A. *Lehrbuch der Geschichte der Philosophie*. 2nd ed. Mainz, 1875.
Symeon the New Theologian. *Slova prep. Simeona novago bogoslova* [Discourses of St. Symeon the new theologian]. Moscow, 1882; 2nd ed., 1892.
Synesius of Cyrene. *Dio Chrysostomus*.
Tauler, Johannes. *Predigten*. 2 volumes. Edited by Walter Lehmann. Jena: Diederichs, 1913.
Thomas à Kempis. *The Imitation of Christ*.
Troeltsch, Ernst. *Zur religiösen Lage, Religionsphilosophie und Ethik*. 1913.
Trubetskoi, Evgenii Nikolaevich. *Mirosozertsanie Vl. S. Solov'eva* [The worldview of V. S. Soloviev]. 2 vols. Moscow, 1913.
Trubetskoi, Sergei Nikolaevich. "Osnovaniia idealizma" [The foundations of idealism]. *Voprosy filosofii i psikhologii* 7:1-5, books 31-35 (1896); repr. *Sobranie sochinenii Kn. Sergeia Nikolaevicha Trubetskogo*, 6 volumes. Moscow, 1907-1912, vol. 2: 161-284.
Trubetskoi, Sergei Nikolaevich. *Uchenie o Logose* [The doctrine of the Logos]. Moscow, 1900. Cited by Bulgakov from the collected works in six volumes, Moscow, 1906-1912.
Uspenskii, Petr Demianovich. *Chetvertoe izmerenie* [The fourth dimension]. 1914.

A Note from the Translator

Uspenskii, Petr Demianovich. *Tertium organum: Kliuch k zagadkam mira* [The third organ. Key to the enigmas of the world]. St. Petersburg: "Trud," 1911.

Vvedenskii, A. I. *"O mistitsizme i krititsizme v teorii poznaniia V. S. Solov'eva"* [On mysticism and criticism in the theory of cognition of V. S. Soloviev]. In *Filosofskie ocherki* [Philosophical sketches]. St. Petersburg, 1901, pp. 39-68.

Wünsche, August. "Kabbala." In *Realencyclopädie für protestantische Theologie und Kirche*. 3rd ed. 1896-1909.

Yogi Ramacharaka. *Hatha yoga*. Ed. Novyi chelovek. Original English, 1904.

Zeller, Eduard. *Die Philosophie der Griechen*. 4th ed. Leipzig, 1903.

Zohar: Sepher ha-Zohar. Translated by Jean de Pauly. Paris, 1911.

Translator's Introduction:
Bulgakov's Journey towards the Unfading Light

By the time Sergius Nikolaevich Bulgakov (1871-1944) came to write *Svet nevechernii* [*Unfading light*], he had already undergone a significant personal and intellectual transformation.[1] Born the son of a cemetery chapel priest in the provincial town of Livny, Bulgakov grew up in an unhappy home: money was tight, his father struggled with alcoholism, and his mother proved to be a poor and anxious manager of the household. The tedium of daily life in Livny, bereft of cultural attractions and compounded by the penury of the Bulgakov family, was somewhat compensated for by the rhythm of the liturgical year and the services celebrated in the parish church of St. Sergius and the cemetery chapel. An ancestral Russian Orthodoxy permeated his early life, and like many of his forebears the young Bulgakov entered a seminary to study for the priesthood; however, three years later in 1888, disillusioned by the intellectual torpor of seminary life and dissatisfied with the rote answers of official Orthodoxy to the questions swirling in his mind, he left the clerical path and entered a secular school where he embraced nihilism. Bulgakov broke his ties with the Church. Although he would later call his fifteen-year estrangement from the Church "my atheism," Bulgakov would insist that at no time did he ever lose his faith. Instead, this period of "unbelief" was for him the negation of belief, but belief all the same.[2] From 1890 to 1894 he studied law and political economy at Moscow University and became an ardent though critical adherent of the thought of Karl Marx. By his own admission, Bulgakov was naturally drawn to literature, philology, and art, but sacrificed these interests in order to pursue studies that would

Translator's Introduction

be of more benefit to his country badly in need of political and economic reform.[3]

Since the 1870s the intelligentsia, whose members came from a broad spectrum of the educated populace and professions, had directed their energies to a thoroughgoing reform of Russian political, social, and cultural life. Chief among their demands were the end of autocracy and the improvement of the economic and educational condition of the vast peasant population through agrarian reform. As a member of the intelligentsia, Bulgakov shared that group's commitment to social reform in Russia, which he expressed initially by turning to Marxism and economic materialism. He published a critical review of volume three of *Das Kapital* in 1895, and authored a more polemical essay in 1896, "On the Regularity of Social Phenomena" in the journal *Voprosy filosofii i psikhologii* [Questions of philosophy and psychology]; this was followed in 1897 by a study "On Markets in Capitalist Conditions of Production."[4] These writings established Bulgakov as a major representative of Marxism in Russia. He traveled to Western Europe in 1898 to conduct research for his dissertation. Shortly before embarking for Berlin, Bulgakov married Elena Tokmakova. Berlin offered Bulgakov the opportunity to meet some of the leading Marxist thinkers in Europe, but as Catherine Evtuhov points out, his encounters with them were far from positive.[5] Indeed the journey to Europe coincided with a personal crisis that marks the beginning of the end of Bulgakov's "atheist" period. His famous mystical encounter with the Sistine Madonna in the Zwinger Gallery of Dresden,[6] coupled with a nagging doubt in the universal truth claims of Marxism, was perhaps a manifestation of his long-suppressed religious personhood even if, as Evtuhov evocatively suggests, such experiences were typical of numerous Russian *intelligenty*[7] who made an intellectual pilgrimage westwards.[8]

His intensifying inner turmoil did not prevent him from making the most of his research opportunities in the West, and in 1900 he presented his finished dissertation, *Kapitalizm i zemledelie* [Capitalism and agriculture], for examination. Though it did not satisfy him or his examiners,[9] it did secure for him a teaching position as professor of political economy at the Kiev Polytechnical Institute and as *privat dozent* at the University of Kiev in 1901. The extent to which Bulgakov had already distanced himself from Marxist thought quickly emerged in a lecture delivered in Kiev in November 1901, "Ivan Karamazov kak filosofskii tip" [Ivan Karamazov as a philosophical type]. Instead of a learned disquisition on pragmatic matters such as grain prices and land redistribution, or a reiteration of the laws of historical development, Bulgakov spoke passionately of the problem of good and evil, of the meaning of human life, and the importance of ethics and personal responsibility in charting a new course for the social reformers.[10] When Bulgakov brought Dostoevsky's philosophical views into the public sphere in his lecture, the prevailing counterweight to Marxism, positivism, and progressivism was Neo-Kantianism; but as sympathetic as Bulgakov might be to that strand of idealist philosophy, the thinker who would most influence his final rejection of materialism and positivism was Vladimir Soloviev, whose works he began to read in 1902 and who was to exert a powerful influence on Bulgakov's subsequent intellectual development.[11] Although he would leave Marxist thought behind, Bulgakov retained its commitment to social change through application of theory to practice. His idealism would be activist, practical, and eventually Orthodox Christian.

On the way to discovering Soloviev, Bulgakov collaborated with other former Marxists such as Nikolai Berdiaev and Petr Struve in producing the collection of essays *Problemy idealizma* [Problems of idealism] and wrote the lead essay, "Fundamental Problems of the Theory of Progress."[12] He joined Struve in publishing the journal *Liberation* and with him was a founder of the illegal political organization "Union of Liberation" in 1903.[13] Also contributing to Bulgakov's intellectual and activist development was his exposure to the thought of Dmitry Merezhkovsky and Zinaida Gippius, founders of the St. Petersburg Religious-Philosophical Society in 1901. The Society's aim was to foster a rapprochement between the intelligentsia and the church. Lasting until 1903, the Society discussed a wide range of topics including church-state relations, Christology, marriage, Tolstoy and the church, and freedom of conscience.[14] Especially important to Merezhkovsky was the development of a new religious consciousness which would overcome the persistent and pernicious dualism of flesh and spirit that he felt underlay the many problems afflicting Russia. For him, transformation of society could come only through a radical transformation of the church.[15]

Although the topics discussed at Society meetings will all surface later in his own writings, including in *Unfading Light*, Bulgakov did not share Merezhkovsky's religious enthusiasm at this time. He wrote an article for Merezhkovsky and Gippius' journal, *Novyi put'* [New path] that brought to the fore his disagreement with Merezhkovsky's approach, maintaining that before any meaningful change could take place in society, the autocracy had to be destroyed and the liberation of the people brought about.[16] The political activism of the Union of Liberation appealed more to Bulgakov, and after the Revolution of 1905 its members formed the Constitutional Democratic (Kadet) Party, which held the most seats in the representative assemblies, the First and Second Dumas (1906-1907). But Bulgakov did not join the Kadets and instead formed the Union of Christian Politics, a movement advocating Christian socialism.[17] It was a short-lived venture. Elected to the Second Duma in 1907 as a deputy for Orel province, Bulgakov had no clear party allegiance. The deepening ideological divide separating the various parties in the Second Duma and its clash with the proposals of Prime Minister Stolypin rendered it ineffectual. A widespread sense of foreboding and imminent catastrophe permeated the intelligentsia. Bulgakov recalled his utter frustration with the Duma in his memoirs.[18] When the Second Duma dissolved in June 1907 after barely five months in session, Bulgakov lost what remaining enthusiasm he had for direct political involvement.

An important factor in his gradual estrangement from the Union of Liberation was the increasingly secular and anti-Christian direction being advocated by leading representatives of left-liberal politics. Earlier, in 1905 Bulgakov supported the call for a council of the Orthodox Church made by the Brotherhood of Christian Struggle and many others, including bishops and priests. Such a council, he felt, was necessary in order to complement the work of the secular representative assembly in support of the much-needed social reforms. In 1906 a preconciliar commission prepared six volumes of information for use at the hoped-for council.[19] The tsar thwarted the council's convocation, but the material gathered by the commission would be put to use when the council finally convened in 1917. In the turmoil of 1905 Bulgakov made the acquaintance of Pavel Aleksandrovich Florensky (1882-1937), with whom he would establish a lengthy friendship. Florensky, a member of the Brotherhood of Christian Struggle, was an eccentric genius, equally at home in abstract mathematics, Orthodox theology, aesthetics, botany, and engineering.[20] Together with Bulgakov, Vladimir F. Érn, Evgenii N. Trubetskoi, Nikolai Berdiaev, Margarita Morozova, and V. P. Sventsitskii he was a founding member of the Religious-Philosophical Society in memory of Vladimir Soloviev, which was organized in Moscow at the end of 1905. Florensky's enthusiasm for Soloviev's notion of all-unity was contagious. In his 1906 essay, "Tserkov' i kul'tura" [The church and culture],[21] Bulgakov jettisons the antipathy towards organized religion and metaphysics common to the intelligentsia in favor of Florensky's notion developed from Soloviev for a symbiotic relationship between the Church and Russian, indeed, universal human culture. In the essay Bulgakov applied the parable of the prodigal son to the contemporary state of Russian culture. He judged it to be deeply divided between secular antireligious humanism and tradition-bound, religious conservatism. Neither the younger son who wandered far from home, representing the liberal intelligentsia, nor the older son representing the status quo could solve Russia's problems by themselves. Both must be reunited in the father's house, the Church, which was solely capable of providing the necessary intellectual, spiritual, and artistic creativity for the resolution of the social crisis. Gone are Bulgakov's previous convictions about the separation of church and state into their proper, independent spheres. Instead he writes, "An economic alliance, a socialist state, is able to remove the external partitions that exist between people and flagrantly violate justice, but it lacks the creative power of unification which is held only in a religious-mystical unity, i.e., the Church."[22]

In 1906 Bulgakov moved his family to Moscow. The following year he was appointed professor at the Moscow Commercial Academy, founded in 1905, and also acquired the position of *privat dozent* in political economy at Moscow University. Bulgakov's ongoing intellectual evolution is documented in the numerous publications he produced from 1904 to 1910. While he retained his interest in social questions, his focus had clearly shifted to a religious and explicitly Christian perspective.[23] As he allowed his ancestral religion to appear more boldly in articles and public lectures, Bulgakov also changed his attitude towards the hated tsar.[24] He too believed that the Russian aristocracy as an institution and the reigning tsar Nicholas II were responsible for the grave social problems afflicting Russia. But the increasing radicalization of the leftists and liberals with their jettisoning of Russian Orthodoxy in favor of a purely secular state no longer resonated in his soul. Quite the contrary, it caused him to uphold the positive value of governance by the tsar, even as he continued to despise Nicholas II, accusing him of promoting the revolution and bringing about the demise of the royal family.[25] He continued to wrestle with the meaning of (political) power as he wrote *Unfading Light*.

Translator's Introduction

Two events in 1909 were especially important for Bulgakov's future. The first was the publication of *Vekhi* [Landmarks], a collection of essays on the Russian intelligentsia by Bulgakov's colleagues, most of them former Marxists.[26] Frustrated by the failure of the 1905 revolution and the successive Dumas to produce real change in society, the contributors brought their criticism of the intelligentsia into the open and zeroed in on what they felt was the most important but unacknowledged reason for the failure of politics to achieve real reforms: the refusal to take seriously the religious and spiritual dimension of the Russian people.[27] That criticism runs throughout Bulgakov's contribution to the collection, "Heroism and the Spiritual Struggle."[28] The second event was the tragic death of Bulgakov's four-year-old son Ivashechka that summer. Bulgakov describes the effect the death had on him in *Unfading Light*. At the funeral Bulgakov had a profound religious experience, mystical and ecstatic, that can be regarded as the final act in his long journey back to Orthodoxy. Death was no stranger to Bulgakov. His first personal experience came when he was twelve years old and watched his beloved grandfather die in the family home. His father's ministry as cemetery priest would have brought the impressionable young Bulgakov into an early familiarity with the Orthodox funeral ritual. Indeed he would remark that "funerals were done well in Livny."[29] He saw many of his siblings die in childhood, and as an adult he watched the pitiable end of his alcoholic brothers; death was a fact of life, not a horror to be dreaded. He would return to reflect on the meaning of death in many of his later works, including *Unfading Light*.[30]

His son's death brought the decade to a close and also marked the end of Bulgakov's old life. Perhaps because Bulgakov's conversion to Orthodoxy occurred in fits and starts over more than a decade, he did not repudiate everything from his recent past as he moved forward. His long association with Marxist thought, especially with regard to economic and labor questions, and his personal experience of poverty carried over into his new life. It is thus not entirely surprising that in 1909 he published "Narodnoe khoziaistvo i religioznaia lichnost'" [The national economy and the religious person], which inaugurated his attempt to create a work ethic based in Russian Orthodox principles.[31] Where two other articles from the same year had seen Bulgakov rethink the social situation of early Christianity, namely "O pervokhristianstve" [On primitive Christianity], and "Pervokhristianstvo i noveishii sotsializm"

Translator's Introduction

[Primitive Christianity and socialism], he now turned to the modern era and the thought of Max Weber in formulating his ideas on labor. These developments, coupled with his renewed interest in Soloviev, form the foundation for his first major work of the new decade, *Filosofiia khoziaistva* [Philosophy of economy],[32] which appeared in 1912. In 1910 Bulgakov founded the Moscow publishing house *Put'* for which he served as editor-in-chief. It grew out of the Religious-Philosophical Society in memory of Vladimir Soloviev and was supported financially by Margarita Morozova. The purpose of *Put'* was to present Orthodoxy in a new philosophical garb and demonstrate its applicability in the contemporary world.[33] The *Put'* authors including Bulgakov participated in a heated debate with German and Russian Neo-Kantians and their simultaneously founded journal *Logos*. They criticized the reduction of philosophy by the Neo-Kantians to mere methodology and technique and argued forcefully for the reintegration of a thoroughgoing metaphysics in contemporary philosophy. The debate fueled Bulgakov's own thinking on Kant and underlies his *Filosofiia khoziaistva* and the sustained critique of Kantianism and Neo-Kantianism in *Unfading Light*.

Whereas his discovery of Soloviev in 1902 had helped Bulgakov enunciate a religiously grounded political activism, his rereading of Soloviev now offered him a solution to the modern philosophical schism between materialism and idealism. And most significantly, Bulgakov embraced Soloviev's notion of Sophia, Holy Wisdom, which he would correct and make the foundation for his remaining intellectual output. His rediscovery of Soloviev coincides with a general renewed interest in Soloviev's ideas. If the turn of the century had valued Soloviev the poet and moral thinker, now it was his religious philosophy that caught the imagination of intellectuals and artists alike.[34] One of the first fruits of Bulgakov's renewed exploration of Soloviev's thought world was his 1910 essay "Priroda v filosofii Vl. Solovieva" [Nature in the philosophy of Vl. Soloviev], which headed the collection *Sbornik Pervyi: O Vladimire Solovieve* [First compilation: On Vladimir Soloviev].[35] Here Bulgakov discusses Soloviev's views of nature as an animated, living organism both individual and collective, which he named Sophia, and how Sophia or the World Soul had operated throughout history. Together with his article "Problemy filosofii khoziaistva" [Problems of a philosophy of economy] published earlier that year, Bulgakov tested the waters for his major theological and philosophical treatment of economy that constituted his doctoral dis-

Translator's Introduction

sertation and appeared in print in 1912, *Philosophy of Economy. Part 1. The World as Household*.[36] Bulgakov rejects Kant's division of human mind into theoretical and practical reason and the complete opposition of subject and object, proposing instead that labor as both cognitive and productive restores these to their unity because both cognition and production have the same subject, the human person. He steers clear of the egotistical individualism of capitalism and the oppressive collectivism of Marxism by positing Sophia as the transcendental subject of economy. Sophia is many things: eternal humanity, world-forming principle, cosmic and earthly, divine and human. Underlying the whole project is an attempt to understand how human beings relate to the external world. The answer is through economy.[37]

As Evtuhov notes, in order to properly understand what he meant by economy one must know that the Russian word, *khoziaistvo*, means both "economy" in the normal English sense, and "household." It also suggests process or activity, so that economy is the activity of labor.[38] She explains that for Bulgakov, human beings interact with the external world through their labor, as individuals and all together, winning from the world their daily sustenance but at the same time contributing to the infusion of the external world with human qualities. Labor should be creative, full of life and joy. Instead, because of the fall, labor became an unwelcome burden that ultimately imprisons the human being in a necessary quest for survival. Marx and his theory of economic materialism focused solely on the condition of the fallen world; but for Bulgakov, there is a deeper reality beyond the merely objective material state that can be restored to the whole of creation through the clarified process of labor. Christ's resurrection was the great symbol for this transformation, and human beings, inasmuch as they share the human nature of Christ, share the common task of realizing this restoration. The world is the creation of God with Holy Wisdom (Sophia) acting as an artisan, and it retains a sophianic quality as something to be realized through human labor. Just as Proverbs 8:22-31 depicts Wisdom at play, full of joy, taking delight in the work of God, so human labor has the potential to be sophianic.[39] It was this vision for Russia that Bulgakov presented in 1912. The banality and oppression that actually gained control of Russia after the Bolshevik Revolution could not have been more different.

Bulgakov became involved in a curious theological-spiritual controversy that caught public attention in June 1913 when the Russian Imperial Navy forcibly removed several hundred monks from the Russian monastery of St. Panteleimon on Mount Athos where they were practicing a suspicious spiritual doctrine known as *Imiaslavie*, Name-Worship.[40] The doctrine owes its origins to the starets Ilarion, a former Mount Athos monk who in 1907 published a book outlining his experiences with the Jesus Prayer, *On the Mountains of the Caucasus*, and sent copies to Mount Athos. Ilarion believed that through his rigorous practice of the hesychast method of prayer of the heart coupled with the recitation of the Jesus Prayer, "Lord Jesus Christ, Son of God, have mercy on me, a sinner," he came into direct contact with God. An adept in the method could reduce the prayer to "Lord Jesus Christ" or simply "Jesus" and enjoy the same mystical rapture. In other words, the divine presence was contained in the name itself. The doctrine received a mixed reception on Mount Athos, with most of its adherents belonging to the Russian St. Panteleimon monastery. By 1909, however, voices were raised against the teaching, and the Athonite communities became deeply divided between the Name-Worshipers and the Name-Fighters *(imiabortsy)*. The Name-Worshipers were accused of heresy, even though the doctrine could be understood as a popularized version of the entirely orthodox teaching on the distinction between the divine essence and the divine energies in God elaborated by St. Gregory Palamas in the fourteenth century. The controversy quickly spread to Moscow, largely through the efforts of Antonii Bulatovich, a priest-monk of the Athonite Andreevskii skete, who published *Apology of Faith in the Name of God and the Name of Jesus* in 1913. Here too opinions were divided. Finally in 1914 Metropolitan Makarii of Moscow and the Holy Synod allowed the Name-Worshipers to remain within the Church but condemned the teaching as "heretical and blasphemous." When the Local Council of the Russian Orthodox Church opened in 1917, Name-Worship was on the agenda for a final resolution. Bulgakov was asked to prepare a brief on the doctrine for the Council's consideration, but no decision could be taken because the council was forced to adjourn prematurely. Grasping the full significance of the issues raised by the Name-Worshipers, Bulgakov set about writing a book, *Filosofiia imeni* [Philosophy of the name], in which he combined contemporary linguistic theory, philosophy, and his own theology to explore the mystical realism of words. It also allowed him to present a sustained exposition of his understanding of prayer.[41] He attends to this problematic in *Unfading Light*. Name-Worship resonated too with poets, musicians, and

Translator's Introduction

painters of the Symbolist movement as they delved into the nature of language and the word.

Bulgakov recalled the beginning of World War I with an initial burst of nationalist pride; however, this euphoria quickly vanished with news of repeated military failures and the radicalization of the political situation in the empire.[42] He continued to write and speak in public, finishing *Unfading Light* at the end of 1916. In the midst of the chaos, a ray of hope for the church emerged when permission was finally given for the convocation of an All-Russian Council of the Orthodox Church. It opened on 15 July 1917 in Moscow. As a delegate Bulgakov played a very important role in the council's work, serving on a number of special committees examining the problem of Bolshevism and the implications of socialism for the church. While the October Revolution was violently sweeping away the old political order, the Council voted to restore the Patriarchate, and installed the metropolitan of Moscow, Tikhon (Belavin) on 21 November as the first patriarch of the Russian Orthodox Church since its suppression by Peter the Great at the start of the eighteenth century. Less than a year later, in September 1918, the Council was forced to close. Bulgakov had been ordained to the priesthood on the day after Pentecost 1918, an event that he remembered with particular delight.[43]

His civic life was not so happy. He lost his position at Moscow University in 1918, and moved to join his family in the Crimea, where for two years he taught political economy and theology at the university in Simferopol. The Bolsheviks captured Simferopol in 1920 and again removed him from his teaching position. He was arrested in October 1922 but for some unknown reason he was allowed to go into foreign exile with hundreds of other undesirable intellectuals. He and most of his family left the Soviet Union on 30 December 1922. Even during these difficult years, Bulgakov continued to write.[44] Bulgakov's flight westward took him to Constantinople in 1923, then to Prague, and in 1925 to Paris where he would serve as Dean and teach dogmatic theology and Old Testament at the newly established Institut Saint Serge. This would be his home until his death in 1944.

The Paris years were very productive: he completed two dogmatic trilogies on Sophiology — the first, *The Burning Bush* (1926), *The Friend of the Bridegroom* (1927), *Jacob's Ladder* (1929); the second, *The Lamb of God, The Comforter, The Bride of the Lamb* (1939)[45] — besides numerous shorter works; he became an active participant in the nascent ecumenical movement, speaking at the Faith and Order Conference in Lausanne in 1927; and was a founding member of the Orthodox-Anglican Fellowship of St. Alban and St. Sergius in England in 1928. His theological writings aroused suspicion among some of the émigré Russians, and in 1935 he was accused of heresy; his own ecclesiastical superior, Metropolitan Evlogii, did not join in the condemnation, which found the normally antagonistic Russian Orthodox Church Outside Russia and the Moscow Patriarchate of one mind in their rejection of Bulgakov. A serious illness in 1926, and then the contraction of throat cancer in 1939, occasioned Bulgakov's writing of an intensely mystical and personal meditation on the meaning of death, *Sofiologiia smerti* [The sophiology of death]. Fittingly, his final work, completed just before his death on 12 July 1944, was devoted to the Book of Revelation: *Apokalipsis Ioanna* [The Apocalypse of John].

Unfading Light is a watershed in Bulgakov's intellectual output. It both sums up everything that precedes it and charts the course for all that follows. The book has been considered a "philosophy of revelation,"[46] "the fullest statement of his socio-cultural criticism,"[47] and an Orthodox foundation for his philosophy of economy.[48] It is the second panel in Bulgakov's metaphysical diptych in which he moves beyond the limitations of strict materialism on the one hand and German idealism on the other. In the first panel, *Philosophy of Economy*, labor — the economic process — emerged as an epistemological category, accounting for how human beings relate with and know the world. Knowledge is something produced by a thinking subject, like any artifact produced by human effort. In *Unfading Light*, religion — religious experience, faith/belief — is a second epistemological category that allows human beings to know God and the world, and themselves in relation to both and to one another. The first book asked "How is economy possible?" and the second, "How is religion possible?" and with both questions Bulgakov dethrones the Kantian intellectual god haunting materialist and idealist temples alike. Uniting the diptych is Sophia, Holy Wisdom. Although *Unfading Light* is not the promised part two of *Philosophy of Economy*, Bulgakov felt that in writing it he had fulfilled his obligations to his readers.[49] Like the earlier book, *Unfading Light* is a product of the Silver Age of Russian culture lasting from 1892 until 1917 (or 1921) in which an enormous explosion of creativity shook every aspect of Russian life — literature, politics, religion, music, art, philosophy, science. Avril Pyman aptly notes that its symbol is the silvery light of the moon,

Translator's Introduction

which, for all its brilliance, cannot entirely defeat the encompassing darkness.[50] Unlike the sun which never changes, the moon waxes and wanes, and throughout the Silver Age a sense of unavoidable decline and loss hangs heavily in the cultural sky.[51]

The book is difficult to categorize, a characteristic of many other pieces of writing from the Silver Age, though Bulgakov is far less experimental than most, including his younger friend Florensky. Still, with its inclusion of lengthy and dry scholarly asides on intricate philosophical and religious matters, its descriptions of personal mystical experiences, closely argued rebuttals of Neo-Kantianism, sharp attacks on contemporary aesthetics, pure theologizing, lyrical peaks and valleys, and prosaic plains, the book does break the definitions of a strictly philosophical, theological, or religious-philosophical monograph. The title itself is typical of the Silver Age, which saw journals and almanacs appear with the name *Apollo, Golden Fleece, Libra,* and *Northern Flowers.* Bulgakov found inspiration for his title in a poem by the nineteenth-century lay theologian — and when he wrote it, Bulgakov too was still a layman — Aleksei Khomiakov, which he cites in his foreword. The phrase "unfading light" refers to Jesus Christ. The French translator, Constantin Andronikoff, pointed out that the phrase occurs frequently in the Orthodox liturgy and goes back to the third-century text of Methodius of Olympus, *The Symposium, or On Virginity.*[52] The adjective "nevechernii" translated as "unfading" literally means "no-evening," i.e., the light does not fade away but retains its radiance throughout. The Russian word for light used here, "svet," can also mean "world," so that in a sense Bulgakov affirms the enduring survival of both the material and the immaterial worlds. An interest in words and their multiple levels of meaning is characteristic of much Silver Age literature, especially Symbolist poetry; while Bulgakov is far from being a poet, he too values the fluid meanings that words may have, and he chooses his vocabulary carefully with this in mind. Form too preoccupied artists of the Silver Age. Though we know that Florensky chose a florid typeface for his *The Pillar and Ground of the Truth* as well as the azure blue cover to represent Sophia, Bulgakov's book does not exhibit a similar concern; nevertheless, three distinct levels of text are marked by three corresponding font sizes — the main argument in normal-size font, detailed lengthy explanatory sections in a smaller font, and footnotes in an even smaller font — so that as he suggests, the reader can choose to ignore the information in the two

Translator's Introduction

smaller fonts without losing the train of thought. This convention seems to have been used by many scholars of Bulgakov's generation, but the modern reader familiar with electronic information technologies will be reminded of links to hypertexts in online documents.

What immediately strikes readers of this book is the astonishing critical breadth of Bulgakov's reading in theology. He was among the first to study the writings of Maximus the Confessor and Gregory Palamas and develop their insights in a productive manner for contemporary theology. Palamas's distinction between the essence and the energies of God is an important precursor for what he himself will say about Sophia in this book and beyond it.[53] But not just the Greek Fathers and the Byzantine tradition underlie his thought; in addition to his erudition in German idealism, Bulgakov is also extremely well read in the Western theological tradition from Augustine onwards, in its mainstream and what may be considered its more esoteric branches. The latter is represented by the Cabbala, Johannes Scotus Eriugena, Meister Eckhart, Jacob Böhme, Angelus Silesius, and John Pordage, all of whose writings Bulgakov mines for veins of ideas that will enrich his own thinking about the central theme of the book, which could be described as the interrelationship of God, the world, and human beings. Cosmology and anthropology are thus important features of this book, and Bulgakov will continue to write about them for the remainder of his scholarly career.

In the lengthy Introduction Bulgakov begins the book with an exploration of the nature of religious consciousness. At the heart of this discussion is the elementary understanding of religion, derived etymologically, as "the identification of God and the experience of a bond with God."[54] In religious experience a bond or connection is established between a human being and the Divine by which one gains certain knowledge of Divine truth. Rational speculation about God remains just that — speculation. Bulgakov offers some lyrical descriptions of his own experiences of the Divine that brought him to appreciate the reality beyond the merely material world and informed his own subsequent spiritual development. All the admirable intellectual efforts to understand religion and religious experience are futile if they ignore or lack an experience of the Divine. He writes, "If people of faith started to tell their own story, what they have seen and come to know with ultimate reliability, a mountain would be formed under which the hill of skeptical rationalism would be buried and hidden from sight.

Translator's Introduction

Skepticism cannot be defeated to the end, for doubt is its element; it can only be reduced to nothing. God is able to annihilate it with his revelation and it is not for us to determine his path or to explain why and when he is revealed. But we know for certain that he can and does do this."[55] Religion is possible because the Divine makes itself known to the human being who recognizes it and exclaims "You exist."

The First Section deals with Divine Nothing. The choice of this term for God is very significant, for as much as through religious experience a person can have certain knowledge of God's presence, God is ultimately unknowable and beyond human comprehension. In light of later criticisms of Bulgakov's theological corpus, it is important to bear in mind that the first major statement he makes about God is apophatic. It is true that he makes a great many positive statements about God, because he believes that religious experience and the nature of the human intellect enable and indeed require us to state what we know of God; however, the first and most important thing we know of God is the Divine Nothing, i.e., that we do not know God. Bulgakov provides a detailed survey of the historical development of negative theology from Plato to Kant before arriving at a dialectical interpretation of Nothing and the contributions of Plotinus, Eriugena, and Böhme. Very important for an understanding of Bulgakov's method and further discussion is his exposition of the fundamental antinomy of religious experience. The Absolute is utterly transcendent to the world and yet in religious experience it is revealed in the Immanent. The Absolute as absolute stands outside any possible conceptualization and yet exists in relation to something Other than it. In revealing itself, the Absolute becomes God, so that the human being can know the Absolute as God and yet remain entirely ignorant of the Absolute as absolute. In other words, the Absolute is relative.

In the Second Section Bulgakov picks up the thread of God as a relational being and looks at what is not God, namely, the World. The World exists as both a creaturely entity and a Sophianic creature. The creaturely nature of the world is known intuitively, through an inner voice that tells the creature "you do not have the root of your being in yourself, you are created."[56] Creation comes about through the free and uncaused sacrifice of the Absolute's absoluteness for the sake of the other, the world. Such an act is a voluntary sacrifice of selfless love, and thus Bulgakov maintains that the world is created not only by God's omnipotence and wisdom but also by Divine sacrificial love.[57]

This discussion of the intuition of creatureliness leads Bulgakov to reflect on creaturely Nothing, and the doctrine of creation ex nihilo of Christian revelation. Bulgakov then considers creation out of nothing from a slightly different angle in order to establish the Sophianic nature of the world. The very essence of God is Love, which has the name Sophia. Love is directed towards some other, and although the Divinity is complete and full in itself, it goes out of itself in a free gift of love to what is not itself, to the non-Divine, in the act of creating. God externalizes the inner Trinitarian love and loves what has been externalized. The object of God's love is Sophia, but Sophia is also the love of love and thus has personal and hypostatic qualities. Since the world is brought into being from nonbeing by Divine Love and in Divine Love, and since Sophia is Divine Love, creation is said to be accomplished in Sophia. This extra-Divine world exists alongside Divinity, simultaneously separated and united with it, like a boundary or border that is neither God nor world, neither Creator nor creature.[58] Sophia is that boundary, "occupying the place *between* God and the world."[59] What or who Sophia is remains only impressionistically defined in this book, but more definition is achieved in the later dogmatic trilogies and in the small book *Sophia the Wisdom of God*. In the present case, Sophia is first of all the Holy Wisdom of Scripture; she is the Eternal Feminine of Goethe and Romanticism; she is absolute and relative, eternal and temporal, divine and creaturely. As Bulgakov himself states, "With her face turned towards God, she is his Image, Idea, Name. Turned towards nothing, she is the eternal foundation of the world, Heavenly Aphrodite, as Plato and Plotinus called her in a true presentiment of Sophia. She is the empyrean world of intelligible, eternal *ideas*, which was revealed to the philosophical and religious contemplation of Plato who confessed it in his doctrine that truly is a sophiology. The created world exists, having as its foundation the world of ideas, which illuminates it; to put it differently, *it is sophianic*."[60] The section concludes with a consideration of matter and corporeality, and the nature of evil.

Having dealt with the nature of the World, Bulgakov turns to the Human Being in the Third Section of the book. If religion concerns the bond between God and what is not God, and if the World itself by virtue of its creaturely status and sophianic nature exists in a bond with its Creator, the fullest expression of that bonding comes in the fullest realization of the creaturely world, the Human Being. Here Bulgakov explores some of the traditional doctrines of Christian anthropology,

Translator's Introduction

viz. the creation of the First Adam as the image of God, the divine likeness, the fall, the incarnation of the Second Adam, and the salvation of humankind. He offers an interesting interpretation of the meaning of sex and sexual differentiation, including the "third sex," no doubt as a response to the disintegration of traditional sexual standards among many of the intelligentsia with whom he associated. This is a topic that resurfaces in *The Burning Bush* and later volumes of his dogmatic trilogies. Another interesting idea that was already broached in the Introduction concerns the possibility of finding Divine truth outside the bounds of the Christian Church, in paganism. Bulgakov devotes considerable space to a subsection on human history, but in fact here he returns to the question of economy once again, this time unraveling the connections between economy, art, and theurgy. He then turns to look at the nature of power, society, and the end of history. In these reflections, Bulgakov refines his earlier views about political authority and the responsibilities of citizens in creating what we might call a just society on Christian and specifically Orthodox principles. This subsection may be a response to Tolstoy's lengthy contemplation of history and power that concludes *War and Peace*.

"The goal of history leads *beyond* history to the 'life of the future age,' whereas the goal of the world leads *beyond* the world, to 'a new earth and a new heaven.' Only in the kingdom of glory, when time ceases, will the goal of the universe come true, while the whole present day is only the pangs of birth. Humankind and every creature will rise in Christ and in him will realize their nature. Only then will the creation of the world be ended, completed by God's omnipotence on the foundation of creaturely freedom."[61] With these words Bulgakov begins his conclusion to the entire work. Briefly and incisively Bulgakov deals with traditional themes of Christian eschatology — hell as a place of torment for unrepentant sinners, heaven as the place of glory for the righteous, the meaning of bodily suffering, the Last Judgment. But much like the great third-century theologian Origen, who felt himself obligated as a member of the church to propose possible interpretations of doctrines as yet undefined, so here and throughout the book Bulgakov offers new ways of looking at old beliefs. Fuller elaboration has to wait until the completion of his two dogmatic trilogies; but the fundamental optimism and joy that runs through all of Bulgakov's theological writings is already in evidence here at the end of *Unfading Light*, expressed as hope for the final salvation of all people and the whole universe, when God will be all in all.

Translator's Introduction

In his preface, Bulgakov described the book as a type of spiritual autobiography or confession in which his lengthy and complicated spiritual journey comes to light. On every page one senses the intellectual and spiritual contest that Bulgakov is going through as he fights his way from the limitations of his own personal history to the freedom of limitless possibilities in the Church. It is tempting to understand this final section of the book as his personal appropriation of the words of Christ from the cross: "It is accomplished." The book is finished, and he has reached the end of his former life; what follows is resurrection and new life.

From the Author

In these "miscellanies,"[1] I would like to display in philosophical thought or to incarnate in speculation some religious contemplations connected with a life in Orthodoxy. Although a task such as this overwhelms by its excessiveness, it also takes possession of the soul with importunity. And such a project does not limit itself to literature; it presupposes a creative act of the spiritual life: a book, but no longer a book, not only a book! Only with the edge of the soul do we touch the life of the Church, burdened as we are by sin, darkened by "psychologism," but even out of such contacts we derive strength that enlivens and renders creativity fruitful. In the light of religious experience, no matter how negligible its measure, "this world" is beheld and evaluated with its anxieties and questionings:

> O Lord! Our path runs between rocks and thorns,
> Our path lies in gloom. You, Unfading Light,
> Fill us with your radiance! (A. S. Khomiakov, *Vesper Songs*)

This light is pursued meagerly and glimmers weakly in the soul through a dark cloud of sin and perturbation; the path through the present towards Orthodoxy and back is difficult. However, can and ought one be liberated from every difficulty? However passionately I may thirst for great simplicity, for its white beam, so do I disavow a false, self-deceptive simplification, this flight from spiritual fate, from my historical cross. And only as a seeker after the religious unity of life, pursued but not found, do I appear in this book. Even if the spiritual essence of the present is ulcerated by problems and perforated with doubts, still in its heart faith does not grow scarce and hope still shines. And it seems that in this agonizing complexity is hidden its religious possibility, a special task is given, proper to historical maturity, and all our problems with their presentiments and portents are the shadow cast by the One Who Comes. To be aware of oneself with all one's historical flesh in Orthodoxy and through Orthodoxy, to comprehend its everlasting truth through the prism of the present, and to see the latter in its light — such is the burning unavoidable need that has been felt patently since the nineteenth century, and the farther one goes the more acute it becomes.

The ideas guiding this philosophizing are united not in a "system," but in a certain *syzygy*, an organic articulation, a symphonic connection. From such a philosophical-artistic plan are demanded, on the one hand, faithfulness and precision of self-reflection in the description of religious experience, in the exposition of "myth," and on the other hand the finding of a corresponding form that is sufficiently supple and capacious for its disclosure. But even when these conditions are present the inner rhythms of thought, its melodic design and counterpoint, the characteristics of the separate parts of a composition remain hard to catch: the philosophical art is among the least accessible arts. This has to be said even about Plato, who showed unattainable models of philosophical poetry in his dialogues, where truth is not so much demonstrated as its genesis is shown. Of course such artistry is not only the inalienable property of the philosophical muse of Plato; in general it is connected with a definite style of philosophizing. Russian religious philosophy also instinctively and consciously seeks such a style, and for it this search is dictated not by exactingness but by inner necessity, by its own type of musical imperative.

In connection with the general plan, the purely investigative part in the exposition is reduced to a minimum: the author consciously waives any aspiration for exhaustive completeness of the bibliographical and scholarly apparatus. The attention of the reader is drawn only to such pages in the history of thought that are of direct importance for the more detailed exposition of the author's own ideas (although with this, of course, care is taken so that there are no substantial omissions in the episodic exposition). In the interests of legibility and the orderliness of exposition two scripts are introduced in the book, with the historical-literary excursuses and comparisons being printed in a

From the Author

smaller font, and they can even be omitted when reading without tearing to pieces the whole cloth of the idea.

This book was written slowly and with lengthy interruptions (from 1911 to 1916), and was already coming to its end under the thunder of the world war. For the humanist worldview, triumphally asserted in "modernity," this war was in truth a spiritual catastrophe, unexpected and devastating. It smashed the dilapidated tablets and overturned commonly venerated idols. By contrast, the religious perception of the world had an inner inkling of the catastrophe as something that was approaching together with the ripening of the harvest of history. In any case events of late have not compelled us to reexamine or change in any substantial way the fundamental lines of the worldview, beliefs, and aspirations that are reflected in this book; indeed they lend them an even greater definition and tragic pathos. The immensity of what is happening is not gaining a hold in the immediate consciousness of participants, and the ordinary "diurnal" consciousness with its attachment to "place" is directly opposed (and in its own manner even rightfully) to the catastrophic feeling of life. Only insofar as we succeed in religious contemplation in rising above our empirical limitedness and weakness do we sense the coming of great eves, the approach of historical completions. "When the branches of the fig tree become soft and send out leaves you know that summer is near" (Matt. 24:32). Historical time has grown dense, and the pace of events is becoming all the more swift. Not by external signs but by the stars rising in the spiritual sky, by inner sight, do we need to get our bearings in this thickening darkness, cut through by ominous flashes of lightning. And if to some it can seem inappropriate in a time of a worldwide earthquake to be occupied with such "abstractions," then to us, on the contrary, a sharpening of the ultimate questions of religious consciousness represents something of a spiritual mobilization for war in the highest, spiritual realm, where external events are being prepared and are also being resolved in advance in a significant measure. In particular that clash of the Germanic ethos with the Orthodox Russian world, which has revealed itself now outwardly, has been coming to a head for a long time; the spiritual war did not begin only now. A hot dry wind has long been blowing towards us from the Germanic West, carrying withering sand, covering the Russian soul with an ashy shroud, damaging its normal growth. This wind, which became perceptible since Peter hacked out his window to Germany, grew menacing towards the beginning of this century. And of

From the Author

course what was more substantial here was not the external "preponderance" of Germany but its spiritual influence, for which its distinctive refraction of Christianity through the prism of the Germanic spirit became defining. This is Arian Monophysitism, ever becoming more subtle and assuming different forms: "immanentism" and "monism" — from Protestantism to the socialist deification of humanity. And for the sake of a conscious opposition it is necessary first of all to know and understand the menacing element, so multifaceted and creatively mighty. Luther, Bauer, A. Ritschl, Harnack; Eckhart, J. Boehme, R. Steiner; Kant and his epigones, Fichte, Hegel, Hartmann; Haeckel, Feuerbach, K. Marx, J. Chamberlain — All of these streams of the Germanic ethos diverging so importantly among themselves, have in "immanentism," however, a common religious basis. So weakly sensed in it is the distance between the Creator and the creation that in a fateful manner it comes close to making the world and humankind into a deity of various nuances and manifestations. But at the same time all this is nothing other than a multifaceted sectarianism of *a Western* type, religiously relative and to a certain degree equivalent in its tonality to our Russian Khlysty [Flagellants].[2] The latter represents an ever-lurking temptation of Orthodoxy and in this sense an apparently normal deviation from it to the side of the mystical deification of humanity, "Christism," i.e., also Monophysitism. If the Western, Germanic sectarianism is conceived and cultivated in *diurnal* consciousness and therefore on the whole suffers from intellectualism, then Russian sectarianism builds its nest in *nocturnal* subconsciousness, its element is hostile to rationality — foreign to intellectualism; in it is revealed the depth of chaos, the primordial abyss, known from of old by the east. And voices so dissimilar and yet religiously consonant call out mysteriously to one another: the thesis and antithesis of sectarianism.

Sectarianism is seduced by the divinity of the world and humankind: anthropology is replaced by anthropolatry, prayer by rapture or meditation, the eye of faith by the intellect, sacrament by ecstasy, religion by mysticism. And yet there is here a dialectically justified stage of religious self-knowledge, although to linger over it and establish oneself in it alone means to fall into religious reaction, in which mystical twilight gathers. In it the ultimate manifestation of the sect's human-god is prepared and ripens, and he must enter into open rivalry with the God-human: little by little this "music of the future" is already being heard. But these pretensions of "gnosis," inasmuch as it wants to substitute for itself the triunity of faith, hope, and love, must be opposed with the greatest resoluteness by the humility of believing love, which alone "will never end, even though prophecies are cut short, tongues fall silent and knowledge is set aside" (1 Cor. 13:8).

And yet the pantheistic truth of "immanentism" must not simply be rejected. Orthodoxy does not consist in denying the world in its authenticity but rather in making the *center* of being human a heart turned towards God and enflamed with prayer, and not autonomous thinking or self-affirming will. Outside this center the world ceases to be the cosmos, the creation and revelation of God, but becomes the instrument for the tempter, a seductive idol. World-denial, with which an insensitivity for history is connected, unfortunately steals altogether easily into Orthodox consciousness, by forming in it too its inclination towards Monophysitism (transcendentalism) or by bringing it closer to the dualism of Manichaeism (Bogomilism). Its antithesis — "immanentism" — is dialectically justified precisely by the presence of such an inclination. To unite the truth of the one and the other, to find not a "synthesis" but a vital unity, in lived experience to know God in the world and the world in God, this is the ultimate task of religious consciousness posed by its history. But before there is a new revelation a new human being is born who hunts for it, whose creativity is the will for this revelation. The paths of this revelation must not be closed, and yet the obedience of faith, the Orthodoxy of the fathers, must be kept ascetically. Is it possible? Is not our spirit split apart by this? Is it not doomed to an interminable decrepitude, to being divided into two, to Hamletism? Is this not simply indecision, standing at a crossroads? We do not have *our own* answer to these reproaches; one cannot even be given *by human* powers, but what is impossible for humans is possible for God. Faith and hope speak to us of miracle, i.e., of a new revelation, a creative act of God in humankind. And we fix our intense gaze on the surrounding gloom. The blacker the shadows fall, gripping the orphaned, weak soul; the deeper the cracks furrow the dried-out earth; all the more obviously does the church leave the historical horizon for the sands of the desert. But all the more frenziedly does the groaning howl burst out of the heart: Yes, come! Command the waves, help the drowning man! Not to us, not to us, but to your name give glory! And in reply are heard in the heart the vows that do not lie, and bowed heads "are raised up." Let these pages too, this lackluster record of great portents, be cast like a letter in a caulked bottle into the raging abyss of history.

From the Author

For the author personally, this book is a type of spiritual autobiography or confession. It is the generalizing comprehension, the sum total, as it were, of *everything* that I have gone through, that spiritual path so broken and complex — too complex! I behold it gratefully here. In the evening hour of life "the bright and morning star" rises calmly on the spiritual horizon and the distant ringing of bells from the temple of never-setting Light can be heard. But the day still wearies with sweltering heat, the rocky trail rises steeply in the mountain, and the road ahead looks difficult . . .

December 1916
Moscow

INTRODUCTION

The Nature of Religious Consciousness

I. How Is Religion Possible?

For the contemporary philosopher who is well versed in "the transcendental method," the meaning of this question ought to be clear, a question that until now, as strange as it may seem, has almost never been posed in transcendentalism. Its formulation initially has in mind an exclusively critical analysis of religious consciousness, the disclosure of premises, judgments, and categories — in a word, everything that is given in this consciousness is apparently presupposed in it and cannot be removed from it. It is therefore a question here of the formal or so to say "transcendental" nature of religion and not of any other content of religious notions; further, it does not deal with the psychological side of religion but with the conditions of the objective meaningfulness of its content, in relation to which psychology is only the milieu, the situation, the actual presence.

The problem of religion, posed "transcendentally," perhaps all the more opportunely leads into a philosophy of religion, being a complete analogy with the fundamental problems investigated in Kant's three critiques. The question that is raised in the *Critique of Pure Reason* is: How is science possible as objective, generally meaningful knowledge, if of course it is possible? Its very existence is established solely by virtue of fact, namely by the presence of mathematical science from which Kant famously "took his cue." Newton undoubtedly was the actual premise for Kant's doctrine of science, and the general question about the possibility of science for Kant was formulated concretely as

Introduction

follows: How is Newton possible if and insofar as he is possible? In answering this purely analytical and critical question, Kant established, so it seemed to him (and to many to this day), the basis for generally meaningful judgments for science, and in his doctrine of experience he attempted to fashion armor that protects against skepticism, the actual conditions of cognition being elevated by him to the class of fundamental, categorial syntheses.

The very fact of science precedes analysis and provides the material for it (critique always arrives *post factum*), but it strives to remove from this fact that which in it is factual, genetic, psychological, and to detach from it that which forms in it a cognitive schema, meaningfulness, sense; in other words, critique considers fact only as *the place of category* or a special case of categorial synthesis. The establishment of categories and their investigation, valuation, and systematization comprises the task of critique but it is by no means capable of generating from itself any sort of fact whatsoever, springing up only by reason of the fact. And strictly speaking, *outside* the relation to this fact its conclusions lose their applicability and general meaningfulness. Kant's schemas are valid for characterizing not the human being in general with all the inexhaustible fullness of its spirit, but only the "scientific human," i.e., only one side of this spirit and its activity.

Our question appears even more analogous to the content of the *Critique of Practical Reason,* which strives to feel out a rational skeleton of ethical experience or to establish a logic of ethics. The actual conditionality of Kant's *second* critique is even more obvious than it was in the first case, for here it is a matter not of cognition, the logic of which seems for everyone more or less compulsory, but of the direction of the will whose nature consists in freedom. Ethics exists only for the one who wants to be ethical, but it is absolutely not written for *insanitas moralis* or for sanctity either, i.e., for all those who find themselves on the other side of good and evil, above or below ethics. Consequently the transcendental characteristic of ethical judgment is part and parcel of the fact of ethics, which can be considered according to its objective meaningfulness or sense, but it can be treated as simple psychologism admitting for itself only a causal or genetic interpretation. If ethical judgments do not have the actual compulsoriness of science or the logical compulsoriness of mathematics, then all those gnoseological, metaphysical, and religious conclusions that Kant draws on the basis of an analysis of ethical experience ("practical reason") are deprived of independent foundation and are supported by ethical intuition. Freedom infiltrates and undermines the hard ground of logical necessity on which Kant strove to erect a dam against skepticism and intuitivism in his *Critique of Pure Reason*.

Our problem has its closest proximity to the content of Kant's *third* critique, namely the analysis of aesthetical judgment, enveloped in an excessively scholastic form that does not correspond to its subject. How is "Geschmacksurtheil," the identification of beauty and the judgment about it possible, of course, so far as it is possible and so far as beauty is accessible to us? What are the inalienable properties of aesthetical judgment? It is obvious that if with a certain logical lawfulness it is possible to negate the compulsoriness of ethics as being rooted in free will, then it is entirely natural to call into question a generally meaningful aesthetics and the objective character of beauty. A huge number of people remain seemingly blind from birth or sound asleep in the realm of beauty, while others deny the objective meaning of beauty, reducing it to the caprice of taste, to pure subjectivism or "psychologism"; a huge number of people are capable of getting bored in front of the "Sistine Madonna" and with Beethoven, and delight in cheap oleography and a sugary waltz. Even if this does not diminish the sovereign nature of beauty and ought not to influence the appreciation of it for those in the know, an element of actual conditionality, of intuitiveness, is of course introduced by this into the transcendental analysis of a sense of beauty. In this sense, the pages that Kant devotes to the analysis of aesthetic feeling symptomatically number among his most interesting pages, because here with full clarity the insufficiency of his rationalism comes to light. Aesthetic feeling is recognized by Kant as "a completely indefinable path of logical proofs *(Beweisgründe)* as if it were only subjective" (*Kritik der Urtheilskraft*, Reclam, 145), and at the same time it lays claim to objectivity and the general meaningfulness of its estimations, which then leads Kant to pose the question: "How are synthetic judgments possible *a priori* in the realm of aesthetics?" Artistic taste therefore becomes for Kant *"Vermögen"* and is considered as a faculty analogous to reason for evaluating *a priori* the communicability *(Mittheilbarkeit)* of feelings that are connected with a given representation (without the instrument of a concept) (160).

But Kant's aesthetic theory does not really interest us here and neither do the principles of the *Critique of the Power of Judgment*. We note only the distinctive use of the transcendental-analytical method which it receives here in the hands of its creator, and especially the extended understanding of it, in view of which it is presented with the task of disclosing the conditions not only of scientific and ethical meaningfulness but also of aesthetical meaningfulness, the analysis of these aspects of consciousness leading not to a subjective-psychological but to a transcendental plane. A transcendental *a priori* is that which is present in any performance of a given activity of consciousness, without which it is in general impossible, namely, not from the aspect of matter or content, but of form or category. The transcendental problem of religion can be posed with the same right as that concerning science, ethics, and aesthetics. The analysis of religious consciousness is bound to reveal the transcendental nature of religion, having unmasked the categories of religious consciousness, and established "synthetic judgments *a priori*" here (as Kant would express it). The question "How is religion possible?" comes to this. In order to pose this question legitimately in the transcendental sense one need not decide beforehand the question about the character of religion and its given content; it suffices merely to have been able to pose the same *if* with respect to religion as is implied with respect to science, ethics, and aesthetics: if it exists. For the transcendental analysis of religion the conditional supposition or assumption of its existence is enough. It is scarcely possible even in our skeptical age to repudiate this modest assumption in advance and *a priori*. Religion is such a universal fact of human life that it is impossible for anyone simply to deny it; if some say that religion in the present day cannot be considered as something proper to all humanity in the same measure, one can surely not forget that this same argument can to a greater degree be applied to aesthetics, ethics, and even science.

Another consideration offers a more probable basis for a skeptical attitude with respect to how the transcendental problem of religion is formulated, to the possibility of a special *fourth* "Critique." One can dispute the autonomous and prototypal quality of religious consciousness, by acknowledging for religion only a heteronomous existence as a derivative attribute or by seeing in it only a transient step in the development of consciousness. An example of just such an attitude is the same Kant who did not include a special "critique of the power of religious judgment" among his systematically planned critiques which, in keeping with his thought, were to investigate all basic directions and exhaust the whole content of consciousness; whereas it is well known that a transcendental description of religion is hidden by him in all three of his critiques.[1] And this is because he did not see in religion an independent realm of the spirit and did not consider religious consciousness to be an entirely special, distinctive element of consciousness in general, but regarded religion exclusively on the plane of ethics, considering it apparently as the music of morality and perhaps its completion. According to Kant, outside of ethics religion does not have and could not have a particular existence; religiousness independent of morality, the immediate reverence of God connected with positive religion, is invariably branded by Kant as "Abgötterei, Fetischmachen, Afterdienst" [Idolatry, fetishism, and pseudo-worship], etc. (see, for example, *Die Religion innerhalb der blossen Vernunft*, Reclam, 193, and *passim*), and in his opinion only the restriction of understanding religion by the limits of pure morality preserves theology from turning into "theosophy or demonology," and "religion into theurgy or idolatry" (*Kritik der Urtheilskraft*, Reclam, 358). Religion outside its moral treatment seems to him to be idolatry — "Abgötterei."[2] Such doctrinal prejudice against the independent treatment of the essence of religion and this dogmatic intolerance with respect to religion, of course, constitute the personal peculiarity of Kant and have no firm support beneath them even in his own philosophizing. In his attitude to the general problem of religion Kant was blinded and hypnotized by his own religious doctrine and thus could not dedicate to the transcendental investigation of this problem that attention which the logic of transcendentalism and simple consistency would have demanded of him. Kant of course is not the only one for whom doctrinal prejudice closes the eyes to the independent problem of religion. Without speaking of the numerous representatives of blind, fanatical atheism, whose practical relationship with religion is expressed in hatred towards it *(écrasez l'infâme),* in the first place one ought to name here the representatives of German idealism, Fichte (of the period of the Atheism controversy) and Hegel, who equally cast religion down from its rightful place and subjugated it to ethics[3] or philosophy. Particularly indicative in this regard is Hegel, for whom religion designates only a step, and not even the highest, in the self-consciousness of the spirit, and thus it is overcome in philosophy.

In order to pose the transcendental problem of religion one needs only to have no prejudice, either metaphysical or speculative, dogmatic or empirical: one needs to look at life with open, simple eyes and allot to the universal-historical fact of religion that attention which naturally belongs to it, if only because of its prevalence.

Introduction

And, first of all, what is religion? In what is the uniqueness of religious experience expressed? What is the quality of *the religious generally speaking*? When answering these questions, in those numerous definitions of religion that are made in religious-philosophical literature, the attempt is made in the majority of cases to establish these or other features (or tasks) of true religiousness, in other words, to express a normative judgment about that which must or can be religion in its most perfect form. On the contrary, our manner of posing the question pursues for the present the purely formal goals of a so-called transcendental analysis of religion. We wish to establish those features without which religion is impossible and *religious* consciousness perishes, consequently those that constitute it. We strive to disclose — *sit venia verbo* [pardon the expression] — the basic categories of religious judgment. The direction in which we ought to search for such a definition is already given in the word itself that expresses the fundamental essence of religion and contains therefore a summary idea about it: *religio* — *religare* — bond, to bind, to unite. In religion a *bond* is established and experienced, the bond of the human with that which is higher than the human. At the basis of a religious relationship lies therefore a fundamental and irremovable *dualism:* in religion, no matter what its concrete form may be, there are always two principles, two poles. Religion (as Feuerbach correctly remarked) is always a bifurcation of the human with himself, his relation to himself as to another, a second, not-one, not-single, but bound, united, correlative. In religion the human is aware of being seen and known before he has known himself, but at the same time he is conscious of himself as remote and torn away from that blessed source of life with which he strives to restore the bond, to establish religion. And so in the most general form one can give this definition of religion: religion is the recognition of God and the experience of a bond with God. If one were to translate this religious formula into the language of philosophy, it would receive this expression: religion is the experience of the transcendent which has become immanent, preserving however its transcendence, the experience of the transcendent-immanent. One need not fear the logical contradiction of these indications, for that which is expressed by them is more pliant and plastic in its living process than are angular, immobile logical definitions. However, here there is no option on the path of precise transcendental analysis — in religion unavoidably has to deal with this conjugation of contradictory logical poles, with their mutual repulsion and constant attraction. In the categories of religion the transcendent-immanent is the basic formal concept in which the bond with the divine is realized. Such is the common human understanding of religion, *communis opinio gentium,* such is its "transcendental" definition, which we are required to analyze further.

In order to affirm its distinctive nature (and not to be only the music of ethics or an immature, incomplete philosophizing) religion must possess its own special organ. Religious experience must differ qualitatively from the closely related and contiguous domains of the life of the spirit. Religion must have as it were its own special logic, establish its own credibility (as is the case for the sense of beauty, an organ of aesthetic perception); it must have the eye of noetic knowing that penetrates higher reality where neither the mental nor physical eye reaches. Religious experience assures the human being of the reality of another, divine world, not so as to demonstrate its existence or by various conclusions to convince him of its necessity, but so as to lead him to a living, immediate bond with religious reality, and show it to him. Only the human being who really has encountered divinity on his life's journey, who has been overtaken by it and on whom it has been poured out with its prevailing force has embarked on an authentically religious path.[4] Religious experience in its immediacy is not scientific, philosophical, aesthetic, or ethical, and in the same way as it is impossible to know beauty with the mind (one can only think about it) so too only a pallid representation of the scorching fire of religious experience is given by thought. In order to comprehend religion, to fathom the *specificum* of the religious in its distinctiveness, one needs to study the life of those who are *geniuses* in religion (just as for aesthetics, surely the laws of beauty are established not by the courses of professors of aesthetics but by the creative works of an artistic genius). The life of saints, ascetics, prophets, and founders of religions and the living monuments of religion — literature, cult, custom, in a word, that which can be called the *phenomenology* of religion — here side by side with the personal experience of each person, is what leads more reliably to cognition in the domain of religion than abstract philosophizing about it.

Calls and Encounters (from an account of a conversion)

I was in my twenty-fourth year, but already for almost ten years faith had been undermined in my soul and after some stormy crises and doubts religious emp-

Introduction

tiness reigned. My soul began to forget religious anxiety, the very possibility of doubts was extinguished, and from a bright childhood there remained only poetic daydreams, the gentle haze of reminiscences always ready to melt away. O, how dreadful is this sleep of the soul, for it is possible not to awake from it for an entire life! Simultaneously with intellectual growth and scientific development, my soul was irrepressibly and imperceptibly submerged in the sticky mud of smugness, self-esteem, banality. A kind of gray twilight set in as the light of childhood was fading away. And then unexpectedly this happened. . . . Mysterious calls resounded in my soul and it rushed to meet them. . . .

Evening was falling. We were traveling across the southern steppe, covered with the fragrance of honey-colored grass and hay, gilded with the crimson of a sublime sunset. In the distance the fast-approaching Caucasus Mountains appeared blue. I was seeing them for the first time. And fixing my avid gaze on the mountains that had opened before me, drinking in the light and air, I harkened to the revelation of nature. My soul had grown accustomed long ago to see with a dull silent pain only a dead wasteland in nature beneath the veil of beauty, as under a deceptive mask; without being aware of it, my soul was not reconciled with a nature without God. And suddenly in that hour my soul became agitated, started to rejoice and began to shiver: *but what if*. . . if it is not wasteland, not a lie, not a mask, not death but him, the blessed and loving Father, his raiment, his love . . . ? My heart pounded under the sounds of the chugging train and we hurried towards that burnt gold and those blue-gray mountains. And again I struggled to capture the fleeting idea, to hold onto the glistening joy. . . . And if . . . if the holy feelings of childhood, when I lived with him, walked before his face, loved and trembled from my own powerlessness to come closer to him, if my youthful ardor and tears, the sweetness of prayer, my childhood purity, which I ridiculed, spat upon, and befouled, if all of this is truth, and all of that is fatal and empty, blindness and a lie? But is that really possible? Did I not know already from seminary that there is no God? Can there even be any discussion about this at all? Can I even recognize myself in these ideas, without being ashamed of my own pusillanimity, without experiencing a panicked dread before "learnedness" and its Sanhedrin? Oh, I was held captive as in the clutches of "learnedness," that scarecrow set up for the intelligentsia mob, the half-educated crowd, for fools! How I hate you, progeny of half-education, spiritual plague of our days, infecting youths and children! And I myself was infected then, and I spread the same infection around me. . . . The sunset had burned out. It was getting dark. And *that* was extinguished in my soul along with its final ray, as if it had not even been born — from deadness, indolence, and dispiritedness. God was knocking quietly in my heart and it heard that knocking; it wavered but did not open. . . . And God departed. I soon forgot about the capricious mood of the evening in the steppe. And after this I again became petty, vile, and banal, as I had rarely been in my life.

How Is Religion Possible?

But soon *that* began speaking again, already loudly, victoriously, imperiously. And you are there anew, o mountains of the Caucasus! I gazed at your ice glistening from sea to sea, your snow glowing scarlet beneath the morning dawn; those peaks thrust themselves into the sky and my soul melted away from rapture. And what had barely sparkled for a moment only to die away immediately that evening in the steppe now resounded and sang, interlacing in a triumphant, marvelous chorale. Before me the first day of creation blazed. All was clear, all became reconciled, replete with ringing joy. My heart was ready to burst from blessedness. There is no life or death; there is one eternal unmoving *today*. The *nunc dimittis* sounded in my soul and in nature. And an unexpected feeling expanded and strengthened in my soul: of victory over death! I would like to have died that minute; my soul asked for death in sweet languor, in order to proceed joyously, rapturously into what rose, scintillated, and shone with the beauty of the primordial. But there were no words, there was no *Name*, there was no "Christ is risen," sung to the world and the heavenly heights. A measureless and imperious *IT* reigned, and this "It" by the fact of its being, by its revelation, reduced to ashes in that moment all barriers, all the little houses of cards of my "learnedness." And that moment of meeting did not die in my soul; this was her apocalypse, her wedding feast, the first encounter with Sophia. I did not know and did not understand then what this encounter bode for me. Life gave a new turn; the apocalypse began to change into the impressions of a tourist and what I had experienced was covered over with a fine film. But what the mountains told me about in triumphant radiance I soon came to know again in a shy and gentle maiden's glance, on other shores, beneath other mountains. That same light shone in the trustful, frightened, and mild eyes almost of a child, full of the sanctity of suffering. The revelation of love told of another world, which I had lost. . . .

*   *   *

A new wave of ecstasy with the world rolled in. Together with "personal happiness," my first encounter with "the West" and first delights before it: "sophistication," comfort, social democracy. . . . And suddenly an unexpected, miraculous encounter: Sistine Madonna in Dresden, you yourself touched my heart and it began to tremble from your call.

En route we hurry one foggy autumn morning to do what tourists do and visit the Zwinger with its famous gallery. My knowledge of art was perfectly insignificant and I hardly even knew what awaited me in the gallery. And there, into my soul peered the eyes of the Queen of Heaven approaching on clouds with the Pre-eternal Child. They had the measureless *power of purity and insightful sacrificial readiness,* knowledge of suffering and readiness for voluntary suffering, and the same prophetic sacrificial readiness was visible in the ma-

Introduction

ture wise eyes of the Child. They know what awaits them, what they are destined for, and they come freely to surrender themselves, to accomplish the will of the One who sent them: She is "to take a sword in the heart"; he goes to Golgotha. . . . I was beside myself, my head was spinning, tears at once joyful and bitter flowed from my eyes, the ice in my heart melted and a kind of knot in my life came undone. This was not an aesthetic emotion, no; it was *an encounter*, new knowledge, *a miracle*. . . . I was still a Marxist then and I involuntarily called this contemplation *a prayer*, and every morning, aiming to find myself in the Zwinger before anyone else, I ran there, "to pray" and to weep before the face of the Madonna; there will be few moments in life more blessed than those tears. . . .

* * *

I returned to my homeland from abroad having lost my footing and already with a broken faith in my ideals. The earth crawled along beneath me irrepressibly. I stubbornly worked with my head, posing "problem" after "problem," but interiorly there was already nothing for me to believe, to live, to love. A gloomy Herzen[5] resignation controlled me. . . . But the more the new gods all betrayed me, the clearer some apparently forgotten feelings rose up in my soul: like heavenly sounds they were only waiting for the spiritual prison, which I had created for myself, to show signs of cracking, in order to burst towards the suffocating prisoner with news of liberation. In all my theoretical strivings and doubts a single motif, one secret hope, now sounded in me all the clearer — the question *What if?* And what began burning in my soul for the first time since the days in the Caucasus became all the more imperious and bright; but the main thing was all the more definite: I did not need a "philosophical" idea of Divinity but a living faith in God, in Christ and the Church. *If* it is true that there is a God, this *means* that everything that was given to me in childhood but which I abandoned is true. Such was the semi-conscious religious syllogism that my soul made: nothing or . . . everything, everything down to the last little candle, the last little icon. . . . And the work of my soul went on nonstop, invisible to the world and unclear even to me. What happened on a wintry Moscow street, in a crowded square, is memorable — suddenly a miraculous flame of faith began burning in my soul, my heart beat, tears of joy dimmed my eyes. In my soul "the will to believe" ripened, the resolution finally to carry through with the leap to the other shore, so senseless for the wisdom of the world, "from Marxism" and every *ism* resulting from it to . . . Orthodoxy. Oh, yes, of course it is a leap, towards happiness and joy; an abyss lies between both shores. *I had to* jump. If afterward it is necessary to justify "theoretically" and give a meaning to that leap for myself and for others, it will require many years of dogged labor in different domains of thought and knowledge, and the whole thing will not be enough, it will be insufficient. But in order to come to believe in a living way, to perceive experientially what enters into Orthodoxy, to return to its "practice," one must still complete a long, long journey, overcome in the self much that stuck onto the soul after years of roaming. I was aware of all this extremely well without losing my soberness for a minute. Nonetheless in essence the question was already decided: from *that* shore I looked at the path lying before me and I was glad to be aware of it. *How* this would be accomplished and when — who could say? Who can say how and when love is born in the soul and bestow on it one's insights? But for some time I knew with complete reliability that this had already happened. And from that time on, a golden chain stretched out in my soul. However, the years passed and I was still languishing behind the fence and did not find in myself the strength to take the decisive step — to approach the sacrament of penance and communion that my soul was thirsting for all the more. I remember how once on Holy Thursday, dropping in on church, I saw (I was then a "deputy") those receiving communion to the stirring sounds of "Of thy mystical supper. . . ." In tears I rushed out of the church and weeping walked along a Moscow street, grown faint from my powerlessness and unworthiness. And so it continued until a strong arm carried me away enraptured. . . .

    Autumn. A lonely, forgotten hermitage in the woods. A sunny day and the familiar nature of the north. Confusion and impotence control my soul as before. Taking advantage of an opportunity I had come here in the secret hope of encountering God. But here my resolution definitively abandoned me. . . . I stood through vespers unfeeling and cold, and after it, when the prayers "for those preparing for confession" began, I almost ran out of the church, "went out, weeping bitterly."[6] In melancholy I walked in the direction of the guest house seeing nothing around me, and I came to my senses . . . in the elder's cell. *It led* me there: I went entirely in another direction as a result of my usual absentmindedness which now was intensified thanks to depression, but in actuality — I knew this then reliably — a miracle happened with me. . . . When the father saw the prodigal son drawing near, he made haste one more time to meet him. From the elder I heard that all human sins are like a droplet before the ocean of divine mercy. I left him then, forgiven and at peace, trembling and in tears, feeling myself borne up inside the churchyard as if on wings. At the gate I met a startled and happy fellow-traveler who had only just seen me leave the church in confusion. He became an involuntary witness of what had happened with me. "The Lord has passed by," he said touchingly then. . . .

    And now it is evening and once again the sun is setting, no longer a southern sunset, but a northern one. In the limpid air the church cupolas appear in sharp outline and the autumn flowers of the monastery stand white in long rows. The woods like banks of clouds recede into the deepening blue distance. Suddenly in the midst of this quiet, from somewhere above, as if from heaven,

Introduction

the church bell chimed, then everything fell silent and only a little later it began ringing out regularly and uninterruptedly. They were ringing for the all-night vigil. As if for the first time, like a newborn, I heard the ringing of the bells, anxiously sensing that the tolling was calling me to the church of the believers. And in the evening of that blessed day, and even more on the following day, after liturgy, I looked at everything with new eyes, for I knew that I too was called and I was really taking part in all of this: for my sake and in my stead the Lord hung on the wood and shed his most precious Blood; for me through the hands of the priest he readies the most holy table; the Gospel reading which recounts the supper in the house of Simon the leper refers to me, as does the reading about the forgiveness of the woman who loved much – the fornicator. And I was granted to taste the most holy Body and Blood of my Lord. . . ."

And so at the basis of religion there is an encounter with Divinity gained in personal experience, and this is the sole source of its autonomy. No matter how the wisdom of this world may preen itself, powerless to understand religion for want of the necessary experience, for its religious vapidity and its deadness, those who have once seen God in their heart possess a completely trustworthy knowledge of religion, and know its essence. The bond between religion and other aspects of the life of the spirit, which undoubtedly exists, does not have a prototypal but a derivative character, not an ontological but a psychological one.

Religion is conceived in the lived experience of God (under whatever appearance this divine revelation may take place). But although he senses God, the human being all the same feels himself in *the world*, in other words, for him a fundamental religious antithesis invariably accompanying religious life is revealed – the juxtaposition of God and the world. As if from a ray of light that fell from the heights and by itself illumined the world from on high, consciousness of the divine world begins to burn in the soul, and at the same time the boundary between the empyrean and the terrestrial is established, separating them but at the same time uniting them. And in this light the world appears in a different way, one receives a completely different taste, a new sensation of being – a perception of the world both remote from God and simultaneously dependent on him. In the human spirit consciousness of the nonabsolute and extra-divine is revealed and consequently, of the relativity and sinfulness of its being, while at the same time the aspiration to be liberated from "the world," to overcome it in

God, is conceived; in other words along with religious self-awareness a feeling of evil, guilt, sin, and of being torn away from God is born in the human being, as is the need for salvation and redemption. To be raised out of the captivity of the world towards God, out of servitude into the kingdom of freedom — every religion awakens such a thirst in the soul, and the deeper the thirst, the loftier and more perfect the religion is. Therefore a religious world perception invariably is accompanied by the familiar disillusionment with this world, by pessimism with respect to its given condition, by that which is sometimes called "world weariness," but at the same time this pessimism is only a shadow that the light of joyous faith casts, promising victory over the world, giving hope of liberation and salvation. The world loses its unconditional quality and its uniqueness: above the world and in the world is God; such is the joyful news of every religion. Hence in general religion — of course, living religion — is the joy of all joys, although it is connected with relative pessimism, an awakening from the sleep of self-satisfaction and world-satisfaction.

Nevertheless, if the conscious need for redemption and salvation psychologically disposes one to religion, as does world-weariness, still by themselves this is not yet religion, just as a question posed, although it presupposes the possibility of a resolution, does not become the answer. For religious self-perception one thing remains decisive: contact with Divinity, faith, "as he is."[7]

The fundamental experience of religion, the encounter with God, possesses (at least at its summits) the sort of conquering power and ardent persuasiveness that leaves every other evidence far behind. One can forget or lose it, but one cannot refute it. The whole history of humanity with respect to its religious self-consciousness turns into some sort of completely irresolvable enigma or simple absurdity if one does not recognize that it rests on living religious experience, i.e., if one does not accept that all peoples somehow saw and knew their deities, knew about them not from "catechesis" alone. In the prophets of Israel we constantly meet such words: *and God said to me*. Have we ever had occasion to ponder these words? Have we tried to understand them, by translating these words even remotely into our own religious experience? "And God said to me!" What is this? Surely not just hallucination, self-deception, charlatanry, or literary device? Or . . . What if it is true . . . what if what is written in these books is true: God spoke and the human being listened, heard . . . God? Of course, he heard not with

Introduction

a physical organ of hearing but with his heart, with his entire being, and the word of God sounded louder than all the thunders of the world, more convincingly and trustworthily than his whole understanding.

From a private letter.... "I do not want to forgive heaven for his sufferings, his crucifixion. How can I forgive what I am unable to understand! And I must not forgive, for God has surely condemned his 'advocates' around Job, who explained everything and debated everything. It seemed to me — and it seems to me now after many years have passed — that God did not want from me an easy reconciliation, for I had to receive a sword in the heart. You are not easy, sacrifice of Abraham! My howl in the face of an innocent victim was wrenched not from a happy but from a harrowed soul: you are just, O Lord, and just are your judgments! But I said this with all my heart! Oh, I did not rebel and did not murmur, for any revolt would have been pitiable and fainthearted, but I did not want to be reconciled, for reconciliation would have been shameful. Father silently answered me: at the head of his body stood the Crucifixion of the Only-begotten Son. And I heard this answer and bowed before him, but innocent sufferings and someone's sarcasm lay like a thick impenetrable cloud between the Crucifixion and his body, and — I know this firmly — here in this cloud is the mystery of my own life too. I knew then that it is very easy, temptingly easy, to endeavor to *forget* about this cloud, to avoid it somehow — since it is unpleasant to carry something in one's soul that is entirely incomprehensible and it is more decent to live in the world with important personages.... Otherwise — only by spiritual struggle, by the cross of my whole life, can I disperse this cloud — it *can* be dispersed, this I also knew reliably, it is the shadow of my own sin, for I myself crucified him with my sins. And he spoke about this to me on that Golgotha night: 'Carry me up, papa, let's go up together!' Oh, let's go, let's go my child, my leader, my teacher, my guardian angel!

"But here begins what cannot be expressed in words....

"My holy one, at the sanctuary of your remains, beside your pure body, my fair one, my radiant boy, I found out *how* God speaks, I understood what 'God spoke' means! In a new and never-before-known clairvoyance of heart, along with the torment of the cross heavenly joy came down into it, and with the darkness of divine abandonment God reigned in my soul. My heart was opened to the pain and torment of people — hearts until then strange and hence closed were exposed before it with their pain and grief. For the only time in my life I understood what it means *to love* not with a human, self-loving, and mercenary love, but with that divine love with which Christ loves us. It was as if the curtain separating me from others fell and all of the gloom, bitterness, offense, animosity, and suffering in their hearts was revealed to me. And in ineffable rapture, frenzy, self-forgetfulness I said then — you will remember this, my fair one — I said: *God spoke to me,* and then hearing you I simply added that *you spoke to me* too. And God was speaking to me then and you were speaking! Oh, now I am living again in gloom and cold, and only by memory am I able to speak about it, but I came to understand what this means: 'God spoke.' Then once and for all I knew that God really does speak and that a man hears and is not reduced to ash. I know now *how* God speaks to prophets. Oh, my radiant angel! This can seem to be madness and self-delusion, abuse and blasphemy, but surely you know that this is not so; I cannot speak falsehood to you. I knew then with ultimate certitude that God spoke to me and thus he spoke to the prophets as well. Oh, he said something different and in another way to the prophets, and they were different — I then knew and sensed an immeasurable abyss between me and them, no less do I know it now. But God is one and his measureless condescension to us is the same; even if between my dark, sinful soul and the holy soul of a prophet there lies a great abyss, still more immeasurable is that abyss which lies between God and every creature — and as a creature I and a prophet are the same thing, and he speaks to the creature. . . . To forget *this* and to doubt *after this* means for me to die spiritually. One can lose one's treasure, be frightened before its defense, but even unworthily cast aside and lost, it is a treasure all the same. . . .

"'I know a man in Christ who was taken up to the third heaven.'[8] Have you read these words? Have you pondered *what* they signify? If this is not delirium or self-deception, if what is written here is true and it happened as written, then what does *this* mean for the one who saw it? With what kind of gaze must he have looked at the world after what was seen, when the heavens opened! . . .

"Oh, my radiant, my fair boy! When we carried you on the steep mountain and then along the hot and dusty road we suddenly turned into a shady park, as if we entered the garden of paradise; after that unexpected turn a church, beautiful like you, which had been waiting for you, immediately looked upon us with its colored windows. I did not know it from before, and like a miraculous vision it appeared before us sunk in the garden under the shadow of an old castle. Your mother fell down with a scream: 'The heavens have opened!' She thought that she was dying and seeing heaven . . . and heaven *was* opened, in it our apocalypse was accomplished. I felt and almost saw your ascension. Oleander pink and white surrounded you like flowers of paradise waiting only to bend over you, to stand guard at your grave. . . . There you have it! Everything became clear, all the torment and sultriness dissolved, disappeared in the heavenly blueness of that church. We thought that events happened only there, below, in the sultriness, and we did not know that this height exists, but it turns out — here we were waiting. . . . And far down below, in the distance, the sultriness, torments, moaning, death remained — and in fact *not this* existed, because that *exists* and is now revealed. . . .

Introduction

"The liturgy was proceeding. I do not know where it took place, on earth or in heaven. . . . 'Escorted invisibly by angelic ranks,' the usual already-familiar sacred words . . . but who is this in the sanctuary on the right . . . can it be heavenly concelebrants? But these dreadful demonic faces, looking at me with such malice unknown to me and exceeding my imagination and . . . also from the sanctuary. . . . But I am not afraid of you for he is ascending to heaven, my fair boy, and you are powerless before his defense, before his light. . . .

"I listen to the 'Apostle' on the resurrection and the universal sudden transformation . . . and for the first time I understand that it will be *so* and *how* it will be.

"Does one need to believe that the liturgy is performed with the ministration of angels when I saw . . . this? Did not the priest Zachariah likewise see an angel around the altar of incense or did not the one serving with the venerable Sergius see an angel performing the liturgy with him (as his vita relates)? But even here is it not impertinent, is it possible to make such comparisons? One must! For, we are not comparing ourselves, not our sinful darkness, but what was seen by divine condescension.

"So this is what that peal was calling me to from the heights which I heard so persistently that summer. You visited us on Christmas Eve, under the peal of bells that were praising Christ who had been born. Your spiritual birth was accomplished on the day celebrating the synaxis of the Baptist, 'the greatest among those born of woman,' the Lord's Forerunner; you belong to his host, heaven's herald. And it seems to me and I believe that at death's bedside with the sorrow of tacit reproach, or with the joy of an eternal meeting, you will become a shining angel of death." . . .

If people of faith started to tell their own story, what they have seen and come to know with ultimate reliability, a mountain would be formed under which the hill of skeptical rationalism would be buried and hidden from sight. Skepticism cannot be defeated to the end, for doubt is its element; it can only be reduced to nothing. God is able to annihilate it with his revelation, and it is not for us to determine his path or to explain why and when he is revealed. But we know for certain that he can and does do this. . . .

Whoever does not allow a special religious attestation and denies a special organ of religious knowledge must come to a halt in astonishment before the universal historical fact of religion, as some kind of general mass hypnosis and insanity.[9] Whoever is unwilling to accept here the uniquely simple and natural (but for some reason metaphysically inadmissible for them) hypothesis of religious realism must contradict it with the theory of mass hallucination and illusion or ... "the invention of priests," *écrasez l'infâme* ... this aim, it seems, justifies every means, but except for the foolish this very means is foolish.

And so in religious experience an immediate contact with other worlds *is given* — and its very essence is in this — a sensation of a higher, divine reality; a sense of God is given, though not in general, *in abstracto*, but precisely for a given human being: the human in himself and through himself discovers a new world before which he trembles from dread, joy, love, shame, repentance. Religion is not only the music of the soul; it does sound for me, but also *outside of* me, above me; it is not subjective but objective, or rather, subjective-objective. Inherent in it is the greater seriousness of realism. Its realism is the main difference of religion from the objectless, subjective, aestheticizing religiosity with which contemporary aestheticizing hyper-refinement is not averse to amuse itself as with a piquant sauce of moods. My religion is not my creation, otherwise it would not be religion at all; it convinces by the power of its immediate credibility, by a different higher persuasiveness than the facts of external reality, e.g., the sensation of this table, of this wall, of this noise. Hence it is impossible to eliminate from religion the reality of God just as it is impossible to eliminate from art objective beauty (which differs as much from prettiness as religion does from religiosity). God *is* — outside me but also for me — far higher than my subjectivity, and yet he communicates with it. This proposition is not only an analytical judgment deduced on the basis of an examination of the concept of religion, but at the same time a religious synthetic judgment *a priori*. YOU ARE — in religion this stands prior to any analysis but at the same time as the object of analysis. In the face of this YOU ARE, this synthetic religious judgment *a priori*, of course, the so-called "proofs for the existence of God" fall silent. They can have a certain significance (whatever that might be) in philosophy, in speculative theology, in general outside the proper domain of religion; in this latter the joyous immediate YOU ARE reigns. On the whole, proofs for the existence of God by their very appearance attest to an approaching crisis in religious consciousness, when for one reason or another the sources of religious inspiration, which is immediately conscious of itself as revelation, run dry or are covered with sand, but that faith which is called upon to say to the mountain "move into the sea" seems to have absolutely no relationship with the proofs. Of course even on purely speculative grounds one should refute the idea of *proofs* for the existence of God, for here, obviously, there is an internal contradiction in the very formulation of the problem: the existence of the absolute which towers above the relative and is free of causality is affirmed by relative notions based on the law of causality and the analysis of causal series. Obviously, we will not encounter God in the field of Kantian experience, for "God is an entirely unnecessary hypothesis for science" (Laplace), and the so-called proofs for the existence of God only lead to a more or less successful postulation of God or to a disclosure from the various aspects of the philosophical concept of God. Religious experience remains the sole path for real, living comprehension of God. YOU ARE, the synthetic religious judgment *a priori*, is the sole support of religion, without which it does not exist, just as art does not exist without beauty or morality without the distinction between good and evil. In the same manner religion becomes independent from ethics, aesthetics, theoretical cognition, philosophy, and science, for it has its own support, its own organ of perception.

But I hear the objection that one is thereby supposing the basis of religion to be "psychologism," a subjective mood, the caprice of imagination to which is attached a transcendental significance. Under the guise of psychologism or logical fetishism, which hypostatizes ideas and moods, religion in our days is frequently shown the door, a formal rejection is issued for it, and it is regarded as finally dissolving into religiosity. There is no satisfactory foundation, however, for this rejection. Religion is psychologism only in the sense that it represents the totality of the facts of psychological life that are realized in a concrete individual psyche. But in this sense absolutely every activity of the spirit can be considered guilty of psychologism. Is not cognition likewise a fact of spiritual life, does not morality have its psychology (more captious criticisms consider morality merely as a psychological fact)? There is nothing easier than "to explain" beauty in the sense of psychologism. And yet, if we apply everywhere a genetic and transcendental examination and distinguish from a fact its sense and meaning, then precisely the same must take place in religion. Here too we distinguish the subjective religious process from its transcendental description and affirm not only the psychological distinctiveness of religion (which would mean to force an open door, for no one denies this at present), but also the independent "faculty of religious judgment." In religion what the human spirit does not comprehend in science, ethics, and aesthetics becomes accessible to it (although each of these taken separately can indicate a path to religion and in fact do this in its own way).

How Is Religion Possible?

Thus, to the preliminary and general question "How is religion possible?" we respond: religion is an immediate recognition of Divinity and the living bond with It; it is possible thanks to the religious endowments of humankind and the existence of a religious organ that perceives Divinity and Its operation. Without such an organ that luxuriant and multicolored development of religion and religions we observe in the history of humanity, and likewise all of its distinctiveness, would, of course, be impossible.[10] Every authentic, living religion knows its own objectivity and rests on it — it deals with Divinity, utters YOU ARE to It; psychologism is only a "religion of mood," i.e., religiosity, which is powerless to rise to the level of religion and shines with the reflected light of something else. GOD is the fundamental content and fundamental "category" of religion.

In order to avoid misunderstanding let us add that for the present we take the concept "divinity, God" in the broadest and most indefinite sense, embracing distinct religions, as a formal category, applied to every possible content. The essential sign establishing the nature of religion is the objective character of its worship, which is connected with the sense of the transcendence of divinity. All historical religions, it seems to us, satisfy this requirement, for such is the nature of religion in general. In this sense the concept of a godless religion contains a *contradictio in adjecto*; it is internally contradictory, for the essence of religion consists precisely in the experiential identification of that which God is, i.e., that above the immanent, given, empirical world a different world transcendent and divine exists, which becomes accessible and perceptible in religion. "Religion in the confines of reason alone" or the immanent religion of subjective idealism is in fact not religion, but only one of its numerous imitations and surrogates.

But I hear the usual objection in such cases: an atheistic religion that affirms as its foundation not God but nonbeing, nothing, is possible and exists, and this religion has worldwide significance and counts hundreds of millions of adherents — Buddhism. It is difficult to judge confidently about Buddhism, so distant and foreign to the Christian world, and in any case it is necessary to distinguish religious practice from theological speculation. It is well known that popular exoteric Buddhism, to which actually this religion owes the breadth of its dissemination, is in no way limited to a single "doctrine of nothingness" but contains in itself elements of concrete polytheism, even fetishism. Beyond this — and this is the most important thing — the Buddhist nothing, nonbeing, nirvana, the all-unity of indifference (*tat twam asi* — this is that) in no way represents only a negative concept but entirely fits our general definition of divinity. For even this nothing is not a perfect zero, but is a positive value in the highest degree: here exactly is understood what exists beneath the veil of maya that only clouds our gaze with the world of phenomena. This positive nothing comprises authentic though for us transcendent reality, with respect to which the religious attitude is typically established. Therefore even this religion is innocent of closed subjectivism, immanentism, and psychologism, no matter how slim its positive doctrine of God might be.[11]

One can also point out that different forms of religious surrogates exist, for example, the religion of progress or of humanity. But even here, insofar as we are dealing with a religious attitude, it is connected precisely with a striving beyond empirical givenness towards some kind of transcendental noumen — the Grand Être of Auguste Comte. One can consider such divinization of a collective concept to be logical fetishism and see in it the lowest level of religious consciousness, but it is impossible to repudiate the religious features inherent in it. Here crude fetishism (extremes meet!) yields a familiar analogy: in a block of wood one honors not the wood but the entity that transcends it, for which the block is in fact a sort of icon.

II. Transcendent and Immanent

A pair of correlative concepts, transcendent and immanent, plays a most substantial role in the definition of religion. These concepts have extraordinarily many meanings; one can expound the whole history of philosophical thought as the history of these concepts or, more particularly, as the history of the problem of the transcendent. In addition, they are correlative: if one pole corresponds to transcendence, immanence is located at the other, and vice versa. Obviously it is necessary to agree beforehand on their meaning. For us the immanent is that which is contained in the confines of a given closed circle of consciousness; that which is found beyond this circle is transcendent or does not exist in its confines. But the transcendent is not nothing, a perfect zero, because otherwise without such a boundary the immanent would not be conscious of itself as immanent, self-enclosed, limited. The transcendent is at the very least a certain frontier domain for the immanent, its boundary. In a certain sense one can consider (gnoseologically) every trans-subjective reality to be transcendent to consciousness: the external world, someone else's I, Mount Elbrus, the Caspian Sea, every unrealized possibility of a new experience. Whatever philosophical refinements this definition may be subjected to, practically, in the immediate feeling of life a certain measure of immanence, actual and potential, is given. Acquiring new impressions from life, be they the Arctic Ocean or the island of Ceylon, Eskimos or Zulus, Brazilian butterflies or crows, the Big Dipper or the sun — in all of this the human perceives himself in an immanent world, one in all its diversity. For him this is *his* world, and therefore the only world for immanent self-consciousness, as the quality-imbued coherence of being. There exists a special cosmic feeling, usually muffled and dimly apprised but which raises its voice at its every irritation. Is this "world" the sole one and is its immanence absolutely closed, or do other "worlds" exist enveloping our immanence with their transcendence and — oh, horror! — bursting into it?

> As the ocean encompasses the earthly sphere
> So earthly life is encircled by dreams . . .
> Night will fall, and with sonorous waves
> The elements beat against their shore.[12]

Are there other worlds? Does the transcendent exist? It is impossible to respond with speculation alone (as usually one is wont to think) or with an immanent experience; one can respond to this only with a new experience, with an expansion and transformation of experience, presupposing of course that our cosmic nature will know by means of a special sense, completely indefinable and reducible to nothing, the domain of a different world "supernatural" for it. The domain of "mysticism" begins here, as does the path of "occultism" or "the science of how to attain cognition of higher worlds" (Steiner). All occultism is the expansion of the immanent into the place of the heretofore transcendent, and by transforming himself a human being becomes an entity of the other world, namely of the one that he comes to know. However, insofar as "spiritual knowledge" is really knowledge, i.e., *the methodical* development of problems, the refinement of observations, the enrichment, improvement, and good ordering of experience, it still has to do with the field of knowledge that is immanent to this world. The "higher worlds" that "spiritual knowledge" teaches us to attain, strictly speaking, are our own world only perceived more broadly and deeply; and no matter how far we may proceed in such cognition it all the same remains within the limits of our world, and is immanent to it.[13] That which is comprehended here, is transcendent only gnoseologically, i.e., in virtue of our limitedness and not according to essence (as trigonometry seems transcendent to us as long as we have not learned it or, rather, until it is awakened in our consciousness: the immanent character of mathematical cognition in this sense was shown with such power already by Plato in his *Phaedo*). On the path of occult knowledge, and in general, of any type of knowledge, with its constant and endless delving deeper into the domain of the divine, it is impossible to encounter God in this world; in this cognition there is an infinity that in the religious sense is bad, i.e., leading away from God, for it does not draw closer to him. Herein lies the profound difference of the occult and the religious paths, which can *in certain conditions* become an opposition; in any case it is impossible to lump them together or substitute them one for the other, as often happens now.

In this manner, although the immanent — "the world" or the "I," the macrocosm and microcosm — likewise has within itself degrees of relative transcendence, of something that has been proposed, but not yet given, nevertheless it is the opposite of the transcendent as such. The transcendent *kat' exochēn* as a religious category[14] does *not* belong to the immanent — to the "world" or the "I" — although it relates to it. There is no path of methodical ascent to it (for the path of religious effort does not have cognition in mind, and is not guided by cognitive *interests*); it is *outside* the proper reach of the human being. One can aspire to it and strain towards it but it is impossible to arrive at it systematically, methodically. The religious path in this sense is necessarily the path of miracle and grace.

God is the Transcendent. He is supernal or supramundane. He is the sole and authentic *Not-I*; inasmuch as *I* (Fichtean) includes everything, the whole world, in itself, he is also *Not-world*, without however this *Not-I* in any way being supposed by our own *I*, as in Fichte, and in this sense it is not some *sub-I* but is the absolute and authentic *Not-I*, i.e., *supra-I, higher-than-I*. One can express this fundamental polarity of religious consciousness, this strained opposition of the transcendent and immanent, in different terms: God and the world, God and nature, God and humankind, God and I, etc. The distance between the world and God is absolute and insurmountable for the world. If it is overcome, then it is so only exceptionally, by interruption, freely, miraculously, and by grace. Any immanence of the Transcendent, the touch of Divinity, is an act truly miraculous and free, an act of mercy and love, but not an act of law and necessity.

God, as the Transcendent, is infinitely, absolutely remote from and alien to the world; there are not and cannot be any naturally determined, methodical paths to him, but precisely therefore he in his condescension becomes infinitely close to us, is the most close, most intimate, most interior, most immanent in us, is found to be closer to us than we are to ourselves.[15] God is outside us and God is in us, the absolutely transcendent becomes the absolutely immanent. Therefore there is not and cannot be any "spiritual knowledge" that leans on *method* for cognition of God (and not only of the divine alone). For before absolute distance, in the face of infinity every finite value and path is annihilated: God can send his angel to Balaam's ass, singe an accursed sinner with the fire and light of his appearance; he can overtake his persecutor on the road to Damascus and nevertheless remain inaccessible to the most intense methodical efforts. For God is Wonder and Freedom, while all knowledge is method and necessity.

By putting it this way we are denying only that a vision of God comes without fail and in conformity with laws for those who seek him. But the quest for God, the preparation of the self, the disclosure of the divine in the self is accomplished by human effort which God expects of us — "the kingdom of God is compelled by force."[16] The whole of asceticism attests to this. It is possible that for a certain epoch of the life of humanity or for a certain spiritual style both philosophy and "spiritual knowledge" turn out to be that kind of preparatory path. However, only the Transcendent recognized in religious experience and existing above the world opens one's eyes to the transcendent in the world; in other words, only an immediate sense of God grants one to see the divine in the world, to come to know the world as a revelation of God; it alone teaches how to grasp the transcendent in the immanent, to perceive the world as the God who is becoming and being revealed. The logic of religious consciousness demands that God be found as the unconditional not-world and the world as the unconditional not-God in order then to see the world in God and God in the world. (Of course, it is a question not of chronological but of transcendental-logical correlation.) One and the same world stands before us at one time like a mechanism, monstrous in its bad infinity, blankly keeping silent about its meaning, at another time like a revelation of the mysteries of Divinity or the source of cognition of God. And cognition of the world — be it natural science (in the broadest, all-embracing sense of the word) or "spiritual knowledge" — in the light of faith in God receives a completely new meaning. The decisive moment remains the encounter with God in the human spirit, the contact of the transcendent with the immanent, the act of faith. *God exists*. This is what resounds in the human heart, the poor, little, puerile human heart; *God exists*, sing heaven, earth, and the world's abysses; *God exists* respond the abysses of human consciousness and creativity. Glory to him!

If the fundamental givenness *of the religious in general* is the transcendent, then *prayer* is the fundamental form of religious achievement *kat' exochēn* [par excellence]. Up until now prayer remains insufficiently understood and valued in its religious-"gnoseological" meaning as the foundation of religious experience. What does prayer represent according to its "transcendental" makeup? First of all, it is the striving of all the spiritual forces of a human being, of the whole human person, for the Transcendent. Every prayer (of course, sincere and ardent, not only external) realizes the command: *transcende te ipsum* [go beyond yourself]. The human makes the effort in prayer to come out of himself, to rise above himself. In prayer the Transcendent becomes the object of human aspiration as such, precisely as God, as something absolutely other, and not the world, not a human being. And at the same time, when a prayer is "heard," when it is ardent and inspired, when its aspiration is attained — it touches the Transcendent, breathes by it, it contains in itself the sufficient, even sole possible attestation of the existence of the Transcendent and of Its condescension to people. It receives the Transcendent as the immanent, by becoming coinherent in the name of God, in which the Transcendent is summoned. The Name of God is as it were the intersection of two worlds, the transcendent in the immanent, and hence beside its common theological sense "name-worship" is in a certain manner the transcendental condition of prayer that constitutes the possibility of religious experience.[17] For God is known experientially through prayer, the heart of which is the invocation of the Transcendent, *naming* him, and he seemingly confirms this naming, acknowledges the name as his, not by simply responding to it but by being really present in it. A religious genius is necessarily an adept of prayer and in essence the whole of Christian asceticism only teaches the art of prayer, having as its highest goal unceasing ("automatic") prayer, the "Jesus prayer," or "mental activity,"[18] i.e., the unceasing striving towards the transcendent Divinity by immanent consciousness. *The Lord prayed*, often and at length, now in a joyous-exultant manner (I glorify You, Father of heaven and earth), now in an intense-agonizing manner (the prayer in Gethsemane), and he taught the Lord's Prayer to his disciples (as John had taught his own). The thunderous fact of prayer — in Christianity and in all other religions — must finally be understood and valued in its philosophical meaning. In the faculty for prayer the human has as it were a special organ of religious perception. It corresponds to the sense of the beautiful or the faculty of aesthetic judgment in aesthetics and the moral will in ethics. It cannot be, by the way, assigned to any separate aspect of psychology, for it is connected with the very foundation of the human person in its unbreakable wholeness.

Where there is no prayer there is no religion.[19] One must not confuse the theosophical surrogates of prayer with prayer itself. "Concentration, meditation, and intuition," which for all that do not deal with God but with the world, immerse the human not in the Transcendent but in the immanent. They want to replace God with the divine: this is deception or self-deception. In addition, on the "occult" path the closest hierarchical step in the order of "evolution" is always the goal of ascension. Prayerful boldness — which is the wonder and grace of prayer — goes directly to the throne of the Most High, passing by all "hierarchies." In turning to the saints for help the latter do not at all appear as those intervening hierarchies that fill up the gulf between the human being and God (for this abyss is not filled up by any "evolutionary" process or hierarchical ascension) but only as powers that are close to us and that *together with* us stand before the throne of the Lord. God's creation stagnating in sins and darkness boldly speaks directly with the Lord in prayer and the Lord is pleased with this boldness. And all "hierarchies," so far as they have meaning in prayer, shine only with the reflected light of the Sun of suns. Such is prayer.

And so, the one who wishes to investigate religion in its "transcendental" characteristics with an unprejudiced and truly critical eye must ask himself: What is prayer? If only he does not give in to the crafty temptation *ratio ignava et obscura* [lazy and obscure reason], or declare all this to be psychologism or psychopathy and does not brush it aside with a disdainful gesture, he will then ask himself: "How is prayer possible?" But Kant the author of Critiques did not want to inquire *lege artis* [authentically] about this, declaring without argument that prayer is "Abgötterei," "Afterdienst," etc. Fichte followed him, seeing in prayer only the abasement of human dignity. In comparison with such a lack of religious taste it is impossible not to note the relative perspicacity of Hegel, who in *The Philosophy of Religion* places a high value on the meaning of "cult" and, naturally, of prayer as part of it (although his general point of view of radical immanentism did not favor the understanding of the central meaning of prayer in religion).

The originality of religion is based on the fact that religion possesses its own means of identifying Divinity, either an organ of the transcendent, its own attestation, or (if we are to extend into the domain of religious life the concept of experience as James does) its own particular experience. "The heart has its laws which the mind does not know," said Pascal, meaning this particular nature of religious evidence and credibility. Usually this religious identification is called *faith*, which therefore receives such a central meaning in the gnoseology of religion: the analysis of the nature of faith is in its own way "a critique of religious reason."

In order to evaluate the meaning of faith, it is necessary first of all to accept that faith, although not subordinated to the categories of logical, discursive cognition, all the same is not reduced to the level of subjective belief, taste, or caprice, for such an interpretation contradicts the very essence of faith: it would be unbelieving faith. Nevertheless faith in its own way is as objective as cognition.

"Does God exist?"

"God lives in my soul."

"No, *does God exist?*"

"He exists in my soul."

I cite this dialogue (which actually took place in 1903 in Stuttgart between me and P. B. Struve) as typical for the way the question of faith is stated. Faith on which religion is firmly established cannot be limited by a subjective mood, "God in the soul"; it affirms that God *exists*, as the transcendent, is outside me and only therefore is in me.[20] In faith the human being does not create God, as unbelief (Feuerbach) says, but God is revealed to the human being and thus the human being finds God in himself or himself in God. Faith from the objective side is *revelation*, in its content as little dependent on a subjective mood as is knowledge, and like the latter is only distorted by subjectivism.[21]

But, skepticism is heard to say, is not this objectivity of faith an illusion, a hallucination, a psychologism? But in that case, as we cross-examine, is it not the same kind of illusion to say, look, this is the sea that I *see,* and this is its sound, which I *hear,* and this is the blue of heaven, which I *contemplate?* Of course, it is possible to admit that I can be mistaken in my sense experience; it is possible that this is not the sea and not its sound, but that it only *seemed* to be so to me, and that there is in actuality no blue of the sky, and I have erred. But I can be certain of this only by relying on sense or aesthetic perception, by correcting and deepening it, but with logical arguments no one can weaken the immediate force and persuasiveness of my impression. In the same manner with arguments of the intellect it is impossible to demolish the immediate evidence of faith as an independent source of religious perception; it is possible to stifle it, to weaken it, but not dissuade from it. This was reflected in word usage, at least of the Russian language, which calls religion *faith.* It is impossible to drive faith out of faith. Reason accepts as truth only that which can be proved, displayed as a necessary link in causation. Logical necessity — such is the basis of knowledge. Faith is a path of knowledge without proof, outside of logical achievement, outside of the law of causality and its persuasiveness. Faith is a *hiatus* in logic, an insane death-defying leap: "be foolish in order to be wise" (1 Cor. 3:18), it says to humankind. Faith is free of the yoke of rationalism (I do not want to say "reason," for it is the expression of the highest reasonableness). The intellect despises faith; in the best case it ignores and does not understand faith.

Such a situation would be unbearable and would completely smash and weaken our consciousness if faith and the intellect had one and the same task, one and the same object. But in reality it is not so. That in which one can believe is impossible to know; it leaves the bounds of knowledge, and that which one knows is impossible to believe in. Who believes in the multiplication table or in the Pythagorean theorem? They know it. And who *knows* God, who includes him in the number of objects of scientific knowledge? They believe in him and know by faith. Faith, according to the definition of the apostle Paul, is "confidence in the invisible as visible, in the expected and hoped for as the real."[22] That which *is not and cannot be* given for rational knowledge, faith can know; it is accessible to it. From this follows the practical maxim: everything that can become an object of cognition must be cognizable. Faith therefore is not at enmity with knowledge; on the contrary, it merges with it lock, stock, and barrel. Although it is "the assurance of things hoped for, the evidence of things unseen" (Heb. 11:1), what is hoped for finally becomes reality, the invisible becomes visible. Faith in this sense is the anticipation of knowledge, *credo ut intelligam* [I believe so that I may understand], although for the present it rests on an insufficient foundation, *credo quia absurdum* [I believe because it is absurd]. Faith leaps across the law of sufficient grounds, of logical verification. Its foundations are insufficient; either they are altogether lacking or they are plainly exceeded by deductions. And yet this in no way means that faith should be completely indifferent towards its groundlessness: it is animated *by the hope* of becoming knowledge, of finding for itself sufficient grounds.[23]

The anticipation of possible experience and the exceeding of its foundations do not at all signify contempt for them. In faith there is freedom but there is no arbitrariness at all; faith has its own "regularity." And first of all faith never arises without some knowledge of the objects of faith, although this knowledge may be insufficient for providing a basis for its content but sufficient for its conception. Faith in God is born from a sense of God that is present in the human, from a knowledge of God. Just as it is impossible to charge an electric machine only by reading about electricity, for a charge is necessary no matter how weak, so too faith is born not from catechetical formulas but from an encounter with God in religious experience, on the road of life. Faith believes and hopes precisely in an expansion and deepening of this experience, which constitutes the object of faith as something unseen and hoped for. But the human being must make the effort himself, must realize this aspiration, which is why faith is a lived task, *spiritual struggle,* for it can become colder or more enflamed, poorer or richer. And thus the object of faith — its dogmatic content — always exceeds the actual religious experience. It is an enormous mistake to think (together with the Doukhobors, Quakers, and similar representatives of related antidogmatic and anarchic currents in religion) that only the real content of *actual* religious experience or *personal* revelation constitute the object of faith, whereas every *tradition* written or oral, liturgical or ritual, as such contradicts living faith. Those who reason in this manner under the pretext of mysticism completely eliminate faith for the sake of religious-empirical evidence; in the face of this distinctive mystical positivism (which, by the way, most often proves to be illusionism) the spiritual struggle of faith and its effort is completely eliminated and therefore faith itself is denied, together with the hope and love indissolubly linked with it, whose place is taken by unconcealed conceit.

On this basis one can and must *learn* faith. Right faith, right dogmas, "orthodoxy" are the task for a religious life, and not only its empirical givenness. Of course, if these dogmas remain on the level of abstract propositions having no persuasiveness for the mind but do not receive the vital power of faith, then they become simply dry straw, which easily burns up. But they receive a vital meaning insofar as they become the object of active and living faith, hope, and love, regulative of religious life. Hence the content of faith always exceeds personal religious experience. Faith is daring and hope. (Below, in conjunction with a doctrine of dogma, we will have to touch on the question of the meaning of tradition for faith.)

As everywhere, so here substitutions are possible. Faith is easily substituted by unbelieving dogmatism, i.e., by nonrational rationalism engendered by laziness of mind, stagnation, and cowardice of thought. The fight with knowledge under pretext of faith flows precisely from such an attitude towards the latter. Faith does not limit reason, which must itself know its limits so as not to stop where it is still able to walk on its own feet.

Although the proper domain of faith is the transcendent Divinity beyond cognoscibility, it extends also into what in principle is not accessible for knowledge, but becomes so merely for the given moment: such are events that have not yet happened but are going to happen, *the future* in general, or events that have happened and lie outside human knowing — *the past.* Finally even the present can be accessible to faith insofar as it is a matter of its laws unfamiliar to the intellect.[24]

However, all the separate beliefs that relate to the domain of the immanent world here and now arise from the central content of faith, and are its separate applications and ramifications; but one thing remains as the principal and in essence sole object of faith: YOU ARE. "It befits one who approaches God to believe that *he exists and* rewards *those who seek* him" (Heb. 11:6). That which constitutes the proper object of faith, in keeping with its own nature cannot become knowledge. Faith is a function of human freedom; it does not compel the way the laws of nature compel us. To impose the truths of faith from the outside would not meet the fundamental requirements of religious consciousness; to coerce our person, whether by logical constraint or force of knowledge, would not correspond to the dignity of the Divinity who respects our freedom. Knowledge belongs "to this world"; it is immanent to it, whereas religion is grounded in the polarization of consciousness, the strained sense of the opposition of the transcendent and the immanent, of consciousness of God and consciousness of the world. Religion signifies by itself not only the bond but also the remoteness of the human being from God. In this sense it is to a certain degree the expression of the sinful falling away of the world from God, of its damaged consciousness of God.

Faith is a function not of some individual aspect of the spirit but of the whole human person in its entirety, in the indivisible totality of all the powers of the spirit. In this sense religion is a *personal* work in the highest degree and thus it is a continual, creative work. It cannot be communicated externally, almost mechanically like knowledge; one can only be infected with it — by the mysterious and untraceable influence of one person on another: herein lies the secret of the significance of religious persons — of prophets, saints, of the very God-human in his earthly life. God does not intrude himself or coerce. He "knocks on the door" of the human heart; whether or not it will open, in all his omnipotence he cannot force it open, for this would mean the annihilation of freedom, i.e., of the human being itself. Only in the kingdom of the future age when "God will be all in all" will he become more immanent to the world than in this age and for that reason the very possibility of religion in its significance as damaged consciousness of God will be abolished. Only then will it no longer be given to human freedom to know or not to know God, to believe or not to believe in him. Faith will become something obvious, similar to natural necessity; it will be freedom's lot only to want God or not to want him, to love him or to have enmity towards him. From this it follows that faith is given only to those who look for it. The one who is fully satisfied with this world and does not thirst spiritually does not understand faith at all, and is organically a stranger to it. In this estrangement from faith is included one of the striking peculiarities of our epoch, thanks to which some, whose minds are grosser, see in faith a type of psychical sickness, while others see psychologism, subjectivism, and mood. In equal measure neither the one nor the other wants to reckon with the gnoseological significance of faith as a special source of knowing, and in religious experience they see only material for "religious psychology" or psychiatry. This state of contemporary humanity has, of course, its spiritual causes but thanks to it one now has difficulty being understood and even simply heard out in matters of faith.

But if faith can be born only among those who look for it (and besides, not always: for the contemporary spirit the loss of the aptitude for finding faith is characteristic, but not for searching for it, as our epoch is full of quests), does this not mean that faith is indeed psychologism and subjectivism? But is the foundation for a similar skepticism really given by this? Even scientific, not to mention philosophical, truth is not revealed to people who are strangers to intellectual life, and artistic creation is likewise inaccessible to people who are deprived of aesthetic perception. Faith not only is born in the freedom of the quest but also, so to say, feeds on this freedom. Hence it is *dynamic*, for it does not give knowledge defined once and for all like worldly knowledge but has a different intensiveness, from simple probability to full obviousness, from an idea merely of the head to a surmounting reality. According to a comparison often repeated in asceticism, God is like fire and the soul is like metal which can stay cold and alien to fire; but once it becomes hot it can become seemingly one with it. Faith has its degrees and ages, its ebbs and flows. Everyone who lives a religious life knows this by personal experience, and this is attested to in religious literature.[25] In a religious life there is no stagnation and immobility just as there are no inalienable achievements and dead points; here everything is always in motion, upwards or downwards, backwards or forwards, and thus there can be no place here for dead, laid-to-rest dogmatism.

Thus faith has two sides: subjective aspiration, the quest for God, religious thirst, a human being's question, and objective revelation, sensation of the Divine world, and God's response. In faith God condescends toward the human being, a ladder is set up between heaven and earth, a double-sided God-human act is accomplished. And this objective content of faith has for the believer full credibility, it is his religious knowledge obtained by the path of revelation. Faith presupposes *mystery* as its object and at the same time its source. This is not that domain of the mysterious for which superstitious people have a weakness, utterly devoid of faith; this is not the domain of mysteries or secrets that are protected from the uninitiated ("*Geheim*wissenschaft," or "*hidden* knowledge" for which, properly speaking, there is in principle no mystery); this is a mystery unconditionally inaccessible to humankind, transcendent to it, and thus necessarily presupposing revelation. "God lives in unapproachable light; no one among humankind has seen him, nor can anyone see him" (1 Tim. 6:16). "No one has ever seen God; the Only Begotten Son, being in the Father's bosom, has made him known" (John 1:18). He "showed the Father," "having revealed his Name to humans" (John 17:6).

Mystery is the transcendent; it can open slightly only in the measure of the entry of the transcendent into the immanent, by an act of self-disclosure, a revelation of the transcendent.[26] Revelation enters as a necessary gnoseological element of faith. Knowledge, no matter how profound and broad it may be, in the final analysis is self-consciousness. When a human being cognizes the world, in essence he cognizes his own self for he himself is this world, as a microcosm. And in this cognition there is no difference in principle between his very elementary act and his ultimate achievements. Knowledge is strictly monistic — in its bounds which are at the same time the bounds of the immanent, there is gnoseologically no place for faith, which has here no ontological basis for itself. Inasmuch as the transcendent is "the transcendental object of religion," *faith* is its irremovable and unsurpassable ground. The transcendent is identified as such only by faith. The transcendent always lies at the boundaries of cognition, outside it, above it. It is mistaken therefore to think that faith corresponds only to an infantile state of religious consciousness, and at a more mature age is replaced and supplanted by knowledge — philosophy and science (although "spiritual") — generally speaking, by gnosis. The relation between faith and gnosis belongs on the whole to the subtlest questions of religious gnoseology. Faith does not deny gnosis; on the contrary it generates it and makes it fruitful. "Love the Lord your God with all your heart, with all your soul (i.e., will) and with all your understanding (i.e., gnosis)" (Matt. 22:37), and of course the spirit, on fire with faith, will bring its fire and light into all domains of its creativity. But the motive, nature, and orientation of faith and gnosis are completely different. Faith is an act of freedom, madness, love, and bravery.[27] It is the tossing of the end of life's thread into heaven in the certainty that it will hang there without any reinforcement. Faith has to do with the inaccessible: "believe what your heart says, *there are no* pledges from the heavens."[28] Faith is the spiritual exploit of the heart, of believing love. It does not need "pledges" and guarantees; they would contradict its essence, for it desires God, loves only God, renounces the world, i.e., all that is given, for the sake of the not-given, the transcendent. It is the highest and final sacrifice of a human being to God — himself, his reason, will, heart, his whole essence, the whole world, all evidence, and is a completely disinterested exploit, giving away everything and demanding nothing. It is the love of humankind for God exclusively and for the sake of God himself; it is salvation from the self, from one's givenness, from one's immanence; it is hatred of the self, which is love for God. It is a mute, imploring, searching gesture, it is a single aspiration: *sursum corda, sursum, sursum, sursum, excelsior!* ... Here a sacrifice is offered by oneself and the world (which here signifies one and the same thing) for the sake of the supramundane and supernal, for the sake of the Father who is in heaven. It is *not a method* of cognition with its sure, calculated tread; it is madness for this world, and God wants it. And this sacrificial act that is accomplished unseen in the soul is a continual sacrifice of faith, which says to an immobile stone mountain "throw yourself into the sea" and says this not for an experiment but only because this stoniness and immobility of the world do not exist for it — such faith is a primary act that cannot be substituted by anything, and only it bestows on religion the aureole of tragic, sacrificial, voluntary surrender of the self to God. And the heroes of faith are great precisely through this sacrifice, the immensity of their surrender. St. Paul the Apostle remembers them in his hymn of faith (Heb. 11). The Church honors them as saints. Only after this sacrificial death does resurrection follow, as day follows night: the joy and victory of faith, a new discovery of one's ruined soul. Outside this moment one is not born for religion: probably, it is entirely possible to be a philosopher, theologian, mystic, Gnostic, or occultist, and ... not to believe in God, not having experienced this free surrender of the self.

In the history of philosophy an extended gnoseological meaning is sometimes added to the concept *of faith;* every intuition establishing the trans-subjective *existence* of the external world or of someone else's I is called by this name. Jacobi[29] advanced the meaning of faith in this sense already in his polemic with Kant; he considered the existence of both the divine and the empirical world to be the domain of faith, and in this manner profaned or so to say secularized the concept of faith.[30] Such a posing of the question flowed from Kant's doctrine of experience understood as subjectivism or illusionism. In order to fill the schemas of concepts with vital content and to catch real and not imaginary fish in the net of reason, it is necessary that cognition have an organ for certifying reality, a sense of the real, which does not break down into separate signs of things but connects them with itself in existence. This empirical sense of reality, resting on intuition, is sometimes called

Introduction

faith or "mystical empiricism."[31] Thus, for example, in his first theory of cognition developed in *Critique of Abstract Principles,* Vladimir Sergeevich Soloviev speaks about faith as establishing the existence of an object and fastening to itself empirical evidence and its logical connection: according to this doctrine, an act of faith is present in every cognitive act.[32] Prince Sergei Nikolaevich Trubetskoi develops a similar point of view in his early gnoseological works (particularly in "The Foundations of Idealism"). Thanks to this terminological confusion it can appear that in both cases — whether the intuition of empirical reality or religious faith is meant — it is a matter of one and the same thing. Besides, strictly speaking, between religious faith and "mystical empiricism" there is on the whole as little common as between faith and cognition, in the makeup of which intuition is, really, a completely irremovable element. It is correct that every reality, be it another's I or the external world, is established not rationally but intuitively, with the intuition of reality having roots in the sense of efficacy, i.e., not gnoseological but praxeological roots.[33] For the intellect (pure reason) such certification can be and is "mystical" and is established "by faith," but this only shows the whole conditional character and insufficiency of an abstract-rational understanding of cognition, for the root of cognition is living-pragmatic; the concept of empiricism must already include beforehand a sign of efficacy that gropes about things and distinguishes the ideal from the real (Kant's "dollars" in the imagination or in the purse). With this praxeological moment an existential judgment is established. One can, of course, call this intuition faith as well as "mystical empiricism," but all the same one must not forget the fundamental difference between intuition and religious faith: such intuition remains entirely in the bounds of empirically given reality, the domain of "this world." It is subject to the whole compulsion of this reality, its ironclad necessity; "to believe" or "not to believe" in the existence of this table does not depend in the least on my will, my person: it is enough for me to feel it or bump against it for the table to stand before me in all its indisputable reality. In the same way, it is not within my power to believe or deny the existence of the person who wrote this unattractive composition. And this revelation of the external world (according to the quite infelicitous and false expression of Jacobi) is equally compelling for every normally organized consciousness. On the contrary, religious faith assures us of the existence of another, transcendent reality and our connection with it. Consequently, its object is *qualitatively* other. It is identified not by the coercion of external senses, not violently, but by the free, creative aspiration of the spirit, *by the quest* for God, by the intense actuality of the soul in this direction. In other words the element of freedom and personhood, i.e., creativity, is irremovable from religious faith: I come forward here not as an abstract, neutral, impersonal, "normally" organized representative of a genus but as a concrete, unrepeatable, individual person. Faith demands love, concentration of will, the effort of the entire person. My faith is not passive perception but active coming out from the self, the divestment from the self of the weight of this world. If we look at how people who have walked the path of faith describe their spiritual struggle, e.g., blessed Augustine *(Confessions),* Thomas Carlyle *(Sartor Resartus),* Blaise Pascal *(Pensées),* Lev Nikolaevich Tolstoy *(Confession),* Fyodor Mikhailovich Dostoevsky *(Pro et contra* in *Brothers Karamazov)* etc., if each of us peers into our own soul crying out to God in the midst of the gloom of doubt, spiritual weakness, and heaviness, we will understand what urgency faith demands not only in the first moments of its conception but in each moment of its existence. Always on the verge of weakening and going out, its trembling fire shines with an even, unfading light only on the summits, among the ascetic heroes. This is why, speaking in general, it is so difficult to define the moment of coming to believe or of losing one's faith, for in reality coming to believe is always and continually happening anew; it is a single act stretched out in time, and like a dark quagmire unbelief always lies in wait for every unbelieving movement, every hesitation on the path of faith.[34]

What has been said gives a basis for a judgment about the limits of religious gnosis, or in general about the Gnostic direction in religion, which has always existed and which in the present day is manifested with the greatest force in metaphysical rationalism on the one hand, and in the so-called theosophical movement on the other hand, or more precisely, in contemporary occultism. Metaphysical Gnosticism received its most extreme expression in the philosophy of Hegel. Hegelian panlogism is at the same time the most radical immanentism known to the history of thought, for in it human thinking passing through a purifying "phenomenological" path becomes human no more but divine, even divinity itself. If logic, according to the well-known expression from *Wissenschaft der Logik* is *"die Wahrheit wie sie ohne Hüllen, an und für sich selbst ist"* [the truth as it is without veils, in and of itself] and in this sense *"die Darstellung Gottes ist, wie er in seinem ewigen Wesen vor der Erschaffung der Natur und eines endlichen Geistes ist"* [the representation of God is how he is in his eternal being before the creation of nature and a finite spirit];[35] if dialectic is the sufficiently safe bridge leading a human towards a superhuman being, to absolute spirit, then obviously the world *is* this very spirit which finds itself on corresponding levels of its own dialectical self-development. For this reason religion, with its incomplete forms of "representation" and faith, is also only a stage of the development of its self-consciousness, which must be surpassed, namely in philosophy. Whence the famous opinion of Hegel, expressed by him already in *Phenomenology of Spirit*, that philosophy is superior to religion, because the mysteries of God and the world are knowable for it in the complete and adequate form of logical thinking; or more exactly, philosophy is the self-consciousness of God. Here, it is true, it is not yet affirmed that the human being is a god (as Hegel's pupil Feuerbach proclaimed); on the contrary, the human being must overcome his empirical humanity, divest himself of it, having become the eye of world reason, of absolute spirit, merged with its self-thinking. But at the same time the process of this phenomenological purification and panlogical ascension is differentiated by continuity and connectedness on all levels; it can be passed through in all directions, similar to how from any point on a circle we can pass through the whole circumference and return to the point of departure, or from the center draw a radius to all the points of circumference. Here there is no polarity of transcendent and immanent, there is no place for super-logical revelation, super-knowledge or ignorance of faith, its *"docta ignorantia"* (according to the expression of Nicholas of Cusa); here there is no mystery either in heaven or on earth, for the human being holds in his hands the principle of the closed chain of the absolute; more exactly, he is itself its link. Hegel's panlogism can be understood only in the sense that for him cognition — of the world and of the self — is at the same time cognition of God. Religion, *the bond* of the human with divinity, has for him the meaning not of the bond of two worlds, but expresses only a definite stage in the development of spirit.[36]

A religious philosophy of occultism undoubtedly has an affinity with Hegelian immanentism as it is being scrutinized. The fundamental idea of occultism, namely that the domain of possible experience accessible to humankind can be quantitatively and qualitatively deepened and broadened by the path of a corresponding psychic training, "a development of the higher faculties," in and of itself still does not lead without fail to immanentism. Occultism is only a special domain of knowledge that differs qualitatively from faith,[37] while all knowledge is self-cognition, i.e., immanent. The human being is considered here as representing the totality of several casings or "bodies" and belonging in this quality to several worlds or "planes." But in connection with this yet another idea creeps in, namely that in passing from one of the lower worlds to a higher one, the human being ultimately attains the divine world. For theosophical Gnosticism, for *"Geisteswissenschaft,"* everything is in principle cognizable, God and the world, just as it is for Hegelianism. There is no place remaining for faith and revelation here, and if it is even possible to speak about revelations of higher spheres in the sense of "initiation," then this initiation, by expanding the domain of experience, does not step over it qualitatively, for these hierarchies likewise still belong to the "world," to the domain of the immanent. One ought to distinguish between the expansion of our experience which reveals new worlds to us (it makes no difference whether it is a world to be studied with a telescope or with astral clairvoyance) and the breach of our experience which is contact with the principle that transcends the world, i.e., with God. Entry into new planes of the world, of course, breaks the previous limitedness; it is destructive for *crass* materialism (although in its place it may perhaps put a more subtle materialism), but occultism can remain atheistic since by expanding the world it locks it up in itself all the more. In general the path of occult and even of mystical comprehension of the world is not necessarily at all a religious path, although it can be united with it. Theosophy (in its more open admissions) lays claim to being a *replacement* for religion, its Gnostic surrogate, and in such a case it changes into a vulgar pseudoscientific mythology. It exploits the mystical curiosity, the Luciferian inquisitiveness of a cold, unloving mind. Commerce with beings from other worlds, if it really is possible and actually takes place, in and of itself is not only incapable of bringing nearer to God but on the contrary even extinguishes religious faith in the soul. The principle of hierarchism, which is advanced unremittingly here, would have a basis only if God entered into the same hierarchy, forming its summit, so that it represented a real and natural ladder of ascent to God. But such a doctrine is pantheistic immanentism and religious evolutionism, which constitute the original sin of occultism. The world (or worlds) represents for it a real evolution of divinity itself; divinity is included

Introduction

here in the mechanism of the world and is accessible to disclosure and comprehension by a methodical, regular path, although for it other methods are required than for the study of the microscopic world, for example. This being the case, occultism with its hierarchies of worlds leads inevitably to *polytheism,* its occult Olympus having a series of steps and gradations, for which reason *polycosmism and polyanthropism* correspond to it: when worlds change, the human being changes too. The present-day human being corresponds to a real stage in the development of the earth; the preceding steps of his existence differ spiritually and physically from the present-day ones, and this must be said even more about subsequent world epochs. A human being is only a link; he used not to exist and must be overcome; evolution leads not to a superhuman being but away from the human and beyond the human. This evolution has no end or limit; the absolute exists for this radical evolutionism only as a possibility of limitless movement, i.e., "bad infinity," whereas religion deals with positive infinity, with the transcendent and absolute God who bestows eternal life on us, giving us repose and saving us from the burning hot wheel "of bad infinity," this rabid, insatiable "evolution."

Consistent Gnosticism, despite all its predilection for the mysterious, is radical immanentism, coinciding in this with Hegelianism. Here the characteristic distinction between faith and knowledge is erased: the temptation of occultism consists precisely in the full overcoming of faith by knowledge (*eritis sicut dei scientes bonum et malum* [You shall be like gods, knowing good and evil, Gen. 3:5] — from which the cult of Lucifer comes, more or less common for all shades of occultism). "Blessed are they who have not seen and have come to believe" (John 20:29) — these words of the Lord to Thomas cannot gain a hearing from Gnostics; for them this is not blessedness but a childlike state at best, the lowest spiritual rank, "the faith of a collier." But the nature of the faith of a collier is no different than that of a philosopher. The heroes of faith, religious ascetics and saints, possessed different cognitive capacities. Sometimes they were not gifted at all in this respect and yet this did not prevent their pure heart from seeing God, for the path of faith, of religious knowing, lies above the path of knowledge,[38] even if it is occult, "the wisdom of this age." *Childlikeness* is proper to faith, not as the absence of maturity but as a kind of positive quality: the kingdom of God belongs to children. "Whoever does not receive the kingdom of God like a child will not enter into it" (Luke 18:17).

III. Faith and Feeling

In his *On Religion: Speeches to Its Cultured Detractors,* in order to convince these "cultured people" Schleiermacher ultimately drowns the masculine nature of religion in feminine sentimentalism. As is known, the principal idea of Schleiermacher is that the proper domain of religion is *feeling,* which by its nature is religious. True, Schleiermacher's rhetorical and vague exposition, especially in the later development of his thought, admits various interpretations which approximate his doctrine at one time to Spinozism (Frank), at another time to Christian orthodoxy; in general he personally did not depart from the latter and he came particularly closer to it in his last compositions. In some places in his work intuition *(Anschauung)* makes an appearance along with feeling; but as Pfleiderer observes,[39] it disappears without a trace. What interests us here, though, are not the nuances of Schleiermacher's doctrine in detail but his central idea — *Gefühlstheologie.*

Let us recall the fundamental features of Schleiermacher's doctrine. According to Schleiermacher, religious life is *the third* aspect of life existing alongside of two others, cognition and activity, and expresses itself in the domain of feeling, for "such is the distinctive domain which I wish to assign to religion, and entirely to it alone ... your feeling ... this is your religiousness ... it is not your cognition or the objects of your cognition, just as it is not your deeds and actions or the different domains of your activity but only your feelings. ... These are exclusively the elements of religion, but at the same time they all belong here; *there is no feeling that would not be religious* (italics mine), or else it bears witness to the morbid and injured state of life which must then be disclosed in other domains. Whence it follows in and of itself that, on the contrary, all concepts and principles without exception are in themselves foreign to religion. For if they must have meaning they belong to cognition and what belongs to the latter already lies in a different domain of life, not in the religious domain" (*On Religion,* trans. S. L. Frank, p. 47).

"Religion has no relation even to this knowledge (i.e., to the sort in which 'natural science rises from the laws of nature to the supreme and universal Steward' and in which 'you will not come to know nature without comprehending God at the same time'), its essence is comprehended outside the participation of the latter. For the measure of knowledge is not the measure of piety" (35). "It is true, for religion, reflection is essential ... but it is not directed ... to the essence of the higher cause by itself or in respect to that which simultaneously is both cause and effect; on the contrary, religious reflection is only (!) the immediate consciousness that everything finite exists only in and through the infinite, everything temporal in and through the eternal. To seek and find this eternal and infinite in everything that lives and moves, in every increase and change, in every action and suffering, and in an immediate feeling to have and to know life itself only as such an existence in the infinite and eternal — that is what religion is. . . . And therefore it is of course life in the infinite nature of the whole, in the all-one, in God, life possessing God in all and possessing all in God. *But it is not knowledge or cognition either of the world or of God;* such knowledge it only recognizes without identifying itself with it" (36). So, feeling is the proper domain of religion. "Thus it (piety) establishes its proper domain and its unique character only in that it wholly goes out beyond the limits of both science and practice and only when it stands along side of the latter is the common sphere of the soul entirely filled, and human nature from this side completed" (38). "True science is finished contemplation; true practice is spontaneous development and art; *true religion is the feeling and taste for the infinite*" (39; italics mine). In this sense Schleiermacher repeatedly compares religion with *music,* the art without words, from pure moods alone (53, 62-63). "The human being does not have to make anything *of* religion but must make and realize everything *with* religion; uninterruptedly, like a sacred music, religious feelings must accompany his active life and nowhere and never may it lose them." Religion shares with music a nonlogical nature; concepts of true and false are inapplicable to it. "Everything is immediately true in religion; for how else could anything arise in it? Only what has not yet passed through a concept, but has arisen only in feeling, is immediate" (56).

Even the ideas of God and immortality, which Schleiermacher considers "elements of religion," are not the main content of religion. For from the one and the other only that which is feeling and immediate consciousness can belong to religion; but God and immortality, as they are encountered in such doctrines, are concepts (101). "And so," continues Schleiermacher, "can anyone say that I have portrayed to you a religion without God when I was studying precisely the immediate and primary existence of God in us in virtue of our feeling? Or is not God a singular and supreme unity? Does not everything particular disappear in him alone? We do not claim to have God in feeling other than through impressions, awakened in us by the world and I was able to speak about him only in this form . . . the one who denies this will be an atheist from the perspective of his feeling and experience" (102, cf. further 103). Therefore in Schleiermacher a tendency towards adogmatism appears that constitutes a natural deduction from his general anti-intellectualism and antilogism in religion. "What we feel and perceive in religious experiences is not the nature of things but its effect on you. What you know or think about the nature of things lies far off to the side of the domain of religion: to welcome into our life and to be inspired in these influences (of the universe) and in what they awaken in us, not isolated by everything singular but in connection with the whole, by everything limited not in its opposition to the other but as a symbol of the infinite — this is what religion is; whereas what wants to go beyond these limits and, for example, delve deeper into the nature and substance of things is no longer religion, but strives in a certain manner to be science.... Indisputably the whole essence of religion is to sense everything that determines our feeling in its highest unity as something one and identical, but to sense everything singular and particular as conditioned by it, *i.e.,* (!!) to sense our existence and life in God and through God" (50-51).

What is striking in all these definitions is that the religion of feeling, founded on a sensation of the infinite, of cosmic unity, does not in any way contain an idea of God, which nevertheless is constantly implied by Schleiermacher and introduced by means of "i.e." as in the cited tirade, thereby becoming a Spinozan equation: deus *sive* natura. But what is natural for the rationalist Spinoza is completely inadmissible for the anti-intellectualist Schleiermacher; without philosophical justification he borrows here from his worldview as a pastor, which by the way *On Religion* teems with. This is camouflaged thanks to Schleiermacher's indisputable personal religiosity and religious temperament. Schleiermacher himself is undoubtedly more religious than his philosophy passing itself off (like Jacobi's doctrine of faith) simply as a *pis aller* [last resort], an attempt to save ancient piety from the onslaught of rationalism and criticism. Schleiermacher's agnosticism resembles in this way the protective coloration appropriated by certain animals (mimicry); his apologetic is guided by the pious desire to entice "its cultivated detractors" with religion, by as easy a means as possible. From this come all the contradictions, which are smoothed over and not made sharper in these speeches. From this comes that confession of faith which, strictly speaking, is pure atheism movingly adorned with religiosity — both Haeckel and Ostwald and the "union of monists" can subscribe to this confession. "The usual representation of God as a separate being outside the world and beyond (?) the world does not exhaust the general subject of religion and is seldom a pure and always an insufficient form of expression of religious consciousness.... This does not represent the true essence of religion, nor does some other concept, but only the immediate consciousness of Divinity, as we find Divinity equally in us ourselves and in the world. To merge in the midst of the finite with the infinite and to be eternal in every moment — herein lies the immortality of religion" (110-11).

It is impossible not to acknowledge that Schleiermacher's doctrine bears clear traces of a duality that permits us to interpret him both as a philosopher of subjectivism in religion (as we understand him here following Hegel) and as a philosopher of faith. The dual influences of Kant and Jacobi were reflected in the young preacher, without being harmonized or reconciled. On the one hand he shared his era's fright before Kant who cooped up the human being in

Introduction

a world of phenomena and proclaimed a religious agnosticism or skepticism on new principles. On the other hand he along with many others (like Fichte subsequently) saved himself from Kant in the opposite extreme, in Jacobi's philosophy of faith in which the true features of religious faith were erased by its excessively broad application to all cognitive acts. For this reason the philosophy of feeling acquires at one time the features of *The Critique of Pure Reason* in its postulates, at another time, features of Jacobi's doctrine. What is of interest for us here is that aspect of Schleiermacher's doctrine in which he is more original, namely, his religious gnoseology of feeling. And above his whole *On Religion* Faust's skeptical pantheistic confession flutters: of half-faith, half-unbelief — on the pretext of incognoscibility.

> Who may name him
> And who confess:
> I believe him?
> Who may feel
> And hazard to say:
> I do not believe him?
> The All-embracer, the All-preserver
> Does he not embrace and support you, me, himself?
> Call it luck, heart, love, God!
> I have no name for it!
> *Feeling is everything,*
> Name is sound and smoke![40]

If one acknowledged that in fact feeling in all its vagueness is the principal or essential organ of religion, this would mean not only to deprive religion of the central, sovereign meaning belonging to it and place it *alongside of* and *on a level with* science, ethics, aesthetics, and in fact even *lower* than them, but, most importantly, to make religion into blind sentimentality, to deprive it of the word, having foisted adogmatism and alogism upon it. Feeling can force its way through, but in and of itself it always constitutes the music of the soul, merely accompanying the one or other representation, volition, and in general a given content of consciousness. Meanwhile, the intention of Schleiermacher's doctrine is precisely to divert religion's domain of feeling into its isolated existence. If one expressed Schleiermacher's theory in contemporary philosophical language, one would call it *militant psychologism,* for "feeling" is affirmed here in its subjective-psychological meaning as *an aspect* of spirit, in keeping with Schleiermacher's persistently repeated definition (see below); at the same time he speaks over and over about comprehending God through feeling, in other words, he ascribes a gnoseological meaning to it, i.e., religious intuition.[41] This confusion of the gnoseological and the psychological is de-

Faith and Feeling

fined nowadays precisely as psychologism. Of course this means leaving religion in a *clair obscur,* somewhere on the border of consciousness, in sweet vagueness. But this vagueness and alogicality of religion is perfect *nonsense,* an unrealizable utopia, and no matter how Schleiermacher himself may refrain from such utterances on the subject of religion, the inevitable result is a dogmatic both minimal and diffuse, but in no way alogical. This brings him closer at one time to Spinoza, at another time to pietism. He speaks in turn about the feeling of the infinite or cosmic feeling, and about the feeling of divinity, or immediately about both (in his last works the feeling of exceptional dependence — *das schlechthinnige Abhängigkeitsgefühl* — makes its appearance as a fundamental sign). Only the complete absence of determinateness and consistency in the fundamental point of view disguises the whole powerlessness of *Gefühlstheologie,* and more importantly, its areligious and atheistic character. For feeling in and of itself, pure feeling, is completely incapable of yielding that without which religion does not and cannot exist: YOU ARE, to feel God, the bond with whom is religion. If there is anywhere that one ought to see the most hopeless immanentism and psychologism, it is in the *Gefühlstheologie* of Schleiermacher, where religiousness, "mood," consciously and knowingly substitutes for religion. This is religious decadence, impressionism, which can be to the liking only of fanciers "of mystical anarchism."

Schleiermacherian "mood" is a sauce for rabbit stew rather than the bagged rabbit itself — according to the famous comparison in Dostoevsky (the conversation between Shatov and Stavrogin in *Demons*). It is not naïve but refined atheism (I understand here, of course, not the personal religiousness of Schleiermacher which is not subject to doubt, but the religious philosophy of his *On Religion*). Generally speaking, in the history of thought it is the ultimate point of religion's humiliation under the guise of its defense, for it is more courageous and natural to acknowledge directly that there is no religion and that it is in general impossible than to banish religion to the darkest corner of consciousness by making use of its twilight. Historically it was quite the reverse; *On Religion* became an event and was an act of courage and enthusiasm on the part of its author who, by the way, submitted in it to the influence of German romanticism, and German pietism even more so. Essentially Schleiermacherian subjectivism is only one of the varieties of Protestant subjectivism (for Protestantism generally speaking is the victory of immanentism, and consequently, of subjectivism), and in this form or another it lives on in Protestant theology. This is manifested in general in its antidogmatism, which it mixes with anti-intellectualism and preaches on the pretext of a battle against the heterogeneous elements of religion. Such is the thought of Ritschl,[42] for example, the most influential and typical tendency in German theology. In accord with Ritschl's basic thought, only "values" established "by judgments on value" belong to the domain of religion, and this religious pragmatism joins with a very skeptical attitude towards dogma, by considering it "metaphysics," prohibited by Kant. In general "mood" and "experience," understood in a completely immanent sense, dominate the religious life of Germany of the nineteenth century; it suffices to name two contemporary representatives of immanentism in religion – Troeltsch and Herrmann.[43]

Schleiermacher's religious alogism, appearing as a result of his immanentism, provoked an angry and sharp critique from the side of the representative of the opposite, panlogical pole in immanentism – namely from Hegel, for whom religion is covered by the domain of logical thinking. In his *Philosophy of Religion* Hegel subjected Schleiermacher's doctrine to a severe but in many ways justified critique. Hegel's radical rationalism, of course, leads him to a complete disregard for feeling (and also for immediate experience in general – let us recall the first chapter of *Phenomenology of Spirit*); he sees in it only subjectivity. Feeling can have the most varied and for all that accidental content: "God, if he is revealed (ist) in feeling, does not have any advantage over the most stupid feeling, but regal flowers grow in the same soil together with a weed" (Hegel's *Religionsphilosophie*, Diederichs, 75). "Therefore if the existence of God is demonstrated in our feeling, it is just as accidental as any other thing to which being can be ascribed. This we call subjectivism, albeit in the most stupid sense." In Hegel's opinion, a human being has feeling in common with an animal, which does not have religion (with Hegel adding that *Gott ist wesentlich im Denken* [God is essentially in thinking]; and since thinking is proper only to humankind, so too is religion proper to him). "Everything in the human being for which thought is the ground can be invested with the form of feeling: law, freedom, morality, etc. . . . but it is not the merit of feeling that its content is true. . . . It is an error to reckon truth and good to feeling" (77). "Soll daher die Religion nur als Gefühl sein, so verglimmt sie zum Vorstellungslosen wie zum Handlungslosen und verliert sie jeden bestimmten Inhalt" [Should religion exist only as feeling, it would die away into what cannot be imagined or operate and would lose any definite content] (78).

Eduard von Hartmann in *Die Religion des Geistes* reproduces and in certain respects deepens Hegel's argumentation from the point of view of his metaphysical doctrine. The principal reproach that Hartmann makes against Schleiermacher's theory is religious alogism, the blindness and amorphousness of naked feeling. "No matter how justified it may be that religious feeling constitutes the innermost kernel of religious life, all the same true religious feeling is only of the sort that is aroused by religious representations of objective (although relative) truth. *Religion cannot exist without a religious contemplation of the world* (italics mine) and this latter cannot exist without the conviction of its transcendent truth" (31). "In order for representations, which are the premise of religious feeling, to become coherent truth, they must be abstracted from their dark, unclear coherence in feeling, correlated among themselves and introduced into a systematic connection – in a word, they must be developed and reworked into a religious world view" (32). Hartmann distinguishes a threefold class of abuse that arises as a result of a one-sided development of feeling in religion: sensible, aesthetic, and mystical. Under the first he understands the excesses of sensibility in religion, under the second – the replacement of serious religiousness with aestheticism, and under the third – mysticism.

Hartmann's remarks touching on contemporary aestheticism as a symptom of religious impotence are extremely apt and justified. "For epochs in which a definite religion declines uncontrollably, it is characteristic that the executions of religious works of art blossom here as never before under different circumstances, whereas the creative capacity for making religious works of authentic grandeur and real depth dies out together with the unclouded trust and unshakeable power of faith. For example, classical church music was never performed more fervently and attractively than now in our unchurchly times, and yet this takes place precisely among the unchurched classes permeated with unbelief" (37). "Fervent and pleasurable occupation with Christian art not only does not speak about a positive attitude towards its religious content; on the contrary, it attests to *such an estrangement and separation* from its living religious content that the penchant for opposition against the art bound with it has already disappeared and has yielded its place to an objective historical-aesthetic attitude" (41). "Therefore aesthetic religious feeling is not authentic and serious religious feeling" (39), which of course is not to deny the auxiliary role of art for religion.

Corresponding to his general intellectualism, Hartmann attacks mysticism with particular fervor, understanding it as a one-sided predominance of mystical feeling. "Mystical feeling is the most undefined and unclear of all feelings; ineffability and inexpressibility, which in the final analysis are proper to every feeling, are incomparably more proper to the mystical. Those immersed in mystical religious feeling seemingly peer into a dark abyss where nothing can be distinguished or recognized; or, what amounts to the same thing, they see a flash of absolute light that seemingly fills everything and that blinds their sight. Mystical feeling has the awareness of containing in itself all religious truth and of not erring in this, but it contains it exclusively as what stimulates feeling, and thus, as an unconscious truth accessible to consciousness only through the affect of feeling" (44). Religion that stops at mysticism and is indifferent towards religious cognition is defective; it inclines towards eudaimonism on the one hand, to the delight in its own mystical ecstasy, and on the other hand is easily subjected to the influence of some such ecclesiastical orthodoxy (in the eyes of Hartmann, a mortal sin). By the way, this does not hinder Hartmann from considering that "mystical and religious feeling is properly a creative principle in religion, similar to aesthetic feeling in art" (44). Hartmann's general conclusion (in the chapter "Die religiöse Funktion als

Gefühl" [The religious function as feeling]) is this: "The value of religious feeling is contained not in feeling as such but in the unconscious process of motivation in which it signals like a symptom of its resonance in consciousness, and the value of this process of motivation consists in the actual result which it produces" (53). Feeling is found, consequently, on the threshold of religious consciousness and prepares the content of its acts; it is, so to say, fuel for the operation of the apparatus but is not the apparatus itself!

The general question about the religious meaning of feeling is of course not exhausted by what has been said. Here we only had in mind to distinguish and contrast a doctrine about feeling as the basis for religion with a doctrine of faith, and we see the principal difference of the former in the subjectivity, formlessness, and amorphousness of religious feeling, its alogicality, which crosses over to antilogicality, adogmatism, and religious blindness. If it is fair to compare feeling in religion with music, then music will not be the highest type of art and activity of the spirit in general because it is wordless, meaningless, alogical. Thus the reduction to music of a different art having its own word would signify its depreciation (although this is extraordinarily widespread in our days).

It may appear unexpected if we place Kant along side of Schleiermacher in "a theology of feeling." Yet, as far apart as they might be in theoretical philosophy, in their understanding of the nature of faith they converge. If Schleiermacher acknowledges feeling as the domain of religion in general, Kant considers for that domain *moral* feeling, which is the organ of *faith*. True, Kant calls the moral will "practical reason" for which its own special canon is established, with this "reason" postulating fundamental religious truths: the existence of God, freedom of the will, and personal immortality; but no matter by what name we might call faith, its essence will not vary from this: only faith pronounces YOU ARE. Postulates only postulate but are themselves powerless to affirm the existence of God; this constitutes, of course, the business of faith. And even Kant himself speaks[44] "about the faith of pure reason" (no matter how contradictory this phrase is, for reason does not believe, it demonstrates — whereas faith is so to say outside reason although it is not contrary to reason). The proximity of Kant to Schleiermacher is determined by the fact that Kant strives to impart to religious (i.e., moral, for him) feeling an alogical or in his language "practical" character. In the domain of concepts (i.e., "of pure reason") nothing must leak out through the chink of faith that is coming to light in practical reason. Kant thereby falls not only into alogism but also essentially into antilogism. But in and of itself, antilogism is logical utopia, something impossible for the human spirit which is illuminated by the light of the logos, an unrealizable task for thought: to reason as if the God identified "by practical reason" did not exist at all for theoretical reason. In reality once God has been found, and it is all the same by which path and which "reason," Kant would need to cross out his whole *Critique of Pure Reason* constructed outside the hypothesis of God and even by its exclusion, and rewrite his philosophical system. Thus water, through whatever crack it might burst, fills the whole indoors and penetrates into every void and pore. Kant wants to keep religious faith on that level of awareness that "practical reason" holds and by making it blind and alogical, to reduce it to the level of Schleiermacherian feeling. Of course this is made easier thanks to the rationalistic prejudice of Kant's doctrine according to which faith is "reason" although of a second sort, i.e., "practical"; consequently over it hangs the control and despotic governance of theoretical reason which has forged the laws of faith and limits its competence. Such legislation of reason in the domain of faith contains in itself an unbearable contradiction that is resolved either by a complete and definitive repudiation of the laws of faith, i.e., of the whole construct of the *Critique of Practical Reason* (the path of the majority of Neo-Kantians) or by its primacy in *all* domains; in such a case it becomes impossible to take the *Critique of Pure Reason* seriously. Kant's doctrine of "rational faith" suffers from incompleteness, it is half-faith, half-reason: although the domain of what is known by reason is overstepped by it, at the same time reason does not want to renounce its dominion and control even in this domain that is foreign to it.[45]

IV. Religion and Ethics

Generally speaking, in reducing the essence of religion to morality, which is so common in the rationalistic tendency of religious thought (Kant, Fichte, Tolstoy, et al.), religion's own proper nature is ignored. It is correct that morality is rooted in religion. The inner light in which good and evil are distinguished in a human being proceeds from the Source of lights. In his undeceived and impartial conscience, so enigmatically free of natural human self-love, the human being perceives that Someone is *con-scious of him,* manages with him his deeds, pronounces his judgment, *always sees him.*

Introduction

You always see me! I know this well, whether I hide myself from You out of shame and dread or embrace You with rapture and trembling. Alas, more often do I remember You only in my thought, but my soul remains cold. And then I am my own and not Yours, the heavens close, and I am left alone in my nothingness, a victim for the insatiable and impotent I. . . . But You call and joyfully I see that only I have departed from You and You always see me.

You always see me: in the terrifying impotence of my upsurges towards You, as in my timid and cool prayer, in the fused torment of a consciousness smashing to pieces and in the burning-hot shame of my sin. You see secret intentions, what I conceal from myself with dread. You know in me both the cold egoist and the doleful coward. You know the crafty sybarite and the mercenary envier. O, it is terrible to think that all that is mine is known to You for You always see me.

You always see me! And You know how I want to love You, though my love is impotent. I want to love only You, nothing apart from You do I want. But I do not know how to want, twisting myself in involuntary effort. But You wait silently and strictly, sadly and patiently. You do not take away my hope, for You believe in me more than I believe in myself. You always see me!

The commands of conscience, which a human being reckons as a law of one's own, receive religious sanction too, and this is the more acute the deeper one's religious consciousness is: they are clothed in the form of religious commandments, the violation of which is perceived as *sin* (and this is already a religious-moral category). "Doing the commandments" becomes the path to God, and at the same time the possibility of religious stumbling for the human, for, according to the word of the apostle Paul, sin is born from law or commandment and outside the law sin does not exist. But morality, which presupposes sinful division into two, the struggle of good and evil in the human being, cannot have an unconditional religious meaning; it is the Old Testament, a period of subjection to law that is overcome (although not abrogated) by the New Testament, by the kingdom of grace. As that which is tied up not with the substantiality but with the modality of human essence, as the fruit of original sin, morality generally speaking does not represent the summit, the absolute limit; it is surmountable. For holiness, although it includes "doing the commandments," is itself already found "on the other side of good and evil." Children, too, whose condition is the living norm of the Kingdom of God according to the Savior, are free of the bonds of morality.

Moreover, religion, which some wish to reduce entirely to ethics, in its integrity is higher than ethics and hence free from it: ethics exists for the human being in certain bounds such as law, but the human being must be able to rise above even ethics.[46] Let them ponder the sense of those stories of the Bible when God, for the purposes of religious economy, or for testing faith, permitted or even ordered acts that wittingly contradict morality: the sacrifice of an only son, the bloody extermination of whole nations, deceit, and theft. Old Testament history is filled with such examples, which is precisely the epoch of subjection to law (and this leads Tolstoy, M. Arnold, and many others astray when reading the Bible, for in their unreligious moralism they see in God a sentimental humanist in their own image and likeness). But although the Bible contains *law*, it is free of moralism and sentimentality; and when the will of God clashes with the voice *of human* morality it is placed clearly *higher* than morality. This means that morality has force only for the human being in his sinful limitedness and does not have an absolute significance. The Good is from God, he is the source of the Good, but God is not the Good if one were to understand it in a restrictive and exclusive sense; God is higher than the Good and in *this* sense remains free even from the Good. The Good is that which God wants *from us*, what *we* recognize as his command. To say it another way, in ethics what is religiously valuable and essential is its sanction rather than its content. Religion makes room for ethics and grounds it but is itself not exhausted by it or even determined by it (it does not "orient" itself by it). Therefore religious "law" is broader than morality, since it includes the ritual and cultic demands in general, which from the point of view of morality are completely unnecessary and are rejected by representatives of ethical religion as idolatry and superstition (*Abgötterei* and *Afterdienst* in Kant).

Ethics is not autonomous but heteronomous, for it is transcendent, i.e., its sanction is religious. It has its roots in religious consciousness. But what happens if the relationship between religion and ethics is turned on its head and it is proclaimed that the Good (in the ethical sense) is God, or to put it another way, that religion is exhausted by ethics? First of all, one ought to observe that to go on talking about religion in addition to ethics which is self-sufficient, to resort to religious sanction where the ethical is quite enough, is as it were unwarranted. However, one does this not so much to add a religious bouquet to ethics as to neutralize religion. Ethics thereby comes to mean a completely independent value and end in itself: that which is found on the other side of good and evil — holiness and childhood — loses all value, for only what passes through the ethical consciousness, only what is carried out for the sake of duty (Schiller was still ridiculing Kant for this) is valued. Here Old Testament legalism rises anew against New Testament grace and advances its own exclusive claims. But in this way the place of ethics in religion is entirely forfeited, so to say, and it receives a subordinate meaning. In this substitution of religion with ethics, the insidious intention of religious immanentism is concealed, namely the latent negation of religion. The transcendent God who is revealed many times and in many ways to humankind is replaced here by the moral law corresponding to the determined condition of sinful human consciousness. In reality, under the label of absolute ethics one definite aspect of human consciousness is deified. Kant's moral theology is precisely that bad anthropomorphism or psychologism in religion on which he declares war as it were, for the creaturely and human here are passed off for the divine; this militant psychologism assumes a character clearly hostile to religion, which is clearly revealed in Kant's religious tracts and especially those of Fichte (of the period of the *Atheismusstreit*). Religious immanentism to which the essence of psychologism in religion is reduced is directed hostilely against faith in a transcendent God and hereby annihilates the original nature of religion, by subjecting fundamental religious concepts to a false and forced interpretation. Ethics turns into pharisaic legalism, proud of its own rigorism and bad infinity in which it sees the exact manifestation of the unconditional quality of moral law. Therefore where the paths of Providence do not coincide with ethics, and where divine love, measurelessly forgiving the prodigal son, does not take legalistic fairness into consideration, ethics unalterably must cast its veto. According to Kant's definition, religion is ethics with the particularity that the commandments of the latter are regarded as the dictates of God. But can and even must one ask what kind of God this is if he only exists in ethical consciousness, which is itself self-sufficient? Is not this idea only an unnecessary doubling of the moral law, and is it not therefore a misunderstanding to distinguish God from an ethical consciousness that establishes a system of moral goals and postulates a moral world order?

Religion and Ethics

Fichte reached this inescapable conclusion "of moral theology" in the famous *Atheismusstreit*.[47] The moral world order for Fichte is "the divine, which we perceive." "This living and acting moral order is God himself; we have no need of another God and we cannot understand any other." "The concept of God as a particular substance is impossible and contradictory." "Beget in yourself a mood in conformity with duty and you will come to know God, and when for your neighbors you are fancied to be still in the sensible world, for your own self you will prove to be in eternal life."[48]

If some, in referring to the autonomy of ethics, identify religion with it, others, in starting out from the same autonomy, want to make it completely independent from religion. Such are the various constructs of utilitarian, evolutionary, and positive ethics. Is such an ethics possible "without the sanction of duty"? Here it is necessary to make a strict distinction between ethics and ethos, or morality and morals, i.e., good breeding, the totality of useful and advantageous habits, a certain dressage that effects so profound a difference between animals — cultured and domesticated. From the totality of similar habits is formed that which in recent times is called "humaneness." Behavior guided by egoism and cold calculation can dictate even party solidarity and economic mutual aid. But if one has in view not morals but morality, then who will resolve to assert that "civilized" nations are better and more moral than uncivilized? Only personal effort, struggle, and spiritual striving, not impersonal dressage, are subject to the domain of ethical evaluation, whereas these domains nearly always get mixed up among themselves and every sort of utilitarian suitability is taken for a moral value.

Morality inevitably breaks down together with the decline of religion, although for the time being this can be disguised as a softening of morals and a raising of personal fitness. For, although ethics does not cover religion with itself, yet it finds its foundation in it and only in it. Autonomous ethics is either a direct taunt at the good, which is what occurs in utilitarianism, or an affectation and pose, for to love the ethical "good," the law, the categorical imperative, is possible not for its own sake but only for the sake of God, the voice of whom we hear in conscience. The religious ideal of righteousness receives a description filled with majestic and very exalted pathos in Psalm 118 (119): *Blessed are the blameless who walk in the path of the Lord's commandments.* Here is given the unattainable ideal of religious righteousness, of virtue *not* for

Introduction

the sake of the Kantian "good," but for God, not in the name of lifeless duty, but entirely out of love for the Creator and his commandments.

Blessed are they who probe his testimonies, they seek him with all their heart (2).

You have commanded that Your commandments be kept diligently (4).

With all my heart I have sought You, do not turn me away from Your commandments (10).

Blessed are You, O Lord, teach me Your statutes (12).

My soul has preferred to long for Your ordinances at all times (20).

I have run the path of Your commandments, for you have expanded my heart (32).

Behold I have longed for Your commandments, in Your justice make me alive (40).

I have been instructed in Your commandments which I have loved greatly (47).

I have raised up my hands to Your commandments, which I have loved, and I have meditated on Your statutes (48).

You are good, Lord, and with Your goodness teach me Your statutes (68).

Good to me is the law of Your mouth more than thousands of gold and silver pieces (72).

Your hands have created and fashioned me: give me understanding and I will learn Your commandments (73).

Let my heart be blameless in Your statutes so that I not be put to shame (80).

My soul vanishes in Your salvation, I have hoped in Your words (81).

For ever, O Lord, Your word remains in the heavens (89).

From generation to generation is Your truth: You have founded the earth and it lasts (90).

If Your law had not been my instruction I would have perished in my humility (92).

I shall not forget Your statutes, O Lord, forever, for in them you have given me life (93).

I am Yours, save me for I have sought Your statutes (94).

Lord, how I have loved Your law, the whole day it is my instruction (97).

How sweet to my throat are Your words, more than honey to my mouth (103).

I am Your servant, give me understanding and I shall know Your testimonies (125).

For this reason I have loved Your commandments more than gold and topaz (127).

Faith and Dogma

Look upon me and have mercy, according to Your judgment of those who love Your name (132).

Direct my steps according to Your word and let not iniquity gain control of me (133).

Deliver me from human slander and I will keep Your commandments (134).

Let Your face shine on Your servant and instruct me in Your statutes (135).

You are just, O Lord, and just are Your judgments (137).

Your word is greatly inflamed, and Your servant loved it (140).

Your justice is justice for ever and Your law is truth (142).

You are near, O Lord, and all Your ways are truth (151).

I have hated and despised injustice, and I have loved Your law (163).

My soul keeps Your testimonies and I have loved them greatly (167).

I have preserved Your commandments and testimonies, for all my ways are before You, O Lord (168).

Let my prayer approach before You, O Lord; in keeping with Your word give me understanding (169).

Let my request come before You, O Lord, and deliver me according to Your word (170).

Let Your hand save me because I have chosen Your commandments (173).

I longed for Your salvation, O Lord, and Your law is my instruction (174).

Let my soul live and it will exalt You, and Your ordinances will help me (175).

I have strayed like a lost sheep, seek Your servant: for I have not forgotten Your commandments (176).

For thousands of years the prayerful flame of this psalm has been setting the soul on fire with its past power. Here is authentic, concrete religious ethics, and in its presence how powerfully one feels the poverty and insipidness of autonomous-ethical constructs — an ethics claiming to be religion or desiring to avoid religion entirely. King David shows up Kant.

V. Faith and Dogma

We have defined the content of faith as the revelation of the transcendent world, or the experience of Divinity. Whatever our judgment about faith in its essence may be, *in itself* the content of faith is precisely

Introduction

this: outside the sensible perception of reality and objectivity of what is experienced there is no place for faith. Faith necessarily senses itself, recognizes itself as revelation, while in a radical manner differentiating itself from the knowledge that is obtained within the limits of this world. Revelation according to its very own concept presupposes that *which* is revealed. Faith contains in itself the identification not only of that which *is* transcendent but also *what* it is; it cannot be limited by naked existential judgment, but includes a certain content: to **YOU ARE** there is always attached a certain predicate, although it may be of minimal content, or to the grammatical subject – a predicate. The deity is revealed to faith not *generally* but concretely and in a qualified manner. In other words, like a trace of itself in consciousness both individual and collective, the act of faith brings with itself and leaves after itself a judgment not only existential but also rich in content – or rather, a purely existential judgment without any rich content would even be impossible, for it would be without a subject. Such existence, drained of all content, would be changed unavoidably into nonbeing as Hegel has shown, and in order not to be subjected to the purgative and murderous karma of a further dialectic process, to which a being abstracted from all content or qualification is doomed in Hegel, it is necessary from the very start to save it from conversion into nothing by means of a defined *what*. This is what faith does. Therefore completely unjustified is that description of faith according to which some limit it only by existential judgment, as some gnoseologists do, the representatives of "mystical empiricism." Faith is not abstract but concrete: this means that *faith necessarily gives birth to dogmas* of one or the other content, or, the reverse, dogma is the formula of that which is identified by faith as transcendent existence.

The act of faith, which leads to the generation of dogma and supposes a definite dogmatic content, necessarily lays claim to the quality of *objectivity* or *trans-subjectivity*; with all its energy it denies psychologism or subjectivism. Dogma is gained through suffering, as is truth that is sought with all the powers of the soul and is not some kind of whim or caprice. In our age it is difficult to assure people that faith is a path devoid of arbitrariness, subjectivism, and caprice for the quest for religious truth, with that which is procured on this path having for itself all the compulsoriness of objective truth, requiring for itself self-sacrificing service. Without this quality of objectivity faith would completely lose its serious and difficult character, and its severity that always brings a tragic breaking of life for the heroes of faith: as they do not behave capriciously, so they do not experience the ephemeral "moods" of exasperated fantasy. The heavy and gloomy aureole of "fanaticism" that usually clothes faith, all this endless history of martyrdom and torture for the faith — these become entirely incomprehensible if one understands faith in the spirit of contemporary decadent "moods." Faith is, perhaps, the most *courageous* power of the spirit, gathering in one node *all* psychic energies: neither science nor art possesses that power of spiritual effort, as can be proper to religious faith. And of course this is possible only because the quality of objectivity is inherent in it to a completely exceptional degree: the most severe and majestic truth gazes through it with its eternal, unmoving eye onto the human being. The power of faith, its genius, so to say, is measured precisely with that degree of objectivity which religiously revealed truth receives in it: such faith is *summoned* to move mountains; from it is required that it place *its own* objectivity of religious truth higher than the objectivity of empirical knowledge that says a mountain is immovable. *Crede **ad** absurdum* [believe **in** the absurd], such is the postulate of faith. "You of little faith!" said the Savior to the apostles terrified during the storm on the lake, and it was indeed natural for them to be terrified, for the immediate danger of drowning was in fact great. The conflict between the content of faith and knowledge that converts the one for the sake of the other into the absurd can arise or not arise, but the objectivity of faith is such that it does not take the possibility of such conflict into account at all. This consciousness of its uniqueness is the inescapable quality of objectivity: truth is not truth if it allows another truth alongside itself or in place of itself; objectivity is jealous and if it is fitting, "fanatical." "Strong as death is love and fierce as the underworld is jealousy." And faith is love, for it is impossible to know truth without loving it: it is revealed only to love. On the other hand, faith is in its essence nothing other than love, but a love that strives, burns, and reduces to ashes everything that is foreign to it. "I came to cast fire upon the earth and how I would wish that it had already flared up!" (Luke 12:49). Fire burns; this is its natural and inalienable quality, and it would be strange to reproach it for this burning heat or to wish that it were deprived of it. Jealousy is the power of love (Fr. Florensky) and love cannot but be jealous, although love turned into jealousy is deprived of its mildness and tenderness and becomes demanding and severe.[49] "I am a consuming fire." "God is a jealous God," God says about himself in the Old Testament.

Introduction

Those hostilely contemptuous of the "fanaticism" of faith usually extol the "fanatics of science." But truth is always intolerant and intractable, and another tolerance costs little. It is too easy to preach tolerance and to be tolerant without having anything for a soul, but try to be tolerant when you ardently believe in a definite truth! Some say: truth does not fear competition, but it is not religion that must fear. It is we who must be afraid, before whom all this "variety" of religious experience lies in an untidy pile, the whole pantheon of gods and religions, the whole assortment of truths that are offered for selection to admirers, where our *truth* lies alongside of all kinds of lies externally and formally enjoying equal rights with it. It is necessary to be a *knight* of the truth, always ready for battle against any belittling of the Beautiful Lady's honor.

So-called tolerance can be a virtue and it becomes an even loftier virtue than intolerance only when it is nourished not by indifferent "pluralism," i.e., unbelief, but when it synthetically (or if you like, dialectically) accommodates in itself relative and limited half-truths and *condescends* to them from the height of its majesty, but in no way being equated with them, not reducing itself to the position of *one of many* possibilities in the "variety of religious experience." As an example one can point to the attitude of the apostle Paul to the Judaism which nurtured him and which he then abandoned (see especially Romans 12): here is an example *of positive tolerance and positive intolerance.*

Love is not "tolerance." Did not the Teacher of love say: woe to you scribes, Pharisees, hypocrites, brood of vipers, whitened sepulchers, all these angry and merciless words, merciless precisely in their truth? Is this really tolerance, in our sour-sweet pluralistic sense? This is surely "riotous conduct" and "fanaticism" in the view of the preachers of tolerance. . . . O God, send us jealous intolerance in the service of Your holy truth!

Insofar as the quality of objectivity is proper to the content of faith, it receives as well the attribute of universality and all-humanity, *catholicity*, which is only a different term for objectivity. If in faith truth itself is revealed for me, if I come out of the shell of my subjectivity and come into contact with something immeasurably vast, then obviously I am coming into contact not with what is in me individually and personally but with what is universal, general, catholic. As a *generic* being, as a *human*, I stand before Divinity; the human essence, the *human* in general, senses itself in me in this act. Herein is the original paradox of religious perception: being the most individual, personally endured, personally conditioned of all the acts of life, it proves to be the most universal at the same time — a clear sign that there is no opposition between the individual and the universal; the truly individual is also the truly universal, or the reverse, the truly universal exists and is known only as the individual.

It is impossible to possess the truth individually: of course in actuality it can be accessible in any given moment only to a limited number of people or even to a single human being, but even he, this one person, has the truth not as *his own* but as common to everyone and in which he only has been made to participate. And if individual truth is on the whole a *contradictio in adjecto* even in the domain of cognition, it is all the more so in the domain of religion where every separate individual perceives himself as a *human being* or as humanity before the face of God. Religion, *religio,* is the connection not only of the human being with Divinity but also of the human being with humanity, or his final and ultimate affirmation in his own humanness, and besides, this connection is stronger and more ontological than any other. Therefore "religious individualism" is burning ice, a round square. Sociologists often do not understand this universal nature of religion. They suppose that humanity is socialized through political, legal, and economic relations and do not notice that before all these particular combinations arise, humanity must already be fastened together and cemented by religion for them to become possible. If nationality is the natural basis of the state and the economy, nationality itself is first of all faith. Only religion is authentically social, and as such it is the basis of the social although, as the most profound basis, it is seen in this meaning all the rarer. Even when they consciously desire to be freed from religion, they still preserve the ideal of "the human" created by and belonging to it, in order to obtain from him "the citizen." On the other hand individualism in religion is an indication of immaturity or unhealthy decline.

At the present time when the taste for serious and courageous religion in general is lost and one cherishes the caprice of subjectivity with its fancifully changing moods more than severe and demanding religion, which does not tolerate childish willfulness, religious individualism finds itself in particular honor: those who still condescend to religion more often than not agree to hold it only individually; personal willfulness in a clear manner mingles with freedom, which is attained precisely by a victory over willfulness. The whole of Protestantism is sick with this kind of individualism, which gnaws away at it like a worm, and it grows weak religiously. It is all the more difficult to believe that the truth is the truth, i.e., that it demands worship for it and selflessness; it is much easier to take this truth as *my opinion* which *I* propose as truth: "this wicked and adulterous generation" makes even from truth a means to gratify its little *I*.

Religious truth is universal, i.e., *catholic (kath' 'olou)*, in conformity with *the whole*, not with particulars; according to its inner striving, in the truth everything is found to be one, or is one in everything: "Let us love one another that with one mind we may confess." As a result of this, truth is *conciliar*,[50] for conciliarity is only a *result* of catholicity, its expression, but in no way its external criterion. It is very important to distinguish catholic conciliarity from collectiveness or external society precisely in view of the fact that this confusion is very widespread. The point is that *the proclamation* of truth, according to Orthodox doctrine, belongs to the *council* which however acts and is authorized by the Church not as a collective, a general eparchial congress or ecclesiastical parliament, but as the organ of the very "Spirit of Truth," the Holy Spirit (whence derives the conciliar formula "it pleased the Holy Spirit and us"). A conciliar declaration of the truths of faith flows from the union in integral and integrating truth: here a majority of votes does not decide (even if externally it is employed as a means of revealing opinions) but a certain lived unity in the truth, an inspiration by it and a communion in it. Hence a quantitative criterion has no decisive significance here: not even one ecumenical council was really universal in the sense that there were representatives of *all* local churches at it, and on the contrary, a council having the external signs of ecumenicity could prove to be *a brigand council* and heretical (Ephesus). And now when the Christian church is split at the very least into two parts, does this mean that catholic truth cannot be declared at all, even if externally an ecumenical council is not possible now? Catholics are not at all wrong in thinking that an external schism of the churches does not bring dogmatic development to a standstill. Otherwise it would be necessary to admit that human squabbles and quarrels very easily block the path of the Holy Spirit's operation on the Church. Their sin and guilt against catholicity does not lie in this at all but in the fact that they have perverted the very idea of catholicity by binding it with an *external* authority like some ecclesiastical oracle: they have subjected conciliarity, mechanically understood as external collectiveness, to a

Faith and Dogma

monarchic representation of this collectiveness — the pope, and thus they have become isolated from the rest of the Christian world in this enclosure of authority and with it they have betrayed catholicity, integrative truth, and ecclesial love. But their antagonists understand catholicity in just as catholic or external a manner and consider the schism of the churches to be a sufficient basis for curtailing the quest for dogmatic truth under the pretext that an ecumenical council is now impossible; for this reason one can rest peacefully. From the concept of catholicity (which corresponds to the immutable promise "where two or three are gathered in my name, there I am in the midst of them" and therefore in them the mind of Christ, i.e., truth itself, rests) it follows that the external measurements of conciliarity have significance for the recognition of truth rather than for its discovery. An ecumenical council — not one in name only but in fact — is possible even now no less than previously. If the gathering "of two or three believers" perceives itself to be really catholic and is so in fact, then the seed of an ecumenical council is hereby already given, while its recognition is the work of subsequent church history.[51]

Thus, true ecumenicity, catholicity, *does not take into account* any external forms or statutes, which are created by and for human beings and which have in themselves nothing indisputable or invariable. The betrayal of catholicity lies precisely in the exaggeration of *its external* attributes. "God does not give the spirit in measures," and when tongues of fire flare up over heads, by whatever external circumstances they did so, it seems credible that religious consciousness becomes ecumenical, catholic. With this reasoning I do not at all mean to undermine the importance and necessity of ecclesiastical discipline or to approve the tendency to dogmatic flippancy into which religious dilettantism easily falls. There is nothing easier than thinking up new dogmas, taking the irritation of one's own fantasy for the blowing of the spirit. A certain distrust of contemporary fashioners of dogma must be respected as an exigency of good religious taste, which enjoins us to be guided by the rule *dogmata non fingo* [I do not make up dogmas], similar to Newton's maxim *hypotheses non fingo* [I do not make up hypotheses]. By the way, invented dogmas are always of short duration and like a toy quickly cease to interest even their very authors.

From catholicity as a general quality of religious consciousness it follows that in religious consciousness, in keeping with its transcendental nature, *the idea of ecclesiality* is already *given* similar to how the

Introduction

idea of the objectivity of knowledge is given in gnoseological consciousness. The search for ecclesiality, for authentic catholicity, constitutes an irremovable feature of religious consciousness; it is the search for the true Church, and the one is indissolubly bound with the other. Religious consciousness is ecclesial by nature. The idea of the church was born not in Christianity; it exists even earlier and outside of Christianity. Therefore one can speak of a church of the Jews, a church of the pagans, a Buddhist church, etc. (although in a formal and so to say religiously transcendental sense). Every religion, as soon as it ceases to be the possession of an individual human being, its founder, and communicates itself to others (and it strives irrepressibly to be communicated), organizes its own community; there is no religion, there is not even the most insignificant sect, that has not organized itself into an *ecclesia* or *ecclesiola*. These circumstances are unusually important for understanding the historical development of religion. They establish the legitimacy and permanence of *ecclesial tradition,* that catholicity which becomes firmly established; in other words, the path towards a positive ecclesiality is outlined. Religions are not put together according to abstract schemas by a single thinker, but represent an original religious-historical monolith or conglomerate having internal coherence and integrity. Existing religions are like ready-made systems of dogmas or original dogmatic organisms living their own particular life. The initiator of a new religion proposes his personal religious experience as its foundation; then this becomes overgrown with the concordant conciliar experiences of its followers. Each religiously alive human being brings pebble after pebble for this building. A collectivity is reborn into catholicity, which is then smelted into ecclesiality. A religion arises, "faith." The religious experience of each separate human being does not allow one to sense *the entire* fullness of religion, but usually there is sufficient of the living contact with religious reality that is given by faith, in *one* only place, and then all the other content of religion, all its promises, are accepted as a postulate, as a hope, as a path. Whoever once has encountered Christ the Savior on their personal path and sensed his divinity has simultaneously received all the fundamental Christian dogmas — his birth from the Virgin, the incarnation, the coming in glory, the coming of the Comforter, and the Holy Trinity. Therefore there is absolutely no need for everyone in their personal experience of faith to have *the whole* content of a given religious doctrine, just as it is not necessary to cover the whole scientific path of hu-

Faith and Dogma

manity in one's personal experience in order to grasp the nature of science; it suffices to come to know it in any particular case.

What has been said leads us to a comprehension of *the historical* in religion. With the twofold nature of religious faith — on the one hand, its intimate-individual character in virtue of which it can be experienced only in the deepest depths of personal experience, and on the other hand, its ardent striving towards suprapersonal catholicity — is established its dual attitude towards the religious empyrean and the historical, concrete forms of religiousness. They can receive a vital significance only after the intimate, personal religious experience opens their living meaning, the catholic nature of religion impelling one especially *to honor* historical tradition. Proper to any religion is a certain old ritualism, an attachment to olden times; not an iota can be changed from the law arbitrarily, by personal whim or taste, without prophetic daring. This is why old churches, old books, old liturgical vessels, old icons naturally inspire for themselves a particular feeling of religious reverence and trepidation. Antiquity is the strength, the power of catholicity, which seems to be concentrated on separate objects as time passes.

Thus religion is historical in nature, or rather it elevates the historical to the catholic. Whoever does not know this, and is squeamish about the historical empyrean under pretext of the freedom of inspiration, is an adolescent in religion. By the way, "enlighteners" who thought up and continue to think up "natural" antihistorical religion, are that kind of adolescent. They do not notice that today's "natural religion" will tomorrow become historical, and even less, that to a certain degree it becomes historical at the very moment when it feels itself to be objective and catholic. Likewise all the persecutors of traditional ritual do not notice that in reality they only introduce a new ritual; thus the Quakers, who reject every external form of prayer, in fact introduced the ritual of naked walls of the meeting-house and "silent meetings." So too Protestantism, after raising an audacious hand against the centuries-old and aesthetically beautiful Catholic ritual, only replaced it with another ritual, poor, dry, and prosaic, within which it is possible to be just as much of an old ritualist as in the most splendid ritual; so also do our sectarians replace the divine beauty of Orthodox liturgical texts with tedious and mediocre "psalms," with a dry Protestant ritual. "Natural," abstract, extra-historical religion is an *Unding* [absurdity], something that does not exist, a negative concept not having a positive content but drawing it only from that which it negates.

Introduction

This is the principal fabrication of religiously mediocre epochs, known already to antiquity with its "euhemerism" and syncretism. "Religion in general" does not exist; there are only definite, concrete religions.

The so-called theosophical doctrine, according to which all religions have a common content and say one and the same thing only with different language, constitutes a special variety of natural religion or "religion in general," and it is necessary to distinguish the *esoteric* doctrine known only to initiates from the *exoteric* doctrine existing for the *profanum vulgus* [vulgar rabble]; differences of symbol and ritual, which are conditioned by historical causes, exist only in the second and not in the first. This doctrine rests on bold analogies and identifications, especially on the convergences of moral doctrines in which it is on the whole easier to find similarities than in dogma and ritual. In this way the original paints of historical religions lose their color; everything concrete passes away into exotericism, and the doctrine of the theosophical society so preoccupied with disseminating a universal religious Volapük[52] is held up as esoteric content (in reality it happens under the guise of a religious Esperanto that brings the propaganda of Buddhism and Hinduism in general to the Christian soil of Europe, but instead of an open manifestation and direct fight with Christianity it prefers the roundabout tactic of its assimilation and neutralization).

The concrete features of religion are established by its positive content, more precisely, by the revelation that it contains (or at least considers that it contains). Religion is not based on a vague and undefined perception of Divinity in general or of the transcendent world in general, to which it is reduced by adogmatic mysticism and *Gefühlstheologie* on the one hand and rationalistic educational activities on the other hand; it is based rather on a certain fully defined *knowledge* of this world, the self-revelation of Divinity. *All religion is dogmatic;* it establishes a relation not to Divinity in general but to a definite God having his own "name." In this sense dogma is an integral part of religion. What is *dogma*? One can differentiate this concept in a narrower and a more expansive sense. In the first sense dogma is a formula that crystallizes in images or concepts a religious judgment. Logical limits established by such a formula usually have a practical origin. Their proclamation more often than not is called for by the requirement of a struggle against some form of heresy. It is for this reason not only a doctrinal definition of the Church but also its *activity* — the condemnation and excision of heresy (e.g., the Nicene formula had an anti-Arian character, that of the Fourth Council, against Macedonius, the Seventh, an anti-iconoclast character, etc.). But in virtue of its indicated origin, a dogmatic formula is only an approximate, though unavoidably one-sided attempt to express religious content in concepts. It is not a dogmatic formula that gives birth to dogma; rather, religious content, or living dogma, generates a dogmatic formula (or formulae).

If the divine world really is revealed to religious consciousness and the transcendent becomes immanent[53] to it in some dogmatic certainty, then obviously there must be a bridge that unites both worlds: there must be things written by which the divine revelations are outlined and a language in which they can be expressed.

But if our words usually serve for the concepts *of this* world, of its subjects and correlations, how can they be suitable for the contents of a different, transcendent world? Does not this transcendence involve both ineffableness and inconceivableness for the human being? We have already said enough about the fact that the divine world cannot be the subject of discursive knowledge and is grasped only by faith. Dogmas, if they are possible, are so not in the sense of logical and dialectical deductions but only as religious knowing. In order to approach an understanding of the nature of this knowing, one must recall the generation of artistic images in painting. An artist is a soothsayer of unearthly reality that is revealed to him in artistic images. The bearer of religious revelation (which can be both a single person and a collective) apprehends the highest reality through the means of religious forms that are akin to artistic ones by their immediacy but differ from them by their religious character. Figurativeness and symbolism unite them, but the content of this symbolism and their source distinguish them.

Religious forms, which realize and express religious content, represent what is usually called *myth*. To myth in religion belongs the role analogous to what is proper to concept or judgment in theoretical philosophy: on its understanding the evaluation of religious dogmatic consciousness depends.

Thus, what is *myth* as a "transcendental" category?

VI. The Nature of Myth

First of all one ought to remove a widespread conception of myth as the product of fantasy and invention. A question so simple and yet so fundamental does not even cross the mind of the partisans of this understanding of myth: "What was a myth for the myth's creators themselves, in whose consciousness it arose? What did they themselves think about the myth that they produced? Some will say, perhaps, that they consciously invented it in order to deceive others. And have they not seriously affirmed that priests invented religion and consequently established it on a conscious and deliberate deception? But in such a case they would have had to deceive themselves first of all, for they did believe in the myths, and they imparted an objective meaning to the myths' content, not considering it in any way to be only the result of poetic fantasy. Only with such a supposition does the role of mythopoesis in the history of humanity become understandable, where the *Dichtung* of myth frequently clarifies the weighty *Wahrheit* of history.[54]

And so first of all one ought to acknowledge that the whole objectivity or catholicity which is proper to "revelation" in general is inherent in myth: in it the content of revelation is substantially expressed or, in other words, the revelation of the transcendent, higher world happens immediately in *myth*. It is the letters with which this world is outlined in immanent consciousness, its projection in forms.

One can say (by applying Kant's terminology) that *myth is a synthetic religious judgment a priori* from which *a posteriori* judgments can then be deduced analytically. Once it has arisen, a myth contains in itself something new, until then unknown to the mythmaker himself, and this content is affirmed as a self-evident truth. This self-evidence is generated precisely by the experiential-intuitive character of its origin. Inherent to myth is its own credibility, which rests not on proofs but on the power and persuasiveness of immediate experience. In myth is ascertained *an encounter* of the immanent world — of human consciousness (no matter how we may expand and deepen it) and the transcendent divine world. The transcendent, all the while preserving its proper nature, at the same time becomes immanent, whereas the immanent opens itself, feeling in itself the inculcation of the transcendent. Activity is necessarily inherent in myth, a certain *initiative* on the part of the transcendent which *desires* this encounter, and the power of a myth's persuasiveness lies in the realism of this encounter. Its objectivity consists in this. It is an event that occurs at the boundary of two worlds that are contiguous in it (Viacheslav Ivanov). It is something "graced" (taking the concept of *grace* in a general and formal sense). If myth is an event, it must be thought especially realistically: to say it differently, in myth it is a question not of abstract concepts but of realities themselves. The content of myth is always *concrete;* in myth it is a question not of God in general and humankind in general but of a definite form or instance of a definite divine revelation. That which underlies myth, its subject, can be designated only with a "proper" name, not a "common" generic name. For this reason, myth is or rather must be the negation of any subjectivism or psychologism (although of course errors and illusions of the mythopoetic consciousness are possible; hence there are subjective or false myths). On the contrary, the awareness that a nonhuman power enters a human being and that events occur in him that exceed his proper measure, alone creates the vital persuasiveness of myth. Here it is not the human being who acts or "sets" *(setzt)*, as takes place in subjective-idealistic constructions; rather, something happens and is set in the human being; higher essences and powers speak in him. The striving of the occultists to hear by means of meditation the voice of things themselves is formally akin to "mythopoesis," as is the faith of Hegel: that after the lowest phenomenological levels of the self-consciousness of spirit are overcome by him by means of philosophical rumination, the Logos itself acts in thought. In particular Hegel wanted to be an authentic mythmaker in logic, for he strove so that in and through it the logical would itself operate which remains transcendent for the human being in his subjectivity or humanity. The pathos of Hegel's logic consists precisely in the experience of just such an encounter of transcendent Logos and immanent thought and in their blending, in making the immanent transcendent or the transcendent immanent, with logic itself receiving a clearly theurgic and undoubtedly supralogical meaning. This mythopoetic pathos of Hegel, perhaps, best of all explains why he put philosophy higher than religion, for he perceived philosophical knowing as an authentic myth, and philosophy as true mythology. With him, logical contemplation becomes an eye for comprehending the noumenal world (whence is understandable Hegel's hostility towards the Kantian doctrine of the thing in itself and its incognoscibility, and in general the sharp and passionate immanentism of his doctrine). From this point of view the weak side of Hegelianism comes down to this: in myth-formation all of the energy belongs to the human being, the mythmaker. Hegel's philosophy is a self-insemination, a parody of conception without seed, mythopoesis in the immanent (for according to Hegel it is sufficient to pass through the regular trial of phenomenology and enter the kingdom of logic, as the Logos has already been attained).

Introduction

In Kant's philosophy, on the contrary, precisely in his doctrine about "ideas" as ultimate concepts, and equally in his doctrine about distinguishing the judgments of practical reason from theoretical reason and "the power of judgment" lies implicitly a whole theory of mythopoesis, although of a negative or agnostic content. According to this theory, the *Ding an sich* [the thing in itself] although transcendent, is all the same impressed in the consciousness as "ideas" or ultimate concepts. But with Kant these ideas differ from myths in that they not only do not witness to the real presence or revelation of the transcendent, but contain even less reality than experiential cognition; they are only schemas, shadowy traces, nothing more. We know to what fatal consequences this agnosticism leads in Kant's theology, where he refers to everything mythical not only without any comprehension but also with malicious disdain, by limiting himself to immanent moral theology. (The false understanding of the nature of myth, connected with a general iconoclast aspiration, distinguishes Luther as well and in general the whole of Protestantism with its immanentism and rationalism.)

And nevertheless even in this doctrine of Kant about ideas as immanent projections of the *Ding an sich* there is a precious seed of the theory of mythopoesis: the *Ding an sich*, transcendent to theoretical cognition, all the same is knowable and indeed by its own special path, distinct from the immanent-experiential; the Kantian postulates of practical reason are his "reasonable" faith, and are likewise nothing other than mythopoesis. In gnoseological language myth is a cognition of that which lies beyond the bounds of the *Ding an sich* for reason, and the Kantian doctrine of the unknowable thing in itself contains therefore a certain philosophical myth of agnostic content. The philosophical contradiction of this Kantian doctrine has always been noted: the *Ding an sich* appears simultaneously both transcendent and immanent to reason; it is for it at once both nothing and something. But this contradiction becomes completely natural if one is to understand the Kantian doctrine in its underlying sense — not as a philosopheme but as a myth or religious perception, for the definition of the transcendent-immanent *Ding an sich*, contradictory from the point of view of speculative philosophy, expresses exactly the essence of religious experience.

Religious mythopoesis must be distinguished from domains of comprehension similar to it. Artistic creativity, insofar as it is based on an authentic "noetic vision," stands in closest kinship with it. Images for an artist have in their own way the same kind of objectivity and compulsoriness as myth. The images control the creative self-consciousness of an artist, and he must master them in his works, creatively consolidate them in the immanent world. His task is to see and hear in a fitting manner and then to incarnate what was seen and heard in some form (it does not matter how: in paint, sound, word, sculpture, architecture); a true artist is bound by the greatest artistic veracity, he may not fabricate anything.[55] Strictly speaking, differences between an artist and a mythmaker do not exist, according to the "transcendental" nature of their knowing. The distinction is here established by their *domain* or subject. We already pointed out that the transcendent in its correlativity with the immanent has different degrees or a different depth, and apart from the transcendent in the proper sense, i.e., the religious domain, there exist many layers of the relative-transcendent that are revealed in the immanent; if we reason in a formally gnoseological manner, in all similar cases we have the presence of mythic insight or mythopoesis. Diverse natural elements (wood-goblins, water-sprites, mermaids, elves, gnomes, etc.) reveal themselves in myth; popular fairy tales in their well-known sphere are these sorts of natural myths, which arise of course at a time of the greatest immediacy and sensitivity to the voices from the domain of what lies beyond the bounds of feelings. Nature in its multivocality speaks in dark traditions and beliefs, in fairy tales, folklore, in the "fantasy" of an artist; sometimes it prophesies directly with its mystical depth. (Thus in ancient and modern times the mysticism of nature emerges; a thinker such as Jacob Böhme, for example, is treated as one of its representatives, a mythmaker of nature whom it is fitting therefore to call not divinely inspired but inspired by nature. Such is F. Tiutchev, the poetic clairvoyant of "chaos.") Generally speaking, the forms of "revelation" and so too its subjects can be diverse: natural, divine, and demonic (which the church fathers named "delusion"); it can proceed from different worlds and hierarchies, and in itself "revelation" with the myth expressing it, understood in a formally gnoseological sense, can have diverse content: good and evil, true and deceptive (for even Satan assumes the guise of an angel of light). Therefore, by itself the "revealed" or mystical character of a given doctrine speaks only about the intuitive means of its reception but says nothing yet about its quality. In principle the possibility of error and deception here is not excluded at all. In this lies the danger of enticement by false revelations, accepted for the truth only because gnoseologically they have the character of revelation; they are not discursive but intuitive. Revelation, mythopoesis, is consequently also that form in which the revelation of the Holy Spirit likewise occurs, but it is itself still not connected with a given form as such for it is entirely possible that for all the formal similarity of a "revelation" the latter proves to be empty and false, deprived of authentically spiritual content. Therefore caution, verification, attentiveness are no less necessary in mysticism and revelation, if not more so than in discursive knowledge. It is necessary to adjust personal intuitions in keeping with church tradition, since only the Church is recognized as "the pillar and ground of the truth," and not the reverse — to verify church tradition according to personal intuition. And here the enormous significance of church tradition already crystallized and cast in dogmas, cult, and daily life, appears anew, traditions *of the historical* church which always moderates self-styled pretensions made in the name of the "mystical church," i.e., frequently in the name of one's own personal mysticism (or what happens even more often and especially in our time, of a single mystical ideology, accepted as authentic mysticism by reason of the paucity of mystical experience). Here as in many cases in religious life we run against an antinomy: naked historicism, external authoritarianism in religion is the ossification of ecclesiality; willful mysticism is its decomposition. Neither the one nor the other is necessary, but at the same time both are necessary: both ecclesiastical authority as well as personal mysticism. To find here the right measure for which there are no external criteria, only an interior one (so to say a religious-aesthetic criterion), is the task of the "spiritual art" guided only by spiritual taste, by a feeling for spiritual time. . . .

The content of myth represents a judgment that confirms a certain bond between a subject and a predicate. In what language is this content expressed? Is it a language of concepts that are subject to a philosophical elaboration not only in their meaning but also in their very origins, or are they signs of a different nature and structure that are found in the same direct relation to philosophical concepts as the forms of art? One can philosophize about them discursively, but in their availability they are *given* to thought. Obviously such is the nature also of the forms of religious myth, its symbolism. The content of myth is expressed in symbols. What is a religious symbol? This question became particularly dear to modern Russian literature (V. Ivanov, A. Bely). Symbolism can have a diverse meaning. Thus in a rationalistic application symbol is taken as a conventional sign, an abbreviation of a concept, sometimes as a whole aggregate of concepts, a constructive schema, a logical draft; it is the condition of conditions and in this sense something nonexisting; it is *pragmatic* in its origins and transparent outside its pragmatism; it arises on definite grounds, clutches at things only in pre-indicated points; its realism is partial, accidental. Such is the symbolism of mathematics to a certain degree; such in particular is the symbolism of scientific concepts. In this sense all science is symbolic but this symbolism proves to be a synonym for pragmatism, subjectivism, and in the final account, skepticism or illusionism. Being pragmatic, science is psychological in its nature, and the whole of it is a vast psychologism although having a basis in the objective essence of things.[56] The opposite of this symbolism of conventional signs and pragmatic schemas is symbolism in religion and art, which equally make use of symbol (which marks their mysterious proximity). Symbolism, according to the well-known definition of V. Ivanov, goes *a realibus ad realiora* [from the real to the more real], from *on* to *ontos on* [being to real being], and for that reason psychologism is foreign to it. Unlike the pragmatic-conventional character of scientific concepts, the content of symbol is objective and weighty, in contrast with concepts as "shells" that do not have their own content or with words that are interiorly devoid of *the word*. It is impossible to lie artistically and it is impossible to act against one's conscience mythopoetically: the human being does not create myth, rather myth is uttered through a human being.

Such is the gnoseological meaning of myth: parallel with discursive thinking and scientific scholarship, alongside of artistic creativity stands religious mythopoesis as a special autonomous domain of the human spirit; myth is the instrument of religious knowing. It is self-evident that what is deposited in the consciousness in the form of myth, by entering into the common human consciousness, affects all the abilities of the soul, and can become the subject of thought, of scientific study and artistic reproduction. But the framework of religious myth, its essential content, is not fashioned by thinking and is not created by imagination; it is generated in religious experience. The content of myth refers to the domain of divine being, on the line of contact with the human. Insight into the divine world is also possible through the membrane of the empirical, from within. In such a case human history, without ceasing to be history, is mythologized at the same time, for it is understood not only by its empirical, temporal expression but also by its noumenal, supratemporal essence; so-called sacred history, i.e., the history of the chosen people of God, is also such a mythologized history. The events of the lives of the Hebrew people are told here in their religious significance; history, without ceasing to be history, becomes myth. But the unique example of that kind of union of the noumenal and the historical, of myth and history, is undoubtedly the Gospel events, the center of which is the incarnate God the Word, who is at the same time the man Jesus who was born at the time of Tiberius and suffered under Pontius Pilate. History becomes here an immediate and supreme mystery, visible with the eyes of faith; history and myth coincide; they merge through the act of divine incarnation.

Myth arises from religious experience, which is why mythopoesis presupposes not the abstract effort of thought but a certain going out of the self into the domain of divine being, some sort of divine operation; in other words, myth has a theurgic provenance and theurgic meaning. This being the case, mythopoesis is not a single act but one that is repeated over and over. According to its theurgic nature myth has a necessary bond with *cult* as a system of sacred and theurgic actions, divine operation and divine worship. This explains the paramount significance of cult for religious consciousness, which is not only practical but also theoretical, even gnoseological. Cult is experienced myth — *myth in action*. Whence the universal significance of divine worship, cult, in every religion, for its living, real symbolism is not only the means for the exercise of piety but also the heart of religion, and its eye is active mythopoesis. The iconoclastic tastes of our age, connected with its abstractness and rationalism, have completely darkened the religious and religious-gnoseological significance of cult for contemporary humankind, which has grown accustomed to pronounce the word *ritual* with haughty and blind disdain. This all depends on that fundamental sin in understanding symbolism in general and cult in particular — anthropomorphic subjectivism or psychologism. Such an understanding of cult leads one to see in its symbolic function only arbitrarily established allegorical symbols or theatrical gestures that awaken a certain mood or express a certain idea (ritual has received almost the same meaning in contemporary Protestantism where even the Eucharist is understood as some sort of symbolic allegory). In such an understanding, divine worship acquires the meaning of a religious spectacle in which didactic plays "are presented" (and instructions and sermons are produced in abundance). In addition the

The Nature of Myth

loss of a taste for the aesthetic of cult makes these "presentations" wearisome and incomprehensible; rationalism declares war on cult for its splendor, beauty, and imagined theatricality (such are the dominating frames of mind of the whole Reformation, especially of Calvinism, Puritanism, and Quakerism). In cult one sees either theatrical ceremonies or "pagan" magism, "mystagogy" (it suffices to read contemporary Protestant theologians, e.g., Harnack's *History of Dogmas*). As a liturgical church par excellence, Orthodoxy is subjected in this respect to special attacks even compared with Catholicism, whose liturgical materials are in comparison not so rich, despite the great splendor of its cult.

In order to understand the meaning of cult, it is necessary to take into account its symbolic realism, its mythopoetic energy. For the faithful, cult is not a theatrical presentation with the goal of creating a mood and it is not an aggregate of willfully selected symbols, but a completely real divine operation, experienced myth, or mythologized reality. True, it is limited by place (a temple, sacred places), objects (sacred things), and time (divine worship, sacred times); it forms therefore only theurgic points on the timeline, but this particularity corresponds on the whole to the nature of religion. Although religion strives to have God as "all in all," to fuse the transcendent and the immanent into one and thereby overcome their reciprocal polarity, still it arises precisely from that tension and exists only by it and together with it. In this sense religion is a certain transitory state — it strives to overcome itself, it perceives itself "as an old testament." When God becomes "all in all" there will be no religion in our sense; it will no longer be necessary to reunite *(religare)* what has been disunited, and there will not be a special cult, for all life will be a divinely operated divine worship. Not for nothing do we read in the Apocalypse about the New Jerusalem coming down from heaven: "I saw no temple in it, for the Lord God Almighty is its temple and the lamb" (Rev. 21:22). Cult creates a portent and a particular experience of the divine in the empirical, where, like everything in religion, it is not abstract, not "in general," but qualified, concrete, in connection with a definite myth — with dogma. Therefore divine worship, cult, is *living dogmatics,* and myths are dogmas in operation, in life. Whence the universal dispersion of cult is understandable, for *there is no religion without cult.* One can present this as an axiom. The diversity of cults corresponds to the diversity of religions, and the migration of religions is accompanied by the migration of cults. One can say that only that is living and vital in religion which is in cult, and what is not in cult dies away or is incapable of life.

Introduction

At the center of divine worship, obviously, is prayer, the meaning of which for mythopoesis is clear from the foregoing. A prayer life receives development and expression in liturgical creativity in which church tradition amasses precious pearls of liturgical poetry and enthusiasm. From this, one can understand the paramount significance of liturgical materials in general, of church hymnody, prayers, and rituals, for mythopoetic self-consciousness. Other aspects of the symbolism of cult, aside from what is expressible in word, have a like significance. In the first place here one ought to put iconography; apart from the religious significance of an icon as such, this myth-object, in which empirical materiality is mysteriously united with transcendent essence, it always has an entirely definite content; this is mythology in paint, stone, or marble. From this stems that paramount significance of iconography for the development of religious life and self-consciousness, for the Christian and for extra-Christian religions in equal measure. Iconoclasm and the decline of iconography signify for the most part the decline of religion too. Generally speaking myth takes possession of all the arts for its own realization so that the written word, a book, is in reality only *one of many* means for the expression of the content of faith (and here the religious limitation of Protestantism is elucidated, which in the whole of its ecclesiastical tradition recognizes only the book, and wants to be a "Buch-Religion" [Book-religion]).

On a level with liturgical material and iconography one ought to place symbolic actions that have a theurgic meaning: the order of divine worship, sacrifices, and sacraments. In the rituals of divine worship naturally arising in each religion, the content of myth is symbolically experienced; dogma becomes not a formula but a living religious symbol. Sacraments, of course, occupy the very central place in cult. In keeping with what has been pointed out, the sacramental character belongs strictly speaking to the whole divine worship, but this sacramentality condenses and so to say crystallizes in the separate acts that constitute the sacraments in the proper sense. *A sacrament* does not at all signify a communication of some sort of mysteries or secrets and it does not have any relation to "arcane knowledge," occultism and magic. A sacrament is as necessary and one may even say gnoseologically irremovable an attribute of religion as is prayer; therefore aside from their religious comprehension, one ought to grasp as well their gnoseological sense. Religion flows out of a sense of the rupture between the immanent and the transcendent, and at the same time an

The Nature of Myth

intense attraction to it: the human being tirelessly seeks God in religion and heaven presses close to earth with an answering kiss. For religion to be possible not only as a thirst and a question but also as a slaking and an answer, it is necessary that this polarity, this tension sometimes yields place to satisfaction, that the transcendent becomes sensible and not only sought after, and administers to itself immanent reality. The sacramental element in a sacrament lies in this vital communion with that world which remains closed for us, and the this-worldly world is then perceived like a vessel for that other world; more briefly, sacrament is the experience of the transcendent in the immanent, a communication of "grace" to creation in definite sacramental acts. And insofar as this feature is inherent in a sacrament, obviously, it constitutes the most interesting point in the general process of mythopoesis. The whole fundamental difference of sacrament from "magism" is clear. Magic is an expanded, refined, and deepened power of the human being over the natural world with the assistance of his higher knowledge; magic is the same as science only on a different level, with other methods. Like it, magism is limited by the domain of the immanent; it is cosmic and natural. It contains no "grace" whatever in the proper sense of this word, aside from the natural grace poured out in the whole world; and it is human inasmuch as it rests entirely on the power of a human being, on his strength and energy. On the contrary, a sacrament is entirely based on grace, and it is realized through the outpouring of the transcendent, supernatural principle into the natural world. By this sign true sacraments are distinguished from false ones that represent nothing other than the variety of magism (natural sacraments). A Christian may properly believe that although the need for sacrament was vividly felt in the pagan world, for by its very essence it cannot be removed from religion, and although the need was met *in its own way*,[57] there were no true sacraments "which nourish unto life eternal." These could only appear in Christianity, after the incarnation of God the Word who gave his Flesh and Blood for eternal life. Their anticipations existed already in the Old Testament church of Israel.

A dogmatic formula is an attempt to state the content of a religious myth in word, to express it in concepts. Dogma, in the sense of formula, always arrives *after* myth, or *out of* myth, i.e., it does not arise in a formula or together with a formula but is only fixed by it, entered in a list. Dogmatics is as it were the bookkeeping of religious creativity, and its formulas are the products of reflection apropos religious givenness. The history of dogma shows that the reason for their establishment and proclamation was the one or other heresy, i.e., deviations not only of religious thought but also and above all of religious life (surely, it is evident for example that Arianism is a completely different perception of Christianity than church orthodoxy). Dogma, in turning down pseudo-wisdom, puts in its place the right formula and this formula is the logical limit, the fence of dogma. It defines that external boundary beyond which it is impossible to deviate, but it is not adequate to dogma at all, it does not exhaust its content: first of all because every dogmatic formula, as already said, is only a logical schema, a sketch of integral religious experience, its incomplete translation into the language of concepts; and then because it usually arises because of heresy — "divisions" (*hairesis* — division), it pursues for the most part critical goals and hence has sometimes even a negative character: "unmingled and indivisible," "one Divinity and three hypostases," "unity in Trinity and Trinity in unity." *Omnis definitio est negatio* [All definition is negation]. This formula of Spinoza is especially applicable to dogmatics, for here *negatio*, hewing dogmas like sparks from a stone, more often is the occasion for *definitio*: the quantity of *possible* dogmatic definitions in Christianity could be significantly greater than those that are formulated at councils.

Dogmas, in coming to life out of dispute, have the character of volitional affirmations. They differ in this sense from theoretical cognition and psychologically converge with that which bears the name "conviction."[58] The forms in which they are cloaked, their logical apparel, are borrowed from the reigning philosophical doctrine: thus, for example — of course not without the special will of God — in the history of Christian dogmatics the influence of Hellenism is said to be very perceptible and beneficial. But from this it in no way follows that they were engendered by it (as Harnack and others suppose). Faith in the resurrection of Christ, "for the Greeks foolishness, for the Jews, a stumbling-block,"[59] as the principal theme of Christian preaching could appear only out of the fullness of religious revelation, as a "myth" in the *positive* significance of this word, and only later on from this seed did the system of dogmas of church doctrine grow. Dogma is the making immanent of the transcendent content of religion, and this draws after itself a whole series of losses, dangers, substitutions; in this logical transcription of myth scholasticism (or "seminary theology") inevitably arises, i.e., a rationalistic processing of dogmas, their accommodation to rational thought, in which their authentic taste and aroma are frequently lost, and "theology" is transformed into "a science like all others," only with its own subject. True, these other sciences, proud of their immanent-experiential derivation, look askance at their poor relative all the time, seeing in it a freeloader. Indeed this standing in the world costs theology itself dearly. One cannot deny, however, that even in this "scientific" work of theology there is a certain use for stock-taking, and the honesty of a Martha who has already ceased to be a Mary is its own.

Between a living religious myth-dogma and its dogma-formula there exists therefore a notorious discrepancy similar to that which exists between a catalogue of an art warehouse and the works enumerated in it or between the program of a concert and its musical execution. This discrepancy is the result not only of the verbal inexpressibility of the fullness of religious experience but also the general inadequacy of the concepts for that which they are called upon here to express. For with concepts that arise as a result of applying categories of discursive thinking, in the supposition of spatiality and temporality, here conditionally are expressed the essences of another world. About God one must speak in numerical, temporal, and spatial terms that belong to our empirical world. God is *one*, God is *triune* in persons: *unity*, *three* are numbers subject to the whole numerical limitation (with the assistance of unity it is quite impossible to express *the one* Divinity, for unity exists only in plurality, and *three* in the Holy Trinity is absolutely not three in the sense of counting: one, two, three, or one and one and one, or one and two). Here number expresses what is a super-number and a super-magnitude, time is that which is supratime, eternity, and space is that which is super-spatial, everywhere. For many this notorious inadequacy of the categories of reason for the subject of religion serves as a motive for dogmatic agnosticism (Kant and his school). But this consideration would have force only in that case if dogmatic concepts were an immediate *instrument of religious cognition;* for such a purpose concepts would be, of course, an unsuitable means. God is inaccessible to reason as a subject of cognition; he is for it a *Ding an Sich* and is found outside the reach of its categories. But dogmas do not claim this, they only assert the fact of revelation, which has already been accomplished in religious myth, and they only translate its content into the language of concepts. *The experiential* derivation of dogma, a religious empiricism of its own kind, by making dogma invulnerable for the critique of rational cognition, at the same time leads to the fact that its expression in concepts generates contradictions and absurdities from the point of view of rational thinking. Are not almost all the fundamental dogmas of Christianity like that, and do not they who consider rational examination the highest and sole criterion of religious truth vainly reject them with such disdain and indignation? An example in person is Leo Tolstoy. His rational critique of dogmatic theology is incontrovertible if one accepted reason as the supreme judge, but it turns into a deplorable misunderstanding if one should reject this premise.

Dogmatics receives from religion a raw mass of dogmas that it is faced with assimilating, classifying, and systematizing as much as possible. The aspiration of reason towards unity, its "architectonic" style, "scholastic" inclinations (indeed scholasticism is in a certain sense a virtue of reason, its conscientiousness — reason must be scholastic) leads to the fact that one or another system, for the most part external and arising out of pedagogical necessities, is imparted to this dogmatic mass; in this way is obtained that which "dogmatic theologies," "systems of dogmatics," *summae theologiae* represent. But if precisely this is how dogmatics relates to the study of myth, then it is possible to ask oneself what kind of value does such a rational stock-taking of super-rational revelations have. Are dogmatics and dogmas needed generally speaking? Is not dogmatization rather a disease of religion, rust that forms on it, and is it not necessary to declare war on dogma in the name of religion? Can one express the unuttered, and need one do so? Have not rivers of blood flowed because of dogmas, has not the church been torn apart because of an iota? Such are the popular objections against dogma, religious, philosophical, everyday. Insofar as they proceed from indifference and laziness of soul, it is possible not to take them into consideration: of course it is more peaceful and simpler to live without taking an interest in the subjects of faith, and even interpreting one's indifference as superiority. The one who has no convictions, who confesses no kind of truth that he would feel obliged to defend with all the powers of his soul, will always be an opponent of dogma, treating with Epicurean levity the "fanaticism" of dogmatics. There is nothing to discuss with this adogmatism of unprincipled and indifferent people: they are lower than dogma and religion, and although in virtue of their quantitative predominance they now set the tone in society's opinion, neither spiritual might nor the content of ideas stands up for them.

Others reject dogma in the name of religious chastity: it seems to them that the faith as expressed in a dogmatic formula is no longer faith, since even "an uttered thought is a lie."[60] But they forget that if in a certain sense this utterance is true, the reverse is also justified: the unuttered is not a thought, and therefore it cannot become truth and the negation of a lie. Everything that is experienced by us in the life of the soul *becomes* a thought, passes through thought, although it is not only a thought and is never expressed in word without a residue. Religious experience, in its fullness shaking our whole essence and not only its intellectual nature alone, unavoidably passes through thought too and strives to be expressed in word. Every experience of God necessarily generates a corresponding thought about God although it is never *only* a thought. Myth in its fullness is not a thought, just as the symbolism of an artistic work is not a thought, but it asks for thought and becomes a thought, taking the form of a word. Inexpressibility is not a synonym for muteness, alogicality, or antilogicality, rather it is the reverse; it is uninterrupted expression that gives birth to verbal symbols for its incarnation. Without this birthing it is a nonincarnated thought, something prematurely born that does not exceed thought but does not attain it. And as nothing can be concealed from the rays of the sun, so nothing can be concealed from the light of reason. Every experience on the one hand is also intellectual. Everything becomes the subject of thought and in this sense everything is thought, everything is word, and has the seal of the hypostasis of the Logos. In this truth, although distorted by one-sidedness, is included Hegel's truth. And this conceivability of all that is, without in any way contradicting that what is cannot be thought through to the end, is the immanent norm of the life of the spirit, and even those who reject it in words cannot violate it, for agnosticism is always already a certain kind of dogmatism, a certain kind of positive dogmatic doctrine about God, albeit of minimal content. Thought is prior to our reason; "in the beginning was the Word," and although our present-day reason is not at all something supreme and ultimate, for it can and must be surpassed, still it is no longer possible to surpass thought — it is the ontological definition of cosmic being, corresponding to the second divine hypostasis of the Logos: "all was through him and without him nothing is which is" (John 1:3).

Therefore we set a conscious (and in this sense "critical") and principled dogmatism against a pusillanimous and barely conscious adogmatism that in its own way is also dogmatic. Religious experience is imperfect, incomplete as long as it has not been expressed in word; myth is not intelligible as long as a thought has not been born of it. For only in thought, in word does religious experience receive certainty, only thus is sentimental vagueness (Schleiermacher) overcome and the final chasing imparted to myth; only in thought and through thought are its objectivity and catholicity definitively recognized. Therefore dogmas constitute the precious wealth of religion, its "uttered word," *logos prophorikos*. Religious consciousness naturally and irrepressibly strives towards dogma. Does not the quest for dogma, "the compiling of convictions," the "search for world-contemplation," form the subject of the constant anxiety and strivings of every living soul, which cannot be satisfied by the spiritual prematurity, amorphous ineffability of feeling? And because of this not only are skeptical Pyrrhonians or Kantians (however impoverished their dogmatics may be) not exceptions, neither are they so to say antidogmatic "mystics." Evidence of this is their writings, where we usually find a mystical system more or less laid bare, i.e., an aggregate of "dogmas." And is it possible to hand on in word what is completely void of thought? The objective, catholic character of religious experience that distinguishes it from the music of frames of mind alone, from subjectivism with its psychologism, demands precisely dogmatic crystallization. The catholic nature of dogma in particular is revealed in the fact that only in word and through word can religious experience be initially communicated to other people, thanks to which *the preaching* of religion is possible, the "service of the word." The courageous and severe nature of dogma commands us not to become mute in the sweet languor of mystical experience, but rather to preach and teach: "having gone therefore *teach* all nations" (Matt. 28:19), the Risen One commanded his apostles. Saul, of course, was not able to express fully in words what he went through on the road to Damascus, but from this unexpressed experience in Saul was born the apostle Paul who went quickly to preach Christ Crucified and became the first Christian dogmatician. And even enraptured to the third heaven he heard *words* there too which although they could not be said in human language, yet were in principle "words" all the same.

On the basis of what has been said, one ought to acknowledge that dogmas are the wealth of religion. Their positive significance, by which is compensated a centuries-old dogmatic conflict that comes to a halt only in epochs of a decline of religious life, consists in the fact that dogmas represent as it were signposts set up along the path of a religious life running correctly, of its normal growth. Dogmas are the hieroglyphs of religious mysteries, which are disclosed only in religious experience and in the measure of that experience. They are therefore norms and tasks for this experience, not individual but ecclesial-catholic. One can never say about a human being who has really come into contact with the life of the church that for him dogmas are only doctrine or rational schemas, logical symbols, for this involvement signifies precisely a real encounter of God with the human being in a living personal experience, personal mythopoesis. Out of this experience, always partial, but allowing indefinite and measureless growth, is drawn the general indication that dogmas really bear witness to religious realities, and consequently, show the true path. No one can ever say about himself that in his personal achievement he holds the whole fullness of church experience, outlined in dogmas, and no one can come in contact with the church's life *outside* his own personal experience, even though it is minimal. Hence the church's wealth of dogmas, as a task, always exceeds the availability of religious experience but at the same time always enters into it and defines it. From this arises the paramount regulatory significance of dogmatics and the pedagogical significance of instruction in the truths of faith in whatever form it should take place. In this way is removed the seeming contradiction between the *personal* character of religious experience, which removes from without a compulsorily given dogmatics (for dogmatics is not geometry), and the *objective* system of dogmas in which the suprapersonal (and seemingly impersonal) catholic consciousness of the church is expressed. The opposite point of view, which negates dogma under the pretext of personal religious experience, radically rejects conciliarity for the sake of religious individualism, anarchism, and impressionism. In the concept of dogma both moments are dialectically reunited in this way: the personal and the suprapersonal, the internal and external principle of freedom and authority, and knowledge and faith. In this way the possibility in principle and even the necessity of a "symbol of faith" is established that is common and obligatory for all members of the Church.

VII. Religion and Philosophy

Dogma is the signalization with concepts of that which is not a concept, for it is found higher than logical thinking in its abstractness; at the same time it is a formula expressed in concepts, a logical transcription of that which is given in religious experience. Therefore dogma, though taking part in thinking, is heterogeneous to it and in this sense transcendent to discursive thinking; it is not its conclusion and outcome. Dogma violates, or rather does not take into consideration the fundamental requirement of logical discourse (formulated with such precision by H. Cohen[61]), namely, continuity in thinking *(Continuität des Denkens),* which rests on the generation by it of its object *(reiner Ursprung).* Thinking creates for itself both subject and problematic. The difficulty of the philosophical problem of dogma consists in this contradiction of its logical description: on the one hand it is a judgment in concepts, and therefore belongs to immanent, self-generating, and continuous thinking, but on the other hand it is transcendent to thought, introduces an interruption in it, violates its self-generation, and falls like a meteorite on the smoothed field of thinking.

The question of the relationship of philosophy and religion rises before us in all its difficulty. Is *religious philosophy* possible, and in what sense is it possible? Is the dogmatism of religion compatible with the most sacred possessions of philosophizing, its *freedom and quest* for truth, with its rule — to doubt everything, to test everything, to see in everything not dogma but a problem, a subject of critical investigation? Where is the place for philosophical searching if the truth is already given in the guise of dogma-myth? Where is the place for freedom of investigation if fidelity to dogma is its guiding norm? Where is the place for criticism if dogmatism reigns? Such are the prejudices against religious philosophy, thanks to which the very question about the *possibility* of religious philosophy or, what is the same thing, philosophical dogmatism, is resolved negatively more often than not (on this account the formula of scholasticism is ironically called to mind: *philosophia est ancilla theologiae,* where *ancilla* is invariably understood as *serva,* not servant, auxiliary and ally, but slave).

The radical difference between philosophy and religion is that the first is an outcome of the operation of human reason with its own powers of searching for truth; it is immanent and human, and at the same time it is inspired with a yearning to outgrow its immanence and its humanity by participating in supernatural, superhuman, transcendent divine being. Philosophy thirsts for truth, which is the chief and sole stimulus for philosophizing. The philosophical idea of God (whatever it might be) is in any case *a conclusion,* the outcome of a system and the *esprit de système* [systematic mind]; it exists only as a feature of the system, as part of it. Philosophically God is defined and proven without fail on the basis of a system, of its structure, its development. "Proofs" for the existence of God, whatever they might be, are all from philosophy and only by a misunderstanding do they turn up in dogmatic theology for which God is given and found higher than or outside of proofs; in philosophy, however, for which God is proposed as a deduction or an outcome of a system, the idea about him is brought into connection with all the ideas of a philosophical doctrine, and exists only by this connection. The logical place of Divinity in the system is determined by the general character of a given philosophical doctrine: from that viewpoint compare Aristotle's system and its doctrine of the divine first cause, the prime mover, with Spinoza's system that is less religious in its general aspiration, or compare Kant, Schelling, Fichte, and Hegel in their doctrines of God.

For philosophy, *God is a problem,* just as everything is and must be a problem for it. In its principled problematism it is free of the *givenness* of God, of a purely religious experience whatsoever; it investigates, doubts, poses questions: *dubito, cogito, deduco!* Of course, in this way philosophy unavoidably strives towards the absolute, towards all-unity or towards Divinity, inasmuch as it is disclosed in thinking; ultimately it too has as its sole and universal problem God, and only God, and it too is theology, or more precisely, a searching for God, an investigation of God and a thinking of God. Philosophy, inasmuch as it is worthy of itself, is permeated by *amor Dei intellectualis* [an intellectual love of God], by a special piety of thinking. But for philosophy only an abstract absolute exists, only a postulate of the concrete God of religion; and with its own powers, without a leap over the abyss, philosophy cannot cross over from an "intellectual God," and "intellectual love for him," to personal love for the living God. *Amor intellectualis* is realized in that its subject becomes a problem for thought; this is the pathos of investigation. Causing problems is the nature of every object of philosophy; here love is expressed in philosophical doubt and reflection, in a question mark which is placed over a given concept and turns it into a problem. Thinking is indisputably the bona fide foundation for philosophy, concerning which philosophy no longer has the possibility of doubting and causing further problems; consequently, thinking is in principle no longer of a problematic nature, rather it is of a dogmatic nature (for the dogmatic is the philosophical antithesis of the problematic). Philosophy says of itself "cogito ergo sum." In its self-certainty, thinking is the subject of faith for philosophy; thinking is more reliable than God and the world are for philosophy, because both God and existence are weighed, made certain, and verified by thinking. Thinking is the Absolute in philosophy, that light in which both the world and God logically spring up.

In this problematism philosophy is essentially an unquenchable and always reigniting "love for Sophia"; if it found satisfaction, it would stand still and put an end to its existence. The subject of its striving is found beyond the limits of its mastery; it is the "ewige Aufgabe" [eternal task] (H. Cohen). And this, above all, is because Truth is not at all the theoretical truth which philosophy seeks. Truth in its divine being is "the Way and the Life." As life, it is its unuttered and not decomposed fullness. As the supreme reality, Truth is both the Good and Beauty in the indissoluble triunity of Life. God is Truth, but it is impossible to say that the truth is God (Hegel); God is the Good, but it is wrong to say that the good is God (Kant); God is Beauty, but it is incorrect to say that beauty is God (Schiller, Goethe). Truth, as the subject of theoretical speculation, is no longer the living truth, it is only an aspect of it, "abstracted" from the indecomposable unity. Truth Itself is *transcendent to philosophy,* which knows only its gleam, its aspect — *verity* — as an eternal searching for Truth. Finding Truth, vitally partaking of Truth would be thereby the overcoming of philosophy, for philosophy itself arises out of that splintered state of existence, its non-verity, where thinking proves to be an isolated domain of the spirit — "abstract."

If it is not truth but only verity, theoretical participation in super-theoretical Truth, which is really accessible to philosophy, this establishes not only philosophy's origin out of the sinful splintered state of being, but also the real link with this Truth, which is revealed in philosophy and speaks to philosophizing reason in a language accessible to it. At the basis of authentic philosophizing lies a revelation of a special type, the "noetic vision" of ideas, according to Plato's eternal pronouncement about philosophy. The basic motives of philosophizing, the themes of philosophical systems, are not invented but are perceived intuitively; they have a supraphilosophical origin that definitely indicates the road beyond philosophy. In keeping with its intuitive basis philosophy converges with art, the intuitive nature of which does not cause any contention. *Philosophy is the art of concepts.* Philosophizing is the reflection of reason on its insights perceived to be true, which play the role of initial axioms and at the same time objects of reflection, critical investigation, analysis, and proof. The fundamental ideas of philosophy are not contrived but are born in the consciousness, like seeds, like germs of future philosophical systems. The diurnal consciousness of a philosopher is fertilized by the nocturnal reveries of a dreamer. An original logical mythopoesis is not foreign to philosophy, and at the basis of really original, creative philosophical systems always lies — *horribile dictu* [dreadful to say] — a philosophical myth. The mythopoetic character of philosophy finds open expression in Plato who passes from the heights of dialectic investigation to myth with an indifference that is seductive for philosophers and with an apparently premeditated disorderliness. And even his most fundamental ideas he frequently expresses with a myth, leaving it to commentators to decide how one ought to treat an exposition of this kind. Is Plato speaking seriously or is he joking? He applies this method in almost all of the most important dialogues of his mature period (the exceptions being only *Parmenides, Philebus,* and *Sophist*). His most intense philosophical speculation makes room for myth, which in no way occupies an accidental place as a literary device but plays a definite role in the development of his thought — sometimes the most fundamental assertions having the significance of a necessary argument are stated in the form of myth. (Let us recall the doctrine of Eros in *Symposium,* the creation of the world in *Timaeus* and *Politics,* the heavenly origin of the soul in *Phaedra,* life beyond the grave in a series of eschatological myths in *Republic, Gorgias,* et al., and immortality in *Phaedo.*) This paradoxical feature of Plato constitutes a real "scandal in philosophy," and everyone copes with it in their own way. All too often the myths are swept aside with a squeamish or condescending grimace. Meanwhile it is impossible to understand and accept Plato otherwise than by looking at this fact directly in the face. The fact of the matter is that in Plato pure philosophizing and dogmatic theology are joined seamlessly, covered by a single cupola: Plato remains simultaneously a mythologist and a philosopher, a dogmatician and a critique-writer throughout, and therein lies the paradoxical nature of his philosophical image, whereas those who hold onto the toga of the founder of the Academy timidly or fastidiously brush aside everything "mythic."

On the basis of what has been said about philosophy and mythology it is easy to give a general answer to the question about Plato's identity and how one is to understand his duality. He was a philosophizing theologian, i.e., a dogmatician, a mythologist, for whom the myths that he expounded represented theological truths of varied worth, accuracy, and certitude. *Plato treated the myths expounded by him seriously and with faith:* that is what one needs to establish with all candor. And yet, apropos the truths that are proclaimed in these myths, and in connection with them, Plato still philosophized, and these bits of his *tou dialegesthai* [discourse] constituted the treasury of Platonism which our time is learning to value all the more. Therefore in Plato a system and *esprit de système* are completely absent, and for this reason he is the father of free philosophical dialectics. Plato is not systematic; rather, he is *thematic and dialectical.* This gives rise to the fragmentariness of his philosophizing, for each of his dialogues, given all their artistic perfection and musical form, is for a system of philosophy only a fragment, an étude, an article, nothing more, without the need of rounding things out, of bringing various ends together into one integral system, for which neither the attempt nor the taste is outlined in Plato. Plato is a philosophical essayist who does not want a system; he loves to philosophize but does not love philosophy. It is unusually instructive to compare him with Aristotle according to the type of philosophical creativity. Although it is impossible not to see the religious motive of philosophy even in the latter,[62] still Aristotle is not in the least a theologian, dogmatician, or mythologist. Aristotle is for the most part a philosopher, *Philosophus,* as they called him in the Middle Ages, whereas on the "divine" Plato there always lay the aureole of something prophetic, mysterious, and mystical. If Aristotle's philosophizing leads him to a doctrine of God, this is only the result of the logic of his philosophizing and not some mythopoetic preconception. The doctrine of God in Aristotle is chiefly a deduction from his philosophy. In it there is not one feature that is not logically justified, demonstrated in one way or the other. Alongside the mythmaker Plato, Aristotle is a representative of pure philosophy, with its striving for system, architectonic completeness, and immanent continuity of rational thinking. And God in Aristotle is only a philosophical idea, a postulate of Divinity, a "proof for the existence of God," outside any personal relation to him.

Plato's very doctrine of *ideas* as the foundation of cognition can be understood as a doctrine about the mythical structure of thought: myth, the touching of the transcendent, "noetic being," logically precedes and gives a basis for abstract rational cognition.[63] All knowledge in Plato is mythologized in this manner and subordinated to mythopoesis, to which knowledge of the transcendent ideas is accessible. An interpretation of Plato's doctrine of ideas in the sense of mythopoesis sheds light on the most central and dark problem of Platonism, which has been posed so acutely in contemporary scholarship (P. G. Natorp, N. Hartmann, and the Marburg school in general):[64] Ought one to understand the ideas of Plato in a transcendental-critical sense, as the formal conditions of cognition and its ultimate limit (Kantian ideas), or in a transcendent-metaphysical sense? What is Platonic "anamnesis"? Is a formal-logical *a priori* understood here which is manifested in each separate act of cognition, or is it a real remembrance about a mythopoetic knowing, with the question *when* the encounter with the transcendent took place — in this life or beyond its limits — having a secondary meaning for the resolution *of this* question?

If what has been said about the intuitive roots of philosophy is correct, to this degree one can and must speak about the religious roots of philosophy, and likewise about the natural and irremovable connection of philosophy with religion. But given this affinity, the radical difference between philosophy and religion remains. The latter is based on the revelation of the transcendent, on the experience of Divinity. This experience is qualitatively different than in philosophy, for it exists not in the guise of theoretical understandings but in its own concreteness, as a lived perception, *experience,* and dogmas are the expression of this experience. Revelations of philosophy are for it only themes and problems, and before critical investigation they have no kind of philosophical significance. The religious importance of dogma does not depend on verification: it *is given* in its authenticity. Religious credibility cannot be replaced by any sort of philosophizing, which can prove only the conceivability, the possibility, and even the logical necessity of Divinity but does not yield experience itself, just as no theory of the sun can replace for me its ray that has acted on my sight and touch. Philosophy and religion therefore can never replace each other or be considered as a consecutive stage of one and the same process. Here we again collide with Hegel's distinctive doctrine about the relationship of philosophy and religion that is of enormous interest in principle.[65]

For **Hegel** generally speaking there is no doubt that God, the subject of religion, also constitutes the sole worthy subject for philosophy.[66] "The subject of religion, as of philosophy, is the eternal truth in its very objectivity: God and nothing but God and the explanation of God. Philosophy is not the wisdom of the world but the cognition of the non-worldly *(Nichtweltlichen)*, not the cognition of the external measure, of empirical existence and life, but knowledge of that which is eternal, which is God and which derives from his nature.... Philosophy therefore explains only itself when it explains religion, and in explaining itself it explains religion. As the pursuit of eternal truth which exists *an und für sich* [in itself], namely as the occupation of thinking spirit and not of arbitrariness or special interest in this subject, it is the same activity as religion.... Religion and philosophy coincide into one. Philosophy is in reality divine worship, it is religion, for it is the refusal of subjective whims and opinions in its occupation with God *(Beschäftigung mit Gott)*" (*Philosophy of Religion*, 7). The philosophy of religion is related to the general system of philosophy in the same manner, that "God is the result of its other parts. Here this end becomes the beginning" (12). "Consequently, philosophy examines the absolute, first of all, as a logical idea, how it exists in thought, how the very definitions of thought are its content. Then, the absolute is revealed in its reality, in its products; and this is the way for the absolute to become spirit for itself. In this manner God is the result of philosophy, about which it comes to know that it is not only the result but also eternally reproduces itself, and is that which arises."

The difference between "positive" religion and philosophy is erased in principle in Hegel's eyes because "two reasons and two spirits cannot exist, divine reason and human reason, divine spirit and human spirit cannot exist that would be completely different among themselves. Human reason, the consciousness of its essence, is reason in general, the divine in the human, whereas spirit, inasmuch as it is the spirit of God, is not spirit above the stars, beyond the limits of the world but God is present ubiquitously and as spirit in all spirits. God is the living God who is active and effective. Religion is the outcome of divine spirit, not the discovery of humankind, but the work of divine influence and impact on it.

The expression that God governs the world like reason would be unreasonable if we did not accept that it also relates to religion and that divine spirit operates in defining and forming the latter.... The more a human being, in his rational thought, forces the matter itself to operate for him, renounces his isolation, and treats himself as the universal consciousness, his reason will not search for its own in the sense of the particular, and the less it can fall into this contradiction; for it, reason, is the matter itself, the spirit, the divine spirit" (17). (Cf. the justified critical observation by A. Drews [1906] apropos this judgment, note 3, p. 398.) If in reason we have God immediately, then "reason is the place in the spirit where God is revealed to a human being" (24), "the ground on which religion alone feels itself at home" (120), "the ground of religion is the rational, or rather, the speculative" (120). "Religion exists only through

Religion and Philosophy

thinking and in thinking. God is not the highest feeling, but the highest thought" (38). In this sense the idea of "revelation" and "revealed" religion is conceived: "revealed *(geoffenbarte)* religion is manifest *(offenbare)* for in it God became fully manifest. Here all is in conformity with the concept: *there is nothing secret in God*" (48).[67]

By comparison with thinking, the lowest form of religious consciousness is that which is usually called "faith" and what Hegel characterizes as knowledge in the form of "representation" *(Vorstellung)*: on it lies the seal of subjectivity, of the undefeated reduplication of subject and object. "Representation signifies that a given content is in me, is mine" (66). "Faith is something subjective to the extent that the necessity of content, its proven quality, is called objective — objective knowledge, cognition" (67). And so-called "immediate knowledge is nothing other than thinking, but taken completely abstractly" (69). Immediate knowledge of God can only say that God *is*. But since being, according to the definition of the *Logic,* is "a universal in an empty and very abstract sense, a pure relation to itself without any reaction inside or from without" (70), then "this empty immediacy which is existence, the summit of dry abstraction, is the most hollow and meagre definition" (70). (It is obvious how much the force of this argument is connected with the solidity of Hegel's *Logic:* the central question about the nature and content of faith is settled with reference to a paragraph on "existence"!) From this Hegel concludes that "the very meagre definition of immediate knowledge of religion . . . does not stand outside the domain of thinking . . . it belongs to thought" (70).[68]

Hegel's fundamental idea about the difference between religion and philosophy is, as we already know, that "religion is the true content, but only in the form of representation" (94); "my representation is the image as it is elevated already to the form of the universality of thought, so that only one fundamental definition is maintained, constituting the essence of the subject and being brought before the conceiving spirit" (84). In representation, abstraction struggles with image, "the sensible is raised to thought only by the path of abstraction" (86), and in this duality and contradictoriness lies the necessity of the transition to philosophy, which is the same thing as religion and acts in the form of thought, whereas "religion, so to say, as involuntarily *(unbefangen)* thinking reason, remains in the form of representation." Only in thinking does one obtain "that identity under which knowledge poses itself for itself in its object"; it "is spirit, reason, objectified for its own self" (121). "In this manner religion is the relation of spirit to absolute spirit. Only in this manner does spirit, as knowing, become known. This is not only the relation of spirit to absolute spirit, but *absolute spirit itself relates itself to* that which we set on the other side as difference; and higher than religion is, therefore, the idea of spirit which relates to itself, and is *self-consciousness of absolute spirit. . . . Religion is knowledge of absolute spirit about itself through the medium of finite spirit*" (121).[69]

Introduction

"Philosophy has as its purpose to come to know the truth, to come to know God, for he is absolute truth; to that extent nothing else is worth the trouble in comparison with God and his elucidation. Philosophy comes to know God essentially as concrete, as a spiritual, real universality, which is devoid of envy but which communicates itself . . . and whoever says God is unknowable, says that he is envious" (394). (This argument, whose whole insufficiency is evident, can be brought forward in defense of the idea of revelation more so than for the confirmation of Hegel's point of view: for him God is given in thinking, *is* thinking, and with that, strictly speaking there is no one or anything to be revealed, and if Hegel himself speaks about revealed religion, he does this in keeping with his usual manner of using empirical givens for threading them into a panlogical schema.) "In philosophy, which is theology, it is solely a matter of showing the reason of religion" (394). "All forms examined above — feeling, representation — can of course have truth as their content, but they themselves do not comprise the true form, which is necessary for true content. Thinking is the absolute judge, before whom the content must certify itself and present its credentials. The reproach is made of philosophy that it puts itself higher than religion. This is actually not true for it has only this same content and not a different one, it only gives it in the form of thinking; *it becomes in this way higher than the form of faith;* the content remains the same" (394). "Philosophy is theology to the extent that it portrays the reconciliation of God with himself (sic!) and with nature" (395).

The distinctive peculiarity of Hegel's philosophical and religious point of view is that thinking is completely adequate to truth, even more, that it is the direct self-consciousness of truth: a thought about divinity, divinity itself, and the self-consciousness of divinity are one and the same. Human consciousness in objective thinking not only outstrips itself but fully transcends itself and becomes not human but absolute. Every tension of the immanent and transcendent, of the one knowing and the one being known, of humankind and divinity, "is lifted" and overcome by divine monism, free from the isolation of the world and the human being: the logic is this — "God is all things in all." It is obvious that philosophy, understood in this manner, ceases to be philosophy anymore and becomes divine activity, divine being, divine consciousness. This is not even religion, for religion presupposes an intense dualism of the immanent and the transcendent, and corresponds to the damaged being that searches for God and as it were is abandoned by God. No, this is suprareligion; it is what is found on the other side of religion when religion is abolished. By interpreting religion intellectually, Hegel takes it only as a form of thought, as a poor, insufficient philosophizing, and in this capacity, of course, he assigns it a lower place because it recognizes truth only in the aspect of "representation," i.e., of a dualistic opposition of subject and object, humankind and divinity. Panlogical idealism here speaks to the end the fundamental thought of subjective idealism, namely, *esse-percipi* [to be is to be perceived]. In Hume it had a subjective-human significance — "to be for the human"; in Berkeley it was interpreted as the activity of Divinity in human consciousness; in Hegel it was transposed already into the language of divine existence: thinking of thinking is the very absolute, one in existence and consciousness.[70]

Striking is this Luciferian ecstasy, which in essence is the pathos of Hegelianism: except for Hegel himself, who can put to the test the blessedness of consciousness and being of God by experiencing his Logic? If he himself really went through it, this is of course an extremely important fact of religious psychology, or more precisely, an extremely interesting religious psychologism. It is one of two things: either the aroma of eternity, the contact of the divine world, is inherent in theoretical thinking to such a degree that its servant truly felt this world in its immediacy by way of thinking (which we do not admit, speaking candidly), or the reverse: we have here an example of an extreme doctrinarism that leads to self-blinding and self-hypnosis, the typical state of philosophical "delusion." Hegelian logical pantheism springs from a basic peculiarity of his worldview, his extreme intellectualism, thanks to which he was fated to speak the final word of rationalism in the form of idealistic speculation. Since thought, conceivability, thinking constitute in Hegel's eyes the sole authentic being, and since the whole alogical side of being, everything that remains above thinking, represents a series of misunderstandings, subjectivism, or as we would say now, psychologism, then for Hegel being is substituted and exhausted by the *concept* of being, and God by *the idea* of God. Armed with "dialectical method," in which apparently the very life of thinking is caught, he converts it into logical magic of his own type, connecting, supposing, lifting, overcoming everything; and he believes in this logical mysticism that the whole past, present, and future are accessible to him, nature living and dead. In reality we know that this philosophical deduction of earth and heaven takes place by means of actual borrowings from empirical being, which in no way at all agrees to be only a concept.[71] For all the value and fruitfulness of independent constructions and observations of Hegel, his system can serve as an example of a complete abolition of religion.

For Hegel philosophical credibility is higher than religious credibility, or more precisely, it constitutes its highest phase, being found with it on one plane. This opinion springs from Hegel's general conviction that *an absolute* system is possible which would be not philosophy but already *Sophia* herself, and precisely as such did he revere his own system. The tragedy of philosophizing is surmounted in it, the knight has discovered his Beautiful Lady (unless he took the portly Dulcinea to be she by mistake), reason has attained transfiguration and been healed from its antinomies. For Hegel his system is the Kingdom of God, which has come in power, and this power in thinking is the church in its logical glory. In such a conviction the Luciferian sickness of this type of philosophy is fully revealed, and Hegelianism is to some extent the limit for this bearing. In contemporary German idealism these motifs resound secretly and hesitantly, although Neo-Kantian immanentism, likewise removing the tragedy of thought, is to that extent a timid repetition of Hegel. In general, "philosophy" in an abstract understanding that thus claims absoluteness is rationalistic immanentism in isolation from the wholeness of religious spirit; it is a specifically Germanic outcome, which has its roots in Protestantism.

In reality, in opposition to Hegel, religious credibility is essentially other than philosophical, as faith is different from discursive thinking and mythologeme from philosopheme. Therefore it is even wrong to pose the question about which of them is superior or inferior; they are not comparable or are comparable only as different aspects of credibility. Of course, for philosophy religion must seem inferior to it, like a nonphilosophy, but this, so to say, professional estimation changes nothing in the hierarchical position of religion, which has to do with the whole human being and not with only one of his aspects, and is a lived relation to the divine world, and not only a thinking about it. But are not the affinity and bond between philosophy and religion almost more substantive than the distinction? In returning to our initial problem — is religious philosophy possible and how is it possible — we must insistently point out that if, really, at the base of philosophizing some "noetic knowing" lies, an immediate, mystical comprehension of the foundations of being, in other words, an original philosophical myth, which nevertheless does not have the clarity and beauty of the religious, then *every authentic philosophy is mythical and to that extent religious,* and thus an irreligious, "independent," "pure" philosophy is impossible. The latter has been invented in our days by people who, although they "occupy themselves with philosophy," by acquiring refinement in philosophical technique, and by whetting the formal instrument of thought, are themselves devoid of philosophical anxiety or philosophical Eros and thus replace the fundamental questions of a philosophical worldview (metaphysics) with philosophical methodology and gnoseology. No matter how revered and important in themselves these questions may be, they alone still do not make a philosopher. To the extent to which they ascend from technical questions to the general one and to questions of principle, they fall under the same law — the religious qualification of philosophy, although it is not always easy to discern this.[72] Only by an investigation of the "scientific" questions of philosophy, i.e., of that which lies beyond the limits of philosophizing itself, can it seem that philosophizing is autonomous and free of any extra-philosophical qualification; at the basis there always proves to be a metaphysical premise that represents only an expression of an intuitive world-perception. Such are gnoseology and gnoseologizing philosophy, this favorite offspring of the present day; in particular Kant, the acknowledged "philosopher of Protestantism," holds such a doctrine. If one is to have this axiomatic or mythical basis for philosophizing in view, then one can call philosophy critical or ideological mythology, and it will be necessary to expound the history of philosophy not as the history of the self-development of the concept (according to Hegel), but as the history of religious self-consciousness, insofar as it is reflected in critical ideology.

With these general considerations an answer is also given to the more particular question, namely, is religious philosophy of a definite type possible, for example, a Christian philosophy (or even more particularly, an Orthodox, a Catholic, or a Protestant philosophy)? The question is resolved without any difficulty in an affirmative sense. For, if in general philosophy, no matter how critical it might seem, is at its base mythical or dogmatic, then there cannot be any grounds for refusing on principle a definite religious-dogmatic philosophy, and all objections are based on the prejudice of an imagined "purity" and "independence" of philosophy from the premises of an extra-philosophical character, which however constitute the true *themes* or *motifs* of philosophical systems. Of course, the one or the other construction can be successful or unsuccessful; it is a question of fact. But a poor system of Christian philosophy does not at all prove that there cannot be a good one or that Christian philosophy is in general impossible.

The chief misgiving this generates among its opponents of principle is that it is subjected here to the danger that the freedom of philosophical investigation suffers, as does philosophical sincerity so to say, and the main nerve of philosophy is killed in the same manner; a bias is created that cheapens philosophical work beforehand. However, do those who assert this take sufficiently into account the fact of universal intuitive substantiation, and, consequently, in this sense, the fact of the inevitable bias of philosophical systems? And do not these same people find themselves in a certain dogmatic prejudice? Surely it is a human being in his ontological fullness who philosophizes and not a fantastic "transcendental" subject that is only a regulatory idea, a section of consciousness, a methodological fiction, although perhaps a fruitful one. One always philosophizes on a definite theme, and only a conscious or unconscious animosity towards Christianity forces one to exclude Christian dogmas from the number of possible themes of philosophizing. But for philosophy these dogmas become precisely only themes, motifs, tasks, and problems, whereas in it they must become the deduction, the end result of philosophizing. There is nothing for philosophical thinking to do with a dogma that is given right away in compelling completeness; the dogma binds it. It must be converted with full philosophical sincerity into a problem of philosophy, into an object of investigation.

The opponents stubbornly and persistently lump together "apologetics" or dogmatics with Christian philosophy. The first is completely deprived of philosophical Eros and with quasi-philosophical means strives to the attainment of a goal that is religious-practical and not at all philosophical. For that reason it is not philosophical but polemical and pragmatic in its very essence. Dogmatic theology is not in any way a philosophical investigation of dogmas, even if it uses philosophy in its exposition, but is only their stock-taking. If for philosophy dogma represents the *terminus ad quem*, then for dogmatics it is the *terminus a quo*. As has already been shown, philosophy is the art of concepts that has its own artists, and the chosen servants of this art cannot lie artistically, which would be inevitable with a premeditated, unphilosophical dogmatism in philosophizing; this would be first of all a manifestation of bad taste, an aesthetic sin. They readily allow that a Christian artist can be sincere in his artistic quests no less than an artist who does not choose religious themes; why then do they have difficulty allowing this with respect to an artist of concepts, i.e., a religious philosopher?

From this it follows that religious philosophy too requires *freedom* of investigation and, consequently, theoretical doubt in completely the same degree as any other philosophy; on its side it even has the advantage of acuity of critical vision because it recognizes its religious conditionality and knows its perilous aspects. Freedom is the nerve of philosophizing. A dogma of faith does not exert pressure upon the freedom of philosophical investigation because its meaningfulness lies on a different plane and is not placed under question by philosophical doubt. It is not *what, but how,* not the theme which is given, but the execution which is set as a task, that has meaning with philosophical elaboration. The freedom of philosophical creativity is expressed in the possibility of *diverse* philosophical systems for one and the same theme, in the possibility of *different* systems of Christian philosophy, which in no way undermines its fundamental meaning. For *a single, absolute philosophical system* that would accommodate absolute truth *generally speaking does not exist.* If only verity is accessible to philosophy but not the Truth itself, which is revealed to the human being in the symbols of religion, then its path is a constant act of comprehending without a final comprehension, an "ewige Aufgabe." The means of philosophy are subject to historical development; they are changeable, and therefore different gnoseological and metaphysical approaches to one and the same theme prove possible. In the dogmatic conditionality of philosophy some see a threat to its freedom because they understand utterly falsely *in what sense and how* dogmas are *given* to the philosopher; it is thought namely that they are imposed from the outside, violently prescribed by someone who has the authority to do so or who appropriates it to themselves. Besides, the perception of a dogma is also a work of freedom, of the internal self-determination and self-creativity of a human being. Therefore a dogma fertilizes but does not coerce, for it is the faith of a human being, his love, his feeling of life, his own self in his free self-determination. For this reason the freedom of philosophy is not emptiness and without motif, creation out of nothing or out of Hegelian being, which is also nothing, out of abstraction that is not abstracted from anything, and is not fertilized by anything. The freedom of philosophy lies in its particular path, quest, comprehension. That which a human being knows as religious dogma he wants to fathom as a philosophical, theoretical truth too, similar to how a sculptor searches for the same in a marble statue. The work of philosophy is done seriously, with lively reason, and only on the condition of intellectual honesty, of sincere seeking and conscientious doubt: it is surely impossible to deceive oneself and one's own reason. Christian philosophy is the philosophizing of Christians who strive philosophically to realize their religious existence and is similar to how any philosophy is the philosophy of someone and about something, whereas "philosophy in general" is a ghost and prejudice, a Hegelian phantom. Therefore the freedom of philosophizing determines not the content but the quality of philosophizing, its tone. Philosophizing, like any creative activity, demands courage from the human being: he must leave the shore and set out swimming into the unknown; the result is not assured. It is possible that he will not return to shore, be lost and even perish in the waves. But only such a journey promises some kind of discovery. The freedom of philosophizing, like any freedom, has in itself a certain risk, but its regal dignity consists in freedom. A collaborator in philosophy is precious for religion, but a slave is useless. Indeed religious faith and mythopoesis cannot be abolished in their domain by any philosopheme, and religion exists with greater dignity outside any philosophy than it does with a philosophy that lacks freedom and is thus insincere, a philosophy that seemingly wants to show with its *apologetics* that religion itself needs an apologia. The task of apologetics, which has imagined itself to be religious philosophy, is therefore in general a false task, equally unworthy of both religion and philosophy, for it unites the absence of religious faith with a free philosophical spirit. Of course, religious philosophy can also have an "apologetic" use; more precisely, it is a powerful means for religious enlightenment, but only when it does not set this as its immediate practical goal. True philosophy is all the same "food for the gods," and all utilitarianism, even the most exalted, contradicts its freedom and dignity.

And so, only in full sincerity, attained only in full freedom, does religious philosophy become possible. And only such philosophy has value for religion. It is possible, however, to raise the question: If in myth religion has a revelation of Truth itself that is accessible to the eye of faith, what meaning does philosophizing about it still have? Does it not become a luxury, the arrogant wisdom of this age with which childlike simplicity must be contrasted? This objection is often heard precisely from those who stand far away from this simplicity and childlikeness and want to offer in its stead laziness and coarseness of mind, obscurantism and despotism. For the childlike simplicity of the children of God who live, the immediate contemplation of heaven has nothing in common with that mannered, pseudophilosophical rustification which in essence does not renounce philosophizing but wants to have it for a cheap price. Philosophy has its requirements, which it cannot and must not waive. It is possible to stand outside philosophy and above it, generally speaking, by being in religion, and it is possible to make do without philosophy at all, but once having passed into its proper domain, one must abandon this vapid rustification. In this disparagement of philosophy one thing is correct, namely, that philosophy does not replace religion, but it has its own independent task, the significance of which one need not exaggerate, but which is impossible to underestimate. The truths of religion, which are revealed and take root in a childlike believing consciousness by means of an immediate and in this sense miraculous way, are then lived out by the human being in his proper human element, in his immanent self-consciousness, regenerating and fecundating him.[73] And the richer, the more ramified, the deeper this experience is, the more vital is the religious truth which otherwise risked remaining a seed without soil or leaven without dough, and dying away because of lack of use. From our understanding of religious philosophy as a voluntary art based on religious motifs, it follows that there cannot and must not be one canonically obligatory type of religious philosophy or "theology": dogmas are immutable but their philosophical apperception changes together with the development of philosophy. All religious dogmas seek new incarnations in philosophical creativity. Therefore the tendency of Catholic theology, which is directed towards making *Thomism* the seeming norm of philosophical creativity, places on Catholic philosophers the burden of unnecessary and harmful dogmatism, inevitably leading to hypocrisy. Wise in this respect was the practice of Hellenistic and Judaic religion, which quite preferred not to have an official theology and were satisfied with immediate dogma in myth, cult, and sacred books. But one can regard religious philosophy too as a special religious ministry, its successful development serving as one of the indirect proofs of the vitality of religion. And let no one point out that there was almost no religious philosophy in the classical epoch of religion — in the century of primitive Christianity, for this brief period of the first faith and joy, illuminated by Pentecost and flooded with its radiance, is the golden age of childhood which is not repeated in history.

Already with the second and third centuries the epoch of theological work of enormous intensity begins, and it continues, now dying away, now flaring up again, to our day.

In a word, faith does not doom to hibernation or inactivity as unwanted, it does not place philosophizing reason under suspicion, but sets it its own task and creates a special stimulus for reality. *Logically* the domain of faith begins where reasons stops, which must use *every* effort to understand *everything* that is accessible to it. The limits to reason are shown not by external authority but by its proper self-consciousness which comprehends its nature. Therefore philosophy does not proceed from dogmas of faith but approaches them as the implied and necessary grounds of philosophizing.[74] For this reason *critical dogmatism* or, what is the same, critical intuitivism, is a type of religious philosophy. Only truth liberates, and when reason has comprehended its own nature, its natural dogmatism, it becomes capable of understanding and valuing its own freedom in a fitting manner. Therefore the critical dogmatism of religious philosophy is, more precisely, can and must be freedom itself and the most critical philosophy.

The words of the apostle Paul about the pagans' natural consciousness of God can be referred to the knowledge of philosophy, for philosophy is "pagan," natural, immanent consciousness of God and self. "When pagans, not having for themselves a law, by nature do the lawful thing, then not having the law they themselves are a law to themselves. They show that the work of the law among them is written on their hearts; their conscience and their thoughts bear witness to this, the one now accusing, now justifying the other" (Rom. 2:14-15). Philosophy marks the quest for God by a human being, left to his own powers, his immanent divinity. For God "from the one blood produced the whole human race . . . so that they would search for God, that they might sense him and find him; although he is not far from each of us: for by him we live and move and exist" (Acts 17:26-27). In the regal freedom bestowed on the human being, in the fullness of his divine adoption, he is granted to make the very being of God into a problem, to search for him philosophically, and consequently the entire possibility is granted of not finding and even of rejecting him, i.e., the possibility of philosophical impiety is implanted together with philosophical piety.

Thus, we distinguish: (1) extra-philosophical, religious mythopoesis; (2) dogmatics, representing the external systematization of dogmas; (3) religious philosophy as philosophical creativity on religious themes; (4) "general" philosophy, which represents the searching of the "natural" pagan mind, but of course still fertilized by some kind of intuition; (5) the canon of philosophy, its poetics and technics, to which the different fields "of scientific philosophy" refer — gnoseology, logic, phenomenology, epistemology.

In our "scientific" age the *science* of religion has received particular development and meaning, noticeably ousting even religious philosophy or replacing it. This attests to the development of the spirit of the scientific character in general and at the same time to the creative decline of religion, by which the collecting of the treasures of others forces one to forget about one's own poverty.[75]

In order to define the relationship of the science of religion to religion itself, one ought to pay attention to *how* religion is perceived by science. It is first of all obvious that only the empirical phenomenology of religion is accessible to it, which is studied like the facts of ethnography or history — recorded, classified, and schematized. Corresponding to the special interests of one or the other science a religious-historical preparation necessary to it is produced, and religious-historical museums are filled with such preparations — dried out plants and flowers, shattered and sorted parts of organisms. An enormous refinement of attention, of course, is achieved in this, but at the basis of all this scientific study lies the vivisection of religion. Therefore it is possible for science to be occupied with religion, with a certain methodological training or school, without having interiorly any religious talents, by treating the facts of religious history like a collector who gathers, for example, Brazilian butterflies or rare beetles. Science incontestably expands *knowledge* about religion and with this, although not outstandingly well, has an effect on religious self-consciousness. But this knowledge about religion remains external: a religious understanding of the facts being studied can be completely absent. Science studies religion with an unbelieving eye, from the outside, and herein lies its advantage (from the viewpoint of the goals of scientific cognition), its impartiality *(Voraussetzungslosigkeit)*, but also its limitation. Of course, the internal is visible through the external. When the purely scientific task of the systematic collecting of material for the history of religion comes to an end, which of course immeasurably expands the limited experience of each separate human being, then the task of religious decipherment and of the religious-philosophical interpretation of the collected facts is inevitably set. In the dominant scientific (religious-historical) direction religious contraband is customarily brought under the flag of science: the representatives of science with their *uncritical dogmatism* bona fide set out as the conclusions of "scientific" investigation their own religion and religious philosophy. The fact of the matter is that science is built according to certain tasks, it poses for itself only definite problems, and correspondingly focuses its attention only on certain phenomena, sweeping others aside (e.g., it is obvious that the whole religious-historical science with its fundamental and methodological rationalism is built on the denial of miracle on principle, and therefore all the elements of the miraculous in religion, without which it is perhaps impossible to understand the latter, it attributes to the domain of legends and fairy tales). For this reason contemporary religious-historical doctrine represents an indissoluble mixture of really scientific, critically produced findings in the domain of the phenomenology of religion and defined religious-philosophical teachings. The basic fact, which the science of religion establishes, is reduced to the multiplicity of religions in the presence of a certain affinity between them, of an external and internal proximity. Both the one and the other, both the variety and the affinity, comprise one of the most important problems of religious philosophy. And only by proceeding from a definite religious worldview is it possible to answer the question about the religious *sense and significance* of this fact.

Science in principle stands in an extra-religious and extra-confessional position (I say *in principle*, because in reality this requirement of principle is never fulfilled and is even unfulfillable, for the servants of science, the scholars, are also confessional and have their own religious or antireligious beliefs). They treat religious monuments like folklore, ethnography, or "culture." The philological-literary study of sacred literature was the triumph of the scientific-critical method applied to sacred literature, especially to the Old and New Testaments, where texts, forms, and in general the whole external, historically conditioned, concrete shell were subjected to comprehensive analysis (not to mention such work as the critical establishment of the text itself). And of course from that point of view there does not and must not exist even the slightest difference between a given literary-historical monument and for example the Gospel. But at the same time it is clear that although the refinement of scientific attention permits one to better study a text of the sacred books, this of course does not remain without result for their religious comprehension, but no scientific analysis will disclose in the Gospel that eternal religious content which is given to the believing heart. There is a radical difference in relation to the Word of God from the side of science and faith, which is established even methodologically, so to speak. The fact of the matter is that if the *method of unbelief*, of cold, rationally inquiring criticism is proper to science, then the *method of reverence* is inherent in religion, incompatible with this cold and rational criticism, and science is not able to see that which exists for religion. The same Gospel that is studied haphazardly by critical science has side by side with this a liturgical, theological use: it is read in church or in solitary prayerful quiet as the Word of God. Therefore, for example, the story about Christ's walking on water, as the object of critical study and as the content of "the day's Gospel," is to a significant degree different things; the critically investigated story of Christ's resurrection, with all the hopeless disagreements of the *"Auferstehungsberichte"* [resurrection accounts], and the joyful news of the Easter Resurrection stand far apart from each other. For the one who believes the Resurrection and has spiritually participated in it, the variants and disagreements of the *Auferstehungsberichte* disappear like the little grass that takes root before Mont Blanc and is visible only to the one who has bent over it. By the way, one has to speak about this invulnerability of faith by science only with the greatest reserve. A weak religious life and a powerful scientism, if they collide, frequently provoke the loss of religious equilibrium. A difference in the methods of criticism and reverence do not prevent their rivalry in the human soul.

The words and characters, inscribed in human language with all historical concreteness and conditionality, are for scientific study only literary-historical monuments, but for a believing consciousness *they are* really the Word of God, and the historical casing only shields their divine content. These words *are transposed* by the Holy Spirit into the Word of God; they have a religious-symbolic nature, i.e., religious reality is inherent to them. The Word of God is a *religious myth in a written word*, constantly radiating its divine light. Now, this light can be invisible to the scientific investigator, whereas it is revealed only to the one participating in the Word of God in the measure of his religious maturity. Therefore the depth of content of the Word of God is infinite and completely incommensurable with the depth of human books, although the latter sometimes surpass it by the splendor of their verbal vestment, which by Divine Providence is modest in the sacred books, and at times beggarly. This idea has been expressed repeatedly in the discernment of the twofold or even threefold sense of sacred Scripture: the literal (which essentially corresponds to the object of scientific study), allegorical (the sense of which, although concealed, is visible to the human eye), and the mysterious, mystical, which is revealed only under enlightenment by grace. The Bible is simultaneously both simply a book, accessible to scientific study, and a monument of Jewish literature, and the Book of books, the eternal Symbol, which is revealed only to faith, only to prayer, only to reverence. People who are experienced in the spiritual life attest that the Word of God has an infinite and constantly deepening content. In a similar manner, dogmas in the form in which *Dogmengeschichte* studies them are only doctrinal theses, *Lehrsätze*, historically conditioned in their emergence, but for the religious consciousness they are symbols of encounters with the Divinity, religious realities.

With respect to the science of religion it is appropriate to pose the same question as we did with respect to religious philosophy: Is the science of religion necessary for religion, does it have a positive religious meaning or worth? An affirmative response is possible for this question too. Once science has appeared with its methods, it would be unnatural if in virtue of the one or the other dogmatic prejudice — clerical or atheistic orthodoxy — it closed its eyes and removed its hands from so essential a domain of scientific study as the phenomenology of religion. From the side of science this would be only an expression of the fullest religious indifferentism and even nihilism, while on the other side, the scientific study of religion is an expression of a distinctive scientific piety. Science brings to the altar the gift that it has: it does not know how to believe, it does not know how to pray, and the love of the heart is foreign to it, but it knows the *amor Dei intellectualis,* and inherent to it is the virtue which corresponds to that love — intellectual honesty, together with the indefatigable quality of the toiler, of the asceticism of labor and scientific duty. And it brings its burden of the law as a gift to the kingdom of grace.

Scientific interest in religion can be a manifestation of religious creativity, similar to religious philosophy. The circumstance that scientific investigation is often connected with frames of mind hostile to religion must not hide the fact that in science religion receives a new domain of vital influence. If one were to look from that point of view at the luxuriant development of the science of religion for the last century, initially one gets the impression of the complete irreligiousness of science, even its barrenness for religion. But this judgment will be shortsighted: one needs to look over the top of the accidental and transient tendencies of the given moment which are quickly mingled with other tendencies, and evaluate the fact of the development of the science of religion in its vital significance. Then it will appear in the appropriate light, namely as a particular manifestation of religious life, although dry and rational, as an intense thought about religion, connected with its study, and indeed both thought and scientific comprehension are also life and do not take place outside the human spirit. We in no way see in science the highest manifestation of the human spirit. But once science in general exists, scientific piety[76] is possible, which to a certain degree the science of religion is (and it is precisely in virtue of this that it can become impiety, if it departs from its straight path because of hostility towards religion).

FIRST SECTION

Divine Nothing

I. The Fundamental Antinomy of Religious Consciousness

The fundamental content of *religious* experience, as contact with the transcendent, outside-the-limits, divine world contains in an obvious manner a contradiction for rational thinking. The object of religion, God, is something that on the one hand is completely *transcendent*, of a different nature, and external to the world and the human being, but on the other hand *is revealed* to religious consciousness, touches it, enters inside it, and becomes its immanent content. Both moments of religious consciousness are given simultaneously, like poles, in their mutual repulsion and attraction. The object of religion, Divinity, is something transcendent-immanent or immanent-transcendent according to its essence. God absolutely towers above the human being, "he lives in unapproachable light, whom no person has seen or can see,"[1] and at the same time he endlessly abases himself, condescends to the world, reveals himself to the world, dwells in the human being ("we will come and make our home with him").[2] The sublimity, the transcendence of Divinity, and the divine condescension and divine hominization or human divinization constitute the fundamental condition of religion. An absolute that was only supernal or transcendent to the world would not be God for the human being, remaining for him completely neutral, equivalent to pure nothing. A God who became completely immanent and only immanent would not be God; it would be a human being or the world, taken in their ultimate depth. Therefore pure and consistent world-divinization or human-divinization is atheism.

Divine Nothing

If we translate this fundamental and elementary fact of religious consciousness into the language of religious philosophy, we will see immediately that before us is a clearly contradictory combination of concepts, leading to antinomy.[3] That which is immanent cannot be at the same time transcendent and to that extent it is not transcendent. That which is transcendent cannot be immanent to consciousness and remain beyond the limits for it. If we take these concepts in static immobility, frozen into logical crystals, the fundamental concept of religion, the idea of Divinity, is in general only a patent misunderstanding, obvious for anyone who possesses training in logic; it is burning ice, a round square, bitter honey. But rational impossibility and contradiction are no guarantee of a real impossibility (belief in this was undermined already by Greek philosophy, by Plato, and Zeno, and in recent days by Hegel who in his *Logic,* no matter how great the errors, forever demonstrated the impossibility of stopping at any of the rational definitions and thereby even revealed the original pathos of contradictions: *der Widerspruch ist das Fortleitende* [Contradiction leads the way forward])! And if religious self-consciousness in its first steps clearly collides with the rational, this is in no manner a definitive sentence for it; on the contrary, it signifies only that the antinomy of religious consciousness must be disclosed and grasped fully in its consequences. Kant's most outstanding service in theoretical philosophy was the ascertainment of the antinomies of the intellect, thanks to which he unavoidably becomes entangled in his own nets. The immanent intellect, which does not know any contiguity with the transcendent world, suddenly becomes transcendent for its own self: it turns out that in its center there is a crack through which its content pours out. True, these antinomies in Kant are felicitously "explained" by reason, but one can consider the competence of the latter in this matter to be doubtful, after the antinomic character of its structure is revealed. What is most important here is that this in no way diminishes the very *fact* of the fatal antinomism in thinking, which plainly shows the inadequacy of thinking to its own proper subject. The intellect proves to be incapable of fully causing being to become immanent for it, having subordinated it to the laws of its thinking: a discrepancy that finds its expression in antinomies is revealed between them and being. An antinomy is a manifest sign of a certain transcendence of the subject of thought for thinking and at the same time the downfall of rational, gnoseological immanentism. Antinomic thinking takes possession of its subject, makes it immanent to itself only partly, only to a certain limit, which is revealed in the antinomy. A subject that was wholly transcendent to thinking could not possibly become an object of thinking; it would be finally inconceivable. And its complete adequacy to thinking would bear witness to its complete immanence. In divine reason in which thinking and being coincide in a single act there are not and cannot be antinomies, unhealthy ruptures, hiatuses that constitute the natural property of human reason.

By the way, this explains the difference between antinomies and contradictions. *Logical contradiction* arises from an error in thinking, from a discrepancy between thinking and its proper norms; it is immanent in its origin and is explained by an insufficient mastery of the subject of thought from the side of logical form. *Dialectical contradiction* in Hegel's sense arises from the general property of discursive thinking, which, being found in discourse in uninterrupted motion, changes position all the time and moves from one point on its path to another; at the same time, if only for a moment, it stops with a firm footing in each of those points and in the same way its race breaks down into discrete instants, into moments of immobility (Zeno)! Of course, with every such delay in the discursive race the whole arbitrariness of every stop is revealed along with the necessity of its "removal" or of further motion towards a new point, again for a new "removal." Dialectics is the discourse of discourses, and only Hegel could see in it the overcoming of discursiveness, something absolute and super-discursive, whereas even Hegel's logic is an enslavement to discourse, notable for its militant character. Therefore dialectical contradiction differs from logical contradiction in that it arises not from a mistake, but from the critical self-consciousness of formal thought, by virtue of which dialectics considers itself as rising above these contradictions.

Antinomy is completely different. It is generated by the recognized inadequacy of thinking to its subject or its tasks; it reveals *the insufficiency* of the powers of human reason which is compelled to stop at a certain point, for it reaches a precipice and an abyss, while at the same time it cannot help but go as far as that point. But some will say: The subject of thinking cannot be inadequate to thinking, can it? For the subject of thinking is thought, it "is generated" by thinking and thus cannot be inadequate to it; in this is the whole pathos of immanentism from Hegel to Schuppe and Cohen. We consider such an understanding to be entirely one-sided; on its account the philosophy of Hegel was chastised, which claimed to deduce all empirical being philosophically and was bankrupted on this pretension. (Kant, the philosophical father of immanentism, was to a certain degree freed from this, for he affirmed the unknowable *Ding an sich* which is nothing but the object of thinking, adequate to it.) The claim of the Neo-Kantians to produce integrally the object of thought by thinking *(reiner Ursprung)* is self-deception, for the conditionally methodological operations of thought, serving only to assimilate its object to thought, are here confused with the object itself. Thought logically splinters and adapts this object to itself, but the object exists before thinking and is independent of it; therefore it is proposed to thinking, it is the problem of problems to which all the separate efforts of thought lead.

Thought is born not out of the emptiness of self-production, for the human being is not God and cannot create anything; it is reflected out of the mass of experiences, out of *experience*, which is in no way a freely posited object of thought but rather one forcibly given. Lived, alogical or supralogical experience precedes gnoseological experience (in the Kantian sense), in which, unattainably for thought, matter is already given which generates thinking, and all this gray mass of experience gradually is overcome and assimilated by thinking. Thinking "generates" its own particular objects by the path of logically overcoming the object vitally given to it, which is not created by it, but which commands it authoritatively. Thus for the purposes of measuring it a mathematician can break down a given area into figures of his choosing and in the process apply suitable formulae — this is the freedom of "production" for his thinking; but all the same he has before him a definite problem given to him that can turn out to be completely unsolvable. Antinomy does not signify a mistake in thinking or even the general falsehood of the problem, a gnoseological misunderstanding, which can be explained and thereby removed. Antinomies are entirely inherent to reason.

Therefore there can be occasions in which thinking becomes fatally entangled in contradictions and falls into antinomy, and it is fully natural that religion belongs to such domains and even *must* belong. If religious antinomies were not available, this would mean that it would be necessary to search for them intensely. For if there is a domain in which the inadequacy of thinking to its object is clear already in the

The Fundamental Antinomy of Religious Consciousness

problem itself, it is of course religion, which rests on the unity of the transcendent and the immanent. Hence theology *more geometrico* [in a geometrical manner], in which everything would be reduced to rational unity and clarity, arouses suspicion toward itself in advance — it is not for nothing that such rational constructs were characteristic precisely of the unreligious century of deism and enlightenment.

And thus, the most general definition of the object of religion leads us to antinomy in which is contained the *coincidentia oppositorum;* the foundation is laid for two lines of thought that scatter in opposite directions. The transcendent God is the eternally unknowable, inaccessible, unattainable, ineffable Mystery to which there exists no approximation. Every attempt to express this mystery in concepts of being, to measure the immeasurable abyss of Divinity, is hopeless in a fatal way, just as a wave is powerless to lift itself with its surge to heaven, no matter how high it may climb. All properties, all words, all qualities, all thoughts borrowed from this world, no matter how we might potentiate and strengthen them, are absolutely unsuited for the description of that which stands beyond the limits of this world. The unconditional negation of all definitions, of every *yes,* the eternal and absolute NOT to everything, to each *something,* is supposed by the Absolute as its sole definition: God is NOT-what (and NOT-how, NOT-where, NOT-when, NOT-why). This NOT is not even *nothing,* insofar as a relation to some sort of *something* is connected with it (for nonbeing is only the fellow-traveler of being, and nothing is the shadow of something, but as an independent concept in general it does not exist); it is *Super-something.* NOT-what does not have any definitions of *something;* it is without qualities,[4] or more precisely, super-qualified.

The transcendence of Divinity can be expressed equally by *NOT-what* and by *NOT-who;* insofar as *what* is an expression of the qualification of being, and *who* of its subjective state or substantiality, the whole domain of being is *who* or *what,* or better, the one and other together. And since every subjective state, every *who* is conjugate with the objective state or *what,* and the division of being into subject and object, *who* and *what,* cuts through it to the very depths, then obviously in grasping the transcendence of Divinity one must negate not only every *what* or *who* but the relation itself, the *link* between them, which flows out of the bifurcation into *who* and *what.* Who *is* what; someone *is* something (or more particular judgments: someone x is the definite someone A, or something y is the definite something B); such are the most general conditions of being. From this it follows that being itself is necessarily a certain who-ness or what-ness and is correlative to them. Thus it is impossible even to say about Divinity in its transcendent aspect that it is, for in saying this, we thereby change it into a certain who and what, or into someone and something, whereas it is NOT-who and NOT-what, and thus generally speaking NOT-is. In other words we have to admit that it is impossible to affirm even being about the transcendent. Whether or not there is something above or outside of being, we cannot know it by our immanent consciousness, for being is the most general definition of immanence, and not for nothing does immanentism of various nuances equally proclaim the formula of idealism: *esse = percipi, sein = Bewusstsein* [to be = to be perceived, to be = consciousness]. Hence those representatives of "negative theology," who in negating every who or what when applied to Divinity nonetheless leave being as its sole attribute, taken in its opposition to nonbeing, illegitimately introduce into the transcendent idea of Divinity a definition borrowed from the realm of the immanent:[5] *Being is not proper to Divinity* (although this does not mean that IT does not exist in the sense of immanent self-consciousness). It is NOT-being, SUPER-being. One cannot say about the Absolute that IT exists, just as one cannot say that IT does not exist: here the human word falls silent, and remains only a taciturn philosophical-mystical gesture, a negation, a naked NOT. About it "there is no other cognition in the soul except the knowledge of the manner by which the soul does not know It" (Augustine).

The absolute NOT of negative theology therefore does not contain any negative affirmativeness which always is correlativity: it is neither *ou* nor *mē* (two nuances of Greek negation, which by their very presence presuppose an entire philosophy and in this attest to the philosophical genius of the Hellenes). Rather this NOT is what negates every expression — the *alpha privative* in *aoristos, apeiros, amorphos* [without limit, without bounds, without form] — not so much the negation of this or that definition as its absence, the expression of the inexpressible, a gesture of the transcendent in the immanent, the limit for thought and for consciousness, beyond which it extinguishes and sinks into night. The *alpha privative* of negative theology is found on a different logical plane than *mē on* or *ouk on* (and so too is the Hegelian *Nichts* or nothing, corresponding only to the meonic state of being, its pure potentiality). For both *mē* and *ou* are for the *alpha privative* of negative

The Fundamental Antinomy of Religious Consciousness

theology already some sort of positive expressions about being, and thereby they relate to the immanent, diurnal, cosmic consciousness that distinguishes the light of being and the shadow of nonbeing, the manifestation of forms and the twilight of potentiality. *Alpha privative* is a gesture, a surge, a motion, not a thought, not a word. It is music, inexpressible in word, an experience that cannot be thought out, an exit *(transcensus)* beyond one's very self.

Thus to think logically to the end the transcendent, which passes beyond the limits of thought, is obviously impossible. Thinking resembles here a serpent that catches itself by the tail, or strives to overtake its own shadow; it can make ever-newer efforts to liberate itself from any given content, to transcend itself, by depleting its energy in the negation of every given. In this sense NOT, as a symbol of the transcendent, is immeasurably more energetic and radical than each particular, objective *not*. Religious transcendence is broader and deeper than gnoseological, noetic transcendence. This transcendence demands the fullest renunciation, death for every living thing, but with the absence of death.[6] In religious philosophy the doctrine of Divinity as the Transcendent received expression in so-called "negative theology" *(theologia apophatikē, theologia negativa)*.

God in his transcendence is endlessly remote from the human being, goes away from him into a mystery beyond limit, by leaving in religious consciousness only NOT, only ABOVE, only emptiness. But religious self-consciousness cannot live, breathe, or be nourished by this emptiness alone — divine communion, divine experience, divine being constitute its vital foundation. Religion is possible only inasmuch as the transcendent Divinity, the ineffable and unthinkable mystery, *is revealed* to humankind, and the Absolute becomes God for humankind (for, according to the expression of Newton, *Deus est vocatio aequivoca*, God is a concept correlative to the one for whom he is God). To say it differently, the Absolute transcendent sets Itself as God, and consequently, accepts into Itself the distinction between God and the world, which includes the human being. God is both the Who and the What for humankind. He is the Subject of revelation and at the same time its Object. Even *being* is inherent in God (though in the highest level); about God one can say: *He is,* He is *ON,* The One Who Is, Yahweh, as he revealed himself to Moses. One cannot say this about the Absolute, for being is a correlative concept; God is *for* humankind or, more broadly, *for* the world. In order that God may be, the world must exist, and it likewise becomes the condition for the being of God. Only God is the basis for religion, which would never arise from the self-contained Absolute alone, from the eternally concealed mystery. That which communicates to religion the feeling of endless depth and ineffable mystery is the *transcendent background of God;* outside religion it appears as that emptiness or "border concept," as the *Ding an sich* in Kant's system. There is no logical bridge between the transcendent or the Absolute and the immanent or God: here there is an absolute hiatus, a bottomless abyss. This has to be recognized simply as a fact in all its triumphal obviousness, but also in its definitive incomprehensibility: it is so. The Absolute in the creation of the world or, to say it better, by the very act of this creation, generates God as well. God is generated with the world and in the world, *incipit religio* [religion begins]. From this begins the possibility of defining God as immanent-transcendent who steps out of his transcendence and absoluteness into immanence and a certain dualism. Here begins the possibility of cognition of God and communion with God; the realm of "positive theology" is revealed *(theologia kataphatikē);* the necessity of dogma and myth appears; finally, the critical establishment of the concept of God arises as a religious-philosophical problem.

It is possible, however, to pose the question whether or not the unity of consciousness is torn asunder by this antinomy. Is there not a bifurcation in it that threatens the human being with spiritual ruin? This would be so if consciousness were only rational-logical, and religious antinomy had a purely rational meaning: then woe to reason and its possessor! Fortunately it is just the reverse: religion is not established on rational comprehension; it stands on its own. On the contrary, the stated antinomy immediately creates for it a constant and irreplaceable impulse; it is the nerve of religion and bestows on it depth and motion. Although unsolvable, it is resolved constantly in religious life, being experienced again and again as the source of religious illuminations in the flame of faith. For the sake of faith it does not have to be understood to the end; faith is the child of mystery, the spiritual striving of love and freedom. It need not fear the rational absurd, for here eternal life is revealed, the boundlessness of Divinity.

And thus by the fundamental antinomy of religious consciousness two paths are marked on it: the path of negative theology and the path of positive theology. We should examine both.

II. Negative (Apophatic) Theology

Deus melius scitur nesciendo [God is better known by not knowing him].
Augustine, *De ordine* II, 6

The general peculiarity of negative theology in the sphere of thinking is its unconditionally negative character; all of its content is exhausted by NOT or ABOVE alone, which it attaches indifferently to all possible definitions of Divinity. All of it is a mute negative gesture directed towards heaven. This NOT is advanced in various doctrines more or less consistently, on which depends the degree of the internal coordination of systems. We ought to observe as a general trait of negative theology that in the majority of cases it grows up in the soil of a heightened mystical feeling, inseparably linked with mysticism. Actually the sheer NOT of apophatic theology would remain only a gaping void if it were not filled with the ineffable and super-rational, almost super-conscious, experience of the transcendent in mystical ecstasy, which inserts in the NOT of negative theology its mystical YES. The negative theology of mystics would in no way differ from the most trivial agnosticism and atheism that smugly and triumphantly put forward their NOT, if it were likewise not founded positively on its own mystical YES, if the day of rational negation here were not anticipated by the night full of voices and experiences of a different world. The idea of negative theology is present as a dialectical moment in religious philosophy as well as in many speculative thinkers. The present historical sketch does not lay claim to completeness but is limited to European religious philosophy: in it are absent the doctrines of the Buddhist East, so rich in motifs of negative theology.

1. Negative Theology in Plato and Aristotle

Plato's doctrine of ideas, the summit of which is the idea of the Good, Divinity itself, necessarily has two aspects, upwards and downwards; ideas have self-existent being in "the intelligible place," representing something transcendent to the world's being as to its coming to be, but they make themselves its foundation. Being is communicated to them, and they to being. Between the two worlds an indissoluble connection exists — of cause and effect, foundation and product, Eros and its subject, etc. In various dialogues of Plato now one and now the other aspect of idealism is emphasized and disclosed — the transcendence of ideas to the world or their immanence. Inasmuch as Plato discloses the first aspect he naturally approaches the sphere of ideas of negative theology and is compelled to flee to descriptions that are primarily negative. Thus already in *Phaedrus* the "supercelestial realm" is described as the colorless and formless and intangible, truly essential essence of the soul visible only to the ruling mind alone.[7] But especially characteristic in this respect is the famous passage in book 6 of the *Republic* concerning the good: "So, call that which furnishes the knowable with verity and gives power to the knower, the idea of the good, the cause of knowledge and truth, so far as it is known by the mind. For no matter how beautiful the one and the other are, knowledge and truth, you will judge justly, by considering the other as even more beautiful: one must esteem the nature of the good even higher. The sun, it seems to me, you will say, supplies visible objects not only with the capability of being seen but also generation and growth and food, though it is itself not generated. . . . Thus too does the good, one must say, supply the knowable not only with the capability of being known but also of receiving being and having essence from it, *whereas the good is not essence but according to dignity and power it stands higher* (transcendent to — *epekeina*) *than essence.*"[8]

One can follow this motif in Plato's other dialogues.[9]

Aristotle subjects the Platonic doctrine about ideas as transcendent essences to criticism; he sees in them only an ideological doubling of reality, which hardly serves for its comprehension. For the Platonic ideas are separated from reality by an impassable gulf and are deprived of active force, of energy. Aristotle contrasts his own doctrine of forms *(morphē)* with Plato's doctrine of ideas; the forms are realized in a certain substrate *(hypokeimenon)*, matter *(hylē)*, with the form being the motive principle leading development to its fullest realization: it is both a given and something proposed for its kind and also the law of its development, the final cause which makes a thing the incarnation of its idea *(entelecheia)*. In this manner according to the sense of Aristotle's doctrine, forms exist not "in the intelligible place" of Plato but only in things. However, independent being belongs to them in the sense that they are the ontological *prius* to things, in virtue of which the possibility *(dynamei on)* passes over into reality *(energeia on)*, with each form having an enduring, eternal existence, and the totality of forms forming their hierarchy or organism. In Aristotle's doctrine of forms we have only a different (in one sense an ameliorated, and in another sense a worsened) redaction of the Platonic doctrine of ideas, without which a thinker could not manage who has understood science as cognition of the universal *(to katholou)* and consequently is himself in need of a theory of this "universal," i.e., a theory of idea-concepts. As reposing in matter or forming it the Aristotelian forms are immanent to the world, but as

Negative (Apophatic) Theology

motive goals, as the ontological *prius* [precedent condition]; they are transcendent to it. Nevertheless one cannot regard even the Platonic ideas in any manner at all as fully transcendent realities that only double it uselessly; on the contrary the world only exists through participation *(methexis)* in the ideas, which constitute what is truly and eternally *(to ontos, aei on)* in what exists and becomes *(gignomenon)*.

Plato's and Aristotle's doctrines in the relation that interests us are contrasted only as two different aspects of one and the same type not in their *what* but according to their *how*. Plato's worldview, if it can be expressed thus, is more sophianic, Aristotle's more theistic. The world of ideas in Plato forms an independent sophianic photosphere that simultaneously conceals and reveals that which is beyond and above this sphere — Divinity itself; the ideas in Plato remain in an unstructured and unorganized plurality, so that even relative to the supreme idea of the good, the idea of ideas, a double meaning is not removed, whether it is Idea in the proper and unique sense or whether it is one of many ideas, although the highest (only the *Timaeus* with its doctrine of the demiurge occupies a special place in this question). On the contrary, Aristotle by ascending along the ladder of forms in their natural hierarchy arrives at the form of all forms which has for its content only itself, the thinking of thinking *(noēsis tēs noēseōs)*, the first moving thing *(prōton kinoun)* that constitutes both the source of every motion and its subject as general striving and love *(ou kinoumenon kinei . . . kinei de hōs eromenon)*; this Form generally speaking is Divinity. Aristotle inordinately combines it with the world, portraying it as a cosmic agent, the prime mover (who himself however remains unmoved). He seemingly lacks an intelligible world of ideas (Sophia) which is located between God and the world in the system of Platonism, wherefore the danger arises for Aristotle of complete religious immanentism, of the dissolution of God in the world, of world-divinization. But for this Aristotle conceives the idea of Divinity too seriously and exaltedly and endeavors to affirm his theism by emphasizing the supermundane transcendent character of Divinity; precisely in the development of this idea he embarks naturally on the path of negative theology.

Aristotle frequently repeats that one must renounce an understanding of Divinity, for every attempt in this direction unavoidably suffers failure.[10] In book 12 of the *Metaphysics,* chapter 7, giving a definition of Divinity as thinking, life, eternity, fullness, and perfection, Aristotle continues in the tones of "apophatic" theology: "It is clear that there exists an eternal, immobile essence *(ousia)* that exists separately from the sensible and independently. But it is also demonstrated that this essence cannot have magnitude, but is indivisible and inseparable. For it brings into motion infinite time, but nothing limited has unlimited power. But since every magnitude must be limited or unlimited, on the given basis it cannot have a limited quantity, nor can it have an unlimited magnitude because unlimited magnitude in general does not exist. Further it is demonstrated that it is not subject to any affect or qualitative change; all remaining motions follow only upon a change of place" (1073a). Aristotle clarifies the question of the relation of God to the world with the following comparison: "One ought to weigh (he says) by which of two means the nature of all good or the best is contained: as something eternally separate, existing independently in itself, or as the order of its parts. Of course it is simultaneously by the one and the other means, as takes place with respect to an army, since for the latter the good lies both in the formation and in the commander, and even more in the latter. For he does not exist thanks to the formation; rather, the formation exists through him" (chapter 10, 1075a). We do not find in Aristotle a closer examination of this question, which is raised rather than resolved by this comparison, and his whole doctrine of God fails by its vagueness and ambiguity.[11]

2. Plotinus (Third Century A.D.)

Plotinus, the head of the Neo-Platonic school, who represents the summit of the metaphysical speculation of Greece, places as the basis of his complex worldview that is far from being vague in details the doctrine of the absolute First Principle, which he most often of all calls the One *(Hen)* and sometimes the Good *(Agathon)*. This divine Fundamental Principle of the world and being is also the common substance of the world, for everything is grounded in the One, has its cause and goal in it, and exists only by its life-creating power. The world is not created by an act of creation, it proceeds from the One, as it were by streaming out of the divine fullness like light from the sun; it is an emanation of divinity, subordinated to the "law of diminishing perfection" (Zeller). Since everything represents the energy of the absolute One only in different degrees of perfection, then with respect to the world this system, according to the just description of Zeller, must be defined as "dynamic pantheism."[12] In Plotinus's system the *nous* plays an intermediate role between the One and the world and forms a second and less pure unity — of thinking and being, but the World Soul serves as the immediate recipient of the influences of the *nous,* having a higher and lower aspect, and it streams already into matter which does not have authentic being and which is meonic *(mē on)* and therefore evil. The One, the Mind, the World Soul constitute the three-level gradation of being (but this threefoldness is not trihypostaseity as is sometimes erroneously thought, confusing Neo-Platonism with Christianity).[13]

In Plotinus the One inevitably receives a twofold description: being the fundamental principle, immanent to all being, it remains at the same time higher than all being, like the simple One transcendent to the world. This unity has of course the meaning not of numerical unity, which is defined in opposition to plurality, but of simple unity, or rather, of super-unity and

Negative (Apophatic) Theology

super-number. One can rightly doubt how much the transcendent aspect of the One in Plotinus is joined with the universal fundamental principle immanent to everything. In this is the fatal duality of dynamic pantheism thanks to which Plotinus's system splits apart from within. But here it is not this peculiarity of Plotinus's worldview that interests us, about which we will speak later, but that description of the One as transcendent which places Plotinus in the series of representatives of negative theology.

We will present that description in Plotinus's own words (*Enneads* VI, book IX, 5-6): the transition to unconditional unity which stands higher than mind is for Plotinus incomprehensible, as it were, a miracle *(thauma to hen)*. "This miracle is the One, which is non-existent *(mē on)* so that it does not receive a definition from another, since truly there exists no corresponding name for it; if it is necessary to name it, it is usually named the One ... it is knowable with difficulty, it is known primarily through the essence *(ousia)* generated by it; the mind leads to the essence and its nature is such that it is the source of the best and the power which has generated what is, but it remains in itself and is not diminished and is not in what proceeds from it; with respect to this we of necessity call it the One in order to designate for ourselves its indivisible nature and by desiring to lead the soul to unity *(henoun)*, but we use the expression 'one and indivisible' not as we speak about a symbol and a unit, for a unit in this sense is the principle of quantity *(posou archai)* which would not exist if the essence did not exist in advance and that which precedes essence. Therefore we must not direct our consideration to that side but must treat it by analogy with the simple, by avoiding the relation to plurality and division.

"How do we speak about the One? And how is it possible to adapt it to thought? In that we suppose it one in the highest degree, similar to how a unit or point is supposed one *(henizetai)*. Here precisely the soul, having decreased quantity and magnitude, gradually stops at the smallest and in this manner remains in some such thing that, although indivisible, was in the divisible and exists in the other. And the very One does not remain in the other nor in the divisible, and it is not divisible as the smallest. It is greater than the other not by magnitude but by power *(dynamei)* so that even that which does not have magnitude exists by power, as also what exists in keeping with it is indivisible and inseparable as power, but not as magnitude. It is necessary to consider it infinite not as immeasurable in magnitude or number, but as immense according to power. For if you begin to think it as God or mind, then it is greater. If in your thinking you bring it to unity, it is also in this respect greater; it is more one *(to henikoteron)* with respect to your thinking than you can imagine God himself, for in itself it is without accidents *(symbebekotos)*. But is it impossible to think the One as such, as self-sufficient? For it must be first of all self-sufficient of another, self-satisfied, foreign to every want; everything multiple and not one has a need, for it came from another. In this manner its essence requires unity, and this latter does not require it, for it is itself. . . . If something must be completely self-satisfied, then it must be one, and it must precisely not experience need with respect to its own self or with respect to the other. It does not seek anything in order to exist or to exist well or in general to have a ground, for once it is the basis of the other then it has its being and well-being not from another – what could have such significance for it outside its own self? Whence the good *(to eu)* for it is not an accident, it is its very self. It has no place, for it does not need a location, as if it were unable to carry itself; that which must be supported is inanimate and is a falling mass, if it does not have a firm support. This is the reason why the other has a firm support through it, by attaining existence and obtaining a place, on which it must be placed according to rank. . . . All that is called needing the good also needs something supporting it, consequently, the One is not the Good. Therefore it desires nothing but is super-good *(hyperagathon)* and good not for itself but for other things, if something is capable of taking part in it. It is not thinking, inasmuch as it is foreign to change and motion, for it is higher than motion and thinking. What would it begin to think? Itself? But then prior to thinking it will be unknowing and needing thinking so that it can know its own self, being at the same time self-sufficient *(autarkēs)*. Therefore, although it does not know itself and does not think itself, there will be no unknowing in it; for unknowing arises in the presence of the other, when one does not know the other. The sole *(monon)* does not know anything and it has nothing that it does not know, and since the One is in communion with itself, it does not need thinking of itself. For communion *(synienai)* should not be added for the concept of the One; rather, both thinking and communion should be removed just as thinking of oneself and the other, for it is not necessary to suppose it like that which thinks but as thinking. Thinking *(noēsis)* does not think but is the cause of thinking for the other. The cause is not identical with the caused, namely the cause is not something out of all the caused. Therefore it is not necessary to call the Good *(agathon)* that which it represents but rather the Good itself *(tagathon)*, higher than different goods."

With such traits the One is portrayed in its negative description. But the fundamental mystical motif of this doctrine also resounds. Plotinus teaches "mental activity" (according to the ascetics' expression), showing the way of mystical comprehension of that which philosophizing reason portrays with such pale and schematic traits. The end of book 9 of the sixth Ennead is devoted to this: "If you vacillate in your opinion that nothing of this exists, put yourself in this *(stēson seauton eis tauta)* and look from there; but look so as not to aim your thought outside; for this does not lie somewhere after you have been freed from the other, but it is inherent in the one who can seize it, whereas it is not inherent *(ou parestin)* in the one who cannot do this. So too it is impossible to imagine something if you are thinking about something else

Negative (Apophatic) Theology

and are occupied with the other, and it is impossible to add anything to the object of thought so that this very object would be obtained — one has to act in this way here too for, by having a representation of the other in the soul, one cannot think it on account of the action of representation, and the soul, enveloped and bound by the other, cannot receive an impression from the representation of the opposite; but, as it is said of matter, that it must be without quality if it is to receive the forms *(typous)* of all things, so too the soul must be formless in a still greater degree, since in it there ought not to be any obstacle for its fulfilment and the illumination of higher *(tēs prōtēs)* nature. If this is so, then, in abstracting from everything external, you must turn primarily to the internal, without inclining towards anything external, and know nothing about everything, and above all, about your own condition, thereupon about the ideas too, to know nothing about your own self and in this manner be submerged in the contemplation *(thea)* of that with which you become one. Then, after sufficient communion as it were you return in order to give news about such communion to others as you are able; perhaps Minos had such communion which is why tradition designates him as the intimate of Zeus; in remembrance he gave reflections of this in the guise of a law, having been fully equipped for legislating from contact with Divinity. It is possible not to value politics for its own sake and at will to remain above it; which is what happens with those who have seen much. In this manner God — says Plato — is not far from anyone but is close to everyone, without their knowledge. But they are the ones who flee *(pheugousi)* from him, or more exactly, they avoid themselves. They cannot therefore master that which they avoid and they cannot search for anything other, for they have annihilated themselves. Indeed a child who is beside himself in madness will not know his own father; whoever has learned to know himself will also know where he is from.

"The one contemplating does not contemplate or contrast what is contemplated as the other, but he himself becomes like the other and no longer belongs to himself; he belongs wholly to that and becomes one with it, united with it like a center to a center; and here complex things constitute one, and duality has place only in the case when they are divided — in this case we speak of the separated. Therefore such contemplation is difficult to describe. How can anyone describe something as other when he saw that which he contemplated not as other but as one with himself? Evidently the rule of such mysteries wants to say this — not to communicate anything to the uninitiated. Since it is not communicable, it was forbidden to reveal the divine to the one to whom it was not given to contemplate. Since then there were not two, rather, the one contemplating and the contemplated were one, as if it was not being contemplated but was united, then the one who in being united with it became one with it, has in himself the image of it by remembering it. But it was itself one, not having any distinction either in itself or with the other, for noth-

Divine Nothing

ing moved in it, no passion *(thymos)*, no desire of some other thing in keeping with his ascent *(tōi anabebēkoti)*, just as no concept, no thought, in general not even himself, if one can express it thus. But as if enraptured and in enthusiasm he rests in solitude, without inclining anywhere and even without turning around himself, standing firmly and as if having become immobility *(stasis)*. He does not think about the beautiful, since he is found already higher than the beautiful, higher than the choir of virtues, similar to a man who penetrated into the very innermost sanctuary and left behind himself in the temple images of the gods, and only in coming out of the sanctuary, does he encounter them for the first time, after inner contemplation and commerce with what is not an image, nor an aspect but is the divine essence itself; images, consequently, would be objects of contemplation of the second order. But this in essence is not contemplation but a special type of vision, ecstasy *(ekstasis)*, simplification *(haplōsis)* and casting off of one's self. . . .

"And he himself does not thereby become essence but higher (transcendent to) than essence *(epekeina ousias)*, as far as he enters into communion with that one" (*Enneads* IX, 10-11).

This description could be completed with other passages from the *Enneads* of Plotinus, but for us what we have cited is sufficient. It is clear that the One remains transcendent to distinct discursive consciousness: it is *epekeina* [beyond] to knowledge, good, beauty, virtue; it is foreign to every predicate, for they are the result of distinction, the properties of "the other," but the One stands on the other side of every distinction. The soul is lifted in ecstasy to experiencing it, to union with it, when, in seeing the divine light, it is poured out into divinity like a drop into the sea. In the words of Porphyry, Plotinus's biographer, in the course of their common life which lasted for six years, Plotinus experienced such a state four times, and every time it was attained without any exertion of powers, "by an indescribable act." Plotinus knew by experience what he was talking about.

3. Philo of Alexandria (First Century)

According to the description of Professor Muretov,[14] one of the best Philo scholars, Philo of Alexandria unites in his theologizing the tendencies of Hellenistic philosophical pantheism and panlogism and the Judaic-rabbinic understanding of Divinity as transcendent to the world. In virtue of the latter tendency Philo proves to be a representative of negative theology in a rather decided form.[15]

"Every qualified determination would introduce a limitation in Divinity and therefore Philo calls God *to apoion* — *the one lacking* qualification,[16] pure and not having any definite sign of existence *(psilēn aneu charaktēros hyparxein)*;[17]

Negative (Apophatic) Theology

Philo says that it is impossible to ascribe to Divinity any properties, for being unbegotten and itself bringing everything into being, it has no need of anything that is proper to creaturely and finite beings" (Muretov, *Doctrine of the Logos*, 110-11).

"As *psilē aneu charaktēros hyparxis*, God cannot be thought as unconditional good or love, as absolute beauty, as most perfect reason; according to his nature God is higher than all these attributes of personal being, better than good itself and love, more perfect than virtue itself, more beautiful than beauty itself; it is not possible to call him reason in the proper sense for he is higher than every reasonable nature *(ameinon hē logikē physis)*; but he is not even a monad in the strict sense, but purer than monad itself, and simpler than simplicity itself;[18] finally one cannot call him life for he is more and higher than life, he is the eternal and inexhaustible source of life."[19]

In connection with this is Philo's doctrine of the perfect incognoscibility and namelessness of Divinity, which Philo calls *akatalēpton, aperinoēton, aperigraphon, akatonomaston* [incomprehensible, inconceivable, indefinable, unnameable], etc. "I do not think," says Philo, "that the One Who Is, however he is in his nature, could be known by any human being whatsoever. As our mind is unknown to us, so the One Who Is is inaccessible to the cognition of people. . . . Thus it is impossible to give him any proper name whatsoever."[20]

Having established the complete lack of qualifications of Divinity, Philo leaves for it the most common determination, namely, *being*. "God is inaccessible to our cognition, saving only according to being *(kata tou einai)*; for what we know about him is nothing but existence *(hyparxis)* alone, and apart from existence we know nothing."[21] "A human being can know about God not how he is but only that he is *(ouch hoios esti all' hoti esti)*."[22] (Cf. Muretov, *Doctrine of the Logos*, 113-15.)

This Philonic idea, which is widely disseminated in Christian theology, is in a certain sense the purest misunderstanding: if negative theology cannot affirm anything about God, then obviously it cannot affirm his being either.

4. The Idea of Negative Theology in the Alexandrian School of Christian Theology (Third Century)

A. Clement of Alexandria

The famous founder of the Alexandrian school, who was educated in Hellenism and raised the authority of Hellenistic philosophy to such heights in the church's consciousness, fully adopted the doctrine of the incognoscibility of Divinity by reason. Chapter 12 of book 5 of the *Stromateis*[23] is dedicated to the development of this idea, which begins with the words of Plato: "God cannot be comprehended by reason and a concept of him cannot be expressed with words." Here, by referring to classical authorities such as Plato, Orpheus, Solon, and Empedocles, as well as to texts from sacred Scripture, Clement explains that "the question about God is united with difficulties." "In fact, with what name are we to call him who is not born, who has no distinctions in himself, no defined aspect, no individuality, no number, but is an essence having no accidents in itself, but equally is not subject to anything accidental? Will you say that God is the whole? It is an imperfect definition because the whole represents a quantity all the same commensurable, but God is the Father of all that exists in general. Do you wish to divide him into various parts? But you are not in any state to do this, for in his essence this One is indivisible. That is why God is without limit and infinite, not at all in the sense that it seems to us — as if we were unable to grasp him with our thought — but rather in the sense that God is not subject to measurement and there are no limits, no bounds in his essence. There are likewise no forms in him, and equally he cannot be named. But if we sometimes name him with such expressions as the One, the Good, Spirit, Being, Father, God, Creator, Lord, we use them not as his name. We fly to the assistance of these beautiful words only on account of the quandary *(aporias)*, in order to guard against other appellations with which the Eternal might be debased. Not one of these locutions taken separately gives a conception of God; whereas together they speak about him as Pantocrator. Things are understood either according to their proper nature or according to their mutual relations among themselves; none of this is applicable to God. He likewise cannot be revealed by proofs, because they are based on previous principles and higher concepts, but nothing can exist earlier than the uncreated Essence. As a result nothing remains for comprehending the unsearchable Essence except his own grace and the revelation of him by means of the Logos who dwells in his womb."[24] In this way the acknowledgment of the incognoscibility of Divinity leads Clement of Alexandria to the affirmation that revelation is the only source of positive knowledge about Divinity.

B. Origen

The ideas of negative theology have a definite place in Origen's doctrine, though it is impossible not to see his proximity to Plotinus in this respect. In the first book of his work *On First Principles,* which contains a general doctrine of God, his transcendence and incomprehensibility are sharply affirmed. "Having refuted, insofar as is possible, every thought of the corporeality of God, we affirm, in conformity with the truth, that God is incomprehensible *(incomprehensibilis)* and inestimable *(inaestimibilis).* Even in the event that we received the possibility of knowing or understanding something about God, all the same, of necessity, we must believe that he is incomparably better than what we have come to know about him. In fact, if we saw a human being who is scarcely able to see a spark of light or the light of the shortest candle, and if we desired to give that human being a concept of the clarity and brilliance of the sun, then without doubt we must have to tell him that the brilliance of the sun is unspeakably and incomparably better and more beautiful than any light seen by him. Such is our mind. Although it is considered very much greater than corporeal nature, yet, in striving towards incorporeality and in becoming absorbed in its contemplation, it is hardly equal to any spark or candle whatsoever – and this as long as it is locked in chains of flesh and blood, and on account of participation in such matter it remains relatively immobile and obtuse. But between all the spiritual *(intellectualibus)* i.e. incorporeal essences, which essence so inexpressibly and incomparably exceeds all the others if not God? Really, the power of the human mind cannot contemplate or comprehend his nature, even though it were the purest and most lucid mind."[25] "There is no nature for which God would be visible, according to St. John; the apostle does not say that God, being visible according to his nature, is inaccessible only to the sight of the weakest creature but that according to his very nature he cannot be seen."[26] "Our mind by its powers *(per se ipsam)* cannot contemplate the Very God, as he is, but it knows the Father of all creatures from the beauty of his works and the splendour of the universe. And so, one ought not to consider God some sort of body or as dwelling in a body, but as simple, spiritual nature *(intellectualis natura)* which does not admit into itself any complexity whatsoever. He does not have in himself anything greater or smaller, but is – from every suitable aspect – *monas* and so to say *henas* – the simplicity of the divine nature would to a certain degree be limited and broken by complexity."[27] In a word, "God is higher than anything thinkable" *(epekeina tōn noētōn)*.[28]

5. Fathers of the Church: St. Basil the Great, St. Gregory the Theologian, St. Gregory of Nyssa (Fourth Century)

The so-called Cappadocian fathers of the Church represent something of a theological middle-of-the-road stance on the question of the comprehensibility and incomprehensibility of God. By not subjecting the question to deeper philosophical analysis and by examining it primarily from a religious-practical side, they consider the idea of negative theology to be self-evident. St. Basil the Great develops his views on this question in his polemic with Eunomius, who affirmed the complete knowability of the essence of Divinity in concepts or, as they are usually expressed in this dispute, in the names of God which correspond to these concepts.[29] Eunomius deems the designation *agennēsia,* ingenerateness to be such a definition of the Divine essence, applying it only to the first hypostasis (from this derive Eunomius' Arian deductions respecting the second hypostasis which does not have this property). Arguing against the doctrine of Eunomius, St. Basil the Great advances the general postulate that "there is not a single name which, having embraced the whole divine nature, would be enough to express it. . . . From the names which have been said of God some indicate what is in God, and others on the contrary, what is not in him. For by these two means, that is by negation of that which is not and by confession of that which is, a certain imprint of God is formed in us as it were." "The essence of God for human nature is unthinkable and completely unspeakable."[30] "What pride and arrogance to think that the very essence of the God of all has been discovered!" "The comprehension of God's essence is beyond not only human beings but also every rational nature." "The very essence cannot be seen by anyone except the Only Begotten and the Holy Spirit, but we, who are led upward by the works of God and from his creations come to understand the Creator, obtain knowledge of his goodness and essence."[31] Responding (in his letter to Amphilochius) to the cunning question of the Anomoeans[32] – what do you worship, that which you know or that which you do not know – St. Basil the Great says: "Whoever affirms that he does not know the essence has still not confessed that he does not know God. . . . We affirm that we know our God by his operations, but we give no promise of approaching his very essence. For, although his operations descend as far as us, still his essence remains unapproachable."[33] "I know that God is. But what his essence is, I set this higher than understanding. How is one saved? Through faith. And faith is satisfied with the knowledge that *there* is a God. . . . Consequently, consciousness of the incomprehensibility of God is cognition of God's essence, and we worship what has been attained not in respect of what kind of essence it is, but in respect of that this essence is."[34]

Eunomius however did not agree with the interpretation of the negative names of God in St. Basil the Great and, not without a certain foundation, objected: "I do not know how through negation of that which is not proper to God he will surpass creation! . . . It must be clear to every intellectual essence that one essence cannot surpass another by that which he does not have."[35] The question of the significance of negative theology in its relation to positive theology thus remained poorly explained in St. Basil.

In his Second Theological Oration, St. Gregory the Theologian says, "I went in order to understand God; with this thought, having renounced matter and the material, and having collected myself interiorly as much as I was able, I ascended the mountain. But when I stretched my gaze, I scarcely saw the back of God (Ex. 33:22-23) and the one hidden *by the Rock* (1 Cor. 10:4), that is, the Word who became incarnate for our sake. And having pressed myself somewhat close I contemplate not the first and pure nature, which is known only by

Negative (Apophatic) Theology

him, that is by the very Trinity, I contemplate not that which dwells inside the first curtain and is concealed by cherubim, but only the extremity and that which extends itself to us. And this is, as far as I know, that greatness or *magnificence* as the divine David calls it (Ps. 8:2[1]), which is visible in creatures, who are created and governed by God. For all of this is the *back of God*, that which, after God, conveys cognition of him to us, similar to how the reflection and image of the sun on the waters shows the sun to weak gazes which cannot look at it because the vivacity of the light staggers the sense.... To understand God is difficult, but to express him is impossible. Thus did one of the Hellenistic theologians (Plato in *Timaeus*) philosophize.... As for me, I think that it is impossible to express God and even more impossible to understand. For a word will be able to explain, if not completely sufficiently then at least feebly, what is comprehended by reason to someone whose hearing is not entirely damaged and whose mind is not dull. But not only people who are grown rigid and bent down low but even the most exalted and god-loving have absolutely no powers or means to grasp by thought such a grand subject, the same as every generated entity for which this gloom — this coarse flesh — serves as a hindrance to understanding the truth. I do not know if it is possible for the supreme and spiritual natures who, being closer to God and being radiated with the whole light, perhaps see him if not entirely then more perfectly and definitely than we do; and besides, according to the measure of their rank, some more or less than others."[36]

Similar to St. Basil the Great, St. Gregory says, "That God exists I do not call incomprehensible, but rather what he is like.... There is a very great difference — to be persuaded of the existence of something and to know what it is. God exists — the creative and sustaining cause of all; our teachers here are sight and natural law.... For us the creative power which moves and preserves the created is clear, although it is not comprehended by thought."[37] "Divinity remains incomprehensible not on account of envy. For envy is far from the divine nature, which is passionless, solely good and sovereign, especially envy towards creation which for God is more precious than the others because what is more preferable for the Word than rational creatures? Besides, our very creation is above goodness."[38] "Since no rational nature, although it strives towards God and the first cause, can comprehend it, according to what I have explained; then, languishing with desire, finding itself as it were in pre-death torments and not bearing these tortures, it sets out on a new voyage in order either to turn its gaze to the visible and from this to fashion something as a god, or from the beauty and harmonious structure of the visible to come to know God, to use sight as a guide to the unseen without losing sight of God in the magnificence of the visible. For this reason some began to worship the sun, some the moon, some the multitude of stars, and some the heaven itself with its luminaries, to which they granted the governance of the world both by the quality and the quantity of movements, and others turned to the elements: earth, water, air, fire."[39] St. Gregory here explains the origin of paganism as "one of the contrivances of the wicked one, who turned good itself into evil, and that there are many other examples of his maleficence. In order to draw people under his authority, he made use of their falsely directed aspiration to find God and after deceiving them with desire and leading them like a blind person searching for the way himself, he scattered them among various rapids and precipitated them into a single abyss of death and perdition."[40]

The general notion of the incomprehensibility of God is expressed as well in St. Gregory's religious poetry. Thus, in the first "Hymn to God," we read, "O, you who are higher than all! For what else is permitted me to speak about you? How can I hymn a word about you? For you cannot be expressed by any word. How can the mind look on you? For you are inaccessible to any mind. You alone are unexplainable because you have produced all that cannot be expressed in word. You alone are unknowable, because you have produced all that is graspable by thought. Everything which is gifted and not gifted with reason returns honour to you. You are the end of everything; you alone are all; you are neither one, nor single, nor all. O all-nameable one! How shall I name you, the one who cannot be named? And what heavenly mind penetrates through the cover beyond the clouds? Be merciful, you who are higher than everything, for what else is permitted me to utter about you?"[41]

The principal occasion for the expression of ideas of apophatic theology in St. Gregory of Nyssa is his polemic with the rationalistic Gnosticism of Eunomius, which he continued after the death of his friend St. Basil the Great.[42] For Eunomius, as we know, there was no doubt of the possibility of the adequate, exhaustive cognition of the divine essence with the help of concepts (names), and the principal such concept was "unbegottenness."[43] In his dispute with Eunomius, St. Gregory takes the generally uncharacteristic position of skeptical nominalism in his theory of cognition (in his doctrine of names). In order to refute the illegitimate exaggeration or rather the false understanding of the correlation existing between the name of God and the essence of God in Eunomius, St. Gregory denies all realism to concepts, names, and turns them into simple signs (like present-day "enemies of the Name")[44] that are invented by human beings. The danger is that with this teaching the foundation of St. Gregory of Nyssa's own sublime system of theology is undermined and thus in the gnoseological theory of names that he advances against Eunomius, one cannot but see polemical enthusiasm and a certain self-contradiction.[45] But irrespective of the nominalistic exaggeration in gnoseology, St. Gregory's fundamental point of view with respect to the inaccessibility of the Divinity to rational cognition completely coincides with the general direction of negative theology in other fathers. "God cannot be grasped by name, by thought, by any other cognitive power of the mind; he remains above the

Negative (Apophatic) Theology

comprehension not only of human beings, but also of angels and every supermundane being. He is inexplicable *(aphraston)*, unutterable *(anekphōnēton)*, above every designation by words; he has only one name which serves for the cognition of his proper nature, namely that he alone is higher than every name."[46] "In human nature there is no power for knowing the essence of God precisely, and perhaps it is too little to speak only of human power; but if someone says that even the bodiless creation is too lowly for accommodating and grasping the infinite nature with knowledge, he will of course not err entirely, . . . and the power of angels does not stand far from our smallness. . . . For great and unsurpassable is the distance by which the uncreated nature is separated from created essence. One is limited, the other has no bounds; one is comprehended by its measure, as the Wisdom of the Creator desired it, the other knows no measure; one is bound with a certain stretch of distance, closed in by place and time, the other is higher than any concept of distance: no matter how much one might strain the mind, it eludes one's curiosity all the same." Generally speaking, "With respect to its essence Divinity remains inaccessible, unthinkable, and exceeds any understanding which can be obtained by means of deduction."[47]

Hereinafter St. Gregory of Nyssa distinctively intertwines in his positive theology the basic motif of apophatic theology in his own dogmatic system, namely, the transcendence of God to creation and his inaccessibility to created consciousness.

6. Areopagitica

The real father of negative theology in Christian philosophy and mysticism is a mysterious author usually dated to the beginning of the fifth century whose work tradition ascribes to Dionysius the Areopagite, an apostolic man converted to Christianity by the apostle Paul in Athens. The composition *On the Divine Names* has particular significance, representing one of the pinnacles of mystical speculation. Standing under the immediate influence of the Areopagite is a thinker such as St. Maximus the Confessor (seventh century) who wrote Scholia,[48] commentaries, on his compositions. The influence of the Areopagite is noticeable on Johannes Scotus Eriugena, on Sebastian Frank, Eckhart and his school, and others.[49] The Areopagite's compositions were written with great enthusiasm, though they are not free of rhetoric. His favorite literary device is hyperbole: theologizing is always defined as *hymnein* [to praise]; concepts are constantly combined with *hyper*, alpha privative, and *auto* (*hē hyperousios hyparxis, hē hypertheos theotēs, hē hyperagathos agathotēs, anaitios autotheotēs*, etc.) [the superessential existence, the super-divine divinity, the super-good goodness, uncaused very divinity, etc.]. The fundamental idea that is developed in *On the Di-*

vine Names is the absolute transcendence and incomprehensibility of Divinity for us. Reason, which is granted its own powers, can and must go only along the apophatic path; positive definitions of Divinity can constitute only the subject of revelation and are contained in the Word of God, where different *names of God* are communicated. The treatise is devoted to an analysis of the meaning of these names. Therefore the apophatic moment is expressed in Dionysius with matchless power and concentration. "In general one ought neither think nor say anything about the super-essential and mysterious divinity *(tēs hyperousias kai kryphias theotētos)* except what is divinely revealed to us in the word of God" *(De div. nom.* I, 1, PG 3, col. 583). Divinity is revealed by grace to humankind in the measure of the capability of the individual spirit, but "the super-essential limitlessness itself is higher than essence (is transcendent to it); higher than minds is the unity surpassing mind; inaccessible to every reasoning is the one which exceeds reasoning; unutterable for every word is the good that surpasses word; the unity which unites every unity, and the super-essential essence, and the mind inaccessible to mind; and the unutterable word, wordlessness, absence of reason, and namelessness, which does not correspond to anything that is; the cause of all being, though it is itself not being, transcendent to every essence" *(De div. nom.* I, 1, PG 3, col. 583).

To express our ideas about the divine we use symbols *(symbolois)* and analogies *(analogos).* "The one, unknowable, super-substantial *(hyperousion),* good in itself *(autotagathon),* which is named the threefold unity, the uniformly divine *(homotheon)* and uniformly good *(homoagathon)* is impossible to express in a word or understand with the mind," and an approximation to understanding must be accomplished by the way of abstraction from all being *(dia tēs pantōn ontōn aphaireseōs)*.[50] Going along this path we inevitably arrive at the apophatic definition that in the language of what is, Divinity is *truly nothing,*[51] *auto to ouden* (namely *ouden* and not *mēden*), as what is removed from all that is *(ōs pantōn hyperousios exerēmenon)* for it is above every quality, motion, life, imagination, notion, name, words, reason, reflection, essence, condition, position, union, border, limitlessness and all that exists" *(De div. nom.* I, 1, PG 3, col. 583).[52] With logical consistency Dionysius establishes the antinomy of religious consciousness that springs from this. "Theologians praise *(hymnousi)* Divinity as nameless *(anōnymon)* and having every name *(ek pantos onomatos)*" *(De div. nom.* I, 6, c. 596). "How can we get to know God who is unthinkable, who cannot be perceived by the senses and in general does not constitute anything of what is? We get to know God, by ascending from the order of creation which he established, which presents images and likenesses of the divine prototypes, by ascending towards that which is found above *(epekeina)* everything by the way of abstraction from everything *(aphairesei)* and of eminence above everything *(hyperochē).* Hence God is known in all things and apart from all things; and God is known in knowledge and in unknowing, and inherent to him are thinking, reason, knowledge, touch, sensation, representation, fantasy, name and all the rest, and at the same time he is not thought, not expressed, not named; he is not something of what is, and he is not known in anything that is; and in everything he is everything, in nothing he is nothing *(en oudeni ouden)* and in everything he is known by all and in nothing by none *(ex oudenos oudeni)"* (De div. nom. VII, 3, c. 872). "He is not this, but he is not that either, he is not in one place but he is not somewhere in another place. But he is all things, being the cause of all things . . . above everything as super-essentially surpassing *(hyperousios hyperon)* everything. That is why everything is stated *(katēgoreitai)* about him at once and he is nothing *(ouden)* of all things" . . . (De div. nom. V, 8, c. 824).

Cognition of Divinity for a human being, and likewise for the ranks of angels and for every creature, is possible only by the path of the condescension of Divinity and the responding ascension of the creature, only through participation *(tais metochais monon)*. "It itself, insofar as It is in itself, in keeping with its proper principle and property, is above mind, essences and knowledge" (De div. nom. II, 4, c. 641). Although the holy Trinity "itself is found in everything, not everything is in it *(kai gar hautē men hapasi parestin, ou panta de autei paresti)"* (De div. nom. III, 2, c. 680). "When we invoke it with sacred prayer and pure mind ready for union with Divinity, then we too are present in it, for it is not found in space so that it would be far from something or would cross over from one thing to another" (De div. nom. III, 2, c. 680). Dionysius speaks about a loving or erotic attraction to God and beauty (consciously identifying *agapē* and *Erōs*): "the divine Eros of the good, is good and it exists through the good. The very Eros of what exists is beneficent and super-predominates in the good superabundantly" (De div. nom. IV, 7, c. 704). "Divine love is expressed in ecstasy, those loving do not belong to themselves but to the beloved" *(Esti de kai ekstatikos ho theios erōs, ouk eon tous einai heautōn erastas, alla tōn erōmenōn)* (De div. nom. IV, 13, c. 712). On the wings of Eros, in the surge of ecstasy, participation in and cognition of God happen — a surprisingly bold idea in an authoritative ecclesiastical writer. Such is the basis of the erotic gnoseology in Dionysius.

In positive theology, namely when he is analyzing the significance and meaning of the names of God, Dionysius invariably points to the Divinity's transcendent nature surpassing every essence; inasmuch as it is disclosed in a given name of God, the alpha privative here yields its place to *hyper*, the method of negation yields to the method of transcendence and hyperbolizing *(per emendationem)*. Thus, the fundamental definition of Divinity as the good is accompanied by the following elucidation: "being only in itself, it does not have essence and far exceeds essence, being non-living it exceeds life, and being non-rational it exceeds wisdom" *(kai en autōi monōi kai to anousion ousias hyperbolē kai to azōon hyperelousa zōi kai to anoun hyperechousa sophia)* (De div. nom. IV, 3, c. 647). In the same way as beauty, Divinity "as all-beauty is above beauty" *(hōs pankalon hama kai hyperkalon)* (IV, 7, c. 701). "God has super-being and above-being in superabundance, by surpassing every being" *(kai gar to proeinai kai hypereinai proechon kai hyperechon to einai pan)* *(De div. nom.* V, 5, c. 820); out of *autoyperagathotēs* [super-goodness itself] flows all being as such (V, 6).

The last chapters of *Mystical Theology* (another treatise of Dionysius) give a sort of summary of negative theology. "And so we say that the cause of everything, in that it is above everything, is not deprived of essence *(anousios)*, of life, of word, or of intellect." On the other hand, "it does not have body, form, quality, quantity, mass; it does not have a place, is not seen, is not accessible to sensible perception; it is not felt or palpable, it does not have disorderliness and perturbation as a result of material attractions, it is not powerless as a result of sensible surges, it does not need light, does not know change, destruction, division, privation, tension, and nothing else from the realm of sensible things.

"If we reason in an ascending direction *(aniontes)* we will say that it is not soul or mind, does not have fantasy or representation, word or understanding; it is not expressed and not thought; it is not number, or order, not magnitude or smallness, not equality or inequality, not likeness or unlikeness; it does not stand and is not moved, it does not rest and does not have power, it is not power or light; it does not live and is not life; not essence, not eternity and not time; it cannot be accessible to thinking; it is not knowing, not truth; not kingdom and not wisdom; not one, not unity *(henotēs)*, not divinity, not goodness, not spirit, as we understand; not fatherhood, not sonship, in general nothing of that which is known to us or others of what is, it is not anything of what is not or what is, and what is does not know it as such *(oude ta onta ginoskei auton hē autē estin)*, and it does not know what is as such; and it has no word *(oude logos autēs estin)*, or name, or knowledge; neither darkness nor light; neither error nor truth; in general it is neither affirmation *(thesis)* nor negation *(aphaeresis)*; by making relative to it positive and negative statements *(ton met' autēn theseis kai aphaireseis poiountes)*, we do not propose it or deny it itself; for the perfect sole cause is above every proposition, and the principle which surpasses perfectly detached from everything (absolute) and is inaccessible for everything, remains superior to every negation" *(kai hyper pasan aphairesin hē hyperochē tōn pantōn haplōs apolelumenou kai epekeina ton holon)* *(De mystica theologica*, cap. IV, V, PG III, col. 1045-48).

The one, multifaceted, unconditional NOT, the absolute NOT, is the content of the negative (apophatic) theology of Dionysius the Areopagite. And, although he is obviously close to Neo-Platonism, he goes further and judges more radically than Plotinus. For, as we already know, in walking down the apophatic path, Plotinus all the same leaves the concept of the One as the definition of the absolute, whereas with Dionysius, in his apophatic aspect, the absolute is neither the One nor Unity, but is fully and definitively NOT-who and NOT-what.

Negative (Apophatic) Theology

7. St. Maximus the Confessor (Seventh Century)

The apophatic moment plays a paramount role in the views of this profound theologian of the Eastern Church, who still awaits appraisal and study. Negative theology forms the underlying basis of positive theology.[53] We come to know God only insofar as he is revealed to us, but the divine essence itself remains beyond the limits of human comprehension. This theme is repeated in various works of St. Maximus, and it would take a special investigation of St. Maximus' doctrine to establish an exhaustive enumeration of similar passages. As we have not set this as our task, we will cite individual opinions.[54]

"God is everything and nothing and above everything: *ho mēden on tōn ontōn alēthōs, kai panta kyrios ōn kai hyper panta ho theos*.[55] "The one, unoriginate and incomprehensible, who fully has all power of being, excludes any thought of time and image, is inaccessible for anyone and cannot be known in natural representations by anything of what is. It is impossible for us to come to know the being of God in itself: he is not beginning, middle or end, or anything else of that which is known naturally as following from him. For he is unbounded, unmoved, unlimited, being immeasurably higher (= absolutely transcendent for) than every essence, power (potency) and activity (energy).... God is not essence (substance, *ousia*) as it is understood simply or in the sense that it is a principle; and he is not potency, as potency is understood simply or in the sense that it is mediating (a middle, *mesotēs*); and he is not energy, as it is understood simply or in the sense that it is the goal of a motion pre-planned in conformity with potency and arising from essence. He is being, having essence and remaining above essence *(ousiopoios kai hyperousios ontotes)*, having power and remaining above power, entirely filled with every activity and inexhaustibility, in a word, he is the active source of every essence, power, activity, beginning, middle and end. All that exists is called conceivable *(nooumena)* for it has principles for its own explanation; God, however, is called not conceivable *(ou nooumenos)* but they only believe in him on the basis of *(ek)* the conceivable; therefore nothing of that which is conceivable can in any respect enter into comparison with him."[56]

St. Maximus considers that every act of thinking presupposes a plurality *(plēthos)* or rather a duality *(duas)*: that which thinks, to which a certain energy of thought and an essence *(ousia)* correspond, and the object of thought *(hypokeimenon)*. In God there can be no place for this division into two; he is *monas* the absolute unit, in him the subject and object of thinking coincide. "God according to his essence *(kat' ousian)* is thinking *(noēsis)*, integral *(holos)* thinking and only this *(monon)*; and he himself is essence, which corresponds to that thinking *(kata tēn noēsin ousia)*, and the whole essence and only it; and he is entirely above essence and he is wholly above thinking, for he is the indivisible monad, indissoluble and simple."[57]

"That which truly is good according to its essence is not a principle or a

Divine Nothing

goal or a cause of being, and it has no relation to that which is the source of motion towards the cause of being."[58] God is entirely transcendent to the world — *hyperousios* — according to a frequently recurring definition of St. Maximus. "*Ho de theos haplōs kai aoristos hyper panta ta onta esti* — God is simply and unlimitedly above all that is." Only faith and love open the heart to the influence of grace, which accustoms the human being to the divine life. "The one who wisely has come to know how one must love *(eran)* God, who is above word and knowledge and every relation in whatever sense and free from nature *(exerēmenou kai physeōs)*, who leaves behind everything sensible and conceivable, all time and eternity *(aiōna)* and place, and is entirely liberated at the last from every activity *(energeias)* which was aroused by feelings or by word or mind, that one will attain in an unspeakable and incomprehensible manner to the divine sweetness which surpasses word and mind; this path and word are known only to the God who gives such grace and to those who are made worthy to receive it from God; here nothing natural or bookish is introduced, since everything that can be said or known is completely overcome and covered by silence."[59]

The inconceivability and ineffability of the content of religious-mystical experience — such is the positive sum of negative theology in St. Maximus the Confessor. Of course, he recalls Plotinus and other Christian and non-Christian mystics. Immersion in the transcendent gives an alogical mysticism, and this even in so powerful a dogmatist, so clear a representative of precisely positive, cataphatic, dogmatic theology as was St. Maximus. According to the doctrine of St. Maximus, however, adogmatic mysticism in no way exhausts religious experience. Accompanying that NOT towards which his negative theology and mysticism lead is the YES of religion, the Word uttered by Divinity and filling the universe with its thunder.

8. St. John Damascene (Eighth Century)

The Exact Exposition of the Orthodox Faith,[60] whose author is usually considered to be St. John Damascene, is clearly connected with the works of St. Dionysius the Areopagite and St. Maximus the Confessor in its doctrine about knowledge of God. This comes to light through the doctrine of the ineffability and incomprehensibility of Divinity. "After the first and blessed nature (Divinity) no one — not only among human beings but even from among the supernal powers, and the Cherubim and Seraphim themselves, I say, has ever known God unless he has revealed himself to him" (1-2). "Of that which pertains to the doctrine of God and the incarnation not everything is ineffable, so too not everything can be expressed in speech; and not everything is inaccessible to cognition, and not everything is accessible to it" (3). "That God *exists*, is clear. *What* he is by essence and nature, however, is completely incomprehensible and unknown" (7). Such definitions as, e.g., incorporeality "do not indicate the essence of God, neither do expressions such as unbegotten and without beginning, unchangeable and incorruptible, and that which is said about God or about the being of God, for this indicates not *what* he *is,* but *what* he *is not.* It is, however, impossible to say what God is in essence. It is much more proper to speak about him through removal of everything. For he is not something of what is, not as one who is not but as one who is above everything that exists and is above being itself. For if knowledge refers to what exists, then what surpasses knowledge will be in any case above even reality. And, on the contrary, that which surpasses reality is above knowledge. Thus, Divinity is limitless and incomprehensible.

"And only this one thing is comprehensible: limitlessness and incomprehensibility in him. And what we say about God affirmatively indicates not his nature but that which is around his nature. If you call him good or just or wise or whatever other thing, you will be speaking not about the nature of God but about what is around his nature. Likewise a certain thing that is said about God affirmatively has the significance of a superior negation, as for example, when speaking about *the darkness* with respect to God, we understand not darkness but that which is not light, but higher than light; and when speaking about light, we understand that which is not darkness" (9). "Divinity is simple and not compound. Whatever consists of the many and the different is compound. And thus, if we call uncreatedness, beginninglessness, incorporeality, immortality, eternity, goodness, creative power, and similar things essential distinctions in God, then what is composed of so many things will not be simple, but compound, which (speaking of Divinity) is a matter of utmost impiety. Therefore one must hold that each thing said about God taken separately does not signify what he is in essence; rather, it indicates either what he is not, or a certain relation with that which is contrasted to him, or something which accompanies his nature or operation" (27-28).

The judgments of the author of the *Exposition of the Orthodox Faith* do not have particular originality or philosophical clarity when compared with the doctrines of Saints Dionysius the Areopagite and Maximus the Confessor, but the lofty doctrinal authority of this work compels us to refer to its ideas with special attention, in particular concerning the question of "apophatic" theology. The cited judgments are even textually close to corresponding passages in the works of the Areopagite, St. Maximus, St. Basil the Great, and others.

9. St. Gregory Palamas (Fourteenth Century)

In the works of St. Gregory Palamas[61] we observe the further development of the idea of negative theology in conjunction with the famous disputes about

Divine Nothing

the light of Mount Tabor. These were conducted between the partisans of St. Gregory (the so-called Hesychasts) on the one hand and the adherents of Barlaam and Akindynos on the other hand, and concluded with the church's condemnation of the latter. The question was posed in this fashion: Does the light which illumined Christ on Mount Tabor and which was seen by the apostles represent the direct *operation* of God, his *energy* (energeia), uncreated and eternal, or is it only a sensible sign in a form accessible for the gross understanding of human beings? Today we would say, does it have ontological meaning or is it only psychologism?

A more general question was raised with it. Does an uncreated and, consequently, eternal, divine energy exist with which God is revealed to individuals, one yet multiform and multifaceted, indivisible and yet divided for those who participate in its gracious influence, or is God immediately revealed to individuals, using for this purpose creaturely means fashioned in time? Relying on the labors of his predecessors, St. Gregory Palamas developed in his works the doctrine of the *transcendent essence* of God, his *ousia*, and his power — *dynamis* and operation — *energeia*, which comes to light in the world. God realizes himself as God in his energy or energies, and the doctrine of his *ousia* is characterized by traits of negative theology, for *ousia* remains fully inaccessible, transcendent for creatures, not only for humankind but also for angels. "Divine super-essentiality *(tēn hyperousiotēta tēn theian)* cannot be either named with a word or understood or contemplated by any means at all; it surpasses everything and is above cognition *(hyperagnōston)*, it abides unattainable even for the unbounded power of supercelestial minds, remaining completely and forever incomprehensible and ineffable for all things. It cannot be named with any name in a language *(kata)* of the present age or of the future; no word *(logos)* generated in the soul or pronounced by the lips is able to express it; no feeling or thinking *(epaphē tis aisthētē ē noēma)* attains to it; it cannot be expressed by any image *(phantasia)*. Unless someone calls it the most incomprehensible totality of negations *(ex apophaseōn teleōtatēn akatalēpsian)*, the most lofty abstraction *(hyperochikos aphairoumenēn)* from everything that is and everything that is said. Therefore it is impossible, in fact *(kyriōs)*, to name either the essence *(ousia)* itself or its nature in the right way, acknowledging this truth to be above every truth. Although at the same time it is the cause of everything, and everything exists from it and on account of it, by existing before everything simply and unboundedly *(haplōs kai aperioristōs)*, it has pre-outlined in itself everything, and it must be named in everything *(ek pantōn)*, but not in the proper sense *(kyriōs)*."[62]

"The essence *(ousia)* of God is completely unnameable, since it is completely incomprehensible.... As unnameable it is at the same time inaccessible to participation *(amethektos)*, for it is above participation *(hyper methexin)*."[63] And the very being of God is known with respect not to essence but only to en-

Negative (Apophatic) Theology

ergy: "the energy is not known from the essence, but the essence is known from the energy, that it *is*, but not *what* it is. That is why God too is known in his being not from his essence but from his providence. On this basis energy is distinguished from essence, for it is what shows, while essence is what is shown through it in its being."[64]

"Every nature is the furthest possible away from and completely alien to divine nature. If God is nature, then everything else is not nature; if everything else is nature, then he is not nature, since what is *(on)*, is not, if the other is what is. If he is what is, the other is what is not.... Although God is and is called the nature of all that is, for everything participates in him and exists in virtue of this participation, still it is not participation *(methexis)* in his nature, but in his energies. In this manner he is both the essence of what is *(ontotes tōn ontōn)* and the form in forms, as the basis of forms *(eidearchis)*, and the wisdom of those who are wise and in general everything in everything *(haplōs kai ta panta pantōn)*; and he is not nature, for he is above every nature, and he is not what is, for he is above everything that is; and he is not what is and does not have form, for he is above form."[65]

The distinction between *ousia* and *energeia* coincides with the boundaries between negative and positive theology: *ousia* corresponds to the transcendent essence of God, *energeia* is his manifestation in the world. "Theotimos: You say that God is communicated by his energy to those who communicate with him *(metechesthai para tōn metechontōn)*? Theophanes: Inasmuch as possible. Theotimos: But with respect to the essence the same God is inaccessible to communion *(amethekton)*? Theophanes: Of course."[66] On this basis, as a negative or limit concept, strictly speaking, *ousia* proves to be one, indivisible and simple, "while divine energy is plural and diverse *(poikilai)*." Energy proves to be the means of communicating *ousia*, and its multiformity is similar to many lamps that are ignited from a fire; it is "not trihypostatic in this sense, but myriohypostatic."[67] And as a result of the indivisibility of Divinity in its *ousia*, each form of divine energy, each of its rays, communicates the *whole* of Divinity: "the incommunicability of the essence *(ousia)* does not at all prevent the communication of the whole God through each of its energies ... for the incorporeal is not divided corporeally. Therefore those who are made capable of perception of the divine and divinizing energy become capable of the perception of God himself."[68] This definition leads, in this manner, to a pure antinomy: "the super-essential essence proves to be completely indivisible, and the divine energy of God is inseparably inseparable *(ameristos de merizousa)*.[69] This being so, the divine energies cannot be attributed to distinct hypostases of the Holy Trinity, but are common to all. "Power *(dynamis)* and energy are common to the trihypostatic nature and operate on the interior and are divided into thousands. For almighty *(pantadynamon)* is the Divinity."[70] In this way, a sharp boundary is drawn between the concept of *ousia* and the concept of the Holy Trinity, as that which is in God himself, and between the divine energies; but in their turn, no less profound a boundary exists between these uncreated *(aktistos)* energies and creaturely, created being, with which the Barlaamites equated them. Energy is Divinity, whole and one in its every ray, Divinity that operates and is revealed *ad extra.*

10. Johannes Scotus Eriugena (Ninth Century)

On the question of negative theology, Johannes Scotus Eriugena, that profound thinker of the ninth century who represents an enormous religious-philosophical interest even for our time,[71] consciously sides with St. Maximus the Confessor and Dionysius the Areopagite who exerted a particular influence on him. In referring to both of these thinkers, he himself distinguishes "apophatic and cataphatic theology."[72] "All designations, by the help of which they clothe Divinity by the way of affirmation, can be removed again by the way of negation. . . . As it is said in the first case, one can in this manner name God without saying that this is strictly speaking accomplished, and on the contrary, in the second case it is said that this does not correspond to reality, although one can thus name God."[73] Eriugena developed his negative theology primarily in the first book and partially in the second book of his fundamental treatise *De divisione naturae,* and he defines its general content in this way, explaining that *"nothing* of all that exists and that does not exist expresses God in his essence, that he himself does not know completely what he is, for in no manner whatever can he be defined according to magnitude or property, for nothing approaches him and he himself is not comprehended by anything, and that strictly speaking he himself is not expressed in himself in that which exists and does not exist — a type of ignorance that exceeds all knowledge and understanding."[74]

Following the path of negative theology familiar to us, Eriugena shows the insufficiency of all definitions of Divinity. "God is called essence, but properly speaking he is not essence, because nothing is opposed to the latter, and he is higher than essence. Similarly he is called good but even this he is not in the proper sense, for evil is opposed to good, and he is more than good or super-good. . . . It is the same way with truth, for lie is opposed to truth and hence God is not truth but more than truth and super-truth. We have a similar case with respect to the remaining divine names. Indeed not in the proper sense is he called eternity, for temporality is opposed to eternity, but he is more than eternal and is super-eternity. We have a similar case with respect to wisdom, which therefore cannot be applied to God in the proper sense because folly and the fool are opposed to wisdom and the wise man; consequently he is more correctly and truly called more than wise or super-wisdom. Likewise he is

Negative (Apophatic) Theology

greater than life, for death is opposed to life. It is the same way with light, to which is opposed darkness."[75]

But even such definitions of Divinity as *super*-essence, *super*-wisdom, and the various word-formations with *super/hyper,* preferred by the Areopagite who so abused them, are obviously only disguised negations: "according to sound they are affirmations, but according to meaning they have a negative significance." For example, "if someone says that something is above essence, he understands not that which is but that which is not."[76]

On this basis it is understandable why in theology God is sometimes designated by the name Nothing. "I dare say that with this name the inexpressible and inaccessible clarity of the unknowable divine Goodness is designated, which is understood super-essentially and super-naturally in its self, and is not, was not, and will not be. It cannot be apprehended in any existing essence, for it surpasses everything. Only by descending in an ineffable manner into the existing does it become comprehensible for the spiritual eye as such, and it alone is found in everything as being, and it is, was and will be. Conceived as incomprehensible, it is called Nothing in the proper sense not without foundation. Insofar as it begins to become visible in its theophanies, it is said that it passes out of nothing over into nothing. Namely, insofar as it must be considered surpassing all essence, it will become known in every essence, and therefore every visible and invisible creature can be called a divine manifestation. For from above to below, i.e. from the celestial essences to the inferior bodies of this world, the whole order of nature insofar as it approaches divine clarity penetrates like the intelligence into what is hidden.[77] Therefore one need not be surprised that in theology the inaccessible clarity of the heavenly powers is often called darkness, for even the highest wisdom itself, to which these powers are close, is often designated as darkness" (III, cap. 19).

Developing this same idea further Eriugena dwells at length (in books I and II) on the explanation of how categories of thinking cannot be applied to Divinity at all (following Aristotle he reckons there to be ten categories: essence, quantity, quality, relation, position, condition *[habitus],* place, time, action, suffering). "For such a nature which cannot be either expressed or thought, the categories are useless for us. . . . If they were applied to Divinity, God would necessarily have to fall under a generic concept, whereas he is neither genus, nor species, nor something accidental."[78]

"If, for example, one inquires about what God is, is one not then seeking a definite condition proper to him? And if one answers that he is this or that, is one not dwelling on a definite and limited condition?" . . . "Indeed, everything about which one can express or think *what* it is, cannot surpass the domain of being, but must by right be regarded either as a part in the whole or as a whole present in its parts or as form in genus, or as the genus present in its forms, or as species in particulars, or as everything encompassing this unity.

Divine Nothing

Besides, this remains far from the simple and indefinable truth of divine nature, to which nothing of all that is corresponds. For it is not the whole or the part, which is why it is called equally part and whole, for by it every whole and every part is created by every means. Likewise divine nature does not exist either as genus or form or species or particular or as a universal or particular essence, but at the same time all of this can be stated about it, for only from it does this receive the capability of existence. It will be the same if one were to call it the totality of all of this, although it surpasses the sum of created things by its unbounded magnitude, for all of this is created by it. How can the divine nature understand itself, what it is, if it is Nothing?"[79] *(Quomodo igitur divina natura seipsum potest intelligere, quid si cum nihil sit?)* From this already-familiar definition of apophatic theology concerning how God is Nothing, not in the sense of negation but in the sense of the insufficiency of any affirmation, Eriugena draws the bold and paradoxical conclusion that *God does not know his own self.* "God does not know what he is, for he is not something; he is unintelligible in every something, both for his own self, and also for every intellect.... God himself does not know at all what he is not, but neither does he know himself as one who is. In this manner he does not know *what* he himself is, i.e. he does not know that he is something, for he recognizes that he in no way at all belongs to that domain which can be known in any such sense and about which one can express or think that it is."[80] Not one of the ten categories that establish "something" as cognizable can be applied to God. "You see why, on what grounds it is said of God: he does not know that everything included in the ten categories exists in his nature, for the latter, obviously, exists solely by its own exclusively sublime and unlimited power. For that which is unlimited in all directions is unlimited according to essence, power and operation, from above and from below, i.e. from beginning and from end. For in essence it is inaccessible, in power incomprehensible, in activity unlimited, without beginning from above and without end from below, in a word, to say it briefly, it is unlimited in every direction."[81]

But at the same time it is clear that "under divine ignorance one ought to understand nothing else but the incomprehensible and infinite knowledge of God himself."[82] "In God there is no ignorance for his ignorance is, on the contrary, ineffable knowledge.... If we say that God does not know what he is, do we not wish to imply that he does not know himself in anything of all that is? For how could he know in his own self something that cannot be in his very self? But the fundamentals of everything that God fashioned in his very self, i.e. the Father in the Son, constitute in him an indivisible one; they do not allow definitions of distinctive components by distinctive differences or accidental definitions, for they admit them only in actions, but not in themselves. What then ought one to think about the ineffable and incomprehensible nature of these very things? Who could imagine here something which is defined

Negative (Apophatic) Theology

by a boundary, extended in space, divided in parts, composed of elements and accidental signs? The divine ignorance is therefore supreme and true wisdom."[83] *(Ipsa itaque ignorantia summa ac vera est sapientia.)* From apophatic theology Eriugena makes a transition to cataphatic theology; we shall encounter his fundamental ideas again below.

11. Nicholas of Cusa (Fifteenth Century)[84]

In the doctrine of that brilliant thinker of the fifteenth century, who is still waiting for a proper study, the idea of God's transcendence, which forms the essence of negative theology, is placed at the foundation of his system, and even his positive doctrine of God is understandable only in the light of this central idea. God is the indifference of opposites *(indifferentia oppositorum),* their coincidence. He is above contradiction. According to a frequently repeated comparison in Nicholas of Cusa, the *coincidentia oppositorum* is the fence of paradise, guarded by Angels and concealing God from creation *(De visione Dei,* 10).[85] As the least crooked line coincides with the most straight, so in God coincide the greatest and the least *(De docta ignorantia,* I, 4), being and nonbeing (ibid., c. 6; *De Possest),* the real and the ideal, the past, present, and future in the absolute *now*. At the same time he is the absolute self-identity *(non illud);* in him there are no differences, each of the so-called divine properties is the condition of the same divine entity. He is oneness, not in a numerical but in a super-numerical sense.

The transcendence and incognoscibility of God constitute the music of the whole system of Cardinal Nicholas of Cusa, who expressively titled his fundamental treatise *De docta ignorantia* and speaks enthusiastically about *sacra ignorantia,* by frequently referring to Dionysius the Areopagite. "Negative theology is so necessary a completion of positive theology," says Nicholas of Cusa *(De docta ignorantia* I, 26), "that without it God would be worshipped, but as a creature. . . . Our sacred science of ignorance *(sacra ignorantia)* has taught us that God is unutterable for he is greater than all that can be named . . . according to this negative theology God is not Father, not Son, not Holy Spirit, but only infinite. Infinity as such is not generated, does not generate and does not proceed. . . . As infinity, considered as such, God is not one or many; from the point of view of negative theology we find in God nothing else but infinity. . . . According to it he therefore is unknowable both in this age and in the age to come, for every creature, not being in the state to receive eternal light, grows dark in comparison with it. God is known only to himself. From what has been said it follows that in theology negations are true, affirmations are inadequate."[86]

"My Lord and God! Help one who is searching for you! I see you in the beginning of paradise and I do not know what I see, for I do not see anything visible; I know only one thing: I know that I do not know what I see, and that I will never be able to find out; I do not know how to name you for I do not know what you are. And if someone tells me that this or that is your name, then because of the fact that he gives a name I already know that it is not your name. For every appellation is a wall above which I see you. If someone gives a concept by which you can be conceived, I know that this concept is not about you, for every concept finds its boundary within the limits of the fence of paradise. And concerning every image and comparison with the aid of which they would begin to think you, I know that it is not an image that corresponds to you. And every mind *(intellectus)* is far distant from you. A high wall separates you from all of this. And if I ascend high up into the air as far as is possible, I see you only as infinity. Therefore you are inaccessible, incomprehensible, unnameable, invisible. Whoever wants to draw near to you must ascend above all concepts, boundaries and limitation. The spirit must be made ignorant *(ignorantem)* and submerge into darkness if it wishes to see you. But what is this ignorance of the Spirit? Is it not a wise ignorance *(docta ignorantia)*? Therefore, o my God, who is infinity, only the one who knows that he does not know you can draw near to you *(qui scit se ignorantem tui)*" *(De visione Dei,* 13).

"Since the greatest is the greatest as such and does not permit opposition, it is clear that no name can be applied to it. For all names arise out of a certain single operation of reason through which one is distinguished from the other. But where everything is one, separate names cannot exist. Hermes Trismegistus justly says therefore that since God is the aggregate of things *(universitas rerum)* he does not have a particular name, for it would be necessary either to call God by every name, for in his simplicity he encompasses in himself the aggregate of things, because a name that is properly characteristic of God must be translated one and all *(unus et omnia),* or rather all in one *(omnia uniter)*.... But oneness is the name of God not in the sense that we understand oneness. Multitude opposes oneness. Such oneness does not correspond to God; only that oneness which is not opposed by otherness, plurality, corresponds to God. Such is the greatest name, which combines everything in the simplicity of oneness, such is the unutterable name which surpasses all reason. For who would be able to comprehend unnameable oneness which infinitely precedes every contradiction, where all without complexity is combined in the simplicity of oneness, without the other and opposition, where the human is not distinguished from the lion, and heaven is not distinguished from earth, and nonetheless each exists in the most mobile manner, not in its own finitude but as the very greatest oneness! Whoever would be able to grasp or name this oneness, which as oneness is everything and as the least is the greatest, that one would reveal the name of God. But since the name of God is the very God, no one knows God except that very spirit which is also the greatest itself and

Negative (Apophatic) Theology

this is the greatest Name. . . . Whence it follows that affirmative names of God are proper to him only in an infinitely small degree *(per infinitum diminute)*, for they are applied to him only in conformity with some sort of creaturely properties. . . . This has force to such a degree that even the name of the Trinity and of the persons of Father, Son and Holy Spirit is applied only in relation to creatures" (*De docta ignorantia* I, 24). One ought to respond in this way even to the question about the being of God: "He does not exist and he does not not exist, he neither is nor is not" (*De coniecturis* 7). The absolute is "above every affirmation and negation," "oppositions take place only in the concrete" (*De docta ignorantia*, I, 4), but not in the absolute. "God is not this and that, he is not there and here, he is as it were everything, but at the same time nothing of everything" (I, 16). "The great Dionysius says that knowledge of God leads more towards nothing than towards something. Sacred ignorance teaches us that what for reason seems to be nothing is precisely the supremely incomprehensible" (I, 17).

Nothing is the absolute, positive NOT; such is the result to which the way of negative theology leads in Cardinal Nicholas of Cusa. But apart from this negative-transcendent aspect, his theology has an affirmative-immanent aspect and here in the dialectical analysis of fundamental concepts, in the investigation of the relationship of the world and creation, is displayed the positive power and originality of this thinker. Separate facets of this doctrine urgently demand a scholarly monograph.

Siding with Nicholas of Cusa is his admirer Giordano Bruno. It is somewhat surprising to encounter the name Giordano Bruno among representatives of negative theology because he has the reputation of being a pantheist. Although the history of thought has emphasized precisely the pantheistic side in Bruno's worldview, in the man himself pantheism was far from gaining the definitive victory, and various currents are in contention. By a strange way Bruno is found to be in manifest dependence on the ideas of Nicholas of Cusa, whose assiduous admirer he was; therefore in his treatise *De la causa principio e uno*, where he expounds a doctrine of the absolute, which strongly recalls the views of Nicholas of Cusa on the *coincidentia oppositorum* and on *Possest*, Giordano Bruno says the following: "What in another case would be opposed and contradictory is in it (in the absolute) one and the same, and each thing is in it one and the same. Thus one needs to go out beyond the difference of times and epochs, as well as of realities or possibilities, because for it there exists nothing either old or new, and in the book of Revelation it is excellently called the first and the last. This most absolute reality, which is identical with the most absolute capability, can be understood in the language of reason only by way of negation, i.e. it is not accessible to comprehension, nor can one understand how it can be everything or how it is. For reason, if it wants to understand, must form in itself a representation conformable with the intellect and adapt itself to it, fit itself with it, become even with it. All of this is impossible here. For reason is never so great that it could not be still greater; the same, being from all sides and in every sense inaccessible, cannot be greater. There exists therefore no such eye that would be able to approach this supremely great light and this supremely deep abyss or find access to it."[87]

12. Jewish Mysticism: Cabbala

The ideas of negative theology enter into the composition of Cabbalistic teaching on the absolute Nothing (Ein Sof). We shall introduce some basic definitions that are relevant to this point.[88] "The Ancient of ancients, the Secret of secrets, has an image and does not have an image. It has an image through which the universe exists (as its revelation), but it also does not have an image, since it cannot be comprehended (in a sufficient way in thinking)" (*Zohar*, de Pauly, III, 288a, Idra suta).

"Before the Ancient of ancients, the Secret of secrets (was revealed) there was neither beginning nor end.... In the book of mysteries is transmitted: The Ancient of ancients, the Secret of secrets, has a certain image and form and insofar as it allows itself to be discerned (to a certain degree). But at the same time it is unknowable for it cannot be sufficiently grasped (by our thinking). It has therefore a certain image and a form, but all the same it does not permit itself (in its most authentic essence) to be discerned to the point that it is something in some class, as the Elder of elders, the Ancient of ancients, the Secret of secrets. According to these signs (of its self-revelation) it is knowable and all the same it is unknowable (in keeping with its true essence)" (*Zohar*, de Pauly, III, 128a, Idra rabba).

"Such is the Beginning of all beginnings (of creative revelation), the profoundly concealed wisdom, the crown of everything exalted (of the suprasensible world of the Sefirot), the Diadem of diadems. They call it *ein* (it is *not*) because we do not know and no one can know what was in this beginning, since this cannot be attained by wisdom (chokma, the second Sefirah), or reason (bina, the third Sefirah)" (*Zohar*, de Pauly, III, 288b).

"There exist three heads, one is included in the other and one is higher than the other. They are (beginning from below): mysterious wisdom (chokma), profoundly concealed wisdom (keter) and never discoverable wisdom (ein-sof). This mysterious wisdom is the principle of every other (inferior, e.g. earthly) wisdom. Above it stands the Ancient, blessed be his name (keter), the basis of mystery. Thirdly, the head, which stands above all others (and reigns over them too): the head which does not exist (as ein-sof). What surrounds it, we do not know" (*Zohar*, de Pauly, III, 288b).

"The Ancient Holy One is concealed, and the supreme wisdom is in-

Negative (Apophatic) Theology

cluded in this cranium such that in the Ancient one can see only a cranium: this is the Head of heads.

"The supreme wisdom is included in this cranium and carries the name of the supreme Brain, of the mysterious World, which gives rest *(apaise)*; no one knows it except its own self. Three heads are included one in the other, and one is above the other. The head is the mysterious invisible Wisdom, which is completely unrevealed; this is Wisdom of all other wisdoms. The Supreme Head is the sacred and mysterious Ancient, the Head of all heads, the Head which is not a head since it is unknown and since what is contained in it will never be knowable; no wisdom and no reason can grasp it. For this reason the holy Ancient bears the name Ein Sof *(Néant),* for the very nothing depends on it" *(Zohar,* III, 288, de Pauly, VI, 83). "The name of the Ancient is concealed for everyone and is unattainable *(insaisissable)*. . . . The holy name is at once concealed and open" *(Zohar,* III, 289a, Idra zouta, de Pauly, VI, 86).

Setting forth the doctrine of "the luminaries" and "Hayoth" the *Zohar* says that above the visible hayoth (the living beings in the vision of the prophet Ezekiel) are the invisible ones, and "above them is the highest firmament, above which no one is able to see because *here everything is above* understanding. Why? Because everything is included in thought, and thought of the Holy, blessed may he be, is hidden, secret, and *too* exalted for it to be possible to attain it and touch the understanding of the human being. Therefore if things subject to thought are unattainable, then with all the more foundation is Thought itself. As regards interior Thought, there is no one who could understand what it is; with all the more foundation is it impossible to understand the Infinite *(Ayn-Soph)* which is intangible; every question and every cogitation would remain futile for grasping the essence of the highest Thought, the centre of everything, the mystery of all mysteries, without beginning and without end, the infinite from which they see only a small spark of light, like the point of a needle and still this particle is visible only thanks to the *material* form which it has assumed" *(Zohar,* I, 2a, de Pauly, I, 129).

In the doctrines of Simon ben Jokhai (in the Idra Kaba) we read:[89] "Before creating any sort of form in this world, before producing any sort of representation, he (God) was alone, without form, not being likened to anything. And who could have understood him as he was when he had no form? En-sof in this state has neither form nor image; there exists no means of understanding him, no method of coming to know him. . . . The Sefirot (the energies of Divinity, its rays) can never comprehend the infinite Ein Sof, which is the very source of all forms and which as such has none itself: in other words, whereas each of the Sefirot has a well-known name, it alone does not have one and cannot have one. God remains always an essence unspeakable, incomprehensible, infinite, being above all the worlds which disclose his presence, even above the world of emanations."

Professor M. Muretov[90] considers the concept of Ein Sof to correspond to the transcendent concept of divinity: "the cabbalistic God is entirely *Deus abstractus*, lacking any definite predicate and not entering into any relation on the outside — not only with people but also with the higher bodiless creatures" (39). As corroboration for this understanding he introduces the following texts from the *Zohar*: "The Eldest and the most incomprehensible has an image and does not have any image: It has an image (Shekhinah) by means of which it created the world and preserves it; but in itself It has no image for it cannot be grasped. It is entirely enclosed in its own self, concealed and inaccessible to anyone. The Eldest is the supreme light more hidden than any darkness — it does not abide in those rays (Sefirot) which are diffused around It. It is the supreme head, the head of all heads, the head which is not head — it is not known what is in this head for it is not perceptible by wisdom or reason. It is impossible for the supreme essence to acquire any definite sign, any definite name. Woe to him who dares to ascribe to Divinity any sort of quality; for qualification is the property of finitude and thus must lead to the Infinite becoming finite.[91]

And so Ein Sof to which belong absolute perfection, absolute unity, immutability, limitlessness, remains at the same time inaccessible for our reason and understanding in its essence; therefore no definition for it can be given, no question can be posed about it, there is no image or resemblance for it. Even the angels do not know God in his might and infinity. Such is the doctrine of the *Zohar*.[92]

The very creation of the world is understood in the *Zohar* as a certain gathering in *(zimzum)*, a formation of the unformed, unlimited, undefined Ein Sof. "Before the creation of the world and the existence of any kind of image, God was without image and likeness. Who could understand God as he was in the beginning? But after he produced the image of a heavenly human being in his chariot he descended into the chariot and was revealed under the image of Jehovah; he wanted to be called according to the attributes by which he rules the world, according to Mercy and Justice. He wanted to be called El, Elohim Sabbaoth, and "The One Who Is." For if God were not disclosed under all these attributes how would he govern the world, now by mercy, now by justice, according to human deeds? How would he extend his light among all the creations and how could they understand him? Woe to the human being who equates God with one of his attributes, still less is it possible to equate God with the image of the human being. The image under which God is revealed is only subjective, inasmuch as the one or other attribute receives its force conformably to the creatures to whom he is disclosed" (*Zohar*, II, 42b, de Pauly, III, 192-93).

A final judgment about whether or not Ein Sof expresses the transcendent essence of God or only a moment of his concealment in creation is extraordinarily difficult: anyone who is familiar with authentic Cabbala, with the nature of its exposition and its method, will understand with what difficulty its teachings will submit to a final formulation. Therefore we intentionally made the texts themselves speak rather than our own descriptions.

13. Negative Theology in German and English Mysticism

A. "German Theology" (Das Büchlein vom vollkommenen Leben von Deutschherr) ca. Fifteenth Century

In this remarkable work of early German mysticism, as if inaugurating its amazing flowering in subsequent centuries, the ideas of negative theology do not as yet receive their development. Nevertheless for the unknown author of *The Little Book on the Perfect Life,* this train of thought is completely natural. He proceeds from the opposition *of the perfect and the imperfect* or creaturely being: the first is *one,* embracing in itself everything, in it there is no subdividing or isolating, while the second is like *something,* this or that. "Isolations *(Besonderungen),*" continues the author, "are comprehensible, cognizable, and uttered; the perfect is incomprehensible, incognizable, and unutterable for all creatures! Thus the perfect is called *Nothing:* since there exists nothing equal to it, the creature as creature is not able to ascertain, comprehend, name or think it."[93] In the further discourses of the Deutschherr, which are in general colored in religious immanentism, the idea of the transcendence of God plays no significant role. Known to the author, as well as to other German mystics, are the works of Dionysius the Areopagite whom he cites. Some people, e.g., H. Büttner, detect in this work the influence of Eckhart and relate the Deutschherr to his school; in our eyes, he stands by himself.

B. Meister Eckhart[94] and His School (Tauler, Suso)

The ideas of negative theology penetrate through and through the speculative system (for here one can speak of a system) of the great German mystic. As applied to God, abstraction from every positive definition as connected with creatureliness runs through Eckhart's system like a red thread, and to this corresponds the principal religious virtue preached by him — *Abgeschiedenheit,* detachment, which is higher than love, higher than humility: "God has no name for no one can express or know anything about him. In this sense a Greek teacher (Plotinus?) says 'What we know or state about the first cause is our own selves rather than the first cause; for the latter is higher than any knowledge and utterance!' And so, if I say 'God is good,' this is wrong, I am good and

Divine Nothing

God is not good! I go even further: I am better than God. For only that which is good can be better and only what can be better can become best. But God is not good, and thus he cannot be better, and if this is so, then he cannot become the best: far away from God are these three definitions: good, better, best. He stands higher than all of them! If I say further, 'God is wise,' then this too is wrong: I am wiser than God! If I say further 'God is something' *that is,* this is wrong; he is something completely superabundant, he is super-essential nonbeing. Blessed Augustine says about this, 'the best that a human can say about God is to know how to be silent from the fullness of the wisdom of interior wealth.' Therefore be silent and do not prattle about God. For when you prattle about him you are lying, you sin. If you wish to be without sin and perfect, do not prattle about God! And you are not able to know anything about God for God is higher than all cognition. A wise man says, 'If I were to have a God whom I could know, I would not honour him as God!' If you know something about him, it is not he. If, however, you 'know' about him, you will fall into the state of ignorance, and through this into the state of a beast! For creatures deprived of knowledge are like beasts. If you do not wish to sink to the level of a beast, then know nothing about the eternally unknowable God. 'Ah, how am I to be then?' Renounce everything that in whatever sense is you, be immersed entirely in the repose of his essence. What was earlier: there he is, here you are – now merges into a single We, where you are there is They – you will know him with an eternal sense: nameless nothing, unrealized 'am,' *ein namenloses Nichts, ein ungewordenes 'Bin.'*"[95] This sermon of Eckhart ("On Renewal in Spirit") ends with the following summons: "You must love God unspiritually, *ungeistig!* This means that your soul must be unspiritual, deprived of every trace of spirituality. For as long as your soul keeps the form of a spirit it has as an object the unformed – *ungestaltetes.* So long as it is like that, it will not possess either oneness or only-begottenness. And so long as it does not possess these it cannot really love God, because true love rests in innateness – *Hineingeborensein.* Therefore your soul must become free from all spirit, it must become soulless, *geistlos!* For if you still love God, insofar as he is God, is Spirit, is Person, in a word, is something formed – *gestaltetes,* reject all this! 'But how then ought I to love him?' You must love him insofar as he is Not-God, Not-spirit, not-person, not formed but one pure, bright oneness, far away from any duality. And in this One we must eternally submerge ourselves, out of being into *Nothing!*"[96]

Such is the favorite motif of Eckhart's pantheistically, Neo-Platonically colored mysticism: turn everything towards the primordial *nothing,* in which resides the oneness of both God and the world in the One. "The perfection of spirit consists in the fact that this *something* which exists here as a created thing, is led towards its *nothing,* towards its eternal prototype. As God is nothing for the spirit, so too this prototype: according to its essence it is God . . .

Negative (Apophatic) Theology

and the supreme blessedness which is accessible to spirit consists in the fact that it spills anew into the nothing of its prototype and completely dissolves in it by its own selfhood. . . . St. Dionysius says about such a state that for all the soul's faculties Divinity reverted to nothing."[97] This discourse on self-annihilation, as one can freely render Eckhart's concept of *Abgeschiedenheit*, is contained in a most concentrated form in an instruction especially dedicated to it (cf. also "On the Contemplation of God and Blessedness," *Vom Schauen Gottes und der Seligkeit*). "Detachment does not want to be this or that, because whoever wants to be 'this' also wants to be something, but it wants to be nothing! This immovable detachment more than anything likens the human being to God. For that by which God is God is in his immovable detachment, and from this is his purity, his simplicity and his immutability. Thus if a human being wants to become likened to God he must become detached."[98]

The most prominent feature of Eckhart's mysticism is that his negative theology in conjunction with the doctrine of *Abgeschiedenheit*, which merges the world and humankind with God, leads him to an acknowledgment not of the transcendence of God but of his maximal immanence: the line between God and creation is completely erased; their distinction is overcome in the oneness that exceeds it.[99] Concerning this see below.

The same motif is encountered in the two most outstanding mystics of Eckhart's school of the fourteenth century, Henry Suso (Seuse) and Johannes Tauler, where it is more keenly expressed in the latter.[100] Heinrich Seuse (whose biography, composed on the basis of notes of his spiritual daughter Elisabeth Stagel, is one of the most fragrant blossoms of Catholic mysticism, reminiscent of the *Fioretti* of Francis of Assisi), that loving and tender *"Diener der ewigen Weisheit"* [servant of eternal wisdom], is little inclined to mystical speculation. When it does occur, he reveals himself to be a faithful disciple of Eckhart, with his sermon on the detached *Nichts*.[101] "The super-sensible *Wo* . . . can be understood as existing, nameless nothingness — *die seiende, namenlose Nichtigkeit*; and then the spirit reaches the Nothing of Oneness — *in das Nichts der Einheit*. And Oneness is called therefore Nothing, for the spirit cannot find a temporal image of that which it is; but the spirit well feels that it is supported by another than itself; because that which supports it is properly more something than nothing; but for the spirit it is of course nothing according to the image of its own being" (I, 161-62). "On this incomprehensible mountain ridge of the super-divine *Wo* a radiant bottomlessness *(Abgründlichkeit)* exists that is perceptible for all pure souls, and then the soul arrives at the hidden unnameableness and incomprehensible estrangement" (I, 161-62).

There is nothing, proclaims Tauler,[102] higher than "the pure, simple submersion in the pure, simple, incognizable, unnameable hidden good which is God"; as Dionysius (the Areopagite) says, "let everything adhere to its (divinity's) *not*." "Dear child, set your resting-place on this unknown God and do not

Divine Nothing

seek either sensation or illumination. Act like a dog: if it comes to where it finds some good meat, it does not dare touch it and flees, because it is used to heavy blows. Later you will understand well, dear child. Only hold on humbly to your pure nothing, which is what you truly are. If even here there is something, it belongs to it and not to you. And do not appeal to anything that can clarify this for you, let it be formless, imageless, super-essential *(überwesentlich)*. . . . Submerge deeper into your unknowing and your non-desiring to know, hold fast with your conscience to the full poverty *(ganz arm)* of your hidden, unknowable God and do not think that you are a human being who in any way whatever knows the great, unknown, hidden God. . . . When God wished to fashion and create all things, he did not have anything before him except nothing *(das Nichts)*. Nothing for his creation is passively more receptive than something." Therefore the whole task of the spiritual life consists *"an einem unergründlichen Entsinken in ein unergründliches Nichts"* [in an unfathomable submergence into an unfathomable nothing].[103] "In this way created nothing is submerged in uncreated nothing: but this is something that it is impossible to understand and to state in words."[104] "True diminution (of oneself) sinks into the divine, interior abyss. Children, lose yourself there completely in the real, true loss of your very selves. *Abyssus abyssum invocat,* the abyss summons the abyss. The created abyss will lead further on account of its depth. Its depth and its known nothing attract the uncreated, open abyss to itself and thus one abyss flows into the other abyss and becomes a single oneness *(ein einiges Eins),* a nothing in another nothing.

"This is that nothing about which St. Dionysius says that God is not all that can be named, known or grasped; the spirit is completely abandoned thereby. And if God had thereby wanted to annihilate it completely, and if it could thereby be fully annihilated, it would become this out of *love for the nothing,* and because it merged with it, for it does not know anything, does not love anything, does not sense anything except the one."[105]

C. Sebastian Frank (Sixteenth Century)

In Sebastian Frank's famous "Paradoxes," the first chapter carries the characteristic title "No one knows what God is." Here we read, "Cicero says (in the first book of *On the nature of the gods*) that if you ask me what or who God is, I will adhere to Simonides. Namely when the tyrant Hieron addressed this question to him he requested a day for reflection. When on the following day he addressed the same question to him, he requested two days. When he doubled the number of days a few times Hieron wondered and asked why he did this, and he replied 'because the more I reflect the darker the matter presents itself to me.' Thus does Thomas Aquinas say that what God is we can neither say nor

Negative (Apophatic) Theology

know. For God is known only to himself, how he is. To an angel, says Thomas, he is known only in a likeness, and to us in a mirror, an enigma. This is the cause: God is neither this nor that, and in general nothing of the things about which one can speak, show, describe, hear and which can be perceived with the senses, shown, seen or expressed. The one to whom he does not speak himself and to whom he does not show himself knows nothing about him."[106] "Hence there cannot be a definition of God. For how can one name or define the One who is all in all and at same time nothing of the things which one could say, show, see, describe etc.? The omnipotent, invisible, incomprehensible, all-seeing, eternal independent good, the essence of all essences, the omnipotent will which properly does not love, is not wise, is not just, is not good etc., but is itself love, wisdom and goodness, the good, eternal light." Frank corroborates and explains this idea with numerous references to pagan and Christian authors (Seneca, Plato, Aristotle, Cicero, et al., Dionysius the Areopagite, Tauler, John of Damascus, Bernard, et al.). Hence "God does not have a name." This idea is elucidated thus: "Names designate a distinction of things in order to differentiate one from many. Since God is one and only, he has no need of a name in order to be differentiated from other things. Likewise, as he is all, and all in all, he cannot have a name, he who is substance, essence and life for all visible and invisible things; indeed of all things which one can name and know – their thing and essence. How can he have a special name differentiating him from others, since he is wholly essence and moreover every essence! . . . No one knows God except God himself. Whoever seeks God, but not in God and with God, I leave to continue searching – he will not find him for a long time. . . . God cannot be known in any way except as by God, i.e., by him himself, by his power which is called the Holy Spirit; hence this remains forever true: whoever seeks God not by God, with God and in God will search on all paths and find nothing."[107]

D. Angelus Silesius (Seventeenth Century)

In the poetic utterances *(Reime)* of this mystical philosopher and poet, published under the general title "Cherubinischer Wandersmann," among the many pearls of mystical profundity are found quite a number of couplets in the spirit of negative theology. We cite some of the most striking ones.[108]

> Gott ist ein lauter Nichts, ihn rührt kein Nun noch Hier:
> Je mehr du nach ihm greifst, je mehr entwird er dir (I, 25).

> Die zarte Gottheit ist ein Nichts und Uebernichts:
> Wer nichts in allem sicht, Mensch, glaube, dieser sichts (I, 111).

Geh hin, wo du nicht kannst: sieh, wo du siehest nicht:
Hör, wo nichts schallt und klingt, so bist du, wo Gott spricht (I, 199).

In Gott wird nichts erkannt: er ist ein einig Ein.
Was man in ihm erkennt, das muss man selber sein (I, 285).

Gott ist ein lautrer Blitz und auch ein dunkles Nicht,
Das keine Kreatur beschaut mit ihrem Licht (II, 146).[109]

The worldview of Angelus Silesius gleams with various tints in its facets; thanks to its poetic form it is not subject to systematization and besides on account of its multifacetedness it gives support for different, sometimes barely compatible constructions. To this one ought to add that Silesius was far from being always successful in mastering form and expressing exactly his true idea. In any case the ideas and tendencies of Eckhart and other mystics were obviously close to him, and in particular this is revealed in respect to what interests us.

E. Jacob Böhme (Sixteenth-Seventeenth Centuries)

It is difficult to distill in a pure state the motif of negative theology from the complex and obscure system of the "Teutonic philosopher." The basis of *"Ungrund"* [groundlessness] or *"Urgrund"* [primeval ground] in Böhme is the full nondisclosure of Divinity which can be expressed only in the language of negative theology. "God in himself is neither nature nor creation, neither this nor that, neither high nor deep. He is groundlessness *(Ungrund)* and ground of all essences, the eternal one, for he is neither place nor ground."[110] "God in himself is free from nature *(naturlos)*, affects and creation. He has no inclination towards anything for before him exists nothing towards which he would be able to be inclined, neither good nor evil. In himself he is groundlessness *(Ungrund)*, without any will turned towards nature or creation, as the *eternal Nothing*. He is Nothing and Everything, and is a single will; neither light, nor darkness, nor love, nor anger, nor eternal one. Hence Moses says 'the Lord is God alone.' For he embraces and finds himself in himself and begets God from God."[111] "If I reflect on what God is, I say that he is one, and with respect to creation the eternal Nothing. He has no foundation or beginning or place and possesses nothing except himself. He is the will of groundlessness *(des Ungrundes)*, he is one only in himself and from the ages he begets in himself only his own self. He is not equal to or like any other thing and does not have his own place where he dwells."[112] "In eternity, as groundlessness, outside (divine, uncreated) nature nothing exists except silence without essence, eternal rest without compare *(ohne Gleichen)*, groundlessness *(Ungrund)* without beginning and end. Here there is no goal, no place, no searching or finding."[113]

Negative (Apophatic) Theology

Most complete is Böhme's doctrine on Divinity in itself, which corresponds to a certain degree to the viewpoint of negative theology, set forth in the composition *De electione* (*Von der Gnadenwahl,* in the collected works edited by Schibler, vol. 4, pp. 467-68). Here we read (§3): "It cannot be said about God that he is this or that, evil or good, that he has in himself distinctions; for in his very self he is without natures, just as he is passionless and unmade. He has no inclination towards anything for there exists nothing before him towards which he could be inclined, neither good nor evil; he is in himself groundlessness, without any will towards nature or creation, like the *eternal Nothing;* in him there is no quality at all *(Quaal)* or anything that could receive an inclination towards him or from him. He is the sole entity and nothing exists prior to him or after him, over which or in which he could derive or receive any sort of volition; he likewise has nothing that could beget him; he is nothing and everything, and is the sole will in which the world and all creation lies, in him all is coeternal without beginning in identical equilibrium, measure and number; he is neither light nor darkness, neither love nor anger, but eternally one whence Moses says, the Lord is the one God (Deuteronomy 6:4)."

§4. "The same unnameable will, without nature and uncreated, which is only one and has nothing either before or after itself, which in its very self is only one, which as nothing is everything, which is also called the one God, embraces and finds itself in itself, and begets God from God."

§27. "If you want to know where God dwells, remove creature and nature, then God is all.... If you say I cannot remove creature and nature from myself for if that happened I would return to nothing, and so I must imagine Divinity conversely, then listen: God said to Moses, you must not make a likeness of God...."

The definitions of God as *nothing* are repeated over and over again almost verbatim or with a few variations, in many places in Böhme's works (cf., e.g., 4, 145, 278, 281, 284-85, 447-48; 5, 22; Claassen 1, 152 et al.).

F. John Pordage (Seventeenth Century)

The remarkable English mystic, close to J. Böhme but completely independent of him, begins his exposition of his own mystical insights (in his treatise *Divine and True Metaphysics*) with a chapter (I) on "the unrevealed Eternity" in which he briefly but with sufficient clarity formulates the fundamental principles of negative theology, which for him are prior to all theologizing.[114]

§1. "Under the name of God and under the name of Eternity I understand the Spirit of Eternity itself. And so, if we consider him as not having revealed his very self, then we cannot say anything about him except that he is eternal unity in simplicity. What this eternal unity and his simplicity are, who can say except God himself? This is the all-sublime and all-surpassing mystery which cannot be found out by any reflection of the intellect, nor by diligent investigation of reason and science, but solely through its own revelation can it be understood. No one can come to know it except it itself: since no creature can comprehend the infinite, unsearchable and incomprehensible Creator. This is the incomprehensible essence of God, it is how he is outside the primordial sphere of the world (Eternity) and how in himself he remains hidden; he is quite unknowable and unsearchable. In this state we cannot say anything about him except that he solely is known to himself; since to any creature no matter what name it might have he is unknown otherwise than only how he reveals himself in the sphere of Eternity, and outside the sphere and above it, he is for every created meaning *the eternal nothing, wholly and completely hidden and as it were entwined and enclosed in his own proper unsearchable mystery;* so that our knowledge of him outside the bottomless sphere of the world of Eternity is *more negative* than affirmative, that is, we come to know more *what he is not than what he is.*" God is comprehensible only in the power and measure of his revelation about himself: "My spirit saw in gladsome terror that outside the limits of this eternal orb (sphere of Eternity) there was nothing but infinite, incomprehensible Divinity, without goal and limits, and that outside this sphere of Eternity one could not see anything about God himself or come to know except only negative knowledge, that is, what he is not" (chapter 5, §6).

The affirmation of the transcendence of Divinity is essentially connected with another basic position of Pordage, namely, the full freedom of God from creation: "What is this freedom of the Holy Triunity? Answer: in this freedom these three are in their own proper eternal unity, simplicity and pure divinity, free from all other essences. They do not touch any essence, neither does one touch them. They are free from the essence of eternal nature, although they are in it and penetrate it. They do not touch it, and it does not touch them; they embrace nature, but nature cannot embrace the divinity of the Holy Trinity since they move themselves in their own proper freedom. They are free from all creatures, and yet they are in them and penetrate them through and through, but they do not touch a single creature and not a single creature touches them; but it remains in its own proper freedom. They have no union or communion with any creatures, except (those) to whom they design to reveal their divinity according to their own proper freedom" (chapter 2, §33).

14. Kant and Negative Theology

We are not setting for ourselves the task of tracing here the fortunes of negative theology in modern philosophy; to do so would essentially necessitate the writing of its complete history; and besides this, it is clear that the metaphysi-

Negative (Apophatic) Theology

cal and even more so the scientific rationalism reigning therein would be least of all favorable to theology. But we do not want to pass over in silence the distinctive position occupied by Kant in this question. Of course the central place belongs here to his all-important concept of the *Ding an sich,* the thing in itself, which is inaccessible to experiential cognition. The thing in itself is transcendent to experience — the categories of the phenomenal world are inapplicable to the noumenal, completely in the same sense and on essentially the same basis on which, for example, Johannes Scotus Eriugena considers the Aristotelian categories inapplicable to Divinity. The thing in itself is a *Grenzbegriff,* a limit concept that surpasses all cognition. It is absolute NOT, the name *of mystery* unknowable to the human being. Inasmuch as this doctrine is directed against the possibility of *any* metaphysics, it is sufficiently disproved by the history of philosophy. But it has another sense too, not only negative and rationalistic but also positive or mystical. When translated into religious language, i.e., the language of negative theology, the Kantian doctrine of the thing in itself, which establishes the laws of faith (practical reason) and opens the doors to mysticism, receives an entirely special significance. It places Kant a head above rationalistic theology with the fundamental criticism of which he advances: for this theology everything is demonstrable, everything is understood, and thus everything is immanent to reason. Breaking down that stone wall of rationalistic self-satisfaction and prejudices was Kant's enormous religious merit. And in this respect Kant stands even higher than his great continuators, not only Fichte, but also Schelling and Hegel. For the latter two each in their own way in fact remove the transcendence of Divinity and the fence of its mystery — the impassable NOT of negative theology. In Schelling's system (and I mean of course his final, most complete and finished system *Philosophie der Offenbarung*) with its doctrine of the self-disclosure of triune Divinity through the world process, the idea of negative theology concerning the transcendence of Divinity corresponds only to a definite moment of divine and cosmic dialectic. In Hegel's system the self-disclosure of Divinity is accomplished in logical thinking, with this thinking essentially being the self-thinking of Divinity, which is why Divinity is immanent to world-thinking. If there is a mystery in Divinity or ignorance about it, it is only because it has not succeeded in completely revealing itself — in generating itself in the world process or basing itself in the totality of logical thinking. Here in principle there is no place for that "inaccessible light" in which God lives. Here there are no boundaries separating the people from Mount Sinai, where even the "friend of God" Moses is given to see only "the back of God." God's nature is not mystery in the usual sense, says Hegel, betraying in these words the basic mystery of his own proper (and also Schelling's) philosophizing — and least of all in the Christian religion: here God let himself be known, he showed what he is; here he is disclosed. He remains a mystery only for sensible perception, representation, for sensible consideration and for intellect.¹¹⁵ In this sense Hegel and Schelling differ from the Wolffian precursors of Kant only by their more philosophical style and subtlety — there where the latter were content with rational constructions, here are erected majestic buildings of metaphysical speculation, but they too are penetrated in no small measure by pretensions to an adequate cognition of Divinity, and thus in a certain sense by religious complacency. In *this* respect Vladimir Soloviev unexpectedly draws near them, and in general sins by the excessive rationalism in his theology.¹¹⁶ Although he characterizes the transcendent absolute with help of the Cabbalistic concept Ein Sof (though we know how problematic that concept is, Soloviev applies it without any elucidation), i.e., in terms of negative theology, but thereupon, illegitimately and without any explanations placing it on the same footing as the first hypostasis, he *deduces* its relation to the world rationally, and consequently, their mutual determination.¹¹⁷ Soloviev plainly confuses or at least insufficiently distinguishes between God as the NOT-what of negative theology and God who has disclosed himself in the world¹¹⁸ — at the beginning of this disclosure.

In this respect Kant proved to be more philosophical in his negative theology than the thinkers cited. God is the inaccessible, transcendent NOT for the creaturely, human self-conscience — this is *one* of the meanings of Kant's doctrine of the noumen (we know that unfortunately it is not the only one and even not the most important; historically it received quite a different interpretation). What has been said does not prevent us from treating sharply negatively what can be called positive theology in Kant, or his "moral theology," where by altering his own superior point of view he returns to rationalism and constructs the most vulgar (in the religious sense) "religion within the limits of reason alone." And in this realm Kant stands already immeasurably inferior to Hegel, Schelling, and Vladimir Soloviev.

III. Divine Nothing

Even a cursory familiarity with the doctrines of negative theology leaves the conviction that they are far from speaking about the Divine Nothing in an identical sense, and ambiguities, multiple meanings, and oppositions are hidden in the twilight half-tones of negative definitions. Therefore the greatest concentration of attention is necessary precisely when analyzing the doctrine of Divine Nothing, for in this primordial intuition is already predetermined the fundamental system of the religious worldview. One can say that religious philosophy knows no more central a problem than that about the meaning of Divine Nothing.

Divine Nothing

The negation of any definition and content, which forms the basis of the negative concept of *negativity as such,* can have a different energy and diverse origin and meaning. It can point to the inexpressibility and indefinability of that which is canceled by negation, and coincides in this sense with the Greek alpha privative: *apeiron, aoriston, amorphon,* etc. (to which the so-called *infinite* judgment in logic corresponds), but it can also designate the absence of definition, indefinability as the state of potentiality, of nonmanifestation, but not as a fundamental indefinability, which would correspond to the Greek *mē,* which in a given case must be translated as *still not* or *for the present not* or even *no longer.*[119] By this twofold *not* of religious intuition two possibilities, two paths of religious philosophy, take shape: the antinomical and the evolutionary-dialectical. The unconditional NOT of negative theology yields no *logical* transition to any sort of YES of a positive doctrine about God and the world. The archangel with his fiery sword of antinomies bars the path to human knowing, by commanding it to bow before incomprehensibility in the ascetic struggle of faith. Therefore the opposition between NOT and YES is not dialectical but antinomical: over the abyss there is no bridge here. By contrast, the meonal NOTHING-SOMETHING hides no antinomy; on the contrary, it actually is negated in rational-mystical gnosis. Here antinomy is substituted for dialectical contradiction: in virtue of internal necessity, of the dialectic of the absolute itself, of a certain metaphysical causality successive links of being are manifested, and in this manner the principle of uninterrupted conformity to laws and its corresponding continuity in thinking triumphs. The archangel with the sword of antinomy becomes invisible; everything proves to be comprehensible, explicable in the face of this monism, which preserves its nature under various guises, and is essentially concealed or exposed rationalism. Here nothing is a certain divine *hylē,* prime matter, in which and out of which *everything* arises regularly and dialectically: divinity, the world, and humankind.

Therefore, depending on one or the other meaning of negation, the union of *not* and *yes, nothing* and *something,* in both instances receives a completely different ontological sense — precisely either antinomical, as a certain *coincidentia oppositorum,* or dialectical, as an internal coherence of co-supposing and mutually conditioning dialectical moments.

If one imparts to the NOT of negative theology the whole unconditional character inherent in it, then one will have to acknowledge first of all that there is not and cannot be any natural transition from this NO-thing to SOME-thing that is accessible to understanding, a path from the maternal bosom of meonal nothing in which *all* is born — or else one must repudiate the initial intuition of the transcendence of God. There is no path from the Absolute into the relative; between the Absolute and the relative yawns the abyss of mystery and "sacred ignorance." At the same time humankind comes to know God in religion, the relative gazes on the Absolute, and thereby finds itself in the Absolute, for there is nothing outside the Absolute; otherwise the latter would be limited by the relative and would not be the Absolute. This completely unique relation between the Absolute and the relative can be defined as the self-consciousness of *creatureliness*, which expresses the relation of the creature to the Creator.[120] The intuition of creatureliness, which has such a paramount meaning in religion, generally speaking is translated with difficulty into the language of religious philosophy, for here the latter must not "deduce" concepts, but provide only a philosophical retelling of religious experience. God created the world, or more exactly, he creates it in a pre-eternal, extra-temporal act; the world is a divine creation. Does this mean that the world is God, or is the being of the world a mode of divine being? No, this indicates precisely the opposite: the Creator abides transcendent to creation because otherwise it will not be his creation but his own essence or nature. To say it otherwise, worldly being is extra-divine; it abides in the realm of the relative and precisely this extra-divineness or relativeness makes the world the world, in opposing it to Divinity. The world is not in any sense at all God, for it is a creaturely-relative being: between it and God lies the creative *fiat*. But does this mean at the same time that the world exists apart from God, outside him, alongside of him? No, the world exists in God and only by God; there is not and cannot be anything lying outside God that would limit him by its being. God would not be God and the Absolute would not be absolute, but relative, if side by side with him but outside of him there was an extra-god or a counter-god. The world is completely transparent for God; it is penetrated through and through by divine energies that form the basis of its being.

The act of creation, which brings the world into being and places it as extra-divine, does not in any way draw it out of the divine bosom. The Absolute posits in itself a relative being or creature, without losing anything in its own absoluteness, but it leaves the relative in its relativ-

Divine Nothing

ity. The philosophical description of the intuition of creatureliness leads to a new, further antinomy: the extra-divine in Divinity, the relative in the Absolute.

If we say that the world is the creation of God we thereby establish that it is not *causa sui* (as Spinoza defines substance); it has a cause and a source of being not in itself but outside itself, in God. And yet at the same time it is impossible to say that God is the *cause* of the world, for this would mean converting the Absolute into the relative, having placed the transcendent in the immanent-uninterrupted series of causes and effects, and interpreting the relations between God and the world in the sense of causal, mechanical dependence, in virtue of which each subsequent thing necessarily flows out of the foregoing. Such a characterization would not at all correspond to the idea of creation, according to which the being of the world or the relative does not at all flow out of and cannot be deduced from the Absolute *logically*, as its causally necessary result; neither compulsory causes of creation nor the necessity of completing itself by the latter can be ascribed to the Absolute in its fullness. In other words, God as the Absolute is completely free of the world; he is "supermundane." To no extent is he conditioned by it and he has no need of it.[121] The creation of the world or the origin of the relative is in no sense causal-compulsory or necessary for the Absolute, as a factor of its life.

God is not the cause of the world, although he is its foundation, and in this sense the world is without cause; but this does not mean that it is absolute and without foundation as *causa sui*. The cosmological antinomy of Kant, according to which it is equally and simultaneously correct and incorrect that the world has a finite cause and that it cannot have one, describes precisely enough the intuition of *creatureliness*. That is why it has a more profound sense and a greater ontological meaning than Kant himself imparted to it, who saw in it only an unavoidable misunderstanding, *transzendentalen Schein* [a transcendental appearance].

From Kant's general doctrine of antinomies, "the *third* contradiction of the transcendental ideas" has a bearing on the *second* cosmological antinomy. It is a question of the final cause of the world relative to which the following thesis and antithesis simultaneously have force (*Kritik der reinen Vernunft*, Reclam, 368-69f.):

Divine Nothing

Thesis	Antithesis
Causality according to the laws of nature is not the only one from which the phenomena of nature can be produced in totality. To explain this it is necessary to accept causality through freedom.	Freedom does not exist, but everything in the world comes to be solely according to the laws of nature.

As proof of the thesis Kant points out that every cause requires for itself a preceding cause, and this ascension from cause to cause will have no end. "Therefore one must accept such a causality through which something happens, without this cause being defined further through some preceding cause according to necessary laws, i.e. through *the absolute spontaneity* of causes which *of themselves* would have begun a series of phenomena that arose according to the laws of nature; consequently transcendental freedom, without which even in the development of nature the order of phenomena is never complete on the part of causes" (370).

As proof of the antithesis Kant points out that freedom, permitted as first causality, all the same does not help the matter because it is incapable of entering into a causal link, being in principle different from it, and hence it either cannot begin a causal series or it tears it asunder. "Nature and transcendental freedom differ as conformity to laws and non-conformity to laws" (371).

Kant resolves the contradiction of thesis and antithesis, as is well known, in the sense that he refers freedom to the intelligible thing in itself, but causality to the world of phenomena, in keeping with his philosophy. Neither the details of Kant's argumentation nor his general explanation interests us here.[122] Antinomy in the understanding of the causal conditionality of creation is revealed by Kant not at all thanks to his gnoseology, in the limits of which it is only formulated; by itself it has a completely independent and more general meaning. Kant's merit is not that he noticed this antinomical quality, for philosophical thought essentially has been dealing with it for as long as one can remember; rather, because he was aware of it so acutely. For Kant it is resolved in the realm of gnoseology; for us its gnoseological realization is derivative. The antinomy expresses the intuition of *the creatureliness* of being.

For rationalist philosophy, for which the highest criterion is the continuity of thinking and the rational overcoming of antinomies, creatureliness is generally speaking a false, because contradictory, idea for which there is no place in critical metaphysics. However, the law of the continuity and noncontradiction of discursive thinking has force only in its own domain, but not where reason turns to its own proper foundations, to the roots of thought and being, with antinomies coming to light that are insuperable for it and at the same time irremovable, and which it must be fully aware of all the same.

The antinomy of creatureliness is only the subsequent disclosing of the primordial antinomy of the Absolute and relative which is expressed in the unconditional NOT of negative theology opposed to every YES linked with it, however, at the same time. Only against the background of the antinomy of creatureliness does the opposition of God and world, Creator and creature, receive an exceptional intensity and profundity. The world as creation receives reality and originality in its relativity, opposes God not as a phantom, illusion, or maya, as if it were only closing the Absolute to its own self; it receives its *realitas* as a gift from the *Ens realissimum*. This is why the relations of God to the world receive a real and two-sided character: of condescension for Divinity and ascension for the creature. Nevertheless, the waves of the world's ocean, no matter how high they might heave, cannot splash up to heaven and touch the Absolute unless the Absolute itself erects Jacob's ladder uniting heaven and earth. On the contrary, immanent self-consciousness alone through self-purification and self-deepening (Eckhart's *Abgeschiedenheit*) is completely incapable, so to say, of absolutizing itself, of overcoming its relativity, of finding itself in God by the path of self-drowning in the Divine ocean and of liberation from every maya. The world and humankind are divinized not by virtue of its creaturely divineness but by virtue of "grace," which is poured out into the world's bosom: the human being can become god, not by its creaturely nature, but only "god according to grace" (in keeping with the familiar definition of the Fathers of the Church).

If the world is contained in God but is not God, for it is separated from God by an impassable abyss of transcendence, then authentic religion can be based on the descent of Divinity into the world, on its voluntary entrance into it, its drawing close to humankind, i.e., on revelation or, to say it another way, it necessarily is a work of grace, of the super-natural or super-worldly operation of Divinity in humankind. It is impossible to penetrate into God or even beyond God only by the way of growing deeper in one's own worldly nature (although it too is the "image and likeness," a certain natural icon of Divinity), without a real *encounter* with the supernal Divinity, without its revelation of itself. With this are set the boundaries of that which can be called natural cognition of God, and likewise of that which is accessible to speculative comprehension. Religion has in its foundations an experiential, one can say, empirical character (of course, the concept of experience is taken here in an extended sense) and hence cannot be established by philosophical "deduction" alone or mystical "gnosis." Therefore God-Creator cannot be "divinity in general" which is accessible to philosophy and "natural religion," but has concrete traits — a name and a face.

One can distinguish three paths of religious consciousness: cognition of God *more geometrico* or *analytico*, *more naturali* or *mystico*, and *more historico* or *empirico* — abstract thinking, mystical self-deepening, and religious revelation, with the first two paths receiving a fitting meaning only in connection with the third, but becoming false as soon as they are affirmed in their isolation. In fact the attempt to exhaust the content of religion by logical analysis of common concepts leads it towards a wasting away and exsanguination — such are the "natural" or philosophical religions, the pathos of which consists in the animosity towards everything concrete-historical (let us recall Tolstoy with his obstinate striving towards an abstract-universal religion: "the *Reading Circle*" etc.); meanwhile living religion strives not towards the minimum but towards the maximum of content. Mystical self-deepening, just as the broadening of scientific or occult cognition, likewise does not contain in itself the key to religious comprehension of the world — and it needs the religious axioms of revelation; only through them do its riches burn with a living flame. There is a typical limit beyond which natural cognition of God cannot pass, no matter if it is philosophical, mystical, or naturalistic: this is the revelation of *person* in Divinity, however intensely it might be postulated. *Impersonalism* is a fatal trait of such doctrines and this is understandable, for person is known only *by encounter*, by the living revelation about oneself. And the first revelation about God, given to Moses, was about him as a Person: the *One Who Is*. This personal character of Divinity is peculiar not only to Judeo-Christianity but also to pagan polytheism — the stamp of the distinctive authenticity of its religious experience. But the Christian dogma of the trihypostaseity of Divinity was revealed to a human being, and not by a human being; only in the light of an already-revealed truth does a human being receive the possibility of beholding the stamp of trinitarity in himself and in all creation. The attempts of a philosophical deduction of trihypostaseity *a priori* (but *post factum* of revelation) only corroborate by their obvious insufficiency and inconsistency the nondeductibility of this truth (naturalistically in Jacob Böhme, speculatively in Hegel, Schelling, and partially in Vladimir Soloviev). This is why "pure" philosophy, which also lays claim to having the decisive voice in questions of religious consciousness, arrives so naturally at the negation of the hypostaseity of Divinity, by seeing in it only an impermissible anthropomorphism or psychologism (here the most militant are the representatives of a "philosophy of the unconscious," Hartmann and Drews).[123]

It is therefore understandable that the fundamental treatise concerning negative theology, the work of the Areopagite, not only bears the expressive title *On the Divine Names*, but also in actuality is dedicated to an explanation of the meaning of the divine names, under which the supernal God is revealed to the world. The NOT of negative theology is indissolubly united here with the YES of revelation. These self-revelations of Divinity, the *divine names*, cannot be deduced logically, mystically, or metaphysically out of the NOT of negative theology, but they are grounded by the inexpressible *mystery* of Absolute NOT-what. Therefore revelation not only reveals but at the same time it points to a mystery that is not and cannot be revealed, and this absolute MYSTERY contains in itself the source "of water that flows into eternal life,"[124] which never runs dry and is never depleted.

How is one to think this revelation of Mystery, this abstraction of the absoluteness of the Absolute, such as the revelation of the Absolute to the relative is? No answer in human language can be given to this. *Not everything is understandable*, but God is in everything and in this is the great joy of faith and submissiveness. We draw near to the abyss where the fiery sword of the archangel again bars to us the further path of cognition. *It is so* — religious experience tells us about this entirely firmly; even religious philosophy needs to accept this as the original definition — in the humility of reason, for the sacrifice of humility is demanded from reason too, as the highest reasonableness of folly. The unutterable, unnameable, incomprehensible, unknowable, unthinkable God is revealed to creation in a name, a word, a cult, theophanies, incarnation. Glory to Your condescension, O Lord!

The transcendence of Divinity or its sublimity is the basis of Judaic monotheism as well as of Christian dogma which is inseparably linked with it and develops it further.

The doctrine of the supermundanity or transcendence of Divinity, of the Divine Mystery, which is slightly opened by Revelation, constitutes the authentic meaning of negative theology among the majority of its Christian representatives, although they are far from always expressing it with sufficient clarity, consistency, and lucidity. Such are the fundamental ideas of Clement and Origen, the doctrine of Saints Basil the Great, Gregory the Theologian, and Gregory of Nyssa, of Dionysius the Areopagite, Maximus the Confessor, John of Damascus, Gregory Palamas, and also Nicholas of Cusa. This becomes clear if one takes these doctrines as of a piece, keeping in mind in these compositions not only negative but also positive theology in their mutual correlation. The greatest misunderstanding apropos of this is historically linked with the Areopagite, readily quoted by thinkers who are actually far removed from him (e.g., Eckhart), thinking him to be a likeminded person. But these misunderstandings disperse, based as they are on a one-sided assimilation of the Areopagite's doctrine, if one takes into consideration his positive theology.

By contrast, it is impossible to say the same thing about the philosophy of Plotinus, which in this decisive point really differs by its ambivalence and indecisiveness; thanks to this it equally could prove to be an indisputable and profound influence on Christian theology (in particular on the Areopagite) and at the same time is a powerful weapon in the philosophical arsenal of religious monism. However, in keeping with his basic tendencies, Plotinus to a large degree belongs to the latter. No less ambivalently sounds the Cabbalistic doctrine of Ein Sof, in which at once are heard the echoes of age-old Jewish dogma and of Neo-Platonism, which is why its significance fluctuates between the sacred mystery of the unpronounceable Name and the Plotinian *One*. The history of thought, however, has emphasized the second understanding — in the spirit of emanative monism (thus this doctrine is refracted, e.g., in Jacob Böhme; perhaps in him one ought to seek the prototype of Spinoza's doctrine of the single substance that exists in many modes and attributes). Of course, the first interpretation would be closer to the spirit of Jewish transcendent monotheism, and it draws Cabbala closer to Christianity towards which it tends with its own most essential doctrines and aspirations (as this has been frequently noted by researchers of Cabbala, e.g., Frank and de Pauly).

What are the results towards which the *second* possibility leads us, which is laid in the doctrine of negative theology about the Divine Nothing?

Divine Nothing, as Something, or as *mē on*, designates the primordial fontal being in its immovable depth, in its noumenal unity, divine fundamental principle. With respect to this Nothing every being

Divine Nothing

— whether divine or of the world and human — is already a certain *what;* in Nothing arises *what, vom Nichts zu Ichts* or *zu Etwas* [from Naught to Aught or to Something] according to Jacob Böhme's favorite expression. In this understanding nonbeing, as the still-nonbeing or the for-the-present-nonbeing, is that meonal darkness in which nevertheless everything is hidden, similar to how with the light of day everything is brought out towards being and is revealed that was concealed beneath the cover of nocturnal darkness. Divine Nothing is precisely this kind of meonal night of nonbeing and nondifferentiation, formlessness and amorphousness, but at the same time the fundamental principle of being (*Grund* or *Urgrund* of the German mystics).

Nothing forms for itself the initial moment of the dialectic of being, to which it is attached and towards which it returns; it corresponds to the greatest generality, nondifferentiation, and nonmanifestation of being, but at the same time it is found fully in its plane, in other words, *nothing exists*. Therefore on the path from nothing to something, from nonbeing to being, there is no leap or *transcensus*, no metaphysical *metabasis eis allo genos* [a change into some other genus], no hiatus yawns, for both nothing and something and both being and nonbeing equally *are being* in the various dialectical moments of its self-determination. Divine Nothing represents an analogy to meonal *Nichts*, with which the dialectic of being begins in Hegel's *Logic*. In Nothing is born everything and in this sense it *is everything* in its unity, *hen kai pan* [one and all]. Not only is the world born but so too is God, for even God here is born in Nothing and out of Nothing; his being is also only a special type of being, relative to the being of the world, co-being to the world. In such an understanding God is still not that ultimate thing beyond which it is no longer possible to penetrate; on the contrary one can do so and thus one must burst open beyond God, be drawn away from not only the world but also from God, *"Gottes ledig werden"* [to become unburdened of God] (Eckhart). And God and the world equally are found on this side of Nothing; they are as it were its hypostases, or more correctly, modes or dialectic moments.

They are found in a defined hierarchical correlation like degrees of the self-revelation of Nothing. Ontologically the world and God are consubstantial inasmuch as they are both modes of Nothing in which everything arises. And if on the path of returning to this Nothing the human must ascend to God (or the gods), and further pass through God and beyond God, then only because it is impossible to be raised to

Divine Nothing

the ultimate degree by passing the penultimate by, whereas god-being is this penultimate degree.

The passage from the original Nothing into something, the distinguishing and forming of the undistinguished and formless is of course also its own kind of *transcensus*, which is described in various ways in different mystical and metaphysical systems. Even an extreme immanentist or evolutionary monist inevitably has to allow such a relative transcendence of the various degrees of being in the self-creation of God and world in Nothing. Here, however, it is essential that these relatively transcendent degrees are dialectical self-positings of one and the same principle which are accomplished inside it, the *transcensus* of its modality, but here the *transcensus* from the absolute to the relative, from the Creator to the creature is neither unconditional nor dialectical but antinomical. Therefore every *something* – be it a god or a human, heaven or hell, angels or demons – has *one* nature or essence, as in the system of Spinoza the single absolute substance exists in an infinite multitude of attributes and modes. "Jupiter is everything that you see," Epicurus supposedly said; if one understands this utterance sufficiently deeply, it will express the essence of every *monoousianism* or monism – materialistic, spiritualistic, idealistic, and mystical.

In absolute Nothing the world and God appear. If the world is not created but arises dialectically in the absolute and is consubstantial with it, then it consequently is eternal and substantial in its foundation; on the other hand God too is not absolute and self-founded in his being, but is generated or originates in the absolute Nothing – the all. This means primarily that *a basis* for God exists, not in God himself but (ontologically) outside him, i.e., above him. God is likewise only the situation or mode of absolute Nothing, so to say, the absolute turned towards the world, its cosmic hypostasis, with the world being some other such mode, and this identical modality of God and world and their consubstantiality in this sense impart to them the character of transience and relativity in an equal degree although in a different sense: "God too passes" according to Eckhart's classic formula. Ultimately a system of general, universal identity is obtained.[125]

A system of religious monism can receive different contours depending on how the question of the origin of plurality – of God and world – is resolved in the single Nothing. Plurality can be resolved into pure illusion, *fata morgana*, deceit of the senses, *maya:* the truth is that there is no world and it is necessary to be liberated from the illusion of

Divine Nothing

it. Such is the philosophy and religion of Hinduism, which has Schopenhauer as its representative in European philosophy — it is not only acosmism but also anti-cosmism. Further, a certain even if degenerated reality produced from the Absolute can be ascribed to the world's being; that is how things stand in the system of Spinoza's static pantheism, and likewise of Hartmann's and Drews's dynamic pantheism: the world emerges, in accord with the doctrine of the latter, as a result of a certain "scandal" in the absolute — the manifestation of the blind and thoughtless will to being that summoned against itself a logical reaction in the entrails of the absolute, with a whole world process being required for the liquidation of this misunderstanding. Therefore simultaneously with the world's being there emerges the "suffering God," and the necessity for redemption from worldly being appears; in a distant perspective one sees silhouetted the return to original nondifferentiation, the absolute night of Nothing. But this hypothesis of a metaphysical catastrophe does not have the greatest philosophical and religious meaning; more significant is another form of dynamic pantheism, according to which the world is an emanation of the Absolute and arises as an outpouring from its superabundant fullness, similar to how water pours out of an overfilled vessel or the sun's light and warmth proceed from the sun. This is precisely the teaching of Plotinus.

A single absolute *One* proves to be simultaneously both transcendent and immanent to the world. The world is the gathering twilight of the absolute that grows thicker the deeper it is submerged in its being. Therefore the system of Neo-Platonism could provide philosophical support for the fallen heathen polytheism: God and the world emanate consistently from the supermundane and super-divine *One*, with its lower stories departing in the darkness of nonbeing, while the upper ones are flooded with blinding light; in heaven a system of divine moons begins to burn, shining, it is true, not with their own but with reflected light, and yet established in the vault of heaven. For what reason and why this emanation of the world takes place from the single Nothing, there can be no answer, and we will not find it in Plotinus's doctrine. The world originates because water cannot but pour out of an overfilled vessel, and a ripened fruit cannot but fall from a branch, but at the same time for Plotinus the world is the place where souls that have grown heavy and fallen away from the bosom of the absolute are corrected and led to understanding. But this provides an answer only about the fates of separate souls, not about the foundations of the world process, nor about the cause of emanation which remains uncaused and incomprehensible all the same, although here precisely is set the task *to explain* the foundations of the provenance of the world. If the world arises only in the process of moving away from the absolute, from its waning, and if its proper nature subsists only in this waning, then evidently the world-creating principle is a progressively augmenting *minus* of the absolute or its submersion in evil: from this one obtains an inevitable anti-cosmism, and only the Hellenic spirit and inconsistency saved Plotinus himself from the Satanic conclusion formulated by Mephistopheles:

> . . . alles, was entsteht,
> Ist werth, dass es zu Grunde geht;
> Drum besser wär's, dass nichts entstünde.[126]

(Plotinus even disputes this idea against the supposedly Christian Gnostics.)

Plotinian emanation differs, however, from Indian acosmism by its realism: the world as the effusion of the Absolute is real so far as the fullness of divine powers that have been poured out into it belong to it; it *is*, it has being, albeit degenerated though not illusory. However, being real in foundation, it remains deprived of any sort of independent task. The Absolute in relation to it remains completely passive; it does not know it, it is the sacrifice of its permissive fullness — in a certain sense the wrong side of it. The world *arises* of necessity in the Absolute, like its shadow, but in this world no sort of perfection happens; ontologically there is in it no history and no eschatology. On the one hand the world is the Absolute itself, as its mode, while on the other hand in the world nothing is accomplished and nothing happens, for it lies not *outside* the Absolute but is it itself, in the state of a certain waning.

Neo-Platonism historically is a hostile competitor with Christianity and, despite the apparent external resemblance, it is actually profoundly opposed to it, and precisely in the very basic and central doctrine of the divine Nothing and the derivative doctrine of the origin of the world from an involuntary emanation of the Absolute. The influences of Neo-Platonism, either conscious or unconscious, possess a great vitality in Christian theology — the Neo-Platonic inclination of thought and feeling is a danger constantly lying in wait for Christian philosophy too. One must know it in order to be on conscious guard against it. Therefore it will be instructive to trace this tendency in Christian philosophy where it has been manifested powerfully and strikingly. As examples of such a tendency, let us consider more closely the corresponding doctrines in Johannes Scotus Eriugena and the German mystics Eckhart and Jacob Böhme.

1. Johannes Scotus Eriugena

In his general doctrine, despite the sincere desire to keep within the boundaries of a Christian worldview, the famous Irishman nonetheless went astray into Plotinian "emanative pantheism"[127] and outlines in advance the future mystical system of Eckhart and Böhme in metaphysical terms. Immanentism or "monism"[128] in Eriugena is manifested first of all in the general conception of the author's *De divisione naturae*. He distinguishes four aspects of *nature* that encompass in themselves Divinity and the creature: nature "not creating and not created" or Divinity outside creation, "nature creating and not created" or Divinity in creation, thereupon nature "created creating," as the aggregate of creative ideas or ideal nature, and finally nature "not creating and created" or the world. All four of these aspects of nature are only different aspects, moments, or states *of a single* nature: all is one, and all is God. Thus Eriugena's metaphysics in principle converges with the doctrine of Plotinus concerning the relation of the One and the world. Here the ontological gulf between God and the creature is filled in and the creature is considered as a mode of the one substance by which the way is paved to future Spinozism. "First, Divine nature is just as created as it is creating. Namely it is created by its own self in the prototypal causes and correspondingly it creates its own self, i.e. it begins to be manifested in its theophanies, by wanting to step out from the most hidden corners of its nature in which it is still unknown to itself *(creatur . . . a seipso in primordialibus causis, ac per seipsam creat, h.e. in suis theophaniis incipit apparere, ex occultissimis naturae suae sinibus volens emergere, in quibus sibi incognita est),* for it is boundless, super-essential, and supernatural and higher than everything that can and cannot be imagined. Consequently when it descends to the fundamental principles of things and as it were creates itself, it begins to be in a certain something *(descendens vero in principiis rerum, ac veluti seipsam creans in aliquo inchoat esse).* But, second, being considered in the final operations of the fundamental causes, it by right can be considered as created and not as creating itself. Namely it is created inasmuch as it condescends to the most external manifestations, further than which it can no longer create anything, whence only createdness has force in it and not creation."[129] In coming out of his own

Divine Nothing

super-essential nature in which God signifies nonbeing, he is created by himself in his own original causes and becomes the principle of every essence and every life.[130]

On the basis of these definitions it is clear that the *nothing* of Eriugena's negative theology signifies not the transcendent and supernal Divinity but the first state of Divinity in its self-disclosure — nothing which passes over into something. To characterize Eriugena's doctrine in relation to what is being considered, of paramount importance is his understanding of the creation of the world out of nothing. In view of the fact that an idea of the creation of the world, strictly speaking, is absent in him, for it merges with the self-creation of God, then the *nothing* out of which the world is created or better "degenerates" is the divine Nothing itself. Eriugena dedicates an extraordinarily large amount of space and attention to the question of creation out of nothing (by attempting to draw to his side the Eastern fathers of the church, such as Saints Basil the Great, Gregory of Nyssa, Maximus the Confessor, Dionysius the Areopagite, some of whose opinions give occasion to a similar reinterpretation, without their being really guilty of immanentism). For Eriugena it is clear that God "makes everything out of nothing, bringing essences out of its super-essentiality, living beings out of its super-vitality, that which is and is not out of the union of all, what is and is not out of the affirmation of everything. The return of all things to the cause clearly teaches this, out of which they arose, when everything returns to God as air to light."[131] It is necessary to understand this nothing out of which God created the world as the "ineffable and incomprehensible clarity of divine goodness inaccessible for every mind" *(ineffabilem et incomprehensibilem divinae bonitatis inaccessibilem claritatem).*[132]

In Book 3 of *De divisione naturae* Eriugena gives a detailed and multifaceted investigation of the question about *nothing* (especially chapters 4-23) from which the world is created, by subjecting to criticism and repudiation the church's understanding of nothing as inferior-being or nonbeing and affirming as the solely conceivable and logical one his own understanding expounded above. The fundamental conclusion that suggests itself from this will be that in nature "God created his own self"[133] or that "we ought not to think the creature and God as two (principles) differing among themselves but as one and the same. For the creature is found in God and God is created in the creature by wondrous and inexpressible ways . . . the trihypostatic supreme goodness . . . is always eternal and always becomes eternal from itself and in itself, but at the same time arose inasmuch as in ever-being it shall not cease to be in becoming — inasmuch as it makes itself out of itself. For this purpose it needs no other matter which was not itself in order to produce in it its own self, and it would prove to be powerless and in itself incomplete, if it should receive help for its own manifestation and perfection from somewhere else."[134]

From what has been cited it follows that properly speaking there is for

Divine Nothing

Eriugena no creation or world as extra-divine (relative) being, for created nature is only a degree in the self-disclosure of Divinity or its mode. The world is eternal in God; it is indeed God. How is one to understand the world existing in time and encompassed by sin? For Eriugena the being of the sensible world begins with the fall into sin of humankind, which occurs not in time but in some extra-temporal act. This world ought not to have existed; sin created it. As a result of this, humankind acquired a sensible body, the division into sexes, and the particularities of organization bound with this were manifested and the world process commenced. The task of redemption is thus nothing other than the universal *restoration* of the original condition, "the return of all things to the cause out of which they came."[135] Strictly speaking this "apocatastasis" of Eriugena is not at all the Christian resurrection with a body, since corporeality generally speaking is considered as the result of the fall; "the spiritual body" of the resurrection is the same intelligible first-formed body which is covered and annihilated by the sensible body. In this respect Eriugena is the most decisive spiritualist, and from his point of view it would be more correct to speak not about the resurrection of the body but about the resurrection *from* the body. Therefore the whole world process for Eriugena is a barren mistake, something completely irrational (an opinion that anticipates the philosophy of pessimism: Schopenhauer, Hartmann, A. Drews). Since the provenance of the world is a process immanent to Divinity, then obviously the fall introduces the drama into the Divinity itself, and it should be concluded that the world process is the mystery of a God irrationally suffering and searching for himself (although Eriugena himself does not draw such a conclusion). Stöckl pronounces the following severe judgment on Eriugena: "One may call Eriugena's doctrine a work of genius, but it is not Christian" (*Lehrbuch,* p. 381).

2. Meister Eckhart

We are far from intending to characterize the *entire* mysticism of Eckhart as non-Christian; quite the contrary, in the writings of this surprisingly rich and deep person of genius there are some invaluable riches of Christian piety which, however, are intermingled with non-Christian mystical motifs and tendencies in a not always distinguishable way. Therefore one can speak only about some Neo-Platonic *motifs* in the works of this great writer. To speak pointedly, a monograph study elucidating the precise *type* of his creative output would be an interesting undertaking. What is it? Is it mystical illuminations or the metaphysical speculation attached to it? Is it philosophy or sermon, or neither the one nor the other but a third, containing a fusion of all of these elements? In any case — and it is necessary to give this the appropriate weight when evaluating Meister Eckhart — the artist of the word and the spec-

Divine Nothing

ulative metaphysician let themselves be known too powerfully and clearly in his compositions for one to take all of his ideas for religious-mystical intuition and revelation, and it is never possible to say confidently whether Eckhart's sermon rests on lived experience or whether it is generated from the artistic images and speculative ideas that caught fire in his soul which he turns into a *task* to be realized by means of mystical experience. An investigation of the chronology of the different works of Eckhart in connection with his spiritual biography and diverse influences that he experienced would be able to shed much light here.

The fundamental idea of Eckhart's theology that bestows on it a non-Christian and Neo-Platonic character is his opposition of *Gott* and *Gottheit*, which are as "different as heaven and earth."[136] God is something produced out of *Gottheit* and completely correlative to the creation; he is the outcome of the differentiation of *Gottheit*. Which is why the character of relativity and transitoriness is so inherent to him, as it is to the creation. *God becomes and passes away* (I, 148). This formula, unusual in its boldness, expresses precisely the thought of the nonabsoluteness, relativity, and even, if it can be so stated, the modality of God; obviously if he is *not* the ultimate, one must then strive *beyond* him, further than him, try *"Gottes ledig werden, Gottes quitt machen"* [to become unburdened of God, freed of God] (I, 175), be liberated from God: *bitten wir dass wir Gottes ledig werden"* [let us pray to become unburdened of God] (I, 172). God arises only together with the world: "All creatures speak about and proclaim God. But why do they say nothing about Divinity *(Gottheit)*? All that is in Divinity is the One about which it impossible to say anything. Only God does *(thut)* something, Divinity does nothing, there is nothing for it to do. God and Divinity differ as do action and inaction" (I, 148, cf. 199). Between God and creation exists only a hierarchical difference, insofar as God is the door for returning to absolute *Gottheit*, but not an ontological difference: as modes of *Gottheit* they are identical. In his "break-through" towards Divinity "I become so rich that God cannot be sufficient for me by all with which he is God, with all his divine acts: for I receive in this breakthrough that in which I and God are *common*" (I, 176). "In this experience the spirit does not remain a creature any longer, for it is itself already 'divinity,' it is *one* essence, one substance with divinity, and is at the same time its own proper blessedness and that of all creatures" (I, 202). Only on that surface of divinity where God is, does the trinity exist which represents as it were his features in creation. And beyond it one can break through: "First of all the soul attains the holy threefoldness *(Dreifaltigkeit)*, which has become *a unity*. But it can become still more blessed: if it pursues simple *(blossen)* unity, about which threefoldness is only a revelation. Fully blessed will it be only when it throws itself into the *desert (Wüste)* of Divinity" (II, 186). It is necessary to abstract every "what" because *Abgeschiedenheit*, the virtue of this abstraction, in the eyes of Eckhart includes all virtues and is even higher than love: "The soul

Divine Nothing

thereby sacrifices everything, God and all creations. It sounds strange that the soul must lose even God! I assert: in order to become perfect it is more necessary in a certain sense for it to be deprived of God than of creations. In any case all must be lost, the existence of the soul must be affirmed in a free nothing! This alone is the intention of God, that the soul should lose its God. For as long as it has God, it cognizes and knows until it is separated from God. Such is the aim of God: to be annihilated in the soul so that the soul might lose itself too. For that which God is called as God he has from creation. Only when the soul has become a creature will it have received God. When it shakes off its creatureliness *(Geschöpf-seyn)* anew, then God remains before himself that which he is" (II, 202-3). But thereby "the soul itself must become divine." The spirit "must be dead and buried in Divinity, but Divinity lives no longer for anyone else but for its own self" (II, 207), and the preacher urges to experience *"diesen göttlichen Tod"* [this divine death] (II, 207).

Gottheit is the fundamental principle *(Wesen)* or nature *(Natur)* of Divinity. The divine hypostases are *"Personen"* about which it is said that *"sie verfliessen in das Wesen"* [they dissipate in the essence] (I, 85) and "having flowed into Divinity the three persons become an indistinguishable unity" (I, 85). Divinity in itself is impersonal; the hypostases arise only as a result of its differentiation, already in "God" or on the border between "Divinity" and "God." It is in this sense that one should understand the statement that there is still imperfection in the soul while "it contemplates God inasmuch as he is trinity" (I, 163): perfection enters only with the contemplation of the *"schlechthin Eine," "ungestaltete Wesen der göttlichen Persönlichkeit"* [the absolutely One, the unformed essence of divine personhood] (I, 163). "You must love God inasmuch as he is non-God, non-spirit, non-person, unformed but only pure, clear, simple unity, far from every duality. And in this one thing we must be immersed eternally from being into nothing" (I, 168). In this sense it is said that "trinitarity is at the same time the world for in it are deposited all creatures. But within, in Divinity, both the one acting and the action remain without change" (I, 184).

The practical aspiration of the religion of *Abgeschiedenheit* is Buddhist nirvana, not only acosmism but also anti-cosmism: to break free from the world arising through the bifurcation of creature and God, into the original divine nothing. Obviously this view makes no room for the idea of history, of the world process, of the world's perfection: the ideal of the restoration of the original state, apocatastasis, is here the naked denial of the world.

Departing from his religious monism, for which Divinity is only the depth of being and not the transcendent principle revealed to the world, Eckhart in fact removes the *revelation* of Divinity in its proper sense, replacing it with the self-revelation of creation (the "breakthrough" through creatureliness); corresponding to this, even the gospel history is interpreted in a spiritualist way. In Eckhart the operation of grace on the natural world is removed just as logically. In one place Eckhart gives this interpretation of the words of the apostle Paul "all that I am, I am through the grace of God": "The words of the apostle Paul," comments Eckhart, "are only the words of Paul; there is nothing about him saying them in the state of grace. For grace worked in him only one thing: his essence was perfected towards the unity of itself. In this its work is exhausted!" (I, 175, cf. 195-96). "Grace itself does not work *(bewirkt)* anything" (I, 196). "The highest work of grace is that it leads the soul to what it is itself" (I, 197).

How portentous was Eckhart's appearance, still in the Catholic era of German history, but already on the threshold of a new time, on the eve of the Reformation! Like the first of his kind he pointed out in advance how the Germanic genius was fatally doomed to pervert Christianity onto the side of religious monism, pantheism, Buddhism, Neo-Platonism, immanentism! Without exaggeration one can say that in Eckhart the whole spiritual development of the new Germany is deposited as in a kernel, with its Reformation, mysticism, philosophy, and art: in Eckhart is included the possibility of Luther, Böhme, Schelling, Hegel, Schopenhauer, Hartmann-Drews, Wagner, and even Rudolph Steiner.[137]

3. Jacob Böhme

How ought one to understand the divine *nothing* in Böhme's doctrine? As a transcendent NO-thing or as the Eckhartian *Gottheit*, or as the Hegelian dialectical nothing out of which everything flows of necessity and in which this everything is woven, or as the Spinozan substance lying at the basis of modes, or as the Plotinian One from which the world emanates? To one familiar with the works of Böhme and the peculiarity of his exposition it will be understandable if we say that an undisputed answer to this essentially fundamental question of principle cannot be given, and the possibility of different understandings even of the very foundations of this doctrine is created, which is still waiting for an attentive and comprehensive investigation and systematization.[138] The "Philosophus teutonicus," who according to the justified estimation of Schelling is "a miraculous appearance in human history and especially in the history of the German spirit,"[139] represents simultaneously a mystic, a clairvoyant of nature, a metaphysician who clothes his mystical comprehensions in a peculiar speculative-mystical system, and precisely a *system,* for "the spirit of system" is unusually strong in Böhme despite the exterior feebleness of his exposition. He is therefore not only a pupil of Paracelsus and a forerunner of Steiner, for he stands in the line of development of occultism, but perhaps, to no less a degree his spirit lives in the metaphysical systems of Schelling and

Divine Nothing

Hegel, Schopenhauer and Hartmann. In his compositions Böhme attempts many times to build and rebuild his system — everything afresh but approximately from the same material — whence there is such an endless mass of repetitions in his compositions;[140] but the material pays insufficient heed to its master, who grows weak under the burden of its abundance, and it remains to a significant degree raw and unprocessed. Obviously, Böhme himself and after him his other followers, e.g., Claassen,[141] was not aware that he was the "philosophus teutonicus," the speculative metaphysician who found himself to a certain degree captive to the "esprit de système." He recognized in himself first of all a spirit-seer, a bearer of "revelations,"[142] and if only one of his compositions, "Aurora," were preserved, his first treatise which has the stamp of freshness and immediacy of "inspiration" and is the most foreign to pretensions of a system, then perhaps it would be possible not to observe one of the basic traits of Böhme's work, noticed with great subtlety by Schelling, namely, his *rationalism*. Oh, of course, this is a rationalism of a completely particular type, *mystical* rationalism (or "theosophism"), where the basic theses rest on the demonstration of mystical experience and cannot be *logically* deduced and postulated. As a mystic and clairvoyant, Böhme is above all an empirical investigator. Those powers and phenomena that Böhme studies are empirically given to him in mystical contemplation similar to how they are given in experimental sciences: just as from electricity it is impossible logically to deduce light or warmth, so in Böhme the elements of God are not deduced but "experimentally" cognized: *Herbe, bitterer Stachel, Angst, Feuer* [harshness, bitter sting, fear, fire], etc. But once established they explain themselves one from the other in a causal-mechanistic manner on the basis of the logical principle of continuity, in a single coherent metaphysical system: in the Böhmian God from his first movement towards revelation to the remote little corner of the universe, from the angel to the last bug, *everything is comprehensible*, everything is explained, everything is rationalized. Here there is no place for antinomy with its logical interruption, or for Mystery. Unalloyed rationalism — here is the other side of that global knowledge or "gnosis" which Hegel thought he possessed on certain grounds, and Böhme on others. This is why Böhme proves to have so much in common with tendencies of contemporary "theosophism," occult or mystical rationalism.[143] That is why his separate insights are dazzling, astounding, and precious — in part but not entirely so; it is necessary to break open the shell in order to get the nut. According to the comparison of Pfleiderer,[144] his system is like a mine in which precious metals are hidden under coarse rocks.

As a metaphysician Böhme poses as his fundamental task the "deduction" of God and the world that rests on mystical experience: By what manner does God arise from Nothing or in Nothing, and the world in God or from God? This problem is entirely analogous to Eckhart's problem (a familiarity

Divine Nothing

with which is definitely felt in the corresponding doctrines of Böhme),[145] namely concerning the origin of God and the world simultaneously in the original, pure Nothing, or concerning the theological *"reiner Ursprung"* [pure origin] (according to the expression of Cohen's "Logic"); however, the radical difference from Eckhart on this point, which determines a series of subsequent differences in Böhme, will be that for him the world arises not parallel with God, as his necessary correlate, but in virtue of the dialectic of God himself or the development of his nature. Therefore we have in Böhme a three-level hierarchy or sequence: *Nothing — God — world;* in Eckhart a two-level hierarchy:

$$\text{Nothing} - \begin{cases} \text{God} \\ \text{world} \end{cases}$$

However, this relation between God and nature forms only the second part of the problem; in the first part both Böhme and Eckhart equally depart from that undifferentiated and unqualified Nothing in which all is formed.

How does Böhme imagine more closely this transition from Nothing to God and through him to creation? Unfortunately Böhme's metaphysics does not give an entirely clear and unambiguous answer, although the predominant impression from it comes down to this: Nothing has here the meaning not of the transcendent NOT-what but of that divine meon or dialectical *nothing* in which the divine *all* comes to light with the immanent regularity of mystical dialectic, as a result of which this *nothing* corresponds only to a definite state or dialectical moment in Divinity. God and nature as "something" are the revelation of "Nothing," *"Offenbarung aus dem Nichts zu Etwas"* [revelation out of Nothing to Something].[146] By what is this transition motivated and is it motivated at all? Here we have only metaphysical expressions, the sense of which is that for Nothing this transition is not free but is compelled by some divine necessity, a need for self-revelation, hunger *(Hunger)*, yearning *(sich sehnen)*, desire *(Begierde)*, i.e., affective states (inasmuch as one can speak of affects in Divinity). "Nothing experiences hunger for Something *(Nichts hungert nach dem Etwas)* but hunger is desire *(Begierde)* as the first verbum Fiat or doing, for desire has nothing that it would be able to make or grasp *(fassen)*. It grasps only itself and contracts *(impresset sich)* i.e. it coagulates *(coaguliert sich)*, it initiates itself in itself, and grasps itself and leads itself out of groundlessness to the ground *(vom Ungrunde in Grund)* and fertilizes itself with magnetic attraction so that Nothing becomes full *(das Nichts voll wird)* and remains all the same as Nothing; this is only a property like darkness; it is the eternal primal state *(Urstand)* of darkness: for where there is property, there is already something, it is not as Nothing."[147] The revelation of God, according to a whole series of affirmations of Böhme, is first of all self-revelation, the revelation of the self for the sake of the very self: "without his revelation God could not be known to his own self,"[148] and "since the eternal good cannot be *(nicht mag)* an insensible es-

Divine Nothing

sence *(ein inempfindlich Wesen)*, for otherwise it would not be revealed to itself, then it leads itself into pleasure *(Lust)* in itself."[149] In this sense one can say that nature is necessary for God or more exactly that it is God explicitly. "In this manner one ought to think of God that he leads his will in knowledge *(Scienz)* towards nature so that his power would be revealed in light and might and become the kingdom of joy: for if nature did not arise in the eternal One all would be silent; but nature introduces itself in suffering, sensitivity and perceptibility so that eternal silence would be moved a little and forces would resound in word. . . . Nature is the instrument of silent eternity by which it forms, makes, divides and gathers itself thereby into the kingdom of joy, for eternal will reveals its word through nature. The word of knowledge *(Scienz)* takes nature into itself, but *it lives through nature* like the sun in the elements or like Nothing in the light of fire, for the flash of fire makes Nothing reveal itself and thereby it is impossible to speak about Nothing, for Nothing is God and everything."[150]

In this manner, according to the just observation of Schelling,[151] Böhme "entangles the Divinity itself in an original natural process," and for Böhme nature is God not only in the sense that it is rooted in God according to its positive existential content, but also in the sense that it is the necessary instrument of his self-disclosure or interior dialectic; "he lives through it," and without this, "God himself does not know what he is."[152] Thus in Böhme the idea of creation and creatureliness is absent strictly speaking, and although in him the expression "creature and creatureliness" *(Creatur und Creatürlichkeit)* is constantly encountered, this concept does not at all have a fundamental metaphysical and ontological sense, but indicates only a definite level in the disclosure of the nature of God (as in Plotinus's system, which nonetheless denies the idea of creation). *Böhme's system is emanational* and in this respect it comes close to the doctrine of Plotinus. The idea of the creation of the world by an incomprehensible and free act of God meets in Böhme a conscious philosophical and religious opponent. He calls "delirium about creation" *(creatürlicher Wahn)* the idea "that God is something foreign and that before the time of the creation of the creature and of this world he took counsel in himself in Trinity by his wisdom as to what he wants to make and to what every being belongs, and in this manner he himself derived from himself the command *(Fürsatz)* where he must determine which thing."[153] "If at some such time he took counsel in himself to be revealed in this manner, then his revelation would not be from eternity, outside feeling and place, and therefore that counsel ought to have had a beginning and become a cause in Divinity, for the sake of which God consulted in his Trinity; consequently in God there must be ideas which appeared to him as it were in the form of images, when he wanted to go to meet things. But he himself is singular and the basis of all things, and the eye of all entities and the cause of every essence; from his property arise nature and creature, about which he began to consult with himself; there is no enemy before him and he alone himself is everything, wanting, power and ability. Therefore, insofar as we want to speak solely and exclusively about the unchangeable essence of God, of what he wants and what he does not want or ever want, we must not speak about his decisions for in him there are no decisions; he wants and does in himself only one thing, namely he gives birth to himself in Father, Son and Holy Spirit, in the wisdom of his revelation; apart from this the one groundless God does not want in himself anything and does not have in himself counsel about the many. For if he wanted in himself many, then he would have to be insufficiently almighty in order to realize this; because in himself he cannot want anything except only himself, for what he wanted from eternity this he is himself, because he is solely one and nothing more."[154]

Corresponding to his worldview Böhme more correctly speaks of the *birth* and not of the creation of nature by God: "Out of the will by which the Divinity encloses himself in trinitarity, from eternity is born the basis of nature, for here there is no command *(Fürsatz)*, only birth; eternal birth is also command, namely God wants to bear God and be revealed through nature."[155] Of course the creative "let there be," *fiat*, which is encountered so often in Böhme, receives a corresponding interpretation not in the sense of command *(Fürsatz)* but in the sense of power of Divinity, its natural might, potency of being, and in this sense in diverse expressions it is defined in many places: "Desire *(Begierde)* from the eternal will of groundlessness is the first form *(Gestalt)* and is *Fiat* or *Schuf*. But the power of free pleasure *(Lust)* is God who brings out *Schuf*, and the one and the other together are called by the word *Fiat*, i.e. the eternal word which created where nothing is, and is the primary condition of nature and all beings."[156] "Fiat is the astringent uterus *(herbe Matrix)* in the first will of the father, and it grips *(fasst)* and holds nature which spirit forms born from Mercury and this is the spirit of God."[157] "The divine *Schuf* as the desire of eternal nature which is called the Fiat of powers"[158] corresponds in Böhme's system to the "let there be" of the Mosaic cosmogony. In this manner, according to the thought of Böhme, nature in essence is not created but, so to say, arises in God automatically with the regularity of a clock mechanism, with which the universe is so often compared in Böhme, and is disclosed in various levels. And from this side in keeping with its philosophical type (although not according to its structure) Böhme's system is close to the pantheistic monism of Spinoza with its single substance undisclosed in itself that is manifested in countless attributes and modes. Only, in Spinoza this monism has a static and immobile character whereas in Böhme it has a dynamic, vigorous character. *Böhmism is dynamic Spinozism;* the conception of the relation of God to the world is one and the same in them both.[159] In ancient philosophy in addition to Plotinus, the hylozoic monism of the Stoics, and in an earlier epoch the teachings of Thales, Anaximander, and in general the Ionic school, represent

Divine Nothing

an analogy with Böhmism. In modern philosophy the spirit of Böhme is most similar to the philosophy of logical automatism, namely to Hegel (of course, even here we have in view the spirit and style of the doctrine and not its dogma). And this affinity was grasped by Hegel himself who speaks of Böhme more than once and with deep admiration.[160] Böhme's system, like Hegel's, is a special form of mystical rationalism in which all antinomies are overcome and the law of "the continuity of thought" dominates. On the contrary, the follower of J. Böhme, Franz von Baader, assiduously dissociates himself from religious monism and interprets the doctrine of his teacher in the sense of the freedom of God from the world and from nature.[161]

Out of *Nothing*, similar to an unrolling spiral which as it unrolls describes a series of circles of ever-increasing diameter (cf. the sketch added to volume four of the collected works of Böhme in Schiebler's edition), is generated the Divine Trinity, God *before* nature, and out of it our world "degenerates" too (*Ausgeburt*, according to the frequently recurring expression of Böhme). According to his original definition Divinity is impersonal: he defines concealed Nothing or *Ungrund* as "will" (*der Wille des Ungrundes*), and this primary will (so reminiscent of the basic motif of the metaphysics of German pessimism of Schopenhauer and Hartmann) is the original source of the self-generation of God; in it the Trinity is generated. "In this eternal generation one must understand three things: (1) the eternal will; (2) the eternal mood *(Gemüth)* of the will; (3) the exodus from the will and *mood*, which is the spirit of will and *mood*. Will is the father; mood is the connectedness *(das Gefassete)* of will as the seat and domicile of the will, or the centre towards nothing, and is the heart of the will; exodus out of the will and mood is force and spirit. This triadic spirit is one essence, and here it is no longer essence but eternal reason: a primordial quiddity *(ein Urstand des Ichts)*, and at the same time an eternal insularity. That which comes out is called the pleasure *(Lust)* of Divinity or of eternal wisdom which is the primordial state of all powers, beauties and virtues; through it the triadic spirit becomes desirous and this desire is the impression, the seizing of its own self: the will seizes *(fasst)* wisdom in the mood, but what is seized in reason is the eternal word of all colours, powers and virtues."[162]

It is obvious that the three outcomes or moments in the god-generating Nothing do not have the character of three persons or hypostases in the one Divinity as ecclesiastical Christianity teaches this. And Böhme himself leaves no doubt about this: "We Christians say: God is threefold but one in essence; it is even usually said that God is threefold in persons, and this is poorly understood by the foolish and partly by the learned, for *God is not a person except as in Christ (Gott ist keine Person als nur in Christo)*;[163] but he is an eternally-generating power and a kingdom with all essences; everything takes its beginning from him. That he is Father, Son and Holy Spirit, as is said about God, is said correctly, but it needs clarification; otherwise the unenlightened soul will not un-

Divine Nothing

derstand. The Father is, first, the will of groundlessness, he is the will towards quiddity *(Ichts)* that is found outside every nature or principle, which is amassed in the pleasure of self-revelation. But pleasure *(Lust)* is the amassed power of the will or of the Father and is His Son, the heart and seat *(Sitz),* the first eternal principle in the will, and that is why he is called Son because he takes eternal beginning in the will, by the self-amassing of the will. In this way will is expressed through a seizing of its own self, like exhalation or revelation: and this issuance out of the will in speech or breathing is the spirit of Divinity *(Gottheit)* or the third person, as the ancients handed down. . . . In any case there is no basis for saying that God is three persons, rather, he is threefold in his eternal generation. He generates himself in triadicity, and in this eternal generation one ought to understand only one essence and generation, not Father or Son or Spirit, but one eternal life or good."[164]

It is clear that a gulf lies between the church's doctrine of the trihypostatic Divinity and Böhme's theology. In him trinitarity is only a threefoldness of moments of self-generation of Divinity, and the sole person he acknowledges in Divinity is Christ, but not as the second person of the holy Trinity who became incarnate in human nature, the hypostatic Son of the hypostatic Father, out of whom comes the hypostatic Holy Spirit, but as the one and sole hypostasis, the monohypostatic moment in the anhypostatic Divinity (whereby personhood is proper to Christ more in his humanity than in his divinity). Despite a certain external resemblance, Böhme's Christology is different from that of Christianity for which hypostaseity is not a "deduced" moment in Divinity, but its vital essence. Of course, even this "deduction," the transition from the impersonal to the personal, is in and of itself a very obscure doctrine in Böhme.

The impersonal character of Böhme's theology is laid bare even more clearly in his doctrine of "nature in God," or "eternal nature," which represents undoubtedly the most original and characteristic part of his doctrine. God in triunity has *everything* only *"in Temperatur,"* i.e., in the state of concordance and indivisibleness, and eternal *Weisheit* [wisdom] is only "a mirror" with ideal reflections of everything. For its own disclosure this *everything* must arrive at the state of differentiation, *"Schiedlichkeit,"* and susceptibility, *"Empfindlichkeit,"* but "the mirror of wisdom" must turn into the "eternal virgin" (Sophia), the susceptibility of everything (so to say, transcendental sensibility). With this is outlined the path towards the subsequent self-disclosure of Divinity, and the *physics of God* begins.

In order for any sort of power to be revealed, there must be a counteraction as the basis for its disclosure; "in yes and no all things exist, be they divine, devilish, earthly or whatever they might be called."[165] In "silence" no revelation happens; "there must be a counter-will, for the clear and quiet will is like nothing and generates nothing. If the will must be generated, it must have something in which it is formed and generates."¹⁶⁶ In divine nature the polarities must be disclosed, heaven and hell, in which Divinity is present either as wrath, *Grimmgott,* "a consuming fire," or as God. "The physics of God" knows seven powers or spirits, and by their aggregate heptad the "body of God" is formed. It is not our task here to examine this most original and interesting, but also most obscure part of Böhme's doctrine, where he is connected especially tangibly with the astrological and alchemistic tradition and works within the frame of the scholarship of his day. Here is a schematic table "of the revelation of the seven spirits of God or powers of nature" composed by Böhme himself.¹⁶⁷

Wrath:
- I. bitter, lust
- II. amassing or the sting of sensitiveness
- III. fear or mood
- IV. fire or spirit

Hellish:
- cruel, cold, avarice
- sting, envy
- enmity
- hypocrisy, wrath

World:
- cold, hardness, bone, salt
- poison, life, growth, feelings
- sulphur, sensitiveness, torment

Love:
- V. light or loving desire
- VI. sound or reason
- VII. body or essence

Heavenly:
- loving fire
- meekness
- divine joy
- heaven

Earthly kingdom:
- spirit, reason, desire
- game of Venus, light of fire
- sounding, shout, distinction
- body, wood, stones, earth
- metal, grass

In eternal nature two realms exist and the possibility of two lives is included: "fire or spirit," which comes to light as "lightning of fire" in the fourth level, by virtue of freedom (again in Böhme freedom is conceived outside a relation to person, impersonally, as one of the powers of nature) determines itself towards divine unity or meekness, and thanks to this the first four elements become either the basis for the kingdom of joy or in rushing towards plurality and self, become a victim of the infernal principle, with each principle individualizing being in its own manner. "God lives identically in all things, but a thing knows nothing about God; and he is not revealed to a thing, whereas it receives power from him, but according to its own property — either from his love or from his anger; and that from which it takes it comes to light on the outside, and if there is good in it then this is as if closed for malice, as you can see in the example of the dog-rose bush, still more in other prickly things: for out of it sprouts a beautiful, sweet-scented flower, and in it lie two properties, amorous and inimical; the one that conquers, bears fruit."¹⁶⁸ The idea that God is in everything although not everything knows this, is one of Böhme's favorites.

The creaturely nature of angels, demons, and people (three *principia*) is generated or created in eternal nature. "Just as the human being is created in the image and likeness of God, so too are angels, for they are the brothers of people"; "the holy soul of a human being and the spirit of an angel have one essence and being, and there is no difference in them except only the quality of their corporeal manifestation."[169] By his insurrection the supreme angel prince Lucifer stirred up infernal fire in himself and became the devil together with his hordes, and the divine matter ("sal nitrum")[170] which he perverted served as the basis for the creation of our world (so that indirectly Lucifer participated in it); at the head is the new angel Adam, who had to replace Lucifer, and after the fall Adam was replaced by Christ. This properly is the "exterior world," "the third principle," in which we live. Creaturely nature, according to the general meaning of Böhme's system, is the final and most peripheral form of revelation or of divine self-generation. The emergence of creation in Böhme's doctrine is described in contradictory concepts: "son and creature" (when applied to angels and humankind), *"Ausgeburt"* [degeneration] and creation, and the like.[171] Especially obscure is the question concerning the relation of eternity to time, to which Böhme continually returns.[172]

In general the very question about the *creation* of spirits – of angels and humankind – remains the least elucidated in Böhme's system, and this makes it equivocal and even multivocal, for on the one hand by explaining "fiat" in the sense of divine determinism, he rejects the indeterminist act of a new creation, but at the same time now and then he speaks about this completely differently[173] or even admits that thanks to the creature's misuse of freedom, namely Lucifer's,[174] God could prove to be compelled to proceed to a new creation, i.e., to the making of the current world on the ruins of the corrupted kingdom of Lucifer so that as a result he destroys this world too.

In general the being of this world "of four elements" *im äusseren Principium* [in the external principle] has a transient and so to say precarious significance; it exists only before the definitive removal of Lucifer, and thereupon the original state of angelic heavenly corporeality must be restored. The spiritual source of the world's affirmation lies in the spirit's being turned towards the many and being averted from the Divine single Nothing,[175] and the flesh of the world must sometime burn up, be drawn away, yield its place to heavenly, angelic flesh. The present world is half the fruit of sin, error, misunderstanding; it does not have its own idea in the creative plan of God. It is only the perverted angelic world of a second principle, of the kingdom of Lucifer, of the realm of the "heart of God." "The external, in the four degenerations *(Ausgeburten)* from the elements, as the essence of the four elements, is initial, final and destructible; that is why everything that lives there must be destroyed, for the beginning of the external world is transient, since it has the goal to revert to ether, whereas the four elements revert anew into one; then God is revealed and the power of God will grow green anew like paradise in the eternal element. Then the essences of the multitude will again enter into the one, but the figure of each essence will remain in the one element."[176] "We are children of eternity, and this world is a degeneration from the eternal, and its perceptibility arises in anger; its root is eternal nature, but degenerated, for it

Divine Nothing

was not thus from eternity; it is destruction, and all must return to the eternal essence."[177] "After this life there is no rebirth: for the four elements with the eternal principle are removed, and the matrix with its division and creation stood in them; after this time it will not have to wait for anything else except for when after the termination of this world this principle will enter the ether; the essence, as it was from the ages, will become free again, it will again receive a body from the proper mother of its quality, for then before it all of its deeds will appear in its mother. For the Day of Judgment is nothing else than the awakening of the fallen asleep and the annihilation of death, which is in the four elements: for the shroud must be removed, but all must again come to life and grow green as it was from the ages. What is born out of death, as out of the four elements, like a beast and all life from the four elements, will no longer receive a body; and as their spirit is born from the four elements, it is destroyed together with the elements and only the figure of elemental essence remains, like four degenerations. But that which is from the eternal, from the one centre of life, exists and remains eternally: and all words and deeds, as having been born from the eternal, remain in the figure." And so the present world arose out of sickness; the flesh is a mask or scab or scale on heavenly flesh. This is why for Böhme the resurrection of the flesh does not exist at all ("since the four elements must be destroyed, this is why corruption exists in the human body"[178]). And if there is no resurrection, there is no transfiguration either; there is only the peeling of a scab and its removal.

One of the fundamental and most profound motifs of Böhme's system, so characteristic for the whole Neo-Platonic inclination proper to German religious thought, is a *repugnance* for the flesh, an insensitivity towards one's own body, so unexpected and apparently incomprehensible in a mysticism of nature and an investigator of a physics of God. This is stated particularly clearly with respect to sex and in a fundamental prudery towards marriage. Connected with this is the ascetical tendency of Böhme's whole practical doctrine, and what is more, a tendency painted with world-negation and nonacceptance of the world.[179] Herein lies one of the most paradoxical traits of the doctrine of the Teutonic philosopher, and Schopenhauer, Wagner, and Hartmann offer their hand to him!

SECOND SECTION

The World

I. The Creatureliness of the World

1. Creation

The world is created by God. It is a creation, and in the Trinity it has the beginning of its being: *Your hands created and fashioned me, I am yours* (Ps. 119:73, 94), says the consciousness of the creation through the lips of the psalmist. Before the face of the unfathomable things of the world, in the limitlessness of the world's expanses and the boundlessness of the world's times, in the immeasurability of the world's depths and the immensity of the world's masses it sounds, this wonderful voice, imperiously whispering: in all of its immeasurableness the world's being does not belong to it, it is *given* to the world. And in the heart of the human being is heard the same unceasing whisper: You do not have the root of your being in yourself; you are created. This voice can be unheard or imperiously and angrily stifled, for belief is free and knows no compulsion. And then inevitably a different, opposing consciousness will be suggested by the voices of the world coming out of the deep: *the world is not created,* it has its foundation in itself, it is its own creation; there is no higher being than the world's and there is nothing that would be higher than being.

Such is the utmost intuition of religious self-consciousness and the initial axiom of faith, which is accepted or rejected in the deepest reaches of integral religious spirit *before* any reflex and *earlier than* any philosophy; the latter only brings to light and realizes diverse possibilities deposited in a decision already made, and gives it a philosophical transcription.

God creates the world — in Absolute super-unity the relative and the plural, the cosmic *hen kai pan* [one and all] arises by an incomprehensible means. This origin cannot be thought of according to the category of causal connection; the world is not a result, and God is not its cause, and this is not only because God, understood as the first cause, is already included in the causal chain, in the realm of the relative, but also because *causa aequat effectum* [the cause equals the effect], the cause explains the result only by finding itself on the same plane with it, while with creation we have *metabasis eis allo genos* [a change into some other genus], a leap from the Absolute to the relative, and the causal explanation is of no use here at all. The idea of the creation of the world by God therefore does not pretend to explain the origin of the world in the sense of empirical causality; it leaves it in this sense inexplicable and incomprehensible. This is why there is absolutely no room for it in scientific thinking, which is based on the immanent continuity of experience and the universality of causal connection; it remains for this useless and foreign to it — it is in this sense wittingly an unscientific idea. The transition from the Absolute to the relative is not accessible to understanding, for it rests on an antinomy which even though it can be recognized, still from that very fact does not become comprehensible for continuous thinking. The character of the relations between the Absolute and the relative, the nature of the relative in the Absolute, is disclosed in the idea of creation.

Religious monism, the doctrine of the origin of the world as the result of an emanation of the Absolute, sacrifices the plural or the relative to the benefit of the Absolute; it requires the suicide of the relative. It does not admit real plurality and the just-as-real relative: for it *pan* [all] is only semblance or misunderstanding; reality belongs to the immovable, inert, all-devouring unity *hen* [one]. But then the question about the independent meaning of the plural and the relative, about its nature and provenance, is raised with all force: By what means do all this foam, waves, and surge come to light on the surface of the Absolute? Let it suffice for the relative to sink into the depths of the Absolute in order to disappear in it, but how was it able to appear on this surface, what meaning in and of themselves do these moments, gleams, and spray have? If we say that being, i.e., relative being in all its plurality, is the aggregate of the modes of the Absolute, i.e., that the Absolute *has* in itself the relative as modes (the doctrine of Spinoza), then in such an identification all we see is evasiveness. But if the relative is only an illusion, then the question arises again: Whose illusion? Who is dreaming? About what? What is the nature of these dreams? Is it possible to think it completely outside of and apart from the Absolute? But then the Absolute is not absolute. Or it remains to admit that the relative is permitted, posited by the Absolute itself, and then we arrive at the idea of *creation*. The world is real in its divine foundation insofar as its being is *being in the Absolute* — in this, ideas of both creation and emanation agree. But in the idea of creation the world is posited at the same time *outside* the Absolute, as the self-existent relative. Between the Absolute and the relative runs the border of the creative "let there be," and therefore the world does not represent a passive outflow, an emanation of the Absolute, like foam in an overfilled cup; rather it is a creatively, initiatively directed and realized emanation[1] — relativity as such.

The divine energies that operate in the world belong to the eternity of the Absolute, and that which belongs to the world itself in its process exists only in the relative: the world rests in the bosom of God like a child in the mother's womb. It lives its own life, its own particular processes run in it which belong to it and not to the mother, but at the same time it exists in the mother and only by the mother. The concept of creation therefore is *broader* than the concept of emanation; it includes the latter in itself, since creation is emanation *plus* something that is created by the creative *let there be!* The Absolute is superabundant, it is the inexhaustible source of super-abounding being which is the outpouring of its wealth and fullness, and in this is the truth of the idea of emanation, which is wholly included in the idea of creation. In the doctrine of emanation (e.g., in Plotinus), nonbeing, which receives this emanation, the darkness which surrounds light remains completely passive, mirror-like, dead; it comprises only a certain minus; it conditions the waning state of the Absolute. The world *arises* here by virtue of necessity, but at the same time it is for itself fortuitousness; it does not have its own task and meaning. In its being it is only *a victim* of the permissive fullness of the Absolute, up to a certain degree its wrong side. The world does not lie outside the Absolute, rather, it is the Absolute; it does not receive self-existence and is not organized in it, rather, as such it remains only the shadow of the Absolute. According to the idea of creation, it is precisely nonbeing, the "nothing" out of which the world is created, that is organized and receives life. The creative *let there be* does not leave it a fortuitous receiver or passive darkness, but makes it a world-forming principle with its own particular creaturely center, "the absolute in process" (according to the expression of V. Soloviev). Therefore in the opposition of creation and emanation the principal debate is not about God but about the world, not about the divine foundation of the world, but about its creaturely nature. Is the world only the medium that passively diffuses and weakens the rays of divine light, or does it by itself gather, reflect, and manifest them? Is there a particular focus of the world, is the world possible side by side with the Absolute, and how and in what sense is it possible? *What* is the world and *is there* a world?

The Absolute, without losing its absoluteness, places in itself the relative, as an independent being — a real, living principle. Thereby duality is introduced in the unity of the indistinguishable and in it the *coincidentia oppositorum* [coincidence of opposites] ascends to the throne: in the Absolute the distinction of God and world appears; it becomes correlative to its very self as to the relative, for God is correlative to the world. *Deus est vox relativa* [God is a relative voice][2] and in creating the world the Absolute places itself as God.

This self-bifurcation of the Absolute as absolute-relative forms the ultimate antinomic limit for thought *(Grenzbegriff)*. Here only reverential silence before the unfathomed mystery transpiring in the inner recesses of the Absolute is suitable and there is nothing more insipid than the various rational deductions of creation, the claims of gnosis, be they metaphysical or mystical.[3] But without laying claim to understanding the mystery, it is still possible to establish its presence. The logic of life and thought necessarily leads us to this as to the sole interpretation of the riddle of our own essence. In the inner recesses of his spirit a human being is conscious of the metaphysical consequences of this (if it can be thus stated) event in the Absolute, of the creation of the world by God, in the duality of his nature, in his absolute-relativity. For the human senses himself as a relative being, a grain of sand flung into the immensity of space and time. But in himself he finds a resilient awareness of his absoluteness, eternity, and godlikeness, a feeling of himself in God and of God in himself that cannot be flooded by the ocean of time and extinguished in the whirlwinds of space. The human being, as a living icon of Divinity, is also this god-world, the absolute-relative.

The Creatureliness of the World

The Absolute leaves the peace of its absoluteness unperturbed by anything, by placing in itself another center, by introducing into itself the principle of relativity. It itself becomes thereby its own potency (or "meon") by giving in itself and through itself a place to the relative, but without at the same time forfeiting its absoluteness. Creation is the Absolute's sacrifice of its absoluteness, summoned by no one or anything (for there is nothing outside the Absolute) and in this sense free and uncaused, rationally inexplicable. Of course, super-rationality does not signify anti-rationality or fatuousness as rationalists like Schopenhauer, Hartmann, Drews, etc., impiously blaspheme the wrong way around. For them the origin of the world is the result of a blind and absurd act of will, as it were a mistake of the Absolute which brought in its train the world process and plunged the Absolute itself into "the tragedy of the suffering God"; moreover this whole history has to end without a trace in the destruction of a futile universe and in a new submersion of the Absolute into a vacant and soporific peace.

The creation of the world by God, the self-bifurcation of the Absolute, is the sacrifice of the Absolute for the sake of the relative, which becomes for it "other" *(thateron)*, a creative sacrifice of love. Golgotha was not only eternally pre-established at the creation of the world as an event in time, but it also constitutes the metaphysical essence of creation. The divine "it is accomplished" proclaimed from the cross, embraces all being, refers to all creation. The voluntary sacrifice of selfless love, the Golgotha of the Absolute, is the foundation of creation, for "God *so* loved the world that he gave his Only-begotten Son," and sent him "not to judge the world, but so that the world might be saved through him" (John 3:16-17). *The world is founded by the cross,* taken upon himself by God in the name of love. Creation is an act not only of the omnipotence and wisdom of God, but also of sacrificial love; it is accomplished for the sake of enjoyment by the being "of the other" which has become in the name of the creaturely "it was very good" an unlimited love for creation. For God *is* Love, and the life of love and its greatest joy is sacrifice. Love has meaning, purpose, and reward *only in itself* and thus does not know the rational *why* — there is nothing holier or more blessed than love. For this reason creation is the absolutely free, having meaning and foundation only in itself, the absolutely independent motion of divine love, love for the sake of love, its holy folly. *Dieu est fou de l'homme* [God is mad for humanity] — Schelling recalls the boldly penetrating expression of the French author: with the madness of love God wants "a friend" (an other), and this friend can only be a human being. It is impious and absurd to speak about "tragedy in God" which by the logic of its development, as if by some "divine fate," leads necessarily to the world process. Creation is freedom from any *why and how*, the cruciform joy of the world's creation voluntarily accepted by God. Tragedy is bound up with doom, with constrained, compulsory necessity, albeit the highest sort. God is at liberty to introduce himself into the tragic process of world history, while remaining in himself and for himself free from it. This is why in the Absolute itself there is no place for tragedy, which is rooted in the antagonism of the shattered forces of relative being.

Creation is therefore an act of the measureless humility of the Absolute, which renounces its own actuality: *love-humility* is the ultimate and universal virtue of Christianity. It is the ontological basis of creation. By giving a place in itself to the world with its relativity, the Absolute in its love humbles itself before the creature — in truth the depths of divine love-humility are unsearchable!

2. Creaturely Nothing

Out of what is the world made? In what is the basis of creatureliness? God fashioned the world out of his own self, out of his essence, answers J. Böhme;[4] the world is a mode of absolute substance — in different ways but in the identical sense reply G. Bruno, Spinoza, pantheists of different nuances, and monists; consequently the inevitable conclusion suggests itself — *the world does not exist* in its own being and relativity. Only the Absolute exists. *The world is created out of nothing* — Christian revelation teaches. Between God and creature, between the Absolute and the relative, there lay *nothing*. *Nothing*ness — behold the basis of creation, the edge of being, the limit beyond which lies dead-end bottomless nonbeing, "the outer darkness," foreign to any light. This feeling of being immersed in nothing, the awareness of one's ontological nothingness, is terrifying and excruciating — a bottomless precipice inspires dread even in fairy tales (this motif is encountered in a Russian folktale). One can be saved from dread before nonbeing only by coming out of the vertiginous abyss and turning one's face towards the Sun, towards the source of any fullness, having transferred one's ontic center out of oneself beyond the limits of the self and into God. Then nonbeing moves away into nonbeing, disappears like a shadow, dissipates like a phantom; there is no longer nonbeing, there are only the triumphant, graciously outpouring rays of being. But when the sun's light grows dim in the soul, when the creature withdraws into itself and stops to feel itself in God — a chilling shiver comes on again, nothing feels like a deathly, gaping hole, like pug-nosed death, and then you begin to seem for your own self to be only an empty shell, having no ontic core. "If you hide your face, they are fretful; if you remove the spirit from them, they pass away and return to their dust; if you send your spirit, they are created, and you renew the face of the earth. May the Lord be praised forever!" (Ps. 104:29-31).

Knowledge about nothing as the basis of the world's being is the subtlest intuition of the creature about its creatureliness. *You are created* means that everything is given to you, even you yourself; what belongs to you, what has come from you is only this underground, affectionately and carefully sheltered by the roses of being. The nature of humankind is marked by genius and nothingness. The underground is the wrong side of being, an imagined greatness that has received reality. Every creature has an underground, although it is able not to know about this, and not to sink into it. This ignorance is the privilege of childhood and the attainment of sanctity; by sinking into it, each person lives through the eerie cold and dampness of the grave. To want oneself in one's own selfhood, to lock oneself in one's creatureliness as in the absolute, means to want the underground and to be affirmed in it.[5] And therefore the real hero of the underground is Satan who fell in love with himself as God, and who was affirmed in his own selfhood and turned out to be captive to his own underground. In his nothing he desired to see the divine all, and he is compelled to retreat into the kingdom of Hades, peopled with phantoms and shadows, as in the chambers of a brilliant god. The beauty of Lucifer and the Demon that so enticed Byron and Lermontov is only a pose; it hides within itself deception and insipidness like expensive and luxurious secondhand clothing, worn over soiled linens, like a life luxuriating in debt and without any hope of repayment, like a dullard feigning genius. Beneath the demonic cloak are hidden Khlestakov and Chichikov;[6] the fairy-like demon turns into a hideous devil with a hoof and a head-cold. Vulgarity is the hidden underbelly of demonism.

There are two abysses in the human soul: dead-end nothing, an infernal underground, and God's heaven which has imprinted the image of the Lord. Known to the human being is the pain of impotence and lack of talent: ashamed of his poverty he grows weak with disgust in the envious and stuffy underground. But saving love gives wings to genius; it teaches how to become God's poor man,[7] to forget his own I and then achieve the measureless endowments of a blade of grass, a sparrow, of each creation of God. It teaches how to rejoice over everything like a child, to give thanks like a son.

Usually we are afraid to draw close to those abysses; we roam along trodden paths of mediocrity in a featureless life. But not for sleepy peace — the human being is created as a son of abysses, swaddled with terror and danger. Fearfully we step away from the precipice, quite wishing to forget about the edge. We do not fall into mortal sin, for we are virtuous in a moderate way, and wanton in trifles, hopelessly reasonable and imperturbably sober. But God does not need our thrift; he calls us to the madness of his love. God manages without us in his work, for he knows his paths, but in the heart of a human being who has closed his heart shut, hell reigns — the impotence of love. The being of humankind is secured on the abysses; one cannot escape from them under the foliage of ordinariness. . . .

But can one speak of the being of nonbeing, about an existing nothing? The fact is that even the ancient elder Parmenides stated:

Never and nowhere is it said that what is not was;
Keep your thought from such a path of trials.[8]

Parmenides teaches us that there is only being, nonbeing does not exist at all; true, he had in view with this his immovable, absolute One, the substance of the world to which alone being belongs, for outside of it there is nothing. Applied to such a concept of the absolute, evidently, the idea of nonbeing has no meaning. But this does not work so simply when applied to the operation of the Absolute, to the creative act by which it summons into existence that which hitherto did not exist, i.e., nonbeing, and creates out of nothing.

Here it is necessary for us once again to dwell on the analysis of *not* when applied to creatureliness. There can be two meanings of this *not* according to the sense of creaturely nothing, to which two types of Greek negation correspond: *ou* and *mē* (*alpha privative* is not relevant at all for this case). The first corresponds to full negation of being — *nothing*, while the second corresponds only to its nonmanifestation and nondefinition — *something*.⁹ This second aspect of nonbeing, *mē on*, strictly speaking refers rather to the realm of being. *Mē on*, as the possibility of possibilities, is the universal mother of being, through whose womb all being passes (it is not for nothing that even such advocates of the universal deduction of all being as Hegel have recourse to *mē*, as does Cohen with this doctrine of "pure origination"). Therefore the whole wealth and fullness of being belong to the *mē on*, although potential and not manifested. One can thus speak about it and about nonbeing only in relation to already-manifested being, but not at all in the sense of emptiness, the absence of being. *Something is,* the *mē on* exists, and between nothing and something lies an incomparably greater gulf than between something and a what, just as a greater gulf separates sterility from pregnancy than pregnancy from birth. The *mē on* is pregnancy, the *ouk on* is sterility. In order that a certain what could arise out of nonbeing, *ouk on* must become *mē on;* it must overcome its emptiness and be freed from its sterility.

And so, once again, in what sense is the world created out of nothing: out of *ouk on* or *mē on*? This dismembered posing of the question already marks out two possibilities, corresponding to the duality of meaning of creaturely *not*. If we allow that the world arose out of divine *mē on*, this will mean that it is not created at all, but is engendered or emanated, generally speaking that it was realized in God in one way or another. The border between the world and God is erased; the world then is the *mē on* of God — we arrive at pantheism with either the acosmism or atheism that springs from it. The other possibility, for us the only admissible one, is that the world is created out of nothing in the sense of *ouk on,* and that is why its investment with *mē on* was the first, fundamental, and essential act of creation. This conversion of *ouk on* into *mē on* is the fashioning of the common matter of creatureliness, of the Great Mother of the whole natural world. In this fundamental and maximum act of creation we have to do with complete incomprehensibility, for it is impossible *to comprehend* by what manner *mē on* arises in *ouk on;* here again is the limit for thought. The creature cannot *grasp* its own proper creation; this always remains a riddle for it, a miracle, a mystery, but *to identify* what has been accomplished is for human consciousness fully in keeping with its powers, and the analysis of this self-consciousness comprises the task for thought too, which must assiduously unravel this knot of ontological interlacements, without tearing the threads to pieces.

The World

But the ancient elder raises his voice anew, insisting that only that which is *to on* (and as its state, *mē on*) exists; there is no *ouk on*, that which is not, at all. How and in what sense can that which is not serve as the basis for creation? Yes, in the Absolute One there is no place for nonbeing as *ouk on* — the wise old man is correct. But we must nevertheless insistently point out that in the Absolute there is also no being which correlative to nonbeing, linked with it, does not exist outside nonbeing; the latter is only posited in being against the background of being as its border. *The Absolute is higher than being;* this is what Parmenides knew, thanks to which he drew it into the dialectic of the relative, i.e., of being.

By the act of creation God posits being, but in nonbeing, or to say it another way, by the same act by which he posits being he co-posits nonbeing as its boundary, milieu, or shadow. *Omnis definitio est negatio,* Spinoza said; every being consists of *yes and no,* according to the brilliant expression of J. Böhme. Therefore although Parmenides remains correct that in the Absolute as that which abides above being even nonbeing does not exist, God indirectly gives being to nonbeing when he posits the relative, i.e., being. *God is the originator not only of being but also of nonbeing.* This formula, dizzying in its boldness and profundity of meaning, belongs to none other than the mysterious author of "the Areopagiticum" and its commentator St. Maximus the Confessor — pillars of Orthodox theologizing.[10] In this they rest of course on the work of ancient thought and above all on Plato who in his surprising *Parmenides,* and likewise in the *Sophist,* gave a masterful analysis of the question about the connection of being and nonbeing.[11] This analysis was partly recaptured in recent philosophy by Hegel and in general constitutes an inalienable achievement of philosophical thought.[12]

Is pure nonbeing outside every positive relation to being, i.e., absolute *ouk on,* accessible to our experience or thinking? One can pursue it as one might chase after one's own back or shadow, but nonbeing exists for us only as the boundary of being, establishing its relativity. Being is submerged in nonbeing and from all sides it is bathed with its waters. Outside such a correlation with being, nonbeing, *ouk on,* cannot be conceived directly but only indirectly, by a certain "illegitimate judgment" — *hapton logismōi tini nothōi,* according to Plato's famous expression about matter in *Timaeus* 52 B. The same Plato observed that "the not existing as such cannot be correctly pronounced or expressed or thought; rather it is unintelligible, unutterable, inexpressible and absurd."[13] The absolute null of being as its sole pure possibility without any actualization remains transcendent for the creature, which always represents the indissoluble alloy of being and nonbeing. But this "outer darkness," this naked potentiality, in the underground of creatureliness, is like some second center (pseudo-center) of being, competing with the Sun of the world, the source of its fullness. For the heroes of the underground it has a unique attraction; it summons in them the irrational, blind will towards nothing, a dizzying yearning for the abyss, similar to what is felt if one looks down from a great height. The kingdom of nihilism, the cult of nothing, hell, exists only at the expense of the positive forces of being, by an ontological theft.

But in general can one manage without the being of nonbeing, i.e., without the collocation of nonbeing with being? Can one place being *outside* its relativity by allowing, as is said, *absolute being?* This is just as impossible as it is to get along without shadows and half-light when perceiving space or geometrical bodies. Nonbeing, nothing, everywhere is translucent in being; it participates in being, similar to how death in a certain sense participates in life, as its wrong side, or darkness in light and cold in heat. All that exists is run through with the dialectic of being and nonbeing, everything simultaneously is and is not, begins and ends, arises in nonbeing and submerges in it, *comes to be*. According to Hegel, being and nonbeing are synthesized in *Werden*, becoming, coming to be: everything *will be*, is found *in becoming, panta rhei* — everything flows, proclaimed ancient Heraclitus, everything only *comes to be*. In Hegel on that score there is the brilliant formula "that there is nothing that is not *a middle state between being and nothing*," and *"becoming is the disappearing of being in nothing, and of nothing in being,* and the disappearing of being and nothing on the whole; but it rests immediately on the difference of the same."[14]

Coming to be (to gignomenon — in Plato's *Timaeus)* is that mysterious, creative synthesis of being and nonbeing which also expresses for itself the essence of creatureliness, of everything relative. Creatureliness is above all and in its essence *mē on, being-nonbeing,* and in this sense one must understand meonal prime matter too, *materia prima,* in which the whole fullness of creaturely being is already included, where *everything* is sown. But alongside of it, in the cold of death, as in the burning rotation "of the fiery wheel of being" the abyss of *ouk on* is felt, the edge of being, the outer darkness, which gazes with its empty eye-sockets. This "dark and difficult form" *(chalepon kai amydron eidos)* as Plato baptized the world's prime matter, was subjected by him to an incomparable analysis in *Timaeus*.[15]

Matter-mother — the meon, is the necessary basis of being, origination, and annihilation. If something comes to be, it necessarily arises out of something and returns somewhere, for the airless realm of pure nonbeing remains beyond the limits of attainability. A mother's bosom is necessary, which is simultaneously the womb (the Platonic *ekmageion*) and the tomb. In other words, it is Great Mother Earth, whose features the Greeks honored under the name of Demeter *(gē mētēr)*; it is that Earth which God created "in the beginning" at the creation of the world (together with "heaven"). Having been seeded by the creative "let there be" it produced out of its bosom all that exists and will receive back into its meonal inner recesses everything that "is earth," that was born from it.

Great mother, damp earth! In you we are born, by you we are nourished, we touch you with our feet, and we are turned back into you. Children of earth, love your mother, kiss her frenziedly, bathe her with your tears, sprinkle her with sweat, drench her with blood, and satiate her with your bones! For nothing perishes in her, she keeps everything in herself, a mute memory of the world; she gives life and fruit to everything. Whoever does not love the earth and does not feel her maternity is a slave and social outcast, a pitiable rebel against their mother, the progeny of nonbeing. Mother earth! From you that flesh was born which became the womb for the incarnated God, from you he took his most pure Body! In you he reposed for three days in the grave! Mother earth! From you sprout forth grain and grape vines, whose fruit becomes the Body and Blood of Christ in the most holy sacrament, and to you this holy flesh returns! You silently keep in yourself all the fullness and loveliness of creation.

Land of My Birth (from the History of a Conversion)

Unexpectedly, far off, the fateful news overtook me. But I hoped that she would not depart from the world without giving a blessing from the grave. I hastened to bid farewell. Long was the sad path from the sparkling, luxuriant south to the quiet, repose, and silence of my family fields. Oh, this hazy, frosty morning with empty fields grown white! Here I languished in private with God and nature, absent from her final hours. A letter arrived, and in it I read "she is laid to rest, beautiful." Oh yes, I knew that this had to be so: the anxious, poignant fire of life was extinguished, her fiery wheel brought her burning course to a stop, she has left necessity, distortion, captivity. And the primordial purity was laid bare, the nature of the soul woven out of a child's trustfulness towards people and a child's faith in God. She always seemed cloudy, but now was clear, always agitated, now calm, always uneasy, today she rests in peace. And the body became joyfully lucid. But how poignant the separation, how important it is to see this, to grasp the mystery of this death. And most of all I wanted to cry like a child, to lament, to kiss. But these cruel hours passed. With sorrowful joy I was seeing the places and faces of home. How newly, how differently I experienced this meeting! But now there is no time for these feelings, for she calls and waits. It is terrible, agonizing to approach one's home church, and the waiting, open grave. I prostrated myself before it, this bright sacred object, overshadowed by the farewell blessing, like a trembling boy on the breast of his mother. . . . "O Lord, grant rest to your departed servant," the funeral hymn burst like a fervent prayerful wave into my half-conscious state — my home Church prayed this for her. And they carried her to the grave to complete the final mystery of life. "You are earth and you will depart unto earth." Oh no, not with sorrow, not with annihilation do the words of the Lord's judgment sound, but with great, measureless joy. Black, loose, and soft the earth fell unheard and tenderly on the coffin lid; like a caring mother she was laying to rest the worn-out wayfarer. The Great Mother opened her womb. And there the bells pealed out the funeral lament loftily, solemnly and entrancingly, sadly and severely, and it seemed that heaven exulted and sang. My soul had grown weak from torment and blessedness. Consciousness took leave. Grief passed over into ecstatic joy. My heart burned and trembled. Hidden strings were laid bare and sounded with a wonderful, unearthly sound: death and birth, marriage and burial, heaven and earth. I took a handful of earth and divided it: one part I committed to her in the grave, the remainder I took away with me, just as a soldier who is leaving on a far and dangerous march will pick up some native soil in his palm. And I placed it in an icon without reasoning and without hesitating, obedient to the instinctive, faithful voice of my heart. As I pray before the icon I bow before this final gift, holy earth, relics, the flesh of resurrection. . . .

Nothing, as being-nonbeing, is the *specificum* of creatureliness, its — strange to say — privilege and ontological distinction.[16] We are not only children of heaven but also children of earth; we have our own personal mother who shields us against the all-consuming fire of the Absolute and generates us towards the autonomy of creaturely being. *Nothing*, in separating the creature from the Absolute, forms as it were its own photosphere around it and gives being to it for its own sake and in itself. The world is autonomous precisely because it is included in nothing, or is created out of nothing. It is remarkable that as soon as the specific feeling of creatureliness or of being created out of nothing begins to grow dull, and the world hereby merges with the Absolute by becoming its mode or hypostasis — it simultaneously becomes ghostlike, loses its autonomy, and pantheism (or cosmotheism) proves to be acosmism. In fact if one were to remove nothing as the basis of creation from thought and feeling, the difference between the Absolute and the world, between the Creator and the creation, vanishes into thin air; the world in itself represents the absolute or, what is the same, absoluteness is ascribed to being, which in reality is correlative to nonbeing, and thus generally speaking is relative. It is obvious, further, that if one is to regard the universe as the Absolute itself ("substance" or divinity), then it cannot be considered as such in its ontic aspect, i.e., in its coming to be, *Werden*. The latter must then inevitably be negated in its ontological authenticity. The real *all*-unity hereby is offered in sacrifice to all-devouring, abstract unity.

The prototype of such philosophizing is given already in the doctrine of Parmenides. In modern philosophy Spinoza's doctrine of the one substance, "in the nature of which existence is inherent" (*Ethics*, theorem 7), deals the most with this, whereas all multiple being turns out to be "modes" of this substance. In a certain sense J. Böhme's system also handles this topic (see above). It is especially instructive to observe the same in G. Bruno, in whose worldview monism still contends with the Christian conception of the world, while lacking the geometric consistency and firmness of Spinozism. In this enthusiast of nature, as soon as this enthusiasm leads him towards pantheism and identifying the world soul with Divinity, the world and its plurality lose their autonomy, acquiring the significance of accidents of a single immovable substance.[17]

The concept of all-unity contains the notion that the opposition of the one and the whole leads nowhere, and this notion is preserved for as long as we take no notice that being exists in nothing, that it is joined to nonbeing and is relative by nature. For this reason, the idea of absolute being, despite its longevity, belongs to a number of philosophical misunderstandings. *The Absolute is higher than being*, it creates being and this creation is creation out of nothing, the placing of being in nonbeing.[18]

The philosophy of monism, which recognizes only the One as a substance closed in on itself, is ignorant of motherhood (and thus, of course, of fatherhood too): for it nothing is born for being, and fierce all-devouring Cronos eternally eats his children. He returns his own seed to himself, without letting it flow out as fertilizing rain on the nothing thirsting for fecundation. In its view the Absolute does not open itself in creation, does not become father of all that is, just as nothing does not become mother, the *mē on* of all, but remains in the "outer darkness" of absolute *ouk on*. And on the contrary, if one were to assume that in placing in itself the relative, or being, the Absolute becomes "the Father of all," then nothing, the nonexisting basis of creation, becomes the Mother, the *mē on* containing everything; it becomes the potential all-unity of the world. The world's independence from God, its extra-divineness or relativity, is established precisely through nothing, its basis, through the connectedness of being with nonbeing. In the Absolute there is no NOT whatsoever, there is only the eternal YES (or rather super-YES); in the relative every *yes* has its *not*.

3. The World as Theophany and Theogony

The mystery of creation, which is revealed in the antinomy of creatureliness, consists in the fact that the creative powers of being, which have as their source the Absolute itself, were poured out into nothing. The world is created by the word of God and lives by the power of God.[19] The whole fullness of being belongs to God, it is his blessedness. The world's *all* in its positive basis is divine; the world abides in God, insofar as the Absolute embraces all in itself. It is impossible to draw the contrary conclusion, which is done in pantheism or cosmotheism, namely that God is the world. However, it is correct to affirm that the world is contained in God, and that God acts in the world. To put it differently, worldly being is divine being, or according to the daring expression of Nicholas of Cusa, *omnis creatura sit quasi infinitas aut Deus creatus* [every creature may be, as it were, infinity or a created God];[20] the world is a "created God." It is the unity of the absolute and nothing, the absolute in the relative or the relative in the Absolute; the absolute brings to a halt, abrogates its actual absoluteness, it makes it potential in order to make room for the relative which thereby participates in the absolute. By creation from nothing the Absolute establishes as it were two centers — the eternal and the creaturely. In the inner recesses of self-sufficing eternity the "absolute in process" appears, a second center. Alongside the Absolute which is super-essentially, being appears in which the Absolute discloses itself as Creator, is revealed in it, is realized in it, and participates in being, and in this sense the world is *God in process*. God *is* only in the world and for the world; in an absolute sense it is impossible to speak about his being. In creating the world God thereby flings himself into creation; he seemingly makes himself the creation. God is drained into nothing, as he converts it into material for his image and likeness. He gives it full freedom of actualization in creatures, while he himself becomes potential. Ignorant of envy, he wants to live in creatures and *become* in them. He honors the nature of the creature which is nothing, more than his own might, for he wants himself in creation, in it — in the other, by wishing to have a friend, independent with respect to himself, although wholly indebted to him for its being. God knows how to wait; for the consummation of the ages, when the Son will subject everything to the Father and God will be "all in all," is separated from the initial *let there be* by a lengthy historical process, which is the gift of God's omnipotence to creaturely freedom. As the prime source of being, God is always in the world, he holds everything in his right hand, but at the same time the world abides outside God, is submerged in creaturely self-existence, i.e., in *nothing*.

In this way the maximum cosmological antinomy is obtained: God, as the Absolute, has in himself the fullness of his life, and absolutely nothing can be added or subtracted (just as how no finite magnitude that itself reverts to zero in relation to the infinite can alter — either increase or decrease — mathematical infinity, ∞). God is an unchanging entity, wholly satisfied and wholly blessed, and the world process neither adds anything to him nor subtracts anything from him. But at the same time God is also Creator of the world. He lives and acts in the world; as God's creation, neither modal nor accidental being belongs to it. Rather, entirely real and nonillusory being does so, for it is real by the realness of its Creator. But, consequently, God himself *becomes* in the world and through the world, he is subject to the process, and one can thus say that God is not complete insofar as the world is not complete, and he is not absolute, for he is still not "all in all." He is correlative to the creature which in virtue of its freedom and its nature can distance itself from God in its nothingness, can close itself off from him by it. In that case God is and remains its living basis, but for nature he is potential and not actual.

Inasmuch as the cosmic process is theocosmic or theogonic, the cosmos is theocosmos or cosmotheos. But this cosmic theogony does not exclude but even presupposes at the same time that the world as the revelation of Divinity is theophany. Therefore the theophanic and theogonic character of the world process not only do not exclude each other but rather they condition each other, because *theogony is real theophany* — the generation of the One Who Is pre-eternally. Here we immediately stumble into a cosmological antinomy that presents itself as a watershed: from this crest slopes go in both directions — towards pantheistic monism and to Manichaean dualism, which accepts alongside God an anti-god, a demiurge, an independent (and evil) principle of the world. The one and the other direction are engendered by the aspiration to rationalize the super-rational: both monism and dualism equally are the outcome of rationalism (even if a mystical rationalism), where God is conceived according to the schemata and categories of eternal being. Thus here only the alternative *either/or* is allowed, where the voice of religious consciousness authoritatively says *both/and*. God is both the Absolute and the Creator of the world, both That Which Is super-subsistently and God as the basis of all being. In the central Christian dogma of the union of two natures in Christ, Divine and creaturely-human, *without division and without merging*, this thought receives an openly antinomical and thus divinely inspired formulation. The Lord Jesus Christ is God, the Second Person of the Blessed Trinity; in him "the whole fullness of Divinity dwells bodily." As God, in his absoluteness, he is completely transcendent to the world, supernal, but at the same time he is completely Human, possessing the whole fullness of creaturely, worldly being, in truth a world-human, itself relative, where divinity and humanity are united in him without division and without merging, in a manner mysterious and incomprehensible for the mind.[21]

The attempt somehow to master rationally the unthinkable mystery of Divinity in the world, to make it comprehensible, inevitably leads either to contradictions or to patent simplification and removal of the problem (as in monism); this is why there never was and never can be a noncontradictory rational metaphysics that has to do with the ultimate problems of the world's being. Philosophy must consciously reckon with the initial antinomies of religious self-consciousness in its constructs — this is what constitutes the religious "critique of reason." Is God transcendent to the world? No, for he abides in the world, in him we live and move and are; he gave a promise to remain with us in the world forever, now and always and unto the ages of ages. But does this mean that God is immanent to the world? Also no. For he lives in unapproachable light; between him and the creature lies a bottomless abyss — *nothing*. Further, is God subject to temporality, do changes occur in him, is anything added to his fullness by the creation of the world and the world process? No, nothing is added, for he is absolute fullness and perfection. But — given this — is divine fullness realized in this world too, is God drawn into the world process with its consummations, times, and seasons? Yes, for the world is still not completed, and God himself raised the cross and was incarnated for the sake of the world's salvation through a human being. Further, does the world limit God, existing outside of him and alongside him? No, for God, as the Absolute, has nothing outside himself. Yes, because God governs the world, but does not reign in it; the Kingdom of God has not yet come in power, and the world lives by its own extra-divine life. On these and similar antinomies the cosmological doctrine of God rests, and there is no need to explain this with the unfailingly logical defectiveness of this or that separate construct and to hope in this that the difficulty will someday be overcome. The task of thought here is precisely *to lay bare* the antinomy, to stumble into its cul-de-sac and to accept with the spiritual effort of the humility of reason that it is above reason: this will be the highest act of understanding. It is not hard to see that the cosmological antinomy cited is only a further disclosure of the basic religious antinomy outlined by "negative theology." God, as "negative theology" knows him, is the Absolute NOT, completely transcendent to the world and to every being; but as God, he is correlative to the world, he participates in being, *he is*. The initial antinomy that *the Absolute is God* is expressed in cosmology as *the all-blessed and self-sufficing God is the Creator of the world.*

However, the "cunning of reason," even when it has perceived the invincible difficulty, all the same attempts to get around it, to use a method already familiar to us of *substituting* antinomy with dialectical contradiction, having turned antithesis into dialectic. In the given case the purpose can be attained by an interpretation of the divine world-creation as corresponding to a certain moment in the dialectic of the Absolute itself, to its inner life, or as a mode of some divine prime essence. But this dialectical-mystical focus, in removing the antinomy, at the same time annihilates the very problem that it wants to solve, be-

The Creatureliness of the World

cause for dialectical monism neither God nor the world, neither the Absolute nor the relative, in their opposition exists. This comes out especially clearly in the doctrine of Meister Eckhart who "asks" to break through beyond God, "to be liberated from God," and at the same time, of course, from the world. God the Creator is for him only a definite and limited stage in the Absolute, and essentially, is not God, but some sort of demiurge, a cosmic hypostasis of the Absolute. This doctrine of Eckhart is a manifest heresy and lie. The same question about creation, about its theogonic and theophanic meaning, underlies the deep philosophical investigation of Schelling in his last system (in *Philosophy of Mythology* and *Philosophy of Revelation*).

On the one hand, Schelling forcefully insists on the full transcendence of God to the world, and in this sense, on his full freedom in the creation (or noncreation) of the world. God, in whose power he happens to place or not to place extra-divine being, *in cuius potestate omnia sunt* (namely *omnia quae praeter ipsum existere possunt*) [in whose power all things are, namely, all things except himself which can exist], this God is the whole *(der Ganze)* God, not only the form *(Gestalt)* of God, but God as absolute person.[22] "It was in God's power constantly to keep by himself only as a possibility this possibility of being-outside-oneself, which appeared to him only as such *(an sich selbst)*, this possible alterity *(Andernheit)*. But it was characteristic for the one in whose power this possibility was, freely to expose this possibility which is strictly a mystery of his divinity (!), not in order that it should thereby receive extra-divine being, which negates God, but so that it would be clearer and more evident, as what is really manifested, and thus it would consequently be overcome and converted into something theurgic and conscious of the divine" *(Philosophie,* I, 304). "If 'the noble spirit of humankind' experiences the need to be understood by another, then so much the more is that need — the only one which, besides, the Divinity who needs nothing has — to place before oneself another in order to convert it into something that knows of itself. . . . Which is why as Plato says it befits the divinity that knows not envy not to remain in that *actus purissimus,* which we could call eternal theogony and which is shown as devouring *(verzehrend)* with respect to everything outside itself, but rather to make this *actus purissimus* a conceivable, discernible fact *(Vorgang),* all the moments of which would need to be united and arranged in the latter, reduced to the unity of consciousness" (304).

But on the other hand, the process of world-creation is, in the eyes of Schelling, also objectively theogonic (as he often defines it), for in it the potencies in God receive being, "are strained" *(Spannung).* In the state of being manifested through the world they correspond to the three hypostases of the holy Trinity. In other words, in the theogonic world process God is generated for his own sake as trihypostatic. In particular "the principle of creation is at the same time the principle of the Son's generation" (323), and therefore of the origin of the separate hypostasis of the Father. One can speak of the eternity of the Son only in the sense that "he is foreknown in advance and loved by the Father. But the Son in this sense is the existing Son only for the Father, he has still not come forward from the Father, and is still not placed outside him as Son. This separation of the Son, which can be properly called birth, can be conceived of only where in general there is talk of separation, i.e., in the principle of creation" (321). Schelling consciously argues against the idea of the eternity of the Son's generation, seeing in this an echo of the disputes with Arius, which had in view another question, namely, about the Son's creatureliness. "Eternal generation," Schelling declares with rationalistic self-confidence, "is a *contradictio in adjecto,* for there is no generation which would not presuppose a relative *non esse*" (331). "The second form *(Gestalt)* of divine being, by being separated from this being, receives the possibility to be a particular person in itself" (333). "Consequently, the second potency, having been separated for itself, still cannot be called God; it is restored in its divinity only when the first and third potencies are restored to themselves anew, i.e., their unity is restored — at the end of creation; and since through the overcoming of the opposite being it also becomes the lord of this being, as initially only the Father was, then it becomes person, as primordially the Father alone was person; and it is the Son, who has equal lordship with the Father. But this is applicable to the third potency as well when through the operation of the second that which exists outside itself is completely overcome and exhausted, and is likewise again restored in being" (333-34). "I ask you," Schelling sums up, "to consider as established the following: (1) The essence of that which the New Testament calls the Son, is eternally in God and is swallowed up in the *actus purissimus* of divine life, is itself with God, *theos.* (2) From that moment *(von da)* when the Father perceives in the forms of his being the possibility of another being, or from that moment when these forms appear to him as potencies, i.e., therefore from eternity, from that moment when he is Father, the second potency presents itself to him as a future Son; he therefore already has in it a future Son whom he comes to know in it in advance, in whom properly he draws up the plan *(Vorsatz)* of the world. This is why the apostle Paul says: in him all is created (Col. 1:16). But here the Son is only in the Father, he has not yet come out of the Father; but (3) even outside *(praeter)* the Father — at first as potency — he is placed only with the principle of creation, he is *the actual* Son only after he has realized himself through overcoming oppositions, consequently, at the end of creation; and as Son he is declared externally (before the world) at a still later moment" (332).

From this the direct conclusion suggests itself that there is still no Holy

The Creatureliness of the World

Trinity, for it is only created or generated in the world process. The epoch of the Holy Spirit has not begun and the epoch of the Son has not ended, and this is why the second is not fully generated, and the first hypostasis with it, and the whole trihypostatic Divinity is found *im Werden.* "At the time of the process of creation there is plurality, but only of potencies, not of persons. God as creator is indeed a plurality, but not of persons *(Gott als Schöpfer ist zwar Mehrere, aber nicht mehrere Personen).* . . . On the contrary, at the end of creation (but only at the end), when the second and third hypostases through the overcoming of opposite being have realized themselves, then there are really present *(da sind)* three persons and not three Gods" (337). The divine hypostases receive in Schelling, according to his own expression, *"die Natur und Funktion kosmischer, demiurgischer Kräfte"* [the nature and function of cosmic, demiurgic powers] (340). Leaving aside the particulars of Schelling's doctrine of trinitarity,[23] it is necessary to acknowledge that with this doctrine he introduces process into the Divinity itself and thereby falls into a contradiction with his own affirmation of transcendence, and thus of the absoluteness of God. Although full freedom in world-creation is ascribed to God by Schelling, it nonetheless comes out that, having abstained from the latter, the Divinity itself remains in *actus purissimus,* proximate to potentiality, and is not generated not only for the world but even for its own self. With this is negated the inner-Trinitarian, inner-divine life in the Divinity outside creation; incompleteness and defectiveness are ascribed to Divinity such that it necessarily needs completion by creation, which is at the same time the self-creation of Divinity. Schelling removes thereby the transcendence and absoluteness of Divinity outside the world and sets out on the path of monism which he repudiated, of a dynamic divinization of the world, for which the world is a becoming or potentializing God (i.e., he proves himself a kindred spirit of Hartmann and Drews whose doctrines are inimical to Christianity). For all his profundity and exegetical skill one has to acknowledge that Schelling introduces opinions about Divinity and the holy Trinity that are completely inadmissible for Christianity, and his whole "deduction" of trinitarity is a sad attempt of presumptuous speculation, of that same treacherous "mystical rationalism" with which he rightly reproaches Böhme. Schelling wants "to explain," and "to deduce" that which the voice of religious feeling and philosophical criticism equally enjoin to *accept* as the fact of divine life, established in religious experience and revelation. Of course, one can interpret this fact philosophically, by giving it a metaphysical expression, by uncovering its philosophical depths — the philosopher can and even must do this, but together with Schelling, who is here wistfully brought close to his rival Hegel, he cannot lay claim to the disclosure of the mystery and genesis of triune life in Divinity, to the establishing of its "philosophical necessity" (317). This is rationalistic lack of taste, which one would least of all want to see in Schelling, and he is paid for it not only with heresy but also with contradiction of his own self. He completely correctly ascertains that "the idea of trinitarity in God is not as it were a separate dogma, a separate thesis in Christianity, but its presupposition or something without which Christianity would not exist in the world" (316); however, this is so precisely because God pre-eternally is the Holy Trinity in his absolute transcendence, and the creation of the world cannot add to or remove anything from this fullness and absoluteness of inner-Trinitarian life. God, as the Absolute, consequently, is the self-sufficing or wholly satisfied, wholly blessed entity, and cannot have either increase or loss, for such an assumption would straight-away lower God to a merging with the world, would lead to divinization of the world or "monism." By introducing process into Divinity itself, Schelling aspires to disclose the seal of trinitarity in the universe, which is visible for every focused mind, even outside Christian revelation. The image of the Trinity is present in the spirit of the human being (Blessed Augustine) — yes, and how else would the Savior's promise be possible that the Holy Trinity will come and make its dwelling in the soul of the one who fulfills the commandments? The seal of trinitarity lies on all of nature (as J. Böhme speaks of this with particular energy); the image of the holy Trinity is imprinted on world history, for the divine hypostases are disclosed in the succession of times. However, precisely that which can be disclosed in time exists from eternity, and Schelling, instead of this, introduces time itself, i.e., the world process, into the inner recesses of Divinity, and defines it with this.

4. Time and Eternity

The mystery of creatureliness is manifested in the contradictory self-consciousness of the creature concerning the *eternity and temporality* of its being. Time is an actual synthesis of being and nonbeing, coming to be, *Werden*. The present, which is always being absorbed by the past and is rushing to the future, is as it were a point having no measurement, moving in the ocean of meonal being: of the half-being of the past and the future, of being that is no longer and being that is not yet. In the intuition of temporality the antinomy of creatureliness makes itself felt — of the divine principle which is submerged in nothing and which has engendered it by itself. For time is the transience and nullity of all that is, but at the same time the possibility of all that was, the *panta rhei* of being. The very consciousness of temporality, with its burning heat and sharpness, is begotten by a feeling of the super-temporality, of the nontemporality of life; it is born only when gazing into time from eternity. Envious Cronos jealously devours his children, by killing, depreciating, overthrowing everything; life is some sort of triumph of universal dying. There is hardly any other thing to which the poets and wise men of the whole world have devoted so much inspiration as to the screams and groanings of temporality. Let whoever wishes to feel this somber lyric poetry with the greatest power become familiar with the majestic "office of burial" inscribed with the name of the inspired hymnographer John of Damascus.

Idiomelon,[24] Tone 1: Which sweetness of life is not privy to sorrow? Which glory stands immutable on earth? All is weaker than the shades, all is more appealing than sleepiness; in a single moment death will receive all these things....

Tone 3: All things human are vain which do not remain after death: wealth does not remain, glory does not exist, for all these things are consumed by approaching death....

Tone 4: Where is worldly passion? Where is thought of passing things? Where are gold and silver? Where are the multitude of slaves and fame? All is dust, all is ash, all is shadow....

Tone 5: I recalled the prophet who cried "I am earth and ash" and again I looked in the graves and saw naked bones and I said "for who is king or soldier, who is rich or poor, who is just or sinner?"

Stikhera:[25] What is our life like? A blossom and smoke, and in truth the morning dew. For come here, let us look clearly at the graves: where is bodily good, where youth? Where are the eyes and fleshly gaze? All has withered like grass, all is consumed....

Come here, brothers, in the grave we shall see ash and dust, out of it were we fashioned, where now do we go? What were we? Which one was poor or rich, which one a lord? Which one was a freeman? Are they not all dust? The loveliness of face has burned up, and death has withered all the color of youth.

In truth all living things are vanity and corruption, appearances are all inglorious things; for we all vanish, we all die; kings and princes, judges and offenders, rich and poor, the whole human nature; for now they who once were among the living are cast down into the grave....

Now do all the bodily organs appear idle which not long before used to move, all are inactive, dead, numb; the eyes have set, the feet are bound, the hands fall silent and the hearing with them, the tongue is stopped with silence and is given over to the grave; truly all human things are vanity.

But out of the depths of despondency, in the midst of doleful silence is heard an incessant whisper, timid and faint, but at the same time confident and not to be stifled: you are eternal and were only born for the sake of time; it is in you, you are not in it, it is you who unroll and wind up its scroll in memory of your spirit, you connect the moments of time in its uninterrupted torrent, you see the past and the future from each moment of the present. Time and eternity are correlative: time would not be felt in its flowing, it would not be summed up from separate broken moments if the super-temporal *subject* of time did not accomplish this. Time is presupposed with eternity;[26] it is nothing other than eternity that stretches into being, having creatively embraced nothing. Therefore temporality is the universal form of being, the quality of creatureliness,[27] to which every creature is subject: angels, humans, and the whole world. Moreover time can be distinguished, temporality receives expression in concrete, qualified times: time for angels, one must suppose, is different from time for humans,[28] and time for a human being is other than for animals. The destructive power of temporality, corruption, can not only undergo development, but also be overcome in time, by being reduced to potentiality, and then time becomes that which Plato considered it (in the *Timaeus*), namely, "a certain mobile form of eternity," *eikōn d'epinoei kiniton tina aiōnos poiēsai*" (37D). Bad time, "the inflamed circle of being," is a fiery wheel, grasped in the clutches of greedy nothing. But according to the measure of how these clutches are unclenched and made insensible, nothing becomes powerless potentiality, the hidden basis of being; and the heavenly music "of eternal life" which constitutes the object of Christian hopes and promises and is known experientially by a saint resounds the more victoriously. Eternity lies not *beyond* time or *after* time, but on a level with it, *over* time, as an ideal for it and *under* time as its foundation which time senses only through the prism of nothing, of nonbeing. At any given instant of being, in its every moment, eternity enlightens, integral and indivisible, where there is no present, past, or future, but where all that happens is extra-temporal. Vertical segments of time penetrate eternity; therefore nothing of that which only once appeared for a moment in time can vanish anymore and return to nonbeing, for it has a certain projection into eternity, it is itself in one of its countless aspects. In this freedom from temporality, in this permanence of what once was the joy of being is included, as is dread before eternity, its threat: at the Dread Judgment nothing will be forgotten or concealed.

What then is time? Is it only the subjective form of consciousness as was proclaimed by Kant? Yes and no. Being the universal "transcendental" form of experience, as it were the prism of consciousness, time is substantially linked with nonbeing, with the submergence of the creature into nothing. Temporality expresses by itself the *condition* of creatureliness in its various modalities and belongs to our "transcendental subject," which expresses the creaturely apprehension of the world. However, the subjectivity of time in this sense does not at all exclude the ontological and fully objective nature of this condition: time does not only appear, it exists and precisely expresses creaturely being. To say it differently, it has not only a subjective nature, but also a subjective-objective nature; in it creatureliness is realized, with the attempt to think through the idea of time leading to the same antinomy as the idea of creation (see above). This is revealed as soon as we try to pose the question about *the beginning* of time: Did time begin in time or what precedes time? The contemporaries of blessed Augustine were interested in these difficulties and they posed sly questions about what God was doing before creating the world. Augustine discusses them in the eleventh book of the *Confessions,* which gives a hitherto unsurpassed analysis of time.

Augustine thoroughly responded to his interlocutors that "before the creation of heaven and earth God was not doing anything, for prior to the creation of heaven and earth there was no time; so is it appropriate to ask 'what was God doing *then?'* Without *time* then is unthinkable."[29] "You do not anticipate time with time, otherwise you would not anticipate all times. But you precede all times past with your eternity without beginning, which is always inherent to you, and with it you experience all future times, which are turned into the past as soon as they appear, whereas *you are the same and your years do not grow scarce.*"[30] "Thus there was never a time when you would be left inactive, because time itself is your production. And there is no time co-eternal with you because you always remain unchangeably one and the same, but time would cease to be time if it did not change."[31] Therefore "the word *before* is inapplicable where there is no time, and their very words that 'you worked nothing before,' have no other meaning than that your creation *is not in time.* Let them understand that there could be no time before creation, but with creation times themselves appeared."[32] Dionysius the Areopagite spoke on this subject approximately in the same sense as Augustine. "God is the king of the ages . . . and he was not and will not be, he did not become nor will he become, all the more he is not; rather he himself is being for essences *(to einai tois ousin)* and not only that which is but also very being of what is, from what is pre-eternally *(proaiōnios)*" (de n. D. V, 4, col. 817). "All time and eternity is from him" (V, 5). "He has superabundant more-than-being and super-being *(to proeinai kai hypereinai proechōn kai hyperechōn)*, he established being as such *(auto phēmi kath' auto to einai proupestēsato)*" (V, 5, col. 820). "We must praise God as eternity *(hos aiona)* and as time, as the cause of all time and eternity, as the ancient of days, as before time and higher than time *(pro chronou kai hyper chronou)* and as the one who sets the times and seasons" (X, 3, col. 910).

The question about the time of the origin of time inevitably arises if one poses the problem of time on the plane of the logic of time, which necessarily requires *before and after:* in them it can never stop in its tracks. Every instant of being thirsts to be fastened to some sort of *before* in order to be set at ease in it, but this very *before* inevitably turns out to be *after,* it seeks its own proper *before,* and thus ad infinitum on both sides. Time always is searching for its end and beginning, but it cannot find them, for thus is its nature.[33] The question about the beginning of time, as about a beginning without beginning, or as about an *after* without any *before,* leads to an irreconcilable antinomy, and it is possible to get out of it only by getting out of time. Temporality must be extinguished and lose its strength, the lines of time must merge into a point, when "time will be no more," as the angel in the Apocalypse swears — only thus can the antinomy of time be resolved.[34]

And yet temporality, as the form of creatureliness, contains in itself flights of eternity that are ineradicable by time. God, by his power summoning the world into being, is also present in time, for in it flows the theophanic process which is at the same time theogonic. And the question that occupied the contemporaries of blessed Augustine, namely, about what God was doing before the creation of the world, is thereby expanded into a more general question about the relation of the Creator to creation or about his real presence in time, about the self-abasement of the Creator through his entry into temporality and so to say the casting off of himself of eternity.

Not only abstract considerations but also the concrete content of the Christian religion enjoins us to acknowledge the whole reality of this entry, whereby the chasuble of eternity is covered over with the rags of temporality. For can one deny the reality of time when in the fulfilled times and seasons God was incarnated, when the nativity of Christ occurred, when his earthly life transpired, and his resurrection and ascension were accomplished? If eternity is clothed in temporality, then time also proves to be fraught with eternity and generates its fruit. It is therefore necessary to accept that between time and eternity there is correlativity — time is grounded by eternity; but in this there exists a hiatus between them, for eternity is transcendent to temporality, it opposes becoming. The presence of God in creation, eternity in temporality, must be understood as theophany, the refraction in the prism of time of what exists eternally, which like the sun sends light and warmth to everything without needing anything itself, without receiving or losing anything. To speak about some sort of profit for God from creation — whether in the sense that Schelling teaches or in some other sense — means to admit the fulfillment of eternity by time, i.e., to deny eternity and in the same way temporality. The temporal can only drown in the ocean of eternity, having been poured out into it, but without having added anything to its fullness. However, being fed by it, it has authentic being, although not without a ground, for its ground is in eternity, but it is all the same real and self-existent, for here the creative power of God operates, erecting the world in nothing; in the creation of the world, in theophany, theogony also takes place. God, by remaining through his essence *(ousia)* higher than the world, is present in the temporal process by his creative power *(energeia),* is born in it: this correlation of eternity and temporality is held on the edge of the sword of antinomy.

5. Freedom and Necessity

The general antinomy of creatureliness finds another expression in the antinomy of freedom and necessity. The very opposition of freedom and necessity is connected with the limitedness and relativity proper to the creature. Freedom is generally speaking a relative concept, and absolute freedom is as contradictory a concept as absolute being. Perfect freedom merges with perfect necessity and in this merging the very distinction itself is canceled, such that the Absolute is transcendent to both freedom and necessity.[35] Their distinction is engendered by the general foundation of creatureliness, *nothing,* the meon, which in its turn has a hidden basis in the pure nothing of oukon, in the limitlessness of nonbeing, *apeiron*. That which sets *peiras* for *apeiron* and creates meon out of oukon establishes the distinction of freedom and necessity: the negative freedom of emptiness is connected by the limits of being which form for it the law, as internal necessity. The positive basis of being is, first of all, the world of divine ideas, God in creation; these ideas are sown into nothing, into limitlessness, and the latter becomes the basis of autonomous being in its independence and freedom: *all exists through God and from God*, but precisely thereby it receives the power to be in itself and for itself, outside of God, as not-God or the world. In the positive basis of its being the world is absorbed by God, flickers out in the rays of his omnipotence: the world does have being that belongs to its own self, for otherwise it would be a god or an antigod; to it belongs only the nothing that assumes and begets towards isolation; but thanks to this negative basis of its being the world also receives extra-divine, autonomous being. This freedom is not at all free ontologically; in its very source, it is not *causa sui*, not substantial, for it is wholly determined from the creative fiat; cosmologically however, as the basis of world being, it is precisely that in which the creature feels itself as itself. Creaturely creativity, which is an actual expression of creaturely freedom, is *not creativity out of nothing but creativity in nothing out of divine something*.

In this freedom of the creature, which rests on creaturely nothing, the divine principles of being do not exist in their power and glory, or in the aspect of eternity, in which they know neither development nor fulfillment, for they do not need them. Rather they are found in temporal becoming as the theme and at the same time the task of the world process, its *given-proposed*, which gives a much more precise formula for the definition of both creaturely freedom and creaturely creativity. That which creation knows in itself as the task of creativity is placed in it by God; in other words, this task is pre-eternally resolved, but it must be resolved in time. The freedom of creation namely is expressed in the realization or nonrealization of the potency of its being. Inasmuch as the world by its existential roots is submerged in God, it is foreign to freedom and the various possibilities of chance and incorrectness connected with it; but inasmuch as it is created and submerged in nothing, it stands under the ambiguous sign of the category of possibility, choice, diversity. As the manifestation of divine powers, the world is itself reality and fullness, but in its creaturely freedom it is still a task, a game of possibilities, an endless possibility of possibilities. *It is not at all possible for the world not to succeed*, or to say it differently, the creaturely meon cannot decompose back into oukon, sink into limitlessness — *apeiron*, nonbeing cannot splash its waves as far as heaven and defeat divine power; however in virtue of its freedom the world can linger in the state of meonality, not attaining a higher level of being. In this the undeveloped meon does not arrive at a round zero which even pure potency is not, but here a distinction is possible in the degree of achievement and the form of becoming, for that which is pre-eternally in God and has no degree is freely realized in the world. This freedom must be imagined with all reality, and so too must time: if in time each of its moments is a window into eternity, as it were its point, then in becoming through freedom we have a real contact of eternity, a birth for it.

Creaturely freedom necessarily is limited, and that in two senses. The creature is an all-unity in which *all* realizes itself through plurality, with unity being the task or norm for it. The milieu of *nothing* differentiates all-unity into plurality; therefore each separate *what* finds itself enveloped by other *whats* into which *all* disintegrates, or to say it differently, it finds *all* as the external limit for itself, or the compulsory givenness, which *opposes,* is *an object* for overcoming. From this arise the conjugation and mutual conditionality of the fundamental definitions of the world being, as freedom and necessity, conformity to law and creativity. Therefore the human being ought not to exaggerate or underestimate its freedom and responsibility, which is defined only by the measure of its positive might, not less but also not more.

The freedom of the creature rests on nothing as its basis: having called nothing into being, divine power limited itself, yielded place to the freedom of the creature. Divine self-exhaustion to the benefit of creaturely nothing forms the positive foundation of creaturely power and freedom. Divine omnipotence and eminent dominion outline a circle of their intentional inaction as the realm of creaturely freedom. By an act of divine condescension — of love for the creature — the sphere of its freedom and might is steadfastly maintained. Still, even the power of the creature is not limitless, and its freedom is not boundless. However great may be the freedom bestowed on the creature as a positive power, it has to do only with the disposal of the divine gift of being, and not with self-creation (opposed to this thought is the absolute idealism of a Luciferian nuance, as for example the *Ichphilosophie* of Fichte). The envious repudiation of this truth is Satanism.

The creature is summoned to being by a creative extra-temporal act that is disclosed in time and by time. Just as it is impossible to think of time outside of eternity and in isolation from it, so too is it impossible to allow that even in one point of being the divine creative act should be absent, having ceased because of superfluity, for this would signify metaphysical annihilation of being, the decomposition of the meon into the oukon, the plunging of the creature into its original, dark nothingness. The world is not reducible to nothingness although it is not absolute; it is infinite although not eternal, inasmuch as time itself is the face of eternity turned toward the creature, a creaturely eternity of its own type. Therefore it is impossible to imagine God as a creator beginning only from a certain time onward which the extra-creative state of God precedes (and is consequently in time). The Lord is always creator, now and forever and unto the ages of ages. Consequently in some sense *the creature is co-eternal with the Creator,* as light coexists with the sun, although eternity is realized for it in temporality. The actuality of God in the world, which makes time real and establishes the times and seasons of worldly events, lays down the foundation *of history*. It eliminates the possibility of a deterministic understanding of the world as a mechanism in which everything is automatically foreordained in advance. On the contrary, as a continually occurring divine creation, as the living garment of Divinity, the world *is not regular* in the sense of mechanical determinism. The world's regularity, established by science, has a pragmatic and schematic meaning only for a given segment of time and *ceteris paribus* besides. In the "laws of nature" there is no such thing that would make them *the solely* possible; they exist because they exist, de facto, until they are abrogated or changed by Divine omnipotence. The sole absolute regularity of the world is the Divine will, i.e., *miracle;* the world is not conformed to law in any deterministic sense whatsoever: mechanical, occult, or metaphysical; rather it is miraculous.

"The laws of nature," the idea of a general world determinacy, some sort of *perpetuum mobile,* is a necessary auxiliary weapon of cognition, its pragmatic crutches, which support the broadening of a human's power and positive freedom. However, these "working hypotheses" have force only for the world of phenomena, for the periphery of being, they themselves having a basis in the deeper layers of being. And especially false is the extension of natural determinism to the very essence of God, which is how a physics of God in Jacob Böhme or in representatives of a philosophy of the occult (Besant, Steiner, et al.) errs. Indisputably everything in nature is filled with divine meaning, all of nature is a symbol of God (as Carlyle felt this with particular intensity), and by entering more deeply into this symbolism the pathos of poets, natural philosophers, mystics, and mages is engendered. But nature, both externally manifested and empirical *(natura naturata)* and as internal and noumenal *(ewige Natur, natura naturans)* does not exhaust God and for that reason does not limit the One who in his absoluteness and transcendence is free from all nature and from all conformity to law, from all physics and history. Conformity to law exists only for the creature and in the end is only one thing — the will of God. But being inviolable for the creature it does not limit the creative absoluteness and the omnipotence of God: God is neither the one nor the other, for generally speaking he *is not,* exceeding all nature. He is not a certain quasi-chemical mixture of "sour, bitter, astringent, sweet," etc., as Böhme's physics maintains. He creatively supposes nature and consequently creates its conformity to law as well. Therefore the Divine creativity is boundless, inexhaustible, never-ending, and measureless. There is no external limit to his omnipotence. God establishes everything by his will. However, God does not turn to creaturely being with his immeasurableness, or more precisely, super-measurability; rather he lays down a *measure* for everything, a regularity invested with the power of compulsion. In summoning nothing to being and giving freedom to the creature, God renounces his omnipotence *in actu* and enters into collaboration with the creature. This union of Divine omnipotence and creaturely freedom, which does not exist outside limitedness, is the foundation of creaturely being. Creation is, therefore, also "an act of providence" for the creature; the Pantocrator is also the Providential One.

However, this providentiality ought not to be understood in the sense of mechanical predetermination, which annihilates creativity and freedom and converts the world into a clock mechanism and the Divinity into an arbitrary and capricious tyrant who fashions living toys for himself. A *pre-*establishment in the course of the world process and in the fates of human beings does not exist, for time is real and that which happens in it *is created* in time, and in its originality it cannot be preordained earlier in some single point of the past: every moment of time is ontologically equivalent and equally real although this does not annihilate their distinction; just the opposite, it is even affirmed. Therefore, if one looks out of the past and the present into the future, in general if one examines the world in time and out of time, it presents itself as an undefined multitude of different possibilities out of which only one is selected and realized by creaturely freedom. And the divine act of providence, once it has permitted creaturely freedom and entered with it into a real reciprocity, influences the world not with mechanically pre-established conformity to law but creatively, always originally and in accordance with the operation of creaturely freedom. *Foresight operates with absolute resourcefulness and inventiveness,* by directing each creative combination of the creature towards the good with the greatest expediency.

The ways of Providence are for us unattainable and unfathomable, but we must believe in their absolute faithfulness and faultlessness. Only in exceptional moments does the hand of Providence become visible in the personal and historical life of humanity, although for the enlightened eye of the saints the world is a continually occurring miracle. The mechanical regularity of the world, the crust of nature, conceals divine Foresight from us, and only with the blood of the heart does one happen to extract from it the spiritual effort of faith and its submission! From this, one understands the fundamental possibility and even necessity of *eschatology,* which is invariably present in the majority of religions. In it is set aside a corresponding place for creatively catastrophic moments of being which in the life of an individual person are birth and death, and in the life of the world, its creation and end, or its new creation ("behold I make all things new," Apocalypse 21:5). In the Gospel it is said that no one knows of the end of the world except the Heavenly Father (not even the Son as one who participates in humanity). Here God operates by a creative *fiat* (or *non fiat*); "What is impossible to humankind being possible for God." By the will a human being cannot add to itself a cubit of growth, it itself is *given* for itself, and only the Maker has power to liberate it from the chain of givenness, to fashion it anew, although thereby the freedom of the creature is not violated. God does not inflict violence upon human freedom. This axiom forces one to acknowledge that neither individual life nor world being comes to a catastrophic halt, while something remains not fully spoken, unrevealed and undetermined. Foresight knows how to wait, sparing the freedom of the creature, but it does not allow useless delays and sluggishness. Therefore even evolution in its natural confines is inviolable and sacrosanct, inasmuch as each one carries in itself the law of its own being and perfection, but at the same time it cannot be acknowledged as a universal and supreme law of being.

In this sense it is necessary to understand the fundamental *possibility of apocalypse,* of promises and prophecies in general, which seemingly contradicts freedom with its indeterminism and plurality of different possibilities. Apocalypse discloses the future deposited in the present but it is not limited by this, for it contains the revelation about what God does with the world through his providential agency and his omnipotence. The divine side of the world process can be accessible only to *revelation*, i.e., to super-natural knowing (in its expression naturally assuming the gnoseological form of *myth*), for "no one knows the things of God except only the Spirit of God." But the question arises: Does not the immanently evolutionary side of the world process presuppose creaturely freedom, and consequently, the presence of different possibilities, so that even its paths are inaccessible to foresight? However, this needs to be acknowledged only for the creature and not for the Creator, for time and not for eternity. Creaturely freedom extends only to the distinction of means or ways of resolving the world's tasks, but not to the very essence of creation — it does not fall to it to ruin or even to corrupt creation substantially. God made the world for certain, with faultless fidelity and not with a merely enigmatic possibility of success or failure; otherwise its Maker would prove to be powerless and imperfect because in this case something new and unexpected for him would have been revealed which he himself was not able to foresee. Such an idea is completely irreconcilable with Divine absoluteness, inasmuch as it grants that even God learns something through the world process, that he develops and matures in it. Then one will have to grant further that time too exists *in itself*, i.e., in isolation from eternity, since in time something super-eternal can really occur which by its novelty completes even eternity. But *everything* temporal is grounded in eternity and there is no present, past, or future: everything *is* immovably and super-temporally in connection and completion — the objective order of temporal becoming, concrete time — "the times and seasons" — is grounded by this connection. For this reason human freedom remains transparent and the future is open for Divinity; there are no different possibilities in it, but there is only reality, the real fates of the creature. The reality of freedom in its authentic realm is in no way negated or diminished by this, for it wholly belongs to the temporal, creaturely world and is inseparably bound with necessity, i.e., with the limitedness of the creature, with its nonabsoluteness. In the eternal foundation of creatureliness the very distinction between freedom and necessity which has complete reality for the creature does not exist at all; it is transcendent to freedom-necessity.[36]

Thus divine revelation, which derives from eternity, is equally possible about the past and the future, for it is the work of God and corresponds to his providential goals. Therefore it is impossible to speak about the *fundamental conditionality* or hypothetical nature of prophecies, to consider them only religiously-pragmatically and not ontologically (the favorite idea of N. F. Fedorov, and by the way, not of him alone). Prophecies are understood here as pedagogical means, threats or warnings, and their existence depends on human freedom. Although many prophecies on the one side really do have that kind of cautionary significance (as for example Jonah's prophecy of the destruction of Nineveh, which is altered by God in view of its inhabitants' repentance), to reduce their very essence to this would signify the weakening of Christian eschatology and the fundamental repudiation of the possibility of apocalypse. The symbolism of prophetic "myths" makes their understanding difficult, and until the "unsealing" of the prophetic books even impossible without a special spiritual illumination, but one needs fundamentally to acknowledge behind them not a conditional but an unconditional meaning; they are not *probabilia*, but the voice of eternity, resounding in time. But this unconditional nature of prophecies is sometimes mistakenly understood as a sort of fate or doom (which is expressed in the religious fatalism of the doctrine of predestination). And what is more, this mistake arises out of the confusion of two different orders of ideas and consists in the translation into the language of temporality and becoming of that which shows itself to be the eternal foundation of the world, in which there is no before or after, indeed not even time itself. In eternity everything is, not predetermined in time but determined by existential nature, equally at the creation of the world and after it ("those whom he foreknew he also pre-established"); however, this does not refer to temporal life in which, conversely, nothing is predetermined or decided, for here freedom operates and on it depends salvation or ruin. We again run against the antinomy of eternity and temporality, and from yet a new side.

II. The Sophianicity of the Creature

1. Sophia

God, as the Absolute, is completely transcendent to the world and is NOT-what. But as Creator he is revealed to the creature, by making a

The Sophianicity of the Creature

place in himself for the relative; by an ineffable act of love-humility he places it alongside of himself and outside himself by limiting himself with his own creation. The Absolute in this way is made God and out of the unconditionally Absolute he becomes the relatively Absolute, or the Absolute for the relative, which is insofar a kind of mirror of divine absoluteness. By revealing himself to the creature God is divested of his absolute transcendence and is manifested in his operation for the creature, in grace or (to use the expression of the dogmatic disputes of the fourteenth century) in his energies. The Divinity in its inner-divine life remains transcendent for the creature, but the operations of the Divinity, its revelations, the divine power which flows out into creation, are the same Divinity, one, indivisible, and everlasting. In this sense the energy of God in its every manifestation, like the operation of God, is inseparable from God, but what appears to the creature is God in creation, the very Absolute-Transcendent. And the operation of the Holy Spirit in the Christian sacraments likewise is God himself, and so too the Name of God, which is a constantly occurring operation of the power of God, the energy of the Divinity, is God. Although from the point of view of the creature God in himself is distinguished from God in creation, yet this distinction is established not by Divine nature but by creaturely limitedness: God is identical to himself both in his supermundanity as the absolute Transcendent, and in his creative energy as Creator and Pantocrator. Through divine revelation the creature receives knowledge about God greater than it can contain, not only by reason of its sinfulness but also by reason of its creatureliness. A mirror reflects, but it does not hold the reflected in it; it witnesses to the being of the object not only in this reflection but also in itself and for itself; it is transcendent to this reflection, while at the same time it reflects the traits of precisely this real-in-itself thing. Therefore the very essence of the reflected thing is completely incommensurable with the reflection; it is transcendent to it and yet precisely and only it is reflected.

The divine energies streaming into the world, the revelations of the Divinity in the creature, introduce thereby differentiation into the Divinity itself, which to that extent already ceases to be a pure NOT for the world, but, in disclosing the inner-divine life, it makes visible what is invisible, introduces into immanent consciousness what is transcendent to it; so to say, it splits up and multiplies the Divinity as a single ray of the sun is split up and multiplied in its reflections and refractions. On the foundation of the operation of God in the creature, what

God is in himself becomes known. Although this cognition in essence is inadequate, that is precisely why it represents the possibility of infinite growth and deepening.

The revelation of the Divinity by mysterious hieroglyphs is traced in creation, which bears its seal, and the Christian faith only uncovers what is written in the heart of the creature. In Christian revelation it is given that the inner-divine life is triunity, one Divinity in three hypostases, which are one in pre-eternally realized Divine love. God is Love, which constitutes not a quality or property, not a predicate, but the very essence of God. And in this Divine Love each Hypostasis, by giving itself in love, finds itself in the other Hypostases, realizes the one Divinity. In the Holy Trinity the absolutely personal character of Divinity, its hypostaseity, is united with the absolutely super-personal character of its trinitarity — "Trinity in Unity and Unity in Trinity." Through the revelation of three hypostases a qualitative differentiation in the life of the Holy Trinity is manifested. Divine Fatherhood, substantiality, source belong to the first Hypostasis; distinction, Logos, knowledge belong to the second Hypostasis, and it is the Heart of God in which the Father loves the Son; the third Hypostasis, the Holy Spirit, feels both Father and Son, in them it finds itself and rejoices in Divine Love. The Holy Trinity is revealed to the world in the triunity of Father, Son, and Holy Spirit as in a connected inner relation and consequently a disclosing act of Divine life. In the very Divinity it is impossible to allow any sequence or gradualness of development, for the Holy Trinity *is* pre-eternally *above and beyond* in a single combined act of Love and Identity. Divine life in the Holy Trinity is closed in itself and absolute. It needs no external fulfillment or disclosure. It is full by itself and if it can become still fuller, then *not for the Divinity* but for *the non-Divinity;* non-Divine or extra-Divine life can be drawn to the fullness and gladdening of Divine life. However, for the Divinity this is in no sense its necessary evolution, or some sort of fate of creation weighing heavily over it, without which its self-disclosure could not occur, but is a gift of free, bountiful love — of goodness, grace, and beneficence. The rays of love are poured out of Divine Fullness; in its superabundance the Divinity comes out of itself and illuminates the darkness of non-Divine nothing, nonbeing. The Divinity, which does not know envy or covetousness and in its infinity and absoluteness knows no increment, wants to summon towards its love even this nonbeing, the non-Divine life. In keeping with its Divine condescension, in the selflessness of love the Divinity wants the non-itself, the non-Divinity, and goes out of itself in creation. But in setting alongside itself the extra-Divine world, the Divinity thereby places between itself and the world a certain border and this border, which according to the concept itself is found *between* God and the world, the Creator and the creature, is itself neither the one nor the other but something completely particular, simultaneously uniting and separating the one and the other (a certain *metaxu* in the sense of Plato).

Holy Sophia is the Angel of the creature and the Beginning of the ways of God. She is *the love of Love*. The divine triunity, God-Love, in its closed, self-sufficient, eternal act of Divine, substantial Love exteriorizes (in the sense of metaphysical exteriorization) the object of this Divine love, loves it, and thus pours out on it the life-creating power of trihypostatic Love. Of course this object of love is not only an abstract idea or a dead mirror, it can only be a living essence, having person, hypostasis. And this love is Sophia, the eternal object of God's love, "of delight," "of joy," "of play." It is impossible to think Sophia, the "Idea" of God, only as an ideal notion deprived of vital concreteness and power of being. That which God essentially and for that reason pre-eternally, extra-temporally conceives (we are well aware of the whole imprecision of these expressions but we use them in the absence of suitable words, for this in human language), one must think in the most real sense, as *ens realissimum,* and precisely such a most real reality does the Idea of God, Divine Sophia, possess. Sophia is not only loved, rather she loves with a corresponding Love and in this mutual love she receives everything and *is Everything.* And as the love of Love and the love for Love, Sophia possesses personhood and countenance, is a subject, a person or, let us say it with theological terminology, a hypostasis; of course she *is different* from the Hypostases of the Holy Trinity, and is a special hypostasis, of a different order, a fourth hypostasis. She does not participate in the inner-divine life, *she is not God,* and that is why she does not convert the trihypostaseity into a tetrahypostaseity, the trinity into a quaternity. But she is the beginning of a new, creaturely multi-hypostaseity, for after her follow many hypostases (people and angels) which are found in a sophianic relation to the Divinity. However, she herself is found *outside* the Divine world, and does not enter into its self-enclosed, absolute fullness. But she is admitted into it according to an ineffable condescension of the love of God, and thanks to this she reveals the mysteries of the Divinity and its depths and rejoices, "plays" with these gifts before the face of God. The life of the Holy Trinity is a pre-eternal act of self-surrender, of self-exhaustion of the Hypostases in Divine Love. Holy Sophia likewise surrenders herself to Divine Love and receives its gifts, the revelations of its mysteries. But she gives herself up differently than the Divine Hypostases, which unalterably remain the consubstantial Divinity, which complete themselves by it and it by themselves. Sophia only *accepts,* not having anything to return; she contains only what she has received. By the self-surrender of Divine Love she commences everything in herself. In this sense she is *feminine,* the one who receives; she is the "Eternal Feminine."[37] At the same time she is the ideal, intelligible world, Everything, the true *hen kai pan,* the all-one.[38]

In the Feminine are the mysteries of the world. In its feminine "principle," *archē (bereshit),* the world is generated before it is created and from this seed of God, implanted in it by a path of disclosure; the world *is fashioned* out of nothing. This generation is, of course, something *fundamentally different* from that generation from his inner recesses by which the Father pre-eternally and atemporally begets his Only-begotten Beloved Son without man and without woman, and in him and through him regenerates God's offspring who are born not of flesh and blood but of God. The generation of the world in Sophia is the operation of the whole Holy Trinity in each of its Hypostases which extends to the receptive essence, the Eternal Feminine. Through this she becomes the beginning of the world, as it were the *natura naturans,* forming the basis of the *natura naturata,* of the creaturely world.

"The fourth hypostasis," by taking into itself the revelation of the Divine mysteries, introduces *through itself and for itself* a distinction, an order, an internal sequence in the life of the Divine Triunity; it apprehends the one and whole Divinity as trihypostatic — Father, Son, and Holy Spirit. As one who receives its essence from the Father it is the creation and daughter of God; as one who knows the Divine Logos and is known by him, it is the bride of the Son (Song of Songs) and wife of the Lamb (New Testament, Apocalypse); as one who receives the outpouring of the gifts of the Holy Spirit, it is the Church, and together with this it becomes the Mother of the Son who is incarnated by the inspiration of the Holy Spirit from Mary, the Heart of the Church, and it is the ideal soul of the creature, Beauty. And all of this at once: Daughter and Bride, Wife and Mother, triunity of Good, Truth, Beauty, the Holy Trinity in the world, is divine Sophia. The second Hypostasis, Christ, is

The Sophianicity of the Creature

primarily turned towards Sophia, for he is the light of the world, all things were through him (John 1), and by apprehending the rays of the Logos, Sophia herself becomes Christosophia, Logos in the world and like him, loved by the Father's Hypostasis which pours out on her the gifts of the Holy Spirit. It is worth noting that in iconography and liturgical texts Holy Sophia at one time comes close to being almost completely identified with Christ, becoming merely a power or attribute (this was how the idea of the Hagia Sophia was understood in Constantinople during the reign of emperor Justinian), at other times with the Mother of God (the celebration of Holy Sophia is externally connected with the Dormition of the Mother of God), with the glorified Church, heavenly and earthly, with the female image of the Bride from the Song of Songs (in certain icons), and even with the cosmos.

What then is this Eternal Feminine in its metaphysical essence? Is it a creature? No, it is not a creature, for it is not created. The beginning of creatureliness is nothing, nonbeing, *apeiron*, emptiness. But in Sophia there is no such *not*, there is only *yes* to everything, there is no nonbeing, which is the bounds of self-isolating, capricious, individual being that tears asunder positive all-unity. Sophia, although she is not the Absolute or God, has what she has immediately from God or *in an absolute manner;* she is free of being submerged in the nothing which is proper to worldly being. Therefore we cannot ascribe to her even the predicate of *being* at least in the sense in which we ascribe it to the creaturely world, although she is the immediate foundation of the creaturely world. As such she borders closely upon it; but, foreign to its limitedness she is the indeterminable and unattainable bounds between being-creatureliness and super-being, the essence of Divinity — neither being nor super-being. She is one-many, everything, one *yes* without *no*, affirmation without negation, light without darkness; *she is that which is not in being,* which means, *she both is and is not,* she participates in the one side of being and with respect to the other she is transcendent to it, she slips away from it. Occupying the place *between* God and the world, Sophia abides between being and super-being; she is neither the one nor the other, or appears as both at once.

The unique nature of Sophia is clear from her relationship to *temporality*. Is temporality applicable to Sophia — time, as the moving form of eternity? On the one hand it appears inapplicable inasmuch as temporality is inseparably linked with being-nonbeing, with becoming, with plurality, and in general is the projection of eternity into nothing.

If every *not* is absent in Sophia then temporality is also absent. She initiates everything, has everything in herself by a single act, in keeping with the form of eternity. Without herself being Eternity, she possesses everything *as an eternal form*. She is not made, and as a result, she did not arise in time; to say it in other terms, with her and in her, time does not yet arise, for she is the idea of God in God himself, but not in creation and not in nothing. In this sense she is supratemporal. But, on the other hand, she *is not Eternity*, for the latter belongs substantially only to God, and is a synonym for his absoluteness, aseity, self-sufficiency. To ascribe to Sophia such Eternity would mean to convert her into a Divine Hypostasis, i.e., to erase any bounds between her and God, whereas this bounds must be established as unconditionally as between God and the creature, although in a different sense. Thus, Sophia is free from time, rises above it, but Eternity does not belong to her. She participates in it as Sophia, as love of Love; however, she participates not by reason of her essence but by the grace of Love — by the influence of divine "energy," not according to *"ousia."* Her original metaphysical nature with respect to temporality and creatureliness is determined by this *middle* position between time and eternity, *"metaxu."* As she does not possess eternity by reason of her nature, Sophia can be found on the plane of temporality in that she is turned towards it. Even more, she can ground it by herself, by giving it a place in herself: time can flow *out of her or in her*, whereas it is not able to start immediately from Eternity.[39] Although Sophia is supratemporal according to her position, she is not transcendent to time according to her nature. Since positive all-unity belongs to her, the whole coherency of being is grounded by her which establishes not mechanical alternation but internal sequence of events, in other words, *objective* time; for time is not bare alternation, the supplanting of the past by the present, the tuft-like brokenness of being. Sophia contains in herself a living and real *synthesis of time* in which the bounds of time are already crossed (although not of temporality in general). If it can be stated in this way, sophianic time is a single, complex, and combined act although it is not supratemporal but above the temporal: this is *eternal time*, one could perhaps say, without fearing a *contradictio in adjecto*, which in fact only appears to be so, inasmuch as *eternity* designates here only the quality of time, its capacity to be synthesized.[40] The same could be said apropos spatiality, which is analogous to time in the respect that moments of combination and separation, yes and no, oneness and plurality are conjugately united in it. Sophia is supraspatial but at the same time she is the basis of all spatiality.

And so, the metaphysical nature of Sophia is not covered at all by the usual philosophical categories: absolute and relative, eternal and temporal, divine and creaturely. With her face turned towards God, she is his Image, Idea, Name. Turned towards nothing, she is the eternal foundation of the world, Heavenly Aphrodite, as Plato and Plotinus called her in a true presentiment of Sophia. She is the empyrean world of intelligible, eternal *ideas,* which was revealed to the philosophical and religious contemplation of Plato who confessed it in his doctrine that truly is a sophiology. The created world exists, having as its foundation the world of ideas, which illuminates it; to put it differently, *it is sophianic.* This is the supreme, richest, and most important truth about the world, the essence of the cosmodicy of Platonism. It is necessary, however, to fix the content of this notion *of the sophianicity* of the world more closely. But for this, one needs to show how and why the sophianic world at one and the same time *is Sophia* and differs from her, *is not Sophia,* what sort of link there is between the world and Sophia and the gulf that separates them. Here we are approaching the problem of cosmodicy equally central for both Platonism and Christian theology. It was revealed to Greek speculation, which in this respect runs parallel to the revelations of Greek art, as the most indisputable truth about the world — that at the basis of phenomena lies the world of ideas beyond the limits, that is, essences. These ultimate essences of things were defined as *numbers* by the Pythagoreans, as *names* in various mystical doctrines, as *ideas* by Plato, as creative *forms* (entelechies) by Aristotle, as *letters* of the Hebrew alphabet in the Cabbala.[41] These various definitions do not contain a contradiction, for they only reflect different means of comprehending one and the same essence. All of philosophy, as well as the art of the Hellenes, is a mental vision of these ideas or a quest for this vision; it is inflamed by authentic love for Sophia — not for nothing has it given itself the name *philo-sophia.* And therein is the secret of its undying meaning for humanity, its freshness and eternal youth.

The most ample of the doctrines concerning the sophianicity of the world produced by Hellenism that have come down to us is Plato's doctrine concerning the ideas or the two worlds. Here its basic difficulties have come to light, which in the eyes of many render it completely worthless. One has to observe that Plato in general does not demonstrate the existence of the ideas; he does not set this task for himself even where induction may perhaps lead to this. The ideas are intuitively identified by mental vision which is painted in the mythological images of *Phaedrus* (246-250) and with erotic ecstasy, the inspiration of Eros celebrated in the *Symposium*. "Let us purify the senses and we will see." With these words of Christian hymnody the basic thought of Platonism can be expressed: the truth is revealed only to love, to erotic folly, to ecstasy. The existence of an empyrean world and the sophianicity of a terrestrial world are therefore immediately attested by religious and thereafter by philosophical contemplation, with philosophy only further unfolding its content and bringing to light its attendant problems.

The basic difficulty, which in this case arose before Plato, consists in the antinomically dual nature, the transcendent-immanent character of the world of ideas. On the one hand it is a kind of *not* with respect to this world, so that when applied to it one has to use the method of negative theology. In this sense one ought to understand the description of the ideas already familiar to us which we find in *Phaedrus*.[42] (The well-known image of the cave in book VII of the *Republic* alludes to this.) Eternal, unconditional beauty, to which the human being is raised through a consideration of earthly beauty is, in accordance with the *Symposium*, "eternal beauty, not created and which does not perish, which does not increase but which also does not fall into decline, which is invariable in every part, at all times, in all respects, in all places and for all people (*aei on oute gignomenon oute apollymenon oute auxanomenon oute phthinon, epeita ou tēi men kalon, tēi d'aischron, oude tote men tote d'ou, hōde pros men kalon, entha de aischron, hōs tisi men on kalon, tisi de aischron*). And this eternal beauty will not present itself to his imagination in the concrete guise of face, hands or any other part of the body, nor in the guise of some sort of conversation or knowledge. This beauty will not cease like something that is found in some other thing, even if e.g. in some sort of living entity, on earth or in heaven, or in some other sort of object, but as something that being homogeneous always exists independently by itself and in itself. And all the remaining beautiful things have such a relation to it that whereas they themselves arise and perish, it definitely neither increases nor decreases at all."

Even eternity is, finally, attributed to this world of ideas, as for example in *Timaeus*: "The model (according to which the world is created) is something that exists in all eternity" (38 B), whereby here are differentiated "that which always is *(on)* and never has origination *(gignomenon)* and the always becoming, but which never is" (27 D). And so the world of that which is *(on)* is transcendent, separate, opposed to the world of that which exists *(gignomenon)*, but on

The Sophianicity of the Creature

the other hand it is for it the cause — *aitia* (*Phaedo*, 100 C), model (*paradeigma* — *Timaeus*, 29 B), and co-participates in it *(metechei, koinōnia)*. Ideas for the world of phenomena have not only artistic-erotic and religious-mystical authenticity but also logical meaningfulness, as common generic concepts *(koinon, to hen epi pollōn, hen eidos hekaston peri ta polla)* whereby these concepts are not only generic names but express the very essences of objects *(ousiai)*. In the disclosure of this logical meaningfulness of the ideas various problems of Platonic dialectics emerge.[43] The world of phenomena not only closes the world of ideas, in that it is itself enclosed in the fetters of corporeality, "as in a shell" (*Phaedrus*, 250 C) or as in a prison, but is at the same time a revelation of that world of ideas, ladders of ascent to the empyrean world. In other words, being transcendent to the world of phenomena, it is immanent to it at the same time, constituting in it that which really is *(ontos on)* in that which is not *(mē on)*.

It is interesting that Aristotle's criticisms of Platonic doctrine made in the *Metaphysics* (books XIII and XIV, and chapter 9 of book I) are based entirely on an unconscious or conscious confusion of two aspects of the world of ideas that flow out of their transcendent-immanent character. According to Aristotle, ideas, first of all, represent useless hypostatizations and doublings of real things. "There are approximately as many ideas, or no less, as there are things, and in investigating the causes of the latter we have crossed over to them from these sensible things. For there is something simultaneous for each separate thing." Ideas must exist not only of present things, but also of things past, and even ideas of negation, the relative, the perishing, death, annihilation *et alia*. The force of this argument lies in the direct identification of concepts that arise in the world of phenomena and apropos of these with ideas themselves, but this straightforward identification in no way emerges from Platonic doctrine, for the world of ideas, although it is immanent to the world of phenomena as its foundation, at the same time differs from it fundamentally. Ideas are submerged in it in becoming and nonbeing; they undergo numerous refractions and reflections while properly constituting the domain of the relative. For this reason although concepts as the logical schemata of phenomena do indeed reflect ideas in multifarious aspects (as Aristotle himself points out), ideas nonetheless are not concepts but only ground them and besides not directly, but obliquely, not immediately, but mediately, by being refracted through the prism of relative human thinking. Aristotle's subsequent argument, that ostensibly according to the theory of ideas there must exist for each thing several and even many ideas, e.g., animal, biped, human, etc., for the human being, is based entirely on this confusion of ideas and concepts. Further there must exist ideas of ideas, e.g., genus or species. Empty logical forms, auxiliary schemata that have only grammatical meaning, are produced by Aristotle without any hesitation in the place of authentic ideas in the Platonic sense. It is of course impossible to deny that

The World

Plato himself did not reach definitive clarity in expounding the question about the relation of ideas to concepts, but he did not give cause for the vulgarization of his doctrine by Aristotle.

Aristotle's other objection to the theory of ideas rests not on the excessive dependence of ideas on the world of phenomena or their complete immanence to it but on the transcendence of the ideas which by itself is not able to explain either being or becoming. "One must arrive at the greatest embarrassment when it is necessary to understand what the ideas offer from the sensibly apprehended for the eternal, or for what arises and perishes, for they are causes either of some kind of movement or of change. But they are completely useless both for understanding other things and for their being, for they are not found in the things participating in them; you see in such a case they would be able, perhaps, to be a cause in the same sense as a touch of white is the cause that something is white. . . . But likewise it is not possible by any means for the other to arise out of the ideas. If they say that ideas are prototypes and the other takes part in them, then these are empty words, poetic metaphors (??). For what is this active principle which influences by gazing on ideas?" And so, the world of ideas is doomed to impotent transcendence to the world of phenomena, since the motive cause of change, of becoming, is absent — *aitia, hothen hē archē tēs metabolēs*.

However, this objection would be irrefutable only in the case that the world of ideas were to represent a self-sufficient divine essence, an assembly of gods without the one God. According to the very profound sense of Plato's doctrine, the world of ideas is nothing other than Sophia, i.e., while it is the living revelation of Divinity it is still not Divinity itself. It does not have its own power, but receives it from God and is the glory of the Word of God. And thus the active relation of the world of ideas to the creaturely world, its transcendent-immanence, can be established only by an act of God's omnipotence that is transcendent even with respect to the world of ideas — the creation of the world. *Archē tēs metabolēs* [*the principle of change*] is the creative *fiat*. True, this latter phase which establishes the hierarchical correlation of Creator, Sophia, and world is far from satisfactorily displayed in the early and middle dialogues of Plato, where one can get rather the impression that the world of ideas, Sophia, is the very highest principle of the world, and that it almost merges with the Divinity. However, Plato's authentic thought (to which there are hints earlier, e.g., in the *Republic*) was thoroughly spoken with a clarity admitting of no doubt in so significant and mature a work as the *Timaeus*. Here with the inimitable, purely Platonic combination of massive mythological images and the most subtle speculative concepts is directly set forth that the world is created by God "who is good and ignorant of envy" (29 D), "according to the model of eternal nature so that it could become like him as much as possible. You see, its model is what exists in all eternity; but its image

The Sophianicity of the Creature

is without ceasing, in the limits of all time, what has been, is, and shall be" (38 B). "If this cosmos is beautiful, and the Maker — its *demiourgos* — is good, this means that he turned his gaze to the eternal *(pros to aidion eblepen);* but if we supposed something different, which is sinful even to state, then he turned to what has happened" *(to gegonōs).* "But it is clear to everyone that it is to the eternal, because the cosmos is the most beautiful of what has happened, and the Maker is the most noble of the causes *aristos tōn aitiōn*" (28 A). In this doctrine Plato comes strikingly close to the narrative of the Old and New Testaments about how "in the beginning (i.e., in the intelligible, sophianic world) God created heaven and earth," and in the beginning "was the Word, and the Word was with God and the Word was God." This beginning,[44] which receives into itself the Word, and in him and through him the gifts of the trihypostatic Divinity, is at the same time the foundation in which creation is initiated; it is according to Plato the "eternal model" of creation. This thought is affirmed in the revelations of the book of the *Proverbs of Solomon,* where the Wisdom of God says of herself "the Lord had me as the beginning of his ways, before his foundations, forever.... I was anointed from the age, from the beginning, before the being of earth.... Then I was in his presence an artisan and I was his joy every day, making merry before his face all the time" (Proverbs 8:22, 23, 30).

In the *Timaeus* Plato finishes his doctrine of ideas, and at the same time an answer is given in advance to Aristotle's doubt; truly it is a historical enigma how Plato's closest pupil could prove to be such an ungrateful and captious critic of Plato's doctrine on the whole. This is all the more startling in that Aristotle's own metaphysical doctrine is only a variant of Platonism, an attempt to resolve certain *of its* difficulties, to avoid *its* aporias. In actual fact, against the imaginary Platonic dualism that disconnects and opposes ideas and phenomena, Aristotle affirms their indissolubility: an idea is a motive principle, a goal, a cause, an entelechy, it is immanent to the thing and yet is for it *prius,* it precedes it ontologically, i.e., it is transcendent to it in a certain sense. To say it differently, it is only from a different end that Aristotle arrives at the same fundamental description of the world of ideas such as he has in Plato, at the recognition of its transcendent-immanence or its immanent-transcendence. Ideas-forms are *seeds* which, each according to its own kind, creatively spring up in becoming, conditioned by Aristotelian *hylē.* Of course, even Aristotle was not able to stop at the plurality of forms that was not reduced to any sort of unity at all, or to take Sophia for the Divinity. Utterly in the spirit of the Platonic *Timaeus* he postulates a supreme form of forms as the motive cause of the world, i.e., God-Creator. Aristotle's doctrine shares the weak side of Plato's doctrine, namely that in it God and Sophia, Creator and world of ideas, are not distinguished with sufficient clarity. Here, evidently, lies the boundary of "natural theology" which is removed only by Christian revelation. Becoming, genesis, is the path from the intelligible idea-potency *dynamis* to the idea which is realized in phenomenon *(energeia)*; in that distinction, fundamental for Aristotle, between potentiality and actuality and both poles of the Platonic doctrine about two worlds, the ideal and the empirical are outlined. The Platonic ideas here are understood primarily as tasks or norms of being; although they are realized immanently, they are given transcendently. Therefore the first cause moves the world not as a mechanical mover but as an object of loving, erotic attraction *(ou kinoumenon . . . hōs kinei de hōs erōmenon)*. Therefore the fundamental discord between Plato and Aristotle, excessively exaggerated by the latter, and besides this, intensified by the enormous difference of creative individualities of both thinkers, concerns not so much the essence of the doctrine as its formulation and elaboration.

In the dispute between Plato and Aristotle the basic problem of cosmology was essentially posed — concerning the sophianicity of the creature. Here the sophianic basis of all authentic being was established in its indisputableness, and alongside of it the extra-sophianic or anti-sophianic shell of coming to be and becoming, of the world of phenomena. The same dispute relative to the sophianic nature of concepts flared up in medieval philosophy under the name of nominalism and realism, and in it the same two poles were emphasized. For both Plato and Aristotle it was equally indisputable that something common exists in concepts, a genus or idea, though neither the one nor the other understood it in the sense of nominalism, i.e., only as abstractions or conventional names — *vox*; rather, they saw in them *realia* of some kind. Together with this it became clear no less for Plato than for Aristotle that one could not conceive of a direct identification of concepts and ideas, but at the same time that it was impossible entirely to tear them apart from each other. In other words it was established that concepts co-participate in ideas and ground the latter, and this co-participation could have different degrees, distinguished by their moving away from the prototypes and submergence in the shades of half-being. The supreme and general ideas, like good and beauty, directly reflect the noetic light; on the contrary, ideas that refer to concrete being such as human, animal, table are only in the ever-weaker reflected lights. In other words, it is possible to reconcile the antithesis between nominalism and realism in the sense of joining both, for the concepts are simultaneously *realia* and *nomina*, albeit in a different degree and intensity. There are not and cannot be concepts that are absolutely anti-ideal and extra-sophianic, *ex nihilo nihil fit*, and even the emptiest and most worthless or false concepts are parasites that sprout up on the living tree of ideas; but likewise there cannot be concepts that are entirely and unconditionally sophianic, for concepts are born from discursive thought which corresponds to the fragmented state of the world, woven out of being and nonbeing, and an authentically sophianic idea is no longer a concept of thought but goes out beyond the limits of reason (about which more below). In the affirmation of the sophianicity of concepts lies the radical lie of Hegel's

The Sophianicity of the Creature

doctrine which from this aspect represents the perversion of Platonism, its *reductio ad absurdum,* and "the wisdom of this age," which gives itself out to be Sophia. (Hegel himself, by the way, does not even speak about Sophia, since there is altogether no place in his system for this concept, but he does speak directly of the Logos; however, this difference has no significance for the question that interests us at present.) Likewise the fundamental error of Schelling's *Philosophy of Revelation,* which leads him to Sabellianism in his Christology, is the confusion of the Logos, the second hypostasis, with Sophia, while all that ought to be understood as sophianic is immediately referred by him to the Logos, to the second and occasionally to the third hypostasis (see above).

The question about the sophianic nature of concepts[45] is only one of the problems that enter into the composition of the general question about the sophianicity of the world. Sophia with respect to the plurality of the world is an organism of ideas in which is contained the ideal seed of all things. In her is the root of their being, and without them and outside them nothing exists. In this sense it is possible to say together with Plato that ideas are the causes of being, but not in the sense of precedence in time, rather as its abiding, supratemporal foundation. The relationship of ideas to things, of Sophia to the world, is the relationship of the supratemporal (and in this sense eternal) to the temporal. Sophia is present in the world as its foundation, but she remains transcendent to the world above all because it is found in time and in becoming, while Sophia is above time and outside every process. But at the same time one cannot separate her from the world in any way, or all the more so place her in opposition to it, for outside of Sophia the world does not exist. That which is genuine in it or which authenticates its being in nonbeing is precisely Sophia. The world of ideas, the ideal *all,* which is actually contained in Sophia, exists for the creaturely world not only as foundation or causality (in the above-indicated sense) but also as the *norm,* the maximum task, the law of life, Aristotelian entelechy with respect to the potential state of being. Every entity has its idea-norm; it searches for and creates itself in keeping with a definite image that is proper to it alone, to its idea, but this is because it has in its supratemporal nature this idea as its single genuine being, *to ontos on,* as its unrepeatable individuality that cannot be confused with anything. And only because precisely this idea is entrusted to it, does it enter into the organism of Sophia through it and in it, by realizing it, and it becomes a participant in the *hen kai pan.*

The World

Here a fundamental and one can even say fatal question of sophianic cosmology arises, which Aristotle essentially posed already: What does this world represent, how is it not a meaningless and unnecessary repetition of the world of ideas, its double? In what does the creative act consist by which the world is created as something new?

This querying is based on a certain misunderstanding. It is possible to speak of repetition or doubling only with respect to the similar in the realm of temporal and spatial being. But what sense does it make to compare that which transpires in time and is realized by the world-creative act as a task and inner law of life, with that which is above time and being itself? The world is nothing sown with ideas; it is *Sophia becoming*. Divine Sophia exists eternally, as the abiding foundation of creation, having inexhaustible might and depth. The proper nature of the world, inasmuch as it differs from Sophia, is precisely its *hylē* (in the Aristotelian sense), nothing, summoned to being, but in itself not having being, with Sophia as the principle of its being. For this reason, those who say that the world is the repetition or doubling of Sophia count as equivalent repeating units that which cannot be thus counted; in common parlance, they are adding together apples and oranges.

But this is a misunderstanding in yet another sense: the world and Sophia do not at all form two principles or worlds that relate to each other in one way or another; it is one and the same world. Sophia is the foundation of the world, its ideal entelechy; she exists not somewhere outside the world but is its basic essence, and in this Aristotle is correct in his ontology. But if we take this world in its state or givenness, then, of course, it differs from Sophia, as unrealized potency differs from its idea. The world is not outside Sophia, and Sophia is not outside the world, but at the same time the world is not Sophia, although sophianicity, which is realized in time, is proper to it.

One has therefore to think of the creation of the world *in the Beginning*, i.e., in Sophia or on her foundation, as *the isolating of her potentiality from her eternal actuality*, by which time and the temporal process are created; the actualization of the potency of sophianicity constitutes the content of this process. Therein is the ontological essence of the world's creation in *the Beginning*, and this very separation of potentiality from actuality that is connected with the creative fertilization of nothing is the incomprehensible mystery of Divine omnipotence. It goes without saying that this potentialization of Sophia exists not for her own sake, not for the sake of her face turned towards the Divinity, and

The Sophianicity of the Creature

not for the pre-eternal Bride of the Word, but for the sake of Sophia's face turned towards the world, i.e., towards temporal being. Therefore one has to affirm simultaneously that the world *is* Sophia in its foundation and *is not* Sophia in its condition. It is obvious that the world cannot be either separated from Sophia or opposed to her; even less can it be regarded as her double. Sophia is the entelechy of the world (in the Aristotelian sense), its potency which becomes energy. In the history of philosophy, the relationship between Sophia and the world can receive and has received diverse metaphysical transcriptions corresponding to the style and design of a given system. For those who above all treasure the orderliness of a system and believe it possible to provide in the concepts of discursive thought an adequate expression of what is, who to a greater or lesser degree are obsessed with a *mania Hegeliana,* the whole task of philosophy consists in the construction of such a system. From our point of view concepts are suited only for *describing* with as much precision as possible, for retelling the content of that mystical intuition in which the sophianicity of the world is immediately revealed to each person in the measure of his spirit.[46]

As the entelechy of the world, in her cosmic aspect Sophia is the world soul, i.e., the principle that links and organizes the world's plurality — *natura naturans* with respect to *natura naturata*. She is that universal soul of the world, instinctively unconscious or super-conscious, the *anima mundi*, which is revealed in the astonishment-eliciting expediency of the structure of organisms, unconscious functions, instincts of the generic principle. Ancient philosophy in the persons of Plato and Aristotle understood this world soul and gave distinct expression to its understanding. This doctrine entered as a necessary element into Christian philosophy[47] and mysticism, and finally, in modern philosophy it is breaking through in the natural philosophy of Schelling, in the theory of the unconscious in Hartmann, in the doctrine of Fechner, Lotze,[48] and in the philosophy of Vladimir Soloviev. In the given state of the world and humankind the world soul operates as the external regularity of cosmic life, with the compulsoriness of a law of physics.[49]

The sophianic soul of the world is covered with many veils like the goddess of Sais,[50] and these veils are themselves worn thin according to the measure of spiritual ascent of humankind. However, the temptation always remains to *remove* a veil and spy what is beyond it, peek at the mystery, transgress against the humility of ignorance or re-

The World

ligious chastity, exceed the measure of one's own age. In this are the temptation of "gnosis" and the spiritual danger of the Gnostic path of occultism. Nature can be violated by humankind within certain limits, and in this is rooted the possibility of black magic and mystical fornication. The one who wants to see in this only Aphrodite Pandemos–the Commoner will have her in that way, for he is like this himself.[51] Here is the greatest spiritual difficulty of our time: on the one hand the time has clearly come for a more spiritual perception of nature than was proper to the modern era with its "natural science"; the necessity of an "occult" comprehension in the broad sense of the word becomes all the deeper and more widespread, but at the same time the religious danger of this path which leads to the betrayal of Christ and to pseudo-Christianity, to submergence in paganism and natural magic, is extraordinarily great.

The world soul, as the force that unites, connects, and organizes the world, displays its operation every time that this very *connectedness* of the world makes itself felt, no matter how this may be realized. It is reflected and refracted differently, through various prisms: phenomenally it is multifaceted though remaining substantially united. It stays one and the same in its foundation even when Adam "gave names" to the living creatures, thereby realizing his own sophianic connection with the world, and when fallen humanity, after expulsion from paradise, was condemned to work the earth cursed by God in the sweat of its brow. The sophianicity of the world has for the creature a different degree and depth: in its highest aspect it is the Church, the Mother of God, Heavenly Jerusalem, the New Heaven and New Earth; in the external, peripheral operation in the cosmos it is the universal connection of the world, simultaneously ideal and real, a living unity of idealness and realness, conceivability and being, which modern speculative philosophy (Fichte, Schelling, Hegel, and Neo-Kantianism) seeks. This living sophianic unity of thought and being grounds human teleology in science, engineering, and economy as well as the possibility of the external mastery of the world, "the world as household." However, they are sophianic in their foundation, but not in their condition, for they perceive the sophianicity of the world palely, externally, insubstantially; thanks to this, the contemplation of the world by science, sophianic in its foundation, is frequently anti-sophianic in practice. Scientific philosophy too, logical or transcendental idealism, is hardly philo-sophianic.

Here a general question arises: How much and in what sense is

The Sophianicity of the Creature

that transcendental or logical consciousness sophianic, the investigation of which has occupied and occupies modern philosophy most of all? One can pose this question differently: Is formal logic the primary expression of the Logos of the world, and is logical consciousness its immediate instrument? One ought to respond to this question negatively: "the logos" of the logic of transcendentalism is *not* the Logos of the world, and the equation of the one with the other is the lie of Hegelianism, proper to all logical idealism. Transcendental-logical self-consciousness or "pure reason" is not the Reason of the world; it corresponds only to a definite sector of the world in its sophianicity, is its foreshortening or projection.

Of course, even "pure reason" is sophianic in its foundation, and it reflects the light of the Logos, though it does not have absolute meaning, but is a condition proper precisely to a given sector of being, and loses its meaning to the extent that it immerses itself into the sophianic basis of the world. "Pure reason" is transient, and its nature is conditional and relative — it is bound with the limitedness and conditionality of our perception of the world of things that are mutually repelled, of the many which does not become the one, but is only unified and connected. Reason is the instrument of that kind of unification. The logical unity of reason corresponds to the external, mechanical unity of the world. "The reason" of philosophy not only does not constitute the highest achievement in the realm of sophianic comprehension of the world, it is in general a transient step. It is relative, not absolute, for thinking is not Logos but only logic, and logic is overcome at the highest levels of penetration into the sophianicity of the world. Logic deceives and is itself deceived *by the absolute form* of its universalism, and of course in its formal universality it obliquely reflects the sophianicity of the world, however, only obliquely. Already when comprehending the dogmas of faith logic changes — thus the doctrine of trinitarity and divine incarnation tears asunder with its antinomies the nets of reason and is therefore so unacceptable for consistent rationalism, which either rejects them altogether as absurd or strives to assimilate them at the price of the perversion of rationalistic accommodation (hence diverse heresies arise, like varieties of rationalism). "The wisdom of this age," as is definitely pointed out in the word of God, differs from the wisdom of the children of God, which for it seems folly. Logical thinking corresponds only to the here-and-now, sinful, shattered state of the world and humanity; it is a sickness or the outcome of immaturity. In *The Dream of a Ridiculous Man,* a work that is striking in its clairvoyance, Dostoevsky hints at this metalogical thinking that is proper to a sinless human being. The spiritual men and ascetic victors of the Church point definitely and repeatedly in their works to this relativity that is the same for thought and the mind; indications of this are found among both mystics and even occultists.

If logic cannot claim any such exclusive connection with the Logos, then philosophy cannot claim such a connection with Sophia. Authentically sophianic in it is not this universal, logical, transcendental consciousness or thinking which is only a provisional means of expressing the world, of assimilating it by thought in a given section of being, in the forms of logical concepts, but precisely this very *philia, erōs,* which lends wings to the soul and elevates it to a noetic vision of Sophia, of the world of ideas. And only that is in philosophy which is revealed to this noetic vision, i.e., precisely that which is not discursive in it but intuitive, and is all the more sophianic. In any case it is incumbent to contest in the most resolute manner the claims of logical idealism of various nuances to absoluteness in the sense of direct participation in the Logos. In their thought processes children are above or below logical reason, but in any case they are outside it, and nevertheless the incarnate Logos of the world himself pointed to them as the norm of perfect being, "for the Kingdom of God belongs to them." And similarly of course one ought not to converge the mind "of minds," of the angelic ranks, with the transcendental-logical mind of philosophy. It goes without saying that an ethic of the mind must have force for humanity, inasmuch as it lives on the plane of the mind, and consequently is to a certain degree doomed to science and philosophy; so too it is obliged to observe logical honesty, to combat intellectual laziness, and to overcome surmountable difficulties conscientiously. Religiously, however, a still more sublime task is set before humankind, namely, to rise *above* the mind, to become *higher than* mind. Precisely this path is indicated by people of a Christian, religious discipline.[52]

Sophia is revealed in the world as beauty, which is the tangible sophianicity of the world. Therefore art knows Sophia more directly and immediately than does philosophy. If religion is the direct self-testimony and self-proof of God, then art, or more broadly, beauty, is the self-proof of Sophia. From the darkening bosom of Demeter rise the vernal flowers; from the embrace of Hades, from dark nonbeing, comes to light the youthful and beautiful Persephone, a sophianized creature. For whom do flowers bloom in their color, which more often than not no human eye sees? For what are birds attired in their bright colors, why have they become so to say living flowers? For whom did the lark and the nightingale compose their songs? Why are tiger and leopard so beautiful in their terrible grace and the lion in his majesty? For what do maiden charms blossom on earth? Is not all of this the radiance of Sophia illuminating inert flesh and "matter" from within? And what else does art want and attain if not that same sophianization of flesh or "matter" (be it a sound, a body, a piece of marble, some paint, or a word)? The artist not only gazes on Sophia with noetic eyes, but with an obedient chisel reveals his vision to the world. The Greeks honored Virginity under various personages: Athena, Diana, and above all Aphrodite to whom the most beautiful works of Greek art are dedicated. Aphrodite, like other goddesses, is one of the natural faces of Sophia, beheld by the Greek genius. And can one define this rapture of beauty in nature or art in any other way than the cosmic amorousness, the erotic pathos of the creature? And this erotic inspiration ascends to the footstool of Sophia's throne, and the "prophetic eyes" are opened. Authentic art, which renders beauty manifest, holds something prophetic within and reveals a higher reality.

Clear from this is the exceptional significance of art, its hierarchic loftiness. In the beauty of nature, as in the creations of art, the partial or preliminary transfiguration of the world makes itself felt, its appearance in Sophia. This beauty lifts with its eros the human being up to the world of the eternal forms of ideas; the tremulous horses carry aloft the faithful coachman towards the life-creating sun, according to the unforgettable image of Plato's *Phaedrus*. Art is the wisdom of the future age, its knowledge, its philosophy. And philosophy is sophianic only insofar as it breathes with this pathos of amorousness, with this sophianic eros which opens the eyes of the mind; to say it differently, insofar as it is art, the fundamental motif of a philosophical system, its theme, is identified by intuition, like noetic beauty, while the system itself is only an attempt to tell of things divine in nondivine language.

But this transfiguration, realized in art, is partial, momentary, and fleeting, and the gloom of the extra- or anti-sophianic state of the world seems all the more opaque. The full transfiguration of the world, its illumination by beauty, the outpouring of the gifts of the Holy Spirit, lies beyond the limits of present-day being. However, it becomes the lot of holy and spirit-bearing men already in this age. The saints see the world differently than we do; it exists for them in sophianic color, in a light-bearing transfigured state. Noumen and phenomenon, idea and matter — for them they flow together into one, and before death they smell the air of resurrection.

The beauty of an object is its sophianic idea, which is translucent in it. And as far as everything existing participates in the world of ideas, everything is fundamentally beautiful, "very good," and can stand in its sophianic idea, i.e., clothe itself in beauty, and be transpierced by its rays. Deformity, stagnation, ugliness belong only to the heavy cover of nonbeing or half-being, materiality and limitedness, that hangs over the postlapsarian world. But this cover is not at all impenetrable. In revealed beauty which exposes the ontic, sophianic basis of the world, all creation is saved. And *all* creation is ideal in its foundation and in its coming transfiguration, although it is extra-ideal, semi-ideal, and even anti-ideal in its current state. An entirely extra-ideal or anti-ideal being does not exist,[53] for this would be pure, empty nothing, nonbeing *before* the world-creation. We can think such a thing only as a limit concept, the edge of being, "the outer darkness," the bottom of Hell, metaphysical nothing, but it is impossible to admit even in thought that the world fashioned by God in Sophia, although perverted in its anti-sophianic state, has been pierced by this emptiness. Rebellious nothing, the chaotic abyss, does not have the power to splash their dead waves through the weir of being that God has erected. The ontological basis of the world consists precisely in the *continuous*, metaphysically uninterrupted sophianicity of its foundation: this same earth of the curse will be paradise indeed when it becomes "a new earth." This does not mean of course that this transition would happen without a catastrophic upheaval dividing different eons; however, this very catastrophic quality presupposes a certain continuity of foundation. A new heaven and earth will not be fashioned again out of nothing, but in them the current earth and heaven will be refashioned, transfigured. Do not the following words of the apostle Paul speak about the sophianic authenticity *of all* creation: "Being found in this tent, we sigh under a burden because we do not want to be unclothed but to be clothed, so that the mortal should be swallowed up by life" (2 Cor. 5:4)?

The great truth "of the occult" worldview consists in the persistent affirmation of this universal animation of the world which excludes dead, soulless, undifferentiated matter that says nothing and has no qualities. The world is a great hierarchy of ideal entities, an ideal organism, and in this understanding of the sophianicity of the "dead" world lies the merit of occultism,[54] bringing it close to the "poetic perception" of nature in general. Pagan natural polytheism shares this trait, to a certain degree, as it represents so to say the religious paraphrase of the doctrine of the sophianicity of the world and the animation of all creatures. It is necessary to say without a moment's hesitation that in this respect polytheism stands closer to Christianity than do mechanistic rationalism and materialism: *panta plērē theōn* [*all things are full of gods*] — this view is closer to the truth than is the doctrine that the world is a mechanism, a sort of hour automat. Ancient occultism and popular polytheism form the authentic basis of Platonic idealism[55] and obtain in its philosophy a luxuriant speculative flowering. That which in philosophy is called ideas, living their own proper dialectical life, occurs in mystical insight as essences, generic and individual at the same time, qualities having not only abstract significance but also concrete being. These Platonic ideas-qualities are known to the mythological consciousness of a people and have been reflected in its sagas, fairy tales, and folklore: from this arise charms, spells, incantations, from this totems and in general the symbolism of wild animals, which has such meaning in all religions, not excluding Judeo-Christianity.

Here we are approaching one of the basic questions of Platonism, namely, the relationship of genus and species, the universal and the particular. Concepts establish the universal which exists in many particulars: human, wolf, fish, animal, etc. Without these universal concepts, cognition and thinking are not possible, as was equally clear to Plato and Aristotle. But in what relation do these concepts stand with the being of things, *ideae* with *res*? Are they abstractions, terms pragmatically and in this sense arbitrarily set by reason, *nomina flaces vocis*, or do the *res* themselves speak in them of their hidden essence? This central question of Platonic ontology, which arose in the medieval dispute of the nominalists and the realists, is now gaining exciting philosophical interest once again, if not in form then in essence. In our opinion both nominalists and realists are correct, though in a different sense. Idea-names, which constitute the ontological foundation of general concepts, are the prototypes of entities in Sophia, outside of which nothing becomes participant in being. Sophia, as the all-unity *(hen kai pan)*, the virginity of the creature, holds everything in herself in a higher confluence and unity. To comprehend this all-unity means to understand the world in Sophia, which is not given to the creaturely eye darkened by sin. However, that which we are not able to behold immediately by reason of its inaccessibility to us we do grasp in the world in its operation, similar to how we see the light of the invisible sun and in this light distinguish objects. The real relationship between ideas and prototypes, between genus and species and individuals, is expressed in the fact that in ideas both the general and the individual exist as one thing, both the generic person of the individual and the collective individuality of the genus are united. In its idea the genus exists both as one and as the fullness of all of its individuals, in their unrepeatable particularities, with this unity existing not only *in abstracto* but also *in concreto*. And what has been said is applicable most of all to that which constitutes the fullness and crown of being, namely, to the human being, and thereafter to the lower hierarchies of living entities subjected to him, to the world of animals, vegetation, minerals. In totems, coats of arms, and sacred images this ideal reality of genus is symbolically expressed: a wolf *exists* not only as the totality of wolves but also as wolfness, as does a lion and lioness, a lamb and lambness; *there is* a rose that blooms in Sophia and a lily of the Annunciation; *there is* gold, frankincense, and myrrh, which are suitable for presentation to the infant boy of Bethlehem, not at all by arbitrary selection but by their inner nature. An icon such as the image of the Theotokos in the fields, surrounded by sheaves of rye, speaks of this, or the so widespread symbolism of animals in iconography.

Humanity is in truth a single Adam both old and new, both first-made and reborn in Christ, and it is necessary to understand in their full significance the words of the Lord Jesus Christ that he himself is present in those who hunger and in those who thirst, in those imprisoned and in all suffering humanity. But at the same time the individualization, the contrasting of separate people as individuals with the Christ-humanity in them, remains no less real. Christ is a human being as such, the whole *idea* of the human, and in this sense the *genus* in the human being; but the latter is realized in being as an indeterminate plurality of individualities in which genus is disclosed. Still, the bases of individuality, namely of the given, and just this, are hidden in genus, are ontologically grounded in it. If it were possible to look from within at the family, the clan, the nation, humanity, all of this would be presented as a single, many-faced, many-eyed entity. In a similar way, they say, it is possible to see all life extended in time as a combined, extra-temporal, single act, or as a synthesis of time.[56]

The Sophianicity of the Creature

The source of the meaningfulness of general concepts is contained in this real unity and ideal validity of all that exists; their value is justified pragmatically through their correlation with reality which may be only indirect. Logic proves to be technical, and technics logical, and therein lies the basis of the possibility of science and its technical application, or to put it differently, the *economic* nature of science. The hypothesis of consistent nominalism according to which general concepts were regarded as human invention, conventional agreement, a fabricated soubriquet, the contrivances of separate people, would make the meaningfulness of concepts completely incomprehensible. It atomizes thinking and proves to be powerless to explain the facts of science. Further, the very possibility of a general concept, of a "common" name, would be an unsolvable riddle: only individual names could be thought up, but not general ones, which need a certain common ideal basis in order to appear. Without this, the shattered logical atoms, individual names, would not lend themselves to any summation and generalization. General concepts are just as intuitive and immediate in their basis as are perceptions of individual being; and outside *general intuition,* inseparable from the intuitions of the individual, general concepts would be impossible. Already by the fact of their existence they testify to the "mental vision" of the ideal essences of being, accessible to humanity under various ways in a concrete-mythological or logical-abstract form. Expressing it with a well-known Platonic term, *participation* in ideas *(methexis)* is proper to general concepts, but thereby neither our scientific or philosophical conception *alone is* entirely adequate to them. It is of course possible to deceive oneself with the hope that, having wandered the path "of phenomenological consciousness," the philosopher already enters into the *topos noētos,* the kingdom of authentic ideas, "Mothers," but for this Hegelian temptation one needs truly to have a certain sophianic blindness.

For Plato an entire series of dialectical problems flowed from this (because of this emerged his transcendental-critical dialogues *Parmenides, Philebus, Sophist*). The doctrine of remembrance *(anamnēsis)* developed in *Phaedo* refers to this. On the one hand, cognition is something present beforehand in the soul, that must only be awakened, made known, realized, but on the other hand the possibility of preliminary oblivion and falling out of consciousness, and consequently an apparently new discovery, is presupposed by remembrance. Full and clear remembrance in general is inaccessible to the prisoners in the cave who find themselves with their back to the sun and only see shadows, but still these shadows attest to the sun and speak of moving objects. An exact transcendentally logical formulation of the relation of ideas to concepts, which simultaneously unites the realist and nominalist understanding, presents exceptional difficulties for philosophy, as was sufficiently revealed already in the mediaeval dispute of the realists and idealists, but equally in modern philosophy, in particular in contemporary Neo-Kantianism. The development of a new philosophy in German idealism is marked, on the one hand, by the attempt of the prisoners to barricade themselves in the cave and make its opening for the sun impenetrable, which is what Kant accomplished in his phenomenalism, or audaciously to force oneself through to the world of ideas by the Luciferian self-confidence of the speculative mind (Fichte and Hegel). This German parody on Platonism does not reckon enough with the fact that Greek intellection was not that abstract philosophizing "of pure" impoverished reason, i.e., torn away from the roots of intuition, which was produced on German soil. The poet, the myth-maker, the mystic and mage are inseparable from philosophy in Pythagoras, Plato, or Plotinus, and as spiritual fathers the pillars of German idealism can take for themselves only... the Sophists, with whom Socrates and Plato clashed not so much on the ground of a definite philosophical doctrine as of the very means of philosophizing, *ars philosophandi*. Socrates contrasted himself with the Sophists, abstract idealists and rationalists who either did not believe in truth at all or who hoped to discover it by the speculative-idealistic path. Against this, Socrates and his great disciple after him set in opposition the fullness of religious, philosophical, and lived experience.

The participation of concepts in ideas, their partial and reflected sophianicity, coupled with extra-sophianicity and anti-sophianicity, the play of light and shadows, grounds the possibility of *error*, of the battle between the truth and falsehood of concepts. The possibility of general concepts is rooted in the noetic vision of ideas, but these general concepts-ideas are seen not in their sophianic harmony or integrity but in a full-scale "depraved" aspect, like the bad plurality of clashing centers, from which the whole mixed character, chaos, and disorderliness of being derives. The source of error, of limitedness, of mistakes is the same on the whole for the whole phenomenality of the world, of bad plurality, which is the *principium individuationis* not in a good but in a bad sense. Error is rooted not in the limitedness of a separate mind whose limitation could be compensated for by the genius of another mind; it has as its source the condition of the world, which "lies in evil." Where then is the cause of this plurality? Where is that *principium individuationis* which at the same time becomes the source of world evil?

2. What Is Matter?

The world has a higher foundation in the realm of ideas or Sophia in which the one and the many, the particular and the universal, one and all harmoniously exist in positive all-unity. But alongside of this the world has a lower "support" — *hypodochē* — which is the "place" of "disintegrated" actualized plurality that finds its unity only in the temporal-spatial process, in becoming, being-nonbeing; layers of being are interlaid here with layers of nonbeing, and being is found in an indissoluble union with nonbeing, like light and shadow. The world is made out of nothing; nothing, pure, empty nonbeing, is the inferior foundation, material, the matter of the world. This is not that nonbeing which we know as a facet of being or at least its shadow. No, here we are talking about the perfect nothing, which God called into being, that darkness which is simply *not-light*, and for that reason even *not-darkness*, for the positive concept of darkness is supposed only by light, since the positive principle of nonbeing is supposed by being. *How* light shone in this "pitch" darkness devoid of light, *how* being was sown in absolute being, is an incomprehensible deed of the all-wisdom and omnipotence of God, of the creative "fiat." We have already pointed out that it cannot be philosophically deduced, for philosophical deduction arrives here and departs from here as from a certain givenness, and at the same time, as from a mystery. It befits atheistic philosophy, which does not acknowledge divine mystery, either to avoid this question altogether, as all modern philosophy essentially does, or to mask its insolubility, i.e., to appeal to a principle that is not susceptible to rational or logical deduction (Hartmann and Schopenhauer). The fact that in Greek intellection such exclusive attention was paid to the question of the prime matter of the world is evidence of Hellenic wisdom and piety; in the doctrines of Plato, Aristotle, and Plotinus it received a complete, exhaustive consideration, to which modern philosophy could add nothing.

The World

Already early Greek philosophy with its cosmologism ran across this problem and gave it different solutions. Matter is characterized as undefined or unlimited *(apeiron)* by Anaximander, the Pythagoreans, and partially by Plato *(Philebus,* 24A). The latter arrives in full earnest at this question in the *Timaeus* where "the dark and difficult genus" forming the third principle of the world, the basis of coming to be *(tou gignomenou),* undergoes discussion. Matter is considered here on the one hand as the unconditional nothing, almost transcendent for thinking, with every attempt at its positive determination being doomed to contradiction; but at the same time this nothing is summoned towards being-nonbeing, to coming to be, and for this reason one can perceive it as the substrate of separate ontic moments, more than this, as the basis of plurality, the general background of being *("pasēs geneseōs hypochēn autēn hoion tithēnēn")* [the matter of all generation, like a wet-nurse]. "It is necessary to call it the always identical *(tauton)* for it never advances out of its potency *(dynameōs);* it always receives everything and never and in no way does it appropriate any form for assimilation of what enters it; for by nature it serves as material for everything *(ekmageion)* which obtains motion and forms from what enters and it is presented through it in diverse moments as different" *(Timaeus,* 50 BC). The very suitability of matter for its role is connected with the fact that it is "free *(amorphon on)* of those ideas which it needs to make room for" (50 D), otherwise it would reproduce them by introducing something from itself. Therefore "that which receives in itself all genus must be foreign to all forms."

On this basis Plato applies the apophatic method already familiar to us to the description of matter as creaturely nothing, by defining it almost with negations alone: "It is a certain invisible sort *(anoraton),* formless *(amorphon),* all-receiving *(pandektēs),* elusive *(dysalōtaton);* we will not call it either earth or water or air or fire or that which has come from them" (51A). This real nothing, subsisting nonbeing, cannot be caught by the senses but only postulated by thought, and that only on the condition that it attempts to come out of itself, as stated by Plato, by means of "an illegitimate judgment" *(logismōi tini nothōi).* In order to do this, one needs to think all nonbeing cleanly away, but all the same in so doing simple, pure nothing, ultimate emptiness, will not be obtained: one has to peak behind the coulisses of being so to say, or by remaining on its facial surface, feel its underside. (An analogous task is given by contemporary artists who try to transmit multidimensional space with a flat drawing; a similar thought captivates the imagination of a child — to see what happens in a room when we are not there.) And all this leads to an antinomy, connected with the concept of creaturely nothing in the same measure as with the concept of Divine Nothing. On the one hand it is nothing, nonbeing, but on the other hand it is the foundation of this world in process, the principle of plurality or the metaphysical (and for that very reason transcendental) place of this world. In precisely this sense Plato defines matter as "a type of space *(to tēs chōras)*, that does not accept destruction, that gives place to all that has generation" (52A). This ideal space forms the metaphysical foundation of that plurality of being in which both temporality and spatiality arise. And so, Platonic matter is located on the very bounds between *ouk on* and *mē on;* it is *ouk on* that is converted into the *mē on* of creation, and in this metaphysical duality is the source of the antinomism of its logical definition. Essentially Aristotle comes close to a similar apophatic description of prime matter *(prōtē hylē)*. For him matter "possessing the capacity to be or not to be each" *(dynaton to einai kai mē einai hekaston)* represents in itself the absence of all qualities – *sterēsis*. The union of the absence of qualities with the capacity for receiving every quality exhausts the description of *prōtē hylē* and brings it close to the Platonic "dark and difficult genus."

We find a more detailed apophatic description of matter entirely in the Platonic spirit in Plotinus, who dedicated the fourth book of the second Ennead (and the sixth book of the third Ennead) to a special study of matter. Here he painstakingly liberates the concept of matter from every qualification, establishing by the same way its alogical nature, which is opposed to whatsoever definition in concepts. Since matter serves for everything, it is itself without qualities *(apoios)*. "It must not be complex, but simple and single in itself, for only so will it be empty *(erēmos)* of everything" (VIII); "it must be suited to everything, as well as to magnitude" (VIII); it has no body *(asōmatos)* and as such it is also without quantity *(aposos);* inasmuch as "quantity is form" (IX), it is "indeterminateness" *(aoristia)* (X). Can one think of indeterminateness, if only by "illegitimate judgment" as in Plato? But the indeterminate is determined by a certain positive judgment, and just as the dark is the matter of every invisible color for the eye, so the soul removes all that in sense-perceptible things is similar to light and, no longer having a determination, it is similar to sight, which is preserved to a certain degree even in the darkness. *It thinks it without thinking, noei ou noousa* (X). "Matter is necessary as a substrate in order to apprehend everything." It has no measure or magnitude, but only the faculty for giving it a place (XI), because it is only an illusory measure *(phantasma tou onkou)*. Matter is devoid of quality, for it is impossible to take negation, deprivation *(sterēsis)*, for a quality (XIII). Matter is unlimited *(apeiron)*. "The unlimited is not only a property of matter, but matter itself is the unlimited," "the unlimited as such *(par'hautēs)* is in opposition to reason" (XV). "*Being does not belong to matter,* it is what truly is not *(alēthinos mē on)*, as the representation and phantom of extension, the striving for subsistence *(hypostaseōs ephesis)*, and does not calm down in rest; it is invisible by nature and flees from what wants to see what exists, when they do not see it; it vanishes upon inspection, gradually accepting opposite aspects: of great and small, insufficient or abundant, a phantom that does not flee and is unsteady. . . . Therefore all of its manifestations are false: when it seems big, it is small, when more, it is less, what it is in the imagination is what

The World

it is not, it flees like a toy which is why that which seems to be occurring in it are toys, images in an image, like an object in a mirror which though located in one place is reflected in another, which seems to be filled, not having anything, but seems to be everything. And those which enter it are a formless phantom and what proceeds from it are phantoms and likenesses, detected by reason of its formlessness, and they seem to have an effect on it, but in actual fact they do not act at all, being powerless and weak and not having stability; and as they have no such thing, they pass by, without cutting it, as through water or as if to send images in the so-called empty space.... Weak and deceptive, matter itself is susceptible to deception; as in a dream, in water or in a mirror these impressions leave it unaffected" (*Ennead* III, book VI, chapter VII). Its indifference is provided for by this featurelessness. But in accepting everything, matter is the universal wet-nurse, *tithēnē*, in accord with Plato's definition. However, "that which enters into matter, as into a mother, does not use it or harm it, and this push is directed not to it, but to one another, for these forces operate on the opposite, and not on the substrate. Matter abides without suffering from the cold that has set in or from the approaching warmth, for the one and the other are neither friendly nor hostile to it. Therefore it is all the more suitable to call it a support and wet-nurse *(hypodochē kai tithēnē)*. Is it a mother, as is said? But it does not give birth to anything. Only they call it mother who define the role of the mother in relation to what is born merely as one who contains but gives nothing to what is born, but so far as that which is born has a body, it is received from nutrition. But if the mother does give something to what is born, then this is not as matter, but insofar as it is a form. For only form is capable of generation, whereas other nature is barren" (XIX).

Plotinus gives essentially the same description of matter as does Plato but in a more verbose and tangled form, bringing to light the antinomy of this concept, which wavers between nothing and something, *ouk on* and *mē on*, and is shot with the colors of the one and the other. The difference between Plotinus's doctrine and Plato's, in conformity with his general metaphysical system, is that alongside of the matter of this world he still postulates an intelligible matter, extra-temporal and eternal, an ideal substrate that receives images of the *mind (nous)* and has, distinct from inferior matter, both authenticity and substantiality (*Enneads* II, book 4, chapters IV-V). Our world, with its matter, represents a descent or a lower level of the higher world, but thereby it produces and reflects it; and therefore matter must be in both worlds, or to say it differently, the matter of the lower world must have a parallel for itself in the higher world.

This concept does not receive further development by Plotinus. His *nous*, the ideal organism of ideas-forms, having a "support" for itself in ideal matter is, in our opinion, nothing other than Sophia, or in a certain sense the very same thing as the Platonic world of ideas. But Plato is to be preferred to Plotinus because in the *Timaeus* he introduces the act of creation as a feature that establishes

The Sophianicity of the Creature

the link between the two worlds, uniting them and at the same time dividing them. Plotinus, who in principle lacks the idea of creation, is compelled simply to double matter and alongside the matter of our world to postulate yet another intelligible matter. Thanks to this doubling a twofold shadow lies on material being. In Plotinus's doctrine much more definitely than in Plato's, matter receives a negative coefficient and is regarded as the principle of evil, as thickening darkness, and as it submerges in it, it gradually extinguishes the light which floods out of the proto-source, the *One*. Matter is passive evil which arises as a result of a weakening of the good, verging on its full absence.

All "material" being, valid in one respect, is at the same time nonbeing in all other respects — *omnis determinatio est negatio* — every determination is delimitation, every delimitation is negation. Being and nonbeing percolate into each other; in every layer and stratum of being the caustic moisture of nonbeing penetrates or can penetrate, decomposing the connectedness and wholeness of its fabric. Therefore every "material" being is individual in a bad sense: here division, fragmentation, is the foundation of individuation. And since every being (in the stated sense) is "material," i.e., every being is coupled with nonbeing, then every being, as something that is subject to division, is individual in a negative sense. The ideal, sophianic world remains on the other side of this being-nonbeing; to say it differently, there is no place for matter — nothing — in it, and if one can speak of its being-essence, then only in the special sense of *suprabeing,* which the shadow of nonbeing does not reach. Therefore here there is no place for negative individuality either, but then the *principia individuationis* are valid in the *positive* sense as autonomous principles of being, as rays in the spectrum of the sophianic pleroma. But in falling into the world of being-nonbeing, the void of materiality, they enter into a bond with the *principia individuationis* in a negative sense.

Ancient philosophy, although it was able to detect nothing as the hidden underlying cause of being, remained powerless before the task of explaining by what means nothing becomes *chōra* [place] or how *ouk on* turns into *mē on,* in other words, how the world of phenomena arises. And this is because here in this question the *limit* of philosophy is reached, the domain of the logical inference of principles ends. Here is the logical hiatus or miracle, the limit event which philosophy cannot explicate but can only establish by interpreting its results. By what means does the world arise, i.e., this mixture of being and nonbeing, by

The World

what means is being created at all, and how are super-subsistent seeds of being immersed in nothing? Ancient philosophy came to a standstill before this problem in natural and legitimate powerlessness, as does any "pure philosophy" that wittingly does not occupy itself with mythologization. Plato replied to this question in the *Timaeus* with the religious myth of the creation of the world by the Demiurge and thereby tacitly certified the impossibility of a purely philosophical response. (He indirectly confirmed this in *Parmenides,* where he showed how the idea becomes entangled in unavoidable dialectical contradictions in analyzing being-nonbeing, and in this sense, *Parmenides* is a dialectical *prooemium* for *Timaeus*.) Plotinus tried to reply to this question likewise not with a speculative but with a religious-mystical doctrine of the One and the emanation of its rays into matter; regardless of the religious value of such a construct, it nonetheless has no philosophical persuasiveness (although it is frequently taken to be philosophical). Here religious intuition or faith comes into its legitimate rights: only *revelation* can inform us about the otherworldly roots of our being, by inevitably expressing itself in the form of *myth* that then can receive a philosophical reworking, and be set as the foundation of a philosopheme.

Both Plato and Plotinus have recourse to myth in equal measure, with the difference that the Platonic myth is more concrete and religious, while that of Plotinus appears to be rendered colorless by mystical speculation. On the contrary, Aristotle, devoid of myth and mythopoesis in the very central point of his system — namely in the doctrine of form and matter in their mutual connection — leaves an entirely substantial emptiness, which philosophical system fears as an interruption in continuity. The question of *the principle of motion,* corresponding to the creation of the world, is left essentially open by Aristotle. Judeo-Christian faith has its divinely revealed myth about the origin of the world in the narrative of the book of the *Genesis* of the human race. "In the beginning God created heaven and earth, and the earth was without form and void, and darkness was over the abyss, and the Spirit of God was borne above the water" (Gen. 1:1-2). *In the beginning,* i.e., in Sophia, through Sophia, on the foundation of Sophia, by Sophia, God *created* heaven and earth by an act of ineffable creativity, incomprehensible in its all-wisdom and omnipotence, the power and nature of which we sense in every breath, in every moment of our being. Heavenly Sophia and earthly sophianicity, perfect actuality and "formless and void" potentiality, divine fullness and hunger for divinity, "light of Tabor" and "darkness above the abyss" — this is the unity of opposites, *coincidentia oppositorum,* transcendent to reason, and it tears it asunder antinomically. But even if this stays a contradiction for reason, it is not able to come up with anything cleverer than this contradiction in order to solve the problem. The intelligible cosmos looks at itself in first-formed Chaos, and becomes its inner potency, and Chaos initiates Cosmos, and becomes chao-cosmos.

The act of creating the world is realized by the making of heaven and earth in the *Beginning,* by the formation of two centers in Sophia. It is one and the same act, for by the very fact that the *earth* is made, *heaven,* its "archetype," already opposes it, being the intelligible foundation of creation. *The Beginning,* i.e., Divine Sophia, in its supernal existence, abides transcendent to the world with its inevitable dualism of heaven and earth, of ideas and matter, but at the same time heaven and earth are made precisely *in the Beginning;* they are grounded in their being in the super-subsistent Sophia. The opposition of heaven and earth is the basis of creation, its initial outcome; its removal, the establishment of a living ladder between heaven and earth, is the final task of the world and historical process: *"Thy will be done as in heaven so on earth."*

Thus, what is this "formless and empty" earth? Is it the "matter" of ancient philosophy, the empty and hollow nothing perceptible only to *logismōi tini nothōi,* a passive and lifeless "place" *(chōra)*? No, the earth is something else and incomparably more. *Earth* is the nothing into which sophianicity has already been poured out, which is why it is potential Sophia. *Nothing* received actual being and became Chaos, a real *apeiron,* about which the mythologies of the Greeks, Babylonians, and other peoples speak. It is the "born Chaos," which stirs beneath being, and sometimes bursts through like a force of annihilation. The creation of the earth lies *outside* the six days of the world's creation, it is its ontological *prius,* and the creative acts of the separate days presuppose as their foundation the first-formed earth: in it light is separated from darkness, the firmament from water; in it the earthly heaven is already made in which the luminaries move and birds fly; on it the earth's water flows together, which "will bring forth" reptiles; out of it is formed the firmament or earthly earth, which will bring forth "a living soul according to its kind, cattle and reptiles and beasts of the earth"; out of it is fashioned the human's body. All this is done by the creative word of God, but already *not* out of nothing, but out of earth, like a gradual disclosing of its sophianic content, its saturation with ideas.[57] This "earth" is therefore as it were cosmic Sophia, its face in the universe, its feminine principle which has power, according to the creative word *"fiat,"* to produce from itself creatures, to give birth from it.[58] It is the Great Mother whom pagans from time immemorial devoutly honored: Demeter, Isis, Cybele, and Ishtar. And in its potency this earth is God-earth; this mother hides in herself since her creation the coming Mother of God, "the womb of divine incarnation," "the heavenly ladder by which God descended," "the bridge which leads those who are of the earth into heaven" (from the Akathist of the Mother of God).

From what has been said it is evident how limited and incomplete the concept of matter remains in Plato and how distorted it is in Plotinus, for whom matter, as a negative principle, as nonbeing, is evil and even the principle of evil. They both prove here to be inferior to Greek popular religion that honored Demeter in a holy manner and established participation in the flesh of the world, a cosmic Eucharistic, in the cult of the Elysian mysteries. Something of the decadence of the intelligentsia peers through here in both thinkers, especially Plotinus, whose limitedness is inseparably linked with his hostility towards Christianity. Both of them, Plato and Plotinus, know only empty matter in their philosophy, but are entirely ignorant of sophianic earth, the mother Demeter, and for this reason their cosmology remains incomplete and defective. In it is missing the necessary substrate of being, of authentic *hypodochē*, for which pure nothing cannot serve. They established pre-subsistent matter, the matter of matter, but rejected the real mother of being, the Earth.

On the basis of what has been said, one can answer more precisely the question of what Aristotelian *hylē* represents, which is formed by the ideas. This is in no case Platonic matter which in general does not exist, for it is outside the limits of being. Being knows only "earth," sophianic and saturated with unbounded possibilities. "Earth" is *all-matter,* but in it *all* is potentially included. Therefore it is impossible to locate in the world empty, unqualified "place" as matter is for Greek idealism. *Matter in general* does not exist at all, for it is only ideally fertilized, initiating matter. Therefore it thirsts not for *formation in general* but for *a definite* form, which it hides in itself like a possibility and will carry in itself like an aspiration. An artist who knows how to understand and respect a material, to capture its style, tone, and idea whether it is wood, marble, metal, paints, sound, or word, knows very well the internal correspondence of matter to form, the voice of matter. Materialism, precisely in its original form which goes by the name of hylomorphism, gives an incorrect philosophical expression to a correct sensation of matter, as an initiating and fruit-

The Sophianicity of the Creature

bearing, qualified principle. Materialism is vague babble about the sophianic saturation of the earth, and with this living feeling of the earth ("of matter") it advantageously differs from idealism, for which matter is an illegitimate concept about nothing, either transcendental *chōra,* or the waning of being, a subsistent minus. Materialists are permeated with piety towards Demeter, although in her most external and gross aspect, while idealists, being deprived of a feeling of matter, do not have even this piety.

Plato and Aristotle equally hold that everything springs up having its entelechy and inner law of being in the heavenly archetype, like a vague attraction or a search for its own proper form: *kinei ho erōmenon,* in the words of Aristotle. The motive principle operates not as an external, mechanical pressure but as the object of erotic attraction. The participation of being in ideas, *methexis,* about which Plato speaks, was explicated by him as the universal all-permeating force of Eros, the great mediator "between god and mortal," *metaxu theou te kai thnētou (Symposium,* 202C). The realm between heaven and earth, or between the divine and the creaturely, the eternal and the temporal, this metaphysical *metaxu,* is overcome by the winged "demon," the son of Poros and Penia, Fullness and Emptiness (for *theos anthrōpōi ou mignytai alla dia touton pasa estin hē homilia kai hē dialektos theois pros anthrōpous* [the divine will not mingle directly with a human being, but thanks to this all commerce and discourse with humans is possible for the gods], *Symposium* 203A). In mythological form Plato here defines the nature of the relations between ideas and their empirical "becoming" as erotic yearning, as the hunger and thirst of emptiness for fullness, and their initiatory force. Matter *loves* its idea-form and strives after it.

The physician Eryximachus speaks about Eros: "On the basis of medicine, of our art, it seems to me, one can see that Eros has control not only over the souls of people, by virtue of beauty, but by virtue of much else Eros also has control over the rest, over the bodies of all living creatures, as well as over what springs up from the earth, and to say it in a word, *over all that exists (en pasi tois ousi);* this god is great and wondrous and has influence over everything *(epi pan teinei)* in both divine and human affairs" (186A). Eros becomes apparent also in the condition of a body — in health and sickness, and for this reason "the healing art is governed by this god," and in gymnastics and agriculture; also governed by him are music, which is *peri harmonian kai rhythmon erōtikon epistēmē* [a science of love concerning harmony and rhythm] (187C), astronomy, and religion. In the speech of Diotima, Eros is primarily described as a general striving for beauty and creativity, the unity and universality of "all-one beauty" *(kalou toiude)* being established. This beauty is, on the one hand, the source of creativity, "of generation in beauty," and on the other hand the ladder of ascent to that knowledge which is something other than knowledge of beauty in itself. It is completely clear that Plato is speaking here about something other than divine Sophia and the sophianic saturation of the creaturely world, and *Eros* is only the mythological transcription of the relation that exists between "earth," matter, and its pre-established form.

And thus *methexis,* the participation of matter in idea, is precisely *Eros,* the Eros of "earth" for "heaven." Idea-entelechy is simultaneously a given as the root of being, and a task, a tendency beyond the limits of what is on hand. It is a pining, a quest for itself in its ideal, eternal essence; it is self-creativity and self-generation. The soul seeks itself like the Shulamite around the city squares of her Beloved. She inquires of everyone whether they have seen the One whom this soul loves. She grows faint from the passionate desire to be united with him, to outstrip herself, "to give birth to herself in beauty." All nature "suffers and moans" from "the vanity and corruption" to which it is doomed in its materiality and opaqueness; all of it is still not that which it is. Like a plant, it wants all the time to come into flower so that in its flowering it can sense, know, its sophianic being. And does not the color of flowers contain a certain living symbolism of the sophianicity of nature, and is not their fruit-bearing force its self-evidence? Everything living strives for grace and beauty, for harmony of motion, for the inner rhythm of its being. And that which is called brutishness and animality in a bad sense is a sickness, a distortion of the animal world. The artist's eye succeeds in glimpsing a nonanimal, almost-human melancholy for itself in the eyes of a creature. And of the purity and "idealness" of the animal world speak most distinctly of all the birds of the sky, its flowers, which praise God by their very being.

The whole creation thirsts for "deliverance" from slavery to "vanity," for sophianic illumination, for transfiguration in beauty, but it speaks of this with a tongue that is mute. And only the human soul, our own soul – poor, intimidated Psyche – do we know with final, intimate, certain knowledge. What can be more certain than that our present I is *not I* at all, for our eternal essence, our divine genius is quite different from our empirical person, our body, character, psychology! *One can never be reconciled with oneself,* and this irreconcilability is perhaps the supreme dignity of the human being. "If it is fitting for me to boast, I will boast of my weaknesses" (St. Paul), and only a complete spiritual collapse would be able to expel this irreconcilability from the heart, extinguish it in the soul. Alcibiades tells Socrates the immortal inspired words repeated by every soul that is put face to face before its own divine essence as before a mirror of its own imperfection and deformity. In these words the pathos of the whole of Platonism is expressed, and in the confessions of Alcibiades-Plato, Psyche herself speaks here, having sensed the eros of her own being: "When I hear him, my heart beats stronger than do those of the Corybantes, and tears flow because of his words; I see that the same happens with many others. Hearing Pericles and other skilled orators I find them eloquent but I have not experienced anything similar: my soul did not become agitated and *it experienced no indignation with its own servile existence.* Hearing this Marsyas, I was often so incited that it was not worth living if I remained as I was" (*Symposium*, 215 E). And in a similar manner does not everyone's soul awaken from the heavy sleep of nonbeing or half-being if they encounter on their path a true "friend," their own Socrates, and in him or through him suddenly catch sight of themselves, having sensed their "servile" state! This bifurcation of consciousness, this feeling that I am not-I, is the most reliable inner evidence of the truth of Platonism, which extends not only to the soul but also to the body. Somewhere in the depths of the soul each person feels themselves to be Endymion, with a lithe, well-built beautiful body that shines through in a Hellenic statue or sculpted dance, and not the lame, "ugly duckling" with a clumsy body devoid of every grace; it is impossible to be reconciled with it, for it is impossible to become accustomed to ugliness.

The human being knows in itself its supreme I as the genius with which each one is endowed, for each human has its special place in the Pleroma of All-humanity; to each human being corresponds its own ray in Sophia. But none are able nor do they know how to uncover in themselves this genius, to dig up the Castalian spring of inspiration,[59] although at times they grow faint from thirst. And everything that they do is *not that*, neither quantitatively nor qualitatively, for, when the soul wants to sing, it expels indistinct and faltering sounds. And only in those in whom humanity has its geniuses and emissaries does this hidden but universal brilliance come to light, which is our real, substantial participation in Sophia. And they stir people with their mere existence like the cry of cranes from the heights of heaven. Everyone wants to fly in the blue heights, and to lack wings is felt to be an insult. Everything is beautiful, everything is genius, everything is sophianic in the foundation of its being, in its idea, in its vocation, but alas, not in its being. And ultimately the task of earthly, human creativity is to find one's authentic, everlasting face, to reveal oneself. Therefore it is erotic in tone, and each creative act is essentially self-creation, self-creativity. All earthly life is summed up in discovering one's own face. And the "science of all sciences," the "spiritual art" of asceticism, sets directly before the human being this task of fashioning "the inner human," of discovering one's authentic essence by the path of long and arduous work on oneself, by spiritual-artistic struggle.

This path is not only the straight path but is essentially the only one, for the remaining paths of creativity lead to the goal only insofar as they coincide with this path in what is most important and substantial. Art, as "giving birth in beauty," is the discovery of the sophianicity of the creature through itself and to that extent in itself, the breach through nothing, through half-being to the essential. But the self-transfiguration of the human being can be limited only by this point of the breach, and the human being remains as it were its own prisoner. And in this way that alluring bifurcation is created in the life of the poet, thanks to which he is simultaneously the herald of the empyrean world and "the most contemptible child of the world." "Beauty will save the world"[60] — this means that the world will become palpably sophianic, but no longer through the creativity and self-creativity of humankind, but through the creative act of God, through the final "very good" for the creation, through the outpouring of the gifts of the Holy Spirit. The revelation of the world in Beauty is that "holy Jerusalem which comes down from heaven from God" and "has the glory of God" (Rev. 21:10-11). Like the force of the continual striving of all that exists towards its Logos, towards eternal life, Beauty is the inner law of the world, a world-forming, cosmourgic force; it holds the world, connects it in its statics and dynamics, and in the fullness of time by its decisive victory it "will save the world."

3. Matter and the Body

In both philosophical doctrines and customary word usage materiality and corporeality are frequently equated. This view is expressed with the greatest force in Neo-Platonism: in accord with the teaching of Plotinus, the body in and of itself is a bad, evil principle. By contrast, in Platonism the understanding of the body as evil, as the fetters and prison for the spirit (expressed with the greatest force in *Phaedo* and partially in *Phaedrus*) still contends with a more positive relationship to it which achieves its peak intensity in platonic eroticism. Therefore one ought to understand the ascetic motif in Plato's doctrine not in the sense of a metaphysical condemnation of the body but as the demand of a practical, religious-ethical asceticism — in the name of the struggle with sinful flesh for the sake of the victory of the spirit which leads to the enlightenment of the body also. Usually these two aspirations of asceticism, on principle opposite each other though having an external similarity, are persistently confused one with the other. For this reason even Christian asceticism does not differ from Buddhist asceticism, and the religion of the salvation of the body is accused of a fundamental hostility towards the body. Not only Plato's own erotic philosophy, at the basis of which lay of course a deep lived experience, saved him from that bad, Buddhist asceticism, but also the bright heaven of Greek religion in which despite all its limitedness, altogether proper to polytheism, the sacredness of the body was deeply felt. This revelation of the Edenic flesh lay at the basis of Greek anthropomorphism and left its mark on the divine works of sculpted art, Hellenic iconography.

The nation-artist to whose mental eyes was revealed the uncorrupted beauty of the body, could not curse and condemn the body definitively, while Plato was too much a son of his people and its religion to commit such a betrayal against the national genius of Hellenism, he who placed the mental vision of this world at the basis of his philosophy. On the contrary, Neo-Platonism, for all its philosophical refinement and saturation by the motifs of occultism and magic, displays the traits of the decadence of the Greek spirit, and even in its yearning for the restoration of polytheism is rather "a tendency of the intelligentsia" uprooted from the soil of positive religion. It is not hard to understand this: the Neo-Platonists contended for a hopeless cause — the religion of paganism was already smashed by the cross, and attempts to save it, no matter how philosophically brilliant, were for all that the result of a spiritual reaction and doomed to failure. "You have conquered, Galilean"; in that dying howl of the reigning adherent of Neo-Platonism and paganism, Julian the Apostate, was expressed the sentence of history. And all philosophical efforts of Neo-Platonism in the struggle with Christianity went to the benefit of the latter, for in Neo-Platonism it obtained a sharpened philosophical weapon that proved useful for Christian theology. (There are no reasons to reject the well-known dependence of Christian philosophy on Neo-Platonism.)

The World

As we already know, Plotinus's teaching on the body is connected with his general emanationist cosmology, according to which materiality is remoteness from the One, *only a minus* and for that reason evil, while the body is matter. It is characteristic for Plotinus's point of view that he is compelled not to distinguish but to merge and equate philosophical matter, which is what nothing and nonbeing are, with the body and to extend the metaphysical-ethical condemnation in its entirety to the body. Precisely this point brings out more distinctly than anywhere else the whole opposition of Plotinus's doctrine to the Christian proclamation of the salvation and resurrection of the body, to belief in the resurrection of Christ and the coming universal resurrection. The union of the soul with the body is in itself already a kind of falling into sin which is described by Plotinus with the following traits: "What is the cause for souls, which had their destiny in that place and wholly belonged there, to have forgotten their god and father and have lost knowledge of him and of their own selves? The principle of evil in them is daring *(tolma)*, becoming *(genesis)*, original isolation *(prōtē heterotōs)*, and the desire to belong to themselves *(heauton einai)*. Since they are evidently happy with their self-authority *(autexousian)*, making much use of the freedom of movement beyond themselves *(par' heautōn)*, they took the opposite direction and distanced themselves quite far and forfeited the knowledge that they themselves are from there (just as children who have become separated from their fathers and have spent much time far away know neither their father nor themselves)" (*Enneads* V, lib. I, cap. I). At its incarnation the soul "loses wings and falls into the fetters of the body," "is buried and remains in the dungeon," "souls of necessity become amphibious, involuntarily leading a life in that place and in these climes" (*Enneads* IV, lib. VIII, cap. IV). "In this the soul commits a double fault: the one consists in the inducement of the soul to condescension, the second in the soul's performance of bad deeds" (cap. V). "The soul becomes bad *(kakē)* in union with the body and is made servile to it and concurs with it in everything" (*Enneads* I, lib. II, cap. III). "They rightly say that the soul becomes vile *(aischran)* through mixture, dissolution, inclination towards the body" (*Enneads* I, lib. VI, cap. V), and therefore that all virtues are reduced to one – to purification *(katharsis)*" (cap. VI). "Courage is apathy before death, death is the separate existence of the soul from the body; whoever loves to be alone *(monos)* does not fear this. If the soul has purified itself, it becomes the idea and logos and is perfectly incorporeal, spiritual and filled with the divine, whence come the source of beauty and everything related" (cap. VI). "For the one for whom life is a good, it is such not because there is a union of soul and body but because evil is averted by good, but death is a greater good. One ought then to say that life in the body is evil in and of itself, but through virtue the good of souls is obtained which are not confirmed in their complexity but already divide this bond" (*Enneads* I, lib. VII, cap. III).

The Sophianicity of the Creature

If the incarnation of the soul is evil or a certain metaphysical faux pas, an accident, then as a result of this even in a favorable case, nothing positive results for the soul, although nothing bad does either;[61] in an unfavorable case the soul becomes dirty, and in order to be liberated from bodily fetters, it must undergo a process of purification which is a multiple reincarnation in different bodies. The character of each reincarnation is pre-established by the deeds of the preceding lives, karma, but their final goal is all the same a disincarnation. It is obvious here how the metaphysical negation of the body is connected with the doctrine of reincarnation, in which the individuality of the body, forever connected with a given soul, is denied. On the contrary the alternating bodies are considered as envelopes or cases for the soul, or even as the separate cells of a correctional institution assigned to criminals according to their conduct. Metempsychosis, which already in Plato sounds like dissonance and seems to be blown on by a non-Hellenic influence, here receives a definitely noxious character. It is easy to grasp that Plotinus energetically repudiates the Christian teaching on the bodily resurrection of the dead. "Sensible perception is a function of the sleeping soul, for the part of the soul which dwells in the body is asleep. The authentic awakening is the authentic resurrection *from (apo)* the body and *not with (meta)* the body. Resurrection with a body is a transition from one sleep to another, as if a mere change of a bed; true resurrection fully liberates from the body which, having a nature opposed to a soul, also has an opposite essence *(ousian)*. Its origination, development, and annihilation are evidence that it is not proper to the nature of true being" (*Enneads* III, lib. VI, cap. VI).

The invective against the body is connected with the metaphysical invective against the world[62] — from the light emanating from Plotinus's One it is principally shadows that fall on the earth. With this is emphasized even more sharply the difference between this doctrine and "the good news" of the Gospel concerning the coming resurrection, "the victory which has conquered the world." In Plotinus that side of Hellenism speaks here which is engraved in the answers of the Athenians to the apostle Paul after his sermon in the Areopagus. These same Hellenists who displayed reverence towards the "unknown God" — *agnōstōi theōi*, akin to the transcendent One of Plotinus, "when they heard about the resurrection of the dead, some began to laugh and others said: we will hear you about this another time" (Acts of the Apostles 17:32); only Dionysius to whose name are ascribed the magnificent Areopagitica became a student of Paul and with that became the forefather of a new Christian Hellenism.

A Neo-Platonic inclination of thought in the question of the flesh is sometimes manifested in Christianity. The task of Christian asceticism is the struggle not against the body but *for* the body, for Christianity sees in the body not fetters but the temple of God.⁶³ We sense an inclination towards a fundamental condemnation of the body, for example, in Origenist spiritualism. In approaching Plotinus in this regard, Origen considers the creation of the world and the clothing of the spirit with flesh as a certain fall — *katabolē*.⁶⁴ In conformity with such an understanding of creation, only *apokatastasis,* the restoration of the world to the original state which it had before the *katabolē,* can be its end. This explanation of the origin of the world recalls the doctrines of the philosophers of pessimism, Schopenhauer and Hartmann, concerning the blind, irrational movement of the will, which without any inner sense generated the world. Of course, such an inclination is poorly reconciled with the general Christian worldview of Origen.

There is a certain analogy with Origenism and Neo-Platonism in the cosmology of J. Böhme, according to which Lucifer is the initiator of our world, who committed through his fall into sin a certain *katabolē* for it and spoiled the "sal nitrum" of his own kingdom. In saving this kingdom and repairing its "sal nitrum," God is compelled to create over again, his final task here being defined as apocatastasis, i.e., the restoration of the kingdom, spoiled by Lucifer, to its original state. Modern German philosophy is also distinguished by an idealistic repudiation of authentic corporeality which is understood only as the transcendental schema of sensible experience or its indissoluble remainder; in spiritualistic systems of philosophy, of the type of Leibnitz or Lotze, it is interpreted exclusively in terms of spirit, as its state, i.e., in and of itself it is declared an illusion.

Christianity contains an entirely different understanding of corporeality. In it the body is granted a positive and unconditional significance. It is not only the result of sin or the falling away into something inferior, *katabolē,* but is the first-formed essence. The fundamental dogma of Christianity concerning the divine incarnation — *ho Logos sarx egeneto,* the Word became flesh — and connected with this the veneration of the Theotokos, the resurrection and the Son of God's ascension in the flesh and his sitting "at the right hand of God the Father" — all of this contradicts the Neo-Platonic, Buddhist, Spiritualist, and Idealist negation of the body in such a clear manner that it is even superfluous to insist on it. What deserves special attention is that in the New Testament Christ is named "the very Savior of the body" — *autos Sōtēr tou sōmatos* (Eph. 5:23) and "the head of the body, the church" — *kai autos estin hē kephalē tou sōmatos, tēs ekklēsias* (Col. 1:18). The church is

The Sophianicity of the Creature

named numerous times "the body of Christ." "Husbands must love their wives like their own bodies: the one who loves his wife loves himself, for no one ever had hatred for his own flesh, but nourishes and keeps it warm, as the Lord does the Church, because we are members of his Body, we are from his Flesh and bones. Therefore does a man leave father and mother and cling to his wife, and the two will be one flesh [Gen. 2:24]. This mystery is great, I am speaking with respect to Christ and the Church" (Eph. 5:28-32). The Church is "his *Body,* the fullness of what fills everything" (Eph. 1:23). Of course it is possible to allegorize absolutely everything in the world, but that is why "one can understand this spiritually" if one desires. However, this would mean not only to do exegetical violence to a given New Testament text, but also to disregard the whole spirit of the Old Testament, with its clear love and affirmation of the body; in particular one would have to entirely allegorize the sacred eroticism of the *Song of Songs,* which is not in any way merely lyric poetry or a didactic tract but is permeated with the most serious symbolic realism. It would be necessary to transgress, further, the doctrine of the Church about the sacrament of marriage; following thereupon one would have to set outside the bounds of what is in principle permitted in Christianity the whole relation of the Church to natural flesh, which finds expression in liturgical sacramental actions, not only in the holy Eucharist but also in the blessing of water, of bread, fruit, houses, etc. Further, the whole of ecclesiastical art would be subject to repudiation — iconography, architecture, music, singing, etc. In a word, one would have to separate from Christianity everything that idealist and spiritualist iconoclasts (in the broadest sense of the word) call religious materialism, or simply "paganism." But Christianity is a religion not only of the salvation of the soul, but also the spiritual glorification of the body. In it alone of all the world religions the body is not persecuted but glorified, for Christ is the Savior not only of souls from sin, but at the same time and in the same way the "Savior of the body." Christianity is the apotheosis of the body and makes a great promise with respect to its redemption.

But what, then, is the *body?* And what is corporeality? More often than not corporeality is defined in negative terms as the antithesis of "the spiritual" or nonspiritual. Such a definition, first of all, is unsatisfactory, as is any purely negative definition, and, secondly, it is not true, if one understands negation as opposition or exclusion. Corporeality in its essence is not at all the antithesis to spirit, for a spiritual corporeality, "a spiritual body," also exists about which the apostle Paul speaks: "If there is a soulish body, there is also a spiritual body — *pneumatikon*" (1 Cor. 15:44), and precisely this corporeality contains the ontological norm of the body. On the contrary, corporeality in the sense of the negation of the spiritual is only a definite state of the body, and an unhealthy one at that, and not its essence. Holy corporeality, the body of the Church, is spiritual and spirit-bearing, and therefore its essence can in no way be defined only as *not-spirit*; rather, it must have a positive definition. One needs to see this essence in *sensuality*, as a special independent element of life, distinct from spirit, but at the same time not at all foreign or opposed to it.

Sensuality differs utterly clearly from both the substantial-volitional core of the person and the thinking that participates in the Logos, the noetic vision of ideas, their ideal contemplation: *alongside* of will and thought is the sensual experience of ideas — their becoming corporeal. Moralists and philosophers, ascetics and mystics have grown accustomed to disdaining sensuality, and the word itself has received associations and aftertastes that are not easily forgotten. For some it is a sinful, carnal captivity of the spirit, something in any case that is subject to overcoming; for others it is a foul though irremovable admixture by which the purity of transcendental and logical schemata become soiled, a necessary springboard for thinking, or the irresolvable sediment that remains at the bottom of a gnoseological retort and is not evaporated from any idealistic reagents. Oh, how easily idealist philosophies would breathe if it were in fact possible somehow to "unthink" and remove blind *Empfindung*, lying like dead ballast in the hold of the *Critique of Pure Reason!* How rounded Fichtean cosmogony would become, which is accomplished by way of the reflection of the I in the mirror of *not-I*, if it were possible to make do with logical impulses alone and if that vexatious "external push" of the coarse world were not needed! How artfully and strongly constructed by Hegel's dialectics the world would be if there were no need still "to deduce" the material "alterity" of spirit, the despicable empyrean from which one has to take out loans! And surely the victory of materialism, that dark Ahriman,[65] over the kingdom of Lucifer would be possible except for that annoying "matter" which obstinately refuses to be enlightened and idealized *to the end*. However, for all their brilliance, logical schemata, capable of containing the whole world, cannot really give rise to a single speck of dust, not ideal, but sensible and real. The *res, being*, is established pre-

The Sophianicity of the Creature

cisely by corporeality or sensuality, and although idealism does not know what to do with it except to remove it with disgust from its bright kingdom, dark Ahriman who controls the key to reality while remaining a logical ignoramus, laughs exultantly. For it is more gratifying to be the last porter on earth than to roam in an idealist Hades like a shadow even of the highest rank.

We have groped our way to one of the fundamental traits of corporeality as sensuality: the reality of the world, the power of being, is established by it. It thereby stands on the very edge of the logical discernibleness of light and darkness; it conceals itself so to say behind an idea as its hidden "support." There is nothing to say about it in word or thought, it would be erroneous to verbalize it; what remains is simply to accept it or state it firmly. Here is why the problem of the reality of the external world represents such a heavy cross for idealist philosophy, for this reality cannot be demonstrated by means of abstract thought; it is only perceptible by sensuality, and therein is the cause of the insolubility of logical and alogical principles, so characteristic for all being. The ideal and the real are divisible only in thinking, but not in actuality. And if reality is established by sensuality or corporeality, which however does not exist outside the idea, then pure idealness is an illusory quality or an abstraction. In walking along this path of thought we unavoidably arrive at the ultimate question of cosmology — concerning the reality of ideas. Is it proper to the highest, intelligible principles of being, to Platonic ideas, both in their divisibility and in their organic wholeness? Are sensible perception and corporeality, which constitute the basis of reality, befitting to them or ought one to understand them only as logical abstractions, once again as *nomina rerum*? Are the ideal first principles of being only ideal schemata which according to content are poorer, drier, more uniform than they are in "mixture" with matter in the realities of our world, or on the contrary does reality in *sensu eminentissimo*, the most real reality, *realitas realissima* belong to them? In an idealist understanding of Platonism one abolishes its whole vital meaning, and it is equated to the contemporary idealism of a Husserlian type, to an inoffensive but powerless "intentionalization" and "ideation." One is left to understand ideas as being provided with the whole fullness of reality, i.e., with sensuality or corporeality. Platonic ideas have a body, no matter how subtle this corporeality may be. And one cannot imagine embodied ideas to be uniform monads lacking qualities which possess the ability merely to push off from each other and in that way to arouse a general feeling of impenetrability, all the while "not having windows" and therefore lacking in qualities in their mutual isolation. Ideas-bodies are concretely qualified, and in no sense do they repeat one another: each idea becomes aware of itself in its own way, i.e., it has an individual body and is a corporeal entelechy.[66]

And so, the ideas not only *know* themselves, but also *feel*. And this spiritual sensuality, the tangibility of the idea, is *beauty*. Beauty is as much an absolute principle of the world as is the Logos. It is the revelation of the Third Hypostasis, of the Holy Spirit. Beauty, as spiritual sensuality, necessarily has as its substrate a certain corporeality which surrenders itself to beauty, apprehends it, and is fulfilled by it. In other words, beauty presupposes *corporeality in general* or *reality in general*, which, by being thoroughly permeated by beauty, makes itself felt as its alogical substrate beyond the limit for ideas. *Reality in general* is identified by a distinctive spiritual touch which corresponds to our dull "muscular" sense of reality. For, such a *general* sense of reality, apart from particular sensations, indisputably exists and is identified metalogically. It constitutes the insurmountable, though not logical, obstacle for idealist metaphysics of Hegel's type, which although in a disguised form, was compelled to capitulate before the alogical side of the logical process. Without this corporeality or reality of ideas there is no beauty, and only thought about beauty would be possible. A certain *apeiron*, covered with ideas-forms and for that reason never betraying its chaotic state, constitutes the hidden underlying cause of all beauty. Chaos in the world of ideas never reveals itself as such, for it is resolved to the very end and without residue into cosmos, but at the same time it is perfectly real. Chaos exists only so that the real cosmos is possible.

We arrive at the acknowledgment of a certain *intelligible matter* which forms the basis of corporeality in Sophia herself, and this *apeiron* proves to be not weakness or defectiveness but on the contrary, might and wealth. It is that matter thanks to which Sophia becomes *ens realissimum, ontos on,* and not an idealist phantom. We have an important presentiment of this truth in the profound doctrine of Plotinus concerning *two* matters: concerning the meonal matter of our world lying in evil and concerning the intelligible matter which is the substrate for *nous*, and gives the possibility of being disclosed to its ideas. According to its meaning in Plotinus, as has already been shown, *nous* corresponds precisely to the Christian Sophia, inasmuch as it lays bare for

The Sophianicity of the Creature

the world the power of transcendent Divinity, the *One;* but, thanks to its "emanative pantheism," the actual hierarchical correlation between the One and the *nous* is obscured, with the latter occupying a sort of intermediate place between the Second Hypostasis, the Logos, and Sophia. Correct also is another idea of Plotinus that is relevant here, namely that intelligible matter belongs to the realm of *nous,* but not the One, i.e., not to the transcendent Absolute. And according to Christian faith, the inner-Trinitarian life of the Divinity, God in himself, represents the absolute, unknowable mystery for every creature. He is entirely transcendent; *no one has ever seen God,* and *God is spirit — Pneuma ho Theos* (John 4:24). To speak about corporeality in relation to the transcendent Absolute, no matter to what degree of refinement and spiritualization, would be both blasphemy and inability to think things through. But God, who is revealed in Sophia, manifests himself in his trihypostaseity as Creator, God-Father, Logos and life-giving Holy Spirit; through giving life, knowledge of himself is given by what is realized in its idea, which it has felt as the vital, operating power of the cosmos, the victory in chaos. The grace of the Holy Spirit shows the holy sensuality, creates holy flesh, *"the very good"* of the world. Beauty is for the most part the revelation of the Holy Spirit. Sophia is the Church which takes into herself the gifts of the revelation of the trihypostatic Divinity, the idea of God; she is according to the word of revelation the "body" of Christ, the "body of God." Consequently, God as Creator has a body in creation. But it does not at all follow from this that the Divinity in its absolute transcendence is corporeal, although equally inadmissible is the opposite affirmation. Here thought must fall silent and lips be closed, mind must become not-thinking, and soul not-sensing. Here is the "fence of paradise," the divine NOT.

And so beauty is a sinless, holy sensuality, the tangibility of ideas. It is impossible to limit beauty by any one sense, e.g., by sight. All our senses have their capacity for becoming aware of beauty: not only sight, but also hearing, smell, taste, and touch, and there is decidedly no foundation to exclude from here any of the existing and possible senses, for the realm of the beautiful is accessible to them all. The spiritual experience of saints bears witness to this for us, as they have acquired the grace of the Holy Spirit and become sophianic in their earthly body. They experienced spiritual delight with all of their senses (see the account of Motovilov, for example, about how Saint Seraphim made the grace of the Holy Spirit tangible for him).[67] From this follows how unfounded is the pseudo-spiritual contempt for the body and sensuality, for which our sinful carnal sensuality is equated with sensuality in general. And it is particularly strange that such confusion frequently occurs precisely by reason of Christian asceticism, which supposedly despises beauty and the body, like Buddhist asceticism. In this they do not understand that the ascetic struggle with sensuality in Christianity arises precisely out of love for noumenal, sophianic sensuality, or spiritual beauty, and enmity with the body is motivated here by a higher love for the body that is expressed most clearly of all in the reverence for sacred relics as a spirit-bearing, enlightened body. It is impossible to despise sensuality — in it one must see "the image and radiance of Divine glory," as divine Sophia is. And as far as our earthly beauty is the sheen of heavenly, sophianic beauty, so is our sensuality that is burdened with heavy flesh a mask, even a grave for spotless and holy sensuality.

An idea senses itself in beauty. In this way it loves its very self, knows itself as beautiful, is attracted to itself with an erotic attraction, in a certain cosmic amorousness. Is this attraction not felt in the intense languor of the universe's splendor, in the blazing of the midday frozen in its lethargy, in the thrilling of the sea sparkling under the burning kisses of the sun, in the slope of mountain heights stretching their snow-white peaks towards heaven? Is not nature in love with its own loveliness and is there not in that loveliness something virginal, bashful, and passionate? Only poets and artists alone see and know this cosmic Aphrodite, her self-adulation, nature in love with its own idea, creation in love with its form. "Let him kiss me with the kiss of his mouth, for your caresses are better than wine. . . . Draw me, we will run after you" (*Song of Songs* 1:2-4). Does not all of nature in its erotic fatigue and its amorous rapture whisper these passionate confessions of the one enamored, when in brief flashes of light it feels itself free from the "vanity subjugating it," as if it had regained consciousness from its lifeless swoon? And does not a poet overhear these sighs and murmuring, does not an artist see these embraces opening out? The attraction of matter to its own proper form-idea, the striving to know itself, to clothe itself in its own proper form, in its essence is an erotic striving, and in the very corporeality of ideas there is something male-female, locked embraces are aglow, lips merge in a kiss. Nature as the Shulamite strives towards the bridegroom, pines for him, seeks him in the squares, and when she finds him, she grows blessedly faint from love. "His left hand is under my head, and his right embraces me" (Song of Songs 8:3). And when *"natura naturans,"* an idea, shines through the *"natura naturata"* turned to stone, the latter breathes with the sultriness of desire, gets excited with the emotion of love. Such is the pan-eroticism of nature. And what we in the world below recognize as the striving of every earthly entity towards its idea, as the eros of creativity, the torment and anxiety of all life, is, in the intelligible world, "in heaven," the pre-eternally completed blessed act, the erotic interpenetration of form and matter, of idea and body; it is spiritual and holy corporeality.

In this spiritual corporeality is rooted the basis of art, for the artist begins to see beauty clearly as realized holy corporeality. He languishes and pines over her like a knight for the Beautiful Lady, always devotedly in love with her. For this being in love, the eros of being, gives birth to his inspiration, although it is given to him to consolidate his insights only in rare and miserly moments, and most often of all it is not given at all. One can be "an artist in the soul" and not have the capacity for this consolidation. One can be constantly agitated and besieged by these images, in love with being in love, but not able to draw out of the self the creative fire, powerlessly burning with an inner flame. But those whom this dark and sad fate has passed by, who know the language of the gods, are the chosen ones of Sophia, the creators of beauty. What is a work of art, from no matter what it might be sculpted, from stone, a word, a sound, paint, or form? What makes art art? Is it a conceptual schema, an abstract idea? No. Is it matter, flesh like any other? Also no. It is the erotic encounter of matter and form, their enamored confluence, a sensed idea that has become beauty; it is the shining of a sophianic ray in our world.

Beauty in nature and beauty in art, as manifestations of divine Sophia, of the Soul of the World, have one essence. As *natura,* simultaneously *naturans* and *naturata,* which constantly realizes itself in its idea, nature is a great and wonderful artist. Art, not as the sum total of technically virtuosic methods, but as life in beauty, is incomparably broader than our human art. The whole world is a work of art continually being realized and attaining completion in the human being in virtue of its central position in the world, for only in it, as in the king of creation, is the cosmos completed.

Sophianic, holy corporeality remains transcendent to our sense experience, and it can be postulated by it only as a necessary metaphysical hypothesis, as its ontological foundation. However, it can become accessible to contemplation or experience under the dawning of the grace of the Holy Spirit, as the experience of the saints attests. But "occultism," which teaches how to perceive experimentally bodies of greater subtlety than our "physical plan" (ethereal, astral, and mental body), does not come close to this experience at all (if only it does not make it more distant), for according to their ontological nature these higher "plans" constitute one thing with the "physical" plan, by forming so to say various degrees of the thickening of corporeality. The "spiritual quality" of these bodies or worlds, about which *"Geisteswissenschaft"* gives an account, has an entirely relative meaning only in comparison with a heavier and less receptive body, material or physical, but these bodies "of the higher plans" are still matter or "earth" (which is why *Geisteswissenschaft*, as we have already indicated, confesses a refined hylozoic materialism). Spiritual corporeality does not yield to "spiritual knowledge." When applied to holy corporeality, the contrast of spirit and body, or spiritualism and materialism, loses all meaning, for it arises only as a result of the incongruity, lack of convergence, and inadequacy of the one and the other. Where a full and complete entelechic, spirit-body state is found, this opposition loses all significance, for as the spirit does not manifest here its spirituality opposed to matter, its hostility to the body, so too the body does not have inertness, materiality, or passive resistance to the spirit. Here there is a full and complete interpenetration of body and spirit in a single life-creating act "of eternalizing life." The experience of our own body can give us a certain analogy, insofar as in harmony with the commands and needs of the spirit it merges with it into one.[68] When we are healthy we do not feel our eyes when they see, our ears when they hear, or our muscles when they move obedient to the will; on the contrary when we are upset, all our organs make themselves known separately. In general we feel our sinful body as the boundary or opponent of the spirit only when it becomes a disobedient instrument, or masters the spirit through lust, but not when it serves us faithfully. From this it follows, by the way, that this selfsame antithesis of spirit and body, so favored by metaphysicians and moralists, conveys not the primordial essence of the body but only its familiar modality, the determined *condition* of corporeality (or what in the given case is one and the same thing, of spirituality), but not its being; from this, one can understand that both spiritualism and materialism are in equal measure inevitably limited and false; they allow one and the same mistake: the confusion of modality, condition, with the very essence of corporeality and the spirituality attendant to it.

Temporality and spatiality, the forms of "transcendental aesthetics," cannot be applied to spiritual corporeality. Temporality is connected with development, becoming, the meonal state and creatureliness in general, and is inapplicable to the supratemporal, which in a single act embraces everything in absolute perfection and completeness. But the same must be said of spatiality. It is conditioned by the mutual impenetrability and repulsion of bodies that cannot immediately occupy one and the same space. Our space represents as it were layers of different density: e.g., light can pass freely through aerial space, through the pores of one expanse of space another one can seep. However, it remains the foundation of spatiality that each definite volume of space, each definite place can be filled by only one substance at a time and that it becomes impenetrable for every other substance for that time.

Spatiality is the impenetrability of matter and is identified practically as boundary or form. This impenetrability is connected with disorganization, with the chaotic state of world matter which has a multitude of unconnected and independent centers and which therefore disintegrates into separate mutually displacing parts (however we may call them: atoms, electrons, centers of energy, and the like). Out of this mutual limitedness arises the external form of any given body, as the limited domain of its being. If one were to remove this cause of spatiality by presupposing the full and complete organization of the world's body where nothing displaces anything, but everything exists in a unity, then, obviously, the reality of space disappears, it becomes pure potentiality. The forms of being will then have the character not of the external constraint of space but only of the qualification intrinsic to it. This internal form, which is realized in the spiritual body, remains inaccessible to our current experience, which is fettered by the real spatiality of the world. And yet we can observe the victory over spatiality from separate incidents in the life of saints who make an appearance far away from where they are located, and who see beyond the limits of what is physically possible. The Gospel narrative about the body of the Resurrected Lord tells us of the same thing: he passed freely through "closed doors" that were impenetrable for the physical body; he appeared suddenly before the apostles and just as suddenly hid himself;

he made his body tangible for Thomas to touch and even capable of taking physical food (honey and fish). Spiritual corporeality is not bound by spatiality[69] as by a boundary, and therefore the external form must yield here to the internal form which, however, is tangible and realized figuratively and corporeally. Spatiality does not by itself establish corporeality, which can become free from its bounds; it is itself connected with a definite state of corporeality, namely with its impenetrability. Even less, however, can one imagine spatiality and temporality idealistically à la Kant, as the form of perception, as if it did not exist at all for the thing in itself. This notion will be true only in the case of transposing it into ontological language: corporeality in itself is free of spatiality and in this sense is supraspatial, but spatiality is its condition or mode. However, from this it does not become a transcendental illusion, for it is the real condition of an authentic reality just as, e.g., sickness in an organism is not an illusion: it does not belong to its being, but is only its condition. One can establish the reality of space, relative though it may be, only by starting out from what lies at its foundation, itself remaining supraspatial, i.e., from spiritual corporeality.

"There are heavenly bodies and earthly bodies" — *kai sōmata epourania kai sōmata epigeia* (1 Cor. 15:40), says the apostle, outlining the whole contrast between holy, spiritual corporeality and earthly, fleshly corporeality. Wherein is this difference? It is obviously connected with the properties of the earth as the matter of earthly corporeality. We know the earth as the universal mother, bringing forth from its womb vegetation, animals, and finally the flesh of humankind. The earth is the common matter of diverse types of flesh about which the apostle Paul says "not all flesh is the same flesh *(ou pasa sarx hē autē sarx)* but there is one flesh for livestock, a different one for fish, a different one for birds" (1 Cor. 15:39). Opposed to heaven, the earth is only the potentiality of spiritual corporeality, its alloy with nothing, a certain primary blending (which Plato speaks about in the *Timaeus*). The meonal foundation of corporeality, which remains only in potentiality in the spiritual body, for it is conquered and entirely overcome by the idea, here in the "earthly body" affirms its actuality, whereas the idea becomes only sought for and proposed; from this arise process, development, becoming. The earth in this sense is *the becoming* spiritual corporeality, it only strives to become the "new earth" which will be manifested at the termination of the world process, when the black and dark mass is transmuted into "the sea of glass, similar to crystal" (Rev. 4:6). Earthly flesh

The Sophianicity of the Creature

is burdened with matter or nothing, i.e., inertness, heaviness, obesity. We observe this mysterious overcoming of matter by idea each time "from the dark block the faces of roses," trees, flowers, and cereals emerge, striving to fashion for themselves a body, to reveal their idea in it. Art achieves the same thing, illuminating matter with an idea.

Finally, the human being produces the same thing in spiritual work and upon himself, by fashioning his higher I and through it changing his own body. Body and matter are in no way identical, as is usually considered; the link of corporeality with matter is an enigma, in its own way no less mysterious than the link of the soul with the body; the bodiless existence of ideas is a fiction and abstraction: *nulla idea sine corpora* [no idea without a body]. The whole earth is a potential body; out of the condition "of invisible and empty" it constantly is clothed in the glory of the six days of creation: everything proceeds from the earth and returns to the earth. The earth in this sense is "God's acre," a cemetery, preserving bodies for the resurrection. Of this earth it is said: "Earth you are and into the earth you will depart." Between corporeality and materiality an antagonism is established that finds religious-practical expression in asceticism. On the soil of this antagonism arises the false opposition of spirit and flesh which is expressed in one-sided spiritualism and materialism. The earth, as flesh, darkens, covers, fights against idea-entelechy, thereby creating a feeling of *fleshiness*, as a sinful principle that limits. The sighing of Plato and the cry of the great apostle refer to this: "Poor man that I am, who will deliver me from this body of death?" So too his testimony about the two laws that live in a human being and fight one against the other. Here lie the ontological roots of morality with its instrument of the categorical imperative, constantly accusing and rendering judgment on the human will that is weakened thanks to the flesh.

The whole world is *one* corporeality and *one* body, in which, however, each corporeal entelechy must become aware of itself entirely individually. Thanks to our sense of spatiality the connectedness of being makes itself felt more weakly than its separation: the impenetrability of space for that reason becomes an axiom for empirical consciousness (this explains, for example, the misunderstandings over how the one and the same Eucharistic sacrifice is accomplished at different times or simultaneously in many places, with the Lord wholly communicating himself to each communicant every time). But the unity of corporeality cannot be entirely destroyed even in the spatial world — it is indirectly corroborated by the functions of nourishing, breathing, the exchange of substances, the universal connectedness of what is.[70] But the individuality of the body is by no means negated by this, although the attempt to define it in the language of material corporeality familiar to us led to antinomies and aporias.[71] The universal penetrability of bodies can harmonize with their dynamic individuality as centers for different incarnate souls, where it is expressed in their intentional connectedness with definite corporeal units (cages). This acknowledgment of the individuality of the body is inseparably linked with the dogma of the divine incarnation. The Lord clothed himself in flesh not only in the sense of a general participation in it but also in the most concrete sense: he was incarnated in an individual body, with it he lived and suffered, and with it he rose, having abandoned an empty grave — the emptiness in the sense of the absence of a body is still emphasized by the burial linens left behind in it and "by the headscarf which was on his head" (John 20:7). Of course all creation rose with him and really will rise with him at some time, for it is all in a certain sense the body of Christ, participating this way or that in his church. But having as his body all flesh, Christ has his own proper Body with which he ascended to heaven and "sits at the right hand of the Father." The proclamation of the resurrection in individual bodies has constituted the core of Christian evangelization since time immemorial (let us recall the preaching of the apostle Paul in the Areopagus of Athens and the skeptically ironic attitude of the Athenian spiritualists of that time: Acts 17:32). This question has been discussed more than once in Christian literature.[72] The acknowledgment of the individuality of the body lies at the basis of the reverence of holy relics as well.

4. The Nature of Evil

The world, created *out of nothing in the Beginning*, i.e., potential and actualizing sophianicity, in its original "goodness" has nothing *anti*-sophianic and contains no evil. For there is as yet no evil in potential nothing, which constitutes the foundation of the created world; on the contrary, it becomes good by participating in the good, by moving from dark nothingness to being. The world *before* the fall represented that sinless potentiality of sophianicity, that metaphysical "earth" on which Eden could spring up. But it had not yet reached the state of

The Sophianicity of the Creature

completion, the actualization of its sophianicity: just like Adam, it was found in an initial, childlike stage of its development, which ought only to have led to the full spiritualization of matter, "the new heaven and new earth." And testifying to this more eloquently than anything is the very possibility of that spiritual and cosmic catastrophe which occurred in the fall and which moved the world off its straight path. *Nothing* was not sensed in the world as the actual principle of creation but remained as its dark, mute foundation. In this was manifested the victory of the goodness of the Creator who summoned to life *nothing* itself. But this foundation of creation hid in itself the possibility of actualization and intervention in the world's destiny, i.e., sin and evil. For this it was sufficient for *nothing* to come out of its potentiality and become tangible as the dark foundation of creation. In itself, of course, *nothing* cannot become the actual principle of creation, the beginning of everything — *ex nihilo nihil fit* — but it can burst into the already-realized creation, become interlaid in it as a force of chaos, and in that case the world receives its current character — a chaos-cosmos. In this way *the possibility* of evil and sin, as the actualization of *nothing*, was given beforehand in creation: goodness and love, which appeared in the creation of the world, did not stop even at being humbled, having given a place to rebellious, chaotic *nothing*, which receives the possibility of self-affirmation only thanks to *everything*, as darkness and shadow receive their being only from light, although they strive to compete with it. The actualization of nothing is therefore metaphysical theft, to which, however, the assent of the Creator of all things was given in advance, for he loved the world in its freedom and not as only an object of his omnipotence. Humbled to the point of respecting the creature, love permits the willfulness of nothing together with creaturely freedom. The actualization of nothing sets the principle for that plural, chaotic being which in all other respects is nonbeing. And already this very *being-nonbeing*, as the general state of creation, is a metaphysical sin about which it is said *the world lies in sin*.

A kind of primordial melancholy and malice exists which is expressed both in "world grief" and in the enmity of everything for everything: *polemos patēr pantōn* [conflict is the father of all things] (Heraclitus), *In Ja und Nein bestehen alle Dinge* [All things exist in yes and no] (J. Böhme). That "minus" exists in the world by which Mephistopheles declares himself as does the "devil" of Ivan Karamazov. The gaping maw of nonbeing draws to itself mysteriously and imperiously. Similar to how on the heights one experiences a tormenting and vertiginous urge downwards, so too does everything living experience the temptation of metaphysical suicide, the urge to get out of "the inflamed circle of being"; yet *in no way can it ever* get to the end, i.e., to full realization, for all the forces of the world cannot eradicate the creative *"fiat"* which rests on each creature. The creature therefore cannot say to itself with full sincerity: die, for already in the very act of affirmation towards nonbeing it realizes itself as being — a living and life-affirming principle. Whence are the insincerity and hypocrisy (in the most profound, final meaning) of metaphysical pessimism, for *no* creature *is able* to desire its own self-annihilation, neither demons nor people. The very cruelest torments — the unsleeping worm and the inextinguishable fire — only affirm the power of being all over again. Need one say that suicide is always and entirely an act of life-affirmation, although sick, capricious, or willful? That will to nonbeing for which Buddhism faintly pines is far removed from it. Metaphysical death — and this is not death but eternal dying — the overthrow into the "pitch darkness" at the very edge of being, can happen for unrepentant sinners only by the will of the Almighty — may he have mercy on what he has made! But even there in the darkness lamentation and gnashing of teeth will be audible, and there the outcast creature will twist and turn convulsively in the clutches of the nothing that envelops it; yet even here nonbeing will not be found, for God's determination is eternal and unalterable. We have the roots of our being in eternity and it does not lie in our power to tear them out; neither are we capable of even wishing this....

The melancholy of life silently bears witness that it is poisoned by nonbeing, and life bears death in itself. Together with sin, death entered the world as a principle hostile to being, destroying it. Before the fall, humankind, and in it all creatures, were created not immortal but also not mortal: nothing, being in the state of potentiality, was still powerless to introduce death into the world, but at the same time it was not already rendered powerless. And as soon as the dike of being had been breached by the act of the fall, nonbeing poured out into the world and flooded all that exists: death became the universal and last enemy. Our forebears lived in childlike ignorance of good and evil and of course they could have completely avoided the experience of evil. The fall or, on the contrary, obedience to the will of God, ought in any case to be reckoned as an act of freedom, and in no way at all one of natural necessity: only the possibility of sin was present in the creature's nature, but not any kind of compulsion towards it. Temptation consisted precisely in the fact that knowledge was to be preferred to obedience, the source of true, positive knowledge. The serpent enticed our forebears with the possibility of becoming *like gods,* i.e., it drew them onto the path of pretentious self-loving plurality, it aroused the desire for *each one* to become a god, and while being a creature to have *everything* for itself, as if from itself. The serpent did not promise that they would in actual fact become gods, for it was clear to their prophetic consciousness which was fed by living communion with God, that God is one; therefore he called them to become *like* gods. And the temptation of the serpent proved to be really realizable because once it burst into the world the element of liberated nothing surrounded every creature with the icy cold of loneliness, it divided the all-one and turned the centripetal force into a centrifugal one. At that point our little *I* was born which swelled up into the cosmic *I* and considered the whole world its throne: in truth "you shall be like gods." For such a poisoned being, which does not have in itself the positive power of immortality, of eternal life in God, *passive immortality,* i.e., the simple absence of death, would be the supreme calamity, hell on earth. The Lord spared his creation and did not grant it such immortality; he sent humankind away from "the tree of life" whose fruits it was not worthy of tasting, and condemned it to returning "to earth" so that at some time once more it would restore to that earth her sophianic power in "the life of the future age." In this manner the one fundamental metaphysical and cosmic catastrophe of the fall, by introducing death into the world, conditioned and summoned the other cosmic catastrophe, but one already good and joyful — the resurrection of the dead, anticipated by the resurrection of the One — the Firstborn of the dead, and the transfiguration of the whole world through the creation of "a new heaven and new earth, in which justice lives."[73]

This fall, which was cosmic in its significance, took place of course not in the soul of the world, as the Guardian Angel of the creature, not in divine Sophia,[74] and not in *"the Beginning."* "Heaven," *kosmos noētos,* the intelligible world, uncorrupted and eternal, abides in a realm beyond sin's reach, above all being; and with sophianic rays, with its subsistent energies it holds the world together, saves it from dispersion, preserves it from the baneful waves of raging chaos, from nothing. The fall happened only in the lowest center of sophianic life, in creation with its ontological center — the human being.

What then is evil? It is obvious that it cannot be understood as a *second* principle of being that exists alongside of the good: such Manichaeism, apart from its religious absurdity, would represent a metaphysical *non-sens*. This dualism would necessarily require a higher, foundational principle, and therefore Manichaeism is nowhere a consistent and ultimately sustained doctrine. It is obvious also that evil as such could not be created by a good and loving Creator, and for that reason it cannot have in itself being or the independent source of life which is nevertheless inherent in the very smallest creature. *There is only good,* and everything that is not good does not exist. But *does not exist* does not signify necessarily *there is not* in the sense of complete absence. Evil can be imagined only as something permitted or which has slipped into the universe as its particular self-determination precisely as an unwarranted actualization of that nothing out of which the world is created. The Maker appointed to this nothing the status of a dark foundation, the passive obedient principle, the reverse and the obverse of being, but creaturely freedom is at liberty to summon to being even nonbeing, to actualize *nothing,* to pour into it its own life. It then receives life indirectly and together with it the power to harm, to become evil, which is therefore a *parasite* of being. But once it has arisen, evil, just like good, becomes multipartite, multiform, and multifaceted; it already exists as both a cosmic principle — evil in nature, and an anthropological principle — evil will in humankind. But in all its guises it has one essence: exclusion from all-unity, extra-sophianicity or anti-sophianicity, individuality, self-love, the confinement of the self in the invisible but impenetrable envelope *of nothing.*

The dominant opinion of ecclesiastical authors of the Eastern Church concerning the nature of evil comes down to regarding it as *nonexisting;* it is the negation or loss *(sterēsis)* of the good. Already in the second century Clement of Alexandria and Origen followed that direction, and in the fourth century it became the dominant one among church fathers: Saints Athanasius the Great, Basil the Great, and Gregory of Nyssa.[75] This doctrine receives its fullest development and deepening in St. Dionysius the Areopagite. All that exists derives from the good, not from evil, and thus evil is not entirely evil, but partakes of the good. "Is not the annihilation of one thing often the emergence of another thing?"[76] In his commentary on this work of the Areopagite, St. Maximus the Confessor says the following: "We have said that if God who exists superessentially *(hyperousios ōn)* is called the one without beginning and the cause of

The Sophianicity of the Creature

all, then matter *(hylē)* is the antithesis, the limit of being and without essence *(eschaton tōn ontōn kai anousion)* similar to how God is super-essential; matter is called both not *(mē)* existing and existing in *(en)* God, arising thanks to his goodness, and through mingling with the sensible it becomes not entirely evil and not entirely good, being revealed through the unstable *(astaton)*. For evil in the unstable has a part of good, for it came out of God and is found in God. Evil as such *(autokakon)* does not exist either in the existing, which one way or other strives towards the good, or in the nonexisting. . . . Evil stands farther apart from good than does the nonexisting, i.e., matter, and correspondingly is more deprived of substantiality *(anousiosteron)* than matter; of itself evil is perfect nothing *(to auto kakon hōs pantē ouden on)*. Briefly stated, evil as such never and in no manner exists. Evil is in matter only by reason of the insufficiency of the good and for that reason it is intangible and invisible."[77]

"Evil as evil," continues St. Dionysius, "does not form any essence or being, it only worsens and destroys the aspect of what exists insofar as it depends on it."[78] "One and the same thing cannot be in the same respect good and evil, annihilation and origination, it does not have independent power and a capacity for destruction *(autodynamis ē autophthora)*. . . . That which exists, exists only by virtue of the good, which is so superabundant that it can fill in even negation and the negative *(sterēsis kai to esterēmena)*; that which is completely deprived of good cannot exist. . . . And origination, which flows out of annihilation, is not the power of evil but the presence of the less good, just as illness is a deficiency of good order in the body." . . . Good gives being even to its own negation *(kai ousioi kai tēn heautou sterēsin to agathon)*. "And so, *evil is not existent — ouk ara on to kakon*."[79] There is no evil in God, otherwise, we would have had to recognize in him enmity and disharmony. There is no evil in angels; they are evil when they punish sinners, but here the punishment is not evil, but that which is punished. By their nature even demons are not evil; they can introduce corruption, but they cannot obliterate being, and their malice consists in the cessation of their participation in the divine gifts. Being evil by nature they would be eternally evil, whereas "evil is inconstant," and "to be always unchangeable *(tauton)* is proper only to the good" (IV, 23). If they are evil not by nature but only by a lack of angelic gifts, evil in them constitutes *"thymos alogos, anous epithymia, phantasia propetēs"* [unreasoning passion, desire without understanding, rash imagination]. The angelic gifts in them have not changed, although they themselves do not see them, but insofar as they exist, they participate in the good, *ek agathou eisi*, and insofar as they are evil, they do not exist, *kath'ho ouk eisin*, and in striving towards the not-existing, they strive towards evil (IV, 23). Human souls also are not evil by nature (IV, 24), for even in them evil is an absence, an incompleteness of the good. Neither are animals evil, and there is no evil in all of nature — it is only in nature's failure to achieve its perfection (IV, 26). "There is no evil in the body, for deformity and disease are deficiency of form and absence of order" (IV, 27); the final abolition *(lysis)* of beauty, form, and order would signify the annihilation of being itself. "For everything: minds, souls, and bodies, evil is the powerlessness *(astheneia)* to master the good proper to it and the falling away from it."[80]

Furthermore, the opinion often expressed by Neo-Platonists is incorrect that "evil is rooted in matter as such, for it too participates in the cosmos, in form and in beauty. Matter existing outside of this is without quality and invisible; how can matter do anything if in itself it has no capacity for perception *(paschein)*? And how can matter be evil if in itself it nowhere and never exists? And if it somehow does exist, then all that exists derives from the good, consequently it too would be from the good, and therefore either the good would produce evil, or evil, in proceeding from the good, would be good. Or two principles exist and they are subordinated to a higher one. If one says that matter is necessary for the completion of the whole world, then how can matter be evil? And how could it give birth to and nurture nature if it were evil?

Likewise limitation and absence in themselves cannot be considered the cause of evil, for a complete negative annihilates the very nature of being – the good, while partial negation does not have power by itself but by virtue of the good being negated by it. "Briefly stated, the good derives from a single and integral cause, evil comes from many particular deficiencies. God knows evil as good *(to kakon ē agathon)* and before him the causes of evil are forces which create good."[81] The cause of good is one. If good is opposed to evil, then there exist many causes of evil, not only causes and forces which call forth evil, but also powerlessness, weakness, discordant blending of the dissimilar. Evil is not motionless, it is not always found in an invariable state, but it is unlimited, indefinable, it is manifested in another that is also unlimited. And the beginning, and the goal of everything, likewise of evil, is the good, for everything exists for the sake of the good, both what is good and what is opposed to it. We do the latter in keeping with certain motives, for no one does what he does having evil in mind, for evil has no substance but only a pseudo-substance *(parypostasin)*, it exists for the sake of the good and not for its own sake. Evil in this sense is an accident *(kata symbebēkos)*, existing for the sake of another and not according to its own cause; while its origination seems right by arising for the sake of the good, in actuality it is wrong, for we accept the not-good for the good. . . . Evil is found therefore outside of the way, goal, nature, cause, boundary, desire, and hypostasis."[82]

The provenance of evil is not from strength but from weakness.[83]

"And so, what is thinkable in contrast with good does not exist essentially, since what does not exist in itself does not exist at all: consequently, evil is not being but the negation of being. We understand evil not as something independent in our nature but we regard it as the absence of good."[84]

According to the definition of St. Maximus the Confessor, "Evil was not and will not be an independently existing thing according to its own nature, for it does not have absolutely any essence, nature, independent substance, power or activity, in what exists, and it is neither a quality, a quantity, a relation, a place, a time, a position, an operation, a motion, a possession, or a passion such that it would be naturally contemplated in whatever has being, and it does not exist at all in all of this according to natural assimilation; it is neither beginning, middle or end." "Evil is a deficiency of the activity of powers inherent in nature with respect to their goal and is decidedly not some other thing. Yet again: evil is the irrational motion of natural powers in keeping with an erroneous judgment towards something else than the goal; I call goal the Cause of what is, towards which everything is naturally drawn."[85]

A similar doctrine of evil was developed in the Western Church by blessed Augustine primarily in his struggle with Manichaeism, which taught the ontological autonomy of evil as a second principle of world being. The subsistent power belongs only to good, the being *(essentia)* and the good *(bonum)* of the world are synonyms. But the world is a being that is not independent, whereas that which is created by God cannot be the same as the Creator himself: *in his enim, quae quoque modo sint, et non sunt quod Deus est, a quo facta sunt* [for in these things which, by whatever way they may be, are not what God is, by whom they were made].[86] By this is substantiated for the creature the possibility not only of the relative path of growth but also the negative path of evil. Evil is something other, as negation *(negatio)*, corruption *(correptio)*, and deprivation *(privatio)* of good-being. It cannot therefore have independent significance, existing exclusively at the expense of the good, "by adhering and sticking to its nature": *ex bono oritur malum, nec fuit omnino unde oriri posset, nisi ex bono* [evil arises from the good, and there was no other place at all from which it could arise than from the good].[87] Consequently, evil can exist only as long as being-good exists; with the annihilation of good-being, evil itself must be annihilated: *bona tamen sine malis esse possint, mala vero sine bonis esse non possint, quoniam naturae in quibus sunt, in quantum naturae sunt, utique bonae sunt* [good things just the same can exist without evil things, but evil things cannot exist without good things, because the natures in which they are, inasmuch as they are natures, are in any account good].[88]

What does the power of *nothing* or evil signify for corporeality? The corporeality of the creaturely world is "earth," mother, but in itself it is still not matter, which exists in it only as a possibility. Ideas-forms, which mother earth begets, are imprinted with the presence of nothing as the dark foundation of the creature: they are fragile, not durable, they are not guaranteed against destruction, they do not have yet the cast of eternity. Otherwise it would have been impossible for sin to spoil the creation to such a degree by introducing into it destruction, disease, and death. *"The earth" became matter,* without of course losing its sophianic saturation and generative power. Death entered the world as the *power* of nonbeing, becoming present invisibly in every creature and inevitably accomplishing its work. For this reason all the processes of life are distinguished by a fatal duality: growth is inseparably linked with destruction, it is movement to meet the unavoidable, inevitable end; with each day and hour of its being and flowering, everything living draws closer to death and destruction, and this inseparability of life and death is one of the greatest enigmas of being. The earth, having become matter, is already incapable of begetting impeccable, immortal, entelechic forms. Inalterably inherent to them are heaviness, inertness, impenetrability – a certain insoluble sediment of "matter in general" lies heavily at the bottom of every form. Plotinus's doctrine of matter as evil is perfectly correct when applied to this condition of being; its fallacy consists only in its condemnation of every kind of corporeality, in its blasphemy against Mother Earth. But the universal feeling of humanity, which is burdened by its fleshly existence, ashamed of its body, sensing it to be like fetters, is a testimony of great portent about the spoiling of natural being, about the sickness of corporeality. It comprises the foundation and essence of Christian asceticism, which does not at all strive towards liberation from the body but towards its apotheosis by the path of victory over the flesh. But although we are ashamed of our carnality, it is through it that we become aware of our corporeality. And we stop feeling this fleshliness of ours, we forget it, when art shows us our authentic corporeality, in a worthy form of being. The inspired sculptures of the Hellenes, which have made a certain impress of the truth about the human body, yield this higher *knowledge* of our corporeality. Why is it that in the presence of great works of art we lose this morbid feeling of shame before nakedness, as if for a moment we feel ourselves to be in Eden? And besides we sense with certainty that these beautiful bodies must be naked, for any clothing would belittle and show disrespect for their beauty.

Who would get the idea in their head *to clothe* the Venus de Milo? By contrast, *outside* this moment of lucidity, the breach of the precepts of modesty, its dulling and loss, attest to the depravity and cynicism of both soul and body. The feeling of shame for one's body, for one's own lack of comeliness which is emphasized only more strongly through the chance flashes of beauty, "by the prettiness," "the nice ones," is one of the deepest and most authentic mystical sensations of the self. It is

The Sophianicity of the Creature

profoundly truthful, for all people in fact find themselves in the situation of Cinderella or the Ugly Duckling with respect to their body; in greater or lesser measure they all pine for their Edenic bodies clothed in beauty and sophianic glory. They know that they have these bodies even though they are powerless to realize them. And from this comes that fatal, magical power of beauty, its poignant enigma (which Dostoevsky felt so ardently). The power of beauty incomprehensibly, irregularly, and entirely irrationally bursts into this world and reigns in it, for beauty is regal and it cannot not reign, and all the world is pulled towards beauty as towards light. It is our own remembrance of Eden, of our own selves in their proper authenticity. But this powerless, and hence illusory, false beauty is deceptive, for it covers over flesh and decay. This is the reason why its flame is so ruinous and incinerating, why it seldom lifts up and saves, but more often ruins: "beauty is a terrible thing; here God fights with the devil" (Dostoevsky).[89] Edenic beauty in non-Eden, in the kingdom of "the prince of this world," is to a certain degree theft and forgery, and thus it bites like a snake and ruins with its sweet poison. Earthly beauty is enigmatic and sinister like Giaconda's smile; here the charms of Venus compete with Elizabeth of Thuringia, and "the adulterous woman" clothed in satanic beauty opposes the "woman clothed in the sun." Both of them compete and agonizingly struggle in the souls of men and women who have lost Eden but have not forgotten it and always pine for it . . . languor on account of beauty, the torment of beauty, is the howl of the whole universe.

And so matter is not the substance of the body as materialists believe, but only its *quality*, the force that makes bodies flesh, and clothes their glory and beauty in a leather garment. But it penetrates *all of* life and not just of the body but also of the spirit. The whole life of the body, all of its functions, receive the imprint of materiality and carnality, which is palpable with particular keenness in the central nodes of life, namely in the functions of nourishing and reproduction, or to say it differently, in those of cosmic and sexual intercourse. This is why the sharp end of asceticism is always directed precisely to that side, and heightened squeamishness strives there also, not knowing how or desiring to distinguish the *condition* from the *essence* of these functions. This metaphysical squeamishness is especially fostered in the philosophy of Plotinus and in the system of Böhme who considers both *the genitalia* and *Mädensack* [sack of worms][90] to have appeared only after the fall. In this, by the way, he has some precursors in several of the ecclesiastical authors. However, the peculiar sensitivity, concealment, and diffidence can be interpreted as an expression of the deliberate sacredness, the deepest intimacy, the special tenderness of this aspect of life; and precisely for this reason it is stricken by sin all the more tangibly.

The materiality of the flesh is also the source of its mortality. It paralyzes the forces of life although it is incapable of completely weakening it. Life will gush again and again like a geyser, breaking into myriads of drops and falling back to the original source. "You are earth and you will go out into earth," was God's sentence against Adam and the whole human race and all creation in him. Here are both judgment and salvation: the return to the earth, the smashing of created form. Death is the ultimate evil, "the final enemy," but it is not the complete extermination of life. For mother earth is inexhaustible in its births; again and again it engenders life, for it is Sophia becoming. "What is returned to earth" only dies away like a seed, waiting for its resurrection. The Son of Man was that grain which lay dormant for three days and three nights in the bowels of the earth in order to beget the fruit of resurrection. And following the First fruits of the dead, the earth will beget anew the dead who were returned to it, now in new bodies that are neither material nor fleshly, and the earth itself will be a "new earth," which it was destined to be by the Creator. Human death is the dissolution of body and spirit. The body returns to earth, and the spirit temporally leads a life without a body where it wanders an unknown path of experience. The death of the other creatures is their return to earth but even it cannot signify their total annihilation, for the whole creation waits for its redemption, "having been subjected to vanity," not voluntarily but compelled by humankind. Before the fall it had that natural immortality which belongs to uninjured corporeality. With its injury nature itself was perverted, the instincts in animals changed, and the "feral" appeared. And why should one believe that in the kingdom of glory they will not receive what they once had but lost thanks to the will of their human king? Why think that transfigured mother earth will forget about these irrational children of hers and not lead them out into life? It is difficult to reconcile oneself to the idea of the glorification of humankind in a deserted world, not inhabited by the transfigured creation that now inhabits even the earth of the curse. And then in the light of transfiguration all the ignominy of their seeming "anti-idealness" and the curse of their "feral state" will fall from them and once more they will become the younger siblings and friends

The Sophianicity of the Creature

of humankind. Even now children, who still retain the sheen of Eden, frequently have their best friends among wild animals. And then it will turn out, perhaps, that others of them, now especially hateful and loathsome by their noxiousness or their ugliness, were only calumniated by the calumniator-devil, and became the victims of his lie and violence, beginning with "the serpent, wisest of the wild animals," who drew to himself a particular curse for his role as the instrument of temptation. And *all* creation down to the last work of God will be saved.[91]

Original sin did not happen in the soul of the world but in its lower center coming to pass, in the domain of creatureliness. It could only harm or poison nature, but not kill it, perverting it in its condition but not in its essence. In other words, original sin brought with it not a substantial but *merely a functional* decay of the world; "the world lies in evil," but it *is not* evil, it is its condition, not its nature. Otherwise would it be possible to confess belief in God who robed himself with this world's flesh, which he made into the clothes of his ineffable Divinity? In determining the *degree* of the world's corruption by original sin a very important nuance of one's sensation of the world is expressed which is far from lending itself always or fully to a distinct formulation, but which exercises the most powerful influence on one's entire worldview. It is fully evident if we compare extreme poles: e.g., naturalism of various shades, which in general is blind towards evil in the world and sees in it chance, misunderstanding, or error (so too modern humanism with its theories of progress: socialism, anarchism, positivism), and anti-cosmism that is blind to the good in the world and sees in it only evil maya (Buddhist asceticism, philosophical pessimism). But different intermediate opinions exist too. In accordance with one opinion, very influential in Christianity, the soul as well as the body was substantially perverted under the influence of sin, with completely new functions and corresponding organs appearing in it, namely, sex and digestion. According to this opinion, present-day sexual organs were missing in our ancestors, and reproduction itself had to be accomplished by a different and unknown path.[92] In accordance with an even more extreme opinion, which belongs to J. Böhme, sex itself is already the consequence of the fall, for the woman was created for the man after his inner separation from *Jungfrau* Sophia; in the original state humankind was above sex. This *Jungfrau* Sophia is the abstract principle of wisdom, the *Spiegel* of Wisdom, and her relation to sex is established only by her name, obviously, which is evoked by the "Book of the Wisdom of Solomon." But there is no necessity at all for this "mirror of wisdom" to be not only "Feminine" but even simply "Virgin." In such an understanding of sex, conception is the most central manifestation of sin, from which a human being is born, and the primordial essence of original sin is sexual desire — the serpent aroused lascivious passion in Eve. The words of the penitential psalm (51) — "in lawlessness was I conceived and in sins my mother bore me" — receive an interpretation in the *narrow* sense, applied to conception itself. The almost substantial corruption of nature is affirmed here: through the gate of sex nothing pure and holy can be born, just because it is sex.

By contrast, the artistic insight of the Hellenes did not know this fundamental squeamishness towards sex and the body, and with Edenic and at the same time childlike naïveté they did not fear nakedness. The church likewise teaches us *not to disdain anything* in nature and not to surrender anything in it to Lucifer. There are no vital functions that it would condemn *as such*. It gives its prayerful blessing to food, and to various needs; in particular it accepts sex on principle, something that is made clear from the sacrament of matrimony.[93] The one or the other understanding of cosmic evil and the influence of original sin has endless importance for the doctrine of our salvation, for in it is decided beforehand the question of the Mother of God and the divine incarnation. Obviously, for those who consider the corruption of nature to be almost substantial and who see in the very birth of a human being the node of sin, the Incarnation is impossible on the basis of a creature's ascent filled by the power of grace. It is realizable only by its absorption, substitution, and actual removal, i.e., this doctrine leads to a more or less clear Monophysitism such as we have, for example, in Böhme who in essence denies the possibility of the Theotokos with his doctrine.

In order to clarify J. Böhme's views one must have in sight his doctrine about "Virgin Sophia," which remained determining for J. Pordage as well.[94] She is the mirror of Divinity in which It sees itself and is revealed to its own self. She corresponds to this definite moment in the self-disclosure of Divinity; namely she stands midway between Divinity, which is defined in its triunity, *in ternario sancto,* and the world both uncreated and created, heavenly and earthly nature. According to the general sense of Böhme's doctrine, Sophia is not revelation but self-revelation of Divinity, a moment of development in Divinity itself. She

The Sophianicity of the Creature

is faceless and impersonal, as Divinity in general is impersonal in Böhme's system; she is "Wesenheit," substance or essence. And thus, according to the first definition of Sophia, she is a passive mirror that does not engender but only reflects: "It was the Spirit of God's dwelling and she was no bearer but is the revelation of God, a Virgin and a cause of the divine essence. She is like a mirror of Divinity, since every mirror keeps still and gives birth to no likeness, but is able to hold a likeness. Therefore this Virgin of Wisdom is a mirror of Divinity in which the Spirit of God sees himself as well as all the miracles of Magic ... and in her the Spirit of God has glimpsed the forms of creatures."[95] This insistent emphasis on the passive mirror-like quality, so to say, the ideal speculative quality of Sophia, forces one to see in her the design of designs, or if it can be expressed thus, the transcendental outline of the world, which does not possess its own life but has an idealistically programmed character. Sophia becomes similar to "clothes by which Divinity is revealed, otherwise its image would not be known, for she is the corporeality *(Leiblichkeit)* of spirit."[96] Therefore the full definition of Jungfrau Sophia will be this: "The wisdom of God is an eternal Virgin, not a married woman, but modesty and purity without blemish; she stands as a likeness of God and is the exact image of the triad; she gives birth to nothing, but the great miracles are in her which the Holy Spirit glimpses and the Word of the Father creates through the bitter uterus as through Fiat, and she is the wisdom of miracle without number. In her the Holy Spirit has seen the likeness of the angels as well as the likeness of human beings, which the Word *fiat* has made."[97] And as in Sophia all creatures are prototypically planned and schematized, so these latter contain in themselves sophianic schemata: "Every divine creature, both angels and human souls, has the Virgin of the Wisdom of God like a likeness in the light of life."[98]

For those who can confuse Böhme's Jungfrau Sophia with the Eternal Feminine, confessed religiously by the Hellenists as Aphrodite, poetically extolled by Goethe, Novalis, V. Soloviev, V. Ivanov, and A. Blok, it is necessary to emphasize persistently that there exists no kind of relation between the one and the other. The concept of the Jungfrau Sophia is sharply distinguished by an extra-sexual feature, or more precisely, one hostile to sex: in general, Böhme's entire system is marked by an absence of eroticism and femininity typical of the Germanic spirit (which reached its apogee in the grand master of Germanic philosophy Kant). "The likeness was in God an eternal Virgin in the wisdom of God, not a woman, and also not a man, but it has been both; just as Adam was both before his Eve which means the earthly human and animal in addition."[99] *"Ewige Jungfrau"* [the Eternal Virgin] is insofar not connected with sex that for Böhme the concept of *"männliche Jungfrau"* [male Virgin] seems entirely natural, which according to Böhme is what the first Adam[100] and the new Adam, i.e., Christ, are. *"Jungfrauschaft"* [Virginity] is the state that precedes the division of the sexes and surpasses it;[101] sex is the consequence of the fall, and the human being is sexless in its original state (for, strictly speaking, it is impossible in Böhme to speak about androgyny or bisexuality, since Sophia stands outside of sex). The formation of Eve from his rib signifies only the removal from Adam of his half, namely, his "womanliness and motherliness," and this did not happen at the very creation of humankind because "the life of both tinctures is only a single human in the image of God, and is not of two sorts in eternity, as male and female."[102] Böhme regards the creation of the woman out of Adam's rib as the result of the already-accomplished fall and as the fragmentation of human nature. The mysticism of husband and wife becoming one, a union "in Christ and in the Church," the positive meaning of the mystery of matrimony, finds for itself no justification in this doctrine. Disgust for sex, which found artistic expression in Leo Tolstoy's "Kreutzer Sonata," distinguishes this doctrine of Böhme.[103] This feature is extraordinarily important for the general world-perception of Böhme, for whom this world, begotten with the interference of Lucifer, deserves not transfiguration but only annihilation. This doctrine of Böhme is profoundly foreign to the spirit of the Cabbala, with which he was undoubtedly acquainted, for the erotic metaphysics of Cabbala despite a certain external similarity with Böhmism (the initial androgyny of Adam) is permeated with a sense of the deepest primordialness and reality of sex.

In Böhme the negative attitude towards the feminine that reduces it to sinfulness inevitably leads him to the typically Protestant reviling of the All Pure Virgin and Mother, "the flower of incorruption," the "lily of the flora of paradise," the supreme blossom of the Feminine. He is compelled to deny the spotlessness of the Mother of God that is inherent to her as well as the special purity of her conception from the "grandparents of God" Joachim and Anne. Here Böhme's basic thought is that Mary did not have sinlessness and purity before the Annunciation, but together with the word of the Archangel the Jungfrau Sophia inhabited her and after having been turned into *männliche Tinctur* [male tincture] she gave birth to the *männliche Jungfrau* Christ; Böhme repudiates the veneration of the Most Holy Virgin herself. "He (Christ) ordered his disciple to take to himself his Mother. His Mother is the Christian church on earth, and the children of God are born in her in spirit.... He subtly points out to us that the exterior human is not the Mother of Christ who gave birth in herself to Christ, for Christ is separated from his exterior Mother and handed her over to John; he extracted eternal nature as the father of eternal birth; thus those act incorrectly who venerate and pray to the exterior Mother of Christ as the Mother of God. All true Christianity is the Mother of Christ, it gives birth in itself to Christ, and Johns, as servants of Christ, are her nursemaid who takes the Mother of Christ to herself as John did" (*Böhme's Werke*, IV, 393, §§ 55, 57-58). In relation to Christ who was born not *from* a human Virgin, "the seed of a woman," but only through a Virgin from Jungfrau Sophia,

The Sophianicity of the Creature

Böhme falls into clear Monophysitism and Docetism.[104] With this, properly speaking, the incarnations of Sophia in Mary and in Jesus merge into one. It is redundant to add that the annihilation of the feminine does not permit Böhme to see the face of the Church as the Bride of Christ, as his Body. (Here the doctrine of Böhme especially invites a comparison with the doctrine of A. N. Shmidt.[105])

Owing to a juridical and thus somewhat monophysitic understanding of redemption among Catholics a doctrine appeared that arose from the aspiration to praise the Most Holy Virgin even more. In fact, the new Catholic dogma of the *Immaculate Conception* of the Most Holy Virgin, as it was promulgated in 1854, received a somewhat different sense. In the bull of Pope Pius IX, *Ineffabilis Deus,* it is stated in the following words: "The most blessed Virgin Mary, in the first moment of her conception, by a special grace of Almighty God and by a personal privilege, for the sake of the future merits of Jesus Christ the Saviour of the human race, was preserved free from any original guilt."[106] According to the meaning of this doctrine, the holy Virgin by the enabling operation of grace is removed from nature as if mechanically for the sake of her predestination. This doctrine comes dangerously close to the viewpoint of Böhme, according to whom Mary apparently is replaced by Jungfrau Sophia at the voice of the Archangel, while her own natural outward form loses its meaning for the divine incarnation after she consents to the inhabitation of Jungfrau Sophia. Catholics, displaying here the general defect of their anthropology, have referred this idea of metaphysical violence against nature and human nature to the very conception of the Mother of God. A question rightly comes to mind: If the spotlessness of the Mother of God is conditioned by an act of grace that has removed her very conception from the power of nature and signifies as it were a new creation, then the omnipotence of God could accomplish this at any moment in the history of the human race and on any of the daughters of Eve. Does not this doctrine remove the meaning of the personhood itself of the most holy Virgin, her freedom and her ascetic effort? Is not the meaning of the whole Old Testament eliminated, which had as its goal the raising of the Hebrew people to prepare for the birth of the Mother of God in it? The Lord's nativity occurred by the supernatural route of "a seedless conception" from the Holy Spirit, for God could not be born like a human being. But he was born from an entirely human mother who possessed everything human.

The World

The Orthodox Church, no less than the Catholic Church, in extolling the "more honorable than the cherubim and more glorious beyond compare than the seraphim," and in honoring her conception with a special feast (9 December), wisely does not define with a formula that which unutterably gleams in the believing heart falling down in prayer before the all-pure Intercessor. However, by observing separate features of her veneration, as far as it is expressed in liturgy, one can reach some conclusions concerning the question that interests us. The Orthodox Church honors the *conception* of the Mother of God proclaimed by the angel to the *grandparents of God* Joachim and Anne (similar to how it honors the conception of the holy prophet John the Forerunner), but at the same time it does not take this conception out of the general order of nature; it does not proclaim it "immaculate" in the Catholic sense.[107] Does this not mean that in the conception and nativity of the Theotokos *nature* was operative, assisted by but not ousted by grace, and it was capable of being raised in the Theotokos to that purity and sanctity which the Church unchangingly praises with the words of the archangel, "Rejoice, Graced One, the Lord is with you, blessed are you among women" (Luke 1:28). "The angel cried out to the graced one, pure Virgin, rejoice" (the paschal post "it is worthy"). In the Mother of God nature, "earth," again attained its summit, that supreme purity and spotlessness of which she has proved to be capable even though assaulted by sin. The building of the Old Testament Church by grace led to the preparation of this purity, to the conception of the most holy Theotokos; in the purity of the Mother of God was concentrated the whole sanctity of the Old Testament, graced and natural; human nature was prepared and adorned in order to receive God in itself. Therefore the appearance of the Mother of God, and consequently the incarnation, was possible only in "the fullness of time," when the natural process of inner rebirth and restoration to health, although assisted by grace, happened, the center of which is the most holy Virgin. The sinful act of Eve turned out not to be irremediable. Mary, the seed of a woman, brought about what Eve had not been called to do. In the person of Mary nature, "earth," proved worthy of receiving heaven, of being joined with it indivisibly and without mingling in the Godhuman. The Mother of God, who surpasses all creatures, is at the same time the *glory of the earth*. Our sage of "motherearth," F. M. Dostoevsky, felt and proclaimed this very thing in his own words: "The Theotokos is the damp mother earth and great joy for hu-

The Sophianicity of the Creature

mankind is contained in this."[108] Mother earth proved to be the mother of the Mother of God.[109]

In contrast to the Catholic doctrine of the Immaculate Conception, the Mother of God proceeded by a natural, human route, and nothing human — not in the sense of possible distortions and sins, but in the sense of nature and temptations — was foreign to her. That is why that mysterious and sacred minute is a turning point in the history of the world when the Virgin said "Behold the handmaid of the Lord," for all of nature, all of humanity said this in her and with her and through her. That is why the humanity which the Lord received from "the pure bloods" of the Mother of God was complete and unquestionable: the Lord Jesus truly became a human being, he assumed the whole fullness of human nature, and for that reason redeemed it with his Blood. Having taken the entire fullness of humanity, he brought to himself the whole weight of its mortal nature and defeated death by his glorious Resurrection. And together with him, who lifted the flesh "with its passions and lusts" high on the cross, nature itself in the person of his most pure Mother co-suffered the redemptive torment through whose soul a sword truly passed. Her Word, "Behold the handmaid of the Lord, let it be done to me according to your word," she put into practice with her whole life and participation in the spiritual effort of her Son's obedience who prayerfully desired "not as I will, but as you will." No creature has known a crueler torment than this torment, and it made the Mother of God "the joy of all who mourn." Together with the Godhuman crucified on Golgotha the natural human essence was co-crucified in the purest and holiest Being, the Ever-Virgin Mother. The Mother of God is not only the sanctification and salvation of the world through the One Born of her, but she herself is the glorification and illumination of nature, which proved to be capable of this and worthy of it. But this means that the power of original sin, although it was great and injurious, remained limited, for in a *substantially* corrupted world a Mother of God could not have been born, and the Savior of the world could not have assumed that flesh. A definitively corrupted world would be worthy of annihilation and of course would find in itself the seeds of death and destruction. God's creation in its deepest fundamental principle can in no way be corrupted by sin so irremediably, so *irredeemably*.

THIRD SECTION

The Human Being

I. The First Adam

1. The Image of God in the Human Being

And God created the human in his image, in the image of God he created it (Gen. 1:27). *And the Lord God fashioned the human out of the dust of the earth and breathed in its face the breath of life; and the human became a living soul* (2:7). The human is created, but in the image of God.[1] It is fashioned from the dust of earth, from general creaturely matter, but the breath of life is blown into it by God himself. God brought its essence out of his very self and as it were shared it. And already in virtue of its origin, the human is a child of God.

We have corroboration of this in the New Testament in the genealogy of Jesus Christ, as it is set out in the Gospel of Luke: "Jesus was the son, as they thought, of Joseph, the son of Heli, son of Matthat . . . of Enos, son of Seth, son of *Adam, son of God — ōn hōs enomizeto, huios Iōsēph, tou Ēli, tou Matthat . . . tou Enōs, tou Sēth, tou Adam, tou Theou*" (Luke 3:23-38). The Son of God according to his pre-eternal birth is depicted as the descendant of the son of God according to adoption, and in the sense of adoption albeit of the Old Testament and under the law, Jesus is considered to be the "son of Joseph."

The image of God in the human must be understood realistically as a certain *repetition*, which on no account is identity with the Prototype; on the contrary, it is insurmountably differentiated from it, but at the same time it participates substantially in it. The reality of this connection between the image and the Prototype is marked by this feature of the biblical narrative: God *breathed* a soul into the human. There is here, consequently, a certain outpouring of Divinity, a kind of creative emanation. For this reason humanity is directly called *the offspring of God — genos theou* (Acts 17:28-29, the speech of St. Paul in the Areopagus). And the Savior refers to the text from Psalm 82:6 in his conversation with the Jews (John 10:34-36), "I said, you are gods and you are all sons of the Most High." When the serpent tempted the human being, it inclined him to misuse precisely his theophoric dignity. Temptation is always relative to the nature of the one being tempted; it presents a distorted and caricaturized elucidation of its real properties! "You shall be as gods." Since you have the image of God as the *repetition* of the Prototype, you will sense it independently, as an essence that *you yourself* possess.

The human is simultaneously a creature and a noncreature, the absolute in the relative and the relative in the absolute. It is a living antinomy, an irreconcilable duality, an incarnated contradiction. And the human finds this antinomic quality in the depths of its consciousness, as an expression of its authentic being. As the image of God, it has formally the nature of Divinity; it is God in potential and only in virtue of this divine potentiality is it capable of "divinization." Neither the inhominization of God nor the divinization of the human would be possible if the very nature of the human was not deiform and receptive of God. And if in the Godhuman in actual fact "the whole fullness of Divinity has dwelt bodily" (Col. 1:19), then this assumes that the human has the *full* image of God and everything that is revealed by Divinity, in some sense in a human manner as well. *Homo sum et nihil divini a me alienum esse puto* [I am a human being and I consider nothing divine to be alien to me]. The possibility of the cognition and revelation of God assumes already a certain godlike being, so far as cognition is a certain real uniting of the knower with the known. And if the Lord Jesus was incarnated as a human being, but not as one of the angels, despite all their proximity to the Throne of God, this then serves as proof that the *fullness* of the image of God belongs only to the human being, and even the powers of heaven do not have it. "For God did not subject the future universe to angels, about which we are speaking; on the contrary, someone somewhere bore witness, saying 'What do humans mean that you remember them? You made them a little lower before the angels; with glory and honor you crowned them and placed them over the works of your hands, and subjected all things under their feet'

[Ps. 8:5-7 (4-6)]. When he subjected everything to him, he left nothing not subjected to him" (Heb. 2:5-8).

God is absolute. Therefore absoluteness in some sense is inherent in his image; the nature of humankind is imprinted by it. God is transcendent to the world, is the absolute NOT, as negative theology knows him. And this trait must be inherent in humankind as the bearer of his image; we find it as the expression of the original self-consciousness and self-determination given by the human spirit to itself. Humankind is transcendent to the world and in this sense is free of the world, is nonworld. It is not exhausted by any *what*, is not defined by any definition, but is, like God, an absolute *not-what*. It places outside itself and opposes to itself any worldly givenness as a certain *what*, while remaining free of it and transcendent to it. Moreover, *humankind is transcendent to its own self* in all of its empirical or psychological givenness, in every self-definition, which leaves the peace of its absoluteness unbroken and its depths not muddied.

> As the immovable deep in a mighty expanse
> Is always the same in the agitation of a storm —
> The spirit is clear and bright in the peace of freedom
> But is the same in passionate desire.
> Freedom, compulsion, peace and agitation
> Pass by and again appear,
> But it is always one, and in the striving of the elements
> Only its power is revealed.[2]

Heraclitus the Obscure foretold of old: "In going to the limits of the soul you will not track them down, so deep is its measure" — *psykhēs peirata iōn ouk an exeuroio, pasan epiporeuomenos hodon houto bathu logon echei.*

The human spirit is inexpressible in any sort of *what*, which languishes in its immensity. Therefore the aspiration *towards absolute creativity*, after the image of God, is inherent in humankind. No manifestation of creativity, which is a creative act as far as it is anchored in a product, no excursion of the spirit out of transcendence into immanence completely exhausts it. As a result creativity cannot grow weak, and although the column of water constantly drops down, breaking up into splashes, still the indefatigable surge of the spirit will send a new stream out of the depths of its waters. Creativity consists in this unceasing self-positing of spirit, while preserving its transcendence. It goes without saying that the image, different from the Prototype, has this trait only as a formal possibility, a thirst, an impulse that is expressed in a gesture that one must not confuse with activity. It would be a great mistake *to equate* them, and while correctly affirming their similarity and correlativity, not to see the chasm that separates potentiality from actuality.[3] It is precisely this potential absoluteness of human creativity, which does not become actual, that gives rise to its tragedy. The human being does not experience it, only being absorbed in self-satisfaction and spiritual laziness. *The quest for a chef d'oeuvre*, despite the impossibility of finding it, the flaming embraces that attempt to hold onto a shadow that always steals away, the depression and the kind of disenchantment that lie in wait for the creative act — what does all of this signify but that the human spirit does not have the power to create its own, which alone would be able to quench its titanic thirst? Pushkin's resignation speaks of the same thing, clear but for that reason no less serious:

> The desired moment has come, my work of many years is finished,
> Why does an incomprehensible melancholy secretly trouble me?
> Why do I stand sadly like an unwanted day-laborer
> Who has received his wage, a stranger to any other work?[4]

The languor of powerless transcendence or nonabsolute absoluteness can be allayed only by a feat of love-humility. In the opposite case, it locks people seemingly with a glass wall in their Luciferian isolation, in the haughty but powerless pose of a challenge to every *what,* to every given, all the while being incapable of expressing oneself with anything. This is the torment of creativity without hope for satisfaction and even without a desire for it; this is severance from being, a rent in the very foundation of creatureliness. We do not know whether this hell in its fullness will be the lot of any living entity, but its rudiments we find in our own nature and in particular in the tragedy of creativity. Hellish acuteness is here paralyzed, however, by the fact that sophianic possibilities of creativity exist. If the creative impulse contrasts itself with every *what* and in this original apophatism outlines itself with a magical circle of anti-sophianicity and transcendence, a hellish grimace, the likeness of hell, results. Otherwise, it is an isolated male principle that wants to give birth from itself without a female principle, in spite of a female, and to find support for itself in this severance of the basic elements of being.

The image of God is realized in humankind not only by the transcendence of its spirit, by negative absoluteness, but also by positive co-participation in the mystery of Divinity, Its trihypostaseity: "Whoever loves me will keep my word; and my father will love him and we will come to him and make our home with him" (John 14:23). Trihypostaseity is traced in our spirit in sacred mysterious letters, and the more we plumb its innermost depths, the more fully we grasp this secret of our being. The triune composition of the soul — will, mind, feeling; Good, Truth, Beauty — in its indivisibility bears witness to this unity (blessed Augustine, V. Soloviev, and others). The prevalence of the doctrine of the trihypostaseity of God in different religions points to the same thing: they are darkened, even distorted expressions of the authentic voice of trihypostaseity in the human spirit. In a similar way the higher generalizations of philosophical thought, which cannot be contained in empty and abstract monism, but which seeks a living and compound plurality, monopluralism, testify to the same. Such is the trinity in Plotinus: the One, Mind, Soul. Although in keeping with its emanationist sense the Plotinian trinity differs substantially from the Christian, it remains a brilliant attempt by philosophy to comprehend the trihypostatic image that lives in the human being. The same can be said of the attempts of philosophical deduction of the Trinity in Schelling, V. Soloviev, and especially Hegel, as far as the natural self-consciousness of the spirit is expressed here from the point of view of logic.

Trihypostaseity is present in the human spirit not only as its basis but also as the internal form of being, as troubled searching and thirst. Disconnected from each other, the "abstract" principles of truth, good, and beauty, like the facets of creative consciousness corresponding to them — cognition, art, and the ascetic effort of the will — are doomed to being tragically unappeased. Each of these aspirations suffers from disconnection and in it finds a boundary. The task of *the whole,* of life in the triunity of truth, goodness, and beauty, which overcomes "abstraction," is its norm. The opening of trihypostaseity in the life of the spirit from faint outline to full concreteness is the source of the eternally beating joy and ever-renewing life that "shines with triune unity sacramentally."

The image of God in a human being is connected not only with the trinitarity of its spiritual composition but also with the *hypostaseity* of the spirit. *A human being is a hypostasis,* a countenance, a person. It has its depth and surface: *beneath* consciousness lies an indefinite quantity of layers of unconscious, or rather, pre-conscious or super-conscious life. A person, a hypostasis, is not exhausted by the present consciousness, which is only a phenomenon or mode of the person, but every content of consciousness is clothed with the form of hypostasis, is experienced as a state of the person. But what is a person? What is the I? No answer can be given to this question other than with a gesture that points inward. *A person is indefinable,* for it is always being defined with everything, remaining however *above* all of its conditions or determinations. Person is the unknowable mystery inherent to each, an unfathomable abyss, an immeasurable depth. It is absolute in its potential meaningfulness (by which the possibility of Fichte's temptation — absolute *Ich-Philosophie* — is elucidated), but always relative and limited in its actuality (by which the lie of this temptation is exposed, which would be legitimate only when potentiality and actuality coincide). The personal character of being, its hypostaseity, we cannot even hypothetically remove from living consciousness (and herein lies the best refutation of "a metaphysics of the unconscious," which wants to oppose to hypostaseity its own depth and foundation). It is simply impossible for a human being to think or feel in reality the state of extra-hypostaseity or unconsciousness; this is the most perfect abstraction, a negative concept. The human knows its hypostaseity or personhood in itself as something completely absolute, eternal in the sense of being extra-temporal, for which it cannot think either creation or annihilation, or in general link it with the flow of temporality. That the empirical person changes and develops in time does not contradict this at all, for there is an extra-temporal point of hypostaseity, "a spectator" who looks *into time outside of time.* The human absolutely *does not believe in* the temporality of its person and its destructibility. The idea of an end — not in the sense of catastrophe, but in the sense of absolute annihilation — *cannot be accommodated* in hypostatic consciousness, which equally does not know either end or beginning. It is not for nothing that the philosophy and mysticism of nonbeing speak not of a total void, but of *nirvana* as some positive and not merely negative nonbeing. When applied to hypostaseity it is incorrect to speak of the *pre-existence* of the human being, for here we have not a temporal sequence but a certain supratemporality, a freedom from time.

The First Adam

It is impossible to think of the annihilation of hypostaseity even among the demons, for hypostasis itself contains the foundation of its own being; it is hypostasis that proclaims about itself: *I am*, and it cannot be annihilated violently, by a negatively creative act. It must annihilate itself and to do so it must desire its own self-annihilation; but this very desire is impossible and contradictory: the desire for nonbeing is being in its intensity, and how will it become the path of its own annihilation? The eternal nature of hypostaseity summons here only eternal infernal torment, the circular motion of a serpent chasing its own tail, a magic circle where all points are simultaneously ends and beginnings.

In what kind of relation to its Prototype is the image of God in the human found? Metaphysics is incapable of giving a *positive* response to this basic question of religious anthropology, and can only outline its maximum negative bounds. The very possibility of repetitions of the image of God, the emergence of new hypostases, is a mystery of Divinity, about which the human is not free to speak. The human is for itself a mystery in its hypostaseity. Is this self-repetition of Divinity, the making of thousands of themes of new hypostases, humans and angels, the creative act of Divinity, either birth or emanation? Human thought is too poor in its rational dismemberment for it to grasp this *with one* concept, and thus here without fearing contradiction all that is left is to turn *either/or* into *both/and*. Multitudinous hypostases are made, born, and emanated. They are *made*, for carrying in themselves the image of eternity, they have it not from themselves, they are not *causa sui*, they do not know eternity actually, but only potentially. But they are free from time and are lifted above it; if one considered creation to be connected with temporality, then they *are not made*. But if on this basis alone we add to them the positive force of eternity, then following the tempter, we declare them to be gods per se. But only the image of eternity is inherent in them, not eternity itself, which is why for the human the *temporal* process is possible and even inevitable, as the actualization of that image. At the same time hypostases can be considered as *having been born* by God, as entities that proceeded out of his inner recesses, for birth is not creation; it differs from it. Finally, the outpouring of the power of Divinity, which occurred when the breath of life was *breathed* into the human by God, is defined most accurately by the concept *of emanation*, which is connected with the concept of birth.

Further, in what kind of relation are these sons of God with the

The Human Being

Divine Hypostases? The Gospel of John distinguishes a twofold birth: "from flesh and blood and the desire of a man," and from God; the second birth gives "power to be sons of God."[5] Although this original divine sonship is paralyzed by sin, thanks to the redemption it is returned to humankind. Of course, this dignity could not be restored if it were not given at the very making of the human who is imprinted more intimately than any with the hypostasis of the Logos, the only-begotten Son of God. That it is precisely the Second Hypostasis who gives the image of the human is attested to by the fact of the divine incarnation: the becoming human of the Second Person of the Holy Trinity, the Lord Jesus Christ. If the human being has the image of God, this means that in some sense beyond precise explanation God has the image of the human being. In the Adam of dust the features of the Heavenly Adam are traced and their final reunion is planned in advance.[6] According to the definition of the apostle Paul, Christ is the Heavenly One, who exists before the ages and before all creation; he is the true first Adam. "The first human is from the earth, one of dust, the second human is the Lord from heaven — *ho prōtos anthrōpos ek gēs choikos, ho deuteros anthrōpos ek ouranou*. As is the human of dust, so are those who are of dust, as is the one of heaven, so are those who are of heaven. And as we carry the image of the one of dust, so shall we carry the image of the heavenly one" (1 Cor. 15:47-49). "Whom he foreknew, he predetermined to be *sharers in the image of his Son, so that he would be the firstborn among many brothers — summorphous tēs eikonos tou Huiou autou, eis to einai auton prōtotokon en pollois adelphois*" (Rom. 8:29).

A central place in the cosmology of the Hebrew Cabbala belongs to the doctrine of the Heavenly Human, Adam-Cadmon; according to this cosmology the whole world has his image, is anthropocosmic.[7] The idea of the human as microcosm, so frequently expressed in philosophical and mystical literature of ancient and modern times,[8] nowhere receives such a profound interpretation as in the Cabbala. Adam-Cadmon is the sefirotic tree, and he contains in himself the whole fullness of divine energies or sefiroth. Each part of his universal organism corresponds to a definite sefirah, and in his image is created the organism of the earthly human, *his body*.[9] A comparison of 1 Corinthians 12:12-17 with this doctrine readily suggests itself.

Christ is the Human from Heaven. This does not mean, however, that only the Second Hypostasis has human form, separately from the First and Third hypostases, for it is impossible to admit such a separation with respect to the Holy Trinity, consubstantial and indivisible. Does not the Lord Jesus say, "I am in the Father and the Father is in Me"? "I have shown the Father." "I revealed his name to people." Furthermore, does not the outpouring of the gifts of the Holy Spirit on believers, beginning at Pentecost, and the very promise of the coming of the Comforter signify a certain co-humanity of the Third Hypostasis? It is fitting to recall also the exceptional descent of the Holy Spirit on the Most Pure Ever-Virgin. The church possesses no dogmatic definition about *how* precisely one ought to understand this descent of the Holy Spirit at the Annunciation. Do we have here the exceptional profusion of grace for the seedless conception of the Divine Son or[10] a kind of image of the divine incarnation?[11]

In its participation in the Human from Heaven the human being encompasses in itself *everything* in positive all-unity. It is the organized all or the pan-organism.

> And as in a dew-drop scarcely noticeable
> You know the whole face of the sun,
> So you will discover the whole universe
> merged in the hidden deep.[12]

The human being is the logos of the universe in which the universe recognizes itself.[13] As one created from the earth, the human being contains the creaturely *all*, but being created *after* all creations, stands above them all.[14] Dominion over all creatures is given to humans: "and they have dominion over the fish of the sea and the birds of the heavens and over wild animals and cattle, and over the whole earth and reptiles which crawl on the earth" (Gen. 1:26). This dominion is based, of course, on the inner superiority of the human being. As the metaphysical center of the universe, as the pan-organism, the human being in some sense *is* this everything subject to him, *has* this everything, *knows* this everything. God brings to the human being all the animals and birds "to see how he will name them and so that just as the human calls each living soul so would its name be" (Gen. 2:19). There is no doubt that this naming of names was not the arbitrary fabrication of nicknames: a name is an expression of the essence identified by the human. For this reason the naming of names was as it were the spiritual conclusion of creation.[15] In its psychic pan-organism the human spirit discovered and identified every living thing. Darwinism notwithstanding, the human being did not proceed from lower forms, but has them in himself: the human being is the *pan-animal* and contains in himself as it were the whole program of creation. One can find in him eagleness and lionness, and other psychic qualities that form the basis of the animal world, of that spectrum into which the white light of humanity can be decomposed. For this reason the whole animal world is actually recapitulated in the human being, while only an insignificant part in this phylogenesis is seen and distinguished.

In this connection one can understand not only the love of humankind for the living creature, so immediate particularly among children, but also the whole symbolism of animals in which human traits are expressed through their shapes (e.g., in the prophet Ezekiel, and in the *Apocalypse,* concerning the Evangelists). The Egyptian religion with its divinization of animals in the forms of deities, sensed with greater keenness the pan-animality of the human being or, what is the same thing, the humanness of the animal world. The bounds that separate human from animal are not unconditional, but relative and constantly shifting — this intuition of Egyptian religion has an internal persuasiveness and is as much its discovery as was the vision of the incorruptible beauty of the human being in the religion of the Hellenes. That same intuition of the pan-animality of humankind is manifested in *totemism,* so widespread in history; by selecting a definite animal as their totem and depicting it on their coat of arms or banners, a given tribe expresses by this means a feeling of deliberate connection with it, a special accentuation of this property in their character. The animal epos, fairy tales, superstitions, and similar things speak of this.[16]

2. Sex in the Human Being

The image of God in the human being is connected with one more mysterious trait. "And God created the human after his image, in the image of God he created it, male and female he created it" (Gen. 1:27). The fullness of the divine image in some sense is here placed in connection with the sexual duality of humankind. In referring to this text the Savior says to the Pharisees, "Have you not read that in the beginning *(ap' archēs)* the Creator made them male and female? And he said: for this reason a man will leave father and mother and adhere to his wife and the two will be one flesh (Gen. 2:24), such that they are no longer

The First Adam

two but one flesh. And so, what God has joined, humankind may not separate" (Matt. 19:3-6; Mark 10:6-9). According to the testimony of the Word of God, humankind *from the beginning* is created as male and female, two in one flesh. But already very early in mystical and patristic literature (probably not without the influence of Neo-Platonism and Gnosis with its eastern roots) a different viewpoint appears. Origen, Saints Gregory of Nyssa and Maximus the Confessor, Johannes Scotus Eriugena and Jacob Böhme, in a somewhat unexpected unanimity, affirm that the creation of the woman is the result of an already-begun falling in sin, its first revelation.

For an illustration of the opinions in ecclesiastical literature, let us compare two different though typical views, namely, those of St. Gregory of Nyssa and of blessed Augustine.

St. Gregory of Nyssa denies the primordial sexual duality of humankind by subjecting the text of Genesis 1:27 to a distinctive exegesis. "It is said *God created the human being, in the image of God he created it;* the creation of the one made in the image is brought to completion. Then what has been said about the organizing is repeated and it says *man and woman he created them*. I think that it is clear to everyone that this must be understood not as referring to the prototype, for *in Christ Jesus,* as the apostle says, *there is neither male nor female*. But the word states that humankind is divided into these sexes. Therefore the organization of our nature is something twofold, the one is likened to divine nature, and the other is divided into different sexes.... I think that in Divine Scripture a certain great and exalted dogma is being taught in what has been said, and it is this: human nature is midway between two things, separated one from the other and standing on the very extremities, between divine and incorporeal nature and between irrational and brutish life, because in the human composition one can observe part of the one and the other of these natures, of the Divine — logicality and rationality which does not admit difference in the male and female sex, and of the irrational — corporeal organization and formation, divisible into male and female sex. The one and the other of these natures are without fail in whatever participates in human life. But the intellectual, as we ascertain from the orderly exposition of the origin of humankind, has precedence in it; added to humankind is communion and kinship with the irrational. For Scripture first says *God created the human being in his image,* indicating by these words, as the Apostle says, that in such a one *there is neither male nor female;* then it names in addition the distinctive properties of human nature, namely, *male and female he created them*" (St. Gregory of Nyssa, *Works*, part 1, "On the Six Days," pp. 139-40).

The Human Being

A distinction in the sexes is made only on the basis of foreknowledge of sin: "God, who by virtue of foreknowledge comprehends in advance where the movement of choice is inclined in keeping with its arbitrariness and despotism (insofar as he knew the future), devised for the image the distinction of the male and female sex, which has no relation to the divine prototype, but, as was said, is appropriated to the irrational nature." In paradise there was no marriage or marital reproduction before sin. One can form an opinion about this state from the Lord's response to the Sadducees: *in the resurrection they neither marry nor are given in marriage* (Matt. 22:30). "The gift of resurrection promises us nothing else but the restoration of those fallen to their original state, for this hoped-for grace is a return to our original life, the leading back into paradise of what was driven out of it. Therefore if the life of those restored has a similarity with the life of the angels, then it is obvious that the life before the transgression was something angelic, and the return to our original life resembles the angels. But although there is no marriage among angels, the angelic host consists of innumerable myriads. Consequently, if owing to sin no transformation and falling away from equal honor with the angels had happened to us, then in the same way we would not have needed marriage for reproduction. But what means of reproduction the angelic nature may have is inexpressible and unimaginable by human guess-work; nevertheless there is no doubt that it does exist. . . . If anyone has difficulty inquiring about the means of human origination and asks, 'would not humankind need the assistance of marriage for this?' then we will ask them about the means of the angels' being: 'why do they comprise innumerable throngs, since they are one essence and numerous?' For we give the customary answer to the one objecting 'how could humankind be without marriage?' when we say 'in the same way that the angels exist without marriage.' But that humankind before the transgression was similar to the angels is proved by its restoration to this likeness. Foreseeing the fall of humankind and in order to secure its achievement of fullness by the gradual increase of the number of those born, God provides for nature a means of reproduction suitable for those who have slipped into sin. Instead of what is proper for angelic grandeur, he implanted in humankind a bestial and irrational means of mutual succession. . . . For the one who took into its nature that fleeting means of reproduction, in keeping with its inclination towards the material, really became bestial" (146-48).

In contrast, according to the opinion of blessed Augustine, marriage existed already in paradise and consequently reproduction "through the union of the sexes" was pre-indicated, although it had to be accomplished by a different means than in the current state of humankind, injured by sin. "At that time the sexual members would be set in motion by the nod of the will, just as all other members of the human body, and then spouse would cling to the bosom of spouse without passionate agitation, preserving complete compo-

The First Adam

sure of soul and body and fully maintaining chastity."[17] In paradise the sexual act itself could not be united with the feeling of bashfulness usual in the present time; at that time the sexual organs themselves were not considered to be shameful, and the very feeling of shame at the sight of the nakedness of the human spirit appeared as the result of the disarray of the harmony between spirit and flesh. Since in the act of falling into sin, spirit lost dominion over the body, and the body came out from under its power and subordination, naturally "the rational soul had to be ashamed; precisely because it was no longer able to restrain weakness and recalcitrance in the body, over which it had received the right to hold dominion."[18] "For the soul, shame is that which opposes the body to it — it is the lower side of human nature, subordinated to it"; in paradise it was obedient to the spirit and "desire did not lead certain members into an aroused state against the will." "If even in the present time among certain people who lead this grave life of corrupted flesh, the body in many motions and dispositions shows a surprising submissiveness exceeding the customary natural measure, then what basis do we have for not believing that before sin, insubordination and punishment of the human being with injury, human members could serve the human will for the reproduction of descendants without any desire?" Then, "a man was able to sow posterity, and the woman was able to receive with her childbearing members which were brought into motion when necessary and only when necessary, by means of the will without any arousal of desire."[19]

In mystical literature one inevitably contrasts J. Böhme's view of sex, in general well known to us already, with that of the Cabbala, which is thoroughly saturated with sex. We shall cite some excerpts from it. *Zohar* II, 70b: "By adding that *the human* is created in the image of God, Scripture hints at the mystery of the male and the female principle. Not only because the human being here below is born by the joint action of father and mother, which is why it deserves the name of human being (Adam), for by this means the generation of its body occurs analogously with the generation of the soul. Likewise is not the lower human generated in accordance with the revelation of the Higher Human Being, always hidden in the highest and original mystery? With regards to the affinity with Elohim, the image of the human being is literally similar to the image of Elohim: hair, forehead, eyes, face, lips, lines of hands and ears — such are the six distinctive signs of physiognomy by which they come to know the human being." Concerning the male-female nature of the human being in the *Zohar* we find the following explanation: II, 99b, "All souls *(neschamoth)* proceed from a great and mighty tree, planted near a river flowing out of Eden, whereas intellectual spirits *(Rouahoth)* proceed from another tree, smaller than the first. The soul proceeds from the higher realm, the intellectual spirit from the lower, and they are united together, according to the image of the union of male and female, and only after they have been united together do they shine and reflect the higher light. When they are united, they are called light *(ner)*, as it is written (Proverbs 20:2): 'The soul of the human being is the light *(ner)* of God.' The word *ner* is formed from the initial letters *Neschama* (soul) and *Rouah* (spirit). Soul and spirit — these are the female and the male. They emit light only when they are united; in separation they do not have the light and do not bear the name *ner.*" "*The man has in his own wife the Shekinah itself,* or rather, he has two companions: a heavenly and an earthly one," and this intimacy is interpreted quite realistically: *Zohar,* I, 50a: "A husband, when he finds himself on a journey, is not alone for he has the *Shekinah* as his wife; when he returns home, he ought to have intercourse with his wife, and for this 'good deed' the *Shekinah* will send most holy souls." "The mystery of this consists in the fact that believing people must direct their soul and thoughts towards the heavenly companion at the moment of union with the here below, because *this is the image of that.*" "In this manner also the man here below is surrounded by two women after the example of the higher."

"Observe that all souls in this world, which are the fruit of the deeds of the Holy Blessed One, before their descent to earth form a unity, and all these souls are part of one and the same mystery. And as soon as they come down into this lower world, they are separated into males and females, and the males and females unite. Observe besides that the desire of the woman for the man produces the spirit of life, and the desire of the man for the woman equally reproduces the spirit. Otherwise, since by the desire of the body the desire of the soul is equally aroused, whence it follows that the generation of man and woman must necessarily call for the descent of the male and the female soul. And while the souls come down into this world, the male and the female souls are united together. They are parted only after their descent into this world, each to its own side, and they go to animate two different bodies, a male one and a female one. And the Holy Blessed One himself again unites them then at the time of marriage. The obligation to unite men and women is not entrusted to any other heavenly head; the Holy Blessed One himself does this, for he alone knows how to do this in a fitting manner." *Zohar,* I, 85b (de Pauly, I, 493) — "Rabbi Abba says: happy the fate of the just, whose souls encircle the holy King before their descent into this lower world. For we know according to tradition that at that moment when the Holy Blessed One sends souls into this lower world, they all are distributed in pairs, they consist of male and female. The male soul is united with the female. This angel bears the name of 'Night.' As soon as the souls are entrusted to this angel, they are distributed; on the one side is the male soul, originally animating the man; on the other side is the female soul, originally animating the woman. And when the time of marriage arrives, the Holy Blessed One, who knows these spirits and these souls, unites them afresh as before; he proclaims their union. Therefore, when the spouses are united, they form only one body and one soul; the right side then is united

The First Adam

with the left in a corresponding manner" — *Zohar* I, 91b (de Pauly, I, 520-21). Correct marriages, which represent the union of kindred souls, are realized only in the context of a righteous life, and in general "les mariages constituent pour le Saint, béni soit-il, un travail ardu" [marriages are an arduous work, for the Holy One, blessed may he be].

It is obvious how closely related this teaching about sex in the Cabbala is to the corresponding ideas of A. N. Shmidt (manuscripts of A. N. Schmidt, with letters to her from V. S. Soloviev [Moscow, 1916]).

In the exposition of the mysterious event in the book of Genesis,[20] at first only a general indication of the creation of man and woman is given (chapter 1), and then is recounted *how* the creation happened, after Adam was led to the thought of his own loneliness through the spectacle of the universal sexual duality of the animal world. The making of the woman was *the completion* of the creation of humankind. The understanding and appraisal of this event has an unusual, exceptional importance: *here* the difference in the sense of the flesh and the world, in a general mystical disposition, takes shape. Of course, the difference of the sexes, immediately expressed in the sexual organs, is not limited by this. The whole organism and each cell in it have the nature of sex. It is necessary for Christian thought to reckon with the fact that the female sex, namely motherhood, is glorified by the Mother of God ("Blessed is the womb which bore you, and the breasts which you sucked," Luke 11:27), and the male sex is glorified by the Savior, on whom the circumcision is carried out on the eighth day in keeping with Jewish law (celebrated on January 1). And whoever wants to belittle and repudiate sex will have to understand the birth of the Savior in a Bogomil[21] fashion as a procession "out of the side" (through the rib) and negate sex in the post-resurrectional glorified body of the Savior, by admitting a radical sinful infirmity of His earthly body. Eriugena, following on St. Maximus the Confessor, stands for such a point of view:[22] if the Savior was revealed to his disciples in a male body, this was only because they would not have recognized him otherwise; but through the transition to a spiritual state the difference of male and female sexes is annihilated in him.[23] It is obvious that it remains to extend the same idea to the Theotokos after her glorification.

But in what sense is the fullness of the image of God in humankind brought into connection with its sexual duality? Eve is fashioned *out of* Adam, who in a certain sense feels himself to be Eve's maker: "Behold this is bone of my bones, flesh of my flesh; she will be called woman *('ishâ)*, for she is taken from man *('ish)*" (Gen. 2:23). Already in their very creation a hierarchical distinction exists between the two sexes which as a result of the fall is heightened disharmoniously ("and your attraction will be for your husband, and he will have authority over you," Gen. 3:16). The hierarchy of the sexes in the New Testament is brought into connection with the relation of Christ to the Church. "Wives, submit to your husbands, as to the Lord, because the husband is head of the wife, just as Christ is head of the Church, he is the Savior of the body" (Eph. 5:22-23). "I also want you to know that the head of every husband is Christ, and of every wife, the husband, and of Christ, God is the head ... the husband is the image and glory of God, and the wife is the glory of the husband. For it is not the husband who is from the wife, rather the wife is from the husband; and the husband was not created for the wife, but the wife for the husband. Nevertheless there is neither husband without *(chōris)* wife nor wife without husband in the Lord *(en Kuriōi)*. For as the wife is from *(ek)* the husband, so is the husband through *(dia)* the wife; and all are from *(ek)* God" (1 Cor. 11:3, 7-12).

God is revealed in and through Sophia who, by receiving this revelation in a feminine way is the "glory of God" *(shekinah* of the Cabbala). Sophia is the feminine principle which receives the power of the Logos, and this unity is described in the Word of God as the "marriage of the Lamb." See to what a sacred mystery the apostle Paul points.

Made two-sexed, but precisely because they appear as a single-sexed entity, human beings also have this sexual duality in their spirit,[24] and know the erotic tension as the deepest foundation of both creation and creative activity. Therefore the human being is worthy to carry the sacred flame of Eros within, and is a child of Porus and Penia. This is why the experience of personal love conceals in itself so endlessly many revelations of the mystery of the universe.

But why would the human, even with its characteristic sexual duality of the spirit, or precisely because of it, not remain that two-sexed-asexual entity, the androgyne, for which J. Böhme and his followers take it?[25] Why does the division into sexes exist? The familiar doubt returns to us: *Why Eve?* Where does wife come from? Is she not indeed the result of sinful sensuality? And another question follows on this one: Is woman *a human being*? Is she not merely seductive lust, captivating falsity, wicked poison? The misogyny that appears in various guises wants to cast woman completely out of the world, as the creation of Lucifer, the daughter Lilith. Therefore redemption is regarded as *deliverance from sex* with the restoration of original androgynism. This view was widespread among certain Gnostics, inasmuch as it is possible to judge from the extant evidence of the Gnostic *Gospel of the Egyptians*. In this text, the Savior, when asked by Salome by what the anticipated will be recognized, replies: "When you trample on the envelope of shame, and when two become one, and the male sex unites with the female, and there will be neither male nor female — *hotan to tēs aischynēs endyma patēsete kai hotan genetai ta duo hen kai to arrēn meta tēs thēleias oute arrēn oute thēly*."[26]

Eve is fashioned out of Adam's "rib." It is a question here of a certain apportionment of the essence of woman from the essence of man. Eve is not made by a new creative act, as was Adam; her emanation does not violate the Sabbath rest by which God rested after the creation of the world and the human being; the breath of life, which had been communicated to Adam earlier, was not breathed by God specially into her. Eve's life is not self-subsistent; she arises in Adam. Eve is present already in Adam's spirit and body by which the sacrament of marriage is grounded: two are one and in one flesh. Like all religious sacraments this one is also an antinomy for reason, flouting the law of identity. And yet, surely the feminine principle could not have been forever left enclosed in Adam, without being apportioned from him, without being clothed in flesh. The necessity of the separate existence of the sexes requires precisely *sensuality*. Those who understand woman as sinful sensuality err in that they take the morbid corruption of sensuality for its essence. Eve could not remain as a merely ideal possibility inside Adam, for then he would not sense her as corporeality, and because of that he would not identify his own proper body. In the person of Eve the immaculate sensuality of the world appeared before Adam, which until then unfolded before him only like a canvas, something alien, external, and to a certain degree ghostly. It was not for nothing that after coming to know the world as he gave creatures their names he sensed his own loneliness in the world where he had been called to become the king, as well as his separateness from it. In Eve the living flesh of the whole world was revealed to him, and he felt himself to be its organic part.[27] In Eve's beauty the sophianic beauty of the world was revealed to Adam. But cannot love even in our sinful world give even now a similar clairvoyance in its flaming moments? And cannot that love song which is called *Song of Songs* refer to the pure love of Adam and Eve, although it has in view immediately that in the image of which marriage exists — the relation of Christ and the Church? It is not to no purpose, surely, that the meeting of the bride with the bridegroom at the crowning is accompanied by the hymn from the *Song of Songs:* "Come, come, bride from Lebanon, come my good one, come my dove!"

As much as in the beloved the whole creation appears for her lover as the image of female beauty, so too does the beloved recognize in this her own femininity and reveal herself to herself. If the sensuality, the corporeality of the world is not a disease or only a subjective state, but an independent element of life, then sex cannot remain only inside the human being, but must be realized in the flesh too, be divided into two in it, so that having felt this division into two, the two may become "one in the flesh." On the contrary, if sensuality and flesh are only a phenomenon, a sinful dream inspired by Lilith, then the sexual duality of the body becomes unnecessary and onerous, and the overcoming of the stagnation and sin of the world must in that case be expressed above all in the healing not of sex but *from* sex, in liberation from Eve by way of her abolition, of the return inside Adam. But then the personal corporeality of the androgyne remains unrecognized in its reality, as something other and at the same time identical. The body loses its plasticity and resilience; it feels itself like a shell, enclosing and burdening the spirit, which strives towards incorporeality. In such a false spiritualism the human being yearns to be divested of its own personal rank in the hierarchy of creation, by moving to the state of incorporeal spirituality which is both alien to it and beneath it. This is why the feminine principle could not remain only in the innermost recesses of the human spirit — and became Eve. False spiritualism in love is just such a mistake of erotic judgment, like bare sensuality, naked lust, for the true object of love is the incarnate spirit or animated flesh.[28] In the present-day sinful condition of humankind this balance is profoundly upset, and nowhere is the tragedy of love so recognizable as in the search for and failure to find this balance, since the temptation to simplify the task, to renounce it, appears involuntarily. Under the influence of natural bitterness from the sinful distortions of love, of sexual *dégoût* (which has very little likeness with ascetic continence), they take up arms against love itself, by cursing her, and frequently at the basis of this enmity towards woman and marriage is the secret sin against love and femininity: *The Kreutzer Sonata!*

"And God blessed them and said to them 'Be fruitful and multiply and fill the earth'" (Gen. 1:28). The first human pair was given the

The First Adam

commandment to reproduce, as a blessing and a command of God. This means that in Adam and Eve God fashioned not only a bridegroom and bride, but also a husband and wife, a father and mother of future children. *New birth-giving* is indicated here as the task of matrimony, as its interior norm, and on this foundation is built the whole sonorous scale of human relations in the family, in which N. F. Fedorov saw with such wise perspicuity the essence of human society: husband, wife, father, brother, sister, grandfathers, grandsons — on all sides the running shoots and branches of Adam's tree.

The joining of the sexes, conception and birth, is the norm of sex according to the primordial determination of God.[29] Sinful humankind does not know this joining in its purity. The power of sin is nowhere told with such acuteness as in the most intimate and tender relations, and its shadows thicken here with disfiguring stains. Thanks to sin an intense and burning antagonism is established between sex and sexual feeling or sexuality. Sexuality is not sex and can even become the negation of its highest principle, but at the same time it is inseparable from sex, which does not exist without it, like fire without burning material. Sex, indivisibly linked with sexuality, gives fire to life and for this reason it is a positive and blessed power (from which one can understand the universal instinctive aversion for "sexual anomalies" or simply for sexual inadequacy, physical and spiritual castration). But at the same time, *the struggle on behalf of sex* is *a struggle against sexuality* and this intimate wrestling in sex itself enlightens it from within; the fight *against* sexuality is enmity against sex also which wants depersonalization instead of a higher affirmation of the person, weakness instead of subdued power. Revolt against sex, even though in the name of the negation of sexuality, attests to a serious injury of the spirit — it is not for nothing that the church so decidedly condemns self-castration (and it is not by chance that with his extraordinary spiritualism Origen performed this on himself, according to tradition). Nonetheless sex, thanks to its sexual murkiness, contains in itself agonizing disharmonies. Of course, in his fiery cry of human powerlessness the great apostle has this aspect of life in mind: "In my members I see another law that opposes the law of my mind and makes me captive to the law of sin which is found in my members. What a wretch I am! Who will deliver me from this body of death!" (Rom. 7:23-24). The life of sex in its actual condition, no matter how it might run, has the seal of tragic hopelessness and antinomic pain (which is symbolized in the tragedy of love-death: Romeo and Juliet,

Tristan and Isolde). The spiritual-corporeal joining of the two in one flesh, as it is given in the norm of creation and of which there is a presentiment no matter how weak in marriage in the measure of the spiritual maturity of the spouses, is connected at the same time with the feeling of disunity, murder, melancholy over the loss of something dear and pure. *"Post coitum animal triste"* [after sexual intercourse the animal is sad]. The serpent poisoned the ecstasy of the flesh with his impure seed.[30] But the esoteric wisdom of the *Cabbala* connects with this ecstasy the ascension into the world above, communion with the Shekinah (herein lies the meaning of circumcision, where the sacred tetragram is allegedly traced on the circumcised organ).

A new birth, connected with such torments and danger for the mother, is not only the redemption for the sinfulness of the joining, but also the normal act of raising souls which have to be born in God's world. At the birth of a new child it suddenly becomes clear and certain that the newly born in actual fact *always* existed in its parents, was eternally with them, and for them it is even impossible to imagine the child as not existing.[31] And the joy of this *encounter* at the birth, when the feeling of mother and father instantly catches fire, does not have worthy words in human language, but in the Eternal Book, in the farewell discourse of the Savior, it is stated *this way:* "A woman, when she gives birth, suffers grief because her hour has arrived; but when she bears a son, she no longer remembers her grief out of joy that a human has been born into the world" (John 16:21). Therefore the *carrying in the womb* is also a mysterious and sacred condition. The gospel story gives the apotheosis of pregnancy in the encounter of the two future mothers, Mary and Elizabeth, flooded with heavenly light; the latter, filled with the Holy Spirit, greets the Ever-Virgin thus: "Blessed are You among women — *en gynaixin,* and blessed is the fruit of Your womb" (Luke 1:41-42). Blessed marriages and chosen conceptions are the religious axis of the Old Testament, the central nerve of its religiosity. But also the depiction of the church in the *Apocalypse,* before its final glorification, affirms this very trait: "And a great sign appeared in heaven — a woman clothed in the sun; the moon is beneath her feet, and on her head is a crown of twelve stars. She was carrying in her womb and she cried from the pains and torments of birth. . . . And she gave birth to a child of the male sex, who is to shepherd all nations with an iron rod" (Apocalypse 12:1-2, 5).

The commandment to reproduce is not connected with the fall; it

The First Adam

is given *before* this, and not of course in order to destroy the chaste purity of the spouses but to realize in and through them the fullness of life. Between virginity and marriage there is in principle no contradiction, and if the fall had not happened, Adam and Eve would have been the first virginal spouses on earth.[32] Disdain for marriage is strictly condemned by church canons.[33] From the priest, the performer of the sacraments, is demanded if not an obligatory entrance into marriage, then sexual normalcy. It was the same in the Old Testament church, where a wealth of children was considered a blessing.[34] The amorousness alone of bridegroom and bride, combined with a negation of marriage (although in the antithetics of love this motif is also present: the lovers in a certain moment of love do not want marriage), cannot be the exhaustive norm of the relations between the sexes. Insofar as this denial is not connected simply with sexual anomalies, an amorousness that chronically fights against marriage leads to a vile captivity to sexual "arousal" against which the apostle Paul wisely warns, by advising that it is better to enter into marriage than to burn, and through this to become a slave to sensual attraction. Ideology though does not alter physiology, which has of course a more authentic ontological-mystical basis. If this preaching is not a tribute to late age and sexual fatigue, it remains powerless or leads to anomalies and vice.

But *a worthy* path of love *is everywhere* difficult, both in marriage and outside marriage, and its antinomies must not be either mollified or eliminated by twists and turns. The apostle Paul does not do this. On the one hand he explains marriage as a "union in Christ and the church," and advises to enter into marriage in order not to burn, but on the other hand he exhorts those who can to remain unmarried because those who have a wife "will have grief on account of the flesh, and I feel sorry for you" (1 Cor. 7:28). "The unwed is anxious for the Lord, how to please the Lord, but the wedded is concerned for worldly things, how to please his wife" (1 Cor. 7:32-33). The tree of life aches in the heart of sex, and here there are no entirely triumphant victors.

Not for nothing does the church in the sacrament of marriage fit it for the journey as for the way of the cross, although with exultant hymns. A love unshared or disconnected kills and consumes with its own fire, and its first ray already burns with the glow of sunset: love is always thinking about death. "Strong as death is love," says the *Song of Songs* of love.[35] The tragedy of marital love is usually manifested when the bride dies in the wife, and the bridegroom in the husband, and love is extinguished. But in the meantime the wife must forever remain for her lover the bride, the enamored woman, and the husband — the bridegroom, the enamored man.[36] This internal norm of love according to which it creates for itself its own law-court contains nothing contradictory in it, just as there is no contradiction, e.g., in the fact that a human being is simultaneously father and son, husband and brother, or mother and daughter, sister and wife.

Love has many faces and many sides, and there is no basis for *setting* its bounds *in opposition* as mutually exclusive. This virginal joining of love and matrimony is the interior task of Christian marriage, and in the sacrament grace is bestowed upon those marrying, in order to revive the health of sex which was lost in the fall. This task is so difficult that even drawing near to it is miraculous. The life of sex with its fiery antinomies and tragic heartbreaks is the most sensitive barometer of a religious life; here, in an intimacy invisible to the world victories and achievements are won, defeat and failures happen. . . . "Having knelt down, he said to them, 'Let him who among you is without sin be the first to cast a stone at her.' When they heard this, their conscience accused them and they started to leave one by one beginning with the eldest until the last one, and only Jesus and the woman remained who stood in the midst" (John 8:7, 9). Who were these zealots of the law — fornicators and libertines? No, they were strict lawyers, guardians of good morals. And yet Jesus was left *alone*. Let each ask in his heart how *he* would have answered the Lord's word — Jesus told the woman "taken in adultery," "Neither do I condemn you. Go and sin no more" (John 8:11). What is this? The Lord does not condemn adultery? He who said "every man who only looks at a woman with desire has already committed adultery with her in his heart" (Matt. 5:28)? Or is this a gesture of sentimentality in reply to the gloating delight of the Pharisees? Of course not! The Lord condemns sin, but he does not cast away the sinner, he does not deprive her of the hope of redemption: go and sin no more! But does not each human soul in the presence of the Lord feel itself to be such a woman, taken in adultery, even though it was committed not in deed but only in word, in a glance, in a thought run through involuntarily? For it is poisoned in its depths, and the trembling element of sex aches in agony. The ascetics knew its fiery power best of all. The restoration of sex to health, its purity and chastity, is not only a *negative* quality of sexual continence, which can be combined with a serious perversion, it is also a positive force — of sinlessness in sex.[37]

The First Adam

That equal fullness of sex, that pairing which is given in the primogenitors, does not exist in all human individuals.

Evidently there exist unpaired beings[38] who are not deprived of sex but have no pair for themselves, no sexual complement. For such "eunuchs from the mother's womb" sex is seductive and foul; in the life of sex they can feel themselves only as bucks or does, and for them it is a collapse. They know erotic flights but without the direct means of the other sex. This is the "angelic rank" which has no *human* sex. "He is of our kind": this is what the Mother of God said about St. Seraphim, and one feels the seraphic, nonhuman whiteness of this "kind." Is it not said of him in the Apocalypse: "and I heard and behold the Angel stands on mount Zion and with him 144,000 who have the name of His Father written on their foreheads" (their special relationship with the hypostasis of the Father is indicated). "And I heard a voice from heaven, like the roar of a great quantity of water and like the sound of mighty thunder, and I heard a voice as if of psaltery players plucking their psalteries: they sing as it were a new song before the throne and before the four living creatures and the elders; and no one could learn this song except those 144,000 redeemed from the earth. It is they who were not befouled — *ouk emolynthēsan* — with women, for they are virgins" (the commerce of the sexes in marriage is in and of itself by no means a defilement, but for those who have the nature of virgins, it *is* a defilement, and they were conscious of their "kind" and conquered the lust of the body). "It is they who follow the Lamb wherever he goes (they form as it were his angelic environment). They are redeemed from the people, as the first fruits for God and the Lamb and there is no slyness on their lips: they are spotless before the throne of God" (*Apocalypse* 14:1-5).

The Savior's conversation with the Pharisees testing him has a substantive meaning for the question of sex. To the question about the permissibility of divorce the Savior replies that marriage is of divine institution and indissoluble (Matt. 19:3-6 = Mark 10:6-7). "The disciples said to him, if such is the relation of a man to a woman, then it is not worth marrying" *(ei houtōs estin hē aitia tou anthrōpou meta tēs gynaikos, ou sympherei gamēsai)*. The disciples' doubt relates to the *feasibility* of this norm of marriage. "He said to them, not everyone can receive this saying *(logon touton)*, but only to whom it is given." This saying is, according to the context, God's determination that there are in marriage "two as one flesh," while "to receive this saying" is not given to everyone. Concerning those to whom it is not given, the Savior continues his words: "For there are eunuchs *(eunouchoi)* who are born this way from their mother's womb, and there are eunuchs who are made such by people; and there are eunuchs who have made themselves eunuchs for the sake of *(dia)* the kingdom of God. Whoever can accommodate it *(chōrein)*, let him do so" (Matt. 19:10-12).

Here three types of celibacy are distinguished: natural or pre-established, actual or "from people," i.e., as a result of the conditions of life that prevent a person from realizing their sexual duality, and voluntary, in accordance with ascetical motives, as the feat of marital fasting. But despite these exceptions, the commandment about marriage is once again confirmed: "Whoever can accommodate it, let him do so."[39] Among the innate and the voluntary eunuchs belong people "of the third sex," both men and women, who recognize amorousness or "spiritual matrimony" but who disdain marriage and especially the generation of children in keeping with various ideological reasons (of relevance here is first of all the chief ideologue of the "third sex," Vladimir Soloviev, with his articles on the Meaning of Love).[40] This militant philandering and spiritual "hetaerism" arises in natures in which owing to the great intensity of psychic life and creativity there results not the spiritual enlightenment of sex, based on victory over sexuality, but its sublimation, whereby even the need for dissipation is far from being always defeated. To put it differently, it is not the *spiritual* victory over sexuality that ascetics know, people of spiritual striving, but its *psychic* refinement. This pretty ugliness, which easily passes over into unnatural inclinations, is usually accompanied by a philandering need for new experiences of amorousness. It is proper to artistic natures, to painters and poets who frequently give birth to their children in an "astral" world, which they confuse with the spiritual. This spiritual mentality is found in connection with a peculiar destruction of spiritual and erotic balance and with the weakening of some vital functions while others undergo a hypertrophied development, with a particular thirst for life, the "metaphysical egoism" of the monad. In separate cases this leads to tragic conflicts between the life of sex and creativity; especially doomed to these are creative women who have to choose between the joys of family and creativity, to take upon themselves sometimes the inordinate burden of "hetaerism" in celibacy.[41] Philandering has its deep roots in the antinomic nature of love, but there are no grounds to see in the third sex and the third way (besides virginity and marriage) some sort of overcoming or victory, or something eschatological.

The First Adam

The full image of the human being is man *and* woman in combination, in spiritual-corporeal marriage. Each individually is a *half-*human, but is an independent person, a hypostasis, and has its own spiritual destiny. But in the innermost recesses of the spirit each human remains all the same two-sexed, because otherwise their life would be impossible. And spiritual sex is in general complex, for each person is an individual and original mixture of male and female elements; and the creative tension, the eroticism of the spirit, is conditioned by this. This immanent conjugal state of the human spirit hides in itself the clue for creativity which is not a volitional act but *spiritual generation,* as the genius of language bears witness, readily applying images from the realm of sexual life to it. The male principle, solar, of genius, logical, is the initiator; to it belongs the theme, motive, impulse, and with it is bound the vision of sophianic essences, the contemplation of ideas. But the creative act is only initiated by him, and not finished; the creation itself is brought forth by the dark feminine womb, "by the earth" of the soul.

> The light from the darkness,
> The faces of your roses,
> Could not rise out of the dark clod
> If their submerged dark root had not dug
> into the gloomy bosom.[42]

This explains the limitedness and fruitlessness of *the methodical* in creativity, insofar as it strives to replace inspiration with workmanship (Salieri against Mozart) and exact method. Creative, fruitful ideas *are born,* they flare up intuitively in the soul (Newton's apple!), method is a means to develop and utilize what is discovered; but it does not replace a human being with a homunculus.

Human creativity in its very essence is marked by the sexual duality of the human spirit, by the mystery of the conjugal state. It is the crossing of two principles, genius and talent, the intersection of the vertical and the horizontal. Genius is a creative initiative, the discovery of new themes, tasks, possibilities; it is a spiritual flight into the "noetic place" where eternal ideas are seen, lightning that penetrates the crust of the world's being. Genius beholds Sophia; she herself is a sophianic ray, her revelation, which is why her attainments are realized as some discovery or gift from on high. Ultimately genius is *person* in its intelligible essence, the baring of its sophianic essence. On the contrary, the carrying-out of a theme, the realization of creative tasks is already the work of talent, of the special giftedness for fulfilling, and without this receptive and generating means even genius will remain fruitless. Creative will has bearing on this, as do obdurate toil and persistent striving to achieve a masterpiece. Although it is sometimes said that genius is toil, in reality this refers to talent, without which the work conceived by genius will not be born. The one and the other element of spirit — genius and talent — are potentially present in every human being and form its spiritual composition, however, with a different degree of obviousness and activity (and in order to understand works of genius one needs to find in oneself echoes for them and as it were accompany genius on its ascent). Genius is the male, initiating principle in creativity, it is spirit; talent is the feminine, receiving, and generating principle, the soul, Psyche. That is why genius is independence itself and originality; whereas talent, as the aptitude for spiritual nurturing, always has before itself a given task or motif, which is carried out with a greater or lesser degree of completion. Therefore it is impossible to have *a will* for genius; on the contrary, one can and must have a will for talent: it is necessary *to make* oneself, to forge one's life. And not only each particular work of creativity, but also the whole of human life must become the discovery of a theme of genius and its talented fulfillment. The saints, who transform their whole life into a fragrant fruit of spiritual creativity, reveal to us the highest achievement on this path also.

Male and female self-consciousness each has its distinctive traits. The man is active, logical, full of initiative; the woman is instinctive, inclined to self-surrender, wise with an illogical and impersonal wisdom of simplicity and purity. An andromorphic woman produces as ugly an impression as does a gynomorphic man. Such *confusion* of the sexes differs from that *complementing* which each sex normally finds in itself. A woman has a male principle, but in her own way, just as a man has a female principle. Whoever honors sex (the "eternally female" and in the same manner simultaneously the eternally male) cannot condone sexual nihilism, which is hidden sometimes under the cover of the equality of the sexes, which in actuality are not equal but deeply different. An imaginary equality inevitably is attended by a desecration of femininity and a reduction of sex to the simple difference of buck and doe; nihilism leads to cynicism.

The sexual duality of the human spirit receives its highest expression in religious self-consciousness, in the turning of the soul towards God, which is usually defined in religious and mystical authors as "spiritual marriage." In finding itself in the Church and merging with it, the human being without distinction of his individual sex, finds itself in the *feminine* element of its soul, and is aware of itself as "the body of Christ." As the church, all humanity without distinction of the sexes is feminine in spirit. This is what the words of the apostle Paul point to, namely that "in Christ Jesus neither the male nor the female sex has force" in their *human* polarization, which here goes beyond these limits. *All* humanity, like the Virgin and the Church in their chastity, are aware of themselves as feminine: "This mystery is great indeed, I am speaking concerning Christ and the Church." On the contrary, the intensity of solely the male principle in the life of the spirit leads to a revolt against God which has its archetype in the uprising of the Daystar, who renounced the feminine element of the spirit, wanted to have everything from himself, in a masculine way, and became the devil.

The human being is created by God as not only a two-in-one entity — Adam and Eve, but also as a polyhypostatic entity, *a family*, as is clear from the blessing of God: "Be fruitful and multiply and fill the earth." This multiplication of hypostases, in keeping with God's determination, must be accomplished through the combination of the sexes: in the loins of the first human pair is found the principle of the single chain of human beings, linking them in one family. The progenitor of humanity himself, Adam, the father of all, and in him Eve too, the mother of every living thing, was born without the seed of an earthly father. He had only a Heavenly Father, although the seed of the whole human race was included in him. For his mother he had the Earth. Similar to him is the Second Adam, who came into the world to regenerate Adam's fallen nature, the true Son of God, and he was also born without an earthly father, and not from the seed of a man. He has an earthly Mother too, the all-immaculate Ever-Virgin, the glory of the Earth.

3. Human and Angel

What is the difference between the nature of a human and an angel? It is impossible to escape this question in a doctrine of the human being. We are unworthy of knowing the life of angels; it may be that surrounded by their chanting hosts we neither hear nor know them. The church reveals to us that they are present with us in intercessory prayer, and the heavenly hosts surround the sacred altar when the bloodless sacrifice is elevated (it is well known from the vita of St. Sergius that one day his disciple saw an angel serving together with the saint of God). Although it is utterly impossible for us to know the proper life of the angels, we do know that angels are *created* by God and although they are incorporeal in the sense that they do not have a human body, they do have a hypostasis: they are not faceless, they are hypostatic powers of God created by the Logos.[43] "For through Him is created everything that is in the heavens and that is on the earth, visible and invisible, whether thrones or dominions or principalities or authorities: all are created through Him and for Him" (Col. 1:16).

Angels have hierarchical distinctions; they form ranks and hosts. In the well-known composition of St. Dionysius the Areopagite, *On the Celestial Hierarchies*, nine ranks of angels are established, with each rank having its own type of spiritual growth. The angelic world is found in a certain mysterious correspondence with the Human from Heaven. According to the word of the Savior, every human being has a guardian angel, a heavenly double. The degree of the angels' proximity to God is inaccessible for humankind. According to their state, the latter are immensely inferior to angels. But according to its nature, and its hierarchic place in creation, in the world, humankind has the *primacy* before angels, and to it belongs in a greater degree the *fullness* of the image of God. The fact that Christ was incarnated as a human and not as an angel, and that he divinized precisely human nature is irrefutable evidence of this. The great complexity of human nature corresponds to its great richness; in it is the source of both human strength and weakness. Thanks to this the sinful moving away from God is not so profound and decisive for it as it is for Satan and his angels. The greater complexity of his nature is expressed also in the great discursiveness, the steeping of human existence in time. We do not have a direct concept of time for angels, but indirectly we can conclude that angelic time is more concentrated, thicker, than the porous, slow time of humans by which the possibility of a prolonged historical process is caused. It was left to the freedom of the angels to be self-determining with respect to God, with an intermediate state of unbelief and ignorance being in general excluded for such perfect spiritual entities: angels know God immediately, they are granted only to love him or to hate him, whereas to *seek* God is proper only for humans. If demons were defined in their falling away from God, angels were consolidated in their angelic perfection, which already excludes the blindness and madness of demons. Evidently it is impossible to speak of a *history* of angels, at least in the human sense of "times and seasons"; rather here it is appropriate to think about a lightning-speed occurrence whose consequences are realized in time. By the way, since they do not have an intuition of angelic time, humans cannot venture a statement about whether a reversal towards the good is possible for the evil spirits, or their repentance. (We have only the definite instructions of the Church that until the end of the world, in this eon, the evil spirits will persist in their malice.)

The principal difference of humankind from the angels is defined by the fact that angels do not have a body similar to the human body, which contains the principles of the flesh of this world. This flesh exists for humankind in its fullness as Eve, woman. *Eve* — here is what distinguishes the image of the human from an angel (which is why monasticism is the rank "equal to the angels"). Even if we were to admit together with other mystics that the spirits of angels have a male or female nature, all the same this does not make up sex in its fullness, for which the being of two essences in one flesh is essential, as is the case with humankind. As a result of their central position in the world, essentially connected with sexual duality, humans have an independent realm where they are summoned to autonomous, regal existence, whereas angels, God's messengers, do not have such a realm. Angels, for all their spiritual height and proximity to God, are *auxiliary spirits, angeloi*, who represent the power of the Divinity, his will. This does not take hypostaseity from them and does not make them faceless and uncreated "powers of God," as Schelling asserts, but it does deprive them of an independent realm, of a special angelic kingdom.

Angelic ministry resembles the priest's standing before the altar of God to perform the sacraments; in the order of Christ's ministry it corresponds to his pre-eternal archpriesthood. But the Godhuman is not only a Priest, he is also King and Prophet, and all these ministries are shared by humanity. The most intimate participation of the angels in the events of our salvation and in the intercessory prayer before God during the celebration of the sacraments is expressed in varied ways in our liturgical texts[44] and also iconography.[45]

And thus the difference between the human and the angel is reduced to their nature and their state. This difference is understood

The Human Being

sometimes in a different way: whoever sees in corporeality a kind of sickness, in the creation of woman, a sign of the fall, and in Eve, the principle of sin, must deny the radical difference in the nature of human and angel, seeing in the human only a failed angel, and in the angel, the normal image of the human which did not diverge from its purpose. Salvation for a human being therefore can only be its dehumanization, the removal of the flesh, the overcoming of sexual duality and the abrogation of the woman, in a word, as it were a novel angelization of its essence. Roughly such an inclination of thought is noticeable in Origen, Eriugena, and especially in J. Böhme (see, for example, his *Aurora*).

In ecclesial self-consciousness, inasmuch as it is expressed in liturgical texts, iconography, and sacred books, the radical difference between human and angel is indisputably asserted. St. Gregory Palamas, metropolitan of Thessalonica (fourteenth century), spoke on this subject with particular certainty.

Here are his opinions.[46] "The intellectual and logical nature of the soul, which has mind and logos, and the life-giving spirit, is alone more conformable to the image of God than are the bodiless angels *(monē kai tōn asōmatōn angelōn mallon kat' eikona tou theou)*; it is ordered by him and has everything immutable, even if it does not keep its dignity and does not correspond to the image of the Maker" (col. 1152). *"There is nothing higher than the human (ouden anthrōpou kreitton)*. . . . For the angels, although they are higher than us by reason of dignity *(tēn axian)*, serve his orders concerning us, and are sent for the sake of the future destiny of salvation" (col. 1165). "The angel's spirit is not animating because it did not receive from God a body from the earth joined with a spirit, in order to have power to animate and preserve it. On the contrary, the rational and logical nature of the soul, being created along with the earthly spirit, received from God the animating *(zōopoion)* spirit, by which it preserves and animates the body joined to it" (col. 1147). St. Gregory sees in the animation of the body by the soul an image of God's omnipresence, which the angels do not have. "Angel and soul, since they are bodiless, are not found in a place, but neither are they found everywhere, since they do not contain everything and are themselves in need of containing. . . . By the fact that the human's soul has mind, logos and spirit which animates the body, it is one, and more than the bodiless angels, it is created by God according to his image." "It is not only because the human is more created in God's image that it has a connecting and life-giving soul, but also through its capacity for ruling *(kata to archein)*. For there is in the nature of our soul something dominant and leading *(to hēge-*

monikon te kai archikon), and there is something servile and submissive: wish, excitement, feeling. . . . Through the capacity of ruling in us *(dia to en hēmin archikon)* God obtained dominion over the whole earth. Angels do not have an attendant body *(synexeugmenon sōma ouk echousi),* which is why they do not have it in subordination to the mind" (col. 1165). "The spiritual nature of angels does not have the same energy of life, for it did not receive a body formed out of the earth by God so as to receive for its sake life-giving power" (col. 1140). "People *alone of creatures have feeling (to aisthētikon) in addition to the faculty of reason and logos,* which being by nature joined with mind invents a multifarious multitude of arts, skills and knowledge: occupation with agriculture, construction of houses and the creation out of what is not *(proagein ek mē ontōn),* although not out of the entirely nonexistent *(mē ek mēdamōs ontōn)* — for this belongs only to God — is proper to humankind alone. . . . Nothing (of this in any sense) *(oudamos)* is proper to angels" (col. 1165). Among the differences between human and angel St. Gregory includes also the *aptitude for agriculture,* for the economic mastery of the earth, as proper only to the human being.

"But, although by reason of the image of God we are higher than the angels, by reason of *the likeness* we are very much lower than the good angels. The perfect likeness to God is realized through the higher enlightenment *(eklampseōs)* of God. The evil spirits are deprived of the latter, because they are in darkness; the divine spirits are filled with it, and hence they are called second lights and effulgence of the first light. In this light the good angels even have knowledge of the sensible *(tōn aisthētōn gnōsin)* which they know not by the power of sensation and not by physical power but they know it by divine power from which nothing present, past or future can be entirely concealed. The partakers of this light, insofar as they have it, also have knowledge conformable with that measure. Through this grace and the light and the union with God angels surpass people. An angel is the first luminous *(phōteinē)* nature after the first cause, from which it receives the luster and second light, flowing out of the first light and participating in it. And the divine minds set in circular motion *(kyklikos)* unite in the radiant outpourings of good and beauty without beginning or end.[47]

4. The Likeness of God in the Human Being

Humankind is created in the image and likeness of God. The image of God *is given* to humankind, it is implanted as the irremovable foundation of its being, while the likeness is that which is realized by humankind on the basis of the image, as the *task* of its life.[48] Humankind could not have been immediately created as a finished entity in which image and likeness, idea and reality, would correspond to each other, because then it would be God, and not by grace and assimilation, but by nature. But then there would be no question of any autonomy of humankind. The discrepancy of image and likeness in humankind, or more exactly, its potentiality and actuality, what is on hand and what is set as a task, constitutes precisely the distinctiveness of humankind which by its hypostatic freedom realizes in itself its own personal ideal image, submerged in a kind of meonality or vagueness. Not only does the human body bear in itself the weight of earthly dust, but also the soul is as it were covered with silt. The bodies of Adam and Eve were beautiful, their organs corresponded to their purpose, and they knew no unhealthy disorders. But they were still not spirit-bearers, their matter was not illuminated from within by spirit or, to put it another way, they were not yet living *relics,* although they were able to become such. Even the body was proposed to humankind as a task of creative struggle and effort, connected with the struggle of the spirit. In both spirit and body humankind was still in a state of pure, innocent childhood. Life in paradise was its first school of life, and up until the approach of a certain spiritual maturity the possibility of evil and sin remained in the human, and each new lesson of self-awareness could prove to be a fatal exam for it. The human being performed his first steps in self-knowledge and self-determination directly under the guidance of God who "spoke" at that time with the human, "visited" paradise, and was in a special proximity to his nature undarkened by sin. Before the fall, Adam was God's *prophet,* harking to divine utterances and inspirations. God settled Adam in Eden to "cultivate and keep it" (Gen. 2:15): the world was given to him not only "for the sake of having a look" (according to the expression of N. F. Fedorov). But the firstborn human exists in God's eyes only with the world and in the world, in which the born king of the universe realizes his rights by free creativity.

Simultaneously with this, God awakens in humankind the consciousness of its creaturely freedom in that he gives it a *law* or *commandment:* "And the Lord God commanded, saying, 'From every tree in the garden you will eat, but from the tree of the knowledge of good and evil you shall not eat, for on the day on which you partake of it, you will surely die'" (Gen. 2:16-17). Least of all can one see in the institution of the commandment any arbitrariness; on the contrary, through it the recognition of the creaturely freedom of the human being is corroborated which is correlative to necessity and finds the occasion to manifest itself thanks to the presence of the commandment, "of the categorical imperative." And the very content of the commandment flows out of the relation of humankind with the world. The commerce of humankind with the world is established not only by knowledge and dominion, but also by sensuality, for the world is like the external body of humankind, as this comes to light in nutrition, in the exchange of substances. And God himself instructs humankind in nutrition, by giving the blessing of food (Gen. 1:29). But in this unity with the world there is also a hidden danger that can threaten the human being even with death, although "God did not create death," but "made the human being for incorruption and fashioned it with the image of his eternal being" (Wisdom of Solomon 1:13; 2:23-24).

The next step of self-awareness for the human was self-definition with respect to all living things. God brings before him all living entities "so that he may see how he will name them, and as the human calls each living soul, so would be its name" (Gen. 2:19). It is a question of course not of an arbitrary fixing of names but of their *finding*. As the pan-animal the human could and had to find *in himself* the ideas or names of all animals and in this way know himself as the vital focus of the animal world, the intercessor of all that lives. And this self-knowledge was, of course, a new step along the path of realizing the likeness of God. The human turned out to be at the height of the situation, for "he spoke the names" (Gen. 2:20) of all creatures and avoided the temptation lying in wait for him here. But precisely for him the danger loomed that he would lose his hierarchical stature through an awareness of his proximity and similarity to the animal world: having drawn excessively close to the animal world, he could fall as far as animality, and darken his spiritual aspect. And of course the danger was all the greater in the realm of sex, where the sexual instinct, aroused by the spectacle of the universal sexual duality of the animal world, and wakened in an unseemly manner, could darken in him the presentiment of his female friend slumbering in his innermost recesses. The first Adam happily passed this temptation both for his sake and for impending Eve: all the animal pairs marched before his eyes, but he did not doubt that here there was "no helpmate like unto him" (Gen. 2:20).

In this act of self-knowledge the human sensed his own incompleteness and imperfection: in him the awareness of loneliness appeared, the thirst for a partner. "And the Lord God brought a deep sleep on the human," *ecstasy — ekstasis* in the translation of the LXX (Gen. 2:21), and during this mysterious sleep induced by God himself, apart from his knowledge or awareness, by an organic isolation of his female essence, a woman was created by God. "God led her to the man" evidently as an unwitting stranger, similar to one of the creatures in the midst of which not long ago there had proved to be no helpmate for him. And behold, Adam proves to have grown so wise and to have fathomed so deeply the mystery of human bi-unity that in a prophetic illumination he bears witness about *who* is standing before him. "And the man said, see, this is bone of my bones and flesh of my flesh" (2:23). His inner voice, the consciousness of himself as a man, said this to him, because he did not know *how* Eve was made. And further with prophetic lucidity Adam states the sacred essence of marriage: "and the two shall be one flesh" (2:24). The creation of the human being *ended* with the fashioning of Eve; a complete human being appeared in the world, man and woman. Humankind received all the fundamental self-determinations of its essence: in relation to the world, to God, to its own freedom, and to its own personal two-sexed essence. And God endowed the first couple with a blessing to reign in the world, to multiply their spiritual powers and to reproduce. "And God blessed them and said to them: 'Be fruitful and multiply, and fill the earth and possess it, and have dominion'" (1:28) over all creatures. "And God saw everything that he had made, and see, it was very good" (1:31).

Adam and Eve, having sensed each other as husband and wife, as two in one flesh, were in a state of harmony and virginity. They were free of evil and burning lust, they were like married children whose joining would be the tribute of pure sensuality consecrating them with a spiritual union. Being husband and wife, they did not become from this, at least in their predestination, buck and doe, which Adam saw in the animal world: "And both were naked, Adam and his wife, and they were not ashamed" (2:25).

The image of God began to shine in humankind with its full light, and in it the likeness of God started to show. *Humankind began* on its own path of becoming like God, by creative realization of its true image. But here a fateful and decisive temptation lay in wait for humankind.

5. The Fall of Humankind

Humankind could grow, realizing in itself the likeness of God, only by the power of love. By sacrificing his hypostasis, by coming out of himself in love, in keeping with the image of the trihypostatic God, a human being finds his essence within. The wisdom of integrity and the integrity of wisdom — *chastity* — becomes the law of life for humankind and is at the same time the condition and the consequence of love. Love for the Heavenly Father, which demands of him a childlike trusting and loving obedience, was for the first-formed human the law of chaste being, by virtue of which he reunited in himself the whole world by becoming its king. As the human grew it would become for him all the more understandable and joyful. In the human himself such a condition was the pure love of spouses who in their mutual relations experienced the erotic ecstasy of the universe. The power of evil was bound to aim its blow precisely against chastity in order to destroy its measure and harmony after having corrupted and perverted the world. Finding themselves in a childlike state, the world and the human being allowed such an attempt to be carried out. Evil could be dangerous precisely at the beginning of the path of human life; on the contrary, each step forward along the path of active chastity lessened the chances of evil. It therefore quickly launched an attack in order to empower the elements of nonbeing, chaos, and dark matter, the overcoming of which was still at the very beginning. To intermingle being and nonbeing in wild chaos would mean to undermine the foundation of the universe, to overthrow and pervert it, to lay bare the pre-existent, inferior abyss in it.

That nonbeing, nothing, was made the matter of being and was summoned to life is the result of the selfless love of God and measureless divine humility; measureless wisdom is manifested in it, as is the omnipotence of God which created the world out of nothing. But the envy and spite permitted by God's longsuffering and which strives to steal the world from God, hastens to take advantage of this, in such a way that from the invisible foundation of creation nonbeing was made into something tangible and poisoned being with itself. This plan could crop up in that sort of creaturely essence which knew the power of nonbeing through its own experience, because it belonged to the creaturely world, for it actualized in itself that power as evil through a blind, rebellious act. At the same time it ought not to belong to our human world; it is found on another plane of being and thus was capable of tempting humankind by slandering God. However, not having direct authority over humankind, it could operate only by suggestion, by subtle and crafty calumnies. Satan can introduce temptation into the world only through a human being, and the victory over a human being is a victory over the whole world, for every creature falls into "groaning" together with humankind (here is why the Antichrist, the complete incarnation in humankind, is the ultimate goal of Satan). Particular victories over separate little corners of creaturely being, e.g., over the serpent, in and of themselves predestined little, and would ruin only those unfortunate creations that proved to be a suitable tool for the action of the devil's malice. The serpent, "being more cunning than all wild animals of the field which the Lord God created" (Gen. 3:1), became such a tool of the devil. The serpent's cunning, which in the gospel is called wisdom ("be wise as serpents" Matt. 10:16), in itself is not at all a negative quality, for the Savior commands the apostles to have it. The idea of this animal also enters the fullness of the pan-animal and is insofar coinherent to humankind. The devil only makes use of the natural properties of this animal that make it a more receptive medium for the purposes of seduction. Of course, being such a medium does not remain without consequence for the animal itself, as is manifestly clear from God's curse on the serpent (Gen. 3:14).

The serpent began his temptation with Eve. Why with Eve? It goes without saying that it was not as a result of Eve's very appearance being somehow connected with sin, but of course as a result of the particularity of her sex, its hierarchical meaning for humankind. Passive receptivity is proper to woman; she is sensuality, generating but not initiating; her power is her weakness. For this reason it was enough to *deceive* the woman, but there was no need to overcome the active opposition natural in the man. In addition the woman, created after the man, was spiritually younger than he, for she did not have the knowledge of the animal world that Adam had acquired before the creation of the woman, when he pronounced the names for animals. Eve, of course, had this knowledge as a possibility in her human essence and she came to know many things from the man. But even here she was more defenseless than Adam, who with his masculine mind was more capable of exposing the serpent's cunning. "And the serpent said to the woman, did God really say you shall not eat from any tree in paradise?" (Gen. 3:1). Already the very *fact* of this conversation, the serpent's question and the woman's artless reply (3:2-3) represented the beginning of the fall; it was her twofold betrayal, both of the man and of God.

The first-created couple could live a full life and come to know God only if united in their love. And that the serpent involved the woman in a conversation about God, that he entered into spiritual

The First Adam

commerce with her on the very ground that wholly formed the possessions of their spousal loving unanimity, was already a spiritual betrayal of Adam on the part of the woman; it was, so to say, spiritual adultery with an enigmatic entity that belonged to the animal kingdom with respect to the flesh, but with respect to the spirit to a strange and hostile world as yet unknown to her. And rather than curtail the discussion, Eve stooped to a conversation with the serpent about God and his justice. It was not of course that she conversed with an animal; on the contrary the sacred privilege of sinless humankind lay in communication with animals. The subject of the conversation was blameworthy and by this very fact the life-giving bond of Eve with Adam was weakened. Fraudulently drawn into the fateful circle of the first isolation — from the man — Eve became alone, weak, deprived of his protection. Such was Eve's first betrayal.

Her second betrayal was her falling away from the love of God, and the unbelief born of this which of course quickly began to seek for "arguments" in its favor. By the very fact that Eve listened to the serpent's question and responded to it she gave witness that she was at least at that moment outside the love of God and that for her God was only a strange commander, a "master," whom she attempted to defend and justify in his manner of operations to the measure of her skills. Then the serpent, seeing that the victim had fallen into his nets, played havoc with them more boldly. He already openly lies ("the devil is a liar and the father of lies," John 8:44) and slanders God, ascribing to him envy towards people and fear of rivalry. He thereby distorts the very essence of God — love-humility, selflessness for the sake of the creature (which he, however, was unable to believe, for blinded by pride he did not understand at all). "You shall be as *gods,* knowing good and evil." The irony of satanic temptation directs Eve on the path of isolation and self-affirmation, calls her to use her hypostasis wrongly, having made of her an autonomous center of being. "And the woman saw that the tree was good for food and that it was pleasing to the eye and desirable, because it yielded knowledge; and she picked its fruits and ate" (3:6). The temptation, which penetrated her heart, came to light straight away in an unwarranted unchaste relation to creation. The woman as if somehow in a new way, with eyes of lust, saw that "the tree was good for food and pleasing to the eye." But in Eden everything was "very good," and Eve's discovery was only that the body ("the tree") could be made a tool of *independent* carnal delights. Evidently, in the first instance it is a question here of some kind of sin in the realm of sex — this is clear from the fact that after eating the fruit the woman began to feel the doe in herself, and then to be ashamed of her body. The loss of chastity was expressed in the awakening of lust not only physical but also spiritual: knowledge acquired by cunning was really knowledge of good *and evil,* of rebelling chaos, and the tree seemed desirable because "it gives knowledge." Satan assumes the aspect of Lucifer, the Gnostic teacher who promises knowledge on the path of a cold development and consolidation of his ego. This temptation also promises nothing that was not already given to humankind in paradise. Tempting here was only the unwarranted, unchaste path to knowledge, the extortion of knowledge, the conceit of gnosis before humbly believing love. Abstract gnosis is a function of ego, whereas God's commandment has ordered to overcome this egocentrism in spousal, cosmic, divine love. The awakening of sensuality and the lust of knowledge had here one source — in the human's abuse of its hypostasis. By turning away from God, humankind turns its face to the world, to creation, and lapses into a lopsided *cosmism* (immanentism); it thirsts only for the world, and not for God. It carries out a betrayal of divine love.

Eve fell. But this falling was not complete and final, for there still remained the man with whom the serpent had resolved not to speak directly. Adam was able not to accept the fruit proffered by Eve, and not give in to temptation, but make an effort to save Eve by the power of his love, all the more because the insufficiency of his vigilance had allowed her conversation with the serpent. Adam would have received, of course, God's assistance in this, and would have saved Eve and humanity from the consequences of her weakness. Adam knew more fully and deeply than she the spiritual measure of the animal world so that he would not consider it possible to learn wisdom and even knowledge of God from a serpent. It was easier for him to scorn the deceit than for the woman. But we ought not forget that the spiritual state of Adam himself was still unstable; with his inexperience he could not understand fully what threatened him if he followed his wife. It is possible that the egoism of love began speaking in him; his wife was found to be closer for him than God, and he had no wish to be separated from her although in shame and sin. If Eve was tempted as a woman, then temptation influenced Adam above all in sexual self-knowledge, altered in him the character of his attraction to the woman, and administered the poison of sinfulness to him. As soon as Adam agreed with Eve interiorly and seemingly was reconciled with her sinfulness, the buck was awakened in him, and the sacred mystery of marriage was overshadowed by the admixture of animal sensuality. The union of wife and husband ceased being a pure image of Christ and the Church, humankind forfeited the interior norm of its being, and then their *nakedness* was revealed to them, not only of the body but also of the spirit, already deprived of wholeness. "Having become like gods," they first of all felt themselves naked, helpless, and confused, and hastened "to hide among the trees" from the face of the Lord, by attempting to sink into the element of worldly life and lock themselves away in it.

"And God said: 'Who told you that you were naked? Did you eat from the tree from which I forbade you to eat?'" (3:11). The Lord does not deny Adam's *nakedness,* which is connected with his creatureliness; but Adam could have been entirely ignorant of it and not sensed it as nakedness. "Adam said, 'The wife whom you gave me, she gave me from the tree and I ate'" (3:12). This answer brings out into the open the darkening of conscience that has already taken place in Adam. Was it so long ago that upon meeting Eve with rapturous love he identified her as his own flesh and blood and solemnly prophesied about the sacrament of marriage? Was it so long ago that he became aware of his very self in her, his wife ("for she is taken from her husband")? But now he coldly and reproachfully speaks to God about her: "The wife whom you gave me," and in Eve he is aware of only a strange entity *given* to him: the image of God in the union of husband and wife has grown pale and been eclipsed first of all. Therefore Adam does not sense what has been done as *the common* guilt of both, and even less does he see the personal guilt of the husband, "the head of the wife," whereas it is precisely Adam whom the Lord at first questions and not Eve, not of course out of ignorance of what has happened. Adam, in denying his responsibility as husband, blames the wife for everything, and indirectly her Maker (presaging with this the path for future misogynists). The wife also became inaccessible to repentance, and like the husband, tries to transfer the guilt — to the serpent. The Lord pronounces the sentence. In it are stated the essence and the dimensions of that change which occurred in the nature of humankind and the world. The whole *path* of human life changed, although of course the Creator's idea did not change, nor did the ultimate goal of the universe: in the darkness of the fall the salvific tree of the Cross began to shine — the new tree of life.

The Lord began his sentencing with the serpent, with the first part (3:14) referring to the animal who sullied himself with the inspiration of evil, while the second part has bearing on the spiritual serpent, the devil, who nevertheless did not succeed in changing God's predestination for humankind and the world; the feminine, which only just fell in the person of Eve, will rise from its lapse in the person of the one who is extolled as "the rising of fallen Adam and the deliverance of Eve's tears." Eve was not utterly ruined by sin; two warring principles appeared in her, and God's Providence, guarding the chosen race, will lead to their final partition by the birth of the Mother of God. Eve's sin proved to be a childish delusion, deception and self-deception, but it was not evil will, the desire for evil and the nondesire for God. It may be that in the childish reason of Eve even a thought such as this was born: the forbidden tree was some slyness or joke of divine pedagogy that would be harmless and merry to guess. In any case the serpent proved to be shortsighted or even powerless: to his lot fell only the temporary dominion of a usurper with the prospect of inevitable failure and inescapable overthrow. He was put to shame namely by the very same impersonal and passive principle of femininity that he especially despised and hated. (Satan is the opponent of the feminine, not in his capacity as the fallen angel but as a fruitless and asexual, polyhypostatic egoist, for in the angelic nature there is no such opposition to woman at all.) It is not by chance that Satan proved to be put to shame precisely by a woman, just as it is not by chance that despite his asexuality it is precisely he who arouses in the first human pair the buck and the doe for which sexual uniting becomes lust, for only in this guise does he know sex and marriage.

God's sentence on Eve was addressed to her as a wife and mother: by her sin she imparted an unhealthy and agonizing character to that which without sin would have served as a source of pure joy — namely marriage and motherhood. Without being abolished in their sacred and mysterious essence, they were changed according to their state: "I shall greatly increase your grief in pregnancy, you shall bear children in pain and your attraction shall be for your husband, and he shall have dominion over you" (3:16). All the normal functions of the woman take on the seal of sickness, poisoned by lust. But only by the path of devout marriages and marital conceptions is it possible to reach that Nativity which "will tread on the serpent's head" and the very sufferings of pregnancy receive a redemptive meaning for the wife, who had seduced Adam, according to the apostle's word: "and Adam was not enticed, but the woman, who having been tempted fell into transgression, but she will be saved through childbearing, if she remains in faith and love and holiness with chastity — *meta sōphrosynē*" (1 Tim. 2:14-15). And the other way around, repudiation of the commandment to give birth, leads to gynocracy in the sense of the lordship of the doe over the woman and the man (with the promotion of the whole arsenal of cosmetics and fashion), to various forms of fornication, hetaerism, and sexual excesses. Either marriage, which also represents a special form of asceticism in sex, or the spiritual practice of virginity in monasticism, the direct path of sexual asceticism: such are the two pre-established norms which point out the path of a pure and worthy sexual life.

In God's judgment upon Adam that change is determined which took place in the position of the human being in the world: from being the king of nature he becomes its slave, and from being an artisan or gardener in God's paradise he becomes a proprietor and tiller of soil. The human being is doomed to *economy;* the "toil in the sweat of your brow" arises and everything becomes economic and laborious. And together with this, death enters the world, and life becomes mortal: "You will return to the earth from which you were taken, for you are dust and you shall return to dust" (3:19). The ties of life that connected being with nonbeing, although not letting it have the power of immortality but merely ignorance of the power that death held over it, weaken, and life wavers in its foundations. It is as if God, in pronouncing his sentence, acknowledges the failure of his purpose — to create the world out of nothing, to confirm immortal life in nonbeing, to endow the creature with freedom which could only ruin it, given its fateful instability. And yet, simultaneously with this sentence God already had a determination about the "seed of the woman," which having conquered death, will fasten together the foundations of life with an indissoluble bond. At the same time death became a boon — salvation from a life on a plague-infested earth, for human nature would not be able to bear the bad infinity of mortal life, the simple absence of death, the immortality of "the eternal Jew," and this very purpose would surely be worthy only of Satan. Death became a necessary act of life, and existence beyond the grave an unknown but salvific path of increase and strengthening of spirit. But at the same time as it is the separation of soul and body, which are intended for joint being, it is an act that is truly contrary to nature, the object of the final horror and final hope. It frightens and beckons with its white mystery — the mystery of new life.

"And Adam named his wife Eve (Life) for she became the mother of all the living" (3:20). Adam resigned himself before the good and wise judgment and understood its nonfinality. He grasped that precisely in Eve, who had tempted him and brought on death, Life was concealed as before, and "a womb wider than heaven" was hidden there that contains the Conqueror of death. And this richly meaningful action of Adam, carried out immediately after God's judgment and before the very expulsion from paradise, showed that the transgressing couple was not subject to despair, but believed the goodness of the Creator and accepted their mission on earth. The prologue in heaven came to an end, and the history of humanity fraught with difficulties began. The heavenly fires go out, the human body grows heavy, everything becomes sluggish and opaque. "And the Lord God made for Adam and his wife leathern garments and clothed them" (3:21). Simultaneously with this they were expelled from paradise after they had expelled paradise from themselves, having lost the capacity to take delight in it. God deprived them of "the fruits of the tree of life," for these would have been able to give them only *magical* immortality; without a spiritual right to it, it would have led to a new fall.[49] In the world, Cain was already preparing to commit fratricide in order to defile the virginal earth with human blood. Paradise was removed from the earth, as the unknown city of God, and the entrance to it was guarded by a cherub "with a sword flaming and turning," and Adam was ordered "to cultivate the earth out of which he was taken" (3:23).

6. Light in the Darkness

The fall was the supreme *religious catastrophe*. The direct and immediate communion with God which was the portion of the primogenitors in paradise was broken. God became distant to both world and humankind (transcendent) and humankind was left alone — as its own lord: "you will be as gods." *Incipit religio*. This beginning of religion is connected with the sinful defectiveness of consciousness of God in a sick and fallen humanity. Although the primogenitors, in experiencing communion with God in paradise, knew the immense gulf separating the Creator from creation, the underground was not laid bare by this awareness in them. They treated the Creator as beloved and loving children, with a trust unclouded by anything and with intimacy. The sharp and painful feeling of creatureliness, offense, and envy were awakened by Satan who summoned in them the rebellion of the underground, the uprising of the creation against its proper foundation. Between God and humankind at that time lay the darkness of the creaturely underground. The effort of humankind to break through this darkness to the light of knowledge of God is expressed in religion. *And the light shines in the darkness, and the darkness did not grasp it.*[50] In paradise humankind did not sense *any distance* between God and itself, and so did not know any thirst for uniting with him. But the pathos of religion is the pathos of distance, and its cry is the cry of abandonment by God. "*Eli, Eli lama sabachthani* — my God, my God, why have you abandoned me?" — this is its ultimate expression. In paradise, if there even was religion, it was qualitatively different from the one familiar to us, for there was in it no quest, no effort, no sweating blood. In paradise there was no temple or altar, for the whole of paradise was a temple. Corresponding to this, in "the new Jerusalem which comes down from heaven, there will be no temple, but God himself will be there, for the Lord God Almighty is its temple and the Lamb" (Rev. 21:22; cf. 22:3).

With the expulsion from paradise the joy of immediate communion with God ceased. "The leathern garments" rendered the radiance of Divinity imperceptible for humans; darkness thickened in human nature. They were aware of being in the *world*, while God had become transcendent, leaving this "world," the land of expulsion, at their disposal. In virtue of its own inertness and heaviness the world seemingly pulls away from God, undergoes "involution," withdraws into itself, and gradually the rays of paradisiacal knowledge of God are extinguished in it and the songs of paradise fade away. It seemed that Lucifer had reason to celebrate, for his purpose — to become the prince of the world, an anti-god, to possess God's creation — was patently realized. The removal of Divinity from the world, its transcendence beyond familiar limits, becomes equivalent to its practical denial; the feeling of the separation of humans from God leads them to divinize the cosmos. *Religion,* which expresses the mutual tension of both poles — this is what remained to humans of the paradisiacal knowledge of God, as remembrance and hope. And the tempter had to extinguish it in order fully to master humankind, having drowned it in the elements of contentment with the world. But the envious self-lover was not able to understand the immeasurableness of love — of divine humility, of God's self-abasement out of love for the creature, as he did not know how to value the gratitude of the human spirit in which the image of God shone with immortal beauty. And God did not leave his creation a victim of solipsistic rapture but came to the salvation of humanity — through religion. Religious revelation began. And the earth became watchful, hearing the call of heaven; humankind felt the heavenly homeland within. Satan was shamed, for never could the human being be emptied to the baseness of complete areligiosity and atheism, and even "modern times," the most godless and weighed down in "involution," have not achieved this spiritual suicide.

In the religious process, which constitutes the essence of the world's history, it is a matter of *salvation from the world*, humanity's recovery of God (*from the depths* I have cried to You, Lord), but also of *the salvation of the world*. The latter can be accomplished only by God; with its own power humankind cannot be liberated from the world, for it is itself the world. Therefore in religion one can distinguish two tasks: divine revelation and divine operation. The first task exhausts by itself the positive content of "paganism"[51] (understanding by this the "natural" religions, i.e., all except Judeo-Christianity), and both tasks simultaneously are resolved in the revealed religion of the Old and the New Testaments.

Banished from paradise, the human *seeks* God, for he is "not far from each of us." Such searching is paganism, which contains or at least can contain positive knowledge of God, something revealed about him. The thirst for an encounter with God in paganism burns even more strongly than in revealed religion; the search is more ardent, more frenzied, more agonizing. Not for nothing does the mist of sorrow, despair, and lack of requital lie above clear Olympus, and thus paganism easily gives in to orgiastic frenzy. The seeming "immanentism" or pantheism — the divinization of the forces of nature, of animals and the human being — must not deceive here, by instilling the notion of some sort of world contentment and balance. Revealed religion could not know such horror of god-abandonment as paganism experienced in convulsive writhings precisely in moments of its religious ascents. The effort of humankind to break through to God was more intense here and, above all, more desperate than in Judeo-Christianity where Jacob's ladder was erected. Not for nothing was it revealed in the fullness of time that pagans proved to be more ready to receive Christ than Jews, for they thirsted and waited for him more intensely: the prodigal son had been homesick and languishing for a long time already.[52] Paganism in its deepest essence is above all else this melancholy of banishment, a cry to heaven: *ah, come!* For that reason tragic concentration and the greatest earnestness are proper to it. But in a fateful way its religious pathos is turned to religious surrogates, to all manner of idolatry, in spite of its own inner aspiration. Least of all can serious religion be content with idolatry, i.e., with the investing of idols with divine power or the powers of nature. In all these objects of worship the pagan sees only living icons of Divinity; for it the whole world is filled by divine power: *panta plērē theōn*. And the gods themselves were like separate splintered rays, multitudinous hypostases of transcendent Divinity. In general, polytheism in paganism is evidence not of the lack of a desire to be lifted up to the One Divinity who remains transcendent, but rather of the *powerlessness* to do so, and is a symbol of the transcendence and inexpressibility of the Divinity. As a result of its facelessness an involuntary multiplicity of faces is obtained. Pure *polytheism* is merely the degeneration of paganism, and to a certain degree its perversion. To say it differently, both in the religious self-consciousness of paganism and in its piety the NOT of negative theology is vitally felt, constituting for it the general religious background and imparting to it a definite aroma, depth, and sublimity.

If it is impossible to regard paganism throughout its entire existence as an out-and-out lie and demonolatry, then how is one to define its truth, or the nature of its original revelations? One can say schematically that in paganism the transcendent is revealed only in the immanent and through the immanent (theocosmism), while in Revelation it comes down itself to the human: there, the ascent of the human, the breach through the thickness of the crust of nature; here, the descent of Divinity, his encounter with humankind. In paganism humankind is left to its own powers — to seek God through the "contemplation of creation," the invisible through the visible. Even the fall could only darken but not paralyze the revelation of God in the world. Humankind, by really having the image of God, thus possesses for itself an organ of divine cognition in its deepened self-cognition: for it *gnōthi seauton* [know yourself] also signifies *gnōthi theon* [know god]. And all nature has the same image, insofar as it is humankind; the whole creation in its sophianicity is full of the revelations of Divinity. These sophianic lights along with the image of God in a human being comprise the objective basis for pagan knowledge of God.

By striving towards the light of Divinity which courses through

The Human Being

the universe, the pagan wants to break through beyond the limits of the world, to perform a religious *transcensus*. On the grounds of this striving a ramified and intense religious life is developed, dogma is laid down, a cult arises and all of its substantial traits: sacred times and places, images, divine worship, rituals, sacrifices, and mysteries. The thirst for mystery, for the encounter with Divinity, for union with it, which is evidence of the seriousness and intensity of religious quests, of course is quite proper to pagan religions as well. There cannot be any doubt that these mysteries did not remain solely an external symbolism, but were a certain mystical action, *were experienced* religiously — outside this presupposition the whole history of religion is transformed into absurdity or paradox. "Initiation" in the mysteries, according to the few bits of evidence that have come down to us, was accompanied by such experiences that separated humans from their past with a new boundary;[53] the significance of these experiences and the sacred horror inspired by them is attested by the severe *disciplina arcani* that invested them with impenetrable secrecy.[54]

But *of what* did they partake and *into what* were they initiated in the mysteries? What kind of "grace" was communicated to the initiates? It is much easier to give a negative answer than a positive one: it was not, of course, the one true partaking of the Body and Blood of Christ for the remission of sins, for this absolute partaking does not exist outside the Church of Christ and the divine incarnation and Golgotha. Nonetheless, the participants in the mysteries did receive *something* — some sort of natural grace, but it is difficult to express what it is in categories of Christian religious thought, and we are not setting this task for ourselves. But we believe that the grace of God is multiform; "God does not give the spirit by measure." From the indisputable fact that pagan mysteries had a natural character, it is still impossible to conclude that they were only natural orgiastic excess. If one admits that a certain objectivity of knowledge of God was inherent in paganism, then one must recognize this in all seriousness and to the very end, i.e., above all when applied precisely to the religious cult, divine worship, sacrifices, and mysteries. But, of course, their efficacy remained limited in a fateful way; it did not provide rebirth but rather only promised it. The deity remained transcendent all the same, and grace operated as if from outside (similar to how it operated through Balaam's donkey). Thanks to a forced enthusiasm, like some theft of grace, mystical possession and its excesses, the condition of religious intoxication to which they aspired by various means arose so easily in paganism. For this reason Christian "sobriety" is in general so uncharacteristic of paganism, even simply religious sobriety which can, of course, be combined with high religious inspiration.

If one acknowledges the religious authenticity of paganism, then one must also accept that in it a positive *religious process* was taking place, a historical "fullness of time" was maturing, or to say it another way, *Christianity was prepared for not only in Judaism but also in paganism.* In it Christianity has its own proper natural aspect, it seems, which one must see sooner or later (up to now, however, this has taken place in an entirely inadequate measure). The fundamental difference between Revelation and paganism, that touches on cognition of God, is in the purity and unalloyed quality of truth, which is proper only to Revelation. Paganism does not know God face to face, but only his natural icon, although even this icon is miraculous and life-giving within reasonable limits of pagan piety. As part of the sophianic pan-organism of the cosmos, humankind is the "noetic" ray of Sophia, and has a definite nature; its idea is the prism through which the world is refracted for it. Connected with this are the concreteness and the limitedness of this perception of the world. In divine Sophia there is no limitedness, for everything exists in everything, but in the world enthralled to sin, this concreteness is always attended by one-sidedness. For this reason every religious revelation in paganism is always a *refraction* of religious truth through a definite prism; its ray passes through glass stained in the familiar manner. From this arise the inescapable *plurality* of pagan religions, and also the *national* character, inherent in them essentially and bringing them close to a national language, folklore, and various forms of national creativity (the fact of religious syncretism, as a late, decadent, and derivative phenomenon, does not contradict this). Paganism, as the religion of *peoples,* bears on itself the stamp of the tower of Babel and the confusion of tongues, in which was expressed an interior reciprocal estrangement in the spirit of humanity. Each people, corresponding to its own intelligible aspect, refracts *in its own way* the spark of the divine Pleroma, and left to its own powers, it fashions *its own* religion and piety. Only Christianity, as the unconditional truth, revealed to humanity by the incarnate Word itself, is free from nationality and in this is ontologically different from paganism.

In keeping with its nature, paganism suffers from *psychologism,* and precisely this property makes it unavoidably plural. This is not that normal psychologism which is connected with individuality that puts its stamp on the general character of perception of the world. It penetrates here into the very depths and becomes the basis of religious cognition. Psychologism when it becomes more profound in this manner becomes cosmism, and takes the human being as a microcosmic entity. Nevertheless it remains submerged in a fateful way in its own subjectivity precisely when it should rise above the world and itself — the act, transcendent in purpose and meaning, remains enclosed in immanence. For immanentism in religion, which paganism is doomed to remain, is precisely psychologism, involuntary and inescapable subjectivism. But having been deepened as far as cosmism, psychologism no longer is definitively enclosed; the rays of objective truth break through it and are translucent through it. Every serious religion possesses a certain degree of truthfulness, and contains some aspect of it. But together with truthfulness, falsity is also proper to it, the distortion of that aspect. This duality penetrates into the proper consciousness of paganism and gives it an inherently tragic element, flowing out of the knowledge of its inconclusiveness and relativity. The initiates in the mysteries came to know that the gods of Olympus were not eternal (Schelling); so too the Germans began to see clearly the "twilight of the gods" and the conflagration of Valhalla. Only Christianity, which can be developed further in its revelation but never be liable to abrogation, is free of this tragic fracture.

This religious psychologism dooms pagan religions to degeneracy through immersion in naturalism and orgiastic excess. A mystically sensitive pagan sensed from the polyphonic chorus of natural spirits, from the beating of the world's heart, the striving of the creature to exceed its given state, to come out of itself and to be infected with this frenzy, the ecstasy of nature. He did not always withstand this mystical pressure: by surrendering to natural orgiastic excess he fell under the spell of natural spirits. Bewitched by them, he lost the capacity for distinguishing natural from religious ecstasy, orgiastic excess from inspiration, and then he became "a pagan" in the bad sense of the word. Paganism to a significant measure is this kind of *possession,* and the apostle Paul warned the Corinthians against this "slavery to the empty and vain elements of the world."[55] A whole abyss lies between Christian ecstasy (as it is described by the apostle Paul in 1 Cor. 14) and pagan orgiastic excess. But at the same time it is necessary to emphasize that in the phenomenology of religious cult, in the ritual of divine worship, sacrifices, offering incense, sacred vestments, honoring of saints and heroes, sacred places and images, in general everything that touches on the organization of religious life, paganism is not at all so far removed from Christianity as one likes to think. Among some people (primarily among contemporary representatives of the "religious-historical" school in Protestantism) this drawing together is made too externally and tendentiously, and by others it is just as tendentiously concealed; a religiously intelligent comparative study of cults is one of the tasks persistently issuing from a correct understanding of the nature of the religious process in paganism.

In view of the tragic duality that doomed paganism to ambiguity and degeneracy, it becomes understandable why it is made the victim of demonic possession: orgiastic excess is replaced by raving, and the elemental spirits are transformed into demons. This ensues together with that religious sightedness which arrives in the world with the incarnation of the Word. "Great Pan" died, but simultaneously a new, transfigured Pan was born. The former naturalism becomes impossible, and dying paganism assumes more and more sinister traits. The pagan gods after Christ are already demons for those who have come to believe in him; prefigurations and forewarnings lost their former meaning after the fulfilment.[56] But the pagans themselves thereby remain to a certain degree innocent of the basic sin of paganism, which weighed on them like a curse of divine repudiation and the weight of expulsion from paradise. Pagan piety, although it comes to know God in the world, is not able to comprehend fully the images and figures through which he is seen. It grows weak under the weight of naturalism, is deafened by the voices of the world, a plaything of its elements. It also grows weak from its polytheism, from being doomed to create ever new and newer gods, masks of the One "Unknown God." The motif of the pantheon, which resounds all the clearer in waning paganism, the striving to collect in it all the venerated gods and not omit a single one (which is why as a reserve or just in case, an altar *theōi agnōstōi* — to the *still* unknown god — was set up), clearly testifies to the loss of faith in separate gods, and to the impossibility of being set at ease in polytheism, which is turned into a bad plurality or bad infinity. Thereby the whole coarseness of the anthropomorphism proper to it is laid bare, and it draws all the more strength in an atmosphere of superstition and decadence. But at its basis lies a deep idea; there is contained the revelation of *the hypostaseity* of Divinity, faceless pantheism is overcome.

This hypostaseity subdivides and multiplies, as if repeating in the reflections of a mirror, and for the given instance it is possible, perhaps, to concur with Feuerbach, that humankind created gods in its own god-bearing image (although this does not mean that it invented them). Alongside of the revelation about the hypostaseity of the Divinity, polytheism also contains a revelation of the sophianicity of nature and humankind. Its language is audible to the listening ear; under the crust of nature is perceptible divine porphyry. Paganism thanks to its mystical vision sees "gods" where only dead "forces of nature" are accessible to our "scientific" consciousness. The world, taken in itself, is a hierarchy of "gods," or a concord in which its many voices merge sonorously and harmoniously into a single chord. With this are defined the mystical depth and authenticity of paganism, as too the relative truth even of its polytheism. But from this also springs its lie, and the religious loathsomeness that the bearers of monotheism, the prophets of Israel, felt so ardently. Here the creature overshadows God and stands between God and humankind.

Paganism as religious naturalism is forever abolished by the Cross, and thus the history of paganism after Christ is the slow but inevitable throes of death. The best evidence of this are the attempts at its restoration, beginning with the Neo-Platonic philosophers or Julian the Apostate who, however much he did not want to be simply a pagan, all the same remained merely an *apostate* of Christianity. To an even greater extent one must say the same with respect to the age of the Renaissance which, for all the sincerity of its attraction to antiquity in its aesthetic, philological, scientific, philosophical respects, remained spiritually foreign to it, if not hostile. Antiquity in the Christian era in general can be interiorly understood not in spite of Christianity but only *through* it and *from* it, whereas the representatives of the Renaissance sought to be liberated from Christianity with its help — indeed, from all religion. Classical antiquity did not know "humanism" in *that* sense, and is entirely innocent of it. In general, paganism, with the exception of separate and limited epochs and social groups, is distinguished by an intense religiosity that disturbs and downright startles when one rubs up against it. To call modern European materialistic civilization with its dominating "scientific" rationalism pagan, as sometimes occurs, is to insult paganism. It is inferior to paganism, and inferior to religion in general, and it still needs to learn much beforehand for it to understand the soul of paganism.

The First Adam

But outside these attempts at an imaginary restoration of paganism, non-Christian religions exist side by side with Christianity. Some of them developed alongside of Christianity and in conflict with it, and thus they have to a greater or lesser degree a character hostile to Christianity — such are Talmudic Judaism and Islam. Others developed outside its visible influence and were sufficiently self-determining with respect to it, although it is natural to assume that rivalry and hostile antipathy are present in their attitudes towards Christianity — Brahmanism, Buddhism, Confucianism, etc. How is one to treat these religions, which if they are not anti-Christian are in any case non-Christian? Is one to search for what is common in each of them so that, having placed this common element in brackets, one may declare it the quintessence of religious truth, as reductionist rationalism does under various banners (theosophy, Tolstoyism)? Or, having acknowledged the fact of *the plurality* of religions in all of its incomprehensibility for us, are we to resign ourselves before the mystery? Every religion is jealous and exclusive by nature, and all the more impossible is any retreat from the absolute truth of Christianity to please non-Christianity. One can and must respect every sincere prayer, and yet a Christian will not begin to pray with a Muslim in his mosque or with a Brahman in his pagoda — such prayer will be felt as blasphemy immediately, any discussions apart. The bounds of beliefs are not established by human will and they must not be transgressed arbitrarily. Here is the mystery of Providence: the truth of Christianity is not revealed to all people in this life. Some try to cope with the difficulty of the question by theories of reincarnation; others declare: *nulla salus sine ecclesia* [no salvation outside the Church], supposing that the mystical boundaries of the Church are known to them in all their precision. But the fact remains in all its incomprehensibility: the preaching of the gospel to the present day in fact has not spread around the globe, and nineteen centuries after Christ the majority of humanity still belongs as if to a pre-Christian epoch. And if we cannot deny the positive religious content in paganism, still less do we have any basis for this with respect to the great world religions, which in their own way seek out God and spiritually comfort their flock. The heroes of religion are always leaders of humanity, and Ramakrishna, for example, belongs not only to India but also to the European world. While one can hold in esteem and value someone else's faith, one needs only to *be* one's own. The true religion is only one, although from this the others do not become a deception; in some other sense they are also "revealed" religions.

The Human Being

In the light of Christian faith those truths which are present in the dogmatic teachings of non-Christian religions, and those traits of authentic piety which are inherent in their cult, can receive a correct valuation. But for the sake of such recognition there is no need whatsoever to endeavor to construct some sort of religious Volapük or to establish an interreligious Esperanto.

7. The Old Testament and Paganism

If we are to understand paganism as a positive religious process, a question inevitably arises: What kind of relation does its "revelation" have with the Old and then with the New Testament? Schelling, to whom belongs the credit for the precise formulation of this question, detects in paganism a revelation of the Second Hypostasis and in the pagan deities he sees aspects of Christ before his advent in the world. He develops this basic idea in his *Philosophy of Mythology* and thereupon in *Philosophy of Revelation* with all of his enormous talent and exceptional insight. However, this idea, which he applies to the solution of particular questions, only appears to be derived empirically from the vast material of comparative mythology, when in fact it is rooted in Schelling's Christology already familiar to us and thus must share with it a common fate.

"In paganism the mediating person (Schelling understands the second potency corresponding to the Second Hypostasis in his metaphysics) operated only as a natural force *(Potenz)*, but since the *true* son, the real Christ, is present *in it* too, then Christ was already in mythology, although at the same time *not as* Christ. The pagans were of course, thus, *chōris Christou*, separated from Christ (Eph. 2:12), namely from Christ as such, and nevertheless it was precisely the very same natural potency which had to die in Christ, the very same through which they were enlightened. For the Father, who made himself inaccessible for extra-divine being, *by an external* manner also withdrew into the consciousness of a little, unseen people, pushed away into a back street of the world.... On the contrary, Christ was the light of the pagans, although in his purely natural influence; properly *he* was the potency of paganism; in it he shaped the ground which sometime must accept the seed of Christianity, for which Judaism was too shallow. Paganism and Christianity were two separate households *(Oekonomien)* which must merge only in Christianity." "Already during the whole time of paganism Christ was in an uninterrupted advent *(in einem beständigen Kommen)*, although He came in fact only when the time was fulfilled."

Interpreting the text of Hebrews 4:15; 5:2, *pepeirasmenon kata panta*, "tempted by everything," Schelling continues: "therefore he knew all the sorrows and temptations to which human consciousness had been liable in paganism. He was already then the suffering Messiah, as the Old Testament depicts him, but suffering precisely because apart from desire he was present in every state of consciousness, though was not himself tainted by them. By his appearance in *humanity*, by his sufferings and death Christ only *performed* the mediation *as* a human, but he is the *eternal* mediator, the mediator between God and human beings, beginning from the epoch of the world *(von Weltzeiten hin)*, and therefore is already the mediator in paganism. Not *in* this action through which paganism arises is he Christ, but he is *already* Christ when he performs this action, for this action (this power over fallen away being) is given to him only inasmuch as he is already Christ, i.e., God's anointed, predestined by God to be heir and lord."[57] "Therefore, Christianity was already in paganism, the latter also had a *substantial* content."[58]

"Whoever recalls the divine condescension in the Old Testament and reckons the divine appearances in them not as simple fables will not deny every and all reality in the *theophanies* of paganism. Pagans were as if driven away *(verwiesen)* from the face of the Father, but precisely to them he gave Christ as Lord, although he operated among them as a natural potency. . . . Not that Christianity came only out of Judaism alone, in a similar degree it has paganism as its premise too; only for this reason is its emergence a great worldwide historical event" *(Philosophie der Offenbarung*, 78).

Corresponding to such an understanding of paganism, the role of Judaism is defined by Schelling primarily in negative traits, as *non*-paganism, "*gehemmtes Heidenthum*" [restrained paganism]. "Judaism was never something properly positive, it can be defined either as suppressed paganism or as hidden Christianity, and precisely this intermediate position *(diese Mitte)* was disastrous for it. The cosmic natural among the Hebrews which they had in common with other peoples, became the envelope of the future supernatural. . . ." "Compared with other peoples, the Israelites were least of all capable of having their own history, least of all filled with that world soul which drew other nations to found great monarchies; they were incapable of acquiring for themselves a great, everlasting name in *universal* history, but precisely for this reason they were all the more equipped to become bearers of divine *(der göttlichen)* history (in contrast to universal history)" (148-49). Schelling advances this kind of position: "Christ was more for pagans than for Jews in a certain sense. . . . Christ in and of himself *(für sich)* is even incomprehensible from Jewry. The latter gives matter (?) for his existence, but he himself is the potency of paganism

The Human Being

foreign to Judaism" (149, note). "When they missed and rejected the transition to Christianity, they excluded themselves from the great course of history. They *had* to find themselves scattered and dispersed in the midst of other peoples, once they ceased to be a people. They were *something* only as bearers of the future. As soon as the goal was achieved, the means became useless ... the Jewish people in the proper sense is *excluded* from history" (150). In these statements, for all their restraint, the typical Germanic religious anti-Semitism peers through (Drews, Chamberlain).

Schelling's idea, which by the way is not his alone, that the epoch of paganism is supposedly the exclusive realm of the Son, while the Old Testament period is the Father's, is incorrect and arbitrary. Here there is insufficient general reference to the fact that the world is the realm of the Logos in a special and exclusive sense. Such immediacy can be affirmed about *all* states and epochs of the world's life, and thus about paganism to the same extent as about Judaism. In general there is no basis for timing paganism to the Second Hypostasis alone. In its religious essence, paganism is the cognition of the invisible through the visible, God through the world, the revelation of Divinity in the creation. And the entire Holy Trinity — not only the Son but also the Father consubstantial with him and the Holy Spirit as well — imprinted its image in the sophianicity of the world, and paganism in *this* respect is the portent of the religious fullness that is coming but has not yet arrived. According to its scope it is much richer in motifs, and in its plan broader than not only the Old but also the New Testament, so far as the latter still contains the promises of the coming Comforter. Paganism has a living presentiment of "the holy flesh" and the revelation of the Holy Spirit. For that reason until now it has not become for us a fulfilled and in that sense promised tradition, "an old testament," and with this, perhaps, is explained the incomprehensible and enigmatic charm it holds over souls even in the Christian era (which it is surely impossible to say about the Old Testament in this sense). True, in paganism nothing can be found in a pure and undistorted guise without refraction through many prisms, but there is in it a sophianic fullness that is still not manifested in historic Christianity (although, of course, only Christianity contains it in all its purity). Paganism has a presentiment of all three divine hypostases. Indisputably, it knows the Father's hypostasis, which it honors under various aspects (Marduk, Amon-Ra, Zeus, Jupiter, etc.). Beyond any doubt it knows the Son's hypostasis un-

The First Adam

der the form of the suffering, dying, and rising God (Osiris, Attis, Adonis-Thammuz, Esmun, Dionysus). Paganism — precisely in virtue of its pantheistic naturalism — senses in advance the outpouring of the grace of the Holy Spirit in the world, which sanctifies its flesh, and the elusive blowing of the Comforter. From this it is understandable and entirely natural if we encounter outside Christianity — in various degrees of approximation — a doctrine of the trinitarity of Divinity, as is well known to historians of religion.

Yet another outstanding feature of paganism deserves special attention, namely that not only male but also female deities are in its pantheon and in general a deity has a sex. The worship of goddesses and the presence of sexual elements in the divinity is usually perceived as a deliberate religious abomination and in any case is regarded as an inadmissible anthropomorphism. That was how the Old Testament related to this: the struggle against the cults of female deities (Astarte) occupies a conspicuous place in the prophets' preaching. Christian apologists were found to be no less irreconcilable here, and modern theologians generally follow their lead. If the names Aphrodite, Demeter, and Isis say so much to the contemporary heart, we are inclined to see literary license in this, the caprice of taste, the aesthetic recidivism of paganism. Meanwhile there is here a serious and deep problem that has as yet not been subject to a fitting discussion in Christianity. Do we really have here only anthropomorphism, religious fornication, the darkening of religious consciousness, delirium that has no relation to any religious reality whatever? Of course, it is understandable why Old Testament religion with its strict and unbending monotheism (Yahwehism) could see here nothing except demonolatry and fornication. It is also obvious that even for those who see in paganism only the exclusive revelation of the Second Hypostasis, only one means of coping with goddesses exists — it is to subject them to an interpretation that neutralizes their sex, as for example Schelling does.[59] But with such an interpretation there nonetheless remains unanswered an even more interesting question: Why do pagan deities not remain asexual or, at least, why is the female element affirmed in some cases, and the male in others?

Of course, we should not forget for a minute to what an extent religious truths were revealed to paganism and the heavenly hierarchies were understood by it imprecisely, obscurely, and distortedly, but even remembering this to a sufficient extent we can all the same recognize that in the worship of the female hypostasis in a deity, sacred and trembling secrets were beginning to be revealed that have not been fully disclosed perhaps even up to now and that fear a premature uncovering. If we are to limit ourselves only to what is revealed and already known to us, we can name at least one of these religious truths, the clear presentiment of which was had in paganism, namely the worship of divine motherhood. Paganism tremblingly glimpsed in advance not only Christ coming into the world, but also his all-pure Mother, the Ever-Virgin Mary, and as it was able, it honored her under various figures. If now those searching "for religious-historical parallels" find a suggestive proximity between Isis weeping over Osiris and the Mother of God bent over the Body of the Savior, it fills us with surprise bordering on reverence, this pagan presentiment of the Mother of God which however was entirely uncharacteristic of Judaism. And right away this side of paganism, which is covered by a greater temptation of sin, filth, and shame, and distorted at times beyond recognition, in the light of *other* presentiments and presages rivets attention on itself with invincible power and, it seems, hides the flame of new life beneath the ashes.

If there are no reasons to consider paganism the religion of the Son, then to the same extent Judaism is *not* the religion of the Father, and in neither the Old nor the New Testament are there any grounds for this equally quite widespread opinion. In fact by what means can Judaism prove to be the religion of the Father if it does not know the Son, who brought the revelation about the Father to the world, who "showed the Father in himself," revealed him to people, gave them "the authority to become children of God," taught them to pray "Our Father," "Abba, Father"? Jehovah, the God of Sinai, is in no way the revelation of the hypostasis of the Father. Is it not said directly that "no one knows the Son except the Father, and no one knows the Father except the Son and to whomever he wishes to reveal him" (Matt. 11:27)? How can one speak of an Old Testament revelation of the Father apart from the Son? In general the mystery of the Holy Trinity remains concealed in the Old Testament although it is completely full of indications and symbols of it; in particular the hypostasis of the Father remains undisclosed, as well as of the Son. The revelation of the Old Testament has a preliminary and preparatory character and pursues a definite purpose: here religious horizons deliberately narrow, even in comparison with paganism. The motifs of "the economy of salvation," the attainment of the predestined goals of divine action, played here a more determining role than the interests of divine cognition. Jehovah was revealed to Moses as the One Who Is eternally (I am who I will be), the living and hypostatic God. But his revelation was not so much about the hypostasis and hypostases as *about hypostaseity* in general, for a hypostasis cannot be disclosed *alone* apart from and independent of the other hypostases. For this reason revelation of the hypostases in general became possible only in Christ in whom was manifested not only the Second Hypostasis, but simultaneously the First and the Third, which is why Christianity is the revelation not only of the Son but already of the whole Holy Trinity, although still not the last and not the definitive one. Old Testament religion taught that one, transcendent, and hypostatic God exists and it demanded exclusive worship of him ("I am the Lord your God, you shall have no other gods except me"), but it did not speak directly of his trihypostaseity, although, of course, this teaching was hidden in it as in a grain of a plant. The three hypostases were still merged into one common hypostaseity, similar to how at a remote distance separate peaks merge into one mountain.

In the Old Testament God was revealed as the One Who Is. He met humankind again, whose solitude in the world was over. But God was revealed to a humankind fallen into slavery to the elements of the world above all else as a supernatural, transcendent Entity surmounting the world. In this is the pathos of Old Testament religion, and in this sense it is really opposed to the cosmism and anthropomorphism of paganism. In Judaism and paganism two antinomically linked sides of religious consciousness, both of its poles, were opposed with the greatest force: the transcendence and the immanence of God to the world, and only Christianity (in the word of the apostle Paul) was able to "reconcile" the split religious self-consciousness through the divine incarnation. Therefore the relationship of the Old Testament to paganism, marked by intolerance and exclusiveness, was determined in a significant degree by motives of religious pedagogy. The sphere of paganism's achievements, with their whole truth and falsehood, breadth and limitation, was above all else *forbidden* to Judaism, and this prohibition did not even allow for a sufficiently close examination of it in order to estimate it more correctly and understand it more broadly. Judaism could only *be seduced* by paganism and from time to time become sick by it in order that after recuperating it would treat the harmful infection even more roughly and unjustly. Let us remember that even the apostles themselves at the beginning of their preaching had great difficulty in overcoming their own prejudices against the "uncircumcised." Christian apologists have inherited from Judaism this relationship to paganism right up to the present day. And until now they look on paganism with the ideas of Judaism, although the prohibition no longer lies on Christianity such as was contained in Old Testament religion, and if it does, then it is completely different.

The transcendent God manifests himself as the lawgiver with respect to the chosen people. Invested with divine sanction, *the law* became the isolating fence that had to separate Judaism from the whole rest of the world. The faith of Israel was not the religion of a good and merciful Father of all peoples, for the reason that it could not and did not want to be international and supranational. Nationalism, and the most ardent and exclusive type besides, was implanted in its very essence, in the idea of election of only one people; compared with Judaism, the religious nationalism in paganism is broad and tolerant. Here, therefore, convergence, merging, "syncretism" proved to be possible between different religions, but it was entirely impossible with respect to Judaism. Old Testament religion had a fully defined task: in the fence of the law, which was only "the shadow of future blessings," in an atmosphere of pure and unalloyed monotheism to raise up the earthly forebears of the Savior, to prepare the appearance of the Most Pure Virgin, as well as John the Forerunner of the Lord and Joseph the Betrothed. In them the living threads of the whole believing righteous Judaism came together as the gospel genealogies of the Savior attest. When this holy and god-chosen birth had been made ready in Judaism, the law accomplished its task. "When the fullness of time came — *to plērōma tou chronou* — God sent His Son, who was born of a woman, *gynaikos*, subject to the law, in order to redeem those under the law, that we might receive adoption as sons" (Gal. 4:4-5).

II. The Second Adam

1. *The Creation of the World and the Incarnation of God*

The creation of the world is an act of divine omnipotence and love-humility. The world is created for the human and in the human, which by its predestination is *deus creatus*, "god by grace." In the unfeelingly cold nothing, God begot the race of the children of God, called to be-

The Second Adam

come gods, not by theft with which the serpent seduced the human being, but by the grace of filial obedience.

The world includes the freedom and the royal dignity of humankind as an unshakeable foundation. If it were merely the "play" of divine creativity, creation would be only an act of God's omnipotence which is free to create and destroy worlds with a wave of the hand. But God's omnipotence is not separable from divine love-humility, and "creative action" without purpose, without meaning, and chiefly, without love is creative action for the sake of creative action, a *jeu divin* [divine play] in raptures with its own might (a feeling that is very natural from a not-omnipotent, envious entity inclined to boastful self-admiration), foreign to God's omnipotence which knows itself and is absolutely tranquil. It is not this *jeu divin* that God's love wants in creating the world, and in Scripture "play" is ascribed not to God but to his Wisdom which by perceiving the revelation of divine creativity, feels joy and rapture through it. In creating, the trihypostatic God summons polyhypostaseity to life; he wants to multiply in the "children of God," to find friends for himself among them. But a son and friend is not a toy or object: once having called him to life, God himself respects his freedom and takes it into account. Having recognized this freedom and introduced it as one of the defining forces in the life of the world, God seemingly limits his omnipotence in its ways for the sake of humankind. The world, created on the foundation of human freedom, cannot be destroyed or annihilated, even if thanks to freedom it "was not successful," whereas people would have turned into children of Satan, or become incarnate devils (Satan was counting on this when he enticed Eve: he dreamed of usurping the world in order to make it a plaything of his ambition, which parodies divine omnipotence, an object of the *jeu satanique*).

The creation of the world was in its very foundation a sacrificial act of Divine love, a voluntary self-depletion or self-effacement of Divinity, his "kenosis," which finds justification only in itself, in the blessedness of sacrificial love. But this general and primordial "kenosis" of Divinity in the creation of the world pre-eternally included a concrete kenosis, the incarnation of the Son of God and the sacrifice on Golgotha. "God so loved the world that he gave his Only-begotten Son, that any who believe in him would not perish but would have eternal life. For God did not send his Son into the world in order to judge the world, but in order that the world be saved through him" (John 3:16-17).

The Human Being

To human freedom, in virtue of which humans could in equal measure be inclined to sin and confirmed against it, it was given to decide if the sacrifice on Golgotha was *really* needed, but as a *possibility* it was decided beforehand in the pre-eternal counsel concerning the creation of humankind: the Father decided to give the Son, and the Son showed obedience to the Father's will right up to the death on the cross. But it was given to the freedom of humankind whether to send him or not to send him to Golgotha. *Such* was the basis of the world's creation, and such is the *price* of the re-creation of the humankind, its second birth.

The idea of the pre-eternal decision for the incarnation of God is expressed frequently in Scripture. "We proclaim the secret wisdom of God, a hidden wisdom which *God predetermined before the ages — pro tōn aiōnōn* for our glory" (1 Cor. 2:7); the mystery of Christianity is confessed *in that way* by the apostle Paul. "Blessed is the God and Father of our Lord Jesus Christ, who has blessed us in Christ with every spiritual blessing in the heavens, since he *chose us in him before the creation of the world — pro katabolēs kosmou —* to be holy and blameless before him in love, having predetermined to make us his sons through Jesus Christ, according to the pleasure of his will, in praise of the glory of his grace by which he has graced us in the Beloved, in whom we have redemption by his blood, the forgiveness of sins by his grace, which he has abundantly bestowed on us in all wisdom and understanding, having revealed to us the mystery of his will according to his pleasure, which he placed beforehand — *proetheto* — in him, in the arrangement of the fullness of time so that everything in heaven and on earth would be united under the head by Christ. In him we have become heirs, having been predestined to this in keeping with the determination of the One who accomplishes all things according to the pleasure of his will, that we might serve to the praise of his glory who earlier hoped in Christ. In him you also, having heard the word of truth, the good news of your salvation, and having come to believe in it, are sealed with the promised Holy Spirit who is the pledge of our inheritance, for the redemption of his lot, to the praise of his glory" (Eph. 1:3-14). The apostle says that he "was given this grace, to announce to the pagans the inexhaustible wealth of Christ and to reveal to all what is *the economy of the mystery hidden from eternity in God — hē oikonomia tou mystēriou tou apokekrummenou apo tōn aiōnōn en tōi theōi —* who created everything through Jesus Christ, so that now God's manifold wisdom be made known through the Church to principalities and authorities in the heavens and *according to the pre-eternal determination — kata prothesin tōn aiōnōn —* which he fulfilled in Christ Jesus, our Lord" (Eph. 3:8-11). In the catholic epistle of the apostle Peter we likewise read: "(you are redeemed) by the precious blood of

The Second Adam

Christ, as of a spotless and pure *Lamb predestined from before the foundation of the world* — *proegnōsmenou pro katabolēs tou kosmou* — but revealed in the last times — *ep' eschatou tōn chronōn* — for you" (1 Peter 1:19-20).

The pre-eternal decision of God, which remained a mystery even for the heavenly "principalities and authorities," could not be unraveled by the tempter, the spirit of envy who in accordance with the same was deprived of every insight into love: judging by himself alone and not admitting anything different or higher, he could count only on the Creator, offended by disobedience, to turn away from the world and cast it off like a broken plaything, and then Satan would reign in it. But he did not know and could not admit that God never leaves the world and humankind to their own fate, for its very creation is already an act of unlimited love of the trihypostatic God. He loved the world with such love that does not stop before the supreme and final sacrifice, before the death on the cross of the Beloved Son. Satan could not even *imagine* this in his haughty egoism.

The incarnation of God was an act of the new and definitive creation of the world that had been damaged in its very nature. The world was completed in the six days of creation in the sense that all the forces and seeds of life were implanted in it, and it could develop further from itself, without a new creative intervention. Therefore on the seventh day God *rested* from the works of creation.[60] But at the same time the world was only *pre-created* in the human being, who had to create himself from his own side with his own freedom and only then enter into possession of the world, having brought to realization the general plan of creation. And when the human's failure on that path was displayed, a new act of creation of the world in the perfect human being through the incarnation was required of God. And this new creation of the world ended with a new, as if second *Sabbath* of divine rest: "This Sabbath is most blessed, on which Christ sleeps, but he will rise on the third day."[61] The incarnate God shared to the end the fate of the world and humankind corrupted by sin, even to the torments and death of the cross,[62] and all the separate moments of the Savior's earthly life are like a single, composite act of divine sacrifice.[63]

The idea of incarnation as kenosis finds multiform expression in Scripture. Philippians 2:6-10 has of course fundamental significance here. "Being in the form of God, he did not consider it theft to be equal to God, but he effaced himself, having taken the form of a slave, and became like unto humans and was in aspect like a human; having humbled himself, he became obedient even to death, death on a cross. And therefore God raised him up and gave him the name above all names, so that before the name of Jesus every knee of those in heaven, on earth and under the earth would bend."[64] He "is the image of the invisible God, born before all creatures. For through him is created all that is in the heavens and on the earth, visible and invisible: thrones, dominions, principalities, authorities — all was created through him and for him. . . . For it pleased the Father that in him all the fullness should dwell and that by means of him he would reconcile everything with himself, on earth and in the heavens, having made peace through him by the blood of his cross" (Col. 1:15-20). "It was fitting that he, for whom and from whom all things are, and who leads many sons to glory, should perfect through suffering the leader of their salvation" (Heb. 2:10). "He must be like his brothers in all things, so that he could be a merciful and faithful high priest before God, for the propitiation of the sins of the people. For as he himself endured having been tempted, so he is able to help those who are tempted" (Heb. 2:17-18). "In the days of his flesh he offered prayers and supplications with powerful cries and tears to the one who can save him from death; and he was heard for the sake of his reverent submission. Although he was Son, he learned obedience through sufferings" (Heb. 5:7-8). "Jesus . . . instead of the joy set before him endured the cross, disregarding its shame" (Heb. 12:2).

According to church teaching, two natures and two wills are united in Christ without separation and without confusion. He is truly God, for "in him all the fullness of Divinity dwells bodily" (Col. 2:9), but he is also truly human, the second Adam: "The first human is dust from the earth, the second human is the Lord from heaven" (1 Cor. 15:47). Only by having become fully human, except for sin,[65] and in this taking on its consequences which weigh on humankind, could the Lord accomplish the salvation of the world. The fundamental dogmatic definition at the same time contains indications of the perfect union in Christ of the absolute and relative, the divine and creaturely, "all the fullness of Divinity" and creatureliness, God and world. This dogma directly and without disguise enunciates an antinomy for reason, for this full union and seeming identification of the absolute and the relative, the transcendent and the immanent, is completely beyond the comprehension of reason, and must be recognized in its antinomic quality as a truth of faith. Attempts to remove and overcome this

The Second Adam

antinomy so as to provide a way out for the requirements of rationalism, having thrown off the yoke of antinomic dogma, lead to the heresy of Monophysitism and Monotheletism. Such for example is the doctrine of Arius, who considered Christ as a creaturely entity, or the doctrine of Apollinarius who dissolved the human element in his divine nature. Christological heresies, belonging to certain basic types, are extraordinarily varied in their forms.

This antinomy of the supracreaturely and creaturely, the divine and human, can also be expressed differently and turn on facets other than those that came to light in the Christological controversies. In particular we collide afresh with the antinomies of eternity and time, theophany and theogony. As God, the Second Hypostasis dwells outside any temporal development, above time and history ("before Abraham was, I am — *prin Abraam genesthai, egō eimi*," John 8:58). Just as it is impossible to admit in eternity or the absolute any sort of process whatever that flows through time, a new becoming and emerging, so is it impossible to speak of a theogonic process, for in God everything pre-eternally *super-exists,* and in relation to the creature and for the creature only theophany is possible. But, since Christ is bound up with time, process, becoming, and history, then human history is in different senses essentially theogonic. Does much need to be enlarged upon for the sake of proving this if the most concrete theogonic act, the Nativity of Christ, forms the divine center of history? ("The Virgin *today* bears *the Superessential* . . . for our sake *is born* a Babe *the pre-eternal God*"; this is how, in complete ignorance of the rational dread before antinomies for reason, the kontakion[66] for the Nativity of Christ announces the event to the faithful.) In general, if we pay attention only to the events of the Savior's earthly life, his resurrection from the dead and ascension into heaven, and the descent of the Holy Spirit on the apostles, it becomes impossible to avoid the conclusion that temporality, process, is introduced here into the life of the Holy Trinity, in which these events are also accomplished in a certain sense, and as a result, just as fullness seemingly reaches maturity, theogony happens. This incomprehensible unity of time and eternity, theogony and theophany, the absolute and the relative, is corroborated precisely by the fundamental Christological dogmas.

Moreover, the basic antinomy that lies in general at the base of religious self-consciousness is corroborated by it to the highest and ultimate degree: the indissoluble bi-unity of the transcendent and the im-

The Human Being

manent, the supermundanity of the Absolute and the revelation of God in the world. In this sense *Christianity is the absolute religion,* for precisely in it the basic religious antinomy comes to light and is experienced with the greatest intensity: here the perfect closeness of God is palpable, but his remoteness is felt with all the more force. In Christ, "without separation and without confusion," the "fullness of Divinity" transcendent to the creation is united with humanity immanent to the world. This union is completed by the ascension of the Lord into heaven together with his glorified Humanity; by this the foundation for the divinization of human beings is laid in the second Adam, their restoration to the dignity of children of God by adoption.

"For you are all children of God by faith in Christ Jesus; all you who have been baptized in Christ have put on Christ as a garment" (Gal. 3:26-27). "For all who are led by the Spirit of God are children of God. Because you did not receive a spirit of slavery so that you should again live in fear, but you received a spirit of adoption by which you cry out 'Abba, Father'! This same Spirit bears witness to our spirit that we are children of God" (Rom. 8:14-16). "And since you are children, God sent into your hearts the Spirit of his Son, who cries 'Abba, Father'!" (Gal. 4:6), and from the heavenly Father "is named every fatherland in the heavens and on the earth" (Eph. 3:15).

The incarnation of God has been realized, Jacob's ladder has been raised between heaven and earth, the salvation of the world is an accomplished fact. Christ became absolutely immanent to humankind and through it to the world. He is the very deep foundation, the most intimate essence of humankind; he is closer to us than we are to ourselves, our empirical, much-changing, and eternally wavering I. He completely supplanted the old Adam and became the new Adam for all humanity.

But this intimate and substantial immediacy of Christ to humanity, which is however closed for it by sin, does not yet give any grounds for the religious familiarity or sentimentality into which the representatives of mystical theology often lapse when they depict communion with Christ as exaggeratedly accessible if not commonplace. Christianity fully maintains a serious and tragic character proper to religion in general, and even more than any other religion it lets one feel the bitterness of the world, instills a certain disenchantment with respect to

The Second Adam

it, while at the same time it compels one to sense a degree of distancing of the human from God. From this are understandable the hostility and irreconcilability towards Christianity of those worshipers of the world who would want to be entirely at ease with and withdrawn into the immediate givenness of the world. And Christ's proximity to humankind cannot refer to the old Adam who still lives a full life in us. Christ became immeasurably close to us and we can tangibly feel and taste this closeness, but at the same time he is immeasurably distant from us and not only by reason of our personal sins, but also as a result of the general state of the world, in keeping with the characteristics of our "eon." For although "the prince of this world" is put to shame, and his power is partly broken, he still possesses the world; the old Adam in the inner recesses of his essence is already replaced by the new, but he still lives in us; death, "the final enemy," is already defeated by the light of Christ's Resurrection, but it mows down a harvest of life as before; the creation still groans, awaiting its deliverance, and the whole world is in agony and suffers from confusion and the conflict of good and evil. Salvation has been accomplished on Golgotha, the world is already subjected to Christ, but according to its condition, in its modality, it still remains alienated from him, and this closeness is only the object of faith and hope, not of triumphant obviousness.

"We are saved in hope. Hope, if one sees it, is not hope, for if someone sees, then what is there for him to hope for? But when we hope for what we do not see, then we wait patiently" (Rom. 8:24-25). Therefore Christianity, although it awakens a religious sightedness that paganism could not give, in the same way it destroys the relative balance that was all the same proper to the latter. Christianity teaches to comprehend the world not only as the garment of Divinity or the cosmos, but also as "this world," a dungeon for the spirit; it instills in the soul a thirst for liberation from the world, a striving to break through beyond its bounds. Therefore pantheism of various shades — not as a religious idea that nevertheless holds a particle of truth within, but as world-perception — remains so distant from Christianity, foreign, even hostile and competitive. And its sentimental, quasi-Christian variety, "panchristism" as a type of some religious naturalism, is a lie and "deception," and this is so despite the fact that the world is now Christosophianic for the saint who has conquered the world and restored in himself sophianic chastity. In Christianity one must attach equally serious importance to the fact that Christ was incarnated, "appeared on earth and lived with humans," suffered and rose, and that he ascended to heaven, is again removed from the world, became transcendent for it again, though not in the previous sense, and dwells in the heavens, "seated at the right hand of the Father."

That is why we expect a second, glorious, and dread advent of Christ which will be a catastrophic break in the life of the world, the end of the current eon. Between the first and the second advent lies an intervening time of a certain if only relative removal of Christ from the world. Therefore, although Christ is now near to people through his Church, and this proximity is made tangibly certain in the Church's sacraments, it is still not that joyful and simultaneously dread proximity in which he will stand with respect to the whole creation after his second coming and the resurrection of the dead. Therefore Christianity cannot in any way, under pretense of panchristism, turn into a fundamental and decisive immanentism and anthropolatry, factually understanding it as a deepened and purified paganism (although it includes the latter, as a subordinate and partial truth, and even discloses its relative truth); but it is equally impossible to understand it according to the type of Old Testament transcendentalism, as a religion of law, obligatory only by its transcendent sanction.[67] It is neither one nor the other, or, it is the one and the other.

2. The Salvation of Fallen Humankind

Fallen humankind preserved in itself the image of God as the foundation of its being, and the intrinsic sophianicity that makes it the center of the universe, but the means of finding its entelechic form, of bringing about the likeness of God, was lost. In it the balance was irrevocably upset precisely in the sphere of becoming like God and thus its very endowments became fateful and dangerous (even for Satan the objective condition for his fall, the temptation of his own power, lay in his exceptional endowments). Therefore with their own powers, no matter how great they might be, human beings cannot pull themselves out of the gulf of sin and render their nature healthy, but are doomed all the more to be stuck in the swamp of sin, drowning in the clutches of greedy nothing. It is a shortsighted error to think that simply in virtue of "evolution" — of time and "progress" — the good will be strengthened in humanity at the expense of evil, and thus humanity becomes

The Second Adam

all the more perfect by force of things, as if automatically. In reality only evil accumulates in that way, while good is realized in the world only by free spiritual struggle. Therefore the divinization of humanity can by no means be achieved through the path of evolution.

This general injured state of life is revealed clearly in death: *nothing* became so actual in humankind that it obtained power to decompose its structure; the wrong side of its being began to come to light — nonbeing. Death was a good deed of the Father who did not wish to give immortality to evil. Over the course of time in the absence of death, corruption and decay would have taken possession of human life to such an extent that no righteousness could have been protected against its influence: sinful humanity, endowed with the gift of immortality, was threatened with turning into devils or at least with approximating that perfection in hell which is inherent only in the father of lies and his minions. Therefore death, which establishes a natural interruption in all human affairs and also places an indelible mark on the whole of human creativity, saves humankind from continuation in the creative work of evil, and in this weakens and paralyzes its power. Deprived of the boon of death, the sinful world, inhabited by corrupted humanity, would satisfy all the more the aspirations of Satan, who could turn it into a swamp of self-satisfied vulgarity and a hell of inescapable agonies.

But was God in any way able to renounce his creation in which he placed his image and breathed the breath of life himself? Obviously, this would be impossible, and for this reason it was necessary *to save* this world and this humanity. But how can it be saved? Evidently, this saved humanity, on the one hand, necessarily must remain itself, *the very same* humanity that cannot be annihilated by God once it has been created. But, on the other hand, this humanity, being subject to the power of sin, cannot be saved, and consequently it must become *different*; having ceased to be itself, it must immediately become *the same and not the same*, other for its own self. Such an antinomic task, which clearly breaks the logical "law of identity," arises in virtue of the logic of salvation, which does not coincide with rational logic, and is determined by the situation of humankind after the fall. Humanity cannot be saved by its own powers or by an external, mechanical power, as a broken object is repaired.

Neither the total annihilation of the old Adam (e.g., during the universal flood) nor the creation of a new humanity having no kind of connection with the old one could be equally reckoned as *salvation*. Precisely *this* humanity must be saved, the old Adam, and besides, *it must save itself*, for only this is compatible with its freedom, but also *it cannot save itself*, for self-salvation exceeds its powers. Therefore only a *human being* could be the savior of humanity, and one who recapitulates in his ontological nature the whole nature of humankind; to say it otherwise, the first Adam, the very root of the human tree. But old Adam fell irretrievably and he waited for his final fate in Sheol; therefore, if he could not be the savior, then one can only conclude that the savior had to be Not-human. Jesus Christ was just such a Human and Not-human, the new Adam, God who became human.

The antinomy of salvation in the history of the religious consciousness of humanity received symbolic expression in the universally disseminated religious act of sacrificial offering. Sacrifice began to be offered outside the enclosure of paradise right away after the expulsion of the primogenitors (Cain and Abel's sacrifices are its established ritual). The sacrifice of repentance and redemption of sin, offered by a human being, has a substitutionary meaning; it is offered by a given person or community as compensation for their sins. It follows that a sacrificial animal, deprived of life for the sin of another, in some sense is identified with them, but also retains its different being, because otherwise a sacrifice would be impossible or could only consist in the self-immolation of the one sacrificing. The idea of sacrifice is therefore a negation of the logical law of identity, for its logic regards the nonidentical as identical. And besides, the religious essence of redemptive or purificatory sacrifice is precisely in this negation of identity. Sacrificing is the central act in divine worship in the pre-Christian world; in particular in the liturgical texts of Old Testament religion it primarily consists of a minutely worked-out ritual of sacrifices. A more substantial meaning in the sacrificial slaughter of the animal is obtained in the shedding of its *blood*, which constitutes the life principle (according to Moses the soul of animals is in the blood). The cult of sacrifices everywhere had a very bloody character; the mystique of blood was experienced intensely and in many forms (we recall the *tauroboleum*, the sacred slaughter of a bull for the purposes of washing with its blood, as was the custom in many mystery cults). This death of the sacrificial animal, with the shedding of its blood, had a direct prototypical significance for the sacrifice of Golgotha, as is explained by the apostle Paul.

The Second Adam

"Christ, the High Priest of future blessings . . . not with the blood of goats and calves but with his own blood once for all entered into the holy place and obtained the eternal redemption. For if the blood of calves and goats and the ash of heifers sanctifies through sprinkling those who have been defiled so that their body became pure, how much more will the blood of Christ who through the Holy Spirit offered himself unblemished to God. . . . The first covenant was confirmed not without blood. For when Moses pronounced all the commandments according to the law before all the people, he took the blood of calves and goats with scarlet wool and hyssop and sprinkled both the scroll and the whole people, saying, 'This is the blood of the covenant that God has ordered for you' [Exod. 24:8]. Likewise he sprinkled the tent with blood and all the vessels for worship. Indeed almost everything according to the law is purified with blood, and without the shedding of blood there is no forgiveness. . . . Christ entered . . . into heaven itself . . . not in order to offer himself over and over again, as the high priest enters every year into the holy place year after year with blood that is not his own; otherwise he would have to suffer again and again since the foundation of the world. But he has appeared once, at the end of the age, to annihilate sin by his sacrifice. The law, having the shadow of future goods, but not the very form of these things, can never, by the one and the same sacrifice offered continually every year, make perfect those who offer them, otherwise they would cease to offer them . . . for it is impossible that the blood of calves and goats should destroy sins . . . and every priest stands daily in service and over and over offers one and the same sacrifice which can never wipe out sins. . . . By one offering he has forever made perfect those who are sanctified." (Heb. 9:11-14, 18-22, 24-26; 10:1-2, 4, 11, 12, 14)

The sacrifice on Golgotha, offered to God on the part of humanity, is the supreme fruit of its repentance and rebirth, for it is offered by the most perfect Human Being. But at the same time it does not belong to humanity, for according to its significance it absolutely exceeds the measure of what is accessible to it, having been offered by God himself, who as the Not-human, at the same time became the perfect Human. The priest's solemn exclamation in the liturgy right before the offering of the Eucharistic sacrifice proclaims this: "offering what is yours from your own to you for all people and for all things." The redemptive sacrifice offered once and for all for eternity has power to be increased and multiplied, being accomplished afresh in the holy Eucharist. Therefore every other sacrifice accompanied by the shedding of blood is forever abolished by it. According to the witness of the apostle Paul, after Golgotha bloody sacrifices can be offered only to demons, and not to

God; they constitute a demonic altar. Likewise the "abomination of desolation, spoken of by the prophets" ascends the throne, even in the Jerusalem temple where the Old Testament altar is destroyed (will there be an attempt made to restore it, sometime at the end of time?)

The fallen human being must die for he cannot not die, but he must also rise in Christ — *the same and not the same* — different from himself, but conscious of his identity with the former, the old and the new. In this antinomy are combined both conditions of salvation: the necessity of preserving the human being once called into existence, and the impossibility of saving him as he is. Thanks to the sacrifice on Golgotha, the old human being is created anew, but remains himself after resurrection: the final separation in him of death and life, being and nonbeing, occurs at the Dread Judgment, which can be regarded in a certain sense as the final, concluding act in the chain of events that constitute in their totality the creation of humankind. Cleft by the final cleaving, the human being remains one and the same, and despite everything, whole.

Christ became a human being in order to be made the new Adam. He had to join the old Adam, walk the path of earthly life and share its burdens and final fate. But for this purpose it was insufficient to appropriate only the separate facets of humanity; it was necessary to accept it wholly, in the greatest fullness and power, with all the sufferings, the torment of god-abandonment and death. And only then, having assumed in himself the whole Adam, having become in truth a human being, having accepted all temptations and being himself tempted, was Christ able to become the new Adam. The new, second creation of the human being, after the relative failure of the first, but with the indispensable condition of preserving Adam and his race, simultaneously required death too, and resurrection, as a living synthesis of the old and the new, across the threshold of which is revealed the definitive completion.

In Christ humanity offered repentance and sacrifice, it was reborn and began to correspond to God's will. It became different, and besides, it became superior in essence (although not in condition) to what it was in paradise, as much as the new Adam is superior to the first. In this regard the Origenist idea of *apocatastasis* must be rejected, the mere restoration of the former without the creation of the new.

The nature of our salvation must be understandable not in the light of a formal-juridical theory of retribution, but in connection with

The Second Adam

a general doctrine on the creation of humankind, with its salvation able to be only a new creation, or more precisely, the continuation of its creation. After the incarnation of God, humanness itself, human nature, became different, for it received the capacity for resurrection and new life thanks to a new creative act of Divinity that poured new powers into it. This point of view accords entirely, by the way, with the doctrine of the apostle Paul about salvation by grace, and by works and merits,[68] where these latter things establish only the degree and form of personal participation in the gracious gift of salvation.

Both the resurrection and the dread judgment extend to *all* humanity, that which knew and which did not know Christ in earthly life (here is the mystery of the preaching in Hades, 1 Peter 3:19-20, and the mystery of the connection with the Church by hidden, invisible paths). *All* people are resurrected, and having been resurrected they will know themselves by the seed of the new Adam whom they will see in the form of the Judge. From the depiction of the dread judgment given in the Gospel (Matt. 25:31-46), it is clear that *all* humanity will be judged according to some immanent norm of *humanness,* which at the same time proves to be the measure of Christ. In this context it will be revealed from the answers of some that although they did not know Christ, they prove to be Christ-bearers in their humanness, reflecting his image. This is that primordial purity, uprightness, and healthiness of human nature which is only damaged by original sin, and is restored by Christ in the redemption. The boundary of the Church runs differently, it seems, than is visible to our gaze, for those ignorant of Christ turn out to be the saved, while those who even performed miracles in his name go to perdition. Nevertheless the new life and the new anthropology are consolidated only in the Church and through the Church, in which Christ dwells, and with him the whole fullness of Divinity. The work of Christ on earth was expressed namely in that the Church was established by him; the beginning of a new, graced life was laid which spiritually restores paradise on earth. The church is not only "a community of adherents," which the great teachers and prophets left after themselves, but a certain Entity, a living organism, the Body of Christ. This does not prevent her from being a hierarchically organized society, with the hierarchy possessing divine authority to perform the sacraments, which was entrusted to her by Christ himself in succession through the apostles.

The very possibility of the church's existence as a society is ontologically based on the emergence in the world of a new mystical center.

The Human Being

In the soul of the world, captive to the "prince of this world," sophianic life, which had been injured by the fall, was reborn with new strength. New strength entered it and "Mary full of grace" was its focus, she over whom "every creature rejoices." But Mary, although the heart of the church, is not yet the church itself, which in its original essence is depicted mysteriously and hidden in the Song of Songs;[69] in the New Testament it is defined already directly as "Bride" or "Wife of the Lamb," and Christian marriage is sanctified in the image of the union of Christ and the Church. If the fall was accompanied by a deep distortion in the life of sex, if it was first of all a sickness of the original marriage, then in the redemption one ought to see the restoration to health of the nature of marriage, thanks to which it becomes ontologically already "in Christ and in the Church," and corresponds to its inner natural norm which stems from the fullness of the image of God in the human being. In the redemption the true marital quality of life is mysteriously restored, and not for nothing was the first miracle, so mysterious and moving, performed at the wedding in Cana of Galilee; not only is old Adam redeemed, so too is old Eve, Adam *and* Eve, as a spousal couple, guilty of the common fall, of the corruption of marriage.[70]

If the new anthropology becomes apparent only in the Church and through the Church, then it is mistaken (even in the sense of a so-called mystical methodology) to seek it outside and apart from the Church, by turning the incarnation into some kind of naturalistic principle, and understanding it almost as a physical energy. Although it has a very profound cosmic significance, penetrating into all the depths of the world, a too one-sided and exclusive cosmism closes the path to its comprehension. The ontology of our salvation is so deep, its work was accomplished at such a depth of being, that on its surface, in the empirical, in the "psychologisms" of life, it at times can even not be felt. For it was not noticed either by Rome or by the whole world of that time that in distant and tiny Judea an event measureless in significance and unique in importance took place — the appearance of Christ. The theosophical notion of a Christ-impulse operating in the world, in the likeness of electricity, heat, or gravity, must be rejected by reason of their naturalistic coarseness. Christ's presence in the world, apart from the graced attestation received through the Church, cannot be revealed by any psychic organs or sensory apparatus; although grace operates in the world, it does so as a force that is foreign to it, supermundane, and inaccessible by means of earthly knowledge.

The Second Adam

The situation of one who seeks Christ apart from the Church in the Christian era is even less favorable than in the pre-Christian era, similar to how a worthy marriage in Christianity is a more difficult task than outside it.[71] "Great Pan has died"; in paganism his days have passed, and if one is to seek God now only in nature, then through it one can hear not "gods," but "wood spirits" who lead astray from the truth, and one becomes a victim of religious deception. It is possible not to know Christ, being foreign to Christianity (as even now are non-Christian religions that belong to a certain extent to a still pre-Christian era); but knowing of him and at the same time denying the Church as the unique path of life in him, a human being becomes the victim of religious deception and self-deception.

Only in the Church does new life exist; living in the Church, and inasmuch as they themselves become Church, men and women receive Christ into themselves. But in so doing, their own essence is not forfeited, indeed it is strengthened. For the Lord Jesus is the perfect Human Being, and therefore everything authentically, ontologically human finds its consolidation through him as the universal Pan-Human. In the old Adam, or in depraved and selfish humanity, true, pure humanness is forfeited, everyone is left enclosed in themselves, humanity exists in a succession of individuals and generations, like a collective but not a community. The single and universal pan-human, gathered and thus catholic humanity, which embraces the living and the dead as well as the as-yet unborn, is ontologically contained in the new Adam, and this is why the Church is the true Humanity, as a positive force. Christ is the Person of all persons, the Hypostasis of all hypostases. In the sinful condition of humankind, the personal principle is impenetrability in virtue of which it completely fills spiritual space with itself, and from the point occupied by it every other person is pushed out. Thanks to this, humanity *is scattered* into persons, is found in disintegration and is capable of forming only a collective or a plurality, even if externally connected and regulated. With the intensity of this personal principle is connected the keenness of life: *höchstes Glück der Erdenkinder ist die Persönlichkeit* [the supreme happiness of the children of earth is the person]! And nevertheless we must agree to sacrifice it, to lose our soul in order to save it from selfishness and impenetrability, to open to it the joys of love-humility. That sick, Luciferian I which is aware of itself in opposition to every other I as to Not-I, must acquire compatibility with it and through it receive a positive and not only a negative definition. If the formula of the first is: *I is not Not-I* and *I is greater than any Not-I*, then the formula of the second is: *I am thou, he, we, you, they*. It is necessary to renounce oneself, not to desire one's own I, to follow the way of the cross or the asceticism of humility, which for that reason has received such significance and such elaboration in Christianity.

There is no task more difficult for human beings than the victory over themselves, for sin permeates every pore of our essence and for a time it is possible simply not to see this. The spiritual dignity of a Christian is expressed distinctively in the ruthless truthfulness of self-consciousness. The spiritual feat of *foolishness*, the complete repudiation of one's psychological guise, the mask of a mummy on a living face, a type of death while alive — such is the limit of this path of self-denial. By remaining entirely foreign to it, by not playing the fool in one's heart, it is impossible to achieve a Christian attitude towards oneself and towards the world, and in essence, achievements on the Christian path are defined by the measure of foolishness, the capacity to deny the wisdom of this world. Foolishness has many facets and many forms, it is not connected with definite forms but it commands not to love one's I, one's self in oneself. It demands a secret sacrifice, one that is uninterrupted and around the clock.

One must hate oneself for the sake of Christ and love him more than oneself, and then in his universal face will be revealed for each one their own face. Each will find themselves in the Other, and this Other is Christ. And finding themselves in the Other, being aware of the source of life in love for them, people will communicate in the mystery of the Holy Trinity, the mutual emptying of the Divine Hypostases in reciprocal love, the blessedness of life in the Other and through the Other. The human spirit is lifted up to unattainable heights and the human person shines in the beauty of that image after which and for the sake of which it is created.

In Christ is included not only the supreme and sole norm of obligation for a human being, but also the law of human existence, although it will be disclosed only at the end of our eon, at the Dread Judgment. Then suddenly *all* humanity will see clearly, and inevitably by the force of circumstances they will be freed from the bygone authority of illusions, psychologisms, the self, belief in the nonexistent as existent. Each one will see themselves in their ontological essence, in their true light, and in this is the immutable foundation of the impartial judgment of Christ. People will learn that true being belongs in the human only to the Christ principle. To the extent that a man or woman has laid the foundation for their own being, realized in themselves the *likeness* of God, unmasked their intelligible face, and come to know in themselves their divine idea, they have the forces of life and growth in the Kingdom of Christ. But those in whom only their self was brought to light do not exist ontologically at all, although this illusion was connected by some threads with their person, which by going off entirely into this illusion remains naked and poor outside it. Then they will have to be agonizingly separated from themselves, i.e., undergo "eternal torments," "the eternal fire," in which the self and its nonexistent deeds are consumed. Such people, who had the possibility of being born beautiful and perfect for eternity and have now already become conscious of this possibility, have made themselves into monsters, offending God with this ugliness.

III. Human History

1. Concrete Time

With the expulsion of our progenitors from paradise, human history is inaugurated. "Adam knew Eve, his wife, and she conceived and bore Cain and said: I have gained a man from God. And she bore his brother Abel" (Gen. 4:1-2), then Seth and so on. So began the gradual birth of humanity in the succession of human generations. That which was to have been accomplished in paradise under paradisiacal conditions of life — for God's blessing "be fruitful and multiply" was given in paradise — now must be realized in the land of banishment. And yet God's benediction preserves its force, and humanity must *be born* in all the many branches of its tree. *History is the birth of humanity* first of all, objective time filled with births, and then with deaths, and interiorly connected by their succession. The changing of generations, the only form in which the single humanity now exists, represents of course a devouring of the fathers by the children, in its own way a dance macabre, a dance of death, but history as concrete time arises precisely in the alternation of generations. The definite characterization of humanity extends not only to separate individuals in their singularity and unrepeatable originality, but also to their aggregates, the aggregate of aggregates, etc. Humanity exists not only as individuals but also as families, tribes, races, nations, and all these units form a single hierarchical organization. Each individual grows up in humanity in a definite "maternal place," occupying a hierarchically determined spot in it, inasmuch as each one is son and father or mother and daughter, and belongs to their own era, nation, etc. Inherent in all these connections is not only empirical being, emergence in time, but also supratemporal essence. They were only able to arise in time because they have their basis in supratemporal time and therefore are given and assigned to time.

Taking as our point of departure this understanding of the hierarchical structure of humanity, we must acknowledge that the succession of people in time, the changing of generations, nations, individual persons, in no case represents something fortuitous and purely empirical, but is determined by the spiritual structure of intelligible humanity. Time is not at all an empty form in which various objects are accommodated without connection and order, neither is it only a form of perception as Kant knows it. Such ideal time is an abstraction engendered through our thinking by means of abstracting from the concrete content, outside of which time simply does not exist. But for Kant true time is just such an abstraction, and the whole ponderous edifice of Kant's *Critiques* rests on it as on a foundation. Objective time is connected, and in this connection it is regular. Similar to how it is impossible to pass from Europe to America by avoiding the ocean, so does the road to the nineteenth century only run through the eighteenth, and precisely the concrete fullness of time creates "the law of history" in that conventional sense in which one can speak of it. Time here is entirely relative to space: similar to how in space occupied by the human body, its every part occupies a definite place, and the head cannot be located where the feet are, so too time represents the extra-spatial projection of the panhuman organism. Of course, although with sufficient certitude, we can only postulate this connection, which is not an object of human sight (save perhaps by virtue of graced insight). We ourselves are still gripped by the flow of time, and neither our own time nor that of universal history has stopped for us; therefore, we cannot contemplate it in its entirety.

In unraveling the projection of time, in searching for a key to the historical cipher, further difficulties and problems rise before us. Our concept of objective time will differ substantially depending, for example, on whether we accept or not a doctrine of reincarnation of souls, i.e., the frequent repetition of the life of one and the same entities; further, whether we see the mystical center of world history in the event of the incarnation or in something different. In addition we must reckon with different possibilities under the filling of objective time, connected with the existence of human freedom. The latter is woven into the fabric of time as one of its shaping forces, but in the presence of variants introduced by freedom the general law of the historical line keeps its force. Objective time contains sufficient foundation for the order of generations and the succession of historical nations, by which the skeleton of history is determined. If history in general is the birth of humanity, then it is realized with an internally defined plan and consistency. History is connected with "times and seasons," having their foundation in the spiritual organization of humanity. Therefore it is not "bad infinity" naturally inherent in formal time, but has a bounds and in particular necessarily presupposes both a beginning and an end, which abstract time does not do at all. "The transcendental" time of Kant, or the abstract form of time, is inevitably conceived as potential infinity, knowing neither beginning nor end; therefore its idea leads reason to an antinomy, detected by Kant himself. On the contrary, concrete time, which history is, has both beginning and end; in other words, it represents an *eon*, a certain completion that is disclosed in time sequentially. We have the fullest analogy to the historical eon in our own personal life, which likewise represents concrete time. By regarding it as abstract time we in essence encounter no logical hindrances for extending this time into eternity, at least from the side of the future, for this abstract time does not know death, which represents a kind of end of time itself. Concretely, human life shows in itself the alternation of ages, necessarily terminating in death, and for this reason time that has suddenly blazed up just as suddenly goes out. In this sense an individual human life is also a certain particular eon, similar to a historical eon.

And thus history is above all else the birth of humanity, the realization of the original creative intention for humankind as a race that accommodates in itself a plurality of individuals. History immediately adjoins the beginning of human existence in paradise through this and insofar as it remains free of the influence of original sin; the means and circumstances of realizing the historical task depend on it, but not the task itself. Thanks to original sin the reproduction of the human race is now accomplished not only through birth but also through death, after which follows resurrection; without it there would be no death, and the first birth would be final. But birth itself, independently of how it is accomplished, is supposed by the reproduction of humanity from one human couple.

The historical birth of a human being, an entity free and godlike, not only supposes birth in the proper sense, i.e., an act of divine omnipotence summoning to existence new lives and realized through the marital union of spouses or in general of persons of different sex, but also the self-creation of the human. The latter is not only born this way or that but it *becomes* its own self only through its free volition, as if giving consent to its own self, determining its own being. Humans are the free executors of their theme, and this realization of the self, the manifestation of their being given and proposed, the disclosure of their essence, the realization in themselves of their own likeness, is a creative act accessible to humankind. So far as this fashioning of their own likeness is the general and irrevocable basis of the creation of humankind, their creative activity and at the same time self-creation, self-generation, determines the most general content of human life. Life is a creative activity and therefore *history is a creative activity*. This property of life is in essence not connected with the actual sinful condition of humanity either, for even in its paradisiacal state humanity had the same basis of being in its creative freedom (thanks to which the possibility of the fall also appeared). To say it another way, human history, as the generation and at the same time the self-generation of humanity, as some sort of completed eon, would have flowed in paradise too, and in the life of our progenitors until the fall we already have this paradisiacal beginning of history. The fall only introduced into history as creative activity a tragic and antinomic nuance, and deprived it of that harmoniousness with which the growth of humanity would have happened, had it not been poisoned by sin.

Up until the fall into sin, there lay before Adam and Eve the possibility of a twofold path of history, as birth and life-creativity: the path of sonship and obedience from which the progenitors deviated in the fall, and the road of good and evil of historical tragedy. For human history is now substantially tragedy, and so it is already in its foundation. To see in history the triumph of harmony being readied or exultant "progress" means to display spiritual blindness and deafness. It is possible to rise above tragedy by religiously and graciously overcoming it — the experience of the saints tells us of this, but this overcoming is accomplished only by way of the feat of the cross, by voluntarily living out tragedy in the sharpest form. One can for a time remain below tragedy by being immersed in bourgeois self-satisfaction, by being deceived by the flowers growing above the abyss; but it is in no way given to anyone to be barricaded against the tragic side of life; everyone inevitably encounters it, even if only in the presence of their own dying. And the same thing is repeated with respect to the historical destinies of all humanity; after the daydreams of self-rapture and sparkling hopes follow painful sobering up and bitter disenchantment! That is why "everything hurts near the tree of life" (K. Leontiev). Ever since they desired a vivid sense of the antinomy of creation and ate of the tree of knowledge of good and evil, this evil became for humankind, if only temporarily, like a second cosmic beginning, a Fate that pressed down heavily and crippled life. It keeps watch over humans before their birth, for the newly born fall into a plague-infested environment, enter a world burdened with sick heredity. The aspects of world Fate are defined as the natural "laws" of world and historical development. Philosophy of history in its essence can and must be a philosophy of tragedy, and indeed itself becomes a tragedy for the kind of philosophy that does not want or know how to accept the ineluctability of antinomy in life and thought.

2. Economy and Art

In the fall the progenitors were subjected to the temptation of lust. Lust for knowledge received apart from love for God and cognition of God, lust for flesh seeking bodily delights independently of spirit, and lust for authority that aspires to power apart from spiritual maturation, took possession of them. Through this the balance of their spiritual powers was destroyed. In their relation to the world they were subjected to the temptation *of magism,* and they hoped to master the world with the help of external, unspiritual means symbolized by the eating of the fruit from the forbidden tree. Laying magism at the basis of their relations to the world, the earth, and the flesh, the progenitors darkened and weakened in themselves their natural sophianicity, in virtue of which it was proper for Adam as a theophoric and god-receptive being to exercise dominion over the world. This power was not the object of concupiscence and an independent goal, but one of the manifestations of his spiritual eminence and holiness. Although in a certain sense one can say that Adam was "a white mage" before the fall, nevertheless for him magic did not yet exist; it arose from the desire to become a mage which is produced by the presence of magism, by the longing for power. In the sinless human being one basic aspiration reigned with which all the remaining ones are in agreement: to love the Father with the will, the mind, and the heart and to come to know him in the world. The temptation of gnosis apart from love remained alien to him. To want the world for its own sake, in the name of power over it, meant to fall into magism, to be changed from a born king and master into a mage, a usurper. But a magic relation to the world supposes not only the aspiration to master it but also its counteraction, not only might but also captivity. To say it differently, magism already implies the emergence *of an economic* relation to the world, a human actuality that is manifested in intellectual, volitional, and physical effort, or in *labor*, and assumes the presence of want or economic need.

God's judgment after the fall expressed the change in human relations to the world that was manifested by the violent entry of an economic element: "The earth is accursed for humankind" (Gen. 3:17). It became a stagnant object of economy opposing humankind, it produces "thorns and thistles" for them, while they are doomed "to be nourished by it with pain" (of course here "nourishment" embraces a whole complex of relations of humans to nature). After admitting the principle of magism into their relation to the world, they surrendered themselves to its authority, and this is confirmed by God's sentence. Nature resembles a hostile force armed with hunger and death, and *all* human life receives the aftertaste of economy, is captive to the vanity of empty and impotent elements.

What is economy in its mystical and metaphysical essence? I have already had occasion to give a forceful answer to these questions in a special study[72] and there is no need to reproduce that analysis here again. We will only stay with the question of the meaning of economy in world history, or of history as economy.

Originally humans were given an existence *free of charge* — through eating "the fruits from the tree of life." Although called to cherish and tend God's garden they were not doomed to idleness, but their labor in paradise was not forced but had the inspired character of loving-creative relation to the world. From "white magi" humans turned into slaves of their labor, and the loftiness of their calling was made dark by their captivity: economic labor is *gray magic* in which the elements of white and black magic are inseparably mixed, the forces of light and darkness, of being and nonbeing, and this mixture already hides in itself the source of constant and agonizing contradictions, puts its very essence on the sharp point of antinomy.

The economic, i.e., active-laboring influence of human beings on nature, is based on their central position in the universe, which is not lost even after the fall. It is sophianic in its deepest foundation, although it is a sophianicity that was clothed in magism and covered with the crust of matter and natural necessity. Everything economic in its coarse or fine sense is utilitarian; it pursues a practical goal that is limited by the interests of terrestrial being. All economic tasks, no matter how broad they might be, belong to the surface of *this* world, the current eon. In all of its ramifications economy is equally subject to the power of nothing, which has actualized itself in the world. Therefore all of its achievements, having a positive basis in the creative forces of being, carry in them an ineradicable seal of this power. This modus of being finds its expression also in the power of temporality, i.e., of history. In this sense one can say that economy is substantially historical; it is connected with temporality, with the changeableness inherent in everything historical.

An internal contradiction, with which "gray magic" is being eaten away, is the discrepancy of its foundation and its actual state — the sophianicity of its root and the anti-sophianicity of its existence. Economy is and can only be creative activity, as is every human undertaking. But economy is at the same time the slavery of necessity, need, and self-interest, incompatible with creativity and inspiration. In its gray color the paints entering into its mixture pulsate by turns: at one time bright tones flare up, at another time dark tones condense. The contradictory nature of economy, on which its fateful limitedness depends, comes to full light in the contrasting of economy and art in their basic aspirations. Both the one and the other are sophianic in their foundation, albeit each in its own way and in a different degree, which is why they cannot be finally parted. They invite parallels as two guises or modes of human creativity. What are these modalities? The aesthetic relation is usually accompanied by a practical disinterest, a lack of self-interest. Art has no business with utilitarian appraisals of this world, for it is fascinated by the beauty of a different, empyrean world and strives to make it tangible. It shows what the soul thirsts and longs for, by revealing the creation in the light of the Transfiguration. Its voice is like a

The Human Being

call from another world, news from afar. For this mysterious force, for this grace of art its object, exactly that in which the heavenly blue was reflected, has a comparatively second-rate significance. A single white ray of beauty exists — the light of Tabor which breaks into the seven-hued rainbow of art. True, art also has its technical side, its economic side. But the achievement of art, the very work of beauty, is *not* a creation of this technique, its regular result, as in economy. By itself even intense economic labor is not capable of producing a work of art, and no effort of will and labor can create an artist.

In its own sphere economy is technical and subject to laws, while art in its own sphere is not subject to laws and is miraculous. A work of art is created by the inspiration of beauty, and it does not admit proof, but convinces by its appearance alone, sovereignly free of logical deductions. Every true work of art is in this sense a miracle, and first of all for the one who accomplished it, for he accomplished it not by his own power, not in his psychological limitedness but by being expelled from it into the mysterious deep of his essence. Only with such vision generally speaking can something *be created* (and not only in art but also in philosophy and science), and on the contrary true creativity is not reached along the economic-technical path with its regular continuity, for nonconformity to laws and discontinuity are its distinctive trait. The charms of art are dispatched rarely and sparingly, but in the depth of every human soul is hidden its thirst, and consequently its artistic endowment. Artistic perception of the world is not the result of aesthetic concupiscence or pretentious mannerism, because it can be combined even with an entirely distinct and modest artistic self-awareness, but it has a deeper foundation in human nature. One can say that *art is a symptom* and a symptom of infinite significance besides. Every human thirsts to see heavenly azure. Plato's Eros is the son of Porus and Penia, and one can experience creative eros not only in the aspect of Porus but also of Penia, of the thirst and torment of a creativity that does not give birth. The hungry are satisfied at the marriage banquet of the Lamb, and only those who do not hunger are not capable of being satisfied.

And so, art is erotic and inspired, economy is prosaic and regular; thus are they opposed in their specific aspirations. But this difference has yet another expression. Economic labor is might — the magic of this world; art, however, is powerless and unrequited in the face of the world. Economy operates actively on the world, with its pick and hoe it loosens and plows up again its "earth," while art leaves it undisturbed and only builds its special world of beauty on the earth or above the earth. "Wealth," "civilization," and its science, industry, war are created by economy; in this sense history is made by it, as philosophizing economic magism, "economic materialism" proclaims. Art remains a fleeting guest in this world, which it only makes uneasy with the news of a different world.

> What use is there in it? Like some cherub
> He brings down to us a few songs of paradise,
> So that having awakened wingless desire
> In us, children of dust, he flies away afterwards.[73]

A ray of beauty gilds those specks of dust that cross its capricious path, but how much more gray and tired life without illumination seems which art is powerless to transform all the same; Salieri the toiler involuntarily begins to envy Mozart "the idle ne'er-do-well." If art treats economy haughtily and contemptuously for its thrifty utilitarianism and lack of creative inspiration, then economy looks patronizingly on art for the impotence of its reverie and the involuntary parasitism in the face of economic need. In the name of its otherworldly kingdom, art frees itself from bearing economic concerns, but at the same time is itself unable to be liberated from economic needs. Remaining on earth and in the conditions of earth, it despises that earth and its labor, without which the growing green tree of human life would wither. Such is the natural antagonism between economy and art — the result of a dual and incomplete world. Pushkin was profoundly aware of this. He put words of perplexity before the unearthly power and earthly impotence of art in his sunny favorite, Mozart, the Muses' naïve and pure chosen one.

> If only everyone felt the power
> Of harmony! But no: then the world
> Could not exist; no one would begin
> To worry about the needs of life here below,
> Everyone would hand themselves over to free art!
> There are few of us chosen ones, idle lucky ones
> Who shun despicable profit,
> We priests of the beautiful alone.[74]

Hostile repulsion and mutual attraction, rivalry, even some seeming envy, exist simultaneously between economy and art. If a certain aspiration for artistic style is inherent in economy in all of its forms, from top to bottom, so art also rivals economy in its might. Before it the temptation to become magical arises, to acquire power over this world, with which it is connected through its matter that receives artistic form. Besides, the servant of art stands in a more intimate relation to it than does a landowner or natural scientist, for they want to gain mastery of it, whereas the artist wants to convince and make it obedient to his design. If he consciously or unconsciously alters the sublime task of art — which is to illuminate matter with beauty, by showing it in the light of Transfiguration — and begins to seek support in *this* world, then art too takes on the features of economy, even if of a special, refined type; it becomes artistic magic; magism bursts into it all the more — whether in the guise of premeditated orchestral sonorities, compositions in paint, verbal consonances, and so on. It is possible to gain mastery of the forces of this world and its charms not only with machines and chemistry, but also with sound and color, just as it is conceivable to shake its physical foundations not only with dynamite but also with music whose different rhythms are perhaps capable of killing like an electric current. Unnoticeably for himself, an artist can perpetrate a substitution and turn his art into a special artistic magic. This temptation of magism has always stood before art, but it gains a particular significance for the present day.

On the other hand economy (in the broad sense) also feels itself to be creative activity and, at a certain prominence of achievement, begins to be a little embarrassed of its thriftiness like the brands of slavery; for this reason it seeks possible approximations to art, it premeditatedly and consciously aestheticizes. But this bond of economy and art is not in any way at all only its own kind of economic decadence; on the contrary it is better to assume that in an age of economism and capitalism it has proved to be abnormally weakened, which explains the springing up of premeditated, far-fetched aestheticism.

Insofar as economy contains an element of creativity, if only of the lowest order, it really does converge with art. It never can be limited to purely utilitarian tasks, but strives towards beauty or at least prettiness as it resolves them. Therefore every economic epoch has its own artistic style, in which the spirit of this epoch is reflected, a national taste, an artistic succession or school and the like. The loss of an artistic style by economy is felt as its spiritual sickness, as a result of which an amplified striving to ennoble and interpret economic labor artistically emerges (as is known, this defines the pathos of the social preaching of J. Ruskin and his disciples). Every epoch has an aesthetic minimum, the observance of which becomes economically necessary, as a familiar artistic taste is economically obligatory. In addition it is possible that economy draws closer to art not from within, seeking a higher measure for itself in it, but it wants to use it for itself externally, having turned it into one of its tools in the goals of "the arts industry." It definitely seeks not beauty but prettiness, aesthetic comfort, serving an exquisite luxury and gourmandism. Such is the aestheticism of daily life, proper to our epoch, for example; but then it just cannot find its own style. Beauty in daily life cannot become customary and routine, which only prettiness can be: beauty is hieratic, it is a holiday, not the workaday routine, and life in this world cannot be a holiday pure and simple. The sublimity and seriousness of the spirit places its stamp of strictness and beauty even on the artistic way of life, while the pursuit of an aesthetic of the everyday is evidence rather of the decline of a feeling for beauty, even with the refinement of taste.

In this mutual pretension of art and economy, in the striving of art to become efficacious, and of economy to become artistic, is recounted their initial unity. In its light they are only different sides of one and the same integral life process, of life in harmony and beauty, and it itself becomes the continually occurring creative activity of beauty, a work of art. Economy here does not differ from art, so that neither economy nor art exists in its abstractions. One can consider the Edenic state of the progenitors before the fall to be like this, and this is what the internal, ontological norm of human creativity is like as well. While still in paradise the human being was entrusted with working and tending the earth, was called from the beginning to activity and creativity in the world. Activity was free of compulsion, and for this reason particularized tasks could not exist for art and economy where there was no art and non-art, or economy and non-economy. Such a synthesis of economy and art, an active, creative life in beauty, was pointed out in advance for Adam and Eve. This original unity of life split apart after the fall, when the captivity of the flesh and the necessity of economy were established, and in the same manner art was doomed to a particular existence. Two channels of thought, two perceptions of the world, took shape: "economic materialism" proper to the "mob," and the idealistic aestheticism of the "poets," and "poet and mob" became hostilely opposed, *both* being right. But the human consciousness is not reconciled with this cleavage of life and yearns for the lost unity and integrity. And each of the isolated elements, economy and art, wants to splash out of their own banks.

> Everything strives in divine valor
> To outgrow itself. . . .[75]

3. Economy and Theurgy

Economy wants to outgrow itself not only by stretching out into the side of art, but also by being stretched in its own proper element, in its dynamic. It strives to become not only *one of* the aspects of life, but the sole or at least the determining one, not acknowledging above itself any extra-economic or supra-economic court. As a result *economism* is obtained as a special way of perceiving the world and a worldview. We have its classic expression in "economic materialism," which is multifaceted and has many forms, even if it is connected with the name of one of its more daring proponents, Karl Marx. The human being feels himself in the world only as a managing subject ("economic man") for whom economy is pure commercialism, while the economic instinct or egoism is assumed as the basis of life. This egoism is only the partial manifestation of the general metaphysical egoism of the creature. Economy, founded on egoism, inevitably suffers from disharmony and conflict, personal and of the group (of the class), and it is impossible finally to harmonize this economic egoism by leading it to the shores of "solidarity," about which socialist thinkers ponder. Economic egoism is an elemental force that necessarily needs not only external regulation but also internal, spiritual-ascetic regulation; left to its own devices and liberated from any restraint, it becomes a destructive force. With respect to economy, both its fastidious negation and complete enslavement by it would be simultaneously incorrect. Economic labor is imposed on us like a penalty for sin, and we must accept it as an "obedience,"[76] obligatory for all humanity. Lordly disgust with respect to economy has nothing in common with that freedom from it which the gospel teaches: it wants not disdain but spiritual overcoming, a way out of this world with its necessity.[77] But economy must not become self-satisfied, being the goal for itself, as economism desires: enrichment for the sake of enrichment. Economy must keep the meaning only of a means for a worthy life, with its religious ideal being here the authentic criterion. By means of this ideal and the self-regulation of economy connected with it, its *spirit* takes shape and defines itself from within them without being fixed to definite forms. The style of economy corresponds to the spiritual style of an epoch (e.g., a fairly transparent bond exists between capitalism and Neo-European humanism).

In economy two tasks are absolved, a twofold struggle is led: against natural and societal poverty, economic and social. The struggle against poverty (in the language of economists "the development of productive forces") is the general obedience of labor imposed on humanity as the "curse" of the earth. "Social politics" is like this, directed towards overcoming or mitigating egoism in human relations. Can both tasks be definitively absolved? Can poverty be defeated "by the development of productive forces" and can the social question be solved by societal reform, as the socialists believe? It is obvious that the second task is subordinate to the first or, at least, cannot be solved separately from the first. But what are the limits for the development of productive forces, and do they exist? Does economy have not only a history but also an eschatology? Can it outgrow itself by passing into a super-economy so that the economic epoch of history ends (K. Marx's *Vorgeschichte*)? May it be that the human being, having economic support in the cosmos and being the demiurge in it, is called to become the cosmourge, the resurrector of deceased life, the guardian of those now present and the godparent of those in the future? May it be that the microcosm — the human being — through economic labor expels death from the macrocosm — the universe — and removes the curse from the earth?

In approaching this series of questions we enter the circle of ideas of the deep Russian thinker N. F. Fedorov. In his *Philosophy of the Common Task*, he essentially gave a grandiose system to a philosophy of economy that is in truth its *apotheosis*. He pointed out to it the possibility of such achievements which no one prior to Fedorov had dreamed of, namely he set for it the task of resurrecting the dead through work, of the economic reproduction and restoration of life. *Fedorov turns economy into theurgy*, or rather, he merges the one and the other to the point of being indistinguishable, insofar as for him resurrecting the dead ceases to be theurgic but becomes entirely economic-magic.

The Human Being

It is necessary to single out the very core of the question concerning resurrecting as it is posed in *Philosophy of the Common Task*. What is life and what is death? A lack of clarity in this fundamental question introduces regrettable ambiguity and indefiniteness to the whole doctrine of Fedorov. In answer to it two possibilities begin to take shape: either the human organism is only a machine, a mechanical automaton and death is only its demolition and corruption, or a spirit lives in it that quickens the body and is united with it, and for that reason death is an unnatural dissolution of the union of spirit and body.

It is fully evident that the first, materialistic hypothesis, strictly speaking does not admit of the idea of resurrecting, i.e., of the return to life *of the same* living creature. The identity of the person resurrected with the previously living one is established by the unity of the supratemporal and immortal human spirit, which quickens the body, while individuality is communicated to the body through the means of the animal soul. Let us allow that thanks to the "regulation of nature" i.e., by the economic path of labor, sons were successful in gathering from planetary space all the atoms of the decomposed bodies of deceased fathers and managed to ignite life in the re-created bodies. And let us further allow that these bodies were exact repetitions of the organism of the deceased according to external and internal composition and that they possessed consciousness of the bond and even of the identity with their previously living doubles. What can be more horrifying than this infernal fabrication, and what can be more baneful than such a counterfeit of resurrecting than these automatically moving dolls that possess a complete resemblance with those organisms once living but now broken and decayed? An overwhelming mystical horror and repugnance arise from the idea that we can meet some sort of automatic doubles, forgeries of our loved ones who are like them in everything; that we can caress them, love them, kiss them: the whole thing is in line with the gloomiest and most fantastic imaginings of an Edgar Allen Poe or E. T. A. Hoffman. It would indeed be a satanic mockery of human love. Resurrecting proposes not only the fullest likeness, but also numerical identity: not two identical copies of one and the same model, in essence entirely alien to each other, but the restoration of the very same, single life only temporarily interrupted. Of course, *such* was the idea of N. F. Fedorov, who was a deeply faithful Christian, and from his faith emerged his "project" and the whole pathos of his doctrine. Therefore a materialistic conception of his idea, its *reductio ad absurdum*, would be repudiated by our thinker with anger and indignation who foreseeing its possibility feared it beforehand. One need not be surprised if the idea of a scientific resurrecting of the fathers has still not appeared even once among materialists who are generally inclined to reverie and have a weakness for utopias. There is not enough interest in this among them, for what sense is there in re-creating a likeness if the original is all the same annihilated by death? True, if they were more consistent and listened more attentively to the

Human History

logic of their own doctrine, they would be able to observe that even in the limits of this life, with the constant renewal of the material organism by the stream of particles flowing in and out of it, and by the constant change of psychic content in consciousness, the unity and continuity of life are established only by its supratemporal principle, connecting its separate moments in a single flowing time; and without this principle the life of an organism would turn into a series of states, constantly changing and strung like beads on the thread of time.

Therefore the idea of resurrecting is possible only in the context of belief in immortality, and Fedorov's idea must be understood in such a way that by means of re-creating the bodies of the fathers through the labor of the sons their departed souls too shall be summoned to new life. In accordance with this understanding, only the body is properly subject to resurrecting, whereas the soul returns to it in virtue of some natural necessity, as soon as it has been restored. A distinctive combination of materialism and spiritualism is obtained to which a purely mechanical conception of both death and resurrection corresponds. According to this opinion, the soul, while it is not yet restored to its body, is in a state of some sort of *anabiōsis*, of pure potentiality. In this situation the possibility is excluded beforehand that the soul, having passed through the gates of death, in general is not able to return to an expired body which is destroyed by death, and quicken it with itself, for *it* has lost the capability of quickening a body; the body alone did not lose the force of life. Therefore the resurrecting of the fathers by the sons is in general impossible once the soul itself must resurrect its body or receive from God the power to do this. No one else can replace it in this. In other words, death, in which Fedorov was inclined to see in general only a type of accident and misunderstanding or a pedagogical method, is an act that crosses too far beyond the limits of this world for it to have been possible to handle it with "the regulation of nature" alone, with methods of physically resurrecting a body, however refined they might be, even with the enlistment of the vital forces of human sperm for the purpose of resurrecting or reverse generation of fathers by sons (for which there are indications in Fedorov's doctrine). The soul can return only to the transfigured body of the resurrection, and it is of no use to sew together again the decrepit and unraveled "leathern garment" of a deceased body from the scraps.

Resurrecting, like birth, is a creative act of Divine omnipotence by which is returned to the soul of the departed its life-giving force, the capability of creating for itself a body, corresponding to its nature; it is the outpouring of the life-giving power of God into the human soul, i.e., a theurgic act. Therefore Fedorov's "project" of an economic, magical resurrecting by work, which represents in this manner a certain *metabasis eis allo genos*, transgresses by an unwarranted mingling of the spheres of economy and theurgy. In this respect, Fedorov's general antipathy towards the miraculous, i.e., the truly theurgic, is typical, in which with his economic point of view he sees first of all something gratuitous. He does not fully value in this situation the whole conditional character and relativity of economy, so essentially linked with the current state of the world, with the malediction weighing heavily on the earth and with the general "groaning of the creation." The lapse into magism was at once the sin by which this dependence of the human on economy was created, and it cannot be overcome by the forces of the same magism on its proper plane. The mortality of life is the result of the unwarranted incursion of magism which disturbs the harmony of life in the spirit-bearing body, whence that inertia of matter arose, which is constantly being surmounted, but can never be overcome definitively by economic labor. Fedorov takes the current state of life as the only possible one on the whole and wants only an expansion of the magical might of the human through the "regulation of nature" directed towards the goals of "the common task," i.e., resurrecting. But he thereby thinks of resurrecting precisely *this* flesh and on *this* earth, otherwise it is hard to understand his idea (although he states his indignation when he met a similar conception of it in a letter of V. Soloviev). Such resurrecting in principle is equivalent to an indefinite prolongation of human life by the removal of death. It is typical that in Fedorov's constructions the experience of life beyond the grave and its meaning are seemingly not considered at all, all those changes the soul endures in its isolation from the body, its growth in this mysterious and unknown state. It is permissible to think that the resurrected Lazarus, although he had passed the gates of death, was by God's pleasure held in something of the *initial* moments of the postmortem path. "Lazarus our friend has fallen asleep"[78] — these words of the Lord are not merely allegory; they point to the special character of Lazarus's death, more like sleep, a temporary halt to life, than the final separation of body and soul.[79] In the opposite case his return to *this* life would be impossible other than on condition that he completely forgot what he experienced beyond the grave. Lazarus came to himself as if from a faint, and the miracle consisted in his unusual return to life. Therefore between Lazarus's death and Christ's death on the cross there is a qualitative difference. The Lord "did not only fall asleep" like Lazarus (or Jairus's daughter), but he tasted death to the end; he went down into hell and passed through all the bounds of life beyond the grave in his three-day abiding in the bowels of the earth. He returned from there, so to say, from the other end, by passing through the whole circle beyond the grave (thus, according to Egyptian belief, the boat of the god Ra sinks into the kingdom of the dead in the west and in the course of the night passes through it in its entirety, coming out in the east).

Immortality is not only the absence of death or its mere removal, something negative, it is also a positive force connected with the spiritual quality of the body where the spirit gains complete possession of the flesh and permeates it; in this way matter, the source of death and mortality, is abolished. Fedorov, going more boldly and radically in the direction of Mechnikov,[80] strives for scientific immortality by accepting in its stead the absence of death or an undetermined continuation of life. He wants the victory over death only as over a moment of mortal life, and not over mortality as its general quality. Fedorov all the time is thinking of the raising of Lazarus, not of the resurrection of Christ, of a revived corpse originally decomposed but newly re-created by means of science, not of the resurrection of the spiritual body glorified and transfigured. For this reason the resurrecting of the fathers, in accord with Fedorov's project, even if it were realizable, is far removed from the resurrection of the dead expected by Christian faith; it is situated on a different plane from it, just as the raising of Lazarus and other miraculous raisings are, although they were accomplished not by natural-magical, economic means but by way of a miracle. The resurrection of Christ receives in Fedorov primarily the projective significance of a pedagogical tool and encouraging example. On the whole the perspective of a resurrection not by work but miraculous and consequently gratuitous can be envisaged only as some sort of failure of history resulting from an unaccomplished "common task": humanity must consciously aspire to make do without the miraculous, transcendent resurrection, by substituting the economic for it. There are many profound truths in what Fedorov says in grounding his ideas about the familial character of humanity, about the love of sons for their fathers, and about the cult of ancestors, as a substantial part of every religion. Incidentally, one cannot but be struck by the closeness of the basic and most intimate motif of Fedorov's religion — religious love for deceased fathers — to the essence of *Egyptian* religion, all of which grows out of reverence for the dead: its whole cult and ritual is an elaborated funeral rite.[81] Fedorov's religion is a seeming Christian variant of an Egyptian worldview.

However, if one takes not the whole content of this profound doctrine in its complete configuration, but only its central idea — "the project" of resurrecting — it is not hard to see that the problem of the *limits of economy* is posed in it. And in solving it, Fedorov falls into obvious Monophysitism, advancing one-sidedly the human element as replacing and ousting the divine force. He wants the human being, by realizing the will of God in creation, to make do as far as possible without God and apart from God, with the rupture of the divine-human unity, indivisible and unconfused. For him God is a transcendent norm, a law, a model, an example, and the human being must make do with its human strengths. For him Christ is only the Son of Man; Christ, "who will come on the clouds of heaven with power and great glory," the judge and resurrector, is more a threat, an undesired *deus ex machina* than the One to whom "the Spirit and the Bride" cry "yes, come!" The economic mage, enlightened by the will to make brothers and raise the fathers, feels himself a theurgist and does not wish for a different theurgy. Raising the dead, set as the ultimate goal for economic will, is on the whole a false task, for in it on the plane of temporality is placed what is *beyond* time, at least, beyond *this* time of our eon. The flesh that is accessible to the influence of economic labor will not resurrect in its current form; the threshold of death or "change" separates it from resurrection, a change that is equivalent to death for those people who have not tasted death. "I tell you a mystery: we shall not all die, but we shall all be changed, suddenly *(en atomōi)*, in the blink of an eye, at the last trumpet" (1 Cor. 15:51-52). Here is that "change" which in essence is a new creative act of God on the human being and which economic labor cannot accomplish, and therefore Fedorov's "project," however far the "regulation of nature" might reach, is unrealizable by human and natural forces.

But the idea of N. F. Fedorov can still be defended, although not in such a straightforward and crude form. It may be that this thought corresponds more to his lofty religious spirit: resurrection of the dead is a divine-human act requiring the joining of divine grace and human action, and by acknowledging fully the divine side of resurrecting, humans must demonstrate their participation in it with their own effort coming from the opposite direction, with their own aspiration for resurrecting. Practically it alone exists for humans as depending on their will and effort. In it people realize their divine power; they show themselves as godhumans, Christs, and the individual Christ, the Lord Jesus, is replaced in this original socioeconomic band of Khlysty by a collective Christ, by humanity which performs the "common task." Separate features of the "project" correspond to this interpretation. So, evidently, it presumes a consistent and gradual raising of the fathers by the sons from generation to generation. Its separate acts are divided, obviously, by a certain interval of time, needed so that those raised could be re-educated and equipped for the new historical conditions in which their resurrection will be found. In a word, resurrecting enters into the historical process; it is evolution, not a catastrophe that appears "suddenly, in the blink of an eye," and interrupts historical time. On the whole it is unclear whether or not there is any place in N. F. Fedorov's notions for *metahistory,* for the "life of the future age," separated by an ontological catastrophe from the present eon. Historical humanity, according to Fedorov's thought, ought not to leave anything to the work of the Son of Man, except for his good example, and Christian revelation of the Holy Trinity for him is reduced to the commandment of resurrecting, to the glory of universal kinship, the supreme form of which is given in the life of the Holy Trinity, as a divine family. This evolutionary monism, although it begins with the doctrine of the incarnation of Jesus, in fact abolishes a living faith in the Crucified God. From it remains only the threatening perspective of a violently miraculous resurrection of the dead at the end of this age, which humanity waits for in the event of its nonfulfillment of "the common task." With such a failure of history people will be raised by God, many to judgment and condemnation. But humanity is warned precisely against this failure; it must make do with its own strengths. In essence this doctrine is the last word of modern European humanism (although Fedorov himself kept aloof from it). In the face of its grandeur the utopias of Mechnikov, Fourier, Marx, and others seem timid and indecisive.

However, the question of the destinies of souls beyond the grave is sidestepped even in this interpretation of Fedorov's doctrine. Without a stretch and forced interpretations it is difficult to combine with this the church's teaching on remembrance of the dead in prayer and its efficacy, on the preaching in Hades, and in general the whole doctrine of the state of the soul beyond the grave which can be established on the basis of church tradition, in particular, the liturgy. The very thought of the deceased being violently awakened from their rest or of the world being flooded by some sort of vampires, incarnated denizens from the astral world, contains something nauseating and mystically loathsome, resembling necromancy. The magnificent scene from the Old Testament automatically comes to mind here: Saul and the Witch of Endor. Saul begs her to summon the shadow of the prophet Samuel, i.e., to perform by means of conjuring and sorcery his apparent raising.

According to the text of the biblical narrative, it seems most natural of all to presume that the Witch of Endor did not possess, of course, the power to raise the dead, but as a medium she could revive an "astral corpse" (larva) by magical means; in this way the impression of resurrecting is achieved. Therefore in its essence necromancy was deception, because no real communication with the world beyond the grave was obtained as a result of it; only its semblance was attained (similar to what may happen in spiritism). But in the given case, to her own horror, in response to her incantation, in keeping with a special regard of God, the spirit of Samuel himself actually appeared to her, from which she immediately reasoned that King Saul himself and not some simple mortal had visited her. He had previously driven "witches and soothsayers" out of his country and appeared to her only under the cover of night, disguised. At first, when the witch expressed fear of incurring punishment from Saul and he assured her of her safety, this did not arouse in her the suspicion that Saul himself was speaking with her. "Then the woman asked, whom do you want me to bring forth for you? And he answered, bring me Samuel. And the woman recognized Saul" (a typical detail: only she, as a "clairvoyant" sees the astral shadow, while at first Saul evidently sees nothing and begins to see only later). "And she cried out loudly" (evidently she herself was struck by the reality of the vision, which she was not expecting). "And the woman addressed Saul, saying why did you deceive me? You are Saul" (this became clear to her from the fact that the authentic spirit of the prophet could appear only to Saul, but not merely an astral specter). "And the king said to her, 'Do not fear, tell me what you see.' And the woman answered, 'I see something like a god coming up out of the earth.' — 'What does he look like?' Saul asked her. She said, 'A very old man is coming up from the earth, dressed in a long robe'" (she really did see something from the world beyond the grave — "coming up from the earth" — and not an astral phantom, which is where her dread came from). "Then Saul knew that it was Samuel, and he fell with his face to the ground and worshiped" (as to a king anointed precisely by Samuel himself, the lucidity that excludes any kind of wavering is here proper to Saul. And on the whole in the tale itself there is not the least indication that Saul was deceived). "And Samuel said to Saul, 'For what purpose are you troubling me to come out?' And Saul answered, 'I am very burdened,'" etc. (1 Sam. 28:11-15).

The souls of the deceased "who rest in God," remain in God's hand like the souls of the unborn. They are beyond the bounds of our time, and go their mysterious way there unknown to us. And the human will is not given to "trouble them to come out," to deprive them of a place of rest by all possible methods of regulating nature.[82] The particular and gradual raising of humanity, generation after generation, even if it were possible in an economic-technical sense, is a religious absurdity.

Let us listen to what is said in the *Apocalypse* concerning the mystery of *the first resurrection*. "And I saw thrones and those sitting on them to whom it was given to judge, and the souls of those beheaded for their witness of Jesus and for the word of God, and who did not worship the beast or its image, and did not receive the mark on their forehead and on their arm. They had revived — *ezēsan* — and they reigned with Christ for a thousand years. The remainder of the dead did not revive until the thousand years were up. This is the first resurrection. Blessed and holy is the one who takes part in the first resurrection. The second death has no authority over them, but they will be priests of God and Christ and they shall reign with Him for a thousand years" (Rev. 20:4-6).

Here it is a matter of some sort of anticipatory "first" resurrection which, although it frees from the "second death," i.e., from the definitive rejection, evidently only anticipates the general resurrection and differs from it qualitatively; at least, those who had part in the first resurrection are not exempt from it. Concerning the latter it says that their *souls revived* and reigned with Christ. One can think that here it is a matter not of a bodily but only of a spiritual resurrection. God leads the souls out of the place of their repose by a creative act, revives them in giving them power in a special way to take part in life, "to reign" i.e., to direct it, being at the same time "priests of God and Christ." By this resurrection of souls their open appearance in a body is in no way assumed as yet for all; on the contrary one can rather think that these revived souls do not yet have bodies and receive power to shape them for themselves only at the universal resurrection. Such is the position of the saints whom the church entreats as alive and able to render their help. In the "first resurrection," which is accomplished in parallel with the confinement of bound Satan, evidently, the manifest participation of the deceased in the affairs of the living will be especially revealed, their leadership and assistance on the paths of history. But all this can remain entirely unnoticed beyond the limits of the Church.

And so, the "first resurrection," about which the *Apocalypse* speaks, represents to a certain degree the antithesis of what Fedorov's project is about, a gradual resurrecting by labor: there, to all appearances, a psychic-spiritual resurrection is proposed, but not yet a bodily one, while here it is precisely a bodily one, and only a bodily resurrection which however must be spiritual. And it is entirely permissible to pose the question: Should one aspire to *such* a resurrecting?

In this way, Fedorov's "project" understood even in the broadest and most undetermined sense as a general idea of the *participation* of the human being in the resurrection of the dead, preserves its basic particularity, and differs from economism and magism. That faith in economy which is displayed in contemporary economism, and in particular in "economic materialism," receives here its most radical expression. *In one* of its facets, namely insofar as it is bound with the economic "regulation of nature," Fedorov's "project" is economic materialism, carried out with such resoluteness that Marx proved not to be up to it by a long shot. Of course, this depends on the fact that Marx, although acknowledged as the father of "economic materialism," did not even set for himself the fundamental question for economism concerning the nature of economy: he conceived it only in technical-legal or mercantile-bookkeeping categories borrowed from political economy. In addition he was dependent on French materialism in his general philosophical views. For this reason Marx was not able to interpret to the end his own economic ideas, something however that N. F. Fedorov was fully up to doing, thanks to the breadth of scope of his religious-economic idea. Fedorov's doctrine is precisely what Marxism has dreamed of confusedly, which constitutes its unconscious but intimate motif. If these ideas in Marxism assumed an ideationally beggarly and off-putting vulgar character, in Fedorov they assumed a nobility and beauty thanks to the lofty religious pathos of his doctrine. But in virtue of this completeness the whole fallaciousness of economic eschatology was made all the clearer, which only in a novel way reproduces the old Jewish messianism, the enticement by the kingdom of this world. It is the seduction of the first diabolical temptation: "If you are the Son of God, order these stones to become bread" (Luke 4:3), i.e., show yourself as the economic messiah, the "son of man," who by the power "of the regulation of nature" restores to life and resurrects. But this appeal here is addressed no longer to the One, not to the Son of God and Son of Man, but to all human sons who are called upon to reveal their divine sonship by the "common task" of the regulation of nature and by its fruit — the revivification of dead matter, the conversion of stones into bread, and raising of the dead by labor.

The Human Being

And so, must the "project of the common task" proclaimed by N. F. Fedorov be definitively and irrevocably rejected as a mirage and "charm"? But the soul resolutely opposes such an attitude toward it, and it would be an act not only of disrespect towards our wise man, but also of misunderstanding of the prophetic and new that he made known to the world. Only, the "project" itself must be understood not according to the letter, but according to the spirit, not naturalistically but religiously-spiritually. In Fedorov a new feeling for life was conceived; a new daring and pathos, a ray of the resurrection caught fire. The whole life of this zealot, devoted to the nurturing *of a single* idea, the "project" of resurrecting, in itself is a *symptom,* and one of paramount spiritual importance besides, and one needs to know how to interpret it. The "project" is not only the last word of economism, which has capitulated before the inertness of sinful flesh, but at the same time a first *prayer* to God for resurrection, a first call of the earth to heaven for the raising of the dead, and one is happy to think that a Fedorov with his "project" has already *existed* in the world. In the Church everyone is alive, it prays for the dead as for the living; however, in this the great gulf separating them is not destroyed, about which the parable of Dives and Lazarus speaks. The "project" of Fedorov is the first word in history concerning the resurrecting of the dead, even if cloaked in an incongruous form. A herald ahead of his time is involuntarily doomed to infelicities when expressing his presentiments. Fedorov belongs to a number of those watchmen who peer intensely into the eschatological gloom: "They shout to me from Seir: Guard, how much night? Guard, how much night? The guard replies: morning approaches, but it is still night" (Isa. 21:11-12).

Together with the feeling of having reached the fullness of time and of the impending end, do not a new prayer and prophetic inspiration for resurrection begin to burn in our hearts? The prayer of the end, "Yea, come, Lord Jesus!" includes in its concrete fullness that cry of the creature, does it not? Does not something similar crop up in the church's experience (although one should not make it crude and anticipate it ahead of time in an artificial and forced way)? And so, *according to the letter* Fedorov's project with its economic enthusiasm of "the common task" had to be rejected, but as a movement of the heart and will, as a prayer and inspiration, it is symptomatically important and dear. Therefore an involuntary contradiction is felt in the final relation to Fedorov's doctrine; for all the unacceptability and even monstrousness of the project it cannot be simply rejected, for something intimate and necessary is bound with it.[83]

As it is connected with the malediction of the earth, economy *does not have* in itself any eschatological tasks that would go beyond the bounds of the mortal life of this age, and its domain pertains exclusively to it. For this reason too it cannot be completed in its own proper limits but must be torn asunder, like human life. This being so, one must not forget that temporality has its depth that also enters into eternity, where time is integrated although by means inaccessible to us for the present. But in the perspective of time economy is bad infinity that has no completion. So far as history is created in economy and through economy (understood in the broad sense), so is the historical *body* of humanity created in and through it, to which it belongs "to be changed" in the resurrection, with the whole world being that potential body for the human being. By economic labor humans realize this world for themselves, organize their world body, and really feel it by actualizing the power that was theirs from the beginning. Even in the role of master a human being preserves a shimmer of the glory of regal Adam. But as a result of his fall he does not so much master the world as the world does him, for the shroud of materiality was hung heavily over the world, and his body was clothed in "leathern garments." In the realm of economic behavior the gospel decrees as the ideal not freedom *in* and *through* economy, but freedom *from* economy; it summons to belief in miracle in spite of the world's inertness, it exhorts us to be the miracle-workers, not the mechanics of the universe, healers, not medics. Economy is only permitted by it — it is reconciled with it as the burden of life of this age, but nothing more. All the efforts of economism are directed by the force of circumstances towards the immortalization of the life of this world, to the denial of the end of the life both of a separate human person, and for the whole world. Scientific economic doctrines, and especially socialist ones, speak of this in various ways: under the guise of freedom in economy through the increase "of wealth" they want to consolidate the economic captivity of the human being, by promising to bring about a contradictory ideal of magical or economic freedom. This is why Christianity does not glorify might as the supreme freedom but weakness, not wealth but poverty, not the wisdom of this age with its economic magic, but "foolishness."

And so, on its own path economy does not have an eschatology, and when it attempts to enter on its path it falls into pseudo-eschatology; it chases a ghost, deceptive and false. This pseudo-eschatology is rooted in an incorrect estimate of economy, oblivious of its conditional character and relativity. Our age, marked out not only by an exceptional flowering of economic activity, but also by economism as spiritual self-consciousness, at the same time is distinctive by its intense economic eschatology. The latter darkens the religious consciousness not only of isolated thinkers but also of national masses, mystically estranged from the earth: such are the socialists, who have become the victim of frantic and blind pseudo-eschatology, in their state of frenzy reminiscent of the messianic expectations of the Jews in the Christian era. Now during the world war this tower of Babel of economism is being pulled down. It is becoming clear to everyone with eyes to see that here the most grandiose of the attempts to erect it until now suffer failure. The magical kingdom from this world has failed once again, and how good that it has failed! "Modern history" has not succeeded, but precisely through this failure, through a deepened experience of good and evil, a general crisis of history and the universe is being prepared. And the failure of all world history is also its greatest success,[84] for its goal is not in but beyond its limits; there the historical element calls and compels.

4. Art and Theurgy

Art stands hierarchically higher than economy, for its domain is situated on the border of two worlds. It gazes on otherworldly beauty and reveals it to this world; it does not feel itself stifled and is conscious of its ability to soar:

> How poor our language is! I want to and cannot . . .
> Convey to either friend or foe
> What rises violently in my breast like a transparent wave:
> Vain is the eternal languor of hearts!
> The wise man bows his venerable head
> Before this fateful lie.
> Only in you, poet, does the winged sound of a word
> Suffice for flight and suddenly fix
> The dark babbling of the soul and the unclear smell of grass.[85]

And not simply fix, but it also illuminates, transfigures in doing so.

> This leaf, because it has withered and fallen down
> Will blaze in hymns with eternal gold. . . .[86]

"Bestow your rose on a poet," and "in a moving verse you will find this eternally sweet-scented rose,"[87] for such is the power of poetry:

> Only you have fleeting daydreams
> Which are seen in the soul by old friends,
> Only you have fragrant roses
> Which are radiant with tears of rapture.

And this is valid of course not only for poetry but for art in general. It can immortalize the temporary, by looking at it in the light of eternity, of sophianic beauty. Beauty itself, of course, is prior to art ("only a song needs beauty, while beauty needs no song"),[88] but art, which reveals it, acquires in that manner an unfathomable depth. Its rhythms go into the breadth and depth, stirring up ever new waves. Beauty has in itself both power and persuasiveness. The power of art is not that it controls beauty but that in its artistic symbols it possesses the key that opens this depth: *a realibus ad realiora* [from the real to the more real]! For this reason a true work of art cannot remain locked up only in itself; in its effectiveness it calls to a life in beauty and gives prophetic witness about it. For this reason art itself does not in any way have a self-sufficing meaning, it is only a path towards the discovery of beauty. It is vital only in this movement, always *ad realiora*. For this reason it is itself also only a symbol, a call, a promise, a grand gesture, but — alas! — one which declines into powerlessness. For art, on a level with a regal vocation, hides in itself the consciousness of its powerlessness. It knows its limit and its relativity, and it must always be aware of it:

> Forget me, frenzied madman,
> Do not ruin my peace,
> I was created by your amorous soul,
> You love not a daydream.
> O, believe and know, faint-hearted dreamer
> That by being tormented and groaning
> The closer you are to your inspired dream
> The farther you are from me.[89]

Thus does "a dream" speak when set before the face of cruel reality, "the prose of life," in response to the poet's appeals. Everything stays in its place: "No, by force one cannot lift the heavy cover of gray skies."[90] And is not beauty a sweet illusion, and poetry a daydream, if art merely stirs up and beckons to the beautiful in the midst of an unbeautiful life, consoles but does not transfigure? From this self-consciousness is born

The Human Being

the cosmourgic yearning of art, the thirst for effectiveness arises: if beauty will sometime save the world, then art must be the instrument of this salvation. In each new creative act the artist opens his embraces ever wider, but the goddess slips away from them like an alluring phantom, leaving him in dumb despair, ready to break his melodious but powerless lyre. If the tragedy of economy which understands its boundaries consists in the awareness that it is prosaic, enthralled, and uninspired, the tragedy of art is its awareness of being powerless, of the terrible discord between the true loveliness of the world revealed to it and the ugliness and deformity present in it. Art does not save, does not alleviate the yearning of earthly being, but only consoles. But are its powerless consolations needed and worthy? One can admire works of art and be enamored of them, but only in order to feel all the more strongly the chains of "contemptible life." And it is impossible to love them with a living human love, for sculpted Galatea in her marble beauty is deprived of the warmth of muscles and blood all the same, and is a counterfeit.

Each creative act strives to become absolute not only according to its source, for it seeks to express in it the person's inexpressible nucleus that transcends every form of unmasking, but also according to its own aspiration, for it wants *to create* the world in beauty, to vanquish and prevail upon chaos through it. Instead, it saves and prevails only upon a chunk of marble (or another object of art) and the cosmourgic waves fall powerlessly in an atmosphere heavy from the exhalations of matter. For this reason the artist, even if magnificent achievements in art are given to him, experiences all the greater dissatisfaction as a creative person.[91] Creativity is a stony path of ascent where the heavy cross is laid on the shoulders of Simon of Cyrene against his will. One can be freed from tragedy and turn down the Lord's cross, refuse to participate in the self-crucifixion of the worldly, unenlightened I, but only at the price of a distinctive spiritual paralysis of the person. Instead of beauty one is left then to be content with prettiness, and once enamored of it, to become deaf to the commands of creativity; from a severe and exacting art one can arrange one's own special tiny little world according to a fastidious "canon" and be content with it. Aestheticism, as an expression of that kind of reconciliation and self-contentment, is the subtlest temptation of the spiritual bourgeoisie. The one who reveres beauty and does not admit its corruption can never quench his thirst, and it does not matter whether he himself possesses a gift for art or not. And he loves art more for that thirst than for the quenching.

Human History

> The Castalian spring with the wave of inspiration
> Gives drink to exiles in the world's steppe.

However as before the not to be muffled melancholy of banishment remains, which will abate only together with life:

> But a third spring, the cold spring of oblivion,
> It quenches more sweetly than all the ardor of the heart.[92]

Such are the confessions of our great poet, who by common opinion is full of joie de vivre and is clear as the sky of Greece, but like it too, knew all the power of insatiable melancholy.[93]

Art wants to become not only consoling but effective, not symbolic but transfiguring. The Russian soul was aware of this striving with special force and gave it prophetic expression in the sage word of Dostoevsky: *Beauty will save the world*. This same belief lay at the basis of V. Soloviev's doctrine concerning effective art, on which he conferred the name *theurgy*; unfortunately it has become firmly established in usage. Through this apparently only verbal definition of the tasks of art as theurgic, Soloviev did much harm to the precise understanding of the essence of the question itself, darkening and even distorting it (in spite of his own personal worldview besides). He directed the spiritual search onto the wrong path, and now it is necessary to return it anew to the point of departure and before all else to pose the fundamental question: Can one speak of theurgy, *theou ergon*, action of God, applied to *human* creativity? Surely one should distinguish the *action of God* in the world, even if it is carried out in the human being and through the human being (which is theurgy in the proper and precise sense of the word), from *human* action which is carried out by the power of divine sophianicity inherent in it. This anthropourgy — *anthrōpou ergon* — is for this reason also sophiurgy, *ergon ek Sophias*. The first is divine condescension, the second, human ascension; one comes from heaven to earth, the other from earth strives towards heaven. And both possibilities, theurgy and sophiurgy, ought to be distinguished as sharply as possible, whereas they are constantly confused, and thereby ambiguity and lack of clarity are created. In fact, what precisely is the topic when the "theurgic tasks of art" are spoken about and in what sense is it both possible and legitimate to assert them?

Theurgy is the action of God, the outpouring of his pardoning and saving grace on the human being. As such, it depends not on people, but on the will of God. In its essence, theurgy is inseparably linked with the incarnation of God; it is God's incarnation continuing in time and being accomplished without interruption, the unceasing action of Christ in humanity: "and lo, I am with you always until the close of the age" (Matt. 28:20). Christ laid an absolute and irrevocable foundation for theurgy and entrusted theurgic authority to the Church through the succession of grace communicated to the apostles: "Jesus said to them, peace be with you! As the Father sent Me, so I send you. And having said this, he breathed and said to them, receive the Holy Spirit" (John 20:21-22). "You will receive power when the Holy Spirit descends" (Acts 1:8). This was accomplished on Pentecost, which is therefore the absolute foundation of Christian theurgy.[94] It is effected in the liturgy, which has its natural center in the sacraments and above all in the Eucharist; incidentally, on the whole one ought to regard all liturgy as a sacrament in the broad sense, for the grace of God streams everywhere here. Theurgic authority belongs to the priesthood, together with the people of the church, although, apart from this pre-established path, grace finds its chosen vessels in the spirit-bearing saints, for, indisputably, great saints and miracle workers like St. Sergius or St. Seraphim, for example, are theurgists in the most authentic sense.[95] The beginning of Christian theurgy was solemnly set at the Last Supper, which anticipates Golgotha.

However, the theurgic character was inherent — but of course only to a certain degree — in Old Testament liturgy as well, so far as the Old Testament church is inseparably linked with Christianity and full of the symbols and fore-types of God's incarnation; it is even not foreign to the pagan cult in the measure in which the vision of God and God's grace were accessible to paganism on the whole, so far as religious authenticity was proper to its mysteries and liturgy. In general, a religious cult is, so to say, the normal if not sole domain of theurgy, while the church's sacraments are its central hearth.

Theurgic authority is *given* to human beings by God, but in no way can it be taken by them of their own volition, whether by theft or vain attempts at personal creativity, and that is because *theurgy, as a task for human effort, is impossible and is a misunderstanding of theomachy*. Although the grace of the sacraments operates without violating the freedom of human beings, by mysterious and unsearchable ways, nonetheless it religiously fecundates and nourishes them, and at the same time it regenerates the world, feeding it with the Body of Christ and giving it His Blood to drink, filling it with the grace-filled substance of the church's sacraments and rites, their theurgic power. Christian theurgy is the unseen, but real basis of every spiritual movement in the world on the path to its perfection. Without its consecrating and life-giving influence, humanity could not draw near to the resolution of those creative tasks that are rightfully set before it on this path, and in this sense *theurgy is the divine foundation of all sophiurgy*. Nothing can replace its power, be compared with it or render it unnecessary, by having shown a new cosmic-human mystery: such a plan is Antichrist's "black mass." Of course, the fog not accidently wreathing precisely this side of the theurgic problem and clouding its real contours must be dispersed with particular insistence. The question must be posed precisely: About *what kind of* theurgy are V. Soloviev and others talking? Does it rest on divine theurgy, as its religious basis, or does it pass it by, and want to make do without it, having accomplished some cosmic Eucharist *in spite of it,* a human action of God, a cosmourgic act? Does this new, still unexplored "theurgy" revoke the divine theurgy as an outlived and decrepit form of religious life, by putting in its place the creative energy of a human being, or does it regard itself as a newly matured fruit on its centuries-old tree?

In a sacrament as a theurgic act, there is a real operation and presence of God, and this constitutes in it the "transcendent" unconditionally miraculous element, which at the same time combines with the cosmic element of human nature. And see, this combination, the encounter and joining of the divine and human-cosmic, is the mysterious and marvelous point of Divine Humanity, really effected in a sacrament. When the priest, by invoking the Holy Spirit upon the offered holy Gifts says aloud: "and make this bread the honorable Body of Your Christ and what is in this cup the honorable Blood of Your Christ, having transmuted them by Your Holy Spirit, Amen, Amen, Amen," an unutterable miracle is then accomplished: Heaven is raised on the Altar, Christ descends and the powers of heaven tremble. . . . *This* cannot be accomplished by any achievements of human creativity, and for that reason there is nothing to recompense. One can understand that unbelief and deified humanity were and are directed against this unconditional theurgic basis, and disputes and disagreements about the meaning of the Eucharist acquire a primary significance. Moral "immanentism" of various stripes was proclaimed by Protestantism, a sui generis mystical impressionism: corresponding to his *frame of mind* the communicant either eats simple bread or receives grace, and the struggle of Protestantism with the Church naturally was focused around the question of the transubstantiation of the holy Gifts. For its part, theosophy interprets the sacraments as magical acts of the focus of occult energies, seeing only the substantial side in a sacrament, although it understands it more subtly. They are possible, and ever new attempts constantly emerge to remove or do without this "rock of faith," which however must remain invariably as the basis of any movement ahead on the path of Christianity.

And so, the theurgic power that is manifested in the sacraments is given and not taken, and here the human being is the receiver and not the maker. Therefore the priest is only the servant of the sacraments, not their executor. This does not, however, presume any passivity or slackness of the human element in him: for the worthy reception of a theurgic act, spiritual sobriety, prayerful fervor, and the concentration of all spiritual powers are demanded. But human energy emanates thereby only in a definite direction — it is exhausted in the feminine striving for self-surrender of the soul to God, of the Church to its Head, in a sacrificial self-crucifixion of the human element. Corresponding to this is the priesthood, the living organ of theurgy, which demands of its bearers faithfulness, self-surrender, and strictness in ministry, for in the theurgic act, in his standing before the Altar, the priest is mystically detached from everything human in himself, is raised above it, and thus always retains that stamp of extra-worldliness, isolation, sacrificial consecration. For the sacrificing priest and the sacrifice are indivisible and identical in a certain degree, and the one offering is in some sense the one being offered with respect to his own proper nature. The Head of the Christian priesthood, the Great High Priest, is at the same time the Lamb, and in his name the priest exclaims as he offers the bloodless sacrifice: "Your own of Your own offered to You for all people and for all." In the priesthood human nature passes through the burning fire of the cherubim's sword protecting the holy altar, and the priest is separated from the people by this curtain of fire, like Moses on Mount Sinai. But in the same way an intense focusing of human powers is expected of him (it is not for nothing that the priesthood, like the Levirate, expects physical and spiritual integrity), for the human being who takes his turn at angelic ministry remains himself all the same, and is compelled to strain his humanity to

Human History

the utmost for this purpose. Serving the sacraments combines in itself sacrificial self-giving with great boldness, for one would scarcely offer without boldness the Sacrifice before which cherubim and seraphim tremble! The theurgic act recalls by this the night struggle of the mysterious stranger with Jacob who forced him to bless him, although he injured his thigh in doing so. To stand worthily not before the altar but only before the sanctuary demands even from lay people an intensity of prayer and a sacrificial self-giving (although in a lesser degree than from a priest). Prayer itself is always a sacrifice to God, a sacrificial giving back of the human element, but to that extent it is also a creative act. Here the straining of all the powers of a spiritual being in a single burst to God is creative effort: *transcende te ipsum*. If sophianic creativity strives for some insight, for artistic achievement, and thus is expressed in *creation,* then prayerful creativity, "spiritual artistry," "mental activity," is realized fully in the *act* itself, in prayer and communion with God. Nevertheless creative human efforts in the theurgy of the sacraments only stipulate the conditions, but are not productive, for an unworthily performed sacrament keeps its terrible power, and on the other hand, it is impossible for anyone to perform a sacrament by any of their own efforts. Here individual daring can be expressed only in the readiness to perform the sacrament, but not in the performance itself, by which the theurgist operates suprapersonally, and thus in a depersonalized manner.

The domain of theurgy is not limited to the priesthood alone; there are other ministries marked with the stamp of divine action.[96] Each ministry, insofar as it is performed with the assistance of God's grace, strives to become theurgic (so that a doctor, although he cures by scientific means, but with prayer, to a certain degree becomes a theurgist). But the prophetic ministry, of course, has particular importance here. What makes a prophet a prophet? Where is the difference between simple inspiration and divine inspiration? A prophet senses in his words and deeds not his own will but the command of God, and precisely this capacity to make himself "a docile reed in the hands of a scribe" distinguishes the ministry of prophet. But with that the prophet is not at all a simple medium; on the contrary the greatest intensity of individual energy is inherent in him — it is enough to call to mind the majestic images of Isaiah, Jeremiah, Elijah, and John the Baptist. The initiative belongs to the prophet — a question addressed to God, human pain, and anxiety. He does not lose his human inspiration or genius; he keeps his person, manner, style. But this human thing does not generate that superhuman something that amazes us in the appearance of a prophet, as a herald of God's will and bearer of God's power. For it is God himself who "again and again and in many ways spoke in the prophets — *lalēsas en tois prophetais*" (Heb. 1:1). Human inspiration in its highest manifestations in a certain sense also attains divine inspiration, insofar as it becomes participant in divine Sophia, the revelation of God in the world. But the prophet has access not only to this divine inspiration through the world and humankind, but also to the direct visitation of the power of Divinity. Here too in an instant of divine illumination a kind of transubstantiation of the human nature, its divinization, is accomplished: when Moses came down from Mount Sinai it was not for nothing that he retained the trace of the radiance of Divinity.

One of the most important deeds of prophetic ministry undoubtedly is the writing of the divinely inspired books, venerated by the Church as the Word of God. The sacred books are first of all simply human books, carrying on themselves the stamp of the person of their author and his epoch; historical science discerns these traits. A given book can stand higher or lower as a literary work, for it is written by a definite person, and the Spirit of God did not turn the prophet into a self-recording mechanism. However, not their human inspiration, imparting to them a natural irresistibility and literary attractiveness, makes them sacred, but the *power of God*[97] present in them, the inexhaustible source of illumination (this is especially clear in the case of the Psalter, which occupies such an exceptional place in the prayer life of ascetics). The Bible is the Word of God not in the sense that it was immediately written by God's Spirit. What a prophet receives from God must be creatively incarnated by him in word, retold, and in this sense the divinely inspired writings of the prophets are all the same a type of literary creative activity. But the human word *is changed* here by the grace of God; it becomes spirit-bearing, theurgic: *the sacrament of the word* occurs. Therefore the Bible though a book is not only a book, it is more than a book. It has an endless depth proper to a religious symbol, and its verbal flesh, by preserving its own character, at the same time becomes a sacred hieroglyph, transparent only for the enlightened eye. In this sense, behind the external, literal content, the flesh of the word, the historical garb, men of spiritual experience discern in it a mysterious, symbolic sense that reveals itself only to awe. Therefore only in the Church and for the

Church is the Bible known as the Word of God, while outside it, it is only a book that possesses a high pedagogical authority and great literary value but is easily turned into a dead letter without life-giving spirit or for that matter representing simply the subject of scientific curiosity.[98] In particular the book of the Four Gospels which in its historical form is the subject of scientific hypercriticism is the Eternal Book only for those who have come to know its vivifying power, falling with an open heart before the spring of living water. And the face of Christ, put together seemingly in mosaic form out of the separate features of the gospel narratives (these features are subjected to historical criticism, which strives to establish "a scientifically reliable" image of Jesus), is not at all a mechanical sum of these components, but is rather an image not made by hands, miraculously impressed on the gospel panel. Similar to the Bible, the theurgic character is also present to a certain extent in church prayers, hymns, and symbols. But here a difference in degree and intensity exists, palpably sensed in religious experience, but not lending itself to formulation.

Prophetic ministry, either in word or action, differently from the priesthood is primarily a personal daring and initiative. Prophets have an individual aspect and a definite task in history which can never be said about separate representatives of the Levirate who merge into one general "Aaronic ministry." The personal daring is present in a saint too, as a bearer of theurgic power, or in a miracle-worker. What boldness before God must one have in order to ask him for a miracle canceling the course of events already mapped out! But at the same time the performance of a miracle by the mercy of God, and not by the power of Beelzebub, presumes the whole power of humility and devotion to the will of God, without which there is no sanctity, no graced spirit-bearing. *Every* Christian is called to holiness; all must aspire to the acquisition of the grace of the Holy Spirit (as St. Seraphim of Sarov defined the goal of the Christian life), although this goal is reached by each one on their own special path, for "the gifts are different and the ministries are different." But the power of faith and prayer is imposed as a duty on each Christian. The word of the Savior is addressed to all: "Have faith in God. For verily I say to you, if anyone says to this mountain, 'pick yourself up and throw yourself into the sea' and does not doubt in his heart but believes that it will happen according to his words, it will be for him whatever he may say. For this reason I say to you, whatever you ask for in prayer, believe that you will receive it, and it will be yours" (Mark 11:23-24). The prayerful boldness of faith is bound with the fullness of humility, for the mountain is not moved into the sea by the will of God for the sake of theurgic experiment or "a sign," and pitying the grieving parents St. Sergius raised by his prayer not all the dead children, but only one. Theurgic energy is poured out in the whole atmosphere of the church, but only the vessels chosen by God who have been purified by ascetic discipline collect its lightning bolts, and find in themselves the power and boldness to accomplish theurgic acts. . . .

The theurgy of the sacraments is closely connected with liturgical ritual and in general with cult, which comprise as it were its flesh. In the liturgical order there is likewise no place for personal creativity as such; here the suprapersonal power of ceremony holds sway. Similar to how a tragedian's mask covers with its ritual disguise the individual face of an actor, and buskins change his figure, so in a liturgical ritual the individuality of the officiant is so to say removed by sacred vestments, fixed exclamations, and actions, and not the person but the order operates. In an equal manner those prayerful hymns, in which the living individuality of their composers was impressed at one time, live in the cult as depersonalized or suprapersonal sighs; they sound so hieratically that they are almost superhuman. And yet we know that liturgical creativity is subject to historical development, with individual inspiration flowing into its supra-individual riverbed, and being accepted by an act of ecclesial sanction. We often know by name separate hymn writers, artists, and architects who have brought their creative gifts here, but these gifts receive their hieratic meaning only after they have been alloyed in the fire of prayer with the common mass of the religious cult, losing their individual face. (One can find a certain analogy for this in folk creativity, simultaneously individual and collective, with the creative individualities not dissolving and sinking but somehow growing organically together with the nameless whole.) Although the order of liturgy possesses a very great hieratic stability, even in it constant movement happens, sometimes told only in nuances and half-tones. Liturgical development is a most faithful indicator of that which happens in the mystical depths of life, but an external observer who searches for "signs" has no access to the sensation of the pulse of prayer, intimate and trembling. This accounts for talk of the immobility of ecclesial life, but equally for far-fetched programmed calls for "a new liturgical creativity" that are religiously powerless.

Human History

It is well known that religious cult in general is the cradle of culture, or rather, its spiritual homeland. Whole historical epochs particularly rich in creativity are marked by the fact that all fundamental elements of "culture" were more or less closely bound with cult, and had a sacral character: art, philosophy, science, law, economy. In particular the highest achievements of art concern the hieratic domain: Egyptian, Assyro-Babylonian, and Greek architecture and sculpture, Christian art of the Middle Ages and early Renaissance, iconography, the plastic arts and dance, music and singing, sacred mystery drama. And around this center were grouped the fields of art more secular, peripheral. From the cradle, art is wrapped with prayer and devotion: at the dawn of cultural history, humanity brings its best inspirations to the altar and dedicates them to God. The bond of culture with cult is on the whole a fact of grandiose significance in the history of humanity, demanding fitting attention and understanding.

An especially close bond exists between cult and art. A noble uselessness common to them draws them together in the face of this world with its utilitarian values, as do their identical economic needlessness and proud extravagance. The fact of cult as well as of art graphically testifies to the truth that a human being does not live by bread alone and is not "economic man" measuring the world by a mercantile standard, but is capable of disinterestedness and inspiration. And in the days when the modern European "economic man" was not yet born, humanity living in huts erected magnificent temples for the gods, in contrast to the contemporary epoch when people know how to build train stations and hotels, but have almost unlearned how to build sacred places.

A question arises involuntarily: Can it be, precisely here, in the nature of the relations that have existed between cult and art, that the religious problem of art has been resolved, and art, being of the temple, was in this way also theurgic? And is this why one needs to search for the resolution of this question that torments our age by returning to the ancient, lost paradise of the organic unity of culture inside the temple fence? That time in the history of humanity, really, can be regarded as a lost paradise of culture when questions now so tragically acute were resolved simply and wisely. But it is impossible to return to a golden childhood, however beautiful it might have been, and the artificial affectation of naïveté or infantile preciousness is insufferable. Indeed on the whole it is impossible to satisfy new inquiries and quests with any reaction or restoration. The restoration of the former position for art cannot be desirable for the present because the relations between religion and art, the demands of cult and the inner aspirations of creativity, at that time were nevertheless characterized by a lack of freedom, although this was not recognized. By consecrating itself to religion, art became its *ancilla,* playing a servile role, and the relation to it was utilitarian, although in the very highest sense. Art had been forged by ascetic obedience, which did not harm it only for as long as it was carried out sincerely and freely, but it became an unbearable hypocrisy and lie when the ascetic ardor was lost. We can observe this in the era of the Renaissance when religious subjects were treated frequently without any religious frame of mind, and in reality problems of a purely pictorial nature were solved in them. In its own day, cult attracted to itself all the arts like a magnet attracts iron. The commonality of tasks and the unity of service established a natural organization of the arts in their cultic combination, but of course, it is erroneous to see here that "synthesis" of the arts by which their particularity is overcome internally and by which the simplicity and unity of white light is restored as a reverse composition of the variegated spectrum. This organization of the arts led at most only to the possibility of the *common* achievements *of shared* arts, with all of them being left as they were, pursuing their particular artistic purpose, although in connection with the unifying tasks of cult. Only for this reason were they later able to become specialized so quickly and easily, transferring out of cult into culture. This became unavoidable and even fully legitimate as soon as the *sincerity* of the relations between cult and art had been destroyed for one reason or another, and calculating utilitarianism infiltrated them, equally alien to the nature of both religion and art. Every heteronomy of goals contradicts the nature of art; it exists only in an atmosphere of freedom and disinterestedness. It must be free also from religion (of course this does not mean from God), and from morality (although not from the Good). Art is autocratic, and by its premeditated subordination it would only show that it does not believe in itself and is afraid of itself. But what is fainthearted art capable of? Then instead of creative quests the convention of stylization makes a home for itself, and instead of inspiration, correctness of the canon.

In the epoch of "cultures," i.e., of every sort of secularization, the domain of cult no longer receives artistic enrichment; it does not know new discoveries. Cult is content with earlier accumulated wealth, which by the way is so great that it completely satisfies its task. For every necessity of everyday life one has to make use of the services of "artistic production" with its more or less superficial aestheticism and stylization, i.e., in essence with fakes and surrogates, to live *without* one's own art. The artist, possessing the sensitivity of an artistic and religious conscience, now feels with particular sharpness that the secret of prayerful inspiration and temple art was lost and is still not found again, and with time he becomes rigid in the inescapability of this torment. In any case the future of temple art is connected only with the general destinies of art.

Having isolated itself from cult, art went its own way and gained the possibility of recognizing its boundaries and sensing its depths. Now it has stopped being heteronomous in its goals. While art remained of the temple and regarded itself only as a means for cult, its soul was entirely set at ease with this recognition. Art knew that it was serving God, and the problem of *justifying* art did not come before it, the requirement to render to itself an account of its ways and goals did not arise. Of all the "secularized" fragments of an erstwhile integral culture-cult, art preserves in itself in the greatest degree the memory of the past in the consciousness of its highest nature and religious roots. The spiritual limitedness of positivism remains alien to it, that world contentment with which both philosophy and science are poisoned — it feels itself a fleeting guest, a herald from a different world, and constitutes the most religious element of extra-religious culture. This trait of art is in no way at all connected with the religious character of its themes — in essence art has no *themes,* but only knows artistic grounds — points on which the ray of beauty catches fire. It is connected with that sensing of the ultimate depth of the world and that trembling which it arouses in the soul. By the choice of the subject for its inspirations art possesses the supreme freedom of infallibility, is found on the other side of good and evil. For it there is no sin and vice, there is no deformity and ugliness, for everything on which the ray of beauty falls becomes transparent and light-bearing in the crystal of creativity. And even the personal gloom of the soul of the artist himself, his sinful foulness, loses its seductive power, passing through the cleansing inspiration of beauty, if only it really touched it with its wing. Art possesses the gift of seeing the world in such a way that evil and ugliness disappear and are dissolved in a harmonious chord. Purely ethical standards are on the whole not applicable to art, and morality raises its voice only where art ends. Therefore true art possesses the privilege of not fearing exposure and on the whole does not know pornography, i.e., the premeditated savoring of vice, and the other way around; the most skillful pornography remains outside art. Free from ethics, in keeping with its spirit and with its internal pathos, art is liable only to mystical and religious judgment. But of course, by remaining free of ethics, art by virtue of its influence promotes the general growth of morality in the human soul.

Epochs of cultural flowering are marked out by the primacy not of ethics but of aesthetics; artistry becomes their guiding perception of life. The thirst for beauty, however, sometimes is too easily satisfied by surrogates, a deadening aesthetic philistinism develops, the aestheticism of the everyday which is taken for a "life in beauty." But the aesthetic perception of the world, artistry, contains in itself a certain lofty, indisputable though not final truth of life, whereas its complete absence not only constitutes ugliness and poverty, but is also the sign of a lack of spiritual wings, of sinful limitedness. Far too few understand that the artistic perception of the world with its criterion is aesthetically the belonging not only of the servants of art but also of its appreciators, but above all and in the highest degree of those who make their own life itself a work of art — the holy ascetics. Whoever does not see this in the spiritual visage of St. Sergius or St. Seraphim and other saints, whoever does not sense the blowing of the most sublime and pure poetry poured out around them, remains alien to the most intimate in them, for in them is a flaming sensation of the beauty of the cosmos, its sophianicity, and there is a sacred irreconcilability towards sin, as ugliness and deformity. Perhaps a certain aridity and matter-of-factness, undoubtedly distinguishing our contemporary ecclesiality, more than anything are connected precisely with its earthbound aesthetic (which is why here they treat with such morbid suspicion the "temptation of beauty" as "decadence"). The incomparable beauty of Orthodox worship and the artistic treasures of its liturgical texts provide the most eloquent testimony of all that such an aesthetic impoverishment in no way constitutes the norm of church life.[99]

The first act of self-consciousness that art performs on the path of its liberation is the declaration of its full freedom and independence from any tasks or norms whatsoever imposed from the outside, no matter how respectable they may be in their own right. As long as art still finds itself prisoner to various "directions," as long as it is tendentious one way or another, not daring to live at its own risk, it still has not been born to self-responsibility. Therefore the slogan *art for art's sake*, throwing down the gauntlet at any utilitarian violence against it, expresses a completely legitimate and dialectically necessary moment in the self-consciousness of art, which must cast off from itself the rusty chains and free itself from sanctimony and conventions and become its own self. For under the guise of "directions" is concealed artistic insincerity, unbelief in its own work, fear of becoming its own self, the heteronomy of art. Autonomous, free art recognizes one task — the service of beauty, and it knows over itself one law — the dictates of beauty, faithfulness to artistic measure. In this way are moved to the forefront purely aesthetic tasks, work on artistic form, which sometimes has been barbarically neglected for the sake of content. Finally the clear awareness is affirmed that form itself is the substantial content of art and that there is nothing outside work on form. The arts, each in their own sphere, elaborate their own forms and establish their canon. In the same way art becomes canonical and subject to laws: the "Alexandrian," "Parnassian," "Academic" naturally arise in the process of the crystallization of the artistic canon. In it a certain petrifaction takes place gradually, against which the young again raise a mutiny so that having achieved a victory and enriched or changed the canon, they themselves become "classics," — *e sempre bene*. In its classical, canonical form art occupies an honorable, official place in "culture," and is satisfied with this honor, aspiring to serene lucidity *à la* Goethe and sublime balance.

What then is the living self-consciousness of art as artistic canon and expertise of form? One thing for it is assured, namely, that the artist *creates* beauty on a level with nature, and up to a certain degree, even in spite of nature; he creates his own world of beauty in the limits of his art. Not far from this is the path to a completely false self-consciousness, that it is not Beauty which creates art by summoning its servants to its altar, but that art itself creates beauty, which is why the artist is a god who builds a rainbow world of dream and fairy tale in his own image and likeness. But in what kind of relation then does this world find itself which is fostered by his creative effort, and how does its beauty relate to the world in which we live and to its beauty? There is *no relation at all* here. Art, understood in this manner, wants only to lead out of this world, to cast a spell, to captivate, by creating its world of sweet daydreams. The artist begins listening to the singing of sirens and becomes a siren himself, but any contact with life calls forth in him a morbid grimace. This subjective idealism in art is nothing other than aesthetic illusionism which does not believe in beauty, and this is why properly speaking it does not believe in art either. Flight from life is here joined with a refined gourmandism, aesthetic gastronomy, blossoming in the hothouse atmosphere of privacy. Art remains a stranger to tragic discord, and Pygmalion, in love with marble Galatea, in essence does not even feel the need to revive her. This art does not sense its task as the exposure of the rhythms of universal beauty, a certain cosmic activity, but only as a delight, "an elevating deception." Idealistic art, by remaining in camera in its self-consciousness, can in fact become desirable for many, for the crowd, and then while preserving the whole privacy of its nature it becomes public property.

For example, contemporary theater, that living incarnation of private-public art, is like this. It does not even believe in itself and even as it wants to look at itself as a serious and vital affair, it is virtually almost *circenses,* an aesthetic attraction. There is no other inquiry except the need for aesthetic emotion in this kingdom of scenic illusion, behind the magical line of floodlights partitioning off "spectators" and "actors." To help this illusion the assistance of several arts is called upon, their own kind of "synthesis." When the ideal of "catholic" art is contrasted with this kind of private-public art, the intention is not at all a new form of aesthetic collectivism or a further level of the socialization of art, but a quite different concept of its nature and tasks. These tasks no longer consist in an "elevating deception" which like any deception is in reality degrading and venomous, but in a creativity that transfigures life. "Catholic" art wants to penetrate to the depths of being, where everyone and everything are one; by striving towards reality, it seeks to remove the spell of floodlights with their deceptive illusionism. The catholicity or sophianicity of art necessarily presumes the overcoming of this natural idealism. Realistic art, for which the *res* itself becomes accessible, in principle is possible only on the condition that it is not the artist who creates beauty, but beauty which creates the artist, making its chosen one its tool or organ. Art does not create but only shows beauty, and lays it bare from beneath the featureless style and ugliness that covers it. It becomes a mirror for the *res* by creating symbols of higher realities. Thanks to its connection with the Cosmos, the reality of which is Beauty, art becomes symbolic. Its lyre is tuned in consonance with cosmic harmony, its sounds make unknown strings quiver, and the waves of these sounds spread far and wide. Symbolic art does not sever the bond of the two worlds as does aesthetic idealism, which is reconciled to only one artistic reverie — it begins to see clearly this bond and is the bridge from the lower to the higher reality, *ad realiora*. This *realiora* art on the whole does not repudiate the artistic canon, the aesthetic of forms; on the contrary, so far as it remains art it knows how to interpret the canon in its own way, and breathe new life into it. It believes in itself because it does not consider itself an empty pastime or human invention, but knows the higher power of art, and this power is Beauty. In this understanding it acquires a gravity unknown to the art that charms and is private.

Once art has become aware of its sophianicity, different questions arise before it besides aesthetic ones. It believes in Beauty and its saving power. But is art itself, which proclaims this gospel of Beauty, really called to save the world by it, to call into being in beauty not only a piece of marble but also the whole heavy formless flesh of the world, to perform a sophiurgic act of world transfiguration? When the matter goes as far as this ultimate but essentially unavoidable question, the living boundaries of art make themselves felt. Aesthetic idealism cannot sense them, which does not want to part with its privacy and does not encroach on any sort of efficacy, but the *realiora* symbolism unavoidably clashes with this question. The point is that symbolism itself, which expresses the higher self-consciousness of free, autonomous art, is still not *realism* in Beauty and cannot attain it. For all that, it remains only "significative," no matter how realist its symbols might be, but it does not become efficacious. The path a *realibus* (or better, *ab irrealibus*) ad *realiora* in art thus remains in a certain intermediate sphere — *metaxu* — but so too it does not reach the *realia*.

The symbolic nature of art is evidence as much of its high calling as of its fateful impotence. Art shows Beauty and captivates with it, but it is powerless to create life in beauty and thereby become authentically catholic, universal. In a certain sense too it remains separated from Beauty, like philosophy from Truth, and only "loves" it, is *philo-kalia*. It is powerless to gather into one the scattered rays of Tabor light, although seeing it in the universe it bears witness to it, and creates in its works prefigurements of the universal Transfiguration. And when yearning for *life* in beauty is stirred up with unprecedented power in the soul of art's servant, a tragic discord begins in him: his art becomes *not enough* for the artist — he begins to demand so much from it that it consumes his spirit in this fieriness. Aesthetic art ceases to satisfy him because it only inflames but does not quench his thirst; it is conventional, limited, powerless. True, aesthetic self-contentment and artistic limitedness become impossible even for *realiora* symbolism, but at the same time, and of course as a result of this, the artistic equilibrium begins to be lost in him: art begins *to dash about*, it searches in different directions for an exit beyond its limits. It attempts to find it by applying new artistic methods or by broadening the diapason of existing ones. In the chase after greater reality, it unites the artistic means of different arts, striving by their "synthesis" to reach unprecedented might. Richard Wagner was the artistic preacher of this kind of synthesis. But these quests lead away onto deliberately incorrect paths. The actual possibilities of art are in general inexhaustible, but for this reason there can be no external, summarizing synthesis of them. Indeed such conglomerations are not needed; unnecessary too that aesthetic violence which this deafening synthesis inescapably is. After all, any art in its depths is *pan*-art, *art in general*, and one need not search for this unity either on the surface or in the phenomenal. (Besides this, the excessive thickening of the aesthetic atmosphere, which is obtained as a result of such a synthesis, can turn out to be auspicious for the development of occult whirlwinds, which in part happens in Wagner: thanks to this, art is replaced by magic and sorcery.)

"Beauty will save the world." But with this it is not at all said that art will do this, for art only participates in Beauty, it does not possess its power. Indeed the consciousness of the artist who has sensed the limits of art is oppressed by this, and this constitutes his tragedy. Antagonism between art and Beauty may even appear: art does not exist outside bounds, no artistic formulation takes place apart from them — *in der Beschränkung zeigt sich der Meister* [in limitation the master is shown][100] — and meanwhile Beauty is a universal force to which measurelessness belongs. Before the face of universal Beauty even art itself becomes aesthetic philistinism to a certain degree, prizing prettiness more than Beauty, attached to its own place and having a definite position in "culture." If such a *temptation* by art arises on the spiritual path of an artist, Beauty itself orders him to offer it in sacrifice, to slaughter it on the altar. Though it be as dear as an eye: if your eye tempts you, pluck it out. In such a case *a crisis of art* ensues. It can turn out to be beneficial, this crisis, according to the law of life. "If a grain of wheat, falling to the ground, does not die, it remains a single grain; but if it dies, it will produce much fruit" (John 12:24). Art falls ill with sophiurgic anxiety; a cosmic storm is stirred up in its soul. This crisis of growth is dangerous and can turn out to be disastrous for art: the refining fire, if it does not melt, then it reduces to ash or disfigures. But the artist, who on the whole does not know sophiurgic anxiety, and who is not attracted *a realioribus ad realissima*, through art to Beauty, proves to be not at the height of his own service. Here history has much to say. We perceive the sunny appearance of Pushkin, the joy and promise of Russian culture, its spiritual center in the first half of the nineteenth century, as belonging to a different historical and perhaps even cosmic epoch; he does not even have anything to do with the fathers but rather with our grandchildren. Pushkin revealed in himself the purest incarnation of a *poet*, clear and integral in his poetic self-consciousness, not knowing creative bifurcation and tragic schism. But precisely Pushkin's poetic self-consciousness is already a lost paradise for our present day (on the contrary significantly closer to it are Gogol "reduced to ashes,"[101] Lermontov and Turgenev). It's no use in saying how already impossible a Goethe is now with that spiritual satiety and Olympian equilibrium, with his aesthetic contentment with the world. It is natural that the spiritual initiator of a new Russia should be the spiritual son of Pushkin, F. M. Dostoevsky, who is entirely enveloped by sophiurgic fire and is filled with this anxiety. So great a poet engendered with inner necessity the one who in his own consciousness no longer thinks of himself *only* as an artist. Next to Dostoevsky of course is V. Soloviev with all his impulses.

The artist who has become aware of the *realiora* of art cannot stop there and not strive further towards the reality itself. He would like for that light of Tabor, the dispersed rays of which he catches in the focus of his creativity, to begin to shine in all the world and show its cosmourgic power in the salvation of the world from "this world" with its deformity and evil. In this very desire in and of itself it is impossible to see something demonic and theomachian (although of course it can become such). In great humility an artist prayerfully invokes the advent in power and glory of that Beauty which art shows only symbolically. In this striving the limits of art as well as of symbolism are clearly transgressed. Art no longer speaks here, but rather that mighty element of the human spirit by which art is generated; not the virtuoso of a definite *ars*, not the professional, but the artist in spirit makes the appeal, the artist-human who has become aware of the creative might of

Beauty through the means of his own art. Therefore the domain of sophiurgy does not coincide with art, at least as it is understood in the generally accepted sense. *Art* itself, its element, is deeper, more general, more original than all particular arts, and if few are born as artists, as servants of these latter things, then through the inspiration of Beauty and participation in it all humanity is called to art. At the basis of art as craftsmanship, therefore, lies art as a higher sense of artistry; it is without a subject or has every subject; it is the contemplation of universal Beauty about which Plato prophesies in his *Symposium*.[102]

In its spirit humankind possesses *all* the arts, which is why it is capable of perceiving them, but in addition to this, it possesses the art of nature — the gift of contemplating the beauty of the world. Evidently, sophiurgic anxiety still strengthens in humankind the self-awareness of this "universal priesthood" in art, of the dormant and unexpended quality of its powers. One can say more: this pan-art (or *beyond*-art) without words, without subject, without skill, possesses a very high consciousness of itself, feels itself incommensurable with respect to separate artistic specializations, and would not consent to exchange its impotence for them, or thirsting for world transfiguration, to be content with . . . advice. But the role of pioneers, awakeners, prophets can belong to makers of art, artists, although they are the ones who can prove to be the most stubborn in an aestheticism that has already become reactionary. *Art is the Old Testament of Beauty*, of the kingdom of the coming Comforter, and of course is itself filled with prefigurements of what lies ahead. But the epoch of art naturally draws closer to an end when Beauty itself comes into the world. However, before this arrival the cosmic darkness thickens, and at the same time a yearning for beauty flares up, the world's prayer for Transfiguration becomes mature. In the sophiurgic thirst for universal Beauty the unquenched truth of paganism, the nonfulfillment of its promises, again announces itself; the captive soul of the world will raise groans and cries. For the Old Testament tablet of Beauty is preserved in paganism as well as in art. The first call to the "wedding feast of the Lamb" sweeps by in the world like a barely audible whisper, and the dried and parched mouth of the creature prays "O Comforter, come and dwell with us!" The Holy Spirit will satisfy expectations and fulfill the promises of art by his grace. Theurgy and sophiurgy combine in one act of transfiguring the creation. It goes without saying that this can be accomplished only in the inner recesses of the Church, under the vivifying operation of the grace of the sacraments streaming in it without interruption, in an atmosphere of prayerful enthusiasm.

What ought the immediate tasks of art that is conscious of its nature and meaning be? Together with this elevated consciousness, art is subject to dangers such as are not found at all on the path of pure aestheticism. They consist mainly in the easiness of *substitutions* connected with an exaggerated or erroneous understanding of its tasks and resources. For art, spiritual sobriety and self-cognition are especially important. And first of all it is incumbent on it to remember that the sophiurgic task is irresolvable by the efforts of art alone and by human will, but presupposes the influence of God's grace. Not the virtuosity of artistic technique, not aesthetic magic, but Beauty itself is the transfiguring, sophiurgic power. And art falls into a notorious mistake if it seeks a resolution of this task only on its own paths, by inventing various sleights of hand and artistic tricks. On this path it can easily wander off into the sphere of magic and even be subjected to the influence of the dark force. Art must in any case remain itself and not lower itself to dubious experiments. The enclosure of strict aestheticism, of an exacting canon (to which of course immobility must be alien) is dictated by self-preservation; this is its own type of asceticism, protecting art from decomposition and formlessness. Art must hide in itself a prayer for the transfiguration of the creation, but it is itself not called to infringe boldly on sophiurgic experiments. Patiently and with hope it must carry the cross of being unquenched in its craving and wait for its hour. With this interior burning, with this craving is created, without doubt, the special *tone* of symbolic art lending it a romantic uneasiness, depth, and hiddenness. It is capable of arousing new, unheard-of forces in art and of creatively fertilizing it. It would be mistaken to define these possibilities in advance because it is impossible to anticipate creativity and inspiration. In only one thing is it difficult to doubt, namely, that art is sentenced to burn still with a religious flame. On this ground a new rapprochement of art with cult is possible, a renaissance of religious art — not a stylization that although virtuosic is deprived of inspiration and is creatively powerless, but a completely free and thus perfectly sincere, prayerfully inspiring creativity, such as was the great religious art of days gone by. Art in any case retains its main acquisition, made in the epoch of "secularization" — its fullest freedom and autonomy. By bringing to the altar, in the enclosure of the church, the sacrifice of its inspirations, it does not become heteronomous at all; it does not limit itself by being locked premeditatedly in the domain of cult, but preserves the breadth of its range, at least as a possibility.

Still, this merely possible religious renaissance in art which may or may not come need not be taken already as the fulfillment of sophiurgic expectations; the latter, on the contrary, cannot not be realized. The revival of religious art, if it does follow, is still by itself in no way an answer to these inquiries, because it still remains *within the limits* of art, while the idea of sophiurgy leads out beyond its limits. But of course prayerfully inspired religious art has the greatest potential to become that spark from which the world flame catches fire and the first ray of Tabor light begins to shine on earth.

And so, what of it? Is the sophiurgic task within the reach of art and should art aspire to it? Yes and no. It must cherish it in the heart, while at the same time recognizing all of its insolvability by the means of art; it must want what is beyond its power and impossible, while striving "to outstrip itself in divine valor." But at the same time it must remain art, for only by being itself is it news of the empyrean world, the promise of Beauty. And its creative impulse, by the will of God, can prove to be the point of departure for sophiurgic activity. There is no more returning to pure art with aesthetic tranquility and limitedness, at least, outside spiritual stagnation or reaction.[103]

5. Power and Theocracy

The historical life of humanity needs organized forms of communal living that are established by a power that commands it and constrains it with force. What then is *power?* What is its religious and mystical nature? In what is its meaning? Why like a dark shadow does it appear with its "sword" everywhere society arises — multifaceted and in many forms but unchangeable in its essence? Why does the amorphous and jelly-like body of the public excrete from itself crystals of power from which its skeleton is then formed? In its origin, no matter how it might be explained in its particulars by "sociologists," power hides in itself something enigmatic: it is not created, but arises; it is not born, but only realized. The potential energy of power, active and passive — both as holding sway and as obeying — is always present in humankind and only waits for a reason to reveal itself. Evidently, power has some sort of relation to the very essence of the human spirit and one must first of all reject the rationalistic fabrications of "the Enlightenment," as if power and right were discovered by someone, invented for a certain need, arose as a result of a "social contract" or free agreement. The deep and dark *instinct* of power, which gives rise to its different forms, is replaced here by rational utilitarianism, and power is something of a type of hired manservant whom one can summon and dismiss. (Such a conception of power has a worthy parallel in the interpretation of religion as the invention of priests or a deliberate deception.) Power emanates involuntarily and arises organically and concretely as *historical* power. Popular consciousness, as long as its depths are not yet covered with the sand of rationalism, unhesitatingly confesses the special *sacred authority* of power. It is initiated in the innermost recesses of the people's soul, and its birth is only recognized and proclaimed by an act of "the people's will." This latter either is aware of itself as the instrument of a Higher Will — and then we have power "by God's mercy" — or it sees in itself the mystical realization of the people's leadership. A certain religious or mystical aureole is invariably present in power as such, which gilds not only the crown of the hereditary monarch but also the lictor's pole-axe of the republican consul. Power reduced in its entirety to the role of a utilitarian means would not survive for a single day, having been made the plaything of conflicting interests, and the modern crisis of power in the age of revolution is linked precisely with the predominance of interests and generally of every sort of utilitarianism in the life of power which is excessive though inconclusive nevertheless.

Humanity possesses the capacity for generating power. It is present not in separate persons who are bearers of power — it is only concentrated in them, its energy condenses in them. In actual fact it is present in all of humanity and is made up of the capacity to command and obey, of authority and loyalty, which are merely the two poles of power, the male and female principle in it. Both the one and the other can be perverted by sinful lust, passing over into love of power and servility. In addition to this, together with all the flesh of the world, weighed down and become material, power in an unenlightened state also has a heavy and hard character. It is displayed with pitiless coercion; the irons of power, like fetters, cut into the shoulders of humanity. Similar to economy which in its present state is bound with the "malediction" of the earth, power carries on itself the stamp of estrangement from God, inherent in all life; it is endured like a burden and captivity, yet forms a necessary enclosure for life. But as the higher dignity of the one who leads economy shines through it, so too power is found in some sort of connection with the regal nature of human beings, with their inherent image of God, although they darken it as much as they express it.

In its essence power consists in *might*, in the capacity for the invariable implementation of the will. Here there is not that barrier of impotence or weakness that invariably stands between a desire and its realization — as if there were no antinomy of freedom and necessity. In this sense power in its fullness (as "sovereignty") is *the image of almightiness*. True, all power is restricted by the actual confines of its manifestation, but beyond their limits it is not power. That is why "the kingdom and the power and the glory," true power, belongs to God alone, whereas earthly power is a symbol of God's omnipotence. However, for God in his forethought for the world omnipotence does not exist *only* as power, as "an abstract principle," in isolation from God's other relations with the world. Divine power is indivisible from divine love, which is revealed in the creation of the world and in its protection. But power is also inherent in the nature of this relation, and already the prevalence alone of such divine appellations as Lord, El, Adonai, Sabbaoth, Kurios, etc. attests that this was always recognized by peoples. And the "meek king," the Lord Jesus Christ, in his earthly root deriving from the royal clan of David, is called King of kings and Lord of lords. He himself confirms his royal dignity with the symbolic entrance into Jerusalem, and with his answer at the court of Pilate, and even with the inscription on the cross, the irony of which proved to be completely ineffective. He is depicted as King and Judge in the gospel account of the Last Judgment. After his resurrection he himself gives witness about himself: "*all power — pasa exousia —* in heaven and on earth is given to me" (Matt. 28:18). And the apostolic letters frequently speak of this: "For this reason Christ died, and rose and came to life, so that he would be Lord over both the living and the dead — *hina kai nekrōn kai zōntōn kyrieusē*" (Rom. 14:9; cf. Eph. 1:20-22; 1 Cor. 15:22-28). The "coming thousand-year reign of Christ" is spoken of in the *Apocalypse*. In the future age "it befits him to reign" in order to subjugate everything to the Father. The "Gospel of the Kingdom" announces the good news of the approach of the kingdom of God coming in power, and the Lord's Prayer teaches us to ask God for its advent. Although this kingdom is "not of this world," all the same in some sense it is a kingdom — after all, one cannot allegorize everything without end.

Human History

God's omnipotence is realized as power only for sin and sinners, in the realm of the extra-divine underbelly of being. On the contrary, it is blended together with divine love for the creature. Christ is the Friend of His apostles and of all who believe; the Holy Spirit, the "Heavenly King," is the Comforter; and God the Father, to whom Christ taught us to pray "Our Father" is the King-Father. *Before* the fall Adam did not know any other power over him but the Father's: God's omnipotence as *Power* became clear to him only after the fall. The ranks of angels too tremble at the divine omnipotence, but they tremble differently than do the demons. The self and self-will having envied God, drew to themselves the operation of his omnipotence as power. That which is given to a creaturely entity and constitutes the sphere of its might is also its power, but this power is not recognized as such by it. Only when a false pretension to what is not intrinsic to it arises within, when it is in fact conscious of both its strength and its weakness, its limitedness, in the same way the "knowledge of good and evil" is awakened in the domain of power. At that moment the human being already knows as power the exceeding strength of God's omnipotence. So too the Angels, praising God, become "heavenly armies" that strike and wage war: "And war broke out in heaven, Michael and his angels fought against the dragon, and the dragon and his angels fought against them" (Apoc. 12:7).

Power was intrinsic to Adam before the fall, corresponding to his central position in the world; he was the king in the universe, the vicegerent of God by right of sonship. This power, although in a damaged guise, remained with him even after the fall. Inherent in Adam would be royal and at the same time fatherly power over humanity, which would have represented a widely ramified family. And this humanity-family, abiding in the love of the Heavenly Father, would not know the chains of statehood or the irons of power, shaping life in its own way. But the union of family, brotherhood, and friendship was destroyed and already Cain's fratricide showed how weak these bonds had become in a humanity injured by sin. Then of necessity power arises for the protection of life, and the apostle considers it to be a divine institution (Rom. 13:1-2).

Power is dual by nature — it knows an active and a passive principle and is made up of ruling and submitting, and in their foundation the one and the other have an irrational and mystical character. Power which is aware of itself as lawful and not usurped, senses in itself the will, the right, and the force to command — with an instinctive sovereignty, without discussion or reflection; equally, loyal obedience must be not ratiocinative, but immediate and in a certain sense without reasoning, blind. Such is the instinct of power, original and dark. The utilitarian-rational realm, however great its meaning may be in the life of power, all the same is not decisive for it. In its constructions, anarchism usually does not consider precisely this instinct of power that generates ever-new forms; it wants to defeat the phenomenology of power without affecting its ontology. Of course, power cannot be only the pure *arbitrariness* of the rulers, and in the coercive form of a law invested with the safeguarding of organized constraint, not all content can be legally included, but only what is accepted or permitted by an actual sense of justice. To say it differently, a "natural law" exists that constitutes the highest norm and task for positive law, "the law of law." Power and law are indissoluble and correlative in their vital merging; if law has its foundation in power, then the latter manifests its life in law: it is the "stated word" of power, its "energy." Nevertheless, constraining rigidity always remains intrinsic to the nature of power. Power represents the *male* principle, isolated and confirmed in its disaffection, to which the element of violence is inherent: it only knows how to subjugate and command, but not how to love and be compassionate. Correspondingly, the submission of the ruled, the passive principle of power, takes on the traits of femaleness, oppressed and enslaved, and just as abstract. Under such a disconnection and polarization of the sexes an eroticism of power becomes ostensibly impossible. But it is not quite so: in its depths power all the same keeps an erotic impulse, and this makes itself felt in triumphant or critical moments in the life of peoples (e.g., war). Then an erotic current runs through and a spark takes fire: power becomes not only necessary but also desired; it will appear in an erotic glow if only for a moment.

    Generally speaking complex relations exist between power and eros and fluctuate between antagonism and convergence. One becomes aware of a constant striving to mitigate, to dampen the male rigidity of power, to convert it into an erotic union, where order would be combined with full freedom, and the mystery of free submission and submitting freedom would be revealed. Power, vested in the steel armor of the state-legal system, settles in vain the unsolvable problem of uniting personal freedom in all of its distinctiveness with a uniform order equal for everyone. This unconscious striving to replace power with an erotic union is present in the many utopian forms of a state. Plato pronounces on precisely this and not something else in the *Republic* when he advances as the ideal of power the rule of philosophers who are supported not by the sword but by the authority of their wisdom and righteousness, and who are strong for being favored and desired: law and the sword are abolished here in the harmony of the reciprocal erotic attraction of all classes. Our Slavophiles cherished a similar super-legal and super-state ideal with respect to the Russian autocracy — and they dreamed of a replacement of the irons of power by its eroticism. Different political dreamers, in particular, anarchists, speak of the same thing, though blindly and deafly. Insofar as these hopes are bound with one or another form of historical power or its evolution, they lapse into utopianism and sentimentalism.

The rupture of the male and the female principle that distinguishes the nature of power and is manifested in its rigid and violent character is rooted in the primordial destruction of sexual balance in humanity, and is not at all connected with one or another particular form of statehood, all of which are the external reaction to the inner evil in humankind, generally speaking. The curse weighs upon power and earth alike. In the sweat of its brow humanity has to carry the burden of historical power with all of its scorpions, in the name of the fact that nonetheless the chief "carries the sword not without reason." Power is a divinely instituted means for the external battle against inner evil, its palliative and symptomatic healing. And yet the striving to overcome power is ontologically right and deeply founded, not the striving for the absence of power promised by anarchy, but for super-power: the sheer negation alone of power is empty and dead, as is any negation. But super-power is nothing other than *divine power,* theocracy, which is the ontological nucleus of power, and thus its hidden task.

Like everything in the world, power strives to "outstrip itself"; it yearns for theocracy. Its absolute ideal is given in Christianity, where "the thousand-year reign of Christ" on this earth is promised as a forewarning, while beyond the threshold of this eon is promised "His kingdom which will have no end." And when the Russian people cherishes the apocalyptic ideal of the "White Tsar," the question here is not the autocratic constitution of the Slavophiles (for this armchair daydream of a Manilov[104] is akin to similar dreaming among anarchists, and in general has nothing apocalyptic in it), but rather a certain overcoming of power. Dostoevsky too by times spoke of it as the dissolving of the state in the Church, and V. Soloviev, as "free theocracy." It is significant that the desire of the Hebrews to have an earthly king, even if the anointed of God, already represented a betrayal of *this* theocracy: "'They have not rejected you,' God said to Samuel, 'they have rejected me so that I should not reign over them'" (1 Sam. 8:7).

Humanity is not internally reconciled with power in its naked guise, with its cruelty and callousness, and it cannot build its relationship with it on bald calculation alone, on a Benthamite arithmetic of benefit. It wants to gild with an erotic aureole the irons of power, it seeks in it the theocratic elements already on hand, it strives towards a super-legal justification of power and law. The element of power in and of itself, as the will to command and the agreement to submit, is something natural-human and median; it belongs to the realm of the relative. In this sense one can also define it as an *animal* principle (in the customary usage of the prophetic books). By the way, "animal" does not mean *bestial*, nonhuman, but only carnal, "psychic," relative. However, something relative is not supported by itself, but seeks justification in the absolute; likewise the animal principle seeks to become godlike through the human, to see itself in theocratic light.

It is well known that in the pagan world a theocratic and sacral character was everywhere ascribed to power. The sacred nature of the power of an Egyptian pharaoh gives us a more grandiose example of this. He was revered as a son of god and as a god, and this conviction defines the religious-political life of Egypt over the course of millennia. From a later time it is enough to recall the cult of the emperors in Rome with which Christianity irreconcilably collided. Faith in the theocratic anointing of power was connected in paganism with its general religious naturalism. As in the living figures of nature it saw icons of Divinity, so too in the natural icon of power it perceived the manifest presence of the power of Divinity, in this way practicing a devout idolatry. So far as earthly power in paganism was immediately equated with divine power, for Christianity it was a *pseudo*-theocracy competing with the singularly divine power of Christ himself (which is why both the pharaoh and the wild animal acquired the meaning of dark, anti-theocratic potencies). But here as in other respects paganism possessed a religious clairvoyance, a capacity to discern the natural icons of Divinity in nature and the human being. Having committed an error in the estimation of particular manifestations of the theocratic principle by virtue of its fateful limitedness, it remained entirely correct in the general definition of the religious nature of power, and its insights here merit deep and penetrating attention.

After Christ the one true King appeared in the world, pagan theocracy connected with the divinization of the head of state became impossible: it would prove to be an abuse and blasphemy, for the whole actual distance between earthly power and theocracy had already been brought to light. Worshiping a "wild animal" as a Deity was now connected not with the perceptiveness but with the blindness of paganism. The opposition of the kingdom of Christ to the kingdom of the beast is one of the fundamental motifs of the *Apocalypse*. While refusing to render divine homage to the emperors, primitive Christianity in no way refused obedience to the beast; on the contrary we know that the apostles summoned Christians to every kind of loyalty.

Once an expanding Christianity through the power of its message became an empire-wide religion, a new question stood before its theocratic consciousness. What is the nature of the power of a *Christian* emperor, and is the animal principle absorbed in it by the divine, or speaking differently, is *it* a theocracy? The attitude to this question proved to be different in the Eastern and the Western church. In the East, royal power began to be regarded as one of the aspects of ecclesiastical service, which on the whole can be different and take many forms, while to each service there corresponds its own special charism. Royal power received the prayerful consecration of the Church in the ritual of coronation to kingship by which a marriage of sorts was established. Therefore, although a certain theurgic quality is inherent in the nature of royal power, it did not force out or supplant the natural, "animal" principle of power. Through this it still did *not* become theocratic, for grace does not force, but only assists those who seek it; rather the inspiration of good as well as evil remained for it equally possible. Here a special, divine-erotic bond with the people was established, tangible only for the Church and existing *above* any legal utilitarianism and state structure, *outside* the relation to forms of a "constitution." The earthly king became in this light something of an icon of the King of kings on which a ray of the White Tsar could flare up in solemn, sacred moments. But in and of itself this power of Christian monarchs still had an *Old Testament* nature, finding its prototype and greatest norm in the Old Testament theocratic kings David and Solomon, who likewise were only foretypes of theocracy and not its fulfillment. Therefore no historical monarch can be considered theocratic; nothing can convert his power into theocracy, or him into a prophesier of God's will, into a prophet or royal theurgist; nothing can bestow on him the authority of impeccability. Christianity does not recognize the duty of blind and unlimited obedience (and even less does it eliminate a conscientious, loyal "opposition"). If even a priest can be forbidden to celebrate the sacraments and actually be deprived of the priesthood, all the more does the supreme bearer of power break his sacred union with the people, once he has committed a serious sin against his service (e.g., by betraying the faith or his people, etc.). Of course, it is a matter for the religious conscience to determine the presence of such a rupture.

Such is the religious conception of royal power in the Eastern church. Therefore one can say that the East did not yield inwardly to the temptation of a pseudo-Christian pseudo-theocracy. It made an appearance here only as a temporary infatuation or abuse. On the contrary, this temptation gained strength in the Western church thanks to the claims of papalism in the realm not only of spiritual but also of secular power. In this way both charisms — kingship and priesthood — seemingly merged in a single theurgic principle. Added to it was the general idea of papal infallibility *ex cathedra,* which was alive of course long before the Vatican dogma. This infallibility fastened together and so to say covered both powers with its cupola. Thanks to the sum total of all these attributes, the pope turned into a universal charismatic which in paganism only the pharaoh, the son of god, the king and supreme priest could feel himself to be. The pope replaces Christ on earth, and his monarchy is already the thousand-year reign of Christ with His saints: such is the unavoidable logic of papalism. In imperial Rome *divus caesar* rises again under the papal tiara; the pagan pseudo-theocracy comes to life.[105] But if Christ's kingdom is already realized in Rome, then surely the One Who Is Coming is an unnecessary hindrance, for his work is already done and lies in the reliable hands of *societas Jesu.* . . . A monstrous substitution results, having fateful consequences for the whole Christian world.[106] For the rebellion against the church — Protestantism — which finds its immediate continuation in the humanist revolution, is in Western Europe the direct offspring of Catholicism, its dialectical antithesis. The result was the beginning of that general "secularization" of life and in particular of power that continues to the present day.

The secularization of power consists in the weakening of the religious fetters that reciprocally bind it and the subjects, in the negation

Human History

of the theurgic principle of power and in its reduction primarily to principles of political utilitarianism, to natural-human animality. Corresponding to this, the human institution of power is set in opposition to the divine right of power. This change in the very perception of the nature of power is connected with the general successes of humanism and the weakening of a religious perception of the world that could not fail to be reflected in a political worldview. That different non-Christian nationalities turned out to be drawn into the orbit of Christian states also contributed to this; as a result, the very character of statehood becomes religiously complex and confused. In the same direction, the realized division of the churches and the splitting-off of Protestant sectarianism had an impact, all of which deprived Christianity of its unity and cohesion as a historical and political force and divided it into different parts competing among themselves. One way or another, the "sacred empire" did not succeed; it proved to be conquered by the weight of the flesh, of sin and a lack of faith. The lofty political ideal of the Russian Slavophiles was found to be suspended in the air, for they refused to see its realization in the Petersburg absolutism of a German model. And least of all does it occur even to one who hates what is coming as its replacement to think now of a reaction or of a restoration of the old state system: the galvanization of a historical corpse will yield an even worse result.

The "secularization" of power steadfastly spreads far and wide, and moreover it operates on both sides. The bearers of former power, losing faith in the church's support for it and in a vital sense of a religious bond with their subjects, became all the more representatives of an entirely secular absolutism fighting against their subjects for their own power on the pretext of a defense of their sacred rights. The sacred empire, on the eve of its collapse, degenerates into a police state, fearing for its own existence. It is a variation of the same political humanism, only under an old mask beneath which there is no longer a living person. Popular masses more and more are imbued with a purely utilitarian understanding of power, but utilitarianism as a basic and decisive criterion in politics is something other than revolution *en permanence,* whether hidden and smoldering under ash, or already burst into flame. Europe, evidently, entered the era of permanent revolution in 1789. But precisely thanks to this utilitarianism *the mechanism* of power, its technique, is being perfected — that which is called in the language of contemporary state law "the legal state." Guarantees of all kinds of "freedoms" are established. Something that absolutism neither knew how nor wished to arrange, what an even earlier epoch did not at all achieve, is being done. But even secularized power cannot hold on by utilitarianism alone — even it needs a distinctive religious consecration, which it finds in the mystical deification of the people, representing a variant of the religion of deified humanity. Overthrowing the thrones that rested upon divine right, the revolution itself rests on "the popular will" which only comes to light through voting, but represents a self-subsisting mystical reality.

In the English revolution, having a religious foundation, the people are still regarded as sovereign *ex iure divino,* whereas in the French revolution as in all subsequent revolutions, it is a question of the enigmatic but for everyone plain reality of the collective, whose will is sacred, and therefore is the highest source of legislation. Its own type of humanistic theocracy arises which sees its task in faithfully defining and realizing the true "will of the people." But how is this to be achieved, and where is one to seek it? The awareness of the clear insufficiency of "ballot boxes" and voting papers for this purpose, fit only for deciding separate practical questions, elicits a lengthy "crisis of the sense of justice" (as Athenian democracy endured in the epoch of Plato, under completely analogous circumstances). The question of the "law of the law" becomes for thoughtful jurists their own form of squaring the circle. For the democratic religion of deified humanity the state is the highest form of life — a pseudo-church. Even more than that: humanity, organized in a state, is an earthly god. This was declared by Hegel and Feuerbach in their own ways.[107] *Legality* proves to be the highest form of human relations. But every spiritual movement in good or evil, in holiness or Satanism, requires for itself a personal incarnation. A newly regenerated cult of statehood in the religion of the democratic deified humanity requires it also. The statehood of the deified people sooner or later must obtain such a personal head who with all his being will accommodate the claims of a kingdom from this world. Thereby the mysticism of deified humanity will be maximally manifested in conscious opposition to Christianity.

In order that a *new revelation* of power could appear, it is necessary for its enigma to stand before religious consciousness in all its acuity. And for this it is necessary that the principle of power should be experienced in all its depth, be known as such, and recognized in its proper nature. And in order to become vitally aware of the problem of theocracy, perhaps it is necessary to be temporarily deprived of theocratic semblances or prototypes, to find oneself placed face to face before power in its human form, in its natural "animality." And in this the positive side of its "secularization" can be expressed also. The *heteronomy* of power, equally characteristic of both pagan pseudo-theocracy and the clerical "Christian state," darkened the nature of power in its autonomy and led to the grave confusion of what is Caesar's and what is God's. In this were ambiguity and indecision which led to falsity and substitutions, to despotism or pseudo-theocracy, i.e., to the triumph of the same "animal" principle, only cloaked with a different official phraseology. Thereby the external victory of "secularization," of the "legal state," was prepared with its human integrity sincerely guarding the "good of the people" and its freedom. But precisely this atmosphere of militant deification of the people, of the kingdom of this world, forces the spiritual suffocation of those who cherish in their soul a religious ideal of power and who do not want *to worship* the "beast," or receive its "mark." One can and must preserve one's loyalty and endure even a hated state system, even highly value its practical achievements, by seeing in it a relative everyday good or just a lesser evil than the antiquated and inveterately lying power of the old style. But to love this power, to feel a religious eros for it, is possible only by taking part in the cult of a democratic Caliban, "offering sacrifices to the beast." One ought to accept a state system that is reduced to political utilitarianism just as one would the burden of economic concerns: acknowledging the integrity of this labor, to bear it ascetically as a vital "obedience"; however, the "integrity," the correctness, is only a religious-moral minimum whereas religion in all of its affairs wants the maximum.

Nevertheless this laicized state system is already its own kind of *negative revelation* of power. This expanded and differentiated body of power is also "the land of the curse," cracked and dried out, and it thirsts for heavenly moisture. The "legal state," with its legal guarantees and all of its earthly wisdom and human-relative truth, does not extinguish the yearning for *a different* kingdom, not only of cold law but of love, for *a different* power — theocratic. But of course this question has meaning only in the Church, and it is a question here not of politics in the usual sense of the word, but precisely of the religious overcoming of "politics," of that *transfiguration* of power which will be its *New-testamental* revelation. Here are possible only expectations and troubling presentiments: where, when, how, visible or invisible to the world — we do not know. Only conjectures and expectations are possible there, about which it is not the place to speak here. The Russian people, filled with apocalyptic trepidation, carries in itself this presentiment — in its idea of the "White Kingdom" through the prism of which it perceived Russian autocracy. The insights of the deepest exponents of the Russian spirit touch upon this: the Slavophiles, F. M. Dostoevsky, V. Soloviev, N. F. Fedorov. Even the irreconcilability with the "animal" principle of the state system in L. N. Tolstoy, in whom all positive ideas are clothed in negation and assume the form of "naysaying," speaks of the same. So too the mystical revolutionary spirit of the intelligentsia with its quests for the invisible coming city,[108] although these are clothed in a foreign and ugly form of social-political utopianism. And indeed on the whole the notorious apolitical stance of the Russian people, having its source not only in the insufficient discipline of the individual and society, but also generally speaking in the absence of a taste for the median and the relative.

And so, the decomposition of the religious principle of power transpires on the empirical surface and secularization triumphs, but in the mystical depths a new revelation of power is being prepared and is maturing — the appearance of theocracy which anticipates its definitive triumph beyond the threshold of this eon.[109]

6. Society and Ecclesiality[110]

Power is the skeleton of human society, which in addition to this has its organs and tissues, its physiology. A public element exists — the existence of society is as basic and irrefutable a fact as is power. Human beings are inseparable from humanity, they are as much individual as generic beings — genus and individual in them are indivisible, conjugate, and correlative. For this reason individualism, which raises a revolt against the generic principle and imagines it can overcome it, in reality expresses only the sickness of generic consciousness evoked by the decline of elementary, natural vitality in connection with the predominance of rationality, of reflection: it is "decadence," which while claiming to be a crisis of the public, in fact signifies only a crisis *in* the public. Against *such* individualism even elementary scientific sociologism is right which knows how to probe the public body, coming to

Human History

know from different sides and with different methods the strength of social cohesion and heredity, and comprehending the character of social determinism in its statics and dynamics. And rebellion against the generic principle is as false and meaningless as is rebellion against one's own body in the name of exaggerated spiritualism.

Humanity exists as family, tribe, classes, nationalities, races, finally, as a single human genus. One thing is indisputable, that it is organized in a definite manner, *it is an organism,* as the sociology of the so-called organic school teaches in a true presentiment of an important mystical truth. This coherence is expressed in politics, economics, customs, social psychology, right up to fashion and gossip. But it is immediately experienced rather as a morbid feeling of disorganization: mutual struggle and egotistical self-assertion reign in society. Here centrifugal and centripetal forces continually compete. Therefore the quest for an organized public is an ongoing concern and labor for all humanity, and it becomes more intense the more complex the expanding social body of humanity becomes, the more tangibly life is socialized. Humanity seeks that kind of social organization under which solidarity might triumph, and egoism might be neutralized: such is the dream of all social utopias. The intense conflict of egotistical self-affirmations here is considered to be some kind of misunderstanding that it is possible to clarify, or an abuse that one can remove or even an immaturity that one can outgrow. By searching for the causes of social evil in the imperfections of this or that social function, sociologists usually do not see at all its general and deep roots; in their understanding of the problem of evil they suffer from sociological colorblindness and limitedness. In these reveries about a normal society one common feature comes to light — the hope of somehow deceiving personal and group egoism, of getting around it, outwitting it with solidarity, satiating it without infringing on anyone's interests. Indeed the slogan speaks of this: liberty, equality, fraternity (without brothers!). The task of an organized society has two sides: not only freedom, but also subordination, not only equality, but also difference, not only fraternity but also compulsory organization. To say it differently, the social ideal strives to realize not universal freedom alone and equality, but true hierarchism, outside of which there is no social cohesiveness. On what then must such hierarchism be confirmed? There can be no reply to this in the sociological order.

A separate human individual is not only a self-enclosed microcosm, but also *part* of a whole, namely one that enters into the structure of a mystical human organism, Adam-Cadmon in the expression of the Cabbala.[111] After the incarnation of God had occurred, the Lord Jesus Christ is this kind of all-perfected, pan-human pan-organism: on entering the Church, which is Christ's Body, a human being enters into the composition of this absolute organism, in relation to which the original mystical unity of Adam-Cadmon is as it were a lower, natural foundation. Humanity exists as a mystical organism which is implanted already in the first Adam. Every human person, having being-for-itself, is its own absolute center; but it does not have independent being, for its center is outside itself, in the whole. The first is the principle of the equivalence of human persons, of the equality according to their spiritual essence, in the image of God. In spirit all are equal, and this equality is vitally recognized in Christianity: "There is neither Greek nor Jew, neither circumcision nor non-circumcision, barbarian, Scythian, slave or free, but Christ is all and in all" (Col. 3:11; cf. Gal. 3:28). On the contrary, a principle not of equality but of difference, of hierarchical structure, is supposed by the mystical organic quality of the human being: "A body is not from one member but from many. If the foot says, 'I do not belong to the body because I am not a hand,' then is that really why it does not belong to the body? . . . The members are many, but the body is one . . . if one member suffers, all members suffer with it; if one member is praised, then all members rejoice with it. And you are the body of Christ, but separately you are members" (1 Cor. 12:14-27). We immediately know ourselves, however, only as persons, as isolated centers of being, and we sense our organic nature only through the social environment as an external givenness, something accidental and forced, not a spiritual community but a collective, having its highest ideal not in love but in solidarity. And only by becoming immersed in ourselves, in our own mystical roots in the pan-organism, do we feel our spiritual community, and come to know ourselves as not-self. This overcoming of our isolation happens in the atmosphere of ecclesial love, in the experience of the church's sacraments, but collectivism no longer covers spiritual community. Here the whole relativity of social inequality becomes clear before the fact of the spiritual equality of people; this is why even slavery in the age of primitive Christianity was not an obstacle to it.

Yet precisely through this aspect Christianity, being catholic, is at the same time extra-social or super-social (and of course sociologism neither completely knows nor understands this). In it really no answer is yet given to the religious problem of society, in which it is a question as much about equality as about the hierarchical difference of humanity. To state the same idea differently, it is a question not only about the spiritual but also the psychic human being whose mystical organic quality enters into its composition. In order to come to know oneself, one must penetrate not only into the depths of the spirit but also feel one's flesh in all its reality. The latter is possible only on condition that humans sense themselves as part of pan-human flesh, having been administered a certain natural sacrament of organic society and become aware of themselves, in spite of their isolation, as a living cell of a living organism. In this context social coherence will appear not as the inert flesh of social matter, crushing and oppressing with its heavy materiality, but becomes a transparent cover under which the motion of the fluids of the pan-human body will be palpable.

Such is the mystical task of religious society. Sociologism in theory and in life, not being aware itself of this, stirs up a thirst for religious society, poses the problem of organic hierarchism, of the sophianic enlightenment of the social body. For long ages humanity lived an immediate social-organic life, and all the societal formations, even the most burdensome, were sanctified by the force of antiquity and were confirmed by religious sanction: castes, slavery, serfdom were regarded as immutable and almost divinely established structures of life, thanks to which they lost part of their toxicity and burden. A theocratic basis was attributed directly to the social order, and behind it stood the force of religious tradition and social conservatism. This elemental stability has in it much that is attractive for an epoch that has hopelessly lost it, and in this is the psychological source of the distinctive romance of patriarchy (Carlyle!). However, such a society, although on the outside cloaked in a religious wrapping without in any way being enlightened on the inside, does not in any manner whatsoever represent a *resolution* of our problem, which is why all these desires of restoration and reaction are sentimental fallacy. The problem was not unmasked and posed in its full acuteness, it was masquerading as a certain heteronomy of a society subordinated to norms of a religious nature. The "secularization" of society brought for it autonomy, but at the same time it set before religious consciousness its problem, which earlier it was unable to sense as such. It did not and could not exist either in the Middle Ages, the epoch of religious patriarchy, or in primitive Christianity, which saw before itself only the all-encompassing darkness of paganism. It was necessary to experience all the bitterness of secularized society and the burning melancholy of religious unresponsiveness; it was necessary to begin seeing sociologically in order to catch sight of the inert social matter with one's own eyes and to sense all the weight of its fetters, so that the first hope for its enlightenment would catch fire in hearts, that a new question would mount up to heaven and a new summons would be heard in humanity — to religious society. Here it is impossible to be content with self-deception and to be reconciled with compromises: we *do not have* a religious society that is connected with the transfiguration of the social element; it does not exist in our religious experience. The spiritual community of faith, of prayer, of love, in general the building blocks of ecclesial catholicity, nevertheless does not contain *this*. It is a question here not of the spirit alone, but also of the flesh, and besides of the social or more precisely of the pan-human flesh, of its salvation and enlightenment, and further of the vision of humanity as a living entity, Adam-Cadmon, the Grand-Être, about which the Jewish Cabbalists, A. Comte, and V. Soloviev speak in unanimous perceptiveness.

What has been until now the attitude of historical Christianity to the problems of society? One motif is indisputably determining in it — the ascetic motif — and for it the norm is ascetic culture and ascetic society (this trait is proper also to Platonism to a certain degree). There is no need *wholly* to give oneself up to the concerns and interests of this world, whatever they might be; it is necessary to observe a certain interior distance with respect to them, to keep one's spiritual freedom. Society must be inwardly, ascetically regulated so that people will not be able to take it "in exchange for their own soul." Therefore, although it is possible, still for the majority (i.e., non-monks) one must take part in the affairs of this world, but without passion, without enthusiasm, and best of all in the name of "holy obedience." One can love as a professional matter that for which one feels a natural calling; for even in society there is a certain element of art, and it knows its own artists and virtuosi, its gifts and talents; however, one can love it only conditionally, and not as "the one thing necessary" solely deserving of love. Putting it differently, it is necessary constantly to be on one's guard against *being seduced* by society. And to a certain degree everything worldly has become "bitter" or lost its savor for one whose heart is pierced by the arrow of Christianity and aches with its sweet pain, who is scorched by its fire. The wisest of the pagan enemies of Christianity, e.g., Celsus, sensed this *estrangement from the world* right away. *Christianity is a sickness* for worldly consciousness. In our days Christianity is having to clash with humanism on these grounds, with its religion of deified humanity, for which "society" approximately corresponds to *sanctity,* for in it is included precisely that "one thing necessary" that has justification and meaning in itself.

By comparison *with such* an attitude Christianity naturally seems cold, restrained, and mistrustful. It uneasily hears the din with which the tower of Babel is again being built, and in the accelerated movement of the chariot of progress it sees a symptom of an impending cataclysm, of the approaching end. It does not believe in this progress; moreover it does not want *this kind* of progress. It is necessary to be fully aware of the profound difference between the so-called *humaneness* which comprises the soul of this progress, and *Christian love,* which can seem not at all humane and even severe in its exactingness (as K. N. Leontiev loved to emphasize in an exaggerated way). For humaneness all suffering is evil; it wants to make everyone content and happy and it believes in the feasibility of this plan. Whereas Christian love knows the purifying power of sufferings, and on the contrary, for it contentment, "satisfaction of the greatest number of needs," according to the hedonistic ideal of happiness, would be spiritual captivity to the prince of this world. For humaneness sin does not exist at all, and evil it knows only as the result of a bad society; for Christianity, social evil is only one of the manifestations of cosmic evil, and not even the greatest, or the ultimate one. Social progress, side by side with the successes of humaneness and partially in conjunction with them, can be accompanied by the subtlest forms of spiritual evil, just as it can itself become in the end a mask for Antichrist.

For this reason, while being implacable towards spiritual evil, Christianity is by no means similarly uncompromising towards external evil and in particular towards social evil understood as derivative. Here it gladly tends towards the practice of opportunism and conservatism. It knows the commandment of *faithful endurance* (which is neither spiritual passivity nor servility), for it does not want to become the victim of provocation of evil. But it is evident that this very commandment is a monstrous temptation for humanism, which for this reason almost always has to *surpass* Christianity in humaneness. Christianity revealed itself to be like this at the beginning of its existence, when even in relation to slavery it displayed its "quietism" and began to teach slaves to carry their yoke patiently "for the sake of the Lord." Then also it displayed its social conservatism, its mistrustful attitude towards external innovations ("let everyone remain in the calling in which they were called"), and this with all of its eschatological qualities. Its irreconcilability with respect to the Roman state arose not from social-political but exclusively from religious motives. And this trait — so to say, of methodological conservatism — became inherent in it and in its whole subsequent history. For Christianity there is no unconditional evil or unconditional good in the social domain, as they exist there for humanism, and for that reason not one of the measures of humaneness that have been realized by the efforts of progress has for it an unconditional value in and of itself, not the abolition of slavery, not the collapse of serfdom, not any constitutions or "freedoms." Indeed they have been frequently realized with the enthusiasm of atheism and with a direct challenge to Christianity, although even this can still not destroy their relative value.

It is obvious that in this situation historical Christianity stands on the edge of a knife and is easily liable to the temptation of perversion. We often observe this in life when patience is replaced by hypocrisy and servility, and independent conservatism by cowardly opportunism, by an obtuse immobility or a proud reactionary stance, and in virtue of this inner laicization a sort of anti-humanism or a reverse humanism is obtained. But Christianity has its own positive motives for social progress, partially coinciding with humanist ones; a dynamic is inherent to it, a movement, and it sets its imperious demands for a social conscience. The motive force of humanitarian progress is not love or pity but a haughty dream of earthly paradise, of a deified human kingdom of this world; this is the modern variant of ancient Jewish pseudo-Messianism. Progress believes that within the limits of history evil can be removed, suffering defeated, and tragedy resolved by the forces of humankind alone. For Christianity mercy, pity, and compassion — in general, *charity* — are the positive motives of society. Charity, however, has essentially only a palliative character, and so Christian politics (or, if one likes, "Christian socialism") is also only organized charity and cannot be anything else, and works of mercy have always constituted the strength of historical Christianity. All special measures, regarded in the category of means, can be considered only according to motives of expediency, which is why Christianity cannot be inscribed with a single and unalterable social politic (it is impossible to say, for example, that Christianity in and of itself would be against socialism as an economic system, or even for it). In this it goes without saying that it has to reckon with the indications of experience and of social medicine, which is what social science essentially is.

Historically, "humaneness" arises in the process of the secularization of Christian ethics, but of course, having been detached from its foundation, it gets an ambiguous and even perverted character, which is why its works too cannot be considered as an unconditional boon (as at one time V. Soloviev evidently allowed).[112] Unconditional good on the plane of the relative, the only place where humanism knows it, does not exist generally speaking, for only the religious coefficient is decisive. A humaneness that asserts itself without Christ and apart from Christ is a religious fraud, a temptation by godless good and godless love, ethical idolatry, and its successes acquire the significance of sacrifices before the altar of deified humanity. It is an anti-Christian pseudo-church under construction, enticing with many signs. It does not, however, follow from this that everything that is opposed to humanism is by that very fact already something good — such anti-humanism (which at one time attracted K. Leontiev) in no way reveals a free attitude toward it. Meanwhile it became usual that precisely such constructs exerted an excessively large influence on the form of ideas of the representatives of the church. This is expressed in their inability to be themselves, in their incapacity to rise up to that spiritual freedom which is inherent in Christianity. Humanism did not create this mighty body of society that occupies so exceptional a place in the humanist religion of deified humanity, but it did attach to the problem of society a specific religious intensity, and one cannot deny that it demands for itself a religious resolution.

One must state forthrightly and with all resoluteness and certitude that in historical Christianity this positive resolution still *does not exist*. True, it blesses and prayerfully consecrates different manifestations of social life and "culture"; by introducing a theurgic element, it fights against theomachian forces operating here. But this prayerful consecration is only "the prayer of a Christian before the beginning of every work," and not an attempt to make religious sense of precisely this specific work which in its essence nevertheless remains religiously unenlightened. Society grows with its own elemental, organic life, similar to the growth of a body, and by this growth recurrent needs and inquiries come to the fore. But it remains impenetrable for religion. The ascetic orientation mentioned above is not capable of assuaging this religious thirst and pain, for it has only a negative character. The positive orientation of Christianity in questions of society is exhausted by the principles of ethics; meanwhile, ethics alone in no way expresses the religious understanding of the question (just as geometry, which has to do only with form, does not meet the requirements for an integral conception of the body). Indeed on the whole a single pure ethics is even uncharacteristic for Christianity. What kind of Christianity, in fact, is the ethical religion of Kant? The resolution of a religious problem solely on the plane of ethics would signify merely its impotence before it. The question remains: What is *the religious nature* of this society in which ethics sees only the material for duty, an inert and unenlightened object for applying the categorical imperative?

But here we really do have a problem, which exceeds our human powers; here a religious event is needed, a new experience and a new word. It is impossible to invent it, and therefore there is no viler taste in religion than to be occupied with inventing religions or producing sectarianism, instead of being concerned with the dignity of religion, waiting and hoping humbly and patiently. Here a religious *metabasis eis allo genos* is needed, the manifestation of a transfigured society, "of holy flesh," of the mystical hierarchy of humanity. Along with the transfiguration of the flesh, the garments of social being "will be enlightened and become white as snow" permeated with the ray of Tabor. But even this problem is out of place in history where it arose, and its answer lies already *beyond* history, or on the very bounds between history and metahistory.

7. The End of History

If one examines history on its own plane and in its immediate achievements, one has to acknowledge that history is a great failure, some sort of tragic misunderstanding. In every respect it leads to agonizing dissonances and tragic dead ends, and not one of the deepest aspirations of humanity is satisfied. And although historical time as something concrete must have not only a beginning but also an end, nevertheless if one adheres to the historical plane, it seemingly does not have its natural end and by not reaching completion, it is doomed to bad infinity.

These very dissonances and antinomies comprise a stimulus for further uninterrupted movement, and it seems that the river of historical time cannot stop in its flow. All historical tasks presuppose uninterrupted "progress," for they cannot be definitively resolved. Can the meaning of history really be expressed as an "eternal cyclical return," as the inevitable result of endless motion?

It appears to be so, however, only if one remains in the realm of the historically phenomenal, but beneath it lies the deep soil of historical ontology. If there, on the surface, history apparently does not know how to come to an end, then here it travels the path of completion, by nearing its ripeness and end. And if from there the end passes itself off as some external, unexpected, violent act, as the personal death of each separate human being is customarily considered to be like, then here the end coincides with the arrival of the greatest maturity; it appears to be justified and regular, just as personal death is sent only when it is timely for the human being. And from this point of view one can say that history has succeeded if it has prepared its regular end and exit *beyond* history: so too "a Christian end of life" is in a certain sense the apotheosis of life and its justification. But the coming of historical maturity is measured, of course, not by the achievements of progress; this is only a symptom, a refracted reflection of that which is happening in the deep, and it covers the meaning of history as much as it reveals it. It matures in divine-human acts of the revelation and incarnation of God. The destinies of history are determined directly or indirectly by the destinies of the Church. The Church is the soul of the world soul and the soul of history.

The ontology of history is also *ecclesial* history, of course not the external "history of the church" as an institution but the inner completion of its destinies. These latter are intertwined with the general course of history, but this bond lies so deep that it is inaccessible to natural humankind unenlightened by the grace of God; it is disclosed in revelation, but even this remains a sealed secret. For the religious consciousness historical epochs are determined differently than for the historian of economy, law, culture, etc. It may be that under the thunders of war and staggering world events, and not unconnected with them, even now something is happening unknown for the world that is more authentic, more definitive, more substantial for its destinies than this war and than all the clamor raised by European "progress." History will be completed not by the fact that the Great Powers will fall and a single world state will be founded with democracy, civilization, and socialism — all of this, taken for itself, is decay and has meaning only by reason of its connection with what is happening in the bowels of the world between humankind and God. The end does not exist for "progress" itself; it is the "eternal Jew" who knows no rest. And if we still hope for something on earth in the realm of religious revelations, it serves as a sign that history has not come to an end internally, independently of the duration of the time remaining for it (for the density or satiety of time is different, and the speed of events changes with its tempo). How do we perceive history? Does ontological time still remain? Is the end near? Only the Father knows the times and seasons, the completion belongs to him, but in keeping with the blossoming fig tree we judge the proximity of summer, and in ourselves a sacrificial readiness for the end and a thirst for the end must ripen. From the human heart must be wrested the prayer for the end: "Yea, come Lord Jesus!" Are we calling him *this way* now? No, although "we bow our heads with hope," all the same we do not call in this way. For we are still full of religious expectations in history, we hope for the Comforter before the coming of the world's agony, before the last effort of the darkness. However, time is short and condensed.

In order to want the end with all one's strength, one needs to have a lively portent of it; its first rays must be taking fire in the world. The Lord on the eve of his sufferings was transfigured before his disciples, and he revealed to them his Glory. And this ray of Transfiguration, this light of Tabor, has not gone out. The whole creation seeks it and yearns for it, and this call for Transfiguration is heard all the more distinctly in the world. The *Apocalypse* still speaks of the mysterious "thousand-year reign of Christ with his saints," of "the first resurrection." Dark is the meaning of this prophecy, and we dare not disclose it. But prophecies are irrevocable, and they *bind* all believers to the Word of God. And surely even before their fulfillment must they not become the subject of prayers, hopes, and yearning? Thus does Christian *hope* speak which keeps us from an unhealthy, excessive pessimism, from poisoning by eschatological fright. Prior to the dread and tragic end of the world, hope's quiet and timid voice speaks; before the world shudders with the throes of death, the ray of the Transfiguration flashes on earth, and the Kingdom of Christ on earth will be revealed, although as a brief preliminary, and to this all history is leading as to its own limit. May it be so, let it be so!

IV. Completion

The goal of history leads *beyond* history to the "life of the future age," whereas the goal of the world leads *beyond* the world, to "a new earth and a new heaven." Only in the kingdom of glory, when time ceases, will the goal of the universe come true, while the whole present day is only the pangs of birth. Humankind and every creature will rise in Christ and in him will realize their nature. Only then will the creation of the world be ended, completed by God's omnipotence on the foundation of creaturely freedom. This joining of divine omnipotence with creaturely freedom, the assumption of the creature's participation in making the world, plays a most important role in the destinies of the world. On the one hand, the world, made by the power of divine love, wisdom, and omnipotence, has its unshakeable foundation in them, and in this sense *the world cannot not succeed,* divine wisdom is not capable of allowing error, divine love does not desire hell as the definitive fate of creation. But, on the other hand, creaturely freedom introduces here the principle of limitedness, erroneousness, infidelity, and insofar as the destinies of the world are entrusted to it, the world *is able not to succeed,* as it has already failed relative to our eon. For the definitive creation of the world it is necessary to fasten together both of these foundations — divine omnipotence and creaturely freedom, inviolably preserved by divine love — into one indissoluble whole and thereby definitively make the divine and human agree. This joining of two natures has taken place in Christ, true God and perfect Human. But if the health and the durability of the world's foundation was secured by this, and a new fall with all of its cosmic consequences was made impossible, then the moral state of each separate human being remains as before entrusted to human freedom.

At the Last Judgment each human being, placed face to face with Christ and in him having come to know the true law of their own life, in the light of this awareness will themselves make an assessment of their freedom corresponding to that "likeness" which is fashioned by the creative work of their life, and they themselves will distinguish in it the transparent, the subjective, "the psychological," from the authentic, the real, and the ontological. Sin produces an agonizing fissure in the essence of a human being, becoming deeper the more powerfully sin controlled the human. The Judgment does not destroy anyone, condemning them to a reversion to primordial nothing, for the image of

The Human Being

God is ineradicable and immortal; rather, it shows to each one their own self in a true light, in the wholeness of their image, given from nature and re-created by freedom, and thanks to this insight, by seeing in themselves the traits of falsehood, they suffer, experiencing the torments of "Hell."

What is the nature of these torments? First of all it is the bitterness of disillusionment, when the subjectivity of that which was presented as objective is apprehended. This perception will transpire by means of a mysterious metaphysical act which is at present incomprehensible for us, which sets an end to the coexistence of good *and* evil in their merging and opposes good as being to evil as nonbeing. In the light of the Last Judgment which this separation is, there will be no place for an illusory quality and chimeras. Then it will become clear for people, how their likeness is unworthy of their image and in what way their creative freedom led them to a dismal emptiness. In this it is possible that they will all the same prefer nonbeing to being and want this emptiness, disappearing into a bottomless pit, shutting themselves up in their creaturely cellar. The torments of utmost disillusionment in oneself and in one's path, but at the same time the reluctance and incapability of accepting this disillusionment, and on top of everything the consciousness of one's highest nature and the agonizingly envious attraction to the divine world torture the soul with sufferings inexpressible in human language. These torments of realized and nevertheless persisting "psychologism" are not limited only to spiritual sufferings, for the human being is an incarnate spirit which is inseparably linked with sensuality, i.e., with a body. Therefore the torments of hell also have a corporeal character; the fire of hell, according to the symbolic witness of the Word of God, consumes not only the soul but also the body. These sufferings cannot destroy the resurrected, glorified, and immortal body, and in essence they do not even touch on it, forming a type of dark cloud over its uncorrupted beauty. However, this cloud will conceal it from its owner, who will see it as a formless and disintegrating corpse.

It is impossible for anyone who understands the spiritual nature of sensuality and the indissolubleness of spirit and body to deny bodily sufferings for the sake of pleasing a haughty spiritualism. In addition, simple consistency would demand simultaneously with torments the denial of beatitude, the glory of the body, and this already leads to an inevitable denial of the whole cosmos, of the whole creation which is

Completion

now groaning and waiting for its deliverance. Such anti-cosmism in any case is far from Christianity with its promises of a new earth and a new heaven. However, bodily sufferings do not pervert the divinely created Body which the just shall see in the beauty of its intelligible idea. Neither evil nor hell exists in general ontologically; it is a sui generis hallucination that arises regularly in sick souls. But precisely for that reason eternity is not proper to it; it has to do with the realm of nonbeing, which has been separated off from being. If the Word of God indeed speaks of "eternal torments," alongside of "eternal life," then of course not for the sake of equating the one and the other "eternity" – the beatitude of paradise, the direct design of God, positively grounded in the nature of the world, and the torments of hell, the result of the power of evil, of nonbeing, subjectivity, and creaturely freedom. Both aspects of "eternity," obviously, must differ among themselves at least as much as Creator and creatureliness are different, Divine omnipotence and creaturely freedom. And of course, "eternity" here is set not in opposition to temporality or limitedness, but *in contrast* to our temporality on the whole. Putting it differently, this means that the life of the future age is not measured by the time familiar to us (it transcends it), but has a different measure. If one understood "eternity" here as it is usually understood, in the sense of bad infinity, this would signify not eternity as a special *quality*, but precisely temporality, only one not having a fixed end. And since in any case it is only on this basis that the torments of hell are called "eternal," it is impossible to draw any conclusion relative to their transient nature, in either the one or the other aspect.

The Gospel parable of the Last Judgment depicts a division of humanity into sheep and goats; it has as its basis the relative preponderance of good and evil in the human being, which exerts influence on one's fate. But this division also takes place in the inner essence of each human being, for there is no one who has not been contaminated by sin, while at the same time there is no one who is completely foreign to any good.[113] Everyone will see themselves as they are, and with this they will see themselves more or less as *a monster*, although in a different degree and a different sense. This is why this judgment is dread *for everyone*, depicted with such threatening features in Christian liturgical texts. There is no righteous person who would not tremble before it: *quid sum miser tunc dicturus*[114] [what shall I say then, wretch that I am]!

But does this mean that there will be no paradise at all, or that it will be populated with outright monsters and invalids? If not, then beyond the limits of the Last Judgment, which shows the creature the impartial truth of God, there is a place for his mercy and the operation of his grace, "which heals the infirm and fills the impoverished." And is there a measure and limit for the power of God's grace, are there irremediable deformities for it? Is it not more correct to think that for the measurelessness of the sacrifice of Golgotha nothing irremediable exists, for there is no measure to divine forgiveness? But people say: there is indeed forgiveness, and it is limitless for as long as a human being is able to merit it by repentance, i.e., until death. But this idea suffers an unquestionable dogmatic repudiation in the face of the church's belief about the efficacy of prayers for the deceased, especially those offered in the celebration of the Eucharist (this belief found a coarsely straightforward expression among Catholics in the doctrine of purgatory). It means that believing love is able to cross even the bounds of death. But where is it said and who will venture to assert that this love loses strength beyond the bounds of the Last Judgment? And do we not read in the apostle other words swelling with anxious hope? "God has shut everyone in disobedience in order to have mercy on everyone. Oh the abyss of the wealth, the wisdom, and the knowledge of God! How unfathomable his judgments, how unsearchable his paths! For who has come to know the way of the Lord? Or who was his counselor? Or who gave to him so that he would have to give in return? For all is from him, by him and for him. To him be glory forever. Amen" (Rom. 11:32-36).

The torments of hell, constituting the reverse side of human freedom, are its *privilegium odiosum* [unpleasant privilege], and in them is expressed the esteem for this freedom rendered by God. For a human being cannot be saved violently and shown favor against one's will: forgiveness from God is insufficient, the readiness to accept this forgiveness, i.e., repentance, is necessary. If human freedom is acknowledged in its full extent, then one has to reckon with it with all seriousness and consistency right up to the torments of hell. For — and it is incumbent especially to remind one who is frightened at them out of a shy and enfeebling sentimentality — they are applied not apart from freedom but precisely with this very freedom, which has become arbitrariness and self-will; they are chosen, not imposed. Of necessity one must conclude from this that liberation from them is impossible without the participation of that same freedom, for the real citizens of hell do not in any way at all want to be liberated from it; on the contrary, they would wish to extend it into the whole universe.

That which torments and is tormented in people is of course their own proper self; it is not something that they have relinquished, that would weigh on them merely by its indelible character. For the past can be blotted out, and the existent can be made nonexistent – the efficacy of forgiveness is based on this; in this is the mystery of the pardon for the prudent thief. The torments of hell come from not wanting the truth which has become already a law for life; non-love for God – this is their foundation. To want "the pitch darkness," *nothing*, if only not to want God – this is the ultimate folly of evil, for which one cannot give any reasons and which cannot be justified; it is the sheer absurdity, the impotent convulsion of evil. In the world where light and darkness, good and evil, being and nonbeing are found in confusion, one can grasp why it is sometimes easy to prefer the underground trench of a mole to the blue of the sky, or the darkness of a cellar to sunlight, for being is inherent in them and consequently something positive, singular, unrepeatable. But in "the pitch darkness" there is nothing positive. Only the unfathomable madness of "the pit of hell" is capable of contrasting God with a perfect and deliberate zero and thereupon preferring this latter to him. But this madness is at the same time impotence, the phantasm of creaturely freedom. It is its naked potency, detained in its potentiality, straining impotently to be actualized. For creaturely freedom itself does not create an ontological foundation for itself, and it is not capable of giving any ontological growth to the divine fullness of being. Its realm is not *being on account of itself* but only *being for the sake of itself*. Therefore one can say that ontologically there is no hell; it does not profane with itself God's world, by presenting only a metaphysical place for nonbeing. It is the state of the creature, insofar as it is connected with human freedom, modality but not substantiality.

The righteous who have comprehended the world in its truth and beauty will not gaze on hell at all, for it does not exist in the eyes of God either. They will know only those who became blind, who persist in the phantoms and do not want to join in the general joy of being. J. Böhme (and following him J. Pordage) lodge hell in the innermost recesses of Divinity, precisely in its three "first principles" where it exists as the *Grimmgott* [wrathful God], and those who determine themselves in this principle also bear the necessary results. Such attribution of hell to the

The Human Being

divine nature must be repudiated along with the fundamental premises of "a physics of God," and Böhme's general monism. But here is contained a correct idea of the possibility for human freedom to provoke by itself such a modality of being which is called hell. In nature itself — although not of God but of the human being and generally speaking of the creation — the possibility not only for beatitude but also torment is implanted, with the individual uniqueness of the human person reaching even for this: every aspect of being has not only its bright side, but also its special underbelly or shadow. For this reason there is also a pseudo-hierarchy in hell; it is a pseudo-kingdom in which the perverted modalities of the divine cosmos combine into a cacophony — the most absurd caricature and parody of divine hierarchy and the music of the celestial spheres.

Therefore, although hell is possible for every form of creation — both of the human being and of the angel — it is inevitable for no one. It is the outcome of creaturely freedom, which would be able not to allow evil in the world, and consequently, hell also. And even injured humanity, thanks to the redemptive sacrifice of Christ, would be able to abolish hell. And if its presence is so definitely pre-established in the Word of God, then it is done, obviously, in virtue of divine foresight which is extended to creaturely freedom, but not in the sense of its inevitability, as flowing out of the will of God. *God did not create hell,* neither did he make death; and similar to death which entered the world through the devil, so too hell originally was begotten by the devil. This is why sinners are dispatched to the "eternal fire, prepared for the devil and his angels." In human freedom, with which the existence of hell is connected, there is nothing immutable or unalterable. At the same time we have no possibility of asserting that God's creation, however clouded and perverted by evil it might be, proved to be irremediably, radically, ontologically perverted — this would mean to ascribe to evil a substantiality, a creative autonomy which it does not have. The heart of being remains untouched by evil, which is only the master of modality. Therefore the devil in his existential foundation is all the same an angel, but one who profoundly and thoroughly perverted his nature. Thus also an ontological basis for his salvation is not forfeited, and a question *of fact* arises: Is repentance possible for him, outside of which there is no salvation at all?

One can suggest only two causes for the eternally abiding existence of hell: a complete incapacity for the good, constituting the natural consequence of a sinful life, and the stubborn, definitive unwillingness for good. As for the first, we cannot indicate the cause for such irreparableness of human nature, for divine grace heals and supplies, it gives strength to life. True, such a spiritual pauper "is saved as through fire," for "his work will burn down" so that "even clothed he will appear to be naked" (2 Cor. 5:3), passing through the most tormenting slashing and cutting off. But is there an irreparable deformity before the face of God? Impenitence, reluctance for paradise, theomachy can prove to be a more invincible obstacle. But this is a work of human freedom that has become arbitrariness and has resolutely opposed the law of life, of necessity. But *such* freedom, i.e., absolute arbitrariness (which is not possible in the present life, where freedom and necessity are mingled inseparably in the life process, as also are being and nonbeing) lacks stability, as a straining self. It is capable of acquiring it only by having ceased to be arbitrariness, i.e., having merged with necessity, and this can happen when sinners hate their sinful will and freely coordinate it with the Divine will, with the universal kingdom of love and beatitude.

This is the reason that the holy angels and human beings who have been favored with contemplating God with their own eyes and with the beatitude of paradise are no longer able to fall into or revert to evil, not because of the freedom *lost* by them, but on account of their passing to another existential *age* and overcoming the freedom rid of necessity (so that the very correlativity of the concepts *freedom-necessity* is abolished which exists only for this eon). Freedom in evil does not at all have the same stability as freedom in good; it is deprived of the ontological brace proper to the latter: one cannot drop anchor and gain a sure footing on it in the emptiness of nonbeing. Therefore freedom in evil presupposes the convulsive willful effort of uninterrupted rebellion, which is why it is possible to break away from it. "Eternal torments" have a merely negative eternity; it is only the shadow cast by the self. It is therefore impossible to acknowledge for them a positive *power* of eternity, and for that reason it is also impossible to affirm their indestructibility, although it is equally impossible to deny it. Here is a religious aporia, and religious chastity and modesty command us to stop in humility before this inaccessible mystery.[115] But here Christian hope remains fully possible, which the ineffable love of God instills, for everything will sink into its watery deep. "Love alone will never cease. Prophecies end, tongues fall silent, and knowledge is set aside. For we know only in part (in setting apart — *ek merous*) and we prophesy in part — *ek merous*, but when wholeness arrives — *to teleion* — the partial — *to ek merous* — will cease" (1 Cor. 13:8-10).

But it is especially unreasonable to apply to the life of the future age the categories of our temporality and in this manner to absolutize the latter. This is done in the doctrine of the reincarnation of souls and eternal "evolution" in general preached by theosophy. The doctrine of the reincarnation of souls is precious to many precisely as a means of coping with the eternity of torments, of removing hell from the universe. But this good purpose is achieved by very bad means, while as a solution for the mystery a dreary rationalism is accepted that destroys the whole difficulty simply by lengthening the time for life thanks to its frequent repetition according to the law of karma. Passing through such a filter the soul will be purified of its impurities and find beatitude. Of course, one can ask oneself the question why then even in a series of lives freedom will not likewise prove to be a demoralizing force, if one does not suppose the compulsory and omnipotent operation of karma. Of course, redemptive sufferings cleanse sinful filth, and no one is granted to escape their good fire. Suffering, however, does not always operate in this way; it can also embitter, and in and of itself reincarnation is powerless to conquer hell.

Against the coarseness of so simplified a resolution and poverty of imagination one should appeal to religious taste. In general we ought not to measure "the life of the future age" with our time, and by the same token we cannot assert that it has a limited or unlimited duration. One ought in general to free this question from the connection with the time familiar to us, because the metaphysical catastrophe, the ontological cataclysm necessarily is accompanied by a change *in the quality of time* as well, and it conceals within itself the means for solving the questions that are unexpected and unattainable for us now. One thing is certain: an ontological essence belongs only to the good and to the beatitude inseparably connected with it, and only it is beyond the distinction of freedom and necessity. Evil is an accident, a modus of creatureliness, an ontological illusion, something that could also not exist, that owes its existence to freedom and thus finds itself in the relative sphere of the opposition of freedom and necessity. Therefore it is ontologically entirely imaginable that evil can be rendered powerless and curtailed and that the bifurcation of freedom and necessity can be overcome. Repentance is presupposed by this, for, of course, no other

Completion

path to the liberation from evil exists, and no matter by what torments this repentance might have been purchased. For all human beings, who know their sinful filth, one thing must be clear: if the torments of hell can pass all people by, they must on no account pass *them* by, for they undeniably deserve them before the judgment of Divine justice. *This is how* personal religious conscience speaks to each individual. But alongside of this the timid voice of hope, the prayer for forgiveness, the voice of the tax collectors cannot be muffled: "O God, be merciful to me, a sinner!" And the Word of God gives hope, for the opposition of good and evil, of paradise and hell is not still the ultimate goal of the universe. For "the Son must reign, only until he casts down all of his enemies beneath his feet. . . . When everything is subjugated to him then the Son himself will submit to the One who subjugated everything to him, and *God will be all in all — ho theos panta en pasi*" (1 Cor. 15:25, 28).

To Him be glory unto the ages of ages. Amen.

Notes

Notes to the Translator's Introduction

1. Bulgakov's own recollections, which form the basis of the present biographical sketch, are available in *Tikhie dumy* [Calm thoughts] (Moscow: Respublika, 1996). Additionally, this sketch owes much to the superb study by Catherine Evtuhov, *The Cross and the Sickle: Sergei Bulgakov and the Fate of Russian Religious Philosophy, 1890-1920* (Ithaca, NY, and London: Cornell University Press, 1997). Readers will profit from Paul Valliere, *Modern Russian Theology: Bukharev, Soloviev, Bulgakov* (Grand Rapids: Eerdmans, 2000). Of interest is the introduction by Rowan Williams in his annotated collection *Sergii Bulgakov: Towards a Russian Political Theology* (Edinburgh: T. & T. Clark, 1999), pp. 1-19.

2. Bulgakov recollects this "atheistic" period in his life in the short text "Moe bezbozhie" [My atheism], in *Tikhie dumy* (Moscow: Respublika, 1996), pp. 319-24. The text was first published posthumously in *Avtobiograficheskie zametki* [Autobiographical notes] (Paris, 1946).

3. "Moe rukopolozhenie" [My ordination], *Tikhie dumy*, p. 346.

4. Evtuhov, *The Cross and the Sickle*, pp. 30-32.

5. Evtuhov, *The Cross and the Sickle*, p. 42.

6. Bulgakov, a convinced Marxist at the time, was overcome by the religious beauty of Raphael's painting, weeping and praying before it on repeated visits. He refers to this event in *Unfading Light*. But even before traveling west, Bulgakov had a religious experience of natural beauty while traveling by train to the Caucasus in 1894. This too is recounted in *Unfading Light*.

7. That is, members of the Russian intelligentsia.

8. Evtuhov, *The Cross and the Sickle*, pp. 43-45.

9. Evtuhov, *The Cross and the Sickle*, p. 36.

10. Evtuhov, *The Cross and the Sickle*, pp. 49-50.

11. Bernice Glatzer Rosenthal, "The Nature and Function of Sophia in Sergei

Bulgakov's Prerevolutionary Thought," in *Russian Religious Thought* (Madison: University of Wisconsin Press, 1996), pp. 154-75.

12. Valliere, *Modern Russian Theology*, pp. 231-37 for a discussion of this period in Bulgakov's life. [Bulgakov's article is available in *Problems of Idealism: Essays in Russian Social Philosophy*, trans., ed., and intro. by Randall A. Poole (New Haven and London: Yale University Press, 2003), pp. 85-125. — Trans.]

13. Valliere, *Modern Russian Theology*, p. 241.

14. Evtuhov, *The Cross and the Sickle*, p. 54.

15. Evtuhov, *The Cross and the Sickle*, pp. 77-81.

16. Evtuhov, *The Cross and the Sickle*, p. 81.

17. Valliere, *Modern Russian Theology*, p. 241.

18. "Agoniia" [Throes of death], *Tikhie dumy*, pp. 331-38. The events and Bulgakov's experiences are vividly described by Evtuhov, *The Cross and the Sickle*, pp. 120-26.

19. For a brief description of these developments see Dimitry Pospielovsky, *The Orthodox Church in the History of Russia* (Crestwood, NY: St. Vladimir's Seminary Press, 1998), pp. 191-98.

20. The best current biography of Florensky is Avril Pyman, *Pavel Florensky: A Quiet Genius* (New York and London: Continuum, 2010). A reliable discussion of his theology is provided by Robert Slesinski, *Pavel Florensky: A Metaphysics of Love* (Crestwood, NY: St. Vladimir's Seminary Press, 1984).

21. See Evtuhov, *The Cross and the Sickle*, pp. 129-31. The essay was published in *Voprosy religii* [Questions of religion], vol. 1 (Moscow, 1906), and included in Bulgakov's collection of essays, *Dva grada: Izsledovaniia o prirode obshchestvennykh idealov* [Two cities: Investigations in the nature of social ideals], vol. 2 (Moscow, 1911), pp. 303-13.

22. *Dva grada*, p. 307.

23. 1904: "O sotsial'nom moralizme (T. Karleil)" [On social moralism (T. Carlyle)]; 1905: "Religiia chelovekobozhiia u L. Feierbakha" [The religion of deified humanity in L. Feuerbach]; 1906: "Karl Marks kak religioznyi tip" [Karl Marx as a religious type], "Khristianstvo i sotsial'nyi vopros" [Christianity and the social question], "Tserkov' i kul'tura" [The church and culture], "Voskresenie Khrista i sovremennoe soznanie" [The resurrection of Christ and contemporary consciousness], "Venets ternovyi (pamiati F. M. Dostoevskago)" [Crown of thorns (in memoriam F. M. Dostoevsky)]; 1907: "Srednevekovyi ideal i noveishaia kul'tura" [The medieval ideal and modern culture]; 1908: "Religiia chelovekobozhiia v russkoi revoliutsii" [The religion of deified humanity in the Russian revolution], "Zagadochnyi myslitel' (N. F. Fedorov)" [An enigmatic thinker (N. F. Fedorov)]; 1909: "Narodnoe khoziaistvo i religioznaia lichnost'" [National economy and the religious person], "O pervokhristianstve" [On primitive Christianity], "Pervokhristianstvo i noveishii sotsializm" [Primitive Christianity and modern socialism], "Geroizm i podvizhnichestvo" [Heroism and the spiritual struggle], "Filosofiia kn. S. N. Trubetskogo i dukhovnaia bor'ba sovremennosti" [The philosophy of Prince S. N. Trubetskoi and the spiritual struggle of modernity]; 1910: "Apokaliptika i sotsializm" [Apocalyptic and socialism], "Razmyshleniia o natsional'nosti" [Reflections

on nationality]. All of these essays and articles are reprinted in *Dva grada*, vols. 1 and 2 (Moscow, 1911).

24. Williams, *Sergii Bulgakov*, pp. 59-61.

25. His complicated and shifting attitude towards royal authority is documented in "Agoniia," *Tikhie dumy*, pp. 331-38, 343-44.

26. Mikhail Gershenzon, Petr Struve, Nikolai Berdiaev, Semen Frank, Bogdan Kistiakovskii, and Aleksandr Izgoev.

27. Evtuhov, *The Cross and the Sickle*, pp. 131-33; Williams, *Sergii Bulgakov*, pp. 61-68.

28. Rowan Williams provides an English translation in his *Sergii Bulgakov*, pp. 69-112.

29. "Moia rodina" [My native land], *Tikhie dumy*, p. 315.

30. Especially important is his essay "Sofiologiia smerti" [The sophiology of death] in *Tikhie dumy*, pp. 273-306.

31. See the excellent discussion of this in Bernice Glatzer Rosenthal, "The Search for a Russian Orthodox Work Ethic," in *Between Tsar and People: Educated Society and the Quest for Public Identity in Late Imperial Russia*, ed. Edith W. Clowes, Samuel D. Kassow, and James L. West (Princeton: Princeton University Press, 1991), pp. 57-74; on Bulgakov, see pp. 61-74.

32. English translation: *Philosophy of Economy: The World as Household*, trans., ed., and intro. Catherine Evtuhov (New Haven: Yale University Press, 2000).

33. Michael A. Meerson, "*Put'* against *Logos*: The Critique of Kant and Neo-Kantianism by Russian Religious Philosophers in the Beginning of the Twentieth Century," *Studies in East European Thought* 47, no. 3/4 (December 1995): 226 (225-43).

34. Evtuhov, *The Cross and the Sickle*, pp. 138-40.

35. The essay was first published in *Voprosy filosofii i psikhologii* 105 (St. Petersburg, 1910), pp. 661-96, and then in the collection of essays on Soloviev (Moscow: Put', 1910), pp. 1-31.

36. Rosenthal, "Nature and Function of Sophia," pp. 158-59.

37. Excellent summaries of the book are provided by Evtuhov, *The Cross and the Sickle*, pp. 158-70; and Rosenthal, "Nature and Function of Sophia," pp. 159-63. For the Kantian aspects of Bulgakov's theory, see Meerson, "*Put'* against *Logos*," pp. 230-33.

38. Evtuhov, *The Cross and the Sickle*, p. 146.

39. Evtuhov, *The Cross and the Sickle*, pp. 146-47, 154-57.

40. Insightful depictions of this moment in Russian Church history may be found in Loren Graham and Jean-Michel Kanto, *Naming Infinity: A True Story of Religious Mysticism and Mathematical Creativity* (Cambridge, MA: Belknap/Harvard University Press, 2009), pp. 7-17, and Evtuhov, *The Cross and the Sickle*, pp. 210-18.

41. He began work on this book in 1920, but it appeared in print only in 1953.

42. "Piat' let" [Five years], *Tikhie dumy*, p. 340.

43. The events leading up to his ordination are recalled in "Moe rukopolozhenie," *Tikhie dumy*, pp. 344-50.

44. Two dialogues, *Na piru bogov* [At the feast of the gods] and *U sten Khersonisa*

[Beneath the walls of Chersonesus], and a book *Tragediia filosofii* [The tragedy of philosophy] survive.

45. Both trilogies are now available in English translations published by Eerdmans: *The Burning Bush* (2009), *Jacob's Ladder* (2010), trans. Thomas Allan Smith; *The Friend of the Bridegroom* (2000), *The Lamb of God* (2008), *The Comforter* (2004), *The Bride of the Lamb* (2002), trans. Boris Jakim.

46. Valliere, *Modern Russian Theology*, p. 268.

47. Williams, *Sergii Bulgakov*, p. 131.

48. Evtuhov, *The Cross and the Sickle*, p. 172.

49. *Svet nevechernii*, p. 354, n. 1.

50. Avril Pyman, *A History of Russian Symbolism* (Cambridge: Cambridge University Press, 1994), p. 2.

51. A brief account of artistic life in the Silver Age is found in W. Bruce Lincoln, *Between Heaven and Hell: The Story of a Thousand Years of Artistic Life in Russia* (New York: Viking, 1998), pp. 267-331. For a full treatment of the Symbolist movement that dominates the period, see Pyman, *Symbolism*.

52. Constantin Andronikoff, "Note du traducteur," in *Lumière sans déclin* (Lausanne, 1990).

53. Williams, *Sergii Bulgakov*, p. 125.

54. *Svet nevechernii*, p. 6.

55. *Svet nevechernii*, p. 14.

56. *Svet nevechernii*, p. 176.

57. *Svet nevechernii*, p. 180.

58. *Svet nevechernii*, pp. 211-13.

59. *Svet nevechernii*, p. 214.

60. *Svet nevechernii*, p. 216.

61. *Svet nevechernii*, p. 410.

Notes to "From the Author"

1. Literally, "collection of variegated chapters," and undoubtedly an allusion to the second-century writer Clement of Alexandria's "Stromata" or "patchwork," which contains a very wide variety of topics pertaining to the Christian life. — Trans.

2. The Khlysty, a sect originating in Russian Orthodoxy in the seventeenth century, are believed to have practiced flagellation as part of their secret religious ritual. — Trans.

Notes to the Introduction

1. Some may object that in Kant's works there is in fact just such a fourth critique, namely in the treatise *Die Religion innerhalb der blossen Vernunft* (written in 1793, that is, *after* all the critiques), which to the greatest extent gives him the right to the

title "Philosopher of Protestantism." In our eyes this composition is the most important for understanding the *spirit* of Kant's philosophy, its intimate religious motive, but he conceived it *not* as a special "critique," which is characteristic for Kant, but only as a systematic application of the conclusions of the three critiques to Christian dogma.

2. Idolatry in practical understanding is ever still that religion which conceives the Supreme Being with attributes such that these must be something other than morality as the sufficient condition in keeping with which a human being would be able to exist in accordance with its will. *Kritik der Urtheilskraft* (Reclam), pp. 358-59, note.

3. In this period Fichte gives this definition of the relationship between religion and ethics: "Morality and religion are absolutely one; both are an apprehension of the supersensible, the first through doing, the second through believing. . . . Religion without morality is superstition which gives the unfortunate one a false hope and makes him incapable of any improvement. Alleged morality without religion may well be an externally honourable way of life, since one does what is right and avoids evil out of fear of the consequences in the world of the senses; but one never loves the good or carries it out for its own sake." J. G. Fichte, *Appellation an das Publikum,* in *Werke,* V, 209; ausgew. W., III, 169.

4. The "Twice Born" in William James. [This term appears in James's *The Varieties of Religious Experience.* It denotes a person suffering from some form of mental illness, typically profound depression, whose urgent quest for meaning delivers him from that unhealthy condition and brings him to a higher plane of reality, in other words, to a new and profound religious experience. – Trans.]

5. Alexander Ivanovich Herzen (1812-1870) was the father of Russian socialism and a major voice for social reform in tsarist Russia. – Trans.

6. The words said of Peter after his threefold denial of Christ, Matthew 26:75. – Trans.

7. The philosophers of pessimism Hartmann and Drews point to the significance of pessimism and the need for redemption with particular insistence. In the eyes of the latter "all religions are essentially religions of salvation," and for the religious-philosophical investigation the task is thus set for demonstrating "how the religious condition must be thought in order to procure for the will to salvation the desired satisfaction without contradiction with itself." A. Drews, *Die Religion als Selbstbewusstsein Gottes* (1906), p. 62. The inordinate emphasis of this motif in their compositions is wholly connected with their general and religious metaphysics.

8. Cf. 2 Corinthians 12:2. – Trans.

9. It is interesting to observe into what interminable difficulties those historians "of culture" fall who lack an inner grasp of religion but who do not have sufficient straightforwardness to completely sweep aside religious beliefs and cult like rubbish and prejudices or the "superstructure" on some sort of "foundation."

10. We are happy to mention that Max Müller arrives at the experiential interpretation of religion as a result of his entire colossal study of religion (in various of his works; see for example *Natürliche Religion,* Leipzig, 1890, lectures II-V). This is his

Notes to Pages 20-22

formula: *nihil est in fide quod non ante fuerit in sensu* [nothing is in belief that was not in sensation beforehand]. By the latter term Müller understands the *experiential* character of religion although of course this experience differs from sense experience.

11. Hartmann justifiably points to this. On the whole we find in his work an extraordinarily precise posing of the problem of religion in its general form: he establishes that "every object of religious function is God; God is not a scientific but a religious concept; science can concern itself with it only insofar as it is the science about religion. We can therefore define religious function as the attitude of the human to God. This definition seemingly loses its force when atheism denies the existence of God and at the same time like Buddhism remains an extraordinarily intense religion; but it is not difficult to recognize that this outward appearance springs only from a preconceived realistic view of the divine essence which does not fit with Buddhist absolute illusionism. And in Buddhism nothing is (1) the absolute foundation of the world, namely the positive cause of the illusion positing the world; (2) the absolute essence (although it is nothing) which lies at the base of the phenomenal world; (3) the absolute goal of the world towards which the world process strives and in which it finds absolute redemption and (4) the bearer and source of the religious-moral world order which is the solely true and constant in the illusion and which alone makes the illusory world process a real process of salvation. In each of these four respects the object of religious function or the subject of religious relation is nothing. In this manner Buddhism is atheism not in the sense that it should deny God, i.e., the subject of religious relation, but only in that it makes nothing, *alpha privative,* a god. If it accomplished the former, it would cease to be a religion; but since it does the latter, it remains a religion and only poses for us the problem of how it is possible to divinize nothing." E. Hartmann, *Die Religion des Geistes,* 3rd ed., pp. 4-5. For this reason Buddhism does not break the rule of "keine Religion ohne Gottesvorstellung" [no religion without a concept of God] (6).

12. A poem by Feodor Ivanovich Tiutchev (1803-1873), written in 1830 while he resided in Munich. — Trans.

13. This idea finds clear expression in the book of Emilio Metner, *Reflections on Goethe,* I (Moscow, 1914), pp. 329-30, 347-401.

14. Philosophers can protest that we apply to religious experiences the terms "transcendent" and "immanent," which have multiple meanings and besides are purely philosophical. They will be right in their reproach only if they do not forget that even for them these concepts do not contain a definite meaning; it is inserted only with a given philosopheme. In other words, the problem of the transcendent (and correlatively, of the immanent) represents the *last* and most generalizing problem of philosophy and consequently already includes in itself a whole system. Therefore it is not connected with a definite *terminological* meaning with the expressions employed by us, and we are free to use them in our own special sense provided of course that we firmly keep the meaning once adopted. Religion, as distinct from philosophy, does not end with the transcendent but *begins* with it, and only in its further development are its sense and meaning gradually disclosed. The transcendent, in the most common meaning, i.e., as exceeding every measure of human experience, con-

sciousness, and being, generally speaking "of this world," is *given* in the initial religious experience, so far as a sense of God is contained in it — this is the fundamental music of religion. Of course one can compose a new term for the designation of this sense, but it seems to us there is no need for this, because in its preliminary and formal definition the transcendent of religion is for the present still not distinct from the transcendent of philosophy: this is more a logical gesture than a concept (and indeed every logical *concept* of the transcendent will unavoidably be like this, i.e., of that which is above concepts).

15. In the mystical writings of Eastern Church authors, Nicholas Cabasilas (fourteenth century) expresses this idea with particular clarity, as does Thomas à Kempis *(On the Imitation of Christ)* among Western authors. Both say this apropos the union with Christ in the mystery of the Eucharist: "Christ stands even closer to those who receive the mystery of the Eucharist than they do to themselves, since He becomes for them a more perfect other, their own I." Bishop Alexis, *Byzantine Church Mystics of the 14th Century* (Kazan', 1906), p. 61.

16. Cf. Matthew 11:12. — Trans.

17. See translator's introduction concerning Name-Worship.

18. The works of church asceticism are filled with a doctrine of prayer, in particular, compositions by Saints Macarius the Great, Simeon the New Theologian, John Climacus, Isaac the Syrian, and Tikhon of Zadonsk. Also those by such church authors as Bishop Ignatii Brianchaninov, Feofan the Recluse, and many others. See also the collections: *Dobrotoliubie in 5 volumes,* "Patristic Instructions on Prayer and Sobriety," collected by Bishop Feofan and others; analogous collections, of course, exist in the Catholic Church. The ecclesiastical literature, one can say, is inexhaustible. One must also refer here to the liturgical wealth of East and West. Even for a superficial "psychological" investigation of religion all of this gives most precious material which, however, is almost untouched. The phenomenological analysis of prayer (for which one can likewise find an abundance of material in religious literature) is entirely lacking. In part this can be explained by the fact that among people who are living religiously there is little taste for or interest in such analysis; among nonreligious people there is an insufficient understanding of and little interest in it.

19. Not for nothing do do-it-yourself and even "atheistic" religions aspire to have at least some sort of cult and, therefore, a practice of prayer. In particular, e.g., a perfectly correct religious instinct guided Auguste Comte when he established a cult for his divinity "Grand-Être." In London I happened to be present at a service of the "Humanitarian Church," which apparently is sometimes called the "atheistic church," where prayers to humanity were recited, and judging by their prayer-book, rituals of baptism, marriage, and other such things had been established.

20. The concept "is" when applied to God is used here only in a preliminary and conditional meaning, in contrast to subjectivism. In what follows we shall see that the category of being in and of itself is inapplicable to Divinity.

21. "Faith is always the consequence of revelation identified as revelation; it is the contemplation of an invisible fact in a visible fact; faith is not the same as *belief* or logical conviction based on conclusions, but a great deal more. It is not an act of one

cognitive faculty estranged from others, but the act of all the powers of reason seized and captivated to its ultimate depth by the living truth of revealed fact. Faith is not only thought or sensed, but, so to say, is thought and sensed together; in a word, it is not cognition alone but cognition and life." A. S. Khomiakov, *Works*, II, p. 62.

22. Cf. Hebrews 11:1-3. — Trans.

23. Thus the coming of the Savior of the world to earth was the object of faith for Old Testament humanity, but here is how the New Testament servant of the Word speaks about him: "that which was from the beginning, what we heard, what we saw with our own eyes, what we observed and what we touched with our hands, the Word of life — for life appeared and we saw and bear witness and we announce to you this eternal life which was with the Father and appeared to us — that which we saw and heard, we proclaim to you" (1 John 1:1-3).

24. In Hebrews 11 faith is given an interpretation in the one and the other sense: "We come to know by faith that the ages are arranged by the word of God, so that from what is unseen the seen should happen" (v. 3); the further content of the chapter speaks about faith as the basis of conduct unmotivated by reason and justified only by faith (see this entire chapter).

25. In the letter to the Hebrews Christ himself is called *the leader and perfecter* of faith. To him belongs in the highest degree the spiritual discipline of faith: "instead of the joy lying before him he endured the cross, and scorning disgrace he took up his seat on the right hand of God's throne" (Heb. 12:2). Of course the mystery of the incarnation remains inaccessible to the human mind: By what manner could God, after being incarnated, so cover Divinity with humanity that he proves capable of performing *the feat of faith in God* and experiencing the human sense of *god-abandonment*? But this points precisely to the very profound *humanness* of faith, its exclusive significance and the permanence of the feat of faith for the human.

26. In this sense a definition of faith is given by St. Maximus the Confessor: *Diversa capita ad theologiam et oeconomiam spectantia*, Centena II, 12-13, PG 90, 1225. "Faith is indemonstrable knowledge *(anapodeiktos gnōsis)*; if knowledge is indemonstrable, faith exceeds, then, nature; with its help by unknown means, we clearly enter into a union with God which surpasses understanding *(noēsin)*. When the mind enters into immediate union with God, the power of thinking *(tou noein kai tou noeisthai)* becomes completely inoperative. But inasmuch as it comes out of it and makes something of the divine things *(tōn meta theon)* the object of consideration, this union is broken which surpasses understanding, and in which, being found in co-union with God, according to the co-participation in Divinity, it itself becomes God and casts off of itself the natural law of its proper nature."

27. According to the definition of Nicholas of Cusa, *"credere est cum ascensione cogitare," "posse credere est maxima animae virtus"* [to believe is to reason with an ascent, to be able to believe is the greatest power of the soul].

28. From Dostoevsky's *The Brothers Karamazov*, book 5, "The Grand Inquisitor." — Trans.

29. Friedrich Heinrich Jacobi (1743-1819) was an influential German philosopher, polemicist, and writer strongly critical of the German Enlightenment and the

philosophical systems that followed: rationalism, transcendental idealism, and romantic idealism. He coined the term "nihilism," which he decried as the end result of all Enlightenment philosophical systems, and argued forcefully against speculative reason and for faith/belief and revelation. Also significant was his claim that every "I" entails a "You" and that both recognize each other only in the presence of a transcendent and personal Deity. – Trans.

30. "Through faith we know that we have a body (!) and that outside of us other bodies and other thinking beings are present. A true, wonderful revelation (!!)" (Jacobi, *Werke*, IV, I, 211).

31. By Lossky in *The Ground of Intuitivism* (by the way, this term belongs to Schelling, *Philosophy of Revelation* I, 115-19, 130, 143).

32. This theory was subjected to analysis by Professor A. I. Vvedensky in his collection "Philosophical études" in the essay titled "Soloviev's mystical theory of cognition." [The information given by Bulgakov is inaccurate. He most likely refers here to the article, A. I. Vvedensky, "On mysticism and criticism in the theory of cognition of V. S. Soloviev," *Philosophical Sketches* (St. Petersburg, 1901), pp. 39-68. – Trans.]

33. See my *Philosophy of Economy*, the chapter on "The nature of science."

34. It follows from this by the way in what kind of illusion certain Protestant sects (Baptists, Methodists) find themselves, who instill in their followers assurance of their already accomplished saved condition; and how much wiser Orthodoxy proves to be here, which cautions against this assurance like a pernicious illusion (seduction) pointing to the necessity of constant struggle with the world, "of salvation" and not "saved condition."

35. Hegel, *Die Wissenschaft der Logik*, First part, 2nd ed. (Berlin, 1841), p. 33.

36. Fichte was infected with a similar intellectualism and not only in the early period (the atheism dispute) but also in the later, the epoch of *Anweisung zum seligen Leben* of 1806. Precisely in this work we find a completely Hegelian idea that religion represents a preparatory step to philosophy, which crowns the spiritual development of the human being. "That which for religion is only an absolute fact becomes genetic for it (Science). Religion without science is a simple and unshakeable faith: science sublates all faith and transforms it into seeing" (V, 472).

37. For example, here is one of many judgments of this kind: "'Secret knowledge' is subordinated to the same laws as is all human knowledge. It represents a mystery for the average human being in the same sense in which letters are a mystery for the one who has not learned to write. *And just as everyone can learn to write, having chosen for this purpose the right path, so too can everyone become a secret pupil and even teacher if they choose for this purpose the corresponding path*" ([Bulgakov's italics – Trans.]; R. Steiner, *The Path to Initiation*, p. 45; see his *Die Geheimwissenschaft, passim*). An even clearer immanent character of occult knowledge is expressed in the following words of Steiner: "The seer investigates spiritual laws in exactly the same manner as a physicist or chemist investigates material laws. He does this in that manner and with that strictness that are suitable in the spiritual domain. But the development of humanity depends on these great spiritual laws. Similar to how oxygen, hydrogen and sulfur will never enter into a union in any future *contrary to* the laws of nature, so too in the

spiritual life he of course will produce nothing opposed to spiritual laws. And whoever knows the latter can in this way have insight into the *inherent regularity of the future*. For the one who is gaining clarity about the actual viewpoint of occultism, the objection likewise falls away that because the position of things in a certain sense is predeterminable, any sort of human freedom becomes impossible. Only that which is subject to some sort of law can be defined in advance. But the establishment of the conditions under which this law can operate is *not* at all defined by law, it can depend on the will of the human being. So it will be with the coming world events and the destinies of humankind. As an adept of mysteries you see them in advance although they must initially be provoked by human volition. The occult investigator in precisely the same way foresees that which will be accomplished by human freedom. . . . Only one substantial difference needs to be clarified in the predetermination by way of physical science or by way of spiritual cognition. Physical science rests on rational understanding, and thus its prophecy is also rational, supported by judgments, conclusions, considerations, etc. The prophecy of spiritual cognition on the contrary proceeds from real higher vision or perception. The adept of mysteries must by the strictest means even flee from any representations based solely on reflection, consideration, judgment, etc." R. Steiner, *From the Chronicle of the World* (Moscow: Spiritual Knowledge, 1914), pp. 138-39.

38. Religious knowledge is described by one of the luminaries of faith in these terms: "The human being has in the one soul a mind, a word [reason] and a single sense although this is divided into five senses in keeping with the five physical needs of the body. With respect to the corporeal, it is indivisibly divided by means of particular senses: sight, hearing, smell, taste and touch; although it is variable, it manifests its activity without change. . . . With respect to the spiritual, there is no need for this general sense to be divided into five senses, as if into five windows . . . but remaining integrally one sense it has with and in itself five senses (or to say it more accurately, more than five) insofar as all of them are one. . . . And so when the one God of all is revealed through a revelation to the one rational soul, every good is revealed to it and it is contemplated (sensed) at one and the same time by all of its senses together. This one good which is at the same time every good is seen by it, is audible, and delights the taste, etc. . . . Thus, the one who is known by God knows that God sees him too. But the one who does not see God does not know that God sees him, since he himself does not see God although he sees everything else well. Thus, those who have been made worthy of seeing all at once with all the senses together, as with one of the many senses, this all-goodness which is both one and many, since it is all-goodness, those, I say, since they have come to know and daily do know with the different senses of one sense different goods together as one, are not aware of any difference in all that has been said, but they call contemplation knowledge and knowledge contemplation, hearing sight and sight hearing." *Discourse of Saint Symeon the New Theologian*, I, 475.

39. O. Pfleiderer, *Geschichte der Religionsphilosophie*, 3rd ed. (Berlin, 1893), p. 309. Cf. in general the whole chapter on Schleiermacher.

40. This is an incomplete citation from Goethe's *Faust*, part I, "Gretchen's Garden." — Trans.

41. Only this duality and obscurity of Schleiermacher's doctrine could support Frank in interpreting "feeling" as religious intuition and not as "an aspect" of the psychic (foreword, xxix-xxx). In so doing he ontologizes Schleiermacher's psychologisms, and depicts the representative of subjectivism and immanentism as the herald "of religious realism."

42. Albrecht Ritschl (1822-1889) was a German Lutheran theologian who understood himself to stand in the tradition of Luther and Schleiermacher. He rejected the use of scholastic philosophy in theology and based his own theological system on the objective fact of the faith of the Christian community. Metaphysics and mysticism have no place in his system. — Trans.

43. The views of Troeltsch are set forth in a series of articles in various Protestant encyclopedias and in the second volume of the complete collection of his works: *Ernst Troeltsch. Zur religiösen Lage, Religionsphilosophie und Ethik*, 1913. For a description of the views of Herrmann, see Herrmann, *Ethik*; and his *Die religiöse Frage der Gegenwart* (in the collection *Das Christenthum*, 1908).

44. "To acknowledge the existence of God . . . is a subjective moral necessity, i.e. a requirement, and not an objective necessity, i.e., a duty, for to acknowledge the existence of any kind of thing cannot be a duty (this concerns only the theoretical application of reason). It is also impossible to understand by this that it is necessary to acknowledge the existence of God as the basis of every obligation in general. . . . For theoretical reason this acknowledgement can be called a *hypothesis;* with respect to the understanding of an object given to us by the path of moral law (the supreme good), that is, with respect to need in the practical direction, it can be called *faith* and indeed the *faith of pure reason,* for only pure reason (both in its theoretical and in its practical application) is the source from which it arises." Kant, *Critique of Practical Reason*, trans. N. M. Sokolov, pp. 130-31.

45. Characteristic of the contradictoriness and duality of Kant's ideas in the question about faith is the chapter in the *Critique of Practical Reason* under the heading "in what manner is it possible to think the expansion of pure reason in a practical respect without thereby enlarging its cognition as speculative reason?" Here the "theoretical" cognition of pure reason still does not gain an increase. "Increase consists here only(?) in that these concepts, previously problematic (only conceivable), are now assertively acknowledged as such in which objects really are inherent, since practical reason inevitably needs the existence of these objects for the possibility of its own, practically unconditionally necessary object of the highest good and through this gives to theoretical reason the right to presuppose them. But this expansion of theoretical reason is not an expansion of speculation, i.e., it does not give a right to make a positive use of these concepts in a *theoretical respect* (??) since here practical reason makes it that these concepts become real and actually receive their own (possible) objects. Since we are in no way given contemplations of them, no synthetic judgment on the grounds of this reality is allowed for them. Consequently, this discovery gives us absolutely nothing with respect to speculation. . . . But theoretical cognition, although not of these objects but of reason in general, (?) all the same is expanded here precisely to the extent that objects are given to these ideas by the path of practical

Notes to Pages 49-62

postulates, and through this, thought, only problematic, receives objective reality. Consequently this is not an expansion of cognition about *given supersensible objects,* but an expansion of theoretical reason and its cognition with respect to the supersensible in general, so far as this impels us to admit *that there are such objects,* although we have no possibility of defining them more precisely, that is, to expand our cognition about objects. For this success, consequently, pure theoretical reason, for which all these ideas are transcendent and have no object, is indebted exclusively to its own pure practical capacity. Here they become *immanent and constitutive* since they are the grounds for the possibility that *a necessary object* of pure reason (the highest good) *becomes real.* Without this, *they are only transcendent and regulative principles* of speculative reason which impel it not to admit a new object outside experience to continue its application in experience to the fullest extent. And if experience receives this expansion, speculative reason with these ideas can proceed to the task only negatively, i.e. by not expanding a concept but by explaining it." *Critique of Practical Reason,* pp. 140-41. Is the domain of reason expanded or not by the achievements of its practical capacity? Kant becomes entangled in contradictions thanks on the one hand to his unwillingness to acknowledge the general cognitive significance of "postulates," and on the other hand, by not having the strength to repudiate them.

46. One of the clearest examples of the surmounting of ethics is war, which is why it is so difficult to accept and justify war ethically, and only its religious justification remains.

47. Forberg's article, "Entwicklung des Begriffs der Religion" [Development of the concept of religion] (1798), which occasioned the "dispute about atheism," and represents the bringing of moral theology as far as the pillars of Hercules, holds the following characteristic question and answer: "How does religion relate to virtue? Answer: As the part to the whole."

48. J. G. Fichte, *Die philosophischen Schriften zum Atheismusstreit. Über den Grund unseres Glaubens an eine göttliche Weltregierung* (1798), Selected Works III, 129-30 (W.W. V, 185-86). *Appellation an das Publikum* (1799), Selected Works III, 169-70 (W.W. V, 210).

49. "Place me as a seal (love is speaking) on your heart, as a ring on your hand: for strong as death is love; fierce as the underworld is jealousy; its arrows are fiery arrows; it is a very powerful flame. Great waters cannot extinguish love, and rivers cannot quench it" (Song of Songs 8:6-7).

50. Bulgakov introduces here the terms "sobornyi" and "sobornost'," all related to the noun "sobor," which poses great problems for translation. In this particular passage, however, it is clear that he has "council" *(sobor)* in mind, and thus my choice of "conciliar" and "conciliarity." — Trans.

51. Was not St. Athanasius the Great with the handful of his partisans the bearer of the authentic catholic consciousness of the Church at a time when its quantitative majority persisted in heresy?

52. Volapük was a language created by the German priest Johann Martin Schleyer in 1879 with the aim of facilitating communication among the various peoples of the world. It presented a regularized grammar, simplified pronunciation, and

orthography. English, with some German and French, provided the raw material for the constructed vocabulary. Esperanto is another such language. — Trans.

53. Cf. Schelling: God is not the Transcendent, as many imagine, but the Immanent, i.e., the Transcendent made into the content of reason. Schelling, *Philosophie der Offenbarung*, I, 170; W.W. II, III.

54. Bulgakov plays on the German phrase "Dichtung und Wahrheit," literally "poetry/fiction and truth," by which Goethe's autobiography is generally known. — Trans.

55. Here for the purposes of illustration I cannot but offer what I heard from L. N. Tolstoy's account: how a certain contemporary of Pushkin recalled that Pushkin himself in conversation with her was carried away by Tatiana who made such short shrift of Eugene Onegin at their final meeting.

56. Cf. the description of science in the chapter "The economic nature of science" in my *Philosophy of Economy*.

57. See Third Section below.

58. Cf. Schelling, *Philosophie der Mythologie* II, 104: "Dogma means, as is well known, the same as the Latin *decretum*, which is of course also used of assertions and doctrines, a decision and only then an assertion. Dogma is something that must be asserted, that does not allow itself to be thought without contradiction (a contrast)."

59. Cf. 1 Corinthians 1:23. — Trans.

60. A line from Feodor Tiutchev's famous poem, "Silentium." — Trans.

61. Hermann Cohen (1842-1918), a German-Jewish philosopher, helped found the Marburg school of Neo-Kantianism. In addition to his studies of the philosophy of Immanuel Kant, Cohen authored several important works on Judaism. In this section of the book, Bulgakov is likely referring to Cohen's *Logik der reinen Erkenntnis* [Logic of pure knowledge]. — Trans.

62. This is well shown in Otto Gilbert, *Griechische Religionsphilosophie* (Leipzig, 1911), pp. 356-456.

63. See Father P. Florensky, *The Essence of Idealism* (Sergiev Posad, 1915), a separate excerpt from the jubilee collection of the Moscow Theological Academy; and his *The Universal Human Roots of Idealism* (1909).

64. Paul Gerhard Natorp (1854-1924) and his pupil Nicolai Hartmann (1882-1950) were important members of the Marburg school led by Hermann Cohen (1842-1918), which created the philosophical movement known as Neo-Kantianism. — Trans.

65. Hegel's *Religionsphilosophie*, cited according to the edition of Diederichs edited by Arthur Drews.

66. Cf. Hegel's *Encyclopädie der philosophischen Wissenschaften im Grundrisse, I. Th. Logik* (W.W. VI, 2nd printing) SS. XXI-II, 3 et al.

67. The idea that in God there is no secret, that He is fully knowable, is encountered often on the pages of Hegel's *Philosophy of Religion*, pp. 334, 335-36.

68. In note 39, p. 419. A. Drews justifiably remarks: "Hegel forgets here that the being of logic designates only the pure concept of being, and not this being itself, that

the affirmation, 'God is a universal,' can be the foundation only for logical, ideal but not real being of God."

69. Not for nothing does Hegel sympathetically cite his mystical forerunner in immanentism Meister Eckhart: "the eye with which God sees me is the eye with which I see him, my eye and his eye are one. In justice I am weighed in God and he in me. If there were no God, I would not exist, and if I did not exist, so would he not exist either" (139).

70. To these general arguments one ought to add the objection that if religion is the lowest level of philosophical consciousness, then it is abrogated and abolished as superfluous after its supreme achievement, and only inconsistency permits Hegel to affirm religion, corresponding to "representation," in its independent significance, alongside of philosophy, corresponding to "concept." Hartmann already points this out in *Religionsphilosophie*, p. 85.

71. A. Drews observes completely correctly in his notes to Hegel's philosophy of religion, "Hegel identifies conscious existence not with the conscious side of being *(Bewusst-Sein)* or with ideal being, but immediately with real being, and passes in this manner to the monstrous assertion that it is possible by means of finite, discursive, conscious being to think out the process of absolute, eternal, preconscious and super-conscious thinking immediately as such. Hegel forgets that the being of logic designates only a pure concept of being and not being itself, that the affirmation 'God is the universal' can be the basis of only a logical but not a real concept of God" (p. 419, n. 39).

72. As, for example, it is difficult to see under the "pure logic" of Cohen the edge of Neo-Judaism concealed in it.

73. Hartmann, among the recent philosophers of Germany who display a much better understanding of religious-philosophical questions, defines the mutual relation between general philosophy and religious philosophy in this way: "Religious metaphysics differs from theoretical metaphysics in that it draws conclusions from postulates of religious consciousness and develops necessary metaphysical premises of religious consciousness from the relationship which is deposited in religious psychology, whereas theoretical metaphysics goes the way of scientific induction. Religious metaphysics is thus the metaphysical part of a religious worldview and according to the aforesaid must coincide with the metaphysical part of a theoretical worldview, although it is acquired by a different path; their accord must be the more exact: the more important the metaphysical part of a worldview is for religious consciousness, the less it contains of religiously indifferent points." Hartmann, *Religionsphilosophie*, 111. The understanding of the correlation between philosophy and religion that is developed in this text gives a different interpretation of it and in a significant measure takes away the very question of the difference between religious and general metaphysics, for in essence they coincide and can be differentiated more readily in the mode of exposition. The particularity of Hartmann's "philosophy of the unconscious" is that it believes itself to be constructed on induction, and thus considers itself the completion of science.

74. Cf. the definition of the mutual relation between faith and "science" in

Schelling (under which he understands philosophy in the first instance): "Faith must not be represented as unfounded knowledge; on the contrary, one ought to say that it is the most well-founded for it alone has that in which every doubt is conquered, something so absolutely positive that any further passage to something other is cut off. Precisely from this it follows that it is impossible *to begin* science with faith as many teach and preach. For the credibility which removes every doubt (and only such can one call faith) is only the *end* of science. First the law, then the Gospel. Reason corresponds to law, faith to Gospel. But as the apostle says that the law was the tutor towards Christ, so the strict school of science must precede faith, although we can be justified, i.e. become truly perfect, only through faith, i.e. through possession of the credibility which removes all doubts. . . . Faith in this manner does not abrogate searching but demands it, for it is the end of searching. But the *end* of searching must exist." Schelling, *Philosophie der Offenbarung*, part 2, 15.

75. Hegel noted such a meaning of the development of the science of religion. "If the cognition of religion is understood only historically, we must regard theologians who have arrived at such an understanding as clerks of a trading house who conduct book-keeping only with respect to someone else's wealth, and work only for others, without acquiring their own property; although they receive payment, their services are only in the maintenance and registration of what comprises the property of others. . . . These theologians have nothing whatever to do with the real content, the cognition of God." Hegel, *Religionsphilosophie*, 22-23. In *Phenomenology of Spirit*, Hegel gave the following apt description of the "historical" direction in German theology which has become so influential in our days: "The Enlightenment *(Die Aufklärung)* contrived with respect to religious faith that its credibility is based on certain *separate historical witnesses* which if one were to consider them to be historical evidence, of course, would not assure their content even that degree of credibility given to us by gazettes that inform about some sort of events; that further their credibility is based on the fortuitousness of the preservation of these witnesses, a preservation on the one hand by means of paper, and on the other hand thanks to art and the honesty in the transference from one paper to another, and finally, on *the correct understanding* of the sense of dead words and letters. In reality it is not at all proper to faith to tie its credibility to such witnesses and fortuities; in its credibility it is an independent relation to its absolute subject, the pure knowledge of it, which does not implicate letters, paper and copyists in its consciousness of absolute essence and is not mediated by such things." Hegel, *Phänomenologie des Geistes, Jubiläumsausgabe*, Phil. Bibl. Bd. 114, pp. 360-61.

76. Scientific piety, which distinguishes the new epoch, is completely analogous with artistic piety, piety in art and through art. Art is also not religion and under no circumstance can it replace it, but it can serve religion by becoming religious, and the epochs of religious enthusiasm are naturally and inevitably impressed with the enthusiasm of religious art. Of course, art is deeper than science and therefore stands closer to religion, but for our analogy this difference has no significance.

Notes to the First Section

1. 1 Timothy 6:16. — Trans.
2. John 14:23. — Trans.
3. The problem of antinomism in thinking is most radically posed in the book of Father Pavel Florensky, *The Pillar and the Ground of the Truth* (Moscow, 1914).
4. Thus does Philo of Alexandria define God *(apoios): Legum Allegoriae.* I, 13: *apoios gar o theos ou monon ouk anthrōpomorphos* [for not only is God without human form but he is also without qualities]. In S. N. Trubetskoi, *Doctrine of the Logos, Collected Works*, vol. 4, p. 123n.
5. For example, Philo of Alexandria, in affirming God's lack of qualities, at the same time ascribes to him being as the sole definition: *ho on* (Life of Moses) 1 (14) 75, IV, 115. In Loofs, *Leitfaden zum Studium der Dogmengeschichte* (1906), p. 63. Cf. S. N. Trubetskoi, *Doctrine of the Logos*, p. 123. Also M. Muretov, *The Philosophy of Philo of Alexandria in Relation to the Doctrine of John the Theologian on the Logos* (Moscow, 1885), pp. 12-13. The same may be found in ecclesiastical authors; see below.
6. This ought perhaps to be the philosophical transcription of *nirvana*.
7. *Phaedrus*, 247 C.
8. *Republic*, VI, 509B.
9. For example, certain motifs of the dialectics of *Parmenides* are relevant here, as the Russian translator of Plato Professor Karpov rightly pointed out (part 3, 341n.): namely the dialectics of the concept of the one *(to hen)* which in one sense is completely transcendent to being and is in this sense nothing, and on the contrary in another sense it contains in itself everything and receives in itself all diversity of forms. If it is said about the first *one* that "for it there is no name, no word, no knowledge of any kind, no feeling, no opinion . . . it is not named and not expressed, and it is not imagined and not known, and nothing of its existence is felt," then about the second *one* is established that "for it there can be knowledge, opinion, feeling . . . there is for it a name and a word — it is named and expressed." *Parmenides* 142 A, 155 D, Russian translation of Karpov, part VI, pp. 276, 303.
10. Cf. *Physics,* 1245 b 17 f. (in O. Gilbert, *Griechische Religionsphilosophie* [1911], p. 381, n. 2).
11. H. Schwarz, *Der Gottesgedanke in der Geschichte der Philosophie*, 1 Part (1913), pp. 58-59, rightly points to this.
12. E. Zeller, *Philosophie der Griechen,* 4th ed. (Leipzig, 1903), Bd. III, Abt. 2, p. 561.
13. Drews makes just such a confusion (tendentious to boot) in his investigation of Plotinus: A. Drews, *Plotin und der Untergang der antiken Weltanschauung* (Jena, 1907).
14. Mitrofan Muretov, *The Doctrine of the Logos in Philo of Alexandria and John the Theologian* (Moscow, 1885); and *The Philosophy of Philo of Alexandria in Relation to the Doctrine of John the Theologian* (Moscow, 1885).
15. "What was dearest to Philo according to his whole standpoint were the negating statements about God which let him appear as the unconditioned one, for the opposition of God and the world is the point from which he proceeds." Zeller, *Die*

Philosophie der Griechen, 3rd part, 2nd section, 4th ed., p. 401. See the comparison of passages from Philo, in the notes.

16. *Legum Allegoriae.* Pf. I, 142: "Whoever thinks that God either has qualities or is not one or unbegotten or immortal or unchanging, offends himself, but not God . . . for it is necessary to think that he is without qualification and immortal and unchanging."

17. *Quod Deus sit Immutabilis.* Pf. II, 412: "They do not compare the one who is with any ideas about what has proceeded, but having freed him from every quality — for one only would correspond to his most high blessedness and ultimate happiness — they take him as a new being without any quality — concerning him they admit only the representation about being, without defining him at all."

18. *Legatio ad Gaium* Fr. 922, C: "The highest good is God and it is beautiful and happy and blessed; if one were to say the truth, then it is better than good, more beautiful than beauty, and more blessed than blessedness, more happy than happiness itself." See also *De. M. op.* Pf. I, 6, and *De vita contempl.* Fr. 890: "That which is, is better than good, purer than one and more primordial than monad."

19. *De Profug.* Pl. IV, 310: "God is greater than life, the source of life, as he says, eternally flowing."

20. *De mutatione nominum.* Pf. IV, 322-38.

21. *Quod Deus sit Immutabilis.* Pf. II, 416.

22. *De praemiis et poeniis.* Fr. 916, B–917, A. See also *Quod pot. Ins. Sol.* Pf. II, 202: "One cannot grasp the incomprehensible nature of God, excepting only his being."

23. In the series *Die griechischen christlichen Schriftsteller der ersten drei Jahrhunderte,* a publication of the Commission of the Russian Academy of Sciences, the *Stromata* of Clement of Alexandria occupy the second and part of the third volume. *Klimentos tōn kata tēn alēthē philosophian gnōstikon hypomnēmatōn stromateis* (Leipzig, 1906). Citation, pp. 377-81.

24. Clement of Alexandria, *Stromateis,* cited with many alterations, according to the Russian translation published in the *Iaroslav Eparchial Gazette* 36 (1891), unofficial part, pp. 565-67.

25. Origen, *On First Principles,* Izd. Kaz. Dukh. Ak. (Kazan', 1899), book I, ch. 1, §5.

26. Origen, *On First Principles,* book I, ch. 1, §8.

27. Origen, *On First Principles,* book I, ch. 1, §6.

28. *Exhortation to Martyrdom,* p. 43. See A. A. Spasskii, *History of Dogmatic Movements in the Era of the Ecumenical Councils,* vol. 1 (Sergiev Posad, 1906), pp. 90-91.

29. In the words of Socrates (*Hist. Eccles. Lib.* iv p. 7, cited in Viktor Nesmelov, *The Dogmatic System of Gregory of Nyssa* [Kazan', 1887], p. 130), Eunomius considered himself in the right to say "I know God just as he knows himself." According to the words of Epiphanius of Salamis, Arius' disciple Aetius said, "I know God as well as I know myself" (Nesmelov, p. 129).

30. *The Works of Our Father among the Saints Basil the Great* (Mosk. Dukh. Akad.), part III, pp. 28, 36 (contra Eunomium).

31. . . . *Basil the Great,* part III, pp. 31, 34, 35.

32. The Anomoeans were a radical sect of Arians who taught that the Son was entirely dissimilar to and of a different essence than the Father. — Trans.

33. ... *Basil the Great*, part VII, p. 139.

34. ... *Basil the Great*, part VII, p. 190. In letter 190 to Amphilochius, St. Basil the Great indicates that we do not know "what a school is" and we do not know the essence of "Timothy," just as in the same reason we know and do not know our own selves.

35. Nesmelov, p. 135.

36. *The Works of Our Father among the Saints Gregory the Theologian, Archbishop of Constantinople*, 3rd ed., part 3 (Moscow, 1899), pp. 14-15.

37. ... *Gregory the Theologian*, p. 16.

38. ... *Gregory the Theologian*, p. 21.

39. ... *Gregory the Theologian*, pp. 23-24.

40. ... *Gregory the Theologian*, p. 25.

41. ... *Gregory the Theologian*, part 5, verse 5.

42. For a general philosophical characterization of this dispute see my [Bulgakov's] essay, "The meaning of St. Gregory of Nyssa's doctrine of the divine names," *Inquiries of Life*, Moscow, 1914, Easter issue. Gregory of Nyssa was Basil's younger brother; Bulgakov seems to confuse him with Gregory of Nazianzen. — Trans.

43. "Like an immature person and in a childish fashion, to no purpose occupying themselves with the impossible as if in some child's palm they confine the incomprehensible nature of God in a few syllables of the word 'ingenerateness,' they defend this stupidity and *think that the divinity is so great and such as can be grasped by the human intellect through naming alone.*" *The Works of Our Father among the Saints Gregory of Nyssa*, vol. VI (Moscow, 1864), p. 299. "Refutation of Eunomius," book 12.

44. See the discussion of Name-Worship in the translator's Introduction.

45. This dualism in the doctrine of St. Gregory is correctly noted in the investigation of Nesmelov, p. 153: "an attentive reading of his (St. Gregory's) works clearly shows that in fact he thought somewhat differently than he spoke in his polemic with Eunomius. All of his historical judgments have their appropriate sense only in relation to the same judgment of Eunomius concerning the complete comprehensibility of God's essence; unrelated to this judgment, they ought to be accepted with the greatest restriction." The polemic of St. Gregory with Eunomius is contained principally in the twelve books of the Refutation of Eunomius, in the Russian edition of his works, occupying volumes 5 and 6 (books 2 and 12 have particular significance). For a distinct and competent exposition of the dispute of Eunomius with Saints Basil and Gregory of Nyssa see Nesmelov, chapters 2-3.

46. "Refutation of Eunomius," book 2 (Nesmelov, p. 153), Russian edition, p. 271.

47. "Refutation of Eunomius," book 12, Russian edition, pp. 291-92, 319.

48. PG 4. The authentic works of Dionysius the Areopagite with paraphrases by Pachimeres are found in PG 3.

49. Dionysius the Areopagite exerted influence on Catholic theology which tends towards an excessive rationalistic clarity, even in the person of its head —

Thomas Aquinas. One can ascertain this, it is true, not with respect to the fundamental structure of his theological system, the *Summa theologiae* (for a generally accessible exposition of Thomas's doctrine see Sertillanges, *Saint Thomas* I-II [Paris, 1912]) but with respect to separate propositions. For example: "It is necessary to use the way of exclusion, in particular when considering the divine essence. For the divine essence by its immeasurableness surpasses every form comprehensible by our mind; in this way we cannot comprehend it through cognition of that which it is but we have only a certain concept of it through cognition of that which it is not." *Contra Gentiles*, book I, chapter XIV. Édouard Leroy, *Dogma and criticism* (Paris: Librairie Bloud, 1907), p. 29. "Concerning God we cannot comprehend that which he is but only that which he is not, and how all the rest relates to him." *Contra Gentiles*, book I, chapter XXX. Leroy, *Dogma and criticism*, p. 129. Here see the comparison of other passages from Thomas Aquinas and his references to Dionysius.

50. Maximus the Confessor comments on the concept *hyperousiotēs* in the following manner (*S. Maximi scholia in lib. de div. nom.*, PG IV, col. 186-88): "If *ousia* comes from the word *einai*, and *einai* presupposes a certain going out, then *ousia* cannot be applied in a real sense to God. For God surpasses *(hyperkeitai)* every essence, himself not being something of what is, but above being, and all being is from him; for only the one God's divinity hidden for all things is the original divine *(thearchikē)* power, which governs the so-called gods and angels, and holy people, and it also fashions *(demiourgos)* those who through participation become gods, really, itself coming from its own self and being divinity without cause" *(ex heautēs kai anaitios autotheotēs ousa)*.

51. St. Maximus comments on the concept *auto to ouden*: "It is necessary to understand that God is nothing *(ouden)* in this sense, that he is nothing *(mēden)* of what exists, for above everything is the cause of everything, whence theologians say that God is everywhere and nowhere. Although he is nowhere, everything is through him, but in him as the not existing, there is nothing *(hōs mē onti mēden)* at all; on the contrary everything is in him as the one who is everywhere. On the other hand everything is through him because he himself is nowhere and fills everything as being everywhere." *S. Maximi Scholia in lib. de div. nom.* col. 204-5.

52. St. Maximus comments in this way on this idea: "He himself is the cause and nothing *(mēden)*, for everything as a result flows out of him, in accordance with the causes of both being and nonbeing; indeed nothing itself is deprivation *(sterēsis)*, for it has being through the fact that it is nothing of what exists; but the not being *(mē on)* exists through being and super-being *(hypereinai)*, being everything as Creator, and nothing as the one who surpasses everything *(hyperbebēkōs)*, and even more being transcendent and super-essential *(hyperanabebēkōs kai hyperousios on)*." *S. Maximi Scholia in lib. de div. nom.*, col. 260-61.

53. For a brief sketch of the doctrine of St. Maximus the Confessor, see the valuable study by Aleksandr Brilliantov, *The Influence of Eastern Theology on Western Theology in the Works of Johannes Scotus Eriugena* (St. Petersburg, 1898), pp. 191-219. S. L. Epifanovich, *St. Maximus the Confessor and Byzantine Theology* (Kiev, 1915).

54. All quotations from the works of St. Maximus the Confessor are taken from

the edition of Migne: PG 90-91, *S.P.N. Maximi Confessoris opera omnia* (according to the edition of F. Combéfis).

55. PG 91, col. 1257 (Ambiguorum liber).

56. PG 90, col. 1084 a, b, d, e (Capita ducenta ad theologiam Deique Filii in carne dispensationem spectantia).

57. PG 90, col. 1167-77.

58. PG 90, col. 1177 (diversa capita ad theologiam et oeconomiam spectantia deque virtute ac vitio).

59. PG 91, col. 1153 (Ambiguorum liber).

60. Quotations are taken from the Russian translation by Aleksandr Bronzov (St. Petersburg, 1894).

61. All references are taken from PG 150, the Works of St. Gregory Palamas. Cf. Bishop Aleksii, *Byzantine Church Mystics of the 14th Century* (Kazan', 1906). For the history of the hesychast and Palamite disputes (along with documentation) see Bishop Porfirii (Uspenskii), *History of Athos,* part 3, section I.1, section III, 1-2 (St. Petersburg, 1892).

62. PG 150, col. 937, *Gregorii Palamae dialogus qui inscribitur Theophanes sive de divinitatis et rerum divinarum communicabilitate et incommunicabilite.*

63. PG 150, col. 1221, *Eiusdem Gregorii physica, theologica, moralia et practica capita* CL.

64. PG 150, 1220.

65. PG 150, 1176.

66. PG 150, 929.

67. PG 150, 941.

68. PG 150, 936. Compare the exposition of Palamas's teaching in Porfirii Uspenskii, *History of Athos,* part III, section 2, pp. 234-37.

69. PG 150, 941.

70. PG 150, 941. Compare the quotation in Porfirii, pp. 266-70, of "The Tale about how the adherents of Barlaam and Akindynos are afflicted with disease." "We say in accordance with the teaching of the saints that the divine essence, as incommunicable and invisible, is more sublime than the illuminations and actions and gifts that are sent out of it, who gives and communicates to the saints the Holy Trinity, Father, Son and Holy Spirit, for all divine energies and gifts are common to the three worshipful hypostases . . . the divine essence is more sublime than the energies and gifts that are communicated from it, as their cause *(aitia)* and source. That is the cause, and these are the results *(ex ekeinēs aitias) (sic!).* . . . Think similarly about the divine essence and the divine energies. However you call them is how you call the divine essence. If the energies are uncreated, then this essence is also uncreated, and if they are created, then it is created too, since energies are indivisible from essence."

71. In Russian see the monograph on Eriugena, Aleksandr Brilliantov, *The Influence of Eastern Theology on Western Theology in the Works of Johannes Scotus Eriugena* (St. Petersburg, 1898).

72. *De divisione naturae,* lib. II, cap. 30, col. 599. *The Works of Eriugena,* collected by Floss; see Migne, *Scriptores Latini,* vol. 122, according to which all references are taken.

There is a German translation by L. Noack, *Johannes Scotus Eriugena. Ueber die Eintheilung der Natur. Philosophische Bibliothek,* Bde 86-87.

73. *De divisione naturae,* lib. I, cap. 14, col. 459; cf. lib. I, cap. 76, col. 522A.

74. *De divisione naturae,* lib. II, cap. 30, col. 599.

75. *De divisione naturae,* lib. I, cap. 14, col. 459-60.

76. *De divisione naturae,* lib. I, cap. 14, col. 462.

77. By the way, according to Eriugena, "even the heavenly powers are necessarily not free from ignorance, and the mysteries of divine wisdom remain unknown to them" (II, p. 28).

78. *De divisione naturae,* lib. I, 33, cap. 15, col. 463. Cf. lib. II, cap. 28, col. 585.

79. *De divisione naturae,* lib. II, cap. 28, col. 589.

80. *De divisione naturae,* lib. II, cap. 28, col. 589.

81. *De divisione naturae,* lib. II, cap. 28, col. 593.

82. *De divisione naturae,* lib. II, cap. 29, col. 598.

83. *De divisione naturae,* lib. II, cap. 28, col. 594.

84. When Bulgakov wrote this section, no complete edition of the works of Nicholas of Cusa existed, though he referred to the *De docta ignorantia,* edited by Paolo Rotta, 1913, and the rare sixteenth-century edition found in the Moscow library of the Rumiantsev museum. He also noted that the extant German translation "of the most important works" of Nicholas of Cusa was out of print: *Des Cardinal und Bischofs Nicolaus von Cusa wichtigste Schriften in deutscher Uebersetzung von F. A. Scharpff* (Freiburg im Breisgau, 1862). He referred to the monograph of the same, *Nicolaus von Cusa als Reformator in Kirche, Reich und Philosophie des XV. Jahrhunderts* (Tübingen, 1871), and K. P. Hasse, *Nicolaus von Kues* (1913) (in the series *Die Religion der Klassiker*); Schwarz, *Der Gottesgedanke in der Geschichte der Philosophie* (1913), Kapitel III, §24. An edition of the translation of his works was being prepared in Philosophische Bibliothek. Since 1932 the critical edition of the Opera omnia of Nicholas of Cusa has been appearing under the auspices of the Heidelberg Academy. A Latin-German edition is available: *Philosophische-Theologische Schriften* (Vienna, 1964-1967, 3rd ed., 1989); a recent English translation is Jasper Hopkins, *Complete Philosophical and Theological Treatises of Nicholas Cusa,* 2 vols. (Minneapolis, 2001). — Trans.

85. Whence in the doorway of the coincidence of opposites, which an angel who is stationed at the entrance to Paradise guards [*Unde in ostio coincidentiae oppositorum, quod Angelus custodit, in ingressu Paradisi constitutus . . .*]; you are within the wall in Paradise. But the wall is that coincidence . . . [*tu es intra murum in Paradiso. Murus autem est coincidentia illa . . .*], *De visione Dei,* chapter 10.

86. *De docta ignorantia,* lib. II, cap. 26, p. 21, cited according to the Basel edition of 1565.

87. Cited according to the German translation of Adolf Lasson: Giordano Bruno, *Von der Ursache, dem Prinzip and dem Einen* (Leipzig, 1902). Philosophische Bibliothek, vol. 21, pp. 70-71.

88. Not possessing sufficient mastery of the Hebrew language I am unfortunately deprived of the possibility of using an original text of the Cabbala and I will take the present excerpts from translations, in particular from Erich Bischoff,

Elemente der Kabbalah, 1 Theil, 1913 (*Geheime Wissenschaften,* 2-er Band); and his *Die Kabbalah,* 1903, as well as from the French translation of the book *Zohar: Sepher ha-Zohar,* trans. Jean de Pauly (Paris, 1911). This translation (in six parts), made up in accordance with competent testimonials, is the fruit of the labor of an entire scholarly life and represents, in truth, a precious contribution to European literature. Differences in the rendering of cited passages by the German and French translators I have taken no notice of (cf. however the comparisons of variants of the translations of several important passages in the notes to the translation by de Pauly, in volume 6, e.g., note 161). Further, some excerpts are cited in the book by A. Franck, *La Kabbale* (Paris, 1843). I also used the German translation of the cabbalistic book *Sefer Jetzirah, Das Buch der Schöpfung,* trans. Lazarus Goldschmidt (Frankfurt, 1884).

89. Cited from A. Franck, *La Kabbale,* pp. 173f.

90. M. Muretov, *The Doctrine of the Logos in Philo of Alexandria and John the Theologian in conjunction with the Preceding Historical Development of the Idea of the Logos in Greek Philosophy and Jewish Theosophy,* I (Moscow, 1885), p. 138.

91. Proceeding from such an understanding, the Sefirot (ten in number) or divine rays which are the personal bearers of the qualities of the Ein Sof itself lacking qualities and the intermediaries of all relations of Divinity with the world, have a creaturely character, according to the opinion of Professor Muretov. "The creatureliness of the Sefirot follows from the fact that they are portrayed in the book *Zohar* as essences limited in their understanding and power — that the self-enclosed *Ein* is as unattainable for them as for other creatures that finally in the book *Zohar* it speaks directly of their creation in time" (*The Doctrine of the Logos,* p. 68). And even "the first revelator and the most universal bearer of the properties of the predicateless *Ein, Metatron,* the firstborn divine son, standing at the head of all the other Sefirot and governing them" (69) for whom are acquired all the predicates of Jehovah, "the name of whom is like the name of God," "despite all his exaltedness over the other Sefirot, in no way at all has a divine nature; he is a creature in the rank of other creatures, although the first and purest ... he is called an angel and is reckoned to the Sefirot, and is called a servant of Jehovah, even though he is older; precisely thus does *Metatron* bear the appellation Adam Cadmon, the first heavenly human, in the sense that he is the first and most perfect creation of God, according to the image of which Adam is created — wherefore the epithet "creates" is often assimilated to *Metatron*" (71). This opinion of Professor Muretov requires verification and in any case it is debatable.

92. Already Azriel, the disciple of Isaac the Blind, affirmed the incomprehensibility and incognoscibility of God as Ein Sof: one ought not ascribe to him attributes or actions or notions or speech or desires or intentions, for every such definition would be a limitation. August Wünsche, *Kabbala* (*Realencyclopädie für protestantische Theologie und Kirche,* 3-te Aufl., 9 Bd., 672, 15-35).

93. *Das Büchlein vom vollkommenen Leben (Eine Deutsche Theologie) in der ursprünglichen Gestalt herausgegeben und übertragen von Herrman Büttner* (Jena: Diederichs, 1907), p. 3.

94. A special excursus will be dedicated to the negative theology of Eckhart and Jacob Böhme in the following section (pp. 167-79), so that here we are providing only

general and preliminary information, for the sake of the completeness of the historical sketch.

95. *Meister Eckeharts Schriften und Predigten,* trans. H. Büttner (Diederichs), vol. I, pp. 165-66. Russian translation, M. V. Sabashnikova (Musaget), *Spiritual Discourses and Sermons of Meister Eckhart* (Moscow, 1912), pp. 146-47.

96. *Meister Eckhart,* vol. I, pp. 167-68; Russian, pp. 147-48.

97. *Meister Eckhart,* "Von zwei Wegen," vol. I, pp. 120-21; no Russian.

98. *Meister Eckhart,* "Von der Abgeschiedenheit," vols. I, IIf., Russian translation, pp. 55f.

99. In connection with the doctrine about detachment Eckhart develops his most important doctrine about God and Divinity, which we discuss in the next section.

100. Heinrich Seuse, *Deutsche Schriften,* ed. W. Lehmann, 2 volumes (Diederichs); Johannes Tauler, *Predigten,* 2 volumes (Diederichs).

101. See, e.g., the discourse "Eine Bekehrung, wo Gott ist and wie Gott ist," and especially "Von dem höchsten Ueberflug, den ein vernünftiges Gemüt erlebt." Vol. I, pp. 153-54.

102. "Von irdischer und himmlischer Ruhe," *Tauler's Predigten,* vol. 2, pp. 3-4.

103. *Tauler's Predigten,* vol. 2, p. 60.

104. *Tauler's Predigten,* vol. I, p. 185.

105. "Vom eignen Nichts," *Tauler's Predigten,* vol. I, p. 211.

106. Sebastian Frank, *Paradoxa,* ed. H. Ziegler (Diederichs), p. 13.

107. Frank, *Paradoxa,* pp. 77, 21.

108. *Des Angelus Silesius Cherubinischer Wandersmann, nach der Ausgabe letzter Hand von 1675 vollständig herausgegeben* (Diederichs, 1905).

109. "God is a pure nothing, no now or here touches him: the more you reach for him the more he escapes your grasp. The tender Godhead is a nothing and supernothing: whoever sees nothing in everything, o man, believe that he sees it. Go where you cannot, see where you cannot see: hear where nothing sounds and rings: then you are where God speaks. Nothing is known in God; he is a unified One: What one knows in him must be oneself. God is a pure flash and also a dark naught: that no creature contemplates with its light." — Trans.

110. Johannes Claassen, *Jacob Böhme's theosophische Werke im Auszuge,* vol. I, p. 156.

111. Claassen, *Böhme's theosophische Werke,* vol. 2, p. 29.

112. Claassen, *Böhme's theosophische Werke,* vol. 2, p. 32. *Mysterium magnum, Werke,* vol. 5, 1, 2-8.

113. Claassen, *Böhme's theosophische Werke,* vol. 2, p. 28.

114. Claassen mistakenly presents Pordage only as a disciple and follower of Böhme (although he considers him "the divine J. Böhme"). Cf. Claassen's introduction to volume 1 of his edition of the selected works of Böhme. *Divine and True Metaphysics* is cited from the new edition being prepared for Put' publishers, which is a reprint, with minor changes, of the edition of the Mason N. I. Novikov, from the beginning of the nineteenth century. [Actually, Novikov's edition appeared in 1787. — Trans.]

115. Hegel's *Religionsphilosophie* (Jena: Diederichs, 1906), pp. 335-36.

116. Therefore it is incumbent on us to distinguish clearly in Soloviev the poet-mystic, with the enormous religious experience of exceptional significance, from the rationalist-metaphysician.

117. See "Philosophical Principles of Integral Knowledge," Collected Works, vol. 1, esp. pp. 320-21, and "Lectures on Divine Humanity," vol. 3, pp. 82f.

118. Here is a typical confusion: "we shall designate this phase of the absolutely existing as Ein Sof or God-Father (primordial god)" (vol. 1, p. 347). Here concepts are united by the conjunction "or" as equivalents that belong to different planes: Ein Sof is the transcendent Divinity *before* disclosure; God-Father is the first hypostasis of the triune God.

119. As is well known, the Greek language knows a third shade of negation, namely, *ou*; it indicates the absence of a given, definite property, and has a concrete content: *not this, not that*. Thus logically *ou* occupies the middle position between *alpha privative* and *mē*. It converges with the first, *alpha privative*, by the decisiveness of its negativity, but it differs from it in the limited scope of its negation. It differs from the second, *mē*, precisely by this decisiveness of negation, in comparison with which *mē* designates only indetermination, but it converges with it by its negative positivity. *Ou* is always correlative to affirmation, as shadow is to light. In the current discussion the central meaning belongs precisely to the opposition of *alpha privative* and *mē*. On the contrary, in the investigation of the problem of matter that stands before us (in the next section) the opposition of *ou* and *mē* proves to be central, and *alpha privative* remains in the shade.

120. Schleiermacher came close to this idea in his definition of religion as "schlechthinniges Abhängigkeitsgefühl" — a feeling of (ontological) dependence as such.

121. The relationship between creature and Absolute can be expressed with the assistance of the mathematical symbol for infinity ∞ thus: ∞ + any finite value or creature = ∞, consequently the creature for infinity in comparison with infinity = 0, having remained *for itself* a value. In the same way the definition of the correlation between the finite and the infinite, which is expressed in the fraction creature/∞ = 0, likewise leads to the zero meaning of the creature before the Absolute, although for itself it has a value.

122. See Pavel Florensky, *The Cosmological Antinomies of I. Kant* (Sergiev Posad, 1909).

123. With arguments such as these Drews raises an objection against the personal character of Divinity: "The spirit is called an individual in its finite limitation and definition by the material organism.... On the contrary, person designates a kind of image of the spirit, when it shows itself in conformity with its essence and consciously strives towards the realization of this as the definition of its being. In this sense the individual is called person inasmuch as it *is* not only spirit but is conscious of and realizes itself as spirit in opposition to its natural conditionality.... There can be no talk of person applied to God. Person is spirit only as something finite, for only such a spirit has corporeality as a premise from which it must distinguish itself as spirit, upholding its spirituality; the absolute spirit in which there is no place for

such differentiation cannot be defined by rational means as person. That which establishes person in a human being is precisely his finiteness, i.e. the unspiritual in him, his material organism, in opposition to which spirit must realize and affirm its independence so that through this it can participate in the highest definition of person.... In this way it is really an advantage for a human being to be a person, for only through this does he become conformed to his own proper and most profound essence.... For absolute spirit, on the contrary, spirituality is its proper nature; in it there is no tension between nature and spirit, in the taking down and reconciliation of which the essence of person consists, because it cannot receive anything from the predicate of person." A. Drews, *Die Religion als Selbstbewusstsein Gottes* (Jena, 1906), pp. 326-28. Having defined person as a symptom of the infringement of spirit by body, Drews manages this phantom of rationalism without difficulty and completely rejects the idea of person when applied to the essence of the absolutely spiritual. In a similar way he makes short work of the Christian doctrine of God-Love, detecting in it an anthropomorphism, for here a human "feeling" is ascribed to the absolute (290f.). Hartmann too declares the doctrine of a personal God to be an anthropomorphism, and Drews's opinions do not add much to his argumentation. Hartmann, *Die Religion des Geistes,* 3rd ed. (Berlin, 1882), pp. 152-53.

124. John 4:14. — Trans.

125. A. Drews distinguishes (in *Die Religion als Selbstbewusstsein Gottes*) two types of religion: *Causalitätsreligion* [religion of causality] to which he relates the religion of the Judeo-Christian type, and *Identitätsreligion* [religion of identity], the religion of the immanent type like Buddhism and the religion of concrete monism which he himself invented. The definition of the first type on the basis of causality, of course, is incorrect, while the definition of the second type on the basis of identity expresses the very essence of the matter.

126. ". . . everything that comes to be is worthy of coming to ruin; therefore it would be better if nothing came to be." From Goethe's *Faust,* lines 1339-41. — Trans.

127. Stöckl thus defines the Plotinian worldview. A. Stöckl, *Lehrbuch der Geschichte der Philosophie,* 2nd ed. (Mainz, 1875), p. 377.

128. This is how Eriugena's Russian investigator A. Brilliantov defines this feature of his doctrine: *The Influence of Eastern Theology on Western Theology in the Works of Johannes Scotus Eriugena,* pp. 248ff.

129. *De divisione naturae,* lib. III, cap. 23.

130. *De divisione naturae,* lib. III, cap. 20.

131. *De divisione naturae,* lib. III, cap. 20.

132. *De divisione naturae,* lib. III, cap. 19.

133. *De divisione naturae,* lib. III, cap. 17.

134. *De divisione naturae,* lib. III, cap. 17.

135. *De divisione naturae,* lib. III, cap. 20.

136. *Meister Eckhart's Schriften und Predigten,* ed. Büttner (Diederichs), I, p. 147.

137. A systematic exposition of Eckhart's religious worldview, together with certain characteristic convergences with the present, is found in H. Schwarz, *Der Gottesgedanke in der Geschichte der Philosophie* (Heidelberg, 1913), ch. 2, §§20-21. Of con-

siderable interest for our topic is the author of *Das Büchlein vom vollkommenen Leben* from the school of Eckhart (in the edition of Diederichs furnished with a very interesting foreword by G. Büttner — in its own way a manifesto of immanentism). Especially deserving of attention are pages 3, 34, 46, 48, 78.

138. As one knows, literature about Böhme is scarce. In addition to the oft-cited investigation of Schwarz, *Der Gottesgedanke in der Geschichte der Philosophie*, ch. 3, §27, one can refer to Elert, *Die voluntaristische Mystik I. Böhmes* (1913), including a bibliography, and A. I. Penny, *Studies on I. Böhme* (1912), among more recent studies. From the older literature see Baader, Schelling, Hegel, Pfleiderer, Claassen, et al.

139. Schelling, *Philosophie der Offenbarung*, Sämmtliche Werke, II Abt. III Bd. (Stuttgart, 1858), p. 123.

140. This trait Schelling calls "the rotation of his mind," in virtue of which he "starts over again in each of his writings, explicates the beginnings that have been explained often enough, without ever advancing or moving forward." Schelling, *Philosophie der Offenbarung*, p. 124.

141. Claassen says: "Böhme was no thinker, no brooder, but a seer." Johannes Claassen, *Einführung in Jacob Böhme* (Stuttgart, 1885), p. 74. But that is just the point: Böhme was at least just as much a thinker and brooder as he was a seer, otherwise not only the interior but also the exterior character of his treatises becomes incomprehensible. In order to feel this difference it is useful to compare Böhme and Pordage, who are very close to each other in the realms of theosophical ideas. Pordage is only a "seer," a "spirit-seer," who unsophisticatedly and without further ado passes on the content of the mystical "lessons" which he received; his individuality as a thinker thereby completely retreats to the background. On the contrary, in Böhme we all the time see the thinker in whom a gigantic logical work takes place.

142. In "Aurora" Böhme mentions that "since I was not in a state to grasp instantly the deep births of God in their essence and to comprehend them in my reason, twelve good years went by until true understanding was given to me." J. Böhme, *Aurora or the morning dawn*, trans. A. S. Petrovskii (Moscow: Musaget, 1914), p. 272, §14. In another place he says "this is said however not in the sense that I could never err at all, for certain things are insufficiently elucidated and they are described as if from a single glance at the great God; for the wheel of nature turns too quickly and the human with his half-dead and sluggish comprehension cannot grasp enough of them" (p. 331, §41). But the intellectual work of Böhme is identified not so much according to this indistinct recognition as according to the general plan of his treatises, which are not very immediate at all but carry in their structure the traces of intense mental work.

143. Schelling gives this description of Böhme's "theosophism": "In the third aspect of empiricism the supersensible is made the subject of real experience thanks to the possible rapture of the human being into God being allowed, and as a result of this the necessary, unerring contemplation which penetrates not only into the divine being but also in the essence of creation and into all the events in it.... We have defined theosophism from the beginning as the opposition of rational philosophy, consequently, of rationalism in philosophy. But basically theosophism strives beyond ra-

tionalism, in reality not being in a state to be liberated from purely substantial knowledge. Precisely knowledge in which rationalism has its essence one ought to call substantial, inasmuch as it excludes every act. For rationalism nothing can arise through action, e.g., free creation; it knows only *essential (wesentliche)* relations. For it everything follows only *modo aeterno*, i.e. purely by logical means, by immanent motion; for it is only a falsified rationalism if for example one explains the origin of the world by the free revealing of the absolute spirit which generally speaking wants to affirm creation through action *(thätliche)*. Full rationalism therefore comes close precisely to theosophism which no less than it is limited by substantial knowledge; theosophism *wants* to overcome it but it does not succeed, as can be seen more clearly than anything in J. Böhme. There is surely no other spirit so tempered in the fire of purely substantial knowledge than J. Böhme; for him God, obviously, is the *immediate* substance of the world; although he *wants to,* he is not able to obtain a free relationship of God to the world, a free creation. Although he calls himself a theosophist, and consequently lays claim to a science of the divine, the content towards which theosophism leads is only a substantial motion, and he imagines God only in substantial motion. By its nature theosophism is no less unhistorical than rationalism. But God truly *is not moved* by positive philosophy, he *acts*. Substantial motion, by which rationalism is limited, departs from a negative *prius,* i.e. from a non-entity, which has to be moved towards being; but historical philosophy departs from a positive *prius* which has no need to be only moved toward being; therefore, with complete freedom, not being compelled to this by itself, it only posits being . . ." etc. Schelling, *Philosophie der Offenbarung,* I, pp. 119, 124-25. Generally speaking Schelling gives a brief but profound philosophical description of Böhmism.

144. O. Pfleiderer, *Geschichte der Philosophie* (Berlin, 1893), p. 23.

145. Schwarz (*Der Gottesgedanke in der Geschichte der Philosophie,* p. 553) even calls Böhme, of course in an exaggerated way, "a new creator and intellectual perfector of Eckhart's thoughts."

146. *Böhme's Werke,* ed. Schiebler, vol. IV, p. 348.

147. *Mysterium magnum,* vol. V, 12, §5; cf. vol. IV, 278, §7; 186, §12; 415 §24; 424 §7.

148. *Mysterium magnum,* vol. V, 24, §11.

149. *Mysterium magnum,* vol. V, 12, §4.

150. *Mysterium magnum,* vol. IV, 477, §§16-17. "Outside nature God is a mystery *(ein Mysterium);* understand as Nothing, for outside nature there is Nothing, i.e. the Eye of Eternity, the unsearchable Eye which stands or looks at itself in Nothing, for it is abyss *(Ungrund)* and the same Eye is the will which is understood as yearning *(Sehnen)* for revelation so that Nothing can be found." *De signatura rerum,* ch. 3, §2, *Böhme's Werke,* IV, p. 284.

151. *Philosophie der Offenbarung,* p. 121.

152. *Aurora,* p. 344, §17.

153. *Mysterium magnum,* vol. IV, 405.

154. *Mysterium magnum,* vol. IV, 473-74, §§2-4.

155. *Mysterium magnum,* vol. IV, 501, §42.

156. *Mysterium magnum,* vol. V, 13, §8.

157. *Mysterium magnum*, vol. IV, 41, §48; cf. 483, §2; 510, §27.
158. *Mysterium magnum*, vol. IV, 495, §13.
159. See for example in Spinoza: "I discovered the nature of God and his properties, namely, that he necessarily exists; that he is one; that he exists and acts according to the one only necessity of his nature; that he constitutes the free cause of all things; that all exists in God and in this manner depends on him, that without him it cannot exist or be imagined; and finally that all is predetermined by God and namely not from freedom at all or absolute benevolence but from the absolute nature of God, in other words, from his infinite might. . . . If things immediately produced by God, were created by God for the sake of attaining their goal, then the very last things, for the sake of which the first were created, would necessarily surpass all others. Further, this doctrine annihilates the perfection of God for if God creates for the sake of some such goal, then he necessarily strives towards that which he does not have . . . consequently God would be deprived of that for which he wanted to prepare the means and desired this." Spinoza, *Ethics*, in the translation of Ivantsov, 2nd edition, part 1, theorem 36, supplement, pp. 51-56. As we see, Böhme too immediately brings forward the last argument against the idea of the free creation of the world. So developed in the Böhmian sense is the following explanation of world evil and imperfection in the divine fullness: "to the question why God did not create all people in such a manner that they would be guided by one only reason I have no other answer than the following: of course, because he had sufficient material for the creation of everything, from the most lofty degree of perfection to the very least; or, more directly speaking, because the laws of his nature are so vast that there were enough of them for the production of everything that an infinite mind may be able to imagine" (p. 62).

160. In his *History of Philosophy*, Hegel sets aside a place for Jacob Böhme in "modern philosophy," in the line of its pioneers *(Ankündigung der neuern Philosophie)*, alongside of Francis Bacon. "Indeed, through him Philosophy came forward for the first time in Germany with a particular character." Hegel, *Vorlesungen über die Geschichte der Philosophie*, 3rd part, 2nd ed. (Berlin, 1844), WW. vol. 15, §270. Likewise not hidden from Hegel's attention was the fact that the Görlitz shoemaker "read a lot, evidently especially mystical, theosophical and alchemistic writings, particularly Paracelsus" (273). "The content of Jacob Böhme's philosophizing," Hegel further writes, "is authentically German; for what marks him out and makes him remarkable is the Protestant principle of inserting the intellectual world in his own mind and contemplating and feeling in his self-consciousness everything which was otherwise on the other side" (273). Hegel found "barbaric" only the form of Böhme's philosophizing, which did not rise to pure concepts but uses for them images, qualities, or elements: "from this aspect Böhme is an utter barbarian" (271). Separate allusions to Böhme are found likewise in the *Philosophy of Religion* and in the second edition of *Encyclopaedia*. Here it is said of Böhme, "the name *philosophus teutonicus* has been rightly assigned to this powerful mind; in part he expanded the content of religion to a universal idea, and in this conceived the highest problems of reason, and sought to grasp spirit and nature in their more definite spheres and formations therein by taking as the foundation that the spirit of the human being and all things which alone

are life were created after the image of God, naturally of no other than the triune God, in order to be reintegrated into it out of the loss of their original image; in part on the other hand he violently reverted the forms of natural things to spiritual forms and forms of thought." Hegel's *Werke*, vol. 6, 2nd ed., XXV-XXVI. Schelling spitefully underlines this convergence between Böhme and Hegel on the ground of religious naturalism (*Philosophie der Offenbarung*, I, pp. 121-22).

161. Baader says, "J. Böhme distinguishes the God-Unit *(Gott-Eins)*, the central God-unity, from his three revelations, of the divine, spiritual and natural realm. But under this central unity he in no way understands its being in itself, undeveloped or non-diffused, but affirms that with the help of this interior self-definition it rules out and excludes from itself all that is not itself" (2, 351). See I. Claassen, *Franz von Baaders Theosophische Weltanschauung als System oder Physiosophie des Christenthums*, II, B., 117. This characterization scarcely corresponds to reality. Baader himself supposes that the creature *(Creatur)* "is not a constituent part of the Creator which forms the periphery and sprouts from it according to the necessity of birthing, but not with absolute freedom similar to a work of art" (7, 89; Claassen, II, 118). "First, the absolute spirit's procession from itself is free, there is no need to confuse it with that interior generation and that exterior generation and conception arising from necessity *(Not)* or instinct. Second, absolute spirit is not divided by its production in its basic essence and does not lose its integrity, just as a word proceeds from me but does not part from me. Third, at the same time nothing is added to absolute spirit with this production, and it has no need of disclosure even for its own proper fulfillment. Fourth, absolute spirit as one which creates is not exhausted in creation, it does not pass over into the latter; as the centre does not pass over into the periphery but, by being differentiated from it, is raised above it. Fifth, absolute spirit realizes its free production only by the fact that it supplies and subordinates to itself a being that although distinguished is not separated from it and is not dependent on it, partly by compelling it to assist itself, partly by making it its instrument" (I, 214, 5; Claassen, II, 119). Baader contrasts creation and emanation (2, 89; Claassen, II, 119) and sees pantheism in the union of God with creation, by considering as false and contradicting every religion the affirmation that "God gives himself content only through creation, and that the all-determining determines, completes and realizes itself only through the act of creation, in becoming the real God out of that which is not God" (I, 396; Claassen, II, 119). On the contrary, Stöckl in his history of mediaeval philosophy considers that "Böhme reduces the origin of the world to a special form of *emanation* from God." A. Stöckl, *Lehrbuch der Geschichte der Philosophie*, 2nd ed. (Mainz, 1875), p. 620.

162. *Mysterium magnum*, V, 7-8, §§2-5. Cf. *De electione*, cap. I, §§5-6: "*The first unoriginate One Will* which is neither evil nor good, gives birth in itself to *the One eternal Good* as a comprehensible will which is the groundless Will's Son, and yet it is equally eternal in the unoriginate will; and one and the same other will is eternal *susceptibility and detectability* since Nothing finds its way to something in its self. And that undetectable, viz. the ungrounded will, proceeds through its eternal find and brings itself into an eternal contemplation of itself. Thus the groundless will is called eternal Father; or the conceived will of the abyss is called his born or sole begotten Son, be-

cause it is the *Ens* [Being] of the abyss in which the abyss conceives itself in a ground. And the procession of the groundless will through the conceived Son or *Ens* is called Spirit, because it brings the grasped Ens out of itself into a weaving or life of the will, as a life of the Father and the Son; and that which Proceeded is pleasure, as the find of the eternal Nothing, since the Father, Son and Spirit always see and find themselves; and it is called *God's Wisdom* or Contemplation." *Böhme's Werke*, vol. IV, p. 468. As a result of the original and complex role that belongs to Böhme's conception of the Son (*Ens, Fasslichkeit, Herz, Licht*, and *Wort* [being, conceivability, heart, light, and word]) the meaning of the Logos by which "all came to be," in a significant measure belongs to *Gottes Weisheit* or Sophia, the relations of which to Logos generally speaking remain unclear. That is why in Böhme it is more correct to speak not about a Trinity but rather a quaternity in God (and a heptad in "Eternal nature").

163. The Son "is called a person because he is an independent essence, which does not belong to the generation of nature, but is the life and reason of nature." *Böhme's Werke*, vol. IV, p. 59, §68.

164. *Mysterium magnum* (1624), cap. 7, §§5-7, II (V, 32-33). It is necessary to note that in *Aurora* (1612), Böhme is still significantly closer to the church's teaching about trinitarity and speaks about three persons of Divinity. (See chapter 3.)

165. Claassen, *Böhme's theosophische Werke*, vol. 2, p. 43.

166. *Mysterium magnum*, IV, 12, §36; cf. 32, §1; 279, §10; 559, §86; 566, §12; V, 16, §22.

167. *Mysterium magnum*, V, 30, §21. One needs to observe that this doctrine is also expounded in Pordage more comprehensibly than in Böhme. See Pordage, *Divine and True Metaphysics*.

168. *Mysterium magnum*, IV, 343-44, §49.

169. *Aurora*, pp. 60, 63.

170. "Sal nitrum" is a term from alchemy connected with the quest for the philosopher's stone and the more familiar term "saltpeter" or potassium nitrate. — Trans.

171. "This world has been created from eternal nature as an *Ausgeburt*." *Mysterium magnum*, IV, 39, §40; 50, §24; 492, §38; 291, §35.

172. "God stands in time, and time in God, one is not the other, but it comes out of a single eternal primordial source" (IV, 295, 14). "Eternity and time are one thing, but in different principles. The spiritual world inside has an eternal principle, while the external has a temporal principle; each has its generation in itself; but the eternally speaking word has dominion over all" (V, 11, §10). "For all things came from eternal spirit, as the image of the eternal; invisible essence which is God and eternity, in its own desire introduced itself into visible essence and was revealed through *(mit)* time, in such a manner that it is in time as life, whereas time is in it as if mute" (IV, 332, §2; cf. IV, 260, §3; V, 19, §12; 27-28, §§8, 10).

173. "The will for this formation (of angels) proceeded from the Father, from the property of the Father it arose in the word or the heart of God from the ages, as the desirous will for the creature and for the revelation of Divinity. For the Father is everything, and all power is in the Father. He is the beginning and end of all things,

and outside him there is nothing, but all that was arose from the Father. *But since from the ages he did not advance as far as the creation of angels, no creation happened before the creation of angels. We may not know the basis and cause for this;* God kept in his power how this happened, that he sometimes moved, for he nevertheless is the immutable God. And we may not investigate further here, because this confuses *(verwirrt)* us. Only about creation do we have authority to speak, for it is a work in the essence of God" (Claassen, *Böhme's theosophische Werke,* vol. 2, p. 64). "The spirits of angels were not forever corporeal but forever they were always essences in the tree of eternal life and their image was perceived eternally in the Virgin of wisdom.... And that is why it is the most magnificent miracle, accomplished by eternity, namely that *the eternal made them incarnate spirits,* which reason does not embrace and sense does not accept, and this is not accessible for us for investigation *(nicht ergründlich). For (created) spirit cannot investigate itself: it sees its depth as far as the abyss, but it does not understand its potter. By contemplation it penetrates into it as far as the abyss, but it does not know its working which is hidden in its own self. We are commanded to abandon penetrating further here and to be silent.* For we are a created thing and must speak only insofar as this touches on creation. Even if we know the *fiat,* still we do not know the first movement of God towards creation. *We know well the division of the soul, but how what stood forever in its essence was moved, we do not know....* This is the mystery of God alone and the creature must remain in humility and submission and not rise any further, for it is still not equal to God. God was to have children but not lords: He is Lord and there is no other. God is spirit from eternity, without foundation and principle. But the spirit of souls and angels has a principle and stands in the hand of God. But the principle towards the motion of the creature which arose in God may not be named" (Claassen, *Böhme's theosophische Werke,* vol. 2, pp. 64-65, 40; Frag. I, 267-79). Logically these elaborated ideas would have had to introduce significant limitations into Böhme's Gnostic system and in this way bring it closer to church doctrine. Obviously Böhme did not achieve such complete clarity in his ideas and "revelations" (Schwartz's judgment based on an attentive study of Böhme agrees with this, I, pp. 578f.). Such a judgment can still be encountered that compels one to recall anew the emanation of the world from God: "Creation is nothing other than the revelation of the all-substantial God without foundation. All that God is in his eternal, infinite generation and domain creation also participates in. But not in almightiness and power, rather *like an apple grows on a tree; it is not itself the tree, but grows from the power of the tree.* In this way all things arose from the divine desire and in essence are created since in the beginning there was no essence but only the *mysterium* of eternal generation. For God begat *(erboren)* creation not in order to become more perfect through it, but for the sake of self-revelation, towards great joy and dominion. Not so that such joy began only with creation, no, it was forever in the great *Mysterium,* but only as a spiritual game in its own self. Creation is also a game out of its own self, as in a model or instrument of eternal spirit which he plays" (Claassen, *Böhme's theosophische Werke,* vol. 2, p. 67. Theos. Er. 4, 1. 3).

174. "You will say now: did the entirely whole God really not know before the time of the creation of the angels that this would happen? No, for if God knew this before the time of the angels' creation, this would be the eternally pre-established will

and not enmity against God; but then God would have created him as the devil originally. However, God created him as king of light, but since he did not obey and wanted to be higher than the entirely whole God, God cast him down from his throne and made in the midst of our time another king from the very same Divinity from which lord Lucifer had been created (understand this correctly: from that *salitre* [curing salt] which was outside the body of king Lucifer) and seated him on the royal throne of Lucifer, and gave him power and authority such as Lucifer had before his fall, and this king is called Jesus Christ" (*Aurora*, p. 199, §§35-36).

175. This life (of creatureliness and dissension) must arrive at nothing . . . in this way in the same life in which I sense my I-ness *(Ichheit)*, sin and death; it must come down into nothing, for in life which is God in me I am inimical to death and sin; and according to life which is still in my I-ness I am foreign to Nothing as to Divinity (dem Nichts als der Gottheit)" (IV, 359, §63). "Freiheit als im Nichts . . . ein Urstand im Nichts" (IV, 348, §12).

176. *Mysterium magnum*, IV, 81, §§120-21.

177. *Mysterium magnum*, IV, 91, §43.

178. *Mysterium magnum*, IV, 83, §39.

179. Schwarz, *Der Gottesgedanke in der Geschichte der Philosophie*, p. 610. We will have to return to this question below in a study of the Virgin Sophia in Böhme's doctrine.

Notes to the Second Section

1. Sometimes the attempt is made to connect the difference between creation and emanation with the opposition of freedom and necessity in God. Schelling particularly defends the freedom of God in the creation of the world. He sees in this idea a necessary trait of theistic philosophy: *Philosophie der Offenbarung* II, III, 310, "The absolute freedom of God in creating is the point of departure. In his power stood that principle of the beginning which was in him as a simple possibility and, consequently, *without* his will there is *nothing*, this principle of the beginning which in the depths of his being he regards as a simple possibility to keep in a hidden state or to raise to reality. This God, in whose freedom is contained the possibility of placing what exists in him of his essence as an opposition, as what exists separately from him and is outside him, this God is the full God, God in all his all-unity, and not only existing in himself, for that one would not be free for himself. The freedom of God has a foundation only in his indestructible all-unity." Schelling often returns to this idea in *Philosophy of Revelation*. The opposition of freedom and necessity in God frequently transgresses by a manifest anthropomorphism (or what is the same, psychologism) and must be in any case protected against this reproach. The system of Prince E. N. Trubetskoi (in his *The Worldview of V. S. Soloviev*) also succumbs to this to a certain degree. For him the opposition of freedom and nature in God plays the same essential role, in conjunction with his admission of unrealized possibilities in the freedom of God. However, the absence of a preliminary analysis of these fundamental definitions affords a charac-

ter of incompleteness to the system of Prince E. N. Trubetskoi, with him standing much closer to Schelling (of course, to *Philosophy of Revelation*) than he himself thinks.

2. Schelling, *Darstellung des philosophischen Empirismus,* Ausgewählte Werke, Bd. II, 549ff. It is interesting that we find this definition of Newton almost word for word in St. Gregory the Theologian: "The name *Theos* is a relative name, as is likewise the name Lord." *Works of St. Gregory the Theologian,* 3rd ed., part 3, pp. 78-79; PG 36, 152.

3. Guilty of excessive "deduction" of creation and consequently of rationalism is Vladimir Soloviev, who reasons about this in the following manner: "If the absolute remained only itself, by excluding its other, then this other would be its negation, and consequently, it would not itself be absolute." *Organic Principles of Integral Knowledge,* Collected Works (St. Petersburg, 1901-07), vol. 1, 1st ed., pp. 320-21. But surely this "other" is completely absorbed and excluded by the concept of the all-one absolute, and in accordance with its concept the absolute has no need (metaphysical) of this other, which in some incomprehensible way or other limits it. "The other" can only be created entirely without compulsion, and is not set according to metaphysical necessity.

4. "God made all things from Nothing, and the same Nothing is he himself, like the living enjoyment in himself of love" (IV, 309, §8). "We cannot say that this world is created out of something, only desire from free enjoyment arose, that groundlessness as the highest good, or essence, as eternal will, contemplates in enjoyment *(Lust)* as in a mirror" (IV, 424, §7).

5. The dual and contradictory nature of creatureliness, woven out of divineness and nothingness, does not admit the immanent divinization of humankind which constitutes the distinctive feature of N. A. Berdiaev's anthropology with its unique mystical Feuerbachianism. See his clever and interesting book *The Meaning of Creativity: An Attempt to Justify Humankind* (Moscow, 1916). In our view both the creative impulse and the frenzy of the "underground" merge indistinguishably in the "creative act" proclaimed by him.

6. Khlestakov, a carousing inveterate liar, is the central figure in Nikolai Gogol's "The Inspector-General," and Chichikov, the epitome of complacency, is the main character of Gogol's novel, *Dead Souls.* The two characters represent precisely the vulgarity Bulgakov refers to in this section. — Trans.

7. Perhaps a reference to St. Francis of Assisi. — Trans.

8. *Ou gar mēpote tout' oudamē phēsin, einai mē onta, alla su tēs d'aph hodou dizēmenos eirge noēma* — this is how the text is cited in Plato's *The Sophist,* 237, A. *Chrē to legein te noein t'eon emmenai, esti gar einai, mēden d'ouk einai.* V, 43-44.

9. In modern philosophy the development between *mē* and *ou* is most distinctly of all expressed by Schelling in his *Darstellung des philosophischen Empirismus (Selected Works,* II, 571): *mē on* is the not-existing which only *is* the not-existing, with respect to which only actual existence is rejected, but not the possibility of existing, since it has before itself being as the possibility of existing, even though it is not the existing, yet not such that it could not be the existing. But *ouk on* is fully and in every sense that which does not exist, or it is that, relative to which is negated not only the *actuality* of being, but also being in general, accordingly even its possibility. In the first sense, through the expression *mē on* only the *status* is negated, the real posing of being, but

that relative to which the negation is made must all the same exist in a certain manner. In the second sense, through the expression *ouk on,* the negation of being *is asserted* and even supposed" (I, X, 283). Schelling explains the difference between *ouk on* and *mē on* with the French words *rien* — pure nothing, and *néant* — relative nothing. According to Schelling's own thought, which is defended in the treatise cited, the world is created by God out of nothing in the sense of *ouk on,* and not *mē on.* Unfortunately he does not entirely remain faithful to it in *Philosophy of Revelation* where he develops the idea of the creation of the world out of itself by God, although in a covert and complicated form (II, III, 284ff.).

10. In the work *On the Divine Names,* St. Dionysius the Areopagite says that "if it is permissible to say so, nonbeing itself strives towards the good which stands above all that exists, it endeavours itself somehow to be in the good," *De divinis nominibus* IV, 3; PG 3, 647. Likewise not only does all that is strive towards beauty, but "it even resolves to utter the word that even that which is not participates in the good and beauty, for it becomes good and beauty when it is glorified in God. *De div. nom.* IV, 7; PG 3, 704. "All that exists comes from good and beauty, all that does not exist superessentially abides in good and beauty." *De div. nom.* IV, 10; PG 3, 708. Commenting on these statements St. Maximus the Confessor says frankly, "*God himself is the cause of nothing* for everything flows out of him as a result, in accord with the causes, both being and nonbeing, for nothing itself is a limitation, for it has being thanks to the fact that it is nothing from what exists." St. Maximus, *Scholia in lib. de div. nom.;* PG 4, 260-61. Further St. Maximus compares creaturely being and nonbeing with the Divine NOT-what of negative theology: "That which is not also exists through being and nonbeing; it is for everything the creator, nothing as transcendent, or rather that which is, is transcendent and super-existential."

11. In the dialogue *Parmenides,* in this "divine game" of the genius who knows his power, the indissolubility of being and nonbeing is expressed dialectically, the being not only of being but also of nonbeing, as well as the nonbeing not only of nonbeing but also of being. "There is the one that does not exist *(to hen ouk on),* for if it does not become that which does not exist, if it loses something from its being to the advantage of nonbeing, then suddenly it will become what exists *(on).* Consequently, in order not to be it must be bound in nonbeing *by the being* of nonbeing *(desmon echein tou mē einai to einai mē on)* similar to how that which exists, in order to be fully, must be bound in being by *the nonbeing* of nonbeing *(to on to mē on echein mē einai);* in the same way, the existing will be in the greatest degree, while the not existing will not be, when the existing participates in the essence of being existing, but it will not participate in the essence of being what does not exist *(metechonta to men on ousias tou einai on, mē ousias de tou einai mē on)* if it has to be completely, and when the not existing does not participate in the essence of not being the not existing *(to de mē on mē ousias men tou mē einai mē on)* but participates in the essence of being the not existing *(ousias de tou einai mē on),* if already the not existing has fully not to be. Therefore, since the existing participates in nonbeing, and the not existing in being, then it is necessary for the one, if it *is not,* to participate in being with respect to nonbeing *(eis to mē einai)*" *(Parmenides,* 162, A B). Quite a lot of attention is dedicated to investigat-

ing the mutual relationship of being and nonbeing and their combination in the *Sophist:* the not existing "in participating in the existing also become existing" *(hoti metechei tou ontos einai te kai onta)* (*Sophist,* 256 E). This analysis is placed in connection with the doctrine of the relativity of being, in virtue of which every being is in one respect being and in another nonbeing, that is revealed in the analysis of motion and change. "We do not share the opinion that negation shows opposition, but only that with the particles *ou* or *mē* which are placed before the words *(onomatōn)* or more correctly before things to which the words that are pronounced after the negation refer, shows a certain otherness" (257 BC). Concerning all the types of being, both together and separately one can say that "in many respects they exist and in many others they do not exist" (259 B).

12. For Hegel, "pure being and pure nothing are the same. The truth is neither being nor nothing but that being does not turn into nothing and nothing does not turn into being, but is passed over." Hegel, *Wissenschaft der Logik* (Berlin, 1841), I, p. 73.

13. *Sophist,* 238 C.

14. Hegel, *Wissenschaft der Logik,* I, pp. 101, 103 (italics Bulgakov). But Hegel extends being, and consequently nonbeing, to God and evidently by recalling Böhme, says: "It would not be difficult to point out this unity of *being* and *nothing* in every example, in everything real or thought. The same must be said that was stated above about the immediacy or mediation of *being* and *nothing,* that nowhere in heaven *(sic)* and on earth is there anything which does not contain both being and nothing in itself." Further Hegel directly applies this to God: "Thus in God himself the quality of *operation, creation, power* etc. essentially contains the determination of the negative — they are a producing of an *"other"* (p. 76). One must recognize that Böhme is guilty of the same fault — the extension of the category of being to God — from whom, of course, one ought not expect philosophical accuracy. Nevertheless, his doctrine of origin in Nothing-Something, as well as the whole doctrine of "nature in God" with its spiritual-physical dialectic, can only be understood in this sense.

15. Plato's famous discussion of matter is intimately connected with the doctrine of the creation of the world. *Timaeus* is the only dialogue of Plato where the world is regarded as the *creation* of the good, of the Creator "who knows not envy." Plato distinguished here (28 D) what always is and has no origin (the world of ideas), what always comes to be but never is (the world of phenomena), and finally the "difficult and dark" form, the purpose of which is to be the substrate *(hypodochēn)* of every origin *(geneseōs),* as it were a wet-nurse *(tithēnēn).*" "Concerning the essence which assumes any bodies, one ought to say that it always remains identical *(tautēn)* because it by no means comes forward from its capacity *(dynameōs).* It always accepts everything into itself, it never in any way acquires any form that resembles what enters it; for it is by nature a receptacle *(ekmageion)* which is set in motion and formed from what enters, and thanks to it presents itself differently at different times" (50 BC). "One can liken to a mother that which receives, that from which (it is received) to a father, and the nature which occupies an intermediate place between them, to generation" (50 D). "This mother and substrate *hypodochēn* of all that appeared visible and perceptible in every way possible by the senses we will not call earth, air, fire or water, or that

which proceeded from them or from which they themselves proceeded; but we will not be mistaken if we have said that it is a certain invisible aspect without form, all-receiving, and somehow untraceably participating in the conceivable and elusive" (51 A). "Finally matter is defined as a type of space *(to tēs chōras)* that does not accept destruction, that gives place to everything that has a birth, but is itself inaccessible to the feelings, is caught by a certain counterfeit judgment, only with difficulty probable" (52 AB). In direct relation to the doctrine of *Timaeus* is the doctrine about the unlimited *(apeiron)* and the limit *(peras)* in *Philebus*. It is known how the Platonic doctrine of meonal matter was interpreted by Aristotle in his doctrine of prime matter *(prōtē hylē)*: the latter lacks every definition, concept, and form *(amorphous, aeidēs, agnōstos, aoristos, arrhythmistos)*. See the *Metaphysics,* book IV, 3.

On the question of being and nonbeing in Plato's doctrine, the study by Nicolai Hartmann deserves very serious attention: *Plato's Logik des Seyns* (Giessen, 1909). Despite the Cohenian objective of this book, it contains fine investigations with respect to the most difficult problems of Platonism and in that respect it even surpasses the capital work of Natorp, *Plato's Ideenlehre* (Leipzig, 1903). Both Natorp and Hartmann dwell on the least studied aspects of Platonism, what one can call its "transcendentalism," and therein lies the undoubted merit of the Marburg school.

16. St. Athanasius of Alexandria speaks about the relationship between Creator and creation: "All that is not created is not in the least similar to the Creator by its essence but is outside him; by his grace and dispensation it is created by the Word. . . . What similarity is there between that which is from nothing and the Creator who produces out of nothing this very being? Or what likeness can the One Who Is have with what is not which already has that lack that it never had being and is located among created things?" *Works of St. Athanasius the Great, archbishop of Alexandria,* part II, 2nd ed. "First Sermon against the Arians," pp. 202-4. PG 26, col. 53. "The nature of created things, as something that proceeded from nothing, taken in itself, is something fluid, weak, mortal. The God of all is by nature good and higher than all goodness. . . . Hence he does not envy anything in being, but wants that all enjoy being. . . . And so, when God observed that every created nature, as much as it depends on the causes lying within it, is something fluid and destructible, and to the end that the universe not be subjected to destruction and not dissolve again into nonbeing, since he created everything by his eternal Word and caused creation to exist, he did not permit it to be attracted and overwhelmed by its own proper nature, from which the danger of arriving again at nonbeing would threaten her, but as the good he governs the universe and supports it in being by his Word . . . so that the creature could stand firmly in being . . . and not be subjected to that to which it could be subjected (i.e. nonbeing)." *Works,* part I, pp. 181-82. "Second Sermon against the Pagans," 41. PG 25, col. 82-84.

17. In the fifth dialogue of his treatise *De la causa, principe e uno,* G. Bruno gives a description of the World Soul or the Universe as the One, immovable and absolute, standing above difference and contradiction (in particular he clearly rests on Nicholas of Cusa's doctrine of the absolute), but thereupon he is presented with the question "Why do things change? Why is matter continually invested with new forms? I

answer that every change aspires not to a new *being* but to a new *aspect* of being. And such is the difference between the universe itself and the things in the universe. For it embraces every being and all aspects of being; out of them each one has whole being, but not all aspects of being, and in reality it cannot have all determinations and accidents. . . . In the eternal, the immovable, i.e. substance, essence, is found plurality, number; as the mode and diversity of essence, it does not become more than one, but only multiform, multi-aspectual essence. All that forms difference and number is only accident, only form, only combination. Each outcome, no matter what kind, is change, while substance always remains the same, because it is only one, divine, immortal essence. . . . This essence is one and constant and remains always; it is one eternally; every motion, every form, all other *is vanity, is as if nothing, indeed nothing is everything outside this unity.*" The relation between the one and the many, the universe and its phenomena, is determined such that the latter "are as it were different methods of manifestation of one and the same substance, the fluctuating, movable, transient appearance of the unmoved, permanent and eternal essence, in which are all forms, images and members, but in an undifferentiated and as it were embryonic state, just as in the seed the arm does not yet differ from the hand, the tail from the head, the veins from bones. But what is born by division and differentiation is not a new and different substance; it only brings into reality and fulfillment certain properties, differences, accidents and levels in each substance. . . . Whence everything that engenders difference of kinds, aspects, that creates differences and properties, all that exists in origins, ruin, alteration and change is not essence, not being, but the condition and determination of essence and being, and this latter is the single endless immovable substrate, matter, life, and soul, the true and the good. Since essence is indivisible and simple, in no way can the earth be regarded as part of essence, the sun as part of substance, since it is indivisible; it is inadmissible to speak about a part in substance just as it is impossible to say that part of the soul is in the hand, another part in the head, but it is entirely possible to say that the soul is in that part which is the head, that it is the substance of the part or is found in that part which is the arm. For part, piece, member, whole, how much, more, less, like this, like that, than this, than that, in accordance with, different from and other relations do not express the absolute and therefore cannot be referred to substance, to the one, to essence, but only through the medium of substance can they be in the one and the essence, *like modes, relations and forms.* . . . Therefore the opinion of Heraclitus does not sound bad when he asserts that all things are the one which in virtue of changeability has all things in itself; and since all forms are found in it, then corresponding to this all determinations refer to it, as do the situations which contradict each other insofar as they are correct. *And so that which comprises plurality in things is not the essence and the thing itself but only the appearance which is presented to the senses, and only on the surface of things*" (after the German translation by Lasson, pp. 100-105). In a fateful manner pantheism leads Bruno to acknowledge the world only as a phenomenon of the Absolute, i.e., to acosmism. The aporia which arise with the definition of the correlation between the single absolute universe and relative being, would come to light with even more clarity if Bruno had moved on to an explanation of the nature of human personhood and individual spirit, which in the name of consistency he would also have to acknowledge as an accident, mode or phenomenon of the single substance (the logic of pantheism usually leads to such apersonalism). The problem *of the reality of the relative* when being is absolutized as the one becomes here interminable and insoluble.

18. This question remains the subject of controversy between the Italian thinkers Rosmini and Gioberti, with the first defining God precisely as absolute being, while the second distinguishes what is and what exists, with what is creating what exists, according to Gioberti's formula. See V. Èrn, *Rosmini and His Theory of Knowledge* (Moscow: Put', 1914), pp. 172-73.

19. As Nicholas of Cusa says: Nam videtur quod ipsa creatura, quae nec est Deus, nec nihil, sit quasi post Deum, et ante nihil, intra Deum et nihil, ut ait unus sapientium: Deus est oppositio nihil, meditatione entis; nec tamen potest esse ab esse et non esse composita (*De docta ignorantia*, Lib. II, cap. II, p. 71). Cited from the new Italian edition of Paolo Rotta (Bari, 1913). [For it seems that the creature itself, which is neither God nor nothing, is as it were after God, and before nothing, inside God and nothing, as one of the wise said: God is the opposition of nothing, by considering being; nor however can it be from being and not be composite. — Trans.]

20. *De docta ignorantia*, Lib. II, cap. II, p. 73. Here we read: Si consideras rem ut est in Deo, tunc est Deus et unitas, non restat nisi licere quod pluralitas rerum exoriatur eo quod Deus est in nihilo. *Nam tolle Deum a creatura et remanet nihil* (p. 78). [If you consider the thing as it is in God, then it is God and unity; it does not remain unless you allow that a plurality of things arises insofar as God is in nothing. For if you remove God from the creature, nothing remains. — Trans.]

21. This makes understandable, insofar as one can speak here about comprehension, the whole paradox of the church's hymnody so monstrous for reason, directly chiding rational thought: "in the grave in flesh, in hell with the soul, as God, in paradise with the thief and on the throne being with the Father and the Spirit, the uncircumscribed filling everything" (Easter hours).

22. *Philosophie der Offenbarung*, I, 311.

23. Eduard von Hartmann, in *Schellings philosophisches System* (Leipzig, 1897), pp. 135-36, with good reason points out, e.g., that the deduction of three hypostases in Schelling nevertheless does not obtain, for the three positions or phases in the development of Divinity are not hypostases. The modalistic character of Schelling's doctrine under examination is also observed by Pfleiderer, who apropos this notes: "Es ist das jedenfalls eher montanistische oder sabellianische als kirchliche Dreieinigkeit" [This is in any case more of a Montanist or Sabellian Trinity than an ecclesial one. — Trans.] (*Geschichte der Religionsphilosophie*, 3rd ed. [Berlin, 1893], p. 351).

24. A liturgical verse having its own melody. — Trans.

25. Stanzas inserted between verses taken from psalms. — Trans.

26. In St. Maximus the Confessor we encounter this formula: "Eternity is time when it comes to a standstill, and time is eternity when it is measured as something expressed in motion such that one can define eternity as time that is deprived of motion, while time is defined as eternity that is measured by motion." *Quaest. ad Thalass.* PG 90, 1164.

27. Although in his emanative system he does not know a concept of creatureliness, Plotinus nevertheless considers time to be a property of inferior, creaturely being from which the realm of divine being is free: "For the first and blessed (principles) no striving towards the future exists, because they are already whole and have all that can be needed for life; hence they do not seek anything, and therefore even the future for them is nothing: there is nothing in which the future must consist. And thus the essence of what exists is perfect and integral, it cannot (fall) to pieces, and indeed it cannot have any completion in anything, and nothing from what is not can be added to it. For not only must all that is belong to everything and to the integral, but in no sense whatsoever can nothing from what is not be participant. Its whole content and nature is as it were eternity, for eternity is *aiōn* forever, is *aei* existing." *Enneads*, III, lib. VII, cap. 3. See also the whole seventh book of the third Ennead "on time and eternity."

28. Blessed Augustine bears witness to this when he says "Although the spiritual world (of angels) is above time, because being created first of all it anticipates the creation of time itself; in spite of this, however, above it the eternity of the very Creator reigns, from whom it too received its beginning through creation if not according to time, which still did not exist, then according to the condition of its being. And so the creation of this world is from you, O our God, but they are not at all what you are, and their essence is completely different from your essence. For although we do not perceive any time either earlier than them or in them themselves, because they always take delight in beholding you with their own eyes and never deviate from you, such that they are not subjected to any change: but mutability is inherent to them *(inest ipsa mutabilitas),* as a result of which they could become clouded in their cognition of you and grow cold in their love of you, if they were not illumined by your light." *Confessions,* book XII, chapter 15. Cited from the edition of the Kievan Theological Academy, *The Works of Blessed Augustine,* part 1 (Kiev, 1907).

29. Augustine, *Confessiones,* XI, 13.
30. Augustine, *Confessiones,* XI, 13.
31. Augustine, *Confessiones,* XI, 14.
32. Augustine, *Confessiones,* XI, 30.
33. See the analogous discussions about time in Schelling, *Philosophie der Offenbarung,* I, 306-9; II, 108-9.

34. "Time is not an object, it is an idea. It is extinguished in the mind," says Kirilov in Dostoevsky *(Demons).* By some contemporary writers time is considered to be a "fourth dimension" (P. D. Uspenskii, *Tertium organum; Fourth Dimension* [1914]; C. H. Hinton, *The fourth dimension and the new era of thought* [Petrograd, 1915]). In admitting the possibility of a spatial perception of time, we do not however see here a doctrine about the metaphysical nature of temporality in its relation to eternity.

35. For this reason the distinction in the very Divinity "of nature" (i.e., necessity?) and freedom, which lies at the basis of the scheme of E. N. Trubetskoi's book, *The Worldview of V. S. Soloviev,* represents for me an illegitimate anthropomorphism that introduces into the Creator the categories of creatureliness.

36. In this manner the reverse correlation to what we have in Kant is obtained: for him freedom exists only for the noumen and it does not exist in the world of expe-

rience, whereas necessity wholly reigns; according to our understanding freedom exists only where there is necessity, i.e., in creaturely self-consciousness; it cannot be ascribed to eternity just as necessity cannot be ascribed to it.

37. In *this* sense (i.e., in no way in a pagan sense) it can, perhaps, be stated about her that she is a "goddess," that mysterious being which our ancestors sometimes depicted on icons of Holy Sophia precisely as a female entity, but distinct from the Mother of God. An example of such word usage we meet in Vladimir Soloviev in the cycle of his sophianic verses where by the way there is this address to *"her"*:

> Near, far, neither here nor there
> In the kingdom of mystical reveries,
> In the world invisible to mortal eyes,
> In the world without laughter and tears,
> There I first came to know you, *goddess*,
> In a misty night.
> I was then a strange child,
> And I had strange dreams.

It is difficult to suppose that the expression "goddess" applied by Vladimir Soloviev to Sophia was here a slip of the tongue or only a poetic image, and not a precise expression of his thought.

38. The theological grounds for sophiology are all the more fully and precisely given in the book of Fr. Pavel Florensky, *The Pillar and Ground of the Truth* (Moscow, 1914), the tenth letter, to which I refer readers. Here is gathered rich iconographical and liturgical material.

39. In Schelling's *Philosophie der Offenbarung* (Stuttgart, 1856-61), I, pp. 306-9; II, pp. 108-9, there are some extraordinarily subtle remarks on how there must be something between eternity and time from which time would be able to begin and that can become what precedes only if what follows appears, but by this sequence objective time will be established. However, because Schelling is in general not familiar with Sophia he is not able finally to deepen his own idea. It seems absurd to absorb time into God and God into the temporal process; this generally speaking constitutes the basic deficiency of his whole conception.

40. Does not the Gospel speak about this kind of eternity: *and these go to eternal torment, while the righteous enter eternal life* (Matt. 25:46)?

41. Compare the doctrine of the creation of the world and the participation in it of separate letters, the doctrine of the heavenly and earthly alphabet, in the book *Zohar: Sepher ha-Zohar*, trans. Jean de Pauly, vol. 1, 2a ff. In Cabbalistic cosmology in general one can see a variant of Platonism or, to say it more generally, an originally expounded doctrine of the sophianicity of the world. In this sense Cabbala essentially approximates to Christianity by developing the Old Testament doctrine of Sophia contained in the Proverbs of Solomon, Wisdom of Solomon, and Song of Songs.

42. See above, p. 112.

43. Compare Fr. Pavel Florensky, *The Meaning of Idealism* (Sergiev Posad, 1915), part 2, pp. 41-134.

44. The Cabbala, commenting on this text "in the beginning *(bereshit)* God made," remarks, "*bereshit* designates *chokma* (wisdom, the second of the three highest sefirot), this means that the world exists through the highest and impenetrable secret of *chokma*," i.e., Sophia. *Sepher ha-Zohar,* trans. Jean de Pauly, I, 3b.

45. Nicholas Malebranche's doctrine of the vision of things in God and divine cognition as the essence of cognition of things presents a grand analogy for the doctrine being developed here (a thorough sketch of Malebranche's doctrine in Russian is in M. N. Ershov, *Problems of Divine Cognition in the Philosophy of Malebranche* [Kazan', 1914]). That which Malebranche asserts is entirely beyond question; however, it is applicable not directly to Divinity simultaneously transcendent and immanent to the world, but rather to its "image and radiance" in the world, to divine Sophia: we come to know things, everything *(pan),* not immediately in God but in Sophia. From this basic feature of Malebranche's worldview flow its fundamental defects, namely nature as that which is disappears in it; for him it is a pagan "chimera." From this is obtained Malebranche's "occasionalism" which deprives nature of any activity and reality and ascribes all active force in it immediately to God. This acosmism in a fatal way leads him to monism, although as a deeply religious nature he loathes it with all the powers of his soul, and he brings his philosophy close to Spinozism. Malebranche's doctrine, undoubtedly, is very profound and correct, in keeping with his aspiration to present himself as a sort of proof from the contrary to the benefit of a sophianic gnoseology.

46. With transcendent-speculative arguments it is impossible *to remove* the intuitively given problem of the sophianicity of the world and to elucidate it in the spirit of gnoseological formalism (the attempt made by the "Marburg school" on Platonism). It is instructive that the very development of New Criticism by virtue of things leads as it were to logical Platonism (Lask, Husserl, Cohen), i.e., it restores in its rights the recognition of the sophianicity of the world although in the most insipid, formally logical aspect.

47. In the works of the fathers of the church the doctrine of the world soul usually merges with the doctrine of humankind and the church, with Christology, anthropology, and ecclesiology. Sometimes a direct polemic is encountered with this idea, which however refers only to its pagan application. Typical in this respect is the polemic of St. Gregory Palamas (fourteenth century) who rejects the astrological world soul, by affirming, however, its existence in humankind: "No sort of heavenly or universal soul exists, but only the rational soul is human: not celestial, but supercelestial, and not thanks to place but in keeping with its proper nature, as the noetic, governing essence" *(oud' esti tis ouranos, ē pankosmios psychē, alla monē logikē psychē estin hē anthrōpinē ouk ouranios, all' hyperouranios, ou topōi, alla tēi heautēs physei, hate noētē hyparchousa ousia).* PG 150, col. 1125, cap. 4.

48. Gustav Fechner (1801-1887) was a German experimental psychologist whose work had an impact on early-twentieth-century philosophers. Herman Lotze (1817-1881) was in his day an extremely influential figure in philosophy and a major representative of "academic philosophy," standing between post-Kantian idealism and the various new philosophical movements of modernism. – Trans.

49. So-called occultism also aims to comprehend the sophianicity of the world soul, or the general regularity of all that exists when it claims to teach not the external but the internal "spiritual" perception of the forces of nature. The fundamental idea of occult philosophy — the animation of all nature and the absence in it of any soulless thing whatsoever, external or foreign with respect to the soul of the world — is entirely correct. The comprehension of the sophianicity of the world yields the possibility, up to a certain point, of comprehending Sophia also, and in her and through her the rays of the noetic light of the Divine by which she herself is enlightened. The religious lie of occultism, insofar as it becomes a surrogate of religion, consists in the tacit and insidious intent to be fenced off from God and the religious, prayerful path towards him through detecting the sophianicity of the world and its divinity. This is the old temptation: *eritis sicut dei scientes bonum et malum* [you shall be as gods knowing good and evil]. "Gnosis," "spiritual knowledge," is again put forward as the means of becoming "gods," being conscious of its sophianicity and the saturation of every sophianic creature with God; thanks to the cognition of the creature, under the pretext of sinking into the divine element of the world, forgetfulness of God is obtained. However, occultism in this sense is religiously false only in virtue of its religious coefficient and not in accordance with its immediate task. In fact a right occultism is possible insofar as such an expression is applicable to that superabundant perception of the sophianicity of nature which is proper, for example, to saints and in general to theophoric people, and can be proper to the nature of humankind. In the case of an unwarranted, wrong relation to it the forces of the world soul become the charms of nature, instruments for sorcery; from there, in the face of a magical relation to nature, a deviation towards religious perversions results.

50. This seems to be a reference to a poem by Friedrich Schiller, "The Veiled Statue at Sais." Sais was a town in Egypt in the western Nile delta. Its principal deity, the goddess Neith, was associated by the Greeks with Athena. — Trans.

51. Thus did the demons pervert in themselves their angelic nature — this is very clearly shown in Pordage's *Godly and True Metaphysics* (Frankfurt and Leipzig, 1715).

52. On the basis of what has been said, our answer to the question of the "transfiguration of reason" is determined which Prince E. N. Trubetskoi raised apropos the views of Father P. Florensky on the antinomical nature of reason. The question is whether reason, the conditionality and relativity of which is revealed in the antinomical quality of its structure, is subject to a graced transfiguration together with the whole world. That which merits eternalization or immortality can be subject to transfiguration; therefore sickness, deformity, and generally speaking that which is connected with temporality and sinfulness are not subject to it — here transfiguration could consist simply in annihilation. Beyond the gates of transfiguration much of what now enters inalienably into the composition of our being will remain and die the ultimate death. And in our reason there is something which belongs to death that will not attain the kingdom of transfiguration, and will not cross beyond these gates. It is precisely what makes it logical, transcendental, and discursive that is mortal in it, but of course, its sophianic root is immortal, found in the general connectedness of

thinking-being. In other words in reason everything sophianic in it belongs to eternity, but that which is extra- or anti-sophianic is subject to death, i.e., the Kantian-Laplace or Fichte-Hegelian reason. And reason itself in its highest rationality and sophianicity is the light of the Logos, is raised above logic, sees and knows its conditionality, relativity, and thus mortality.

    53. For this reason I refuse to accept the category of completely anti-ideal entities, as it were clots of nonbeing alone, which Prince E. N. Trubetskoi establishes (*The Worldview of Vladimir Soloviev,* vol. 1, pp. 298-300) and to which, evidently, the opposite category of completely ideal entities must correspond. Everything in the world is ideal or sophianic in its basis, but can be anti-ideal in condition and in any case inadequate to its idea. It is impossible to make an exception even for parasites and intestinal worms, which Prince Trubetskoi considers to be obvious examples of the anti-idealness of being, for in keeping with their high structure and the expediency of their composition, they are just as sought out by Providence as is every creature; likewise to deprive ichthyosaurs of authentic being, as Vladimir Soloviev did, simply because they no longer exist and because they were so enormous and awkward, is hardly a sufficient philosophical ground. And if bacteria, parasites, and similar things in the morbid state of the world have received such a doleful assignment, how are they worse off than wild animals or even people turned wild? In their own way they merely share the common fate of the world lying in evil. The unconditional anti-idealness of whatever sort of living entities cannot be admitted at all without acknowledging that the spirit of malice has the capacity not only to pervert, ruin, "slander" the world, but within certain limits to make its own anti-cosmos. It is well known that J. Böhme responded to essentially the same question with his doctrine of the distinction of three principles in God, with his special category of creation corresponding to the first of them, the principle of anger, fire, and darkness; and the parasites of Prince Trubetskoi together with bats, frogs, and other impurity are ascribed by him precisely to this kingdom of gloomy fire. Here the hellish principle is introduced, as a principle of creation, which then is only weakened by the principle of light, i.e., by the already purely divine principle of being. J. Böhme correctly emphasizes the feature of the qualitative difference of creatures. If every creature is original in its idea and distinctive in its freedom, then it preserves individuality in its sinful condition, i.e., it perverts itself in its own way. And in this sense one can admit in separate creatures an especially intense anti-idealness of being. But this still does not make them metaphysically anti-ideal entities, and a bug is estimable by the sophianic mystery as are a dove and roses, although in its creaturely malice it has perverted its essence to a special loathsomeness or has undergone an especially serious illness. Dostoevsky has wisely felt this. "Every entity must consider itself superior to all others. A bug for certain reckons itself higher than you; if it can, then for sure it would not be a human, but would remain a bug. A bug is a mystery, and mysteries are everywhere" (material for the novel *Demons,* from the conversations of Stavrogin with Shatov).

    54. Under occultism I understand here not so much contemporary, schooled occultism fostered by special training, but the general natural faculty of humankind to penetrate through the crust of phenomena, especially proper to peoples in earlier

epochs of development and which is reflected in fairy tales, epic literature, folklore, beliefs, and superstitions.

55. P. Florensky points to this with particular energy in the pamphlet "The Universal Human Roots of Idealism" (Sergiev Posad, 1909).

56. This is the answer to one of the objections of Aristotle against Plato, when he points out that one must inevitably acknowledge the idea of the "eternal Socrates," i.e., the idea of the individual, whereas it is essentially general. Of course one can speak of the "eternal Socrates," by understanding the eternal in Socrates, i.e., his ideal general and thus generic content and his qualitatively determined person that enters into the composition of a generic organism. But this does not mean that the empirical traits of the earthly life of Socrates would be eternalized in the world of ideas, for they belong not to eternity but to temporality; they can be eternally impressed only in a single compound act, the synthesis of time.

57. St. Gregory of Nyssa develops the idea that in the creation of the world one needs to distinguish two acts — general and particular creation — "in the beginning" and in the course of the six days, with general creation corresponding to the making in the oukon of the meon-mother of being, and the second, the manifestation of all that is found in the condition of meonal formlessness. From the words *the earth was invisible and unstructured* (Gen. 1:2) it is clear that "all was already in possibility at God's first aspiration towards creation, as if from some sort of enclosed power sowing being in the universe, but in reality each thing still did not exist separately . . . the earth was and was not, because qualities had not yet gathered to it. According to the translation of Symmachus this passage reads: "the earth was idle and without difference." St. Gregory of Nyssa interprets the word "idle" to mean that "it was still not in reality, it had being only in possibility, and the word 'without difference' means that qualities had still not been divided one from the other and could not be recognized each in its particularity and in and for itself, but all appeared to the gaze in some combined and undivided quality, and were perceived as being subject to neither color, nor form, nor volume, nor weight, nor quantity, nor any other similar thing, taken separately in itself" (*Works of St. Gregory of Nyssa*, part I, *Hexaemeron*, pp. 21-23).

58. The Cabbala depicts in its realistic language the correspondence of earth and all that derived from it in this manner: "And the One who is on high is the Father of all, it is he who created everything; it is he who fertilized the earth, which became pregnant and gave birth to these 'products.' It was fertilized as a cow is fertilized by a bull" (*Sepher ha-Zohar*, trans. Jean de Pauly, I, p. 268).

59. The Castalian Spring at Delphi was visited by those seeking answers from the Delphic oracle; it became a symbol for a source of poetic inspiration. — Trans.

60. A phrase from Dostoevsky's novel, *The Idiot*, often cited by Bulgakov. — Trans.

61. By the way, in this respect Plotinus's judgments do not always agree among themselves: despite the fact that the life of an incarnate soul is evil, it performs a kind of practical exercise in virtue in the soul, it learns, and this understanding of earthly life relates Plotinus with theosophy. Here is the most important place that refers to this: "If thanks to an accelerated departure the soul is liberated from the body, it suf-

fers no sort of loss; and it came to know the nature of evil in order to have the forces locked in it opened and the energies of creativity revealed which would have remained vainly abiding in peace in the incorporeal, for they would never have been able to cross over into action; and what it has would remain hidden from the soul" (*Enneads* IV, lib. VIII, cap. 5).

62. Nevertheless Plotinus still remains enough of a Hellene that the attitude of certain Gnostic sects towards the universe, which certain historians, among whom is Zeller, extend to Christianity (see Zeller, *Die Philosophie der Griechen* II (Leipzig, 1903), part 2, sect. 607), elicits a protest from him: "This would be the same as if two people were to inhabit one and the same beautiful house, where one reproached its layout and builder but nevertheless remained to live in it, while the other, on the contrary, did not reproach it but explained that the builder had erected it very skillfully but that he was waiting for the time to come when he would leave it and would not need a house. . . . We must, while we have a body, remain in the dwelling prepared for us by the good sister the soul" (*Enneads* II, lib. IX, cap. 18).

63. The greatest champion of the fundamental dogma of Christianity, the incarnation of Christ, Athanasius of Alexandria, is at the same time the principal defender of the ontological authenticity and holiness of the body. He says, "The Lord's principal purpose was the resurrection of the body, which he had to accomplish. For this served as a sign of the victory over death in order to show it to everyone and to convince everyone that the annihilation of corruption is accomplished by him and incorruption is already bestowed on bodies." *Works of St. Athanasius the Great,* part 1, "Sermon on the incarnation of God the Word," §22.

64. Origen, *Works,* 1st ed., *On First Principles* (Kazan', 1899), book III, chapter 5.4, pp. 284-85. "In my opinion, it is impossible to ignore that circumstance that Holy Scripture calls the creation of the world by a certain new and special name, *katabolē*. In Latin this expression is imprecisely translated with the term *constitutio*. In Greek *katabolē* rather signifies to cast down *(dejicere),* i.e. casting downwards *(deorsum jacere)*. . . . I think that the end and completion *(consummatio)* of the saints will consist in their invisible and eternal state. . . . In a like state, one must think, were the creatures beforehand. But if they had such a beginning, as the end which lies in wait for them, then without a doubt they were in an invisible and eternal state from the beginning. If it is indeed so, then obviously the rational entities descended from the higher state to the lower and besides not only souls who merited this descent by the variety of their motions, but also those entities which were brought down from the higher and invisible state into this lower and visible one for the service of the whole world, although not according to their own desire: *for creation was subjected to futility not by its will, but for the one who subjected it unto hope* (Romans 8:20). Thus precisely the sun, the moon, the stars and the angels received the commission to serve the world and those souls which because of the least deviations of the mind, received the need in those coarse and fleshly bodies: for the sake of precisely these entities, for whom this was necessary, this visible world was arranged. And so, with the word *katabolē*, evidently, is indicated the bringing down of all the entities in general from the higher to the lower state."

Blessed Jerome's version of this passage contains the same thought. The idea of the incorporeality of creatures in their original state is clearly expressed in *On First Principles,* book I, chapter 7.4-5, where it is said that the vanity to which the creature is subjected is "nothing other than bodies, for although the body of the saints is ethereal, it is all the same material." Compare III.5.4; III.6.1; and the *Commentary on John* 1:17. The devil, who in the book of Job is called a dragon, was the first entity enclosed in a body. This dragon fell away from God and as punishment for his fall he was robed in a body. He attracted to himself many other entities. Originally "the saints led a completely immaterial and incorporeal life *(aulon pantē kai asōmaton)*." Compare the *Commentary on Matthew* 15:35, and the comparisons in the notes to the Russian translation of *On First Principles,* XLIX, 115.

65. In Zoroastrianism, Ahriman is the principle of evil, the personification of evil, or the evil spirit, paired with the spirit of goodness, Ahura Mazda. — Trans.

66. In speaking of corporeality we are discussing only the general philosophical side of the question and leave unexamined the various "plans" of corporeality. Meanwhile here one can undoubtedly distinguish bodies of a different subtlety, i.e., not only physical, but also "astral, mental, and ethereal," and perhaps other bodies. For the philosophical understanding of corporeality these distinctions are not substantive and bodies of different "plans" merge in the general concept of body.

67. *On the Goal of the Christian Life: Conversations of Saint Seraphim of Sarov with A. N. Motovilov* (Sergiev Posad, 1914). Idem, S. Nilus, *The Great in the Small* (Tsarskoe Selo, 1902, 1905).

68. According to the doctrine of the Yogis, conscious mastery of the instinctive functions of the body, with the aid of a corresponding regimen and exercises, can be carried significantly further than now takes place among the majority of people. See Yogi Ramacharaka, *Hatha Yoga,* ed. Novyi Chelovek, and other publications of this series.

69. Even the broadening of experience according to occultism allows one to surmount spatiality: the "astral" body is not bound by space, and on this is based the possibility of an "astral outflow," the appearance of doubles and various telepathic phenomena.

70. See chapter 3 of my *Philosophy of Economy,* on food and labor, for the meaning of these functions.

71. The negation of the individuality of the body on the basis of its universality comprises the chief flaw in the discussions of Leroy on the resurrection of Christ: Édouard Leroy, *Dogma and Criticism* (Paris: Librairie Bloud, 1907), pp. 146-243. As a result, Leroy arrives at a spiritualism hostile to the body and in essence he denies the Resurrection of Christ as a concrete fact. Simple consistency would demand that he go further and deny the concrete divine incarnation, i.e., the very basis of Christianity.

72. In his dialogue "On the Soul and the Resurrection, a Conversation with His Sister Macrina," St. Gregory of Nyssa gives the following answer to some misunderstandings connected with the question of the individual character of the bodies of resurrection. "The soul knows the natural property of the elements, which flow together into the composition of the body with which it was united, even after their dis-

solution. And although naturally these elements, by reason of the opposite qualities placed in them, have been drawn far apart from each other, the soul keeps each of them from mixing with the opposite one; nevertheless the soul will subsist in each element, with cognitive power touching and adhering to what is peculiar to it, until the disconnected elements again flow together into one aggregate for the restoration of what had decomposed. This is the resurrection in the proper sense and is called such. . . ." "The soul remains in those elements with which it was originally united even after the dissolution, as if it was posted as the guard of its property, and in keeping with the subtlety and ease of movement of the spiritual power it does not abandon what strictly belongs to it when that is being dissolved with the same; it is not subjected to any error when it is being fragmented into small parts of elements, but penetrates its own, which are mixed with homogeneous ones, and it does not grow weak in its powers, passing with them, when they overflow in the universe, but it always remains in them wherever and however nature might arrange them. If the force which orders the universe gives a sign to the decomposed elements to reunite again, then just as different strings fastened to one lead all together and at one time follow after what is being dragged, so because of the attraction by the single power of the soul of diverse elements at the sudden flowing together of what strictly belongs the chain of our body will be linked together by the soul, whereby each part will again be joined together in harmony with its original and customary state, and will be clothed in its familiar form" (Gregory of Nyssa, *Tvoreniia izhe vo sviatykh ottsa nashego Grigoriia Nisskago* [The Works of St. Gregory of Nyssa], 8 parts [Moscow, 1862-72], part 4, pp. 254-55). In a further development of his ideas St. Gregory makes clear that here he has in mind not the restoration of a body in that form which it had before death, and in general not a material body *(sōma)* but some sort of dynamic body *(eidos)* through which "the restoration of our nature in its original state" will occur (pp. 314, 322), that was proper to humankind before the fall. Consequently the "garments of leather" are discarded which in St. Gregory's understanding signify the lower, material corporeality, and a higher, though entirely individual, corporeality is restored. Cf. Nesmelov, pp. 598-606.

73. 2 Peter 3:13. – Trans.

74. Some ambiguity and vagueness on this basic question is characteristic of the teaching of V. Soloviev, who ascribes the fall at one time to the world soul, and at another time to Adam.

75. See Leonid Pisarev, *The Doctrine of Blessed Augustine of Hippo on the Human Being in Relation to God* (Kazan', 1894), part 2, chapter 1, pp. 99-100.

Clement of Alexandria, *Stromateis*, IV, 13: "Of course sin lies in the energy and not in the essence, and therefore it is not the work of God."

Origen, *Homily on John*, II, 7: "All evil is nothing although it is also the nonexistent; the good is identical to what exists, whereas evil or bad is opposed to the good as what does not exist is opposed to what exists, from which it follows that the bad and the evil are nonexistent; evil is being deprived of what exists."

St. Athanasius the Great, *Against the Hellenes*, 4: "What exists I call the good, inasmuch as it has for itself models in the existing God, and what does not exist I call evil." See the Russian translation, part 1, p. 130.

St. Basil the Great, Homily 2 on the *Hexaemeron*, 4, 5: "Evil is not a living and animated essence, but a condition of the soul that is opposed to virtue and occurs in the careless through the falling away from the good. Hence don't go inquiring after evil in the external, do not imagine that there is some sort of original evil nature."

St. Gregory of Nyssa, *Homily on Matthew:* evil is nothing in essence. "Evil does not exist in and of itself, but is revealed with the deprivation of the good; good always unalterably remains firm and immovable and is constituted without any preliminary deprivation of anything. Thus, that which is imagined according to its opposition to the good in essence does not exist, since what does not exist in and of itself does not exist at all: consequently, evil is not being but the negation of being." *In eccles. Hom. II,* cited in Nesmelov, p. 410.

76. St. Dionysii Areopagiti, *De divinis nominibus,* IV, 19; PG 3, col. 717.
77. *St. Maximi scholia in lib. de divinis nominibus;* PG 4, col. 73.
78. *De divinis nominibus,* IV, 20; PG 4, col. 273.
79. *De divinis nominibus,* IV, 20; PG 4, col. 273.
80. *De divinis nominibus,* IV, 27; PG 4, col. 728.
81. *De divinis nominibus,* IV, 27; PG 4, 30, col. 729.
82. *De divinis nominibus,* IV, 27; PG 4, 30-31, col. 732.
83. *De divinis nominibus,* IV, 27; PG 4, 32, col. 732.
84. See Nesmelov, pp. 407-10, 500.
85. "Questions and Answers for Thalassius," PG 90, col. 253; Russian translation, S. L. Epifanovich (Bogoslovskii Vestnik, 1916), II, pp. 31-32.
86. *De civitate Dei,* XIV, 13, 11 (Pisarev, p. 103).
87. *De nuptiis et concupiscentia,* I. II, c. 28 (Pisarev, p. 103).
88. *De civitate Dei,* XI, 16. See the study by Leonid Pisarev, *The Doctrine of Blessed Augustine of Hippo on the Human Being in Relation to God* (Kazan', 1894), part 2, ch. 1, pp. 101f.
89. This is an inexact quotation from "Confession of an Ardent Heart" in Book 3 of *The Brothers Karamazov,* where Dmitry says, "The terrible thing is that beauty is not only frightful but mysterious; there the devil fights with God and the field of battle is the human heart." — Trans.
90. This is Böhme's term for intestines. — Trans.
91. Of course, it is impossible to speak about the individual immortality of animals, for in general the concept of individuality in the human sense is not applicable here. Here one ought to think rather about a certain generic life that is realized in many individuals.
92. E.g., St. Gregory of Nyssa says apropos the resurrection: "and what is received by us from the skin of the irrational things — carnal merging, conception, birth, impurity, suckling, food, disgorging, gradual arrival at completed growth, maturity of age, old age, sickness, death" — none of this is subject to resurrection. *Works,* part 4, 315-16.
93. In the "order of service for crowning" the latter is regarded as an ecclesiasti-

cal and human solemnity, with any sort of disdain for sex and matrimony as such being absent. On the contrary the service recalls the wedding in Cana of Galilee, which is sanctified by the presence of the Lord himself, it remembers the Old Testament patriarchs who were reckoned as being in the genealogy of the Lord Jesus, and requests single-mindedness and chastity for the betrothed (a clear sign that there exists no contradiction between chastity and marriage): "show their marriage honorable, preserve their bed unsullied, bless their cohabitation to remain spotless," "join them ... since they are joined by you as husband and wife, espouse them in single-mindedness; crown them in one flesh, bestow on them the fruit of the womb, the blessing of children." And as is known, those being wed are led around the ambo in crowns, accompanied by the same hymns as at an ordination to the priesthood; this alone shows how highly marriage is valued by the church.

94. John Pordage, *Godly and True Metaphysics* (Frankfurt and Leipzig, 1715), pp. 119-24.

95. *Über die Menschwerdung*, ch. 1, 1, 13; cited by Werner Elert, *Die voluntaristische Mystik Jacob Böhmes* (Berlin, 1913), p. 64. "Es ist des Geistes Gottes Wohnhaus gewesen und sie ist keine Gebärerin gewesen, sondern die Offenbarung Gottes, eine Jungfrau und eine Ursache der Göttlichen Wesenheit. . . . Sie ist als ein Spiegel der Gottheit, denn jeder Spiegel hält stille und gebieret keine Bildniss, sondern er fährt Bildniss. Also ist diese Jungfrau der Weisheit ein Spiegel der Gottheit, darin der Geist Gottes sich selber siehet sowohl alle Wunder der Mariae . . . und in ihr hat der Geist Gottes die Formungen der Creaturen erblicket." [Bulgakov provided the original German in the body of his text. — Trans.]

96. *Böhme's sämmtliche Werke*, ed. K. W. Schiebler, vol. IV, *Von dreifachen Leben des Menschen* (Leipzig, 1832), cap. 5, §50, p. 71.

97. "Die Weisheit Gottes ist eine ewige Jungfrau, nicht ein Weib, sondern die Sucht und Reinigkeit ohne Makel, und stehet als ein Bildniss Gottes, ist ein Ebenbild der Dreizahl; sie gebiert nichts, sondern es stehen in ihr die grossen Wunder, welche der h. Geist erblicket, und das Wort des Vaters durch die herbe Matricem, als durch Fiat schafft, und ist die Wunderweisheit ohne Zahl. In ihr hat der h. Geist erblicket die Bildniss der Engel, sowohl die Bildniss des Menschen, welche das Verbum Fiat geschaffen hat." *Böhme's sämmtliche Werke*, §44, p. 70.

98. "Jede göttliche Kreatur, als da sind Engel und Menschenseelen, haben die Jungfrau der Weisheit Gottes gleich ein Bildniss ins Lebenslicht." *Böhme's sämmtliche Werke*, §57, p. 72; cf. chapter 18, §53, p. 260.

99. "Die Bildniss ist in Gott eine ewige Jungfrau in der Weisheit Gottes gewesen, nicht eine Frau, auch kein Mann, aber sie ist beides gewesen: wie auch Adam beides war vor seiner *Heven, welche bedeutet den irdischen Menschen, darzu tierisch*." *Böhme's sämmtliche Werke*, chapter 6, §68, p. 96.

100. See *Myst. Mag.* 56, "wie Adam vor seiner Eva war: da er weder Mann noch Weib war, sondern eine männliche Jungfrau." [How Adam was before his Eve: he was neither man nor woman, but a male Virgin. — Trans.]

101. Christ became a human without the aid of a man, so that he would lead us out of this loathsomeness before God (of animal mixing). He became such a virginal

child, with both tinctures in one another (as in Adam before the fall) that he brought our division into one in himself. Christ was therefore born of a Virgin, so that he would hallow again the womanly tincture and sojourn in the male so that the man and the woman would again become an image of God and no longer be man and woman, but male Virgins, as Christ was. Christ "sundered husband and wife and brought Virginity back, as two tinctures in one inseparable, eternal union of love" (Johannes Claassen, *Jacob Böhme, sein Leben und seine theosophischen Werke im geordneten Auszüge mit Einleitungen und Erläuterungen* [Stuttgart, 1885], pp. 3, 23). "When on the cross Christ redeemed our virginal image again from husband and wife and tinctured it with his heavenly blood in divine love, he said after he had accomplished it, 'it is accomplished'" (203).

102. Claassen, *Jacob Böhme*, p. 203.

103. "Therefore, o human, behold how you make use of animal lust: it is in itself an outrage before God, whether in marriage or outside marriage" (Claassen, *Jacob Böhme*, p. 209). Böhme himself had a wife and children, as we know. But what else but disgust do matrimony and childbearing suggest in such an attitude, which is the metaphysical murder of wife and children?

104. "Although the earthly one was not a true virgin, still she was made a virgin in the benediction by the heavenly, divine one.... So only the earthly died in her, the other lived for ever, and thus she became again a chaste and modest virgin, not in death but in the benediction.... She was indeed a virgin, but the true virginity was hidden in her and held with earthly desire. When God revealed himself to her, she put on the pretty virgin of God and became a male virgin in the heavenly part" (Claassen, *Jacob Böhme*, pp. 3, 12). "The pure, modest virgin, in whom God was born, is the eternal, pure, modest virgin before God. Before heaven and earth were created, she was a virgin and in addition entirely pure without any stain. This pure, modest virgin of God entered into Maria at her incarnation, and became her new human in the holy Element of God.... *She was however not called a holy, pure virgin according to her earthly birth: the flesh which she had from Joachim and Anne was not pure from stain; but, her sanctity and mercifulness is according to the heavenly virgin*" (15). "*She is not the Mother who bore God (as Jews and Turks accuse us of teaching), rather, God bore her anew in her seed and blessed her*" (22).

105. Anna Nikolaevna Shmidt (1851-1905) worked principally in her native Nizhnii Novgorod as a journalist. Her fame rests on her mystical writings, in particular some correspondence with Vladimir Soloviev in 1900. Bulgakov took an interest in her views and wrote a study of her ideas, "Vladimir Soloviev i Anna Shmidt" [Vladimir Soloviev and Anna Shmidt], *Tikhie Dumy*, 51-81. — Trans.

106. Heinrich Denzinger, *Enchiridion Symbolorum et Definitionum*, 1st ed. (Würzburg, 1854), p. 357.

107. In the service for the Conception of the Theotokos (the monthly menology, December), in the verses to the "O Lord I have cried" we read: "The prophetic utterances are now being fulfilled. For the holy mountain is raised in the womb, the divine ladder is implanted, the great throne of kings is readied; the place is adorned for God's entrance; the burning bush begins to blossom, the myrrh receptacle of the

sanctuary begins to flow. . . . The great and all-glorious mystery unknown by angels and human beings and hidden from the ages, today in the womb of chaste Ann is carried as the child Mary the Daughter of God who is made ready for the dwelling of the King of all ages and the renewal of our race. . . ." Sedalen: "A new heaven is built in Ann's womb by the order of God almighty, from it shines forth the sun that never sets." Canon, ode 1: "Today we celebrate your conception, O divinely wise Ann, for you conceived her who contains him who nowhere can be contained." . . . "Glorious Ann now conceives the pure one who has conceived without the flesh the Lord most blessed." . . . "From corrupted entrails, O Virgin, you have shone forth, for in the uncorrupted womb you carried the sun of glory, and you were as we are except for the twisting and confusion (of sin)."

In the excerpts cited are included the fundamental motifs on which this service is built; here there is not a word about an "immaculate conception" and in no way is its natural characteristic denied, but the conceived Ever-Virgin is hymned.

108. From Dostoevsky's novel, *Demons*. — Trans.

109. The church sings from the stikhira of the Nativity of Christ at vespers: "What shall we offer you, O Christ, that you have appeared on earth as a human for our sake? *Each of those created by you* offers you thanksgiving: Angels a hymn, the heavens a star, the magi their gifts, the shepherds wonder, the earth a cave, the desert a manger; *we offer a Mother Virgin*. You who are before the ages, O God, have mercy on us."

Notes to the Third Section

1. "I am the image of your unspeakable glory, even if I bear the wounds of transgressions. Of old you created me out of what is not and honored me with your divine image." From the Canon of Burial.

2. A variant (or an inexact citation) of a poem by Vladimir Soloviev from 1875. — Trans.

3. This confusion of image and Prototype, of ego and Ego, distinguishes the fundamental motifs of Fichte's metaphysics, who equates the human I, taken in the greatest intensity, with the divine I. The intuition of the transcendence of the spirit in relation to all of its determinations or products lies at the basis of the philosophy of creativity in N. A. Berdiaev (*The Meaning of Creativity* [Moscow, 1916]), but he sees insufficiently the difference between image and Prototype, between the unlimited creativity of humankind on the basis of sophianicity and the absolute divine creative act. Therefore the result is an objectless and for that reason powerless although pretentious, creative gesture.

4. Pushkin's poem "Trud" [Labor], written after he completed "Eugene Onegin." — Trans.

5. John 1:13, 12. — Trans.

6. The church sings, "Adam of old was deceived and, desirous of becoming

God, he did not become him; God becomes human, so that Adam can be made God." Stikhira on "praise" for the feast of the Annunciation.

7. In one of the ancient liturgies, the human being is characteristically called *kosmou kosmos* (the cosmos of the cosmos).

8. The doctrine of the microcosm is encountered in the extant astrological books by Manilio and Firmico, and equally in the hermetic books; it is contained in the principal work on Egyptian astrology of Nekhepso and Petosiris (Dieterich, *Eine Mithrasliturgie*, p. 55). The doctrine of the solarity of the eye as the condition of sight, praised by Goethe, apart from Plato (*Republic*, VI, 508a) and Plotinus (*Enneads*, I, 6, 9), is encountered in Poseidonius (*Sext. Emp.*, VII, 93: *to men phōs hypo tou phōtoeidous opseōs katalambanetai, hē de phōnē hypo tēs aeroeidous akoēs* . . . [*for light is received by the flame-like sense of sight and sound by the sky-like sense of hearing*]. The same idea comes up in the pseudo-Aristotelian work *Peri kosmou*, c. 1. In Manilio in the well-known verses II, 115, we read: *Quis caelum possit nisi caeli munere nosse/et reperire deum nisi qui pars ipse deorum* [*who can know heaven unless he has known the favor of heaven/and who can find god unless he is himself part of the gods*]? The image of the *phōtoeidēs opsis* comes up in him too, IV, 886ff. Finally, let us cite an orphic verse (fr. 280), *tōi lamprōi blepomen tois d'ommasin ouden horōmen* [*we see with brightness but in wise do we see with the eyes*]. In Dieterich, *Eine Mithrasliturgie*, p. 56-57.

9. In one of the late cabbalistic schemata the following correspondence is established for (a) the divine names, (b) the ranks of angels, (c) the heavenly spheres, (d) the parts of the body, and (e) the commandments:

(1) Sefirah Keter, "Corona": (a) 'Ehēyeh (I am who am, Exod. 3:14); (b) Ḥayyōt (living creatures, Ezek. 1:5); (c) fiery heaven; (d) brain; (e) first commandment.

(2) Sefirah Chokma, "theoretical" reason: (a) Yah (Exod. 26:4); (b) Ôphanîm (wheels, Ezek. 1:16); (c) first motion; (d) lung; (e) second commandment.

(3) Sefirah Bina, "practical" reason: (a) Yhwh; (b) Erellim (powers, Ezek. 33:7); (c) firmament (zodiac); (d) heart; (e) third commandment.

(4) Sefirah Nezed, "love": (a) El; (b) Chaschmalim (sparkling entities); (c) planet Saturn; (d) stomach; (e) fourth commandment.

(5) Sefirah Gebura, "fortress/strength": (a) Eloah; (b) Seraphim; (c) Jupiter; (d) liver; (e) fifth commandment.

(6) Sefirah Tiferet, "sovereignty/dominion": (a) Elohim; (b) Schin'annim (the many); (c) Mars or the Sun; (d) gall; (e) sixth commandment.

(7) Sefirah Netsakh, "strength": (a) Yhwh Ṣebaoth; (b) Tarschischim (strictness); (c) Sun or Mars; (d) spleen; (e) seventh commandment.

(8) Sefirah Khod, "magnificence": (a) Elohe Ṣebaoth; (b) sons of God (Job 1:6); (c) Venus; (d) kidneys; (e) eighth commandment.

(9) Sefirah Jezod, "foundation": (a) Elchai, the living God; (b) Ischschim (fiery flame, Ps. 104:4); (c) Mercury; (d) male member; (e) ninth commandment.

(10) Sefirah Malkut, "kingdom": (a) Adonai (Lord); (b) cherubim; (c) moon;

(d) female organ; (e) tenth commandment. See Bischoff, *Die Elemente der Cabbalah*, I. Th., 181; compare his *Die Cabbalah*, 1903.

10. As A. N. Shmidt asserts with her enigmatic daring.

11. It would be instructive to conduct a very careful analysis of how this dogmatic question is understood in Orthodox liturgical texts in order to hear the evidence not of school theology but of the prayerful heart prostrate before the Patroness of the world. Undoubtedly, liturgical theology can shed light on the question more deeply and vitally than the rational definitions of dogmatics. (Even after a cursory glance numerous liturgical parallels leap before one's eyes relative to the basic moments in the life of the Savior and the Mother of God, which correspond to the church feasts of the Nativity of the Mother of God and of Christ, the Entrance into the temple of the Virgin Mary and the Visitation of the Lord, the Resurrection of Christ and the Dormition of the Mother of God; in particular the service of the Dormition "Praises of the most holy Theotokos" represents a direct parallel to the "Praises" from Orthros on holy Saturday.)

12. From the poem "Good and Evil" by Afanasii Afanasievich Fet (1820-1892). — Trans.

13. "With a single logos, fire arranged everything in the body in accord with its own proper nature: (it made the body of the human) a likeness of the universe, the small (microcosm) corresponds to the great (macrocosm) and the great corresponds to the small." The imitation of Heraclitus in Hippocrates: *The Pre-Socratics*, trans. A. Makovel'sky, I, 173. Is not a similar idea about the sophianic universality of the human pan-organism expressed in the dark fragment of Empedocles? "We know earth by earth, water by water/the divine ether we know by ether and the destructive flame by fire. Love by love and sad discord by discord." *The Pre-Socratics*, II, 217.

14. According to the doctrine of the Cabbala, before the creation of the human being the earth did not yet yield fruits: "Only when the human being had been created did the generative power of the earth become visible to the world... none of the works of heaven and earth were revealed prior to the creation of the human being; heaven contained its rain, and earth contained its productive power which it had.... But as soon as the human being appeared in the world, everything appeared together with it. When the human being sinned, everything was taken out of the world, and the earth became accursed.... The powers of the earth became hidden as was the case before the creation of Adam." And so it remained until the circumcision of Abraham and the establishment by this of the covenant with God. *Sepher ha-Zohar*, trans. de Pauly, vol. II, 3-4.

15. Even in the *Koran*, with all of the weakness of the anthropological principle in it, we read this account: "Behold, your Lord said to the angels: I shall place a deputy on earth. They said: Will you really place on it the one who will do obscenities on it and will shed blood, whereas we send up praise to you and hallow you? He said: I know what you do not know. And he taught Adam all the names, then concerning them he proposed to the angels, having said, proclaim these names to me if you are just. They said: praise to you! We have knowledge only of what you have taught us; You are knowing and wise. He said: Adam, announce to them their names! And when

he proclaimed to them their names, he said: did I not tell you that I know the secrets of the heavens and the earth, and I know what you will make known and what you will conceal. And behold, we told the angels: kneel before Adam, and they knelt, except for Iblis; he refused, magnified himself and became one of the unbelievers." *The Koran*, the legislative book of the Mohammedan faith, trans. from the Arabic of Gordii Sablukov, 2nd ed. (Kazan', 1895). Chapter 2: "The Cow," pp. 28-32.

16. In the Cabbala the idea about the humanness of all that exists, of course, occupies a central place. "The form of the human includes in itself all things, and all that may exist has its stability only through it" (II, 135a). "The human figure includes in itself all that exists in heaven and on earth, the higher and lower entities" (III, 144b). "No form, no world had stability before the human form existed. For it includes in itself all things, and everything that exists has stability only through it. One only needs to distinguish between the 'higher' (heavenly) and 'lower' human. The latter could not exist without the former. Every formation of everything reposes on the image of the human" (III, 144a). "The human being is the union and the highest final point (crown) of creation. Because he was made only on the sixth day. As soon as the human being entered creation, everything was completed, the higher and lower world, for all is united in the human. He unites all forms" (III, 148a). "The diverse parts of our body correspond to the secrets of a higher wisdom. All of this is only like clothing. For inside is the secret 'of the heavenly human'" (I, 191a).

"When God wanted to create the human being, Law said to him: if you create the human and he ends by falling in sin, how will he find the power to bear the penalty which you prescribe for him? The Holy One, may he be blessed, answers him: I created repentance before the foundation of the world. At the moment of the creation of the human being, the Holy One, blessed may he be, says to the world: World, world! Know that you, like the laws that govern you, exist only by virtue of the Law; therefore I created the human being and settled him in your midst, so that he would devote himself to the study of the Law. If the human being will not do this, I shall return you to the state of tohu-wa-bohu. In this way your existence depends on the human being.... Observe that each human who devotes himself to the Law *supports the world* and all the deeds of creation fulfill their function in a corresponding manner thanks to him. From every member of the human not one exists which would not have its equivalent in the universe. The human consists of members; each of its members has its rank; one is necessary for life, another is simply useful, and all members in union form one body. Likewise in the universe: it consists of members of different ranks, and *all of these members form one body.*" *Sepher ha-Zohar*, trans. J. de Pauly, vol. II, 131-32. Cf. 423-24, 625.

17. *De civitate Dei*, XIV, 26. See the thorough exposition of this question by Leonid Pisarev, *The Doctrine of Blessed Augustine, Bishop of Hippo, concerning the Human Being in His Relation to God* (Kazan', 1894), part I, ch. III, pp. 70f.

18. Pisarev, 72: *De peccat. merit.* II, 22.

19. *De civitate Dei*, XIV, 23, 17, 24.

20. After the narrative of the commandment given to Adam with respect to the tree of knowledge of good and evil, the narrator continues: Genesis 2:18 — "And the

Lord God (Yahweh Elohim) said: 'It is not good for the human to be alone; let us make for him a helpmate who corresponds to him.'" Further on, as if preparing the human being for the creation of woman, God brings to him all creation in order to call him to an awareness of his loneliness in the world by the spectacle of universal sexual duality. Genesis 2:20-24: "And the human called the name for every animal and bird of heaven and all the beasts of the field; but for the human no helpmate was found who was like him. And the Lord God induced a deep sleep in the human; and when he had fallen asleep, he removed one of his ribs and covered the place with flesh. And the Lord God fashioned a woman from the rib which he removed from the human, and he brought her to the human. And the human said: 'Behold this is bone of my bones and flesh of my flesh; she will be called *woman* for she was taken from (her) man. Therefore a human will leave his father and his mother and cling to his woman; and the two will be in one flesh.'" In the text of this narrative there is no hint that the creation of woman was provoked by the falling into sin. It is typical that in the Greek translation LXX, *sleep* is designated as *ecstasy* — *ekstasis*.

21. The Bogomils were a dualist religious sect originating in the Balkans in the tenth century and preaching a strict dualist form of religious doctrine. They rejected most of the teachings of orthodox Christianity. — Trans.

22. *De divisione naturae*, lib. IV. Cf. A. Brilliantov, *The Influence of Eastern Theology on Western Theology in the Works of Johannes Scotus Eriugena* (St. Petersburg, 1891), pp. 178-83, 209-12, 334-39.

23. *De divisione naturae*, II, 10, c. 537D.

24. In Michelangelo's painting of the ceiling of the Sistine chapel we have some profound insights into the mysticism of sex. In the "creation of Adam, the primogenitor awakened into being looks with languor at the Creator, and in the folds of His fluttering clothing is already present the soul of the as yet uncreated Eve who fastens her eyes steadily on Adam as if calling her husband to herself, instilling in him a yearning for her. And the unborn souls of future children of Adam throng together with Eve. The astounding master attests by his perceptiveness that Adam never existed without Eve and his children, that polyhypostatic humanity whose father he was, and the virginal youth is already husband and father in potential. He further depicts the creation of Eve out of the flesh of Adam: here Adam is seized by a deep and blessed sleep, full of reveries about Eve who proceeds out of him in that ecstasy outside his awareness, as if by a vegetative process. Then we see Eve already bewitched by the serpent: like a bird wounded by a shot, she is powerless before the lust that possesses her, gripped by the parching thirst of sin, and Adam grown heavy is no longer able to help her. He has likewise been transformed from a virginal husband into a lascivious buck. And see, enveloped by shame, darkened and made heavy, they are driven out of Eden." *Incipit tragoedia*. Thick gloom falls on the earth and the fires of Old Testament hopes merely flicker in it.

25. To their number has been added in recent times N. A. Berdiaev, *The Meaning of Creativity*, pp. 180f.

26. Cited by Clement of Alexandria in *Stromateis* III, 13, 92. See E. Preuschen, *Antilegomena* (Giessen, 1910), p. 2. The following utterance of the Savior is cited there

(*Stromateis* III, 9, 63): "I came to destroy the deeds of woman" — *ēlthon katalysai ta erga tēs thēleias*. Hippolytus makes a typical reference to these passages in respect of the Naassenes in *Philosophumena* V, 7: "Attis was castrated, i.e. he was freed from the lower earthly parts of creation and passed over to the eternal higher essence in which, they say, there is neither male nor female, but a new creature, a new human who, they say, is *male-female* — *arsēnothēlys*."

27. Nourishment, the participation of the flesh of the world, is connected with marriage, for it also attests the fleshly sensuality of humankind. The commandment concerning food, according to the first chapter of Genesis, is given immediately following the blessing for reproduction and possession of the earth, the one connected, of course, with the other (vv. 28-29). In the second chapter the commandment concerning the tree of knowledge of good and evil, it is true, precedes the creation of the woman, but this can scarcely be regarded as a change in the meaning of the narration of chapter one, but rather as an indication of the peril from temptation, possible through the woman.

28. The Cabbala gives this explanation of marriage: "All spirits and souls, before they set off into the (lower) world, consist of a male and a female part which (above) are united in one entity. When they come down to earth, both halves are separated one from the other and thereupon they take up their abode in two different bodies (divided by sex). But when the time for marriage comes, the Holy Blessed One, knowing all spirits and souls, unites them (by marriage), as they were before and then they form one body and one soul. But this union (of right souls) is determined corresponding to the conduct of the human being. Only if the human being is pure and his deeds are pleasing to God, will the union fall to his lot which he possessed before birth" (*Zohar*, I, 91b). In the opposite case he receives for a spouse a soul that does not correspond to him (striking on this point too is the proximity between the Cabbala and the teaching of A. N. Shmidt).

29. A. N. Shmidt studies this with exceptional perspicuity in her anthropology, which errs surely only by the insufficient acknowledgment of this norm for humanity in its earthly being.

30. According to the teaching of the Cabbala, Eve's falling into sin is that she "had intimate relations with the serpent" (*Zohar*, II, 636, 299a). A. N. Shmidt's understanding of the fall is close to this. Likewise, only after he repented did Adam begin to live with his wife, but not with the female demons with whom he had entered into a bond after the fall. Cf. *Zohar*, II, 605, 256b.

31. For this feeling too one will find a lot that is explained in the teaching of A. N. Shmidt.

32. In our days V. V. Rozanov has imparted original revelations in the mysticism of sex. He represents in this realm an astounding phenomenon of a kind of mystical atavism. He is a type of experiment of sexual vivisection, and at the same time an experimenter in the dark and eerie realm where not everyone dares to venture. He is a living remembrance of that state in the life of sex when the primogenitors "were naked and were not ashamed." In his impudence and naïve shamelessness with which he carries out his self-baring and directs his inquisitive eye to places normally closed by

modesty, not only is there an original amoralism reported, but another, important awareness of the noumenal *righteousness* of sex (present in the Old Testament and thereupon in the Cabbala) also shines through which one can say is precious in its mystical immediacy. This is the gleam of the Edenic marriage of Adam and Eve. The one-sidedness and poverty of Rozanov's comprehension of sex is that he knows it only in coitus; he understands it only naturalistically and biologically, although in this he deepens biology mystically in ways not even dreamt of by biologists. Rozanov knows the sex of the body and corporeal joining, but he distinguishes poorly the sex of the soul from the conjugality of the spirit, because for him the nature of "the third sex" ("queer souls") remains closed; in it he sees exclusively the sexual abnormality "of the Uranians,"* homosexuality, defectiveness of sex. Knowing sex exclusively in the aspect of marriage, Rozanov hostilely ignores sex *before* marriage and *outside* marriage, but in particular, the amorousness of bridegroom and bride, and thus he does not know the tragedy of love: there is nothing for him to say about the fate of Tristan and Isolde. The squeamish negation of marriage in the name of amorousness represents the same Rozanovism but in reverse, taken with a minus, and therefore of course it cannot be regarded as its overcoming. It is more probable to see the latter in the deep doctrine about sex in A. N. Shmidt, where identical attention is given to the sex of the body and of the soul. [*Uranians is the English form of the German *Urning*, a term invented by Karl Heinrich Ulrichs (1825-1895) for men sexually attracted to other men. — Trans.].

33. *Rule of the Apostles* 51: "If a bishop, priest, deacon or anyone of sacred rank distances himself from marriage, meat and wine, not for the sake of the work of continence, but by reason of repugnance, having forgotten that all is very good and that God in creating humankind created them male and female, and in this manner slanders abusively the creation: either let him be corrected or let him be reduced from the sacred rank and expelled from the church. The same holds for the laity." The Rule of the Council of Gangra, I: "Whoever reproaches marriage, and disdains a faithful and pious wife who has sexual relations with her husband, or reproaches her that she cannot enter the kingdom, shall be anathema." Rule 10: "If anyone from those who are living virginally for the sake of the Lord shall exalt themselves above those who have contracted marriage, they shall be anathema." See P. Florensky, *Stolp i utverzhdenie istiny* [The pillar and ground of the truth] (Moscow, 1914), pp. 294-95.

34. According to the teaching of the Cabbala, failure to fulfill the commandment to reproduce is one of the heavily punishable transgressions. *Zohar* II, 100b: "Souls come down below in a chronologically pre-established order; the soul of a mother arrives before that of a son, and his soul before that of a grandson etc. But sometimes this chronological order is overturned, namely when a human being without any foundation has neglected to fulfill the command to be fruitful and multiply. In this case the soul of the human reverts to earth in the guise of a mother, and the soul of a mother reverts to earth in the guise of a son." "Souls which quicken men derive from the Tree of Wisdom, which is the male principle, and souls which quicken women derive from the Lower tree, which is the female principle. A human being who dies without children brings judgment on his soul because it cannot be raised up to

the higher world, to the level of Joseph where the Tree of Wisdom is found. In order to save her child, a mother undertakes a new descent to earth but under the form of a son, while the soul returns under the form of a mother. The mother's descent and the transformation of the male principle into the female and back is absolutely unavoidable in similar cases, for the soul of the human who died without children can no longer enter into the body of a man if it does not have a soul-sister who existed before as the spouse. For each human being, dying without children, is separated from its spouse forever; its soul no longer is joined with the soul of the spouse. This transformation of the male principle into the female is so unhealthy that if people were able to compose an idea about this for themselves, they would understand that no physical pain compares with it."

35. In the *Zohar* we find an interesting interpretation of this text of the *Song of Songs: strong as death is love*. The scripture wants to say, like the force of a human in the moment when the spirit leaves the body. Tradition informs us that in the moment when a human is ready to breathe his last breath, each of his members receives the filling in of a significant force because the spirit, foreseeing its imminent separation, flees from one member to another, like a ship without a rudder; which is why the human never has so much power as before the end. *And strong as the netherworld is jealousy*. For love that is not accompanied by jealousy is not love. Similar to how the guilty fear descending into the netherworld is the man permeated by love: he experiences dread of losing the object of love. In accord with another explanation, this comparison has the following meaning: similar to how those descending into the netherworld know about all the sins for which they are punished, so too does the person who loves with jealousy notice the bad deeds on the side of the beloved subject, and this observation strengthens his love" (*Sepher ha-Zohar*, de Pauly, II, 245a, 568-69).

36. Beatrice, who died early, was not the wife of Dante, who had a family. Does this division of wife and "donna" respond to the interior nature of love, or is it only the human weakness of Dante? Surely if Dante only preserved faithfulness of heart to Beatrice, as he testifies by his poetry, then the wife was for him only a concubine, and therefore he himself, by having a concubine, to that extent betrayed the covenants of his love — and its image would be, of course, more integral and purer without this betrayal. In the age of knighthood the "beautiful lady" generally speaking had no relation to the wife, and her adoration got along superbly with the coarseness of morals and the principle of might makes right. Love remained "idealistic," but idealistic flights were powerless. Is not this "idealism" in love the spiritual cradle of philosophical idealism with its typical loss of reality?

37. From the numerous witnesses about this in ascetical literature we shall cite only one as an example. "An angel commanded Abba Pafnutius, who considered himself to be completely free of carnal desires, to conduct the following test on himself: 'Go and lock in your embrace a naked beautiful maiden, and if by holding her to yourself you feel that the peace of your heart remains unperturbed, and in your flesh no rebellious upheaval occurs, then a visible flame will alight upon you quietly and without harm. . . .' The elder, who was startled by these words of the angel, resolved not to subject himself to such a dangerous temptation, but, after asking his con-

science, and testing the purity of his heart, he knew that the power of his chastity could not equal the power of such a trial" *(Writings of St. John Cassian the Roman).*

38. "The queer spirits," according to the terminology of A. N. Shmidt, *From the Manuscripts of A. N. Schmidt, with Letters to Her from V. S. Soloviev* (Moscow, 1916).

39. This understanding is corroborated in Mark's parallel wherein a general judgment about "eunuchs" is absent, but the commandment of marriage is confirmed with the same words.

40. One ought especially to name Z. N. Gippius among our contemporaries; in recent times N. A. Berdiaev has associated himself in his own way with this.

41. An expressive example of this conflict is given by the life of S. V. Kovalevskaia, who was overtaxed by it and fell victim to the tragedy of female creativity.

42. From a poem by Vladimir Soloviev. — Trans.

43. In his doctrine of angels (*Philosophie der Offenbarung,* II, 284ff.) and corresponding to his general views, Schelling denies the created status of angels *(nicht erschaffen)* and sees in them only "potencies" or ideas: "Every angel is the potency-idea of a definite creation of the individual" (286). His doctrine of Satan corresponds to this: "The evil angel potencies which are no longer under the dominion to which they had been subjected" are contrasted with good angels who "are by nature good and without will" (284-85).

44. We will take only the ordinary liturgy: "the Cherubicon," "singing the victorious hymn"; in the liturgy of the pre-sanctified gifts, "now the heavenly powers are serving invisibly with us"; at the liturgy of holy Saturday, "let all human flesh keep silent . . . for going before him are the angel choirs, with every principality and authority, the many-eyed cherubim and the six-winged seraphim." The doctrine of angels according to the data from Orthodox liturgical texts is an as-yet-unfinished task.

45. Depictions of angels are located on the north and south doors of the sanctuary. In iconography the typical motif of "the liturgy of the angels" exists. The priestly phelon [chasuble] suggests the winged nature of angels.

46. PG 150, St. Gregorii Palamae. *Capita physica, theologica,* etc. Cf. Bishop Aleksii, *Byzantine Church Mystics of the Fourteenth Century,* pp. 23-25.

47. Cited by Bishop Aleksii, *Byzantine Church Mystics,* pp. 26-27; PG 150, cap. 62, 63, 66, 77.

48. The distinction between the image and the likeness of God was made already by Origen: "When Moses tells of the first creation of the human being, he says *and God said let us create humankind in our image and likeness.* Then he adds *and God created humankind, in the image of God he created it, male and female he created them and blessed them.* He said *in the image of God he created it* but he kept quiet about the likeness. With this he demonstrates nothing other than that the human received the dignity of the image in the first creation, while the perfection of the likeness is received at the end, i.e., the human himself must acquire it for himself through his own personal diligent labors in imitation of God, since the possibility of perfection is given to him at the beginning through the dignity of the image, while he must receive the perfected likeness at the end himself, through the fulfillment of works. But the apostle John defines more openly and clearly the supreme good when he proclaims in the following

manner: "Children, we do not yet know what we shall become; but if it is revealed to us about the Savior, then without a doubt you will say, we shall be like Him" (1 John 3:2). With these words the apostle indicates very definitely both the end of everything, which he calls as yet unknown to him, and the likeness of God, for which one needs to hope and which will be given in conformity with the perfection of merits. So too the Lord himself in the gospel indicates that the likeness will be realized but it will be realized by reason of his petition; He himself vouchsafes to ask this of the Father for his disciples, saying, *Father, I desire that where I am they will also be with me. As I and You are one, so let them be one in us* (John 17:21, 24). These words show that the likeness itself, if it can be thus stated, will be perfected and from the likeness it will be transformed into unity, without a doubt because in the perfection or in the end God will be all in all." *Works of Origen*, 1. *On First Principles* (Kazan Theological Academy, 1899), book III, chapter 6 §1, pp. 291-92; PG 11, col. 333-34.

49. As a indication of the danger of new Luciferian temptations in the context of immortality, one ought to understand the sad irony of God's words: "And so Adam became as one of us, knowing good and evil; and now may he not stretch out his hands and not take even from the tree of life, and not eat of it and not begin to live eternally" (3:22).

50. John 1:5. — Trans.

51. In his speech in the Athenian Areopagus addressed to pagans, the apostle Paul gives this picture of the religious process: "From the one blood God produced the whole human race to inhabit the whole face of the earth, having fixed the predetermined times and limits of their habitation, *so that they would search for God, whether or not they might sense him or find him* although he is not far from each of us: for we live and move and exist through him, as certain of your poets said: we are his race" (Acts 17:26-28). A similar idea is expressed [by Paul in his writings]: "That one can know God is clear to them [pagans], for *God appeared to them.* For *what is invisible of Him,* the eternal power and Divinity, *is visible through contemplation of creation*" (Rom. 1:19-20). "But they, *having come to know God, did not glorify him,* and they did not thank him but wasted their time in their imaginations *and they exchanged the truth for a lie and served the creature instead of the Creator*" (1:21-25).

52. For this reason one can understand the appearance of such figures as Cornelius the centurion in paganism: "pious, God-fearing with all of his household, giving alms to many and always praying to God" (Acts 10:2). The apostle Peter says concerning this, "In truth I know that God is no respecter of persons, but in every nation the one who fears God and walks in justice is pleasing to him" (Acts 10:34-35).

53. Here is the famous description of the experiences during initiation into the mysteries of Isis by Apuleius (*Metamorphoses* X, 23): "I went as far as the verge of death, I entered the threshold of Proserpina and when I passed through all the elements, I turned back again; at midnight I saw the sun, shining with a clear white light; I stood before the highest and lowest gods face to face and prayed to them with the very greatest intimacy." Aristotle (see Synesius, *Dion* 48) put it thus: "those who have to receive initiation must not learn anything, but experience in themselves and be led to such a frame of mind, of course, insofar as they prove to be receptive for it."

54. Cf. the account of Pausanius (*Descr. Gr.* X, 32, 23) concerning an uninitiated, who by chance saw the mysteries of Isis in Titereus and told about this, then died after the account; here too is a similar account about a case that took place in Egypt.

55. "Know that when you were pagans — *ethnē* — you went to the mute idols since *somehow you were led to them* — *hōs an ēgesthe apagomenoi*" (1 Cor. 12:2). "But then, not knowing God, you served *gods which in essence were not gods* — *tois physei mē ousin theois*. Now having come to know God, or better, having been known by God — *gnontes theon mallon de gnōsthentes hypo theou* — why do you return to the powerless and poor elements again to whom you wish to enslave yourselves anew?" (Gal. 4:8-9).

56. It seems to us that this is how one must understand the passage in 1 Corinthians 8:4-5 where the apostle Paul gives this definition of pagan gods: "We know that idols are nothing in the world and that there is no other god but the One God. For, although there are so-called gods — *eiper eisin legomenoi theoi* — whether in heaven or on earth, since there are many gods and many lords, we have one God and Father from whom is everything, and we are for him, and one Lord Jesus Christ, through whom everything is, and we are through him." Here the reality of gods is not denied in any sense at all, but at the same time they are recognized as having lost power for those who know the true God. The gods that are confirmed *against* Christ are already demons. In this sense the apostle continues: "The pagans, in offering sacrifices, offer to the demons, not to God. But I do not want you to be in communion with demons. You cannot drink the cup of the Lord and the cup of demons" (1 Cor. 10:20-21). But the same apostle, having to do not with Christians who had relapsed into paganism, but with pagans who still did not know Christ, deals completely otherwise with their altars and piety. Let us recall the beginning of his address in the Areopagus: "Athenians! In every way I see that you are especially devout. For in passing through and examining your sacred places I found an altar on which was written — To the unknown God. Him whom you honor without knowing him I proclaim to you" (Acts 17:22-23). And the same apostle exclaims, "Can God only be among the Jews and not also among the pagans — *ethnōn*? Of course, among the pagans too" (Rom. 3:29). And the very difference and opposition of Jews and pagans is temporary and abrogated by the Cross: "Christ is our peace, who made *one from both* — *poiēsas ta amphotera hen* — and destroyed the barrier standing in the middle, having abolished the enmity by his Blood, and the law of commandments by teaching, so that *out of two he made in himself one* — *tous duo ktisē en autō eis hena*, a new human, by establishing peace and *in one body he reconciles both* — *tous amphoterous en heni sōmati* — with God by means of the cross, which put to death the enmity in it" (Eph. 2:14-16). To regard pagan deities as demons is characteristic of Old Testament Judaism in its exclusivity — Ps. 96:5, "For all the gods of the pagans are demons, the Lord created the heavens." Cf. Psalm 105:37; Deuteronomy 32:16-17.

57. Schelling, *Philosophie der Offenbarung, sämmtliche Werke*, II Abth., B. IV, 74-75.

58. Schelling, *Philosophie der Offenbarung*, II Abth., B. IV, 76-77.

59. "Among the questions which a theory of mythology must answer is this one: where in mythology is the distinction of male and female deities from? We can reply: a female deity is always either the consciousness of the god that is parallel to it,

stands on a level with it and is simultaneous, or the consciousness of a higher god who is only coming. In the first case it is like a spouse, in the second, like a mother of the god" (Schelling, *Philosophie der Offenbarung*, I, 41, 2-13).

60. Genesis 2:2-3.

61. *Kontakion* and *ikos* for Holy Saturday.

62. "You came down to earth to save Adam, and not finding him on earth, O Master, you went down even unto hell seeking him." Matins of Holy Saturday, the Praises, first stanza, 25th strophe.

63. We have an interesting liturgical illustration of this idea in the little-known fact that the services before Christ's Nativity include conscious and deliberate parallels with the services of Holy Week, primarily Good Friday and Holy Saturday, and separate and very typical hymns are reproduced here only with necessary and minor alterations. I shall cite two examples. "I lift my morning prayer to you who by your mercy have emptied yourself without changing and who bear the form of a slave from the Virgin, O Word of God. Grant peace to us who have fallen, O lover of the human race!" (Irmos, fifth ode). "You bear the form of Adam, who are completely in the image of God, and you wish to be held in hands, you who hold in your hand everything by your power, said the Pure and All-Immaculate One, prophesying: how shall I wrap you in linens like a newborn? How shall I nourish you with my breasts, you who nourish everything? How shall I not be amazed at your poverty beyond comprehension? How shall I call you my son, when I am now your servant? I sing you, I bless you, who bestow great mercy on the world." "The All-Immaculate one, seeing the newborn who took flesh from her, the pre-eternal God, holding him in her arms and often embracing him, and filled with joy she prophesies to him: God most high, invisible king, how shall I look on you? I cannot understand the mysteries of your measureless poverty. For this very little cave, someone else's, makes room for you who are born, and without canceling my virginity you keep the womb as before your nativity, and give great mercy" (Stikhera for 24 December; cf. the corresponding hymns for Holy Saturday).

64. The interpretation of this text has always attracted the attention of theologians. In a philosophical sense Schelling's interpretation is of great interest by reason of the expression *morphē theou* [form of God], which corresponds to his general Christological construction. Schelling, *Philosophie der Offenbarung*, 25th lecture. The mystical side of the question is disclosed by P. A. Florensky, "He did not consider it theft" (Sergiev Posad, 1915).

65. For this reason the expression in Philippians 2:7, "made in human likeness and in aspect became like a human" cannot be understood in a docetic fashion; it has in view to highlight that the nature of Christ apart from nonparticipation in sin was not human only but also divine. That "assimilation" is understood here entirely realistically is attested to by subsequent words in the same text about obedience even to death on a cross.

66. A type of liturgical hymn sung in the Orthodox Church. — Trans.

67. We have a reactionary restoration of this transcendentalism in Islam, and in this is its main pathos, essentially anti-Christian. God has no children; this is stub-

bornly repeated in the Koran in every fashion; neither Son nor sons, but between Allah and the creature is an absolute, insuperable distance. Here are some illustrations.

"Infidels are they who say that the Messiah, the son of Mary, is God. The Messiah said, 'sons of Israel, worship God, my Lord and your Lord!' Whoever thinks up co-participants in God, God will deprive of paradise. . . . They are unbelievers who say that God is himself three, whereas there is no god but the one God. . . . The Messiah, the son of Mary, is only an envoy, like those who were before him and now are not" (Chapter 5, "The Table," 76-77, 79). "See, God will say, 'Jesus, son of Mary, did you say to the people, in addition to God venerate me and my mother as two gods?' He will say: 'Praise to you, you would know; you know what is in me, but I do not know what is in you, for you alone know fully the mysteries. I said to them only what you commanded me: worship God, my Lord and your Lord'" (116-17). "It is not proper to God to have children, praise be to him. When he decides there should be some such essence, he will say only 'Be!' And it receives its being" (Chapter 19, "Mary," 36). "In his power is everything that is in the heavens and on the earth; everything is subordinated to him. He brings creation to life and over time he turns it back into nothing: this is easy for him. . . . He has set before you as an example your very selves: of the slaves over which your right hand holds sway, are there any who are co-participants with you in that which I have allotted you so that in this they were equal with you?" (Chapter 30, "Romans," 25-27). Cf. Chapter 4, "Wives," 169-70 and others. Cited after the translation by G. Sablukov.

68. Likewise in daily prayers, at vespers and matins, we pray in these words: "And again, Savior, save me by your grace, I beg you: for if you save me by works, there is no grace or gifts, but debt all the more . . . but whether I want or not, save me, Christ my Savior, forestall soon, for soon I will have perished" (Matins). "I know, Lord, that I am unworthy of your philanthropy, but am worthy of every condemnation and torment. But, Lord, whether I will or not, save me. For if you save a righteous man, it is nothing great; and if you have mercy on a pure man, it is nothing marvelous; for they are worthy of your kindness. But may your mercy work a miracle on me a sinner" (Vespers).

69. The mystical understanding of the Song of Songs, according to which the life of the church is depicted in it, became customary among Christian authors. We will recall only the interpretation of St. Gregory of Nyssa. Evidently, here we clash with the central problem of the mystic A. N. Shmidt.

70. The idea of Eve's redemption along with Adam's appears with particular clarity in iconographic representations of the Resurrection of Christ and his descent into Hell, where Adam and Eve *together* meet the Savior, having received the joyful news of redemption; the same idea is repeated many times in Orthodox liturgical texts.

71. Sexual dissipation and refined forms of fornication in Christian lands are widespread, probably more so even than in non-Christian ones. It is often observed, e.g., that the morals of uncivilized pagans or of Muslims who live side by side with Christians are purer and stricter than the latter. Minors are alien to the vices of adults, but in return they are not capable of achieving their virtues.

72. *Philosophy of Economy*, Part 1: *The World as Household* (Moscow: Put', 1911). The basic ideas of this study receive further development and deepening in the present work, but those questions are also considered which were destined for the *second* part of *Philosophy of Economy*, namely ethics and the eschatology of economy. For this reason, although formally the present work is not the promised second part, in essence I consider my obligation to the readers of *Philosophy of Economy* here to be in fact fulfilled.

73. From Pushkin's poem "Mozart and Salieri." Russian text in A. S. Pushkin, "Motsart i Salieri," *Sobranie sochinenii*, vol. 6 (Moscow, 1969), p. 161. — Trans.

74. "Motsart i Salieri," p. 168.

75. A quotation from V. Soloviev's translation of the poem "Weltseele" [Soul of the world] by J. W. Goethe. — Trans.

76. Bulgakov uses a term from monastic life for a task assigned to a monk by his religious superior or spiritual confessor, which he is asked to accept out of obedience to the higher authority. — Trans.

77. Cf. in my collection *Two Cities*, "Christianity and the Social Question," "Economy and the Religious Person," etc. Cf. also the sketch "Basic Motifs of a Philosophy of Economy in Platonism and Early Christianity."

78. John 11:11. — Trans.

79. It is remarkable that the same feature is repeated in the account of the raising of Jairus's daughter: "Jesus said to them, 'Leave from here, for the girl has not died, *rather she is sleeping.*' And they laughed at Him" (Matt. 9:24; Mark 5:39; Luke 8:52).

80. Ilia Iliich Mechnikov (1845-1916) was a biologist, zoologist, and protozoologist who was awarded a Nobel Prize in 1908 for his work on white blood cells, which he was the first to discover (in 1882). He had a keen interest in the prolongation of life and proposed many dietary solutions based on his scientific research towards that end. — Trans.

81. Egyptian religion is based on belief in an existence beyond the grave and in resurrection for a new life beyond the grave. The cult of the gods and the deceased, of Osiris and Osirises (for each deceased person was regarded as a hypostasis of Osiris), merges into one ritual. The attentive manufacture and solemn burial of the mummy, which even in the tomb is revived by the double of the deceased — the *ka*, with the whole complex liturgical ritual and an entire arsenal of magical incantations (according to the *Book of the Dead*) — all of this receives its meaning as a preparation of the body for its raising and life beyond the grave. According to the myth of Osiris, he was torn to pieces, but his body was gathered by Isis and restored and revived by Horus who in that way was the resurrector of his own father; likewise every son in the ritual of "opening the mouth" performed over the mummy, returns life to the deceased — Osiris. The exceptional attention is understandable which the Egyptians paid to the habitations of the world beyond the grave, the manufacture of sepulchers, the so-called mastaba, pyramids, for this was equivalent to the building of temples and responded to the most intimate and important side of their reverence for gods.

82. "Blessed is the path on which you walk today, O soul, for a place of refresh-

ment has been readied for you." With these words the Church bids farewell to the dead at their burial.

83. A comparison of Fedorov's "project of the common task" and the dream of Scriabin about the creation of the *Mysterium* automatically suggests itself, or rather about the artistic training for such a *Mysterium,* which must put an end to this eon and be revealed as the bounds between two cosmic periods. For all the utopian quality of his aspirations, revealed best of all through his untimely death, this plan which inspired his whole artistic creativity, is not a simple fantasy; it is a *symptom* full of deep meaning, for it testifies to the appearance of new calls, portents, and presentiments in the contemporary soul, and above all else in the Russian soul, as the most open to the future and especially sensitive to the signs of the end.

84. In the Koran such words are repeatedly encountered which in their own way express Hegel's idea of the *List der Vernunft* [The cunning of reason]: "They were cunning, and God was cunning, but God is the most clever of all the cunning" (Chapter 3, "The Family of Imran," 47).

85. From a poem by Afanasii Afanasievich Fet. — Trans.

86. This and the following lines are from Fet's poem "Poetam" [To poets]. — Trans.

87. Both phrases are from Fet's poem "Esli raduet utro tebia" [If the morning gladdens you]. — Trans.

88. From a poem by Fet, "Tol'ko vstrechu ulybku tvoiu" [I only meet your smile]. — Trans.

89. The first two stanzas from Fet's poem "Forget Me, Frenzied Madman." — Trans.

90. The first line of a poem by Vladimir Soloviev, written in 1897. — Trans.

91. The disclosure of the disharmonies of creativity in various respects is the chief worth of N. A. Berdiaev's book, *The Meaning of Creativity.*

92. The four lines are from A. Pushkin's poem, "Three Springs." — Trans.

93. The poetic confession of the great master, Michelangelo, filled with tragic yearning, echoes them:

> My eyes no longer see mortal things;
> If my soul were not created in the image of God,
> It would have to be satisfied with external beauty
> Which is pleasant for the eyes, but since it is delusive
> The soul is lifted up towards universal beauty. (Ed. Carl Frey, LXXIX)

94. Theurgic authority was preliminarily entrusted to the apostle Peter, and in his person to the Church at the solemn moment of the first confession of belief in Christ on earth, pronounced on the way to Caesarea Philippi: "I will give you the keys of the kingdom of heaven: what you bind on earth shall be bound in heaven, and what you dissolve on earth shall be dissolved in heaven" (Matt. 16:19).

95. An aspiration to replace theurgy with magic and to present the theurgist only as a mighty mage, a "Gnostic," exists in theosophical literature; it is based solely on natural convergence of the external form of his actions with the magical. But the

difference here is that the theurgist operates by God's power, and the mage by natural-human power.

96. The general ministry of the apostle Paul has to do with this. "The gifts are different, but the Spirit is one and the same; the ministries are different, but the Lord is one and the same; and the operations are different, but God is one and the same, who produces everything in everyone. But a manifestation of the spirit is given to each one for benefit. To one is given the word of wisdom by the Spirit, to another the word of knowledge by the same Spirit; to one the working of miracles, to another prophecy, to one discernment of spirits, to another different tongues, and to another the interpretation of tongues. One and the same Spirit produces all these things, allotting to each one in particular, as it pleases Him. . . . And others God has placed in the church, first of all, as apostles, secondly, as prophets, thirdly, as teachers; further those having powers, as well the gifts of healing, of assistance, of direction, and different tongues" (1 Cor. 12:4-11, 28). As charismatic gifts, they are all theurgic too.

97. One ought not confuse the theurgic power, present in the Bible, with those properties of verbal magic which are connected with a certain rhythm, poetic speech, etc. One can encounter this typical confusion in the writings of the occultists for whom on the whole theurgy in the present meaning of the word does not exist. But the magical operation of a word has to do with the natural-human sphere and not the theurgic.

98. The church's establishment of a canon of sacred books is only an authoritative acknowledgment and imperative sanctioning of their theurgic might. Here something happens analogous to what occurs at the canonization of saints and the recognition of their remains as holy relics: the power of sanctity and incorruption was present earlier, while here the universal recognition of this fact occurs which is expressed in the prayerful invocation of the saint.

99. Significant in this regard is the appearance of K. N. Leontiev, an aesthete among aesthetes, and yet who found for himself religious and aesthetic refuge in the bosom of Orthodoxy, in the quiet of Athos and Optina, in obedience to elder Ambrose, and who ended his days as the monk Clement. I am no longer speaking of such artistic individualities as V. Soloviev and F. Dostoevsky possessed. The strengthening of the aesthetic current in Orthodoxy is observed in our own day as well.

100. An aphorism of Goethe, popular among theosophists. — Trans.

101. Perhaps a reference to Gogol's short story, "St. John's Eve," in which the sinful peasant Petro is reduced to a heap of ashes because of a pact with the devil. — Trans.

102. See pp. 222-23 in this translation.

103. For the question under consideration here, the phenomenon of A. N. Scriabin is highly demonstrative and instructive. This sophiurgic anxiety appeared in him with enormous power, not allowing him to be satisfied with art as such, but compelling him to aspire *beyond* art, to seek to overcome it. At the same time this aspiration was the well out of which the spring of his musical inspirations flowed, because they were engendered in tireless searches for themes of the coming *Mysterium*. If one regards its idea as a creative dream, an ideal projection, it expresses symbolically a

sophiurgic aspiration unattainable in art (and *that is how* his untimely death explained it). If one sees here a "project" of miracle performed by art, with the role of theurgist or mage being assimilated to the artist himself, then one has to see here a typical substitution of the sophiurgic task with aesthetic magism, with the temptation of a false messianism leading to deified humanity and its emulation of Lucifer (not without the clear influence of theosophical ideas).

104. Manilov is a character from Nikolai Gogol's *Dead Souls*, known for his futile and complacent daydreaming. — Trans.

105. It is erroneous to equate the authority of royal power in the sphere of church governance with papalism as a variation of it — caesaropapism. Infallibility in political and ecclesiastical questions was never recognized by the Church for royal power; to it belonged rights only in the sphere of church governance, and these naturally flow from the relation of the king to the Church in its earthly, historical body, but are in no way expanded to doctrine or to the hierarchy as such. Therefore caesaropapism here could be only an abuse when the false claims of power did not encounter enough opposition in the people of the church, and not as a norm or lawful act.

106. It is curious that the greatest analogy with Catholicism in this respect is *Islam*, with its idea of the theocratic caliphate in which the head of state is at the same time the vice-gerent of the prophet and thus unites in himself the fullness of secular and spiritual power. It is not accidental, perhaps, that during the era of the crusades two political Islams clashed around the Tomb of the Lord, one Muslim and one Catholic, which attacked a prostrate Byzantium in equal measure.

107. Cf. my essay "The Religion of Deified Humanity in L. Feuerbach," *Dva Grada*, I, as well as in a separate edition.

108. In recent years D. S. Merezhkovsky has joined this camp literarily.

109. This chapter was already undergoing corrections when the revolution broke out and the collapse of the Russian autocracy occurred. This event right away changes the perspective and transfers us to a new historical (or perhaps apocalyptic?) epoch; a new act of the universal-historical tragedy begins. But I am leaving this chapter almost without alterations in the form in which it was written in the summer of 1916. Now it would have been constructed in a different key, but it would not have been essentially altered. For however grandiose this event may be for Russia and for the whole world, it has no decisive significance for the problem of power and its religious perspectives. In addition, for a long time I have had to reckon internally with the painful sickness of Russian autocracy and with the perspective of its possible disappearance from the historical horizon and of its own sort of "priestlessness" in the hierarchy of power.

110. In view of the fact that the greatest part of my printed works and academic courses in one way or another are connected with questions of society, I consider myself in the right to be especially brief here and not to repeat what has already been said. Cf. my books, *From Marxism to Idealism, Two Cities, Philosophy of Economy*, etc.

111. A. Comte's "Grand-Être" corresponds to this in the language of positivism, which V. Soloviev explicated in his own way.

112. In the essay "On the Decline of the Medieval Worldview"; on the contrary,

in "Three Conversations," he is freed from this point of view, for here Antichrist is the hero of humanism.

113. Concerning this inner cleaving of the human the apostle Paul says "If anyone builds on this foundation (which is Christ) out of gold, silver, precious stones, wood, hay or straw, the work of each will be revealed, for the Day will show it, because it will be revealed with fire, and fire will test the work of each, what sort it is. The one whose work that he builds survives, will receive a reward. But the one whose work burns will suffer loss; but he will be saved, but as if through fire" (1 Cor. 3:12-15; cf. 2 Cor. 5:1-4).

114. A phrase from the "Dies irae." — Trans.

115. The positive meaning of the Church's condemnation of Origenism, which is far from clear on the whole, in our view consists in the removal of its too straightforward and exigent dogmatization, not to mention its evident inclination to the side of non-Christian spiritualism. It is possible to understand it not as the establishment of a definite dogmatic opinion, which in general does not exist even up to the present day, but as a pedagogical measure of church discipline.

Index of Names

Aetius, 453n29
Akindynos, 132, 456n70
Alcibiades, 248-49
Aleksii, bishop, 456n61, 495n46
Angelus Silesius, 147-48
Apollinarius, 347
Apuleius, 496n53
Aristotle, 81, 84, 111-14, 135, 147, 221, 223-29, 235, 239, 241, 244, 247, 472n15, 480n56, 496n53
Arius, 200, 347
Arnold, M., 49
Athanasius the Great, 270, 448n51, 472n16, 481n63, 483n75
Augustine, 35, 108, 111, 144, 202, 205-6, 273, 289, 295, 296, 475n28

Baader, Franz von, 175, 465n161
Bacon, Francis, 464n160
Basil the Great, 121-25, 131, 160, 166, 270, 454n34, 454n45, 484n75
Berdiaev, N. A., 439n26, 469n5, 487n3, 491n25, 495n40, 501n91
Berkeley, G., 89
Bernard, 147
Bischoff, E., 457-58n88, 489n9
Blok, A. A., 279
Brianchaninov, I., bishop, 443n18

Brilliantov, A., 455n53, 456n71, 461n128
Bronzov, A., 456
Bruno, G., 139, 186, 194, 457n87, 472-73n17
Büttner, H., 143
Byron, G. G., Lord, 187

Cabasilas, N., 443n15
Carlyle, T., 35, 210, 419, 438n23
Chamberlain, H. S., 338
Cicero, 146-47
Claassen, J., 459n114, 462n141, 465n161
Clement of Alexandria, 119-20, 270, 440n1, 453n23, 483n75, 491n26
Cohen, H., 80, 82, 105, 172, 189, 449n61, 449n64, 450n72, 477n46
Comte, A., 20, 420, 443n19, 503n111

Dante, A., 494
David, king, 53, 123, 406, 411
Dionysius the Areopagite, 125-28, 130-31, 134, 137, 139, 143, 145-46, 147, 160, 166, 205, 253, 270, 271, 312, 454-55n49, 470n10
Dostoevsky, F. M., 232, 275, 282, 385, 401, 409, 416, 444n28, 475n34, 479n53, 480n60, 487n108, 502n99
Drews, A., 86, 159, 163, 167, 170, 185,

505

Index of Names

201, 338, 441n7, 449n68, 450n71, 452n13, 460-61n123, 461n125

Elert, W., 462n138, 485n95
Empedocles, 120, 489n13
Epicurius, 162
Epiphanius of Salamis, 453n29
Érn, V. F., xxiii, 474n18
Ershov, M. N., 477n45
Eryximachus, doctor, 247
Eunomius, 121-22, 124, 453n29, 454n45
Ezekiel, 141, 294

Fechner, G., 229, 477n48
Fedorov, N. F., 214, 303, 316, 371-80, 416, 501n83
Feofan the Recluse, 443n18
Fet, A. A., 489n12, 501n85, 501n88
Feuerbach, L., 6, 26, 36, 334, 414, 469
Fichte, I. G., 5, 22, 26, 42, 47, 50-51, 81, 151, 209, 230, 238, 256, 290, 441n3, 445n36, 479n52, 487n3
Forberg, F. K., 448n47
Fourier, C., 377
Francis of Assisi, 145, 469n7
Frank, S., 125, 146-47, 160, 439n26, 447n41

Gilbert, O., 449n62
Gioberti, 474n18
Gippius, Z. N., 495n40
Goethe, J. W., 82, 279, 397, 401, 446n40, 449n54, 461n126, 488n8, 500n75, 502n100
Gogol, N., 401, 469n6, 502n101, 503n104
Gregory of Nyssa, 121, 124-25, 454n42, 454n45, 480n57, 482-83n72, 484n75, 484n92, 499n69
Gregory Palamas, 131-32, 160, 314, 477n47
Gregory the Theologian, 121-22, 160, 469n2

Haeckel, E., 41

Harnack, A. von, 71, 74
Hartmann, E. von, 44-45, 159, 163, 167, 170, 171, 175, 179, 185, 201, 229, 239, 254, 441n7, 442n11, 450n70, 450n73, 461n123, 474n3
Hartmann, N., 85, 449n64, 472n15
Hasse, K. P., 457n84
Hegel, G. W. F., 5, 26, 35-38, 41, 44, 54, 65, 77, 81, 82, 85-94, 104-6, 108, 151-52, 158, 161, 170-71, 175, 189-91, 201, 226-27, 229-31, 237-38, 256, 258, 289, 414, 445n36, 449nn67-68, 450nn69-71, 451n75, 462n138, 464-65n160, 471n12, 471n14, 479n52, 501n84
Heraclitus, 191, 267, 287, 473n70, 489n13
Hermes Trismegistus, 138
Herrmann, W., 44, 447n43
Hieron, 146
Hinton, C. H., 475n34
Hippocrates, 489n13
Hippolytus, 492n26
Hume, D., 89
Husserl, E., 257, 477n46

Isaac the Blind, 458n92
Isaac the Syrian, 443n18
Ivanov, V., 64, 68, 69, 279

Jerome, 482n64
Johannes Scotus Eriugena, 125, 134-37, 151, 165-67, 295, 457n77
John Cassian, 494-95n37
John Climacus, 443n18
John Damascene, 130-31
Julian the Apostate, 251, 334
Justinian, 219

Kant, I., 1-5, 18, 25, 33-34, 41-42, 44, 46-47, 49-50, 52-53, 64-66, 75, 78, 81-82, 85, 90-91, 104, 106, 110, 150-52, 155-56, 205, 238, 279, 360-61, 424, 440-41n1, 447n44, 447-48n45, 475n36, 479n52
Khomiakov, A. S., 443-44n21

506

Index of Names

Laplace, P. S., 18, 479n52
Lask, E., 477n46
Leibnitz, G. W., 254
Leontiev, K. N., 363, 421, 423, 502n99
Lermontov, M. I., 187, 401
Leroy, E., 455n49, 482n71
Luther, M., 66, 170, 447n42

Macarius the Great, 443n18
Malebranche, N., 477n45
Marx, K., 10, 370-71, 377, 379
Maximus the Confessor, 125, 129-31, 134, 160, 166, 190, 270-71, 272-73, 295, 299, 444n26, 455n50, 470n10, 474n26
Mechnikov, L., 375, 377, 500n80
Meister Eckhart, 143-46, 167-70
Michelangelo, 491n24, 501n93
Motovilov, A. N., 259
Müller, M., 441-42n10
Muretov, M. D., 118-19, 142, 458n91

Natorp, P., 85, 449n64, 472n15
Nesmelov, V., 454n45
Nicholas of Cusa, 36, 137-40, 160, 195, 444n27, 457n84, 472n17, 474n19
Novalis, 279

Origen, 120-21, 160, 254, 270, 295, 303, 314, 354, 481n64, 483n75, 495-96n48, 504n115
Orpheus, 120
Ostwald, W., 41

Paracelsus, 170, 464
Parmenides, 188, 190, 194
Pascal, B., 26, 35
Paul, apostle, 48, 56, 78, 96, 125, 170, 200, 234, 248, 253, 256, 264, 266, 286, 292, 300, 305, 311, 332, 341, 344, 352, 353, 355, 496n51, 497n56, 502n96, 504n113
Peter, apostle, 344-45, 441n6, 496n52, 501n94
Pfleiderer, O., 39, 171, 474n23

Philo of Alexandria, 118-19, 452n5
Plato, 22, 82-85, 104, 111-14, 117, 119-20, 123, 147, 190-91, 199, 204, 217, 221-29, 233, 235, 238-47, 251, 253, 264-65, 366, 402, 409, 414, 469n8, 471-72n15, 480n56, 488n8
Plotinus, 114-18, 120, 128, 130, 143, 160, 163-64, 165, 173-74, 183, 221, 238, 239, 241-46, 250, 252-54, 258-59, 274, 275, 289, 475n27, 480-81n61, 481n62, 488n8
Poe, E. A., 372
Pordage, J., 149-50, 278, 431, 459n, 462n141, 466n167, 478n51
Porphyry, 118
Poseidonius, 488n8
Preuschen, E., 491-92n26
Pushkin, A. S., 288, 367, 401, 449n55, 487n4, 500n73, 501n92

Rimsky-Korsakov, N., 367
Ritschl, A., 43, 447n42
Rozanov, V. V., 492-93n32
Ruskin, J., 369

Salome, 301
Samuel, prophet, 377-78, 410
Saul, king, 377-78
Schelling, F. W. J., 81, 151-52, 158, 170-71, 173, 185, 199-202, 207-27, 229-30, 289, 313, 332, 336-39, 449n58, 451n74, 462n140, 462-63n143, 468-69n1, 469-70n9, 474n23, 476n39, 495n43, 497-98n59, 498n64
Schiller, F., 50, 82, 478n50
Schleiermacher, F., 39-44, 46-47, 78, 447nn41-42, 460n120
Schopenhauer, A., 163, 167, 170-71, 175, 179, 185, 239, 254
Schuppe, V., 105
Schwarz, H., 452n11, 461n137, 462n138, 463n145
Scriabin, A. N., 501n83, 502n103
Seneca, 147
Seuse, H., 145

Index of Names

Shmidt, A. N., 281, 299, 486n105, 489n10, 492nn28-31, 492-93n32, 495n38, 499n69
Simeon the New Theologian, 443n18
Simonides, 146
Socrates, 238, 248-49, 480n56
Solon, 120
Soloviev, V. S., 152, 158, 184, 229, 279, 289, 299, 308, 374, 385, 387, 401, 410, 416, 420, 423, 460n116, 469n3, 476n37, 479n53, 483n74, 486n105, 487n2, 495n42, 500n75, 501n90, 502n99, 503n111
Spinoza, B., 41, 43, 74, 81, 155, 160, 162-63, 170, 174, 183, 186, 190, 194, 464n159
Stagel, E., 145
Steiner, R., 21, 170, 210, 445-46n37
Stöckl, A., 167, 461n127, 465n161
Struve, P. B., 26

Tauler, J., 145, 147

Thomas à Kempis, 443
Thomas Aquinas, 146, 455n49
Tikhon of Zadonsk, 443n18
Tiutchev, F. I., 67, 442n12, 449n60
Tolstoy, L. N., 35, 47, 49, 76, 158, 280, 335, 416
Trubetskoi, E. N., Prince, 468-69n1, 475n35, 478-79n52, 479n53
Trubetskoi, S. N., Prince, 34

Uspenskii, P. D., bishop, 456n61, 456n68, 475n34

Wagner, R., 170, 179, 400
Witch of Endor, 377
Wünsche, A., 458n92

Zeller, E., 114, 452n15, 481n62
Zohar, 140-42, 297-99, 458n88, 476n41, 477n44, 480n58, 489n14, 490n16, 492n28, 492n30, 493n34, 494n35

Index of Scripture References

OLD TESTAMENT

Genesis
1:1-2	244
1:2	480n57
1:26	293
1:27	285, 287, 294, 295
1:28	302, 318
1:28-29	492n27
1:29	317
1:31	318
2:2-3	498n60
2:7	285
2:15-17	316
2:18	490n20
2:19	293, 317
2:20	317
2:20-24	491n20
2:21	317
2:23	300, 318
2:24	255, 294, 318
2:25	318
3:1	320
3:2-3	320
3:5	38
3:6	321
3:11	323
3:12	323
3:14	320
3:16	300
3:17	364
3:19	325
3:20	326
3:21	326
3:22	496n49
3:23	326
4:1-2	359

Exodus
3:14	488n9
24:8	353
26:4	488n9
33:22-23	122

Deuteronomy
32:26-17	497n56

1 Samuel
8:7	410
28:11-15	378

Job
1:6	488n9

Psalms
8:5-7	287
51	278
82:6	286
96:5	497n56
104:4	488n9
105:37	497n56
118	51
119:73	181

Proverbs
8:22-23	225
8:30	225
20:2	298

Song of Songs
1:2-4	260
8:3	261
8:6-7	448

Isaiah
21:11-12	380

Ezekiel
1:5	488n9
1:16	488n9
33:7	488n9

Index of Scripture References

APOCRYPHA

Wisdom of Solomon

1:13	317
2:23-24	317

NEW TESTAMENT

Matthew

5:28	306
9:24	500n79
10:16	320
11:12	443n16
11:27	340
16:19	501n94
19:3-6	295, 307
19:10-12	308
19:36	307
22:30	296
22:37	32
25:31-46	355
25:46	476n40
26:75	441n6
28:18	406
28:19	78
28:20	386

Mark

5:39	500n79
10:6-9	295, 307
11:23-24	392

Luke

1:28	282
1:41-42	304
3:23-38	285
4:3	379
8:52	500n79
11:27	299
12:49	55
18:17	38

John

1	219
1:3	77
1:5	496n50
1:12	487n5
1:13	487n5
1:18	32
3:16-17	185, 343
4:24	259
8:7	306
8:9	306
8:11	306
8:44	321
8:58	347
10:34-36	286
11:11	500n78
12:24	401
14:23	289, 452n2
16:21	304
17:6	32
17:21	496n48
17:24	496n48
20:7	266
20:21-22	386
20:29	38

Acts

1:8	386
10:2	496n52
10:34-35	496n52
17:22-23	497n56
17:26-27	96
17:26-28	496n51
17:28-29	286
17:32	253, 266

Romans

1:19-20	496n51
1:21-25	496n51
2:14-15	96
3:29	497n56
7:23-24	303
8:14-16	348
8:20	481
8:24-25	349
8:29	292
11:32-36	430
12	56
13:1-2	407
14:9	406

1 Corinthians

1:23	449n59
2:7	344
3:12-15	504n113
3:18	27
7:28	305
7:32-33	305
8:4-5	497n56
10:20-21	497n56
11:3	300
11:7-12	300
12:2	487n55
12:4-11	502n96
12:12-17	292
12:12-27	418
12:28	502n96
13:8-10	434
14	332
15:22-28	406
15:25	435
15:28	435
15:39-40	264
15:44	256
15:47	346
15:47-49	292
15:51-52	376

2 Corinthians

5:1-4	504n113
5:3	433
5:4	234
12:2	441n8

Galatians

3:26-27	348
3:28	418
4:3-5	342
4:6	348
4:8-9	497n55

Index of Scripture References

Ephesians

1:13-14	344
1:20-22	406
1:23	255
2:12	336
2:14-16	497n56
3:8-11	344
3:15	348
5:22-23	300
5:23	254
5:28-32	255

Philippians

2:6-10	345
2:7	498n65

Colossians

1:19	286

1 Timothy

2:14-15	325
6:16	32, 452n1

Hebrews

1:1	390
2:5-8	287
2:10	346
2:17-18	346
4:15	337
5:2	337
5:7-8	346
9:11-14	353
9:18-22	353
9:24-26	353
10:1-2	353
10:4	353
10:11-12	353
10:14	353
11	33, 444n24
11:1	28
11:1-3	444n22
11:3	444n24
11:6	29
12:2	346, 444n25

1 Peter

3:19-20	345, 355

2 Peter

3:13	483n73

1 John

1:1-3	444n23
3:2	496n48

Revelation

4:6	264
12:7	407
14:1-5	407
20:4-6	378
21:5	212
21:10-11	250
21:22	71, 327
22:3	327

Index of Liturgical Texts

Akathist of the Mother of God, 246
Annunciation service, 488n6
Conception of the Mother of God, 281, 282
Divine service before the Nativity of Christ, 206, 347, 487n109
Easter Hours, 474n21
Evening prayer (vespers), 11, 499n68
Funeral service, 193, 375
Holy Saturday service, 489n11, 495n44, 498n61

Marriage rite, 193, 255, 301, 305-6, 484-85n93
Morning prayer (matins), 498n62, 499n68
Nativity of Christ service, 206, 347, 487n109
Prayers from the Divine Liturgy, 282, 353, 386, 495n44

www.ingramcontent.com/pod-product-compliance
Lightning Source LLC
Chambersburg PA
CBHW021349290426
44108CB00010B/164